D1499703

THE GROWTH AND FLUCTUATION OF THE BRITISH ECONOMY 1790–1850

THE GROWTH AND FLUCTUATION OF THE BRITISH ECONOMY
1790–1850

AN HISTORICAL, STATISTICAL, AND
THEORETICAL STUDY OF
BRITAIN'S ECONOMIC DEVELOPMENT

ARTHUR D. GAYER

W. W. ROSTOW

ANNA JACOBSON SCHWARTZ

with the assistance of
ISAIAH FRANK

WITH A NEW INTRODUCTION BY
W. W. ROSTOW
and
ANNA JACOBSON SCHWARTZ

VOLUME I

BARNES & NOBLE
BOOKS
10 East 53d St. New York 10022
(a division of Harper & Row Publishers, Inc.)

Published in the U.S.A. 1975 by:
HARPER & ROW PUBLISHERS, INC
BARNES & NOBLE IMPORT DIVISION

The Growth and Fluctuation of the
British Economy 1790–1850
prepared under the Auspices of the
Columbia University Council for Research
in the Social Sciences
and first published in 1953
by The Clarendon Press, Oxford
This edition first published in 1975
by The Harvester Press Limited, Hassocks, Nr Brighton

'The Growth and Fluctuation of the British
Economy 1790–1850' © The Clarendon Press
1953, 1975
Introduction to the new edition © W. W. Rostow
and Anna Jacobson Schwartz 1975

ISBN 06–492344–4

Printed in Great Britain by Unwin Brothers Limited
Old Woking, Surrey
Bound by Cedric Chivers Limited
Portway, Bath

NEW PREFACE (1975)

This is the second occasion that the co-authors of this preface have had to reflect on the project which ardently engaged us in the late 1930's. Like our prefatory addendum of 1952 (pp. viii-xiv), the present task is touched with sadness, for Arthur D. Gayer, who conceived, organized, and directed the project, following on from his Oxford doctoral thesis of 1930, did not live to see it published. It was, as his 1941 preface indicates, a work of "close and harmonious co-operation," on which we look back over some thirty-five years with satisfaction and, even, nostalgia. It was, for all participants, a true human and intellectual adventure to bring together a mass of raw statistical data never before organized; newly created commodity and share price indexes; a rigorous application to the statistical data of the cyclical and trend analysis developed by the National Bureau of Economic Research; a short-period historical narrative; and, then, in Part I of Volume II, a synthesis of all this with the best theory of cycles and of trends we could devise.

Since the 1930's the historical study of business cycles has not flourished. We moved into a world of war and then of postwar control of aggregate demand by fiscal and monetary policy. The world's citizens came to regard unemployment not as an act of God but of man; and they properly imposed that perspective on their political leaders. What are here called major cycles disappear. The central short-term problem became how to reconcile steady high levels of employment with relative price and balance of payments stability, a problem thus far handled with indifferent success in technically advanced democracies and Latin America. The social sciences, including economic history, turned away from cyclical analysis.

Nevertheless, there have been several studies since 1952 which bear on this book. In 1959 R. C. O. Matthews published his intensive analysis of the 1830's: *A Study in Trade-Cycle History: Economic Fluctuations in Great Britain, 1833-1842*. Partly in response, Peter Temin wrote his essay on *The Jacksonian Economy* (1969), presenting an essentially monetary interpretation of the transatlantic boom. He challenged the view that the expansion in money supply which supported it was the result of the political war on the Bank of the United States, and instead attributed it to an abnormal international flow of reserves into the American banking system—of Mexican silver rather than of specie from the Bank of England—an interesting but debatable conclusion. None of the other cycles of the period covered here has been subjected to such lively re-exploration and debate.

Derek H. Aldcroft and Peter Fearon, however, edited with a lengthy introduction a collection of papers on *British Economic Fluctuations, 1790-1939*, published in 1972. This includes a critique of the present study by Matthews as well as an essay by one of the co-authors (Rostow) which drew on the present study.

T. S. Ashton, in a remarkable piece of pioneering, brought his unique wisdom and feel for the eighteenth century to bear on earlier cycles in *Economic Fluctuations in England, 1700-1800* (1959). He confirms the cyclical pattern we found in the decade of overlap (1790-1800) between his book and ours; but he mobilizes some interesting supplementary evidence.

As we sensed in 1952, however, interest in this period shifted from cycles to its place in the study of long-run economic growth. That interest, in turn, generated research in two directions. First, the statistical pattern in which modern British growth unfolded after 1800. At the initiation of Simon Kuznets, Phyllis Deane and W. A. Cole produced their statistical and analytic study: *British Economic Growth, 1688-1959, Trends and Structure* (1962, 1967). More than a third of that pathbreaking effort, however, is devoted to the origins of industrialization in the eighteenth century. And it is that second problem, reaching back to Gregory King's social accounts of 1688, and, even, earlier, which, it is fair to say, has most engaged economic historians of the past generation interested in modern Britain.

The monographic literature running up from the past to 1790 and a little beyond is too vast to be dealt with here. But its content is suggested by some of the titles in the valuable series of volumes of which Peter Mathias has been the general editor, published under the rubric, Debates in Economic History: R. M. Hartwell (ed.), *The Causes of the Industrial Revolution in England* (1967); E. L. Jones (ed.), *Agriculture and Economic Growth in England, 1650-1815* (1967); W. E. Minchinton (ed.), *The Growth of English Overseas Trade in the 17th and 18th Centuries* (1969); D. C. Coleman (ed.), *Revisions in Mercantilism* (1969); François Crouzet, *Capital Formation in the Industrial Revolution* (1972); A. E. Musson (ed.), *Science, Technology, and Economic Growth in the Eighteenth Century* (1972). In a similar vein, but with a wider geographical perspective, Barry E. Supple edited *The Experience of Economic Growth* (1963), containing *inter alia* five essays under the rubric "The Pioneer of Economic Growth: Great Britain."

This concentration on the way Britain moved into industrialization resulted, of course, from a re-thinking of the growth process as men's minds turned, during the 1950's and 1960's, to the problems and destiny of the developing regions of the world. Reflecting that interest, Phyllis Deane's volume of summary is entitled, for example, *The First Industrial Revolution* (1967).

Part of this re-thinking of early modern British economic history was focused around propositions put by one of the present authors (Rostow) notably in *The Stages of Economic Growth* (first edition, 1960), some of which were foreshadowed by an article in the *Economic Journal* in 1956, "The Take-Off into Self-Sustained Growth." This led to a vigorous debate at the 1960 meeting of the International Economic Association, held in Konstanz, a full record of which was published in 1963 (W. W. Rostow [ed.], *The Economics of Take-off into Sustained Growth*). One question at issue relates to the present study:

to what extent was there discontinuity in the British economic performance in the last two decades of the eighteenth century; and does the degree and character of that discontinuity justify designating the period 1783-1802 as a take-off into self-sustained economic growth. The issue is also addressed in Appendix B (pp. 199-207) of the second edition of *The Stages of Economic Growth* (1971), where it is noted that the grounds for controversy had considerably subsided in Miss Deane's post-Konstanz writings. We all now agree, I believe, that the expansion from 1783-1802 was unique; this was the interval when the critical new inventions went into effect with powerful spreading effects; but this explosive expansion was the result of a long, dynamic period of preparation (or preconditioning)—the latter a proposition never in question.

One aspect of the debate with Miss Deane, on which all hands acknowledged the data were inadequate, has been pursued by other scholars; that is, the extent to which the coming of the industrial revolution in Britain brought with it a rise in the investment rate. The character of the preliminary new findings is well reflected in J. P. P. Higgins and Sidney Pollard (eds.), *Aspects of Capital Investment in Great Britain, 1750-1850* (1971), the report of a conference held at the University of Sheffield, 5-7 January, 1969.

To this debate and fresh research the present study contributed less than it might have done for a particular reason. The collection and analysis of the statistical data begins with the year 1790. As the historical narrative notes at several points, 1790 falls in the middle of a powerful expansion whose prior trough is 1788. That trough, in turn, is a minor setback in the postwar expansion of the British economy beginning in 1784. If we had it to do over again, we surely would have begun with 1783 or 1784; and in all probability, we would have prefaced the narrative with an account of the previous decades, with the coming to fruition from about 1760 of the germinal inventions whose introduction into the production process is a central feature of the boom reaching its peak in 1792: Cort's puddling process; the new textile machinery; and Watt's steam engine. It is explicitly noted (for example, p. 16) that: "This was the period when the new developments in textiles, iron, power, and agriculture which often define 'the industrial revolution,' were first put into effect." But our emphasis in the 1930's clearly differs from that we might have brought to the subject matter twenty or thirty years later.

One aspect of British economic development in the nineteenth century dealt with here has come under special scrutiny; that is, the railways, whose evolution is tracked (in the *Investment* sections, Volume I, Part I and pp. 434-9 of Part II) from modest beginnings at the turn of the century to the great railway boom of the 1840's. Stimulated by R. W. Fogel and A. Fishlow's work on the American railways—in turn, responding in part to observations made in *The Stages of Economic Growth*—G. R. Hawke has examined meticulously *Railways and Economic Growth in England and Wales, 1840-1870* (1970). He seeks, in the end, to measure the direct and indirect contribution of the railways to British national income, indulging in a bit of counter-factual history at the end.

The shift from an interest in short-run cyclical analysis to long-run growth is wholly understandable. Economic history, like the other social sciences, has been and, in the authors' view, should be, in degree, responsive to the problems of the active world. It is a field with a proud record of enriching men's insights not only on where they have come from but on where they are and where they should go. But in moving from cycles to growth, it is our feeling that analysts have made less use of short-period historical narrative than they might have done. This judgment is based on a proposition about theory and a proposition about method.

So far as theory is concerned, the Marshallian long period—the coming in of new technologies and other structural shifts on the supply side—does not occur smoothly. It happens from day to day, year to year, cycle to cycle. Long term growth in the period examined here is, in large part, the cumulative result of what happened in the upswings of the major cycles—not completely because the minor cycles and even recessions also saw some structural change. If one wishes fully to understand the process of growth, one must be willing to study its unfolding over short periods of time, when the reasons for shifts in the pattern and scale of investment and the inter-connections among the sectors of the economy are often much more clear than it is when the sweep of growth is reduced to average percentage rates of change in the various parts of the economy. Keynes, was, technically, quite wrong when he asserted that in the long run we are all dead: the Marshallian long period is with us every day of our lives in modern economies, with changing production functions.

In terms of method, the measurement of growth merely in terms of overlapping decadal averages or other devices for smoothing short period variations conceals as much as it illuminates. And it is not wholly compensated for by regression or other forms of correlation analysis. These sophisticated tools are legitimate; but they can lead to false conclusions unless supplemented by a detailed short-period analysis of how things actually moved. In any case, the co-authors retain as one of their most valuable lessons from work on this study, the memory of how important it was, in interpreting the meaning of the average measures emerging from the National Bureau analysis (Volume II, Part II), to command the intimate insights the historical narrative provided (Volume I, Part I). The intensive study under way in Britain on the eighteenth century and in the United States on the pre-1860 period, for example, would, in our view, be strengthened if scholars would proceed beyond Ashton's pioneering study of eighteenth-century fluctuations and the old (1935) but valuable pioneering study by W. B. Smith and A. H. Cole, *Fluctuations in American Business, 1790-1860* (1935).

Two other trend investigations of rather different style are currently being conducted. One is work on post-World War II economic growth in seven countries (France, Germany, Italy, Japan, Sweden, United

Kingdom, United States), viewed as a continuation or modification of longer-term experience, under the aegis of the Social Science Research Council Committee on Economic Growth, with Simon Kuznets and Moses Abramovitz sharing general responsibility for co-ordinating the studies. The rough organizing framework is the proximate growth sources roughly in the form familiar from Denison and others. In each case, the authors try to discover the major causes shaping long-term trends, the difference between prewar and postwar experience, and, usually, changes in growth experience within the postwar period. A notion of both the common elements and the variation between the studies is afforded by two that have appeared: J. J. Carré, Paul Dubois, and Edmond Malinvaud, *La Croissance Française* (1972), and Kazushi Ohkawa and Henry Rosovsky, *Japanese Economic Growth* (1973).

The other trend investigation currently under way is the work of Milton Friedman and one of the authors (Schwartz), under the auspices of the National Bureau of Economic Research. It is a comparative study of monetary trends in the United States and the United Kingdom since 1880, and their relation to income, prices, and interest rates. To isolate longer-term relations, the basic level observations are either the average of a cyclical expansion or cyclical contraction; observations of rates of change are the slopes of least-squares lines connecting three successive phase averages. The purpose of the study is to test some general propositions in monetary theory and some of the empirical generalizations suggested by the Friedman-Schwartz study of U.S. monetary history (1963). One of these generalizations is that long swings in growth rates for the U.S. economy and other economies are best interpreted as episodic rather than as reflecting an underlying cyclical mechanism. The monetary data support the episodic interpretation.

One challenge laid down in the 1952 addendum (pp. xiii-xiv) is now being taken up by one of the authors (Rostow). It is noted (p. xiii): "The analysis of growth rates and their determinants requires not only an approach in terms of the whole effective trading area, but it also demands a perspective covering very long periods of time, certainly, for most purposes, periods longer than the sixty years examined here." A study is now under way, going beyond *The Stages of Economic Growth*, of the evolution of the world trading area from the eighteenth century to the present and its interplay with the stories of growth in the major nations and regions.

With respect to the basic theoretical analysis presented in this book, further study and reflection have led to an amiable divergence of view between us that should be shared with our readers.

One of us (A. J. S.) has concluded that at least three aspects of the analytical approach of the study require modification in light of recent theoretical and empirical research: (1) the role assigned to monetary policy; (2) the interpretation of the behaviour of interest rates; (3) the emphasis on *relative* price rather than price *level* changes.

The study is a faithful reflection of the outlook of the economics profession on at least the first two issues in the aftermath of the economic debacle of 1929-33. The efficacy of monetary policy was questioned. No distinction was made between nominal and real interest rates. It was accepted that central banks could control interest rates through increasing or decreasing the supplies of credit and money and by changing their own discount rates. Changing interest rates, it was thought, might influence private business investment spending and thereby aggregate income. With respect to the third issue, our stress on relative prices illuminates developments in individual sectors of the economy, but our neglect of absolute prices obscures the understanding of the long-term swings in the British and world price levels over 1790-1850.

(1) The revival of interest in money in the past two decades has stimulated an outpouring of research. Studies of the determinants of the supply of and demand for money and of the effects of changes in money supply in the leading developed and developing countries have demonstrated that persistent deflation and inflation reflect primarily wide variations in the average rate at which national money supplies grow; and that fluctuations in the rate of growth produce fluctuations in employment and spending. It is surely plausible that regularities that have been observed between changes in monetary growth rates and subsequent business cycles in the short run and in rates of price change in the long run from post-Civil War years in the United States to post-World War II years in many countries around the world also characterized British experience in the six decades before the mid-nineteenth century (Friedman and Schwartz, "Money and Business Cycles," *Review of Economics and Statistics*, 1963; A. J. S., "Secular Price Change in Historical Perspective," *Journal of Money, Credit and Banking*, 1973).

For Great Britain, estimates of the stock of money are unavailable for the period covered by the study. Of the three variables useful to regard as the arithmetic determinants of the stock of money—the stock of high-powered money, the ratio of the public's deposits to its currency holdings, and the ratio of the deposit liabilities of the commercial banking system to its reserves—estimates of the stock of high-powered money could be derived. In the United States, it is the major variable accounting arithmetically for changes in the stock of money, and it is likely so also for Great Britain. Changes in high-powered money during the period of suspension were produced mainly by Bank of England issues, thereafter by gold flows as well as by Bank of England issues. The reaction by the Bank to losses of gold or inflows of gold triggered changes in its issues which ultimately affected the rate of growth of the money stock.

Changes in the deposit ratios over the long run no doubt also influenced the rate of growth of the British money stock. In the short run, bank failures in Great Britain, as in the United States, must also have reduced the public's confidence in banks and led them to attempt to convert deposits into currency, thus producing downward pressure on the money stock. Banks in turn might be expected to react by seeking to strengthen their reserves and in time succeeding in doing so, thus adding further to downward pressure on the stock of money.

From 1797 to 1821, Great Britain had an independent national money, convertible into neither gold nor silver nor the money of any other country at any fixed ratio—the counterpart of U.S. experience from 1862 to 1879. In both cases, the stock of money could be determined internally. From the close of the Napoleonic Wars in Great Britain and of the Civil War in the United States, each country prepared for resumption. In both, the major requirement for resumption was that internal prices should decline so that they would bear about the same relation to prices in the rest of the world as they did before suspension of specie payments. In both countries, the drastic and sustained price decline occurred as the quantity of money contracted relative to real output. From 1821 to 1850, British money was convertible into gold at a fixed ratio, as U.S. money was from 1879 to 1914. In each country, the stock of money and internal prices had to be at levels that would produce a rough balance in international payments without abnormal gold movements. The stock of money was a dependent variable, though there was some leeway in short periods.

Changes in the stock of money, however produced, impinge on the public's desired money holdings. Research on the demand for money has shown that it depends in a stable way on income, other asset holdings, interest rates that can be earned by holding alternatives to money, and expectations regarding the change in prices of goods and services. If the money stock grows faster than does the amount households and firms want to hold, individually they will try to reduce their money balances to desired levels by purchasing assets, paying off debts, or making unilateral transfers, using either redundant money holdings or current flows of income. These attempts to convert excess money into goods, services, or securities increase the flow of expenditures and income. Opposite effects result when the money stock grows slower than does the amount the public wants to hold. Thus money supply changes lead to changes in output, employment, and prices. The adjustment of money balances continues until the real value of the money stock—nominal money holdings divided by the price level—is again equal to what the public wants to hold.

For business cycle analysis, the evidence provided by this approach is that change in the rate of monetary growth causes a change in the rate of growth of nominal income in the same direction, after a lag that is variable in length—from six to nine months to more than a year. The change in the rate of growth of nominal income usually shows up first in real output and, after a longer lag, in prices. Major and minor cycles in Great Britain may be defined not only as we have in this study, but also by reference to systematic differences in the pattern of monetary growth rates in the two classes of cycles—similar to the differences identified for U.S. cycles since 1867.

(2) A resurgence of research in the determinants of interest rates has paralleled the resurgence of research in the determinants and effects of money. Changes in money supply have three different effects on changes in interest rates. The first is the familiar liquidity effect, the short-run tendency of an increase in money-supply growth to reduce

interest rates. This effect is short-lived and is overtaken by the second effect, the tendency of a rise in the monetary growth rate to produce a subsequent rise in nominal income and thereby to increase demands for credit and money and raise interest rates. The income effect thus offsets the decline in interest rates due to the liquidity effect and restores interest rates to their initial level. The third effect is that of price expectations. Nominal rates of interest will be higher than the real rate if it is expected that prices will rise. Lenders will demand an inflation premium above the real rate to protect themselves against the expected loss in purchasing power, and borrowers will be willing to pay it since they will expect to repay the loan in depreciated money. Hence nominal interest rates tend to be higher during periods of secular price rise than of price fall.

Since interest rates tend to move within a relatively limited range, a common fallacy is to assume that the top of the range is proof of tightness; the bottom of the range, proof of ease. Yet a high interest rate when demand is strong may not be restrictive, while the same rate with weak demand may be highly restrictive—the income effect dominates the liquidity effect. Similarly, sustained movements in interest rates, either upward or downward, may reflect price expectation effects, not the liquidity or income effects.

(3) The emphasis on relative prices in the present study and the cost explanation offered fail to account for price level movements. Changes in relative prices tell us nothing about changes in the price level. The price of commodity X, for example, can double with respect to commodity Y by the absolute price of X doubling and the price of Y staying the same, or by the absolute price of X staying the same and the price of Y halving, or by any of an infinite number of other combinations. No amount of information on the factors affecting the relative prices of X and Y can explain which of these alternatives will occur. That is the role of price level analysis.

The cost-push or cost-pull explanation offered in the present study for secular price change stresses demand and supply conditions in individual markets. Rises in costs are associated with poor harvests, obstructions in supply conditions—including wartime blockades—increases in foreign exchange, insurance, freight and interest costs. Declines in costs are associated with good harvests, improved transportation facilities, discovery of new foreign sources of supply, technological improvements, and reduced foreign exchange, insurance, and interest costs.

These factors are all highly relevant to the price of one item *relative* to the price of others. But, for movements in general prices, the cost explanation begs the question of the source of the autonomous increase or decrease in costs. The explanation is generally *ad hoc*, relying on different factors in different circumstances and typically confusing effects on relative costs with effects on absolute costs. Moreover, even if this basic defect is overlooked and we suppose an autonomous increase or decrease in money costs, a valid application of the cost explanation would have to demonstrate how the increase in money costs increased either money supply or velocity or both or how a decrease in money costs decreased either money supply or velocity or both. We gave no such demonstration.

The secular price episodes in the period 1790-1850 occurred at approximately the same dates in numerous countries. Relative price changes and the cost explanation do not illuminate the reasons for this phenomenon. Even within a single country there are lags in the propagation of inflation and deflation, how much more so across national boundaries. Prices of traded goods tend to be kept in line with world prices by international competition, but the prices of non-traded goods relative to traded goods depend on the relative productivity of such goods. That can vary from country to country, leading to the unwarranted conclusion that secular price behaviour can be understood only by reference to developments in individual countries.

However slow, delayed, and sophisticated the adjustment may be, the mechanism for the diffusion of secular price change is the mutual adjustment of price levels between countries by international trade and the redistribution of the world stock of monetary reserves. A change in the quantity of money is the means whereby prices in one country are kept in line with prices abroad. Changes in the quantity of money in any one country are produced by changes in that country's prices relative to foreign prices. Changes in the quantity of money then produce changes in the country's absolute price level. That is the lesson of economic history and of current events.

These changes in the analytical framework do not affect the validity of the basic research that undergirds these volumes, but would obviously alter the cast of the present analysis. From the perspective of the foregoing paragraphs, attention to monetary relationships in the study of British business cycles in the nineteenth century and to the three monetary effects on the cyclical and secular behaviour of interest rates would entail revision of some of the conclusions of these volumes. The present analysis of secular change of real output would be less affected. While monetary changes influence output change in the short run, in the long run the rate of monetary growth affects prices primarily. Real output growth in the long run is determined by real factors. The suggested changes in the analytical framework thus offer a challenge to the scholars of today to reinterpret our basic data, thereby both testing the developing framework and correcting and refining our conclusions.

The other co-author (Rostow) would hold to the portrait drawn here of the relation between price movements and the monetary system. Given the extraordinary weight of a few prices (notably, wheat) in the over-all price index, he would not accept the distinction between individual and general price analysis. He believes still that the British monetary system played a limited and essentially passive, responsive role in determining the outcome for the economy as a whole. In this view, he is strengthened not only by John Clapham's conclusions arising from his study of the Bank of England (referred to on p. ix) but also from all he has subsequently learned about the British monetary system in the nineteenth century. A different public policy or, even, a different concept of the Bank of England's role in Threadneedle Street might have produced a different result. But W. W. R. still believes Alfred Marshall had it right, for his time and place, when he said: 'I am never weary of preaching in the wilderness "the only very important thing to be said about currency is that it is not nearly as important as it looks." '

A final observation, looking to the future. Not only the analysis of cycles, but the analysis of trend periods has dropped from fashion since this study was completed. There has been little fresh work on protracted trends, transcending business cycles, in prices, relative prices, interest rates, real wages, and the pattern of investment of the kind undertaken in Volume II, Part I, Chapters IV and V. It is a subject which, in its time, engaged many fine minds, among them Kondratieff, Spiethoff, Schumpeter, and Mitchell. Here two trend periods are considered: 1790-1815; 1815-1848. The literature on the subject deals also with the trend periods on either side of 1873 and 1920 (see, for example, W. W. R.'s *Process of Economic Growth*, Chapter VI). As we look ahead, it may well be that we entered in 1971 another protracted period when the pressure of population and income increase will raise, relatively, foodstuff prices; the pressure of demand will, relatively, raise prices for the sources of energy; the pact of industrial expansion will raise disproportionately the price of certain raw materials; investment patterns (including investment to generate new technologies) will have to shift to assure adequate supplies of such commodities as well as to assure the air and water supplies taken virtually for granted in the first two centuries of industrialization. If this should happen, it may have consequences for interest rates, real wages, and income distribution not unfamiliar to students of trend periods of the past. Trend period analysis may, once again, become fashionable as well as relevant.

New York City   Anna Jacobson Schwartz
Austin, Texas   W. W. Rostow

DIRECTOR'S PREFACE (1941)

THESE volumes have been in preparation for some five years. The general study of British business fluctuations during the first half of the nineteenth century has, however, been of especial interest to me for a longer period of time. In 1930 my doctoral dissertation at Oxford University was entitled 'Industrial Fluctuation and Unemployment in England, 1815–1850'. At the completion of that study I was by no means satisfied that I had exhausted the fruitful possibilities for research in the subject, but felt that no worker could single-handed pursue it further in a really satisfactory manner. Teaching duties and other research obligations consumed my time in the years intervening until 1936, when the Columbia University Council for Research in the Social Sciences made available to me funds to organize a broader research project in the same field.

It soon became evident that the data were far more abundant than I had expected. The task of collecting and organizing them was time-consuming to a degree beyond all original calculations. In the nature of the case, furthermore, lines of investigation other than those I had initially envisaged assumed importance and called for treatment. But not for these reasons alone did the study become a prolonged undertaking. Because of the character of the materials and the type of analysis employed, there was no choice but to proceed slowly and laboriously. The grant originally made in 1936 was renewed annually by the Columbia Research Council. It is indeed a pleasure to acknowledge the indulgence and generosity of the Council in agreeing to successive extensions of the life of the project, and in making available very substantial funds, in the aggregate, for its consummation.

I am more deeply indebted than I can say to Dr. Wesley C. Mitchell for his unfailing encouragement and interest in the study, and for his consistently helpful advice and kindly guidance. With his co-operation and that of Drs. Arthur F. Burns and F. C. Mills, the privilege of unlimited consultation with the members of the staff of the Business-cycle Project of the National Bureau of Economic Research was accorded me and my collaborators. Dr. Burns was most generous to us with his own time and always ready to discuss our problems with us. Messrs. Julius Shiskin, Denis Volkenau, and H. I. Forman, and Miss Sophie Sakowitz of the National Bureau also gave us assistance on many details of the cyclical analysis of time series.

During two summers spent in England in 1937 and 1938 I had the benefit of advice from many quarters. Helpful suggestions were made to me by Sir William Beveridge, Professors T. S. Ashton, J. H. Clapham, T. E. Gregory, F. A. von Hayek, John Jewkes, D. H. MacGregor, and Drs. Leo Liepmann and H. A. Shannon. Two of Professor Hayek's assistants, Dr. Marie Dessauer and Mr. A. Maizels, prepared some very useful memoranda for us. Mr. H. C. B. Mynors of the Bank of England kindly supplied us with indispensable data on the Bank's operations.

I also wish to express my warm thanks to Dr. Frederick R. Macaulay and Professors Herbert Heaton, Charles A. Cole, and David Owen, who read portions of the manuscript. Messrs. Louis M. Hacker and Rufus S. Tucker, and Professor Norman J. Silberling were of much help on certain historical and statistical problems.

In making the study my associates and I consulted many other persons, and our obligations both for specific facts and for general enlightenment are so numerous as to be embarrassing. We must perforce, for lack of space, forego the pleasure of making acknowledgement by name here to all the individuals who generously responded to our demands upon them. But in certain cases at least our debt is recorded at appropriate points in the body of the text.

The general direction of the study has throughout lain in my own hands and ultimate responsibility for its contents therefore rests with me. I was fortunate, however, in enlisting the aid of a very able staff of collaborators, chief amongst them Dr. W. W. Rostow, Mrs. Anna Jacobson Schwartz, and Mr. Isaiah Frank. The study is our joint product. We worked in close and harmonious co-operation for various periods throughout the investigation; we participated in varying measure in the collection and analysis of the data; and we passed upon and worked over the successive drafts of each other's work, embodying the substantial comments and suggestions of the others. But primary responsibility for various portions of the work belongs, respectively, to my collaborators as indicated below. Dr. Rostow became associated with the study in the summer of 1939, fresh from an extensive study of his own on British business fluctuations in the later nineteenth century. His association with us was indeed a fruitful one. Dr. Rostow is responsible for Volume I, Part I; Chapter III of Volume I, Part III; and Part I of Volume II. He contributed in a vital way to the general character and stamp of the study. Mrs. Schwartz, a former student of mine at Barnard College, began working with me when the project was first organized, and continued to do so throughout its course. Nearly all the collection and statistical analysis of the data were done by her or under her direction. She is primarily responsible for Volume I, Part II, Chapters II and III, Sections 1, 4–7, 9, and 10; Volume I, Part III, Chapters II and IV; and the volume of statistics on the British economy. Mr. Frank, then a graduate student at Columbia, joined my staff soon after Mrs. Schwartz and was with us continuously until the Fall of 1939, and intermittently thereafter. Main responsibility lies with Mr. Frank for Chapter III, Sections 2, 3, and 8 of Part II of Volume I. Primary responsibility for Chapter I of Volume I, Part II and Chapter I of Volume I, Part III, is shared jointly by Mrs. Schwartz and Mr. Frank, and for the analysis of cyclical patterns in Part II of Volume II by Mrs. Schwartz and Dr. Rostow. To all my collaborators I offer my heartiest thanks.

All of us, in turn, owe a heavy debt to our staff of assistants, conspicuously Miss Elma Oliver and Mr. Stanley Rosch, who performed the bulk of the statistical analysis during 1938–40 and distinguished themselves by their reliability and resourcefulness. They were succeeded by Mr. Harry Eisenpress, to whom the accuracy of these volumes owes much by reason of his unstinting and painstaking work. Others who have worked with us for shorter periods include Dr. Ernest Doblin, Miss Hanna Stern, Mr. David Schwartz, and Miss Rosemary Riley. We have also had valuable assistance in England from several staff members residing there. Nearly all the transcription of the share prices was done by Dr. and Mrs. S. Moos. The search for various other data was pursued with persistence and patience by Mrs. Eileen Conly Winton, a former graduate student at Columbia. Finally, we should like to express our appreciation to Miss Esther Rosch for her cheerful and efficient typing of a trying manuscript, and to Mr. H. I. Forman, to whom belongs the credit for the excellence of the charts.

For the facilities they afforded us in consulting their files, and for making available the original price data collected by Professor Norman J. Silberling, we are indebted to the Harvard Committee on Economic Research: Professor Arthur H. Cole and Miss Dorothy Wescott showed us unfailing courtesy and consideration. Dr. Selma Fine, Mr. Benjamin Higgins, Dr. Paul M. Sweezy, and Dr. Elizabeth B. Schumpeter kindly made available to us unpublished manuscripts in their possession. Dr. Schumpeter also gave us assistance in connexion with certain obscurities in the British foreign trade data. We also wish to express our appreciation to the staffs of the Barnard College library and the various other Columbia University libraries for their helpfulness.

Finally, it is appropriate that, having left Barnard College, I should place on record my debt for having been allowed for so many years to use not only my own office, but, on occasion, adjoining ones in Milbank Hall, to shelter the project. Mr. J. Swan, Comptroller of the College, and Dr. Clara Eliot, in charge of the statistical laboratory, were most hospitable. These volumes appear now prefaced from another address, but it was in Milbank Hall that nearly all the work on them was done.

A. D. G.

QUEENS COLLEGE
NEW YORK CITY
February 1941

ADDENDUM (1952)

DR. GAYER died on 17 November 1951 as the result of an automobile accident in New York City. It is thus the sad duty of his co-authors to bring the original preface up to date for publication.

More than a decade will have elapsed between the virtual completion of this study and its publication. The delay was mainly caused by the preoccupation of the authors with other tasks, during and after the war. The study, as it stood in 1941, contained large portions which were finally judged of primary interest only to specialists and which could be made available to them in forms more economical than full publication.[1] The segregation of such portions of the study, the re-editing required, and final publishing arrangements have, in the circumstances of the authors, produced substantial delay.

The study was constructed with an awareness of the relation between the implicit or explicit conceptions that historical analysts bring to their materials and the results which emerge. It is evident that, if the job were to be done now, its character and emphasis might be somewhat different. This would apply, in particular, to the analytic portions of the text, notably Volume II, Part I. One quality of the study has induced the authors to leave it largely as it was first completed : namely, the fairly clean separation of the facts from the judgements made upon them. The *History* (Volume I, Part I), the formal statistical analysis of Volume II, Part II, as well as the microfilm presentation elsewhere of the raw statistical evidence, give to others an opportunity to work independently over the materials on terms equal to those of the authors. This was the intent ; and, barring the inevitable reflection of individual judgement in the selection of facts for the *History*, we believe this objective to have been achieved.

Only one limited portion of the study has appeared separately ;[2] and one of the authors has used these materials as a foundation for a part of his later work.[3] The bulk of the history and analysis appears, however, for the first time.

---

[1] Volume I, Part II, of the study is a summarized version of a much longer original text. In addition, three major portions of the study are being reproduced in microfilm and will be available in that form upon application to the Columbia University Council for Research in the Social Sciences. The microfilmed materials include: the monthly data on share prices from which the indexes presented here have been constructed, together with detailed discussion of their institutional background ; the monthly data on individual commodity prices, which served as a base for the new price indexes ; and a volume of statistics on the British economy over the years 1790–1850, including discussion of sources, continuity of data, reliability, and so forth. An Appendix to Volume II presents the tables of contents of this microfilmed material.

[2] A. D. Gayer, Anna Jacobson, and Isaiah Frank, 'British Share Prices, 1811–1850', *Review of Economic Statistics*, xxii, 1940.

[3] W. W. Rostow, 'Business Cycles, Harvests, and Politics: 1790–1850', *Journal of Economic History*, i, No. 2, Nov. 1941 ; 'Adjustments and Maladjustments after the Napoleonic Wars', *American Economic Review*, Supplement, Mar. 1942 ; and portions of Chapters I and II, *British Economy of the Nineteenth Century*, Oxford, 1948. The article originally published in the *Journal of*

Since 1941 important work has been published on the period covered by the study. Perhaps most directly relevant is the late Sir John Clapham's *The Bank of England, A History*.[1] Chapters IV–VIII of his Volume I and, especially, Chapters I–IV of Volume II cover, from the Bank's surviving books and papers, the story of the years 1790–1850. Clapham states that he attempted only a 'light background of general affairs, economic or political' and that he resisted 'the temptation to wander into attractive bypaths'.[2] It was to be expected, however, that such a work, written from a massive knowledge of the whole economic history of the era, would illuminate the position of the Bank in the economy as well as the workings of the economy itself. Clapham's chapters covering the period of this study, aside from their value in their own right, are a valuable supplement to the *History* presented here in Volume I, and especially to the financial sections of the historical chapters (numbered, in each case, 5). Had Clapham's work been available it would have been extensively used.

Apart from its value as a supplementary account of the money market[3] and for the occasional introduction of a new strand in the story,[4] Clapham's volumes on the Bank strengthen our general analysis at several important points. He confirms the limited role of the Bank in financing general credit expansions;[5] he deprecates the importance of strictly monetary factors in the price decline after the Napoleonic Wars;[6] he makes clear that the most important of the Bank's cyclical functions was its lending to ease the crises of confidence that often followed the upper turning-point.[7] Further, Clapham leans heavily, in his general view of events, on the part played by good and bad harvests and on their effects, through the level of grain imports, on the money market and the national credit position.[8] Thus, in one of its aspects, *The Bank of England* may be regarded as supplementary and mainly confirmatory evidence on the character and mechanisms of monetary factors in business fluctuations from 1790 to 1850.

Apart from his volume on the Industrial Revolution, referred to below, two recent papers by Prof. T. S. Ashton have borne on the period and issues of this study: 'Some Statistics of the Industrial Revolution in Britain'[9] and 'The Standard of Life of the Workers in England, 1790–1830'.[10] The first presents a series showing the number of patents registered each year from 1756 to 1830. Whether or not ingenuity thrived more in depression than in prosperity it is evident that fluctuations in patents are

Economic History is reprinted as Chapter V, in the latter volume. In addition, various portions of *The Process of Economic Growth*, New York, 1952, reflect the present project.

[1] Cambridge, 1944, two volumes.

[2] Ibid., Preface, i. vii.

[3] See, for example, the vivid description of the crisis of 1793, ibid. i. 257–65.

[4] See, for example, the question of the Irish loan early in 1797, ibid. i. 270–1.

[5] See, for example, ii. 20–22, on the boom of 1808–10, and p. 185, on the expansion of the forties.

[6] ii. 72–79.

[7] See, for example, i. 262–5 (1793); ii. 21 (1810); ii. 89–91 (1825); ii. 199–211 (1847).

[8] See, for example, ii. 66–67, 146, 177, 198–9.

[9] *Manchester School*, May 1948.

[10] *Tasks of Economic History*, Supplement ix, 1949.

closely related to general fluctuations in long-term investment. In the period of overlap with this study they appear to follow sensitively what are here described as major cycles; namely, cycles marked in their expansion phases by large increases in long-term investment.[1] Peaks in patents come in 1792, 1802, 1813, 1818, and 1825. With the single exception of 1813 (for which period the major cycle peak is here taken at 1810) the conformity is exact. Like other reflectors of long-term investment, patents respond to minor cycles, but on a lesser scale.

In this paper, as well as in his discussion of the workers' standard of life, Ashton alludes to the view that the fall in export relative to import prices after the Napoleonic Wars reflected a deterioration in the real economic position of Great Britain. Ashton notes that the relative decline in the export index results mainly from a disproportionate fall in cotton textile prices; and that this decline, in turn, resulted from a fall in the real costs of British textile manufacture. Ashton holds that the textile price decline was the proper result of improved technology; and to this factor one might add the disproportionate fall in the price of raw cotton imports, which carry a lesser weight in total imports than manufactured cotton textiles in total exports. Ashton's argument thus illuminates the fallacy of applying the concept of the net barter terms of trade to historical periods, where short-period conditions do not apply, as a measure of the gains or losses of trade.

Ashton's thoughtful exploration (in his second article) of the differing impact of money wage and cost of living changes on different groups within the British population may be regarded as a distinct refinement on the view presented here, which is principally based on overall statistics and general qualitative observations. His long-held position that the forces operating on real wages after the Napoleonic Wars were broadly making for improvements in welfare is supported by the evidence of this study.

A brief essay by Mr. Ward-Perkins also bears on the period covered here.[2] He examines the causes of the crisis of 1847, contrasting contemporary fears and judgements with a more modern perspective. He emphasizes the cushioning effects of continued railway building after the upper turning-point and relies rather heavily, in this phase of his argument, on the short-period course of Hoffmann's index of producers' goods output.[3] Readers may wish to compare his account with that presented in Chapter VI of the *History*, where somewhat greater emphasis is placed on the influence of the American cyclical pattern in determining the course of the British economy from 1845 to 1848 and where, generally speaking, a somewhat gloomier view is taken of Britain's economic position in those years.

Walther Hoffmann's volume on British industrial growth since 1700,

---

[1] For a definition of major and minor cycles see below, Vol. II, pp. 534–40.

[2] 'The Commercial Crisis of 1847', *Oxford Economic Papers*, New Series, ii, No. 1, Jan.

1950. [3] See below, Vol. I, p. 324 n. 5. The revised index available to Ward-Perkins eliminates the spurious decline in 1845 shown in the earlier figures.

published in 1940, recently became available to us.[1] It contains a revised version of the indexes of production that appeared in *Weltwirtschaftliches Archiv* in 1934 and which were used in our study. The changes in the index numbers are minor, and it is doubtful whether the measures of average cyclical behaviour of the series, presented below in Part II of Volume II, would be significantly altered by the substitution of Hoffmann's final figures. The more detailed information now at hand on the sources and components of the indexes has not changed our judgement of their reliability: they are more useful as measures of total production movements covering periods of at least a decade than of movements of relatively brief duration.

Similarly, Lord Beveridge has published a second, supplementary article on British business cycles[2] which did not become available until after the analysis of his work had been completed. Although Beveridge's revisions, notably in his iron series and construction sub-index, somewhat strengthen his results, they remain subject to the general reservations made in the Appendix to Chapter III, Volume II.

A statistical contribution of some importance has been Mr. Albert Imlah's recalculation of import values for the first half of the century, permitting new estimates for the net barter terms of trade as well as for the trade balance.[3] Although clearly an improvement on Schlote's figures, used here, it is not believed that their application would have required any fundamental change in the analysis presented in Volume II.[4]

In addition to these specialized contributions there has been Ashton's *The Industrial Revolution, 1760–1830*,[5] as well as Prof. J. U. Nef's essay, 'The Industrial Revolution Reconsidered'.[6] Ashton only touches lightly on the pattern of cyclical fluctuations and formal measurements of trend.[7] There is a sense, however, in which his deceptively thin volume, dealing with the response of individuals and institutions to the challenge and threat of a rising population, is pitched on a level of analysis more fundamental, if less technical, than that attempted here. In one of its aspects it might be regarded as an appropriate introduction to the present volumes. On quite different lines, Nef argues against the view that the Industrial Revolution constituted a fundamental break in the evolution of the Western World. His plea for a reordering of values in modern civilization, in the light of their pre-Industrial Revolution bases, places the issues of growth and fluctuation examined here in a setting even wider than Ashton's.

[1] *Wachstum und Wachstumsformen der englischen Industriewirtschaft von 1700 bis zur Gegenwart*, Jena, 1940.

[2] *Oxford Economic Papers*, Sept. 1940.

[3] 'Real Values in British Foreign Trade', *Journal of Economic History*, viii, No. 2, Nov. 1948; and 'The Terms of Trade of the United Kingdom', ibid., x, No. 2, Nov. 1950.

[4] See especially, Vol. II, below, pp. 797–9; also W. W. Rostow, 'The Historical Analysis of the Terms of Trade', *Economic History Review*, Second Series, vi, No. 1, 1951.

[5] London, 1948 (Home University Library).

[6] *Journal of Economic History*, iii, No. 1, May 1943.

[7] See especially, Chapter VI, 'The Course of Economic Change', pp. 142–61.

The changes in economic thought and techniques of analysis over the past decade which might be thought to bear on this study are at once more considerable than those in historiography and more difficult to identify with precision and confidence.

The reader will, of course, now have available an authoritative statement of the technique of statistical analysis developed by the National Bureau of Economic Research, as well as a preliminary statement of certain results covering later periods for Great Britain, the United States, and certain other countries.[1] Working with less full and refined statistical data, the authors of the present study have sought to answer in approximation, for their country and period, larger and more final questions than Burns and Mitchell, at the present stage of the work of the National Bureau. The National Bureau techniques are here used simply as one major instrument in an eclectic analysis. A comparison between Volume II of this study and the more austere interim statement of the National Bureau may be of interest, with respect to both method and, to some extent, conclusions.

In economic theory there have been, since 1941, major developments in at least three directions, impossible as well as inappropriate for us to annotate here. First, the analysis of short-period income fluctuations, crystallized in Keynes's *General Theory*, has been considerably refined both in conception and in empirical application. Second, the short-period theory of international trade has been transformed in harmony with income analysis, opening, again, new areas for empirical research. Third, economists have moved towards a more mature consideration of long-run, dynamic problems, responding in part to Keynes's reflections on secular stagnation, in part to the emerging character of post-war issues and of the inter-war years as seen in retrospect.

Recent developments in income analysis might well have influenced the character of Volume II, Part I, if it were now to be rewritten afresh; although the lack of continuous and reliable national income statistics will remain a grave limitation on speculation of this character over the first half of the nineteenth century. Nevertheless, with respect to the international as well as domestic aspects of the British economy over these years, recent developments in economic thought and method should suggest new possibilities of analysis not exploited in the present study; and, in any case, the partisans of one or another conception of the business cycle and its mechanisms will undoubtedly wish to rework from the evidence their counter-interpretations to Volume II, Part I, Chapters I–III.

But beyond that, could, for example, one establish from piecemeal evidence whether the proportion of the national income invested changed over these years? Did the changing character of the population and income distribution yield a changing average propensity to consume? And in an-

---

[1] Arthur F. Burns and Wesley C. Mitchell, *Measuring Business Cycles*, New York, 1946, and Wesley C. Mitchell, *What Happens during Business Cycles: A Progress Report*, New York, 1951.

other direction, could correlations of some meaning be established between changes in an index reflecting fluctuations in national income and in the volume of imports ? Could the rate of increase of the volume of exports be systematically related to rates of growth in income in the main British markets ?

It is our feeling that the greatest possibilities for further work lie in fitting these years into the concepts and sequence of long-run dynamic development, viewed for the world trading area, taken as a whole. The reader will note in Volume II, Part I, the extent to which the course of the British economy depended on population growth and movements overseas, the opening up of new areas, and international flows of capital. Even during the years of war Britain's evolution cannot be understood except as part of a distorted but real international economy, in which the flows of produce from the New World, re-exported somehow to ally and even enemy, were a central feature. Similarly the nature of the great expansions of the 1820's and 1830's are ultimately to be understood only in the light of an analysis which would include the full range of forces operating in Latin America and the United States. The less volatile development of the European economy is similarly relevant to the trend increase in British foreign trade in that direction. Even when the principal direction of British investment was internal, as in the railway boom of the 1840's, this phenomenon must be seen in the context of the disillusions resulting from the heavy export of capital of the previous decade. In terms of industries, the extraordinary development of the British cotton industry is, evidently, a consequence of events throughout the world trading area: in the southern United States, with respect to raw material supply ; in the northern United States and on the continent, with respect to competition or the lack of competition ; throughout British markets, with respect to the rate of growth of demand. This study has examined only the British roots for phenomena which are the consequence of complex inter-actions between the British and other economies. If the historian is to assist the economist in learning to treat the demand for capital as a dependent rather than an independent variable, a national approach to modern economic history must, to some important extent, be abandoned.

The analysis of growth rates and their determinants requires not only an approach in terms of the whole effective trading area, but it also demands a perspective covering very long periods of time, certainly, for most purposes, periods longer than the sixty years examined here. The slow-moving interacting economic, social, and political forces which determine changes in the average rate of growth, for an economy as a whole and for its particular sectors, are unlikely to be seen in proper perspective unless the analyst is prepared to study the curves of growth over a substantial course. Further, analysis of this type is likely to require the elaboration, in coming years, of conceptions, if possible quantitative conceptions, which would permit some ordering of the complex and ramified determinants of growth. It is the authors' hope that, despite its evident limitations as a growth analysis, this study may prove useful and even stimulating to those who may be concerned with the extension of knowledge in these directions.

. . . . .

The index for these volumes has been prepared by Dr. Morris Beck, to whom we wish to acknowledge our indebtedness. Throughout the preparation of these complex volumes for publication we have been sustained at every point by the Clarendon Press and by the Columbia University Council for Research in the Social Sciences which never lost interest in the venture it fostered more than fifteen years ago.

A. J. S.
W. W. R.

NEW YORK CITY
CAMBRIDGE, MASS.
  March 1952

CONTENTS

VOLUME I

PART I

A HISTORY OF BRITISH BUSINESS FLUCTUATIONS

PART II

BRITISH SHARE PRICES AND JOINT-STOCK ENTERPRISE

PART III

BRITISH COMMODITY PRICES

VOLUME II

BRITISH BUSINESS CYCLES AND TRENDS

CONTENTS

PART II

STATISTICAL MEASUREMENT AND ANALYSIS

LIST OF FIGURES

VOLUME I

VOLUME II

CORRIGENDA

Volume I, page 10, note 1, l. 2, *for* Part I of the *History read* Volume II

Volume I, page 219, note 1, l. 1, for *Statistical Illustrations of the British Empire*
read *Statistical Tables of the United Kingdom.*

LIST OF TABLES

VOLUME I

VOLUME II

GENERAL INTRODUCTION TO THE STUDY

A STUDY of the growth and fluctuations of an economy must of its nature deal overwhelmingly with quantitative data. In one aspect this study may be regarded as an attempt to organize and to interpret the statistical material relating to the economic position of Great Britain from 1790 to 1850.

1. Choice of Period. The period covered affords a fairly satisfactory interval for unified investigation. By its close Great Britain, clearly the dominant economic power of the world, was about to launch into a quarter-century of international railway construction and triumphant free trade. Recovery from the depression of 1845–8, the end of the Corn Laws and Navigation Acts, the opening up of California, and the self-conscious sense of progress reflected at the Crystal Palace in 1851 underline the usefulness of the mid-century as an historical turning-point. The symbolic quality of these events is strengthened by the inauguration, at about that time, of new trends in such strictly economic variables as the direction of investment, interest rates, commodity prices, and the trade balance.

The case for choosing 1790 as the initial date is less clear-cut. The whole period from the end of the American war in 1783 to the outbreak of the French wars a decade later is the proper setting for the opening of the study; and the first sections of the *History* (Vol. I, Part I) do attempt to indicate broadly the character of the economic system upon which the French wars had their impact. In those years many of the inventions which sometimes are taken to define the 'industrial revolution' were first put into operation; the United States re-emerged as a significant British market; and the distinctively late-eighteenth-century canal boom occurred during the general business expansion which reached its peak in 1792. The principal reason for choosing 1790 in preference to 1783 (the end of the American war) or 1788 (the cyclical trough preceding the peak in 1792) is, simply, that many statistical series first become available in 1790.

2. Relation to Economic History and Business Cycle Analysis. The study consists of the following five main sections:

Vol. I, Part I. *A History of British Business Fluctuations*
Vol. I, Part II. *British Share Prices and Joint-stock Enterprise*
Vol. I, Part III. *British Commodity Prices*
Vol. II, Part I. *British Business Cycles and Trends: General Analysis*
Vol. II, Part II. *British Business Cycles and Trends: Statistical Measurement and Analysis*

The study is historical in the sense that it seeks to throw new light on familiar events and to present new historical evidence. It is, however, designed, at least equally, to contribute to the analysis of the nature of business fluctuations and trends. A peculiar importance attaches to a study of fluctuations in Britain from 1790 to 1850; for, sometime within those years, it is generally assumed, the business cycle emerged in its more or less modern form. Implicit in the framework around which the *History* in Vol. I is constructed, and explicit in the theoretical and statistical investigations of Vol. II, is the assumption that theoretical concepts developed in modern business-cycle theory are relevant to an analysis of the course of events in our period; and, in general, that assumption seems to have been valid. To the economist, then, this study may, in substantial part, appear as an exercise in the application of theory, and, more specifically, of business-cycle theory.

Among current analysts of business cycles there is, on one point at least, a heartening unanimity. All are aiming, ultimately, to explain their nature in the broadest and most general theoretical terms. But they agree that any final theoretical formulations must be consistent with the fullest historical and statistical data; and that the techniques of the historian and the statistical analyst must be thoroughly exploited in the process of distilling the theoretical hypotheses. Among such investigators there have been, first, those who have begun with a consideration of existing general theories of the business cycle; e.g. Gottfried Haberler (*Prosperity and Depression*). Haberler has made it clear, however, that he regards this as a mere preliminary task. In the introduction to his study of business-cycle theories he indicates elaborate historical and theoretical investigations as the next step. On the other side there have been those who have begun, primarily, with a refined treatment of available statistical and historical evidence, notably, of course, Wesley Mitchell and the National Bureau of Economic Research. Such workers have employed theoretical concepts widely in fashioning their statistical tools, and in formulating their evidence in its preliminary forms. But they have modestly refrained from dealing with the most general hypotheses, whose formulation constitutes their final goal.[1]

Within the limits of the data we have attempted to employ and to combine both outlooks. A maximum amount of the empirical evidence has been collected and refined; and it has been ordered in the light of the most general theoretical concepts that seem to bear on it. This study cannot, of course, pretend to have answered finally any of the ultimate questions which concern either the 'theoretical' or the 'empirical' investigators of

---

[1] The focus of the technical procedure of the business-cycle analysts of the National Bureau lies in ascertaining average or typical cyclical behaviour. The reliability of an average measure is, of course, increased as the number of individual cases on which it is based is multiplied. This study, extending as it does over a period of sixty years lying beyond the range of the National Bureau's investigation, provides essential observations for either corroborating their conclusions as to cyclical behaviour, or for bringing to light structural changes in the nature of business cycles themselves. In employing the concepts developed by contemporary theorists, moreover, we have applied them to historical situations and economic data for which they were not specifically designed to account. Any broader validity to which these theories may lay claim must rest on some such independent application and testing.

business cycles. It covers a limited period in history, and a limited area; the data that it employs are, in many respects, inadequate; and, finally, the problems of the British economy in 1790–1850 differ to a considerable extent from those which have engaged the attention of recent analysts of business fluctuations. And yet, it is hoped, this study represents an essay in a type of collaboration between historical, theoretical, and statistical analysis towards which the science of economics now clearly tends.

3. Sources and Nature of Data. With the exception of the new materials which entered into the construction of the indexes presented in Parts II and III of Vol. I, and the original weekly Bank of England returns, the statistical data employed were, very largely, found scattered through the parliamentary papers. Only those who have worked with these sources can appreciate fully the difficulties involved in creating internally consistent series from the data presented there. They have, nevertheless, long been available, and our contribution has been essentially one of collection, organization, and evaluation. The series systematically collected[1] cover continuously the entire period or a substantial part of it. But, especially in the *History*, statistical evidence is occasionally used which is available only for short periods. Such materials were drawn from the *Annual Register*, from contemporary periodicals and pamphlets, and from a variety of secondary sources.

To some limited extent we have been able to use statistical series discovered or constructed by other students of the period. Shannon's figures for brick production and the income-tax returns recently published by Hope-Jones are examples of the former; while Schlote's corrected foreign trade series, Hoffmann's and Kondratieff's production indexes, and the wage and cost-of-living indexes of Bowley, E. B. Schumpeter, Tucker, and Wood illustrate the latter. It has usually been possible to find and to examine the component series from which existing indexes have been constructed. The nature of our analysis has been such that these individual series have been used as well as, and, to a large extent, in preference to the indexes. It will, however, be evident to readers that the latter serve, in many cases, a highly useful purpose.

As an historical effort, the search for statistical data has been gratifying with respect to the number of series, their accuracy, and their range. But by standards of current business-cycle analysis the gaps are serious, notably with respect to national income and its components, unemployment, wages, certain branches of production, and investment. The greater number of our series, moreover, are in annual form, which prevented fully sensitive measures of timing. These circumstances did not, however, preclude an attempt to present a fairly full view of the movements of the economic system. Qualitative evidence, especially on the character and volume of investment and the severity or mildness of unemployment, has

---

[1] Separately available; see above, p. viii, n. 1.

at times proved extraordinarily helpful in filling in an otherwise incomplete picture.

The descriptive chapters of Vol. I employ extensively parliamentary reports and non-statistical (as well as statistical) primary materials. Most of the materials themselves are familiar to historians of Britain in these years. The principal justification for this volume lies not so much in the presentation of new evidence as in the mobilization of existing materials to bear on the peculiar issues of business fluctuations and trends. It is significant that isolated passages from existing monographs and considerable sections of parliamentary reports which had hitherto been largely ignored were found relevant to the subject-matter of this investigation; while, constantly, familiar evidence emerged in a new light.

4. Analytic Procedures employed. Statistical data, such as form the groundwork of this study, are meaningless unless they are ordered in two directions: their significance in the context of the economic system from which they emerge must be established, and judgement must be made as to their meaning in terms of economic analysis. There is available, for example, a series representing the number of bricks produced charged annually with an excise duty. When the internal consistency and inclusiveness of that series had been established, judgement was required first as to the significance of brick production in Great Britain during the period under analysis, and second as to the significance of its movements as an indicator of construction and domestic investment generally. Adequately to trace its year-by-year course required a parallel examination of almost all other series relating to the economic position of the society, as well as a knowledge of events for which there is or can be no continuous quantitative evidence. But even a full history of brick production (in conjunction with a general history of the economy) would not yield precise evidence as to its typical behaviour in the course of business cycles or an exact measurement of its trends over various periods. That need was fulfilled by the application of the statistical procedures developed by the National Bureau of Economic Research.

In choosing a statistical procedure the National Bureau's method of cyclical analysis recommended itself chiefly for three reasons. First, the measures are computed in such a way that almost direct use of the original data is made and a minimum violence is done them. Except for the elimination of seasonal variations in monthly data, no attempt is made to rid the series of 'other component movements' in order to arrive at cyclical residuals. Second, by utilizing the method a precise, quantitative description of all the significant cyclical and trend characteristics of a series may be obtained. The computations, moreover, though elaborate, are mathematically simple, and the measures they yield easy to comprehend. Third, the method facilitates comparisons of the cyclical behaviour of a large number of time series by applying to them all a uniform set of reference-cycle dates. These dates mark the turning-points in general business activity. The reduction of the original data, expressed in diverse units, to relatives of their average values during the periods thus marked off puts all the materials into comparable form. The resulting measures, in conjunction with the year-by-year history and the general institutional background to the series, finally made possible generalization as to the nature of British business cycles and trends.

The successive stages involved in moving from the raw data to the general analysis in themselves reveal how the conventional statistical, historical, and theoretical procedures have been utilized. At least five such stages can be distinguished:

1. The transcription (from contemporary records such as parliamentary returns or other sources) of the original series, checked for internal consistency, and, where alternative sources were available, for accuracy.
2. The estimation of the importance to the economy of the variable represented by the series—the number of persons and the variables related to its fluctuation; in short, its institutional setting.
3. The placing of the movement of the series in its full historical context, in conjunction with other statistical and qualitative data, i.e. the history of its movement.
4. The application of a statistical procedure designed to measure the typical pattern of cyclical behaviour, and the relative consistency of that pattern as well as trend movements.
5. The final ordering of the series and other evidence in the light of the most reasonable theoretical propositions.

5. Organization and Contents of the Study. Each of the major units into which the study is divided is, in one sense, a separate piece of research, although closely related to the other units.

Part I of Vol. I is a general economic history of Great Britain from 1790 to 1850, written from the perspective of business fluctuations. Its form and scope are discussed at greater length in a special introduction. It attempts to bring together in a coherent narrative the most relevant statistical materials as well as a large body of qualitative evidence. It supplies, within the limits of the data, an historical explanation of the short-period movements of the economy, tracing, among other series, the course of the newly constructed commodity and security price indexes. Here the individual cycle or even the particular year is the analytic unit.

Part II of Vol. I presents new indexes of security prices, 1811–50. The raw data from which they have been constructed, drawn from Wetenhall's contemporary *Course of Exchange*, have long been available, but have hitherto remained unused. In Chapters I and II two general indexes are presented, including and excluding mining shares, and eight sub-indexes, comprising shares of canals, docks, waterworks, gas-light companies, mines, railways, insurance companies, and banks. Aside from their value as a separate historical contribution, such indexes were deemed a necessary tool, hitherto lacking, for the treatment of business fluctuations over this period. Their interpretation demanded, however, detailed knowledge of the institutional history of the special activities they reflect. The results of such particular institutional investigations are presented, in compressed summary form, in Chapter III.

Part III of Vol. I presents monthly price indexes developed from the abundant price data collected by Professor Silberling. At least three reasons justified the construction of new indexes, despite the existence of several alternatives : no existing index contains all the commodity prices available ; none is weighted ; and none has been calculated in monthly form. The new indexes comprise weighted groups of imported, domestic, and all commodity prices. The *Price* sections of the *History* (Part I of Vol. I) seek to place the movements of the new indexes in the context of the economy as a whole, and their principal movements are separately discussed in Chapter III, Vol. I, Part III.

Part I of Vol. II is partially dependent on the conclusions of Part II and was, in time, a subsequent construction. Part II contains an analysis and interpretation of the cyclical and trend behaviour of the greater part of the statistical data available. It deals, on a level of statistical generality, with materials which have already been regarded historically in the *History*. In the *History*, however, each movement is viewed, essentially, as unique. The statistical techniques of Vol. II, Part II, are designed to extract from the data measurements of average behaviour. A combination of these two perspectives, that of the historian and the statistician, is designed to set the stage for the generalized theoretical analysis of Part I of Vol. II. These latter chapters on cycles and trends represent conclusions at the highest level of generality attempted in this study.

6. Relation to Previous Work on the Period. In tracing the British economy from the early stages of the process of industrialization through the years of warfare with the Continent and the three decades of subsequent adjustment and advance, we are treating a period that has claimed the attention of numerous distinguished students of economic history. There have been, first of all, the historians of technical and institutional development, notably Cunningham, Clapham, Ashton, and their numerous followers, including the historians of particular regions and industries. Then there have been the continental historians of financial crises : Bouniatian, Juglar, Lescure, Tougan-Baranowsky, Wirth. Employing Tooke's great study of prices and some of the parliamentary papers, these analysts described, in terms of their own particular cycle theories, the sensational course of events in 1792–3, 1809–10, 1824–5, and the other periods of crisis and panic.

The events of the World War of 1914–18 and its heritage of economic problems stirred a different line of inquiry. By analogy, the financial history of the Napoleonic Wars and the subsequent period of monetary readjustment commanded the attention of both economists and historians. From that interest stems the work of Silberling, Hawtrey, Viner, and others. With the publication of Schumpeter's recent *Business Cycles* still another view of the years 1790–1850 has been propounded. Like his predecessors, Kondratieff and Spiethoff, Schumpeter sees in those years the unity of a single long-wave process.[1] Finally, there have been the chroniclers of the period, principally Smart, Thorp, and, above all, Thomas Tooke.

Among these works our most direct debt is to Tooke. For, while the others have suggested lines of inquiry and, occasionally, furnished useful data, the availability to us of more complete statistical evidence has largely placed them in the category of secondary sources. We have, wherever possible, gone afresh to the original data; and, in all but few instances (e.g. regional histories), the materials from which previous writers have worked were available in addition to considerable further evidence on those aspects of their problems that fell within the scope of our work.

Tooke's six volumes, however, constitute an enlightened and well-informed commentary on the principal economic events of our entire period. His central concern was, it is true, the short-run movement of individual commodity prices. But his peculiar theoretical bias, emphasizing, as it did, the supply and demand conditions in individual markets, led him to bring to bear on price movements forces stemming from foreign trade, long-term investment, and the whole monetary system. For purposes of this study it was fortunate that Tooke was deeply suspicious of a simplified quantity theory of money. He lacked, patently, detailed or continuous information about the state of individual industries; he was not primarily interested in the course of labour's position; even his most detailed data—on prices and the Bank of England—are sparse by today's standards. And yet we have in his work the commentary of a man who lived through a considerable number of the years about which he wrote, who played an active role in its economic processes, and who was passionately interested in the mechanism of its institutions. The debt we owe to his work is amply revealed in footnote references.

This study asks a set of questions quite different from those addressed to the data, for example, by Professor Clapham in the first volume of his *Economic History of Modern Britain*. His concern, and the traditional interest of most economic historians, has been the changing modes of economic organization, the rise and fall of particular institutions, the development of technology, the role of economic legislation. General economic histories have been, essentially, compendia of discrete monographs, even though unified by some general over-all conception. It has been of the essence of most modern economic history that it deals with the secular development of sections of the economic system or with isolated events.

[1] Strictly speaking, Schumpeter has dated a long-wave from 1786 to 1842, reckoning the British railway boom of the forties as part of the succeeding wave.

Our bias has been consistently that of the economist-historian rather than that of the descriptive-historian of institutions. The terms 'business cycles' and 'trends' are, in themselves, abstractions of the economist. They do not exist in the same simple sense that the cotton industry existed or the Corn Laws. They involve immediately a conception of the economic system as a whole, and draw into operation the full arsenal of the economist's vocabulary. Factors are judged more or less relevant as they seem to bear on general economic fluctuations. And although considerable attention is given to long-term movements (i.e. trends), even there the perspective is largely that which arises from the economist's short-period standards of relevance.

This study is in no sense a substitute for the kind of investigation typified by Clapham's work. It is rather a complement to such history. Although this study draws heavily on institutional material, there are, perforce, large gaps in the background. With the possible exception of the descriptive background to the new share index (Vol. I, Part II, Chapter III), only those aspects of institutional history immediately relevant to the story of business fluctuations and trends are introduced. Regional history, a detailed chronology of technical developments, secular changes in the mode of life, and the other familiar and important categories of economic history are subsidiary to the central interest of the study.

The work of this study has raised for its authors innumerable problems of method. These have ranged from matters of detailed statistical procedure to the broadest issues of historiography. Although some, at least, of these problems were new, the solutions reached or attempted are better seen in the text itself than in an abstract introduction. The field of economic history, as we now know it, had its inception in a rather barren controversy over method. The battle-cries of the mid-century German seminars, of Thorold Rogers, Ashley, and even Clapham in his younger days, remain merely a chapter in intellectual history. It is a lesson we have accepted, that their contributions to both the body of history and to historical method lie implicit in their work rather than in their *ex cathedra* utterances about the nature of economics and economic history.

The reader interested primarily in the scope of the study and its general results, rather than in the detailed research, should find useful the introductions and the summaries preceding the chapters in the *History*, Vol. I, Part I. Vol. II, Part I, containing our theoretical conclusions, is based, as explained above, on the statistical analysis of individual series, the results of which are given in Part II of that volume. This section will probably be of interest primarily to technical students who desire to follow in detail the steps in our statistical procedures. Those concerned only with the broad conclusions will be assisted by the first chapter in this portion of the text describing the method of analysis, and by the summaries of the relationships revealed by the statistical measures which precede the subsequent chapters.

PART I

A HISTORY OF BRITISH BUSINESS FLUCTUATIONS

INTRODUCTION

1. The Problem of Short-period Historical Analysis. Part I, as its title indicates, is essentially an historical construction. It attempts to describe continuously the movement of the British economy from 1790 to 1850, from the perspective of business fluctuations. There is, however, no set of accepted conventions for a narrative of this kind as there is for institutional or political history. Basic problems of definition and relevance have been, in this field, largely neglected.

A reason for this is, perhaps, the relatively late development of general theories which attempted to interrelate the action of all the principal economic variables as they bear on business fluctuations. Without some such theory, however broad or simple its terms, the problem of a continuous short-period narrative is intractable. One is faced with a mountain of trade reports, a morass of statistical evidence. One can write of the money and capital markets, of specific industries, of labour; one can speculate about price movements over long periods, and of the secular development of the economy as a whole. The distinguished list of monographs available on this period attest to the fruitfulness of such research. But in themselves, or even when placed side by side, they do not yield a continuous, interrelated narrative. For a significant grouping of the data, from this limited point of view, one must look to the theorist.

The business-cycle theorist would appear, at first sight, to be in no position to speak with authority to the historian. The violence of controversy occasionally seems to indicate, at best, a narrow range of agreement. But even the more severe professional disagreements, on closer examination, are seen to turn on matters of emphasis or formulation. Almost all theories deal with the same variables, and even with the same relations among them. A sufficient area of common ground exists to pose a series of questions which, when answered, even in first approximation, define the position of an economy at any moment and indicate the factors most relevant to its progress or regression. This *History* is constructed on a framework designed to conform to such a least common denominator of current business-cycle theory.

2. Organization of Part I. A cumulative narrative describes each cycle, tracing successively the impulses to expansion (or contraction) derived from foreign trade and new investment; the repercussions of such impulses on output, prices, and employment within the chief industrial areas; the effect of expansion (or contraction) on the demand for short-term funds; and the resultant position of labour. Within each of these sections the treatment of the material is as flexible as the data demand.

No attempt is made in the *History* to abstract a pure 'business cycle'. The recurrent characteristics of ebb and flow should emerge if, in fact, the *History* asks the appropriate questions. An orderly presentation of its contribution to business-cycle analysis belongs to Vol. II of this study, where the historical material is combined with more refined statistical measures.

The position of the sections devoted to *Foreign Trade* and *Investment* is based on the assumption that, for Great Britain, in the years covered, these factors constituted the mainsprings of business fluctuations. Their action, as one would expect, was not necessarily discrete: loans, for example, to the United States or to South America might result directly in an expansion of commodity exports to those areas. During the Napoleonic Wars government subsidies to various German principalities were paid, largely, in exports. There is as well some analytic justification for treating foreign trade before new investment. In each of the major booms, large-scale new floatations appeared relatively late in the upswing, after several years of previous expansion, based largely on increased commodity exports, financed on short-term credit.

Data on investment are, of course, neither continuous nor inclusive. The index of brick production (compiled by Shannon) and the official registry figures for new ships alone cover the period without a break. Nevertheless, one can identify in each boom the principal types of new investment and their relative importance. It is impossible to arrive at any figure for gross capital formation; but the magnitude and directions of new investment can be roughly charted. The growing role of railway construction can be clearly traced, for example, in 1824–5, 1835–6, 1844–7. The sections on *Investment* also contain a description and discussion of the movement of the security indexes compiled in the course of this study (Vol. I, Part II), as well as of Consols, Bank Stock, and India Stock.

In the sections on *Industry and Agriculture* attention is focused almost exclusively on coal, iron, wool, and cotton. These were, for purposes of business fluctuations, the most significant sections of British industry; and continuous evidence on them is most readily available. They include, moreover, the parts of the economy where technical advance was most rapid, and an account of them throws light on the whole question of the 'industrial revolution'. Strictly speaking these sections also contain considerable data on investment; i.e. the construction of new plant, the opening of new mines, the installation of new processes. Although full quantitative evidence is rarely, if ever, available on these developments, the major periods of large-scale industrial investment can be roughly defined.

The sections on *Finance*—charting the demand and supply of short-term funds and consequent rates—have been placed after the account of foreign trade, long-term investment, and industry. Despite the greater availability of information on the money market, and the dramatic quality of events there, its role in shaping the nature of business fluctuations was relatively secondary. At certain points in the cycle money-market conditions, and more particularly the elasticity of the supply of loanable funds, were of considerable positive importance: notably in the early stages of recovery, when easy money was virtually indispensable, and during the financial crises which climaxed the major booms. But the works of Tougan-Baranowsky, Wirth, Bouniatian, Juglar, and Lescure over-emphasize the role of the money market. Only when concerned with the history of financial crises, *per se*, do such data justify the share of attention they have traditionally received. And the *History* is in no sense merely an account of financial crises.

The position of *Labour*, in the *History*, is viewed in relation to the economy as a whole. An attempt is made to trace the movement of money and real wages, and to account for those elements in strikes, labour organization, and labour legislation that can be related significantly to business fluctuations. One asks, in short, what the state of the labour market was and to what extent it can be connected with the picture of the economy previously drawn. With no anti-humanitarian overtones, the *History* is concerned with labour primarily as a commodity.

The text contains two further sections: *Prices* and an *Introduction*. The sections devoted to *Prices* trace the movements of the new indexes constructed in the course of this study (Vol. I, Part III) and offer a limited and immediate explanation of their chief fluctuations. These sections are placed early in the sequence of each chapter for no very strong analytic reason, but rather for the convenience of those readers whose primary interest is in the movement of the newly constructed price indexes. These sections also serve to introduce immediately fluctuations in the yield of the domestic harvests since they determined short-period changes in the price of wheat, and heavily affected the domestic price index. The *History* as a whole might, in one sense, be considered as background to the price indexes, for the principal developments in foreign trade, in the long- and short-term capital markets, within industry, and in the markets for labour are all determinants of the prices of individual commodities, and thus of the indexes. A further treatment of individual prices appears in the sections on *Industry and Agriculture*. Where data are available, the parallel or divergent course of prices and production is traced in each industry.

The opening section of each chapter—the *Introduction*—is designed to facilitate the reading of what is, at best, a difficult narrative. Each chapter covers roughly a decade and is, in turn, broken into two parts, in most cases according to the cyclical pattern. There are, thus, two *Price* sections, two on *Foreign Trade*, &c., within each chapter. Each of the two parts of a chapter covers an interval of from four to eight years. The reader, then, is forced mentally to shuttle back and forth over these short periods, carrying over, from one section to the next, the relevant portions of the argument. The *Introduction*, in giving a condensed view of the entire decade, is meant to facilitate that process.

The obvious alternative to this formulation of the data would have been some form of annals. A year is, however, a less useful analytic unit than the cycle. Annals, further, would have precluded the use of statistical series, at least in the manner in which they have here been employed; and they would have inhibited the more expansive and co-ordinate discussion of developments which occurred within given markets over a period longer than one year. Either type of organization would have led to some discontinuities; but, on the whole, the device of sections, each covering roughly a business cycle, was deemed to involve the less serious objections. An appendix to Part I presents a brief note on annals covering the sixty-year span, as well as indexes of cyclical fluctuation.

Agriculture, for Britain during this period, was obviously of great importance. Even in 1850 Britain grew an overwhelming proportion of the wheat consumed at home. The fluctuation of the wheat price affected directly the income of the agricultural population and the real wages of the industrial population; and, perhaps more important for cyclical fluctuations, the changing quantity of foreign wheat required often significantly tightened or eased the money market. The position of agriculture is described along with industry in the section entitled *Industry and Agriculture*. The movement of the wheat price and an account of the changing supply of British wheat appear in the *Price* sections; for the newly constructed domestic index is heavily weighted with wheat. In its consequences for the money market the state of agriculture appears also in *Finance*; for retail prices, and thus real wages, in *Labour*.

As an historical effort the *History* is, of course, limited, at times severely limited, by the nature of the data available. *The Economist*, a chronicle in itself, covers only a few years within the period. Qualitative data must be gleaned from a variety of sources, differing in reliability, detail, and inclusiveness; evidence before the parliamentary commissions, the *Annual Register*, *Hansard*, and, after 1834, the reports of the Poor Law Commissioners; from Macpherson, Tooke, Porter, and the economic pamphleteers; from the industrial historians who wrote in the thirties and forties, when Britain first became self-conscious about her recent industrial development, notably Galloway, Baines, Scrivenor, and Bischoff; from the excellent conventional institutional studies which are, however, not focused primarily on the problem of business fluctuations, Clapham, Mantoux, Cole, Heaton, Ashton, Jenks, Hunt, Sweezy, among many others; and from the continental historians of British crises, who were useful, although the data they employed were, for the most part, available and were consequently approached afresh.

This brief cataloguing of types of non-statistical sources indicates the heterogeneous character of the data. The basic source material has by no means been exploited exhaustively. There are contemporary periodicals, company records, and large sections of the evidence and reports of the parliamentary commissions which contain unused materials that bear on business fluctuations. Despite its length and compression the *History* is, in a sense, journalistic. Only the major lines are sketched in: the economist's questions are answered only in first approximation, at best.

The statistics form the backbone of the *History*. Other data are either corroborative commentary on them or designed to permit statement on matters for which statistical evidence is not available: e.g. the tone of the capital market, the attitude of entrepreneurs towards wage movements, the repute of types of new issues, the state of industrial expectations, the organization of labour, institutional and political developments, and, at times, the relative severity of unemployment. Direct quotation has been used extensively in presenting the non-statistical evidence. There are certain obvious disadvantages in breaking the text in this manner; but the statements of contemporaries convey more strongly than any paraphrasing the temper of the markets described—the atmosphere within which the principal movements developed.

The statistics in the body of the text are presented with the understanding that the reader has already in mind the broad outlines of the cyclical pattern as briefly sketched in the *Introductions*. The extent of the conformity is roughly noted, and corroborated, where possible, by other evidence, often merely a chance phrase in the *Annual Register* or in Tooke. Serious divergences from the expected pattern are more assiduously pursued. For the more important movements of the series some sort of historical explanation can be found: e.g. a loss of bullion at the Bank can be traced to demands from particular directions; a sharp movement of an individual price, not shared by others, can be allocated to some peculiar conditions in its own markets. These are, of course, explanations of a highly restricted order, but they are a necessary condition to generalization about causal processes on a more abstract level.

In order to assist the reader in seizing quickly upon the main short-period quantitative movements in the economy, the text is interspersed with charts covering the time periods separately analysed. These charts vary somewhat in their content, depending on the issues of particular importance at different times and on the data available. The principal statistical series continuously available are, for the most part, presented. The charts are located as close to the relevant passages of the text as has proved technically possible. The *Introductions* contain a chart of the abstract business-cycle pattern whose construction is explained in an appendix to Part I of the *History*. The other statistical data are presented, as the accompanying ratio scales indicate, so as to reveal percentage rather than absolute changes in the figures.

The *History* is, then, an analysis of material relating to the more important markets in the economy. Its construction is based on this assumption: that if one can establish, even crudely, the amount and direction of exports and of new investment, the trade balance, the condition of the banking system and the principal rates of interest, the movement, in the major industries, of output, employment, and prices, and the money and real wages of labour, one has assembled the materials for a coherent interconnected account of a moving economic system. The whole, in this case, should be something more than the sum of its parts.

Part I concludes with an appendix, 'The Business-Cycle Pattern in Great Britain, 1790–1850'. This section is designed to form a link between the history of Vol. I and the statistical and theoretical analyses of Vol. II. The dating—annual and monthly—of cyclical peaks and troughs is given and doubtful cases are discussed. The establishing of such dates is a necessary preliminary to the statistical analyses of Vol. II. Two business-cycle indexes are then presented, which convey a statistical picture of the amplitude and rate of movement between turning-points. Finally, a number of disagreements between Thorp's widely used *Annals* and our cyclical dating are examined. In a sense this whole appendix constitutes a distillation of all our data as it bears on the historical pattern of general business fluctuations.

Chapter I

1790–1801[1]

INTRODUCTION

THE first chapter of the *History* has been somewhat arbitrarily ended in 1801. Although it can be marked off as a minor cyclical low-point, that year was distinguished by no major crisis. It neither ended nor began a distinctive set of trends. Its justification as a point of demarcation is rather that it permits a continuous analysis of periods on either side of the Act of Suspension of 1797. The coming of the Peace of Amiens in the autumn of 1801 and, quite unconnected with it, a temporary respite from chronically bad harvests also justify a break at that time.

Part I of the chapter covers the period 1790–3. The years before the outbreak of the Revolutionary wars afford a view of the British economy in the latter years of the eighteenth century, under peace-time conditions. The peculiar consequences of the war can be better judged by comparison with more normal years. But more particularly the crisis of early 1793 marks the end of a cyclical upswing. The usual consequences of a period of credit expansion in its latter stages may be traced back into 1792. There would probably have been a 'crisis of 1793' even if war had not broken out.

The year 1790, when the newly constructed price indexes begin, comes after several years of increasing trade, both at home and abroad. The boom was associated by contemporaries with the end of the American Wars; and there was no clearly defined break in the upward movement between 1783 and 1792 although several series (wool production, brick production, bankruptcies) exhibit low points in 1788. There is, in any case, a marked acceleration after 1788, with increasing exports from Britain to the United States the outstanding feature of the boom. A period of easy money at the Bank and the rapid growth of new country banks made short-term capital cheap and easily available in Britain. Stimulated by increased output and incomes, afforded by rapidly expanding export markets, a variety of new internal developments were undertaken, especially canals, turnpikes, and land inclosures. But one can also trace, in 1790–3, the early application of new industrial methods in textiles, mining, iron manufacture, and other industries.

By 1792 the credit facilities of Britain appeared to be under strain. An increasingly large burden was being thrown upon the Bank of England.

[1] Cyclical pattern:

	Trough	Peak
Circa	1788	1792 (Sept.)
	1794 (June)	1796 (May)
	1797 (Sept.)	1800 (Sept.)
	1801 (Oct.)	

Market interest rates rose, bankruptcies began to increase. The outbreak of war under these conditions precipitated sudden panic, with both banks and individuals striving to make all available assets as liquid as possible. A government offer to support the credit structure, however, immediately restored confidence. By the end of 1793 the banking system had recovered and industry was slowly reviving, partly under the impact of the large loan-financed expenditure that the government was already undertaking, but more immediately through a resumption of the increase in exports. Excepting agriculture, new domestic investment did not appear again on a large scale until about 1798.

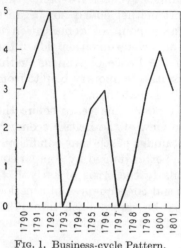

FIG. 1. Business-cycle Pattern, 1790–1801

The prices of imported produce and non-agricultural domestic commodities show the increase to be expected in the latter stages of a boom. The British harvests dominate the domestic price index. An abundant crop in 1791, after two bad years, produces a fall in the index until about the middle of 1792. Mediocre harvests in 1792 and 1793 cause a rise thereafter. But in general the position of labour was improving, with a sharp rise in its calculated real wage, in 1791–2.

The first nine years of the war present a complex problem to the historian. An unbalanced budget, heavy expenditure abroad, and bad harvests are combined with a previously unparalleled boom in foreign trade, and, after 1797, a rapid continuation of internal industrial development. From the perspective of trade fluctuations a feature of the period is the failure of any one of the four crises that occurred within it (1793, 1797, 1799, 1801) to induce a prolonged deflation. There are (except in 1793 and 1797) virtually no complaints of unemployment. In part this may be attributed to the relatively small amount of employment dependent on long-term capital investment in a still predominantly agricultural and commercial economy; for, although the textile industries were subject to sharp fluctuation, especially in the export branches of the trade, a brief period of decline was sufficient to permit a depletion of stocks and a resumption of increase. But in part the continued excess of government expenditure over revenue must be held responsible for the failure of any of these crises to introduce an extended general contraction. This view gains force when it is realized that not only Britain but the greater part of the Continent of Europe was under the same sort of stimulus. A considerable part of Britain's war-time expenditure took the form of capital export, and there were as well autonomous inflationary movements in various of the continental states. It is thus not surprising that the principal impulses to expansion rose from the side of the export markets.

To the historian of labour the early years of the war are notable for the widespread unrest of the British working classes. The coincidence of bad harvests with the upward pressure on prices of a war-time boom made for a drastic reduction of real wages, especially in 1795–6 and 1799–1800. The State acted at once to relieve the cause of the unrest and to repress its manifestations. The Speenhamland system was introduced in 1795, the Combination Acts were passed in 1799–1800.

So much attention has been given the suspension of specie payments in 1797 that it is worth pointing out that all the consequences of an un-balanced budget, and especially the tendency for prices to rise, were evident as strongly under the gold as under the paper standard. There is no question but that the removal of the restraint gave the Bank and the government greater freedom of action than they would otherwise have enjoyed. The fact that the exchanges could be ignored proved of great importance, especially in the period from about 1808 to 1815. But until 1801 the chief result of suspension seems to have been in removing the fear that it might happen. Before 1797 the Bank had strictly limited its commercial advances, at times to the point of arbitrary rationing. With hoarding at an end, and the support of the banking community given its notes, the Bank of England, while maintaining a fairly high level of reserves, was able to expand its loans. And this occurred, until 1801 at least, without a serious weakening of the foreign exchanges.

The cyclical pattern that can be traced in these years includes a clearly marked cycle from 1793 to 1797, with a peak in 1796. In 1798 recovery was again under way. The ensuing cycle was marked by larger increases in domestic investment than its predecessor. There was a mild set-back in 1799 due to a brief crisis in the Hamburg trade, and again in 1801. The latter recession can be discerned in many of the annual series, and is a more general movement than that of 1799. Perhaps the most accurate view is of a cycle from 1797 to 1801, with a peak in 1800. The return of peace, however, in the latter months of 1801 prevented the decline from proceeding to any great lengths. The year 1802 was clearly prosperous; 1803 a year of depression, as war was resumed.

The central interest of most economic historians of this period has been the consequences of the war and war-time finance on the British economy. From the perspective of the years after 1918, the movement of the ex-changes, the abandonment of the gold standard in 1797, and the heavy increase in the government debt have commanded, by analogy, the major concern of recent investigators. Their bias has been supported by the fact that the financial problems attracted, in their own day, an overwhelming share of attention. The government, in going off and then returning to a gold standard, was raising dramatically the whole question of the relation of money to prices and output. The speculation of contemporaries is a fruitful literature. But here the procedure will be first to outline the movements of production and commerce, blocking in only the more essential elements in the financial framework within which they developed; and then to turn to the operation of the monetary mechanism.

PART I: 1790–3[1]

1. Prices. From 1790 to 1792 the domestic price index falls, while the index of imported commodities rises sharply. This is to be attributed essentially to the fact that the prices of foodstuffs were declining, while a world-wide boom was raising the prices of those commodities dependent rather on the state of commerce than on the weather. The fall in the price of wheat from 1790 to 1792, however, is accentuated by the fact that both 1789 and 1790 were years of deficient harvests and high grain prices.[2] In the latter months of 1790 wheat imports were permitted on a large scale and the price declined. It continued to fall through 1791, a year 'of great abundance',[3] until May 1792. The price of wheat was 56·0 in May 1790, 37·0 two years later (shillings per quarter). The harvests of neither 1792 nor 1793 were particularly good, and agricultural prices rose.[4] The annual average domestic price index was, in 1793, above the figure for 1790 (87·1 and 91·6, respectively), although the average wheat price was not (50·5 and 47·7, respectively). This is accounted for by the rise, from 1790 to 1793, of domestic prices other than wheat, due primarily to widespread internal prosperity.

Import prices, from 1790 to 1792, rose in two waves, from February to November 1790, and from August 1791 to February 1792. The persistence of the general upward stimulus, however, is indicated in the annual averages of the index: 1790, 87·5; 1791, 94·6; 1792, 99·0. The markets in which import prices were determined were large and well organized, and subject to speculative fluctuation. Irregularity in the rise of such prices in the course of expansion was to be expected. With the outbreak of war, despite the onset of general depression, import prices again rose sharply (peak, April 1793), the average figure for 1793 being 100·6. Expectations engendered by the outbreak of war and by a rise in freight and insurance rates seem to have been responsible for this brief speculative movement, which was not sustained.[5] From April 1793 the index declines to June 1794.

---

[1] A list of sources cited is given at the end of Part I of the *History*. Footnote references are, therefore, confined to author or short-title and page, after initial reference has been made.

[2] Tooke, *A History of Prices*, i. 80–81.

[3] Ibid., p. 81.

[4] The fall and the rise in the price of wheat produced its usual repercussions. The low price of 1791 called forth 'complaint on the part of the landed interest, and was the occasion of a fresh corn bill' (idem). By the end of 1792 some of the citizenry of Leicester had rioted, 'under the pretext of being aggrieved by the high price of provisions' (*Annual Register*, Chronicle, 1792, p. 19). The Corn Law of 1791 provided for corn imports only when the domestic price was 50s. or over. In 1794 the price of wheat rose above 50s., and remained above it until long after the end of the wars. In 1804 the import limit was raised to 65s.

[5] Tooke, i. 177–9.

Many non-agricultural domestic prices also reflect the cyclical pattern, as indicated in the following tabulation:

	Jan. 1790	Jan. 1791	Jan. 1792	Peak 1792–3
Copper (pence per lb.)	9·2	9·2	9·8	(Apr.–Dec. 1793) 11·5
Hides (pence per lb.)	12·5	15·0	16·8	(Jan. 1792) 16·8
Iron bars (£ per ton)	15·1	15·9	16·1	(Jan.–Dec. 1793) 16·9
Lead pigs (£ per ton)	19·5	18·8	21·2	(Jan.–Sept. 1792) 21·2
Leather butts (pence per lb.) . .	13·8	15·8	18·5	(Nov.–Dec. 1792) 20·0
Rape oil (£ per ton)	35·5	28·9	31·5	(Feb.–Mar. 1793) 43·0
Hard soap (shillings per cwt.) . .	55·0	54·0	60·0	(Jan. 1792) 60·0
Tin (shillings per cwt.)	76·0	76·0	86·0	(June 1793) 105·0

These prices, while they share the general upward trend, exhibit wide divergences in the extent of their movement, the timing of the upper turning-point, and their response to the outbreak of war.

2. Foreign Trade. The boom of which the sequence of 1790–3 is a part began roughly in 1788, although the entire decade of peace, from 1784 onward, was one of increasing prosperity. The stage had been set by a period of easy money as the Bank of England replenished its reserve, which had fallen dangerously low by the end of the American wars: 'There was a steady and uninterrupted influx of gold into its coffers during the five following years (1784–9).'[1] In 1789 the bullion held at the Bank amounted to £8·6 million. Discounts at the Bank, however, declined from 1785 to 1789. With market rates falling, borrowers preferred to avoid the inflexible 5 per cent. minimum at the Bank. It was the country banks that bore the brunt of credit expansion until its final stage.

It seems probable that the primary stimulus to recovery came from the expansion of foreign trade. The official values (i.e., volume indexes) of imports and exports (including re-exports) moved as follows:[2]

(In £ millions)

	Volume of total imports[a]	Volume of total exports		Volume of total imports[a]	Volume of total exports
1787 .	. 15·5	8·5	1791 .	. 17·1	11·9
1788 .	. 15·7	8·8	1792 .	. 16·9	13·2
1789 .	. 15·3	10·0	1793 .	. 16·9	10·8
1790 .	. 16·5	10·5			

[1] Tooke, i. 193–4.
[2] Werner Schlote, *Entwicklung und Struk-turwandlungen des englischen Aussenhandels von 1700 bis zur Gegenwart*, p. 133.
[a] For footnote see p. 12.

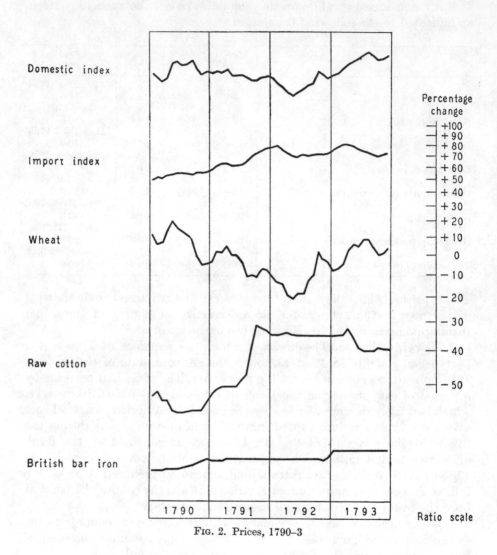

FIG. 2. Prices, 1790–3

[*Footnote to p. 11*]

  a The import figures were affected by fluctuations in the quantity of grain imports, which moved irregularly. (The figures given from 1788 through 1791 represent total imports into Great Britain including imports from Ireland; from 1792 the series excludes imports from Ireland.) Wheat and flour imports (in 1,000 quarters): 148·7 (1788), 112·6 (1789), 222·6 (1790), 469·0 (1791), 21·1 (1792), 475·8 (1793). The fall in total imports in 1789 and 1792, as well as the maintenance of their high level in 1793, the year of crisis, are possibly to be explained by reference to these figures.

The United States, to Britain's surprise and gratification, continued as a major market despite their new political status. Both in relative increase and in absolute quantity the export figures to the United States are the outstanding feature of British foreign trade during these years:[1]

Official Value of Total Exports from England

(In £ millions)

	U.S.A.	British W. Indies	Asia	Germany	Holland	France
1788 . . .	1·7	1·4	1·4	1·4	1·1	1·2
1789 . . .	2·3	1·4	2·0	1·6	1·5	1·3
1790 . . .	3·3	1·6	2·4	1·7	1·2	0·8
1791 . . .	4·0	2·2	2·3	1·8	1·2	1·1
1792 . . .	4·1	2·4	2·4	2·1	1·3	1·2
1793 . . .	3·3	2·2	2·7	2·4	1·5	0·2

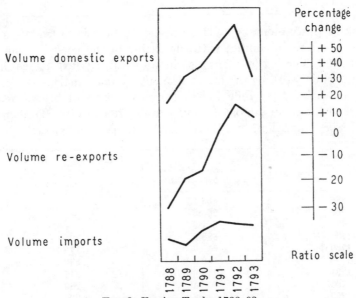

Fig. 3. Foreign Trade, 1788–93

The repercussions of the outbreak of revolution in 1789 and of war, early in 1793, are evident in the figures for France. The important role of the United States, the West Indies, and the Asiatic markets is also clear. On the Continent, the increase in German purchases was alone on a comparable scale. Already Hamburg was beginning to feel the influx of wealthy refugees from revolution. The generally stagnant figures for Holland indicate the results of their departure from Amsterdam.

[1] D. Macpherson, *Annals of Commerce*, vol. iv, annual tables. All future references to Macpherson in the text are to vol. iv.

3. Investment. The boom within Britain, following a pattern which was to become familiar throughout the nineteenth century, seems to have got under way somewhat later, possibly as a result of the increase in confidence and incomes created by activity in the export markets. Information as to new investment is sparse. It is clear, nevertheless, that the building of canals and of turnpikes and the inclosing of farm land constituted major forms of enterprise at home.[1]

	Bills of inclosure, No.	Navigation and canal bills		Turnpike bills, No.
		No.	Sums authorized	
			£	
1788 . .	35	3	115,000	—
1789 . .	33	3	133,500	1
1790 . .	25	8	377,400	3
1791 . .	40	10	803,700	4
1792 . .	40	9	1,063,600	4
1793 . .	60	26	3,159,700	6

The peak in parliamentary bills representing new investment in 1793 is not to be taken as in conflict with the dating of the peak in general prosperity in 1792. The lag (evident also in later railway floatations) indicates mainly the slow working of the parliamentary machinery.

Building activity, as reflected in the production of bricks, responded similarly, with output almost doubling from 1785 to 1792. Timber imports show a lesser expansion, but share clearly the peak in 1792 :

	Production of bricks (in millions of bricks)	Quantity of fir timber imports (in 1,000 loads of 50 cu. ft.)
1785 . .	463·1	—
1786 . .	565·6	—
1787 . .	651·9	—
1788 . .	629·2	205
1789 . .	650·7	179
1790 . .	730·5	230
1791 . .	778·9	217
1792 . .	858·4	289
1793 . .	848·2	200

[1] On canals, see below Part II. The figures here are from Appendix G, Parliamentary Papers, 1819. It is significant that the Committee of 1797 pointed to canals, turnpikes, and inclosures as measures of 'expensive enterprise of a private nature' (*A.R.*, Chr., 1797, p. 99: *Annual Register* henceforth referred to in this manner). The boom produced as well two attempts to develop primitive areas. These are indicative merely of the pervasion of an enterprising spirit rather than of a significant trend. The larger was the Sierra Leone Company whose announced purpose was 'introducing cultivation and fair commerce among the natives of Africa'. Its capital stock amounted to £242,899. An unsuccessful attempt on a much smaller scale was made to establish a colony of settlers on Bulama, an island, also in West Africa. By the end of 1793 the original 200 settlers had 'dwindled away' and the colony was abandoned. (Macpherson, p. 239.)

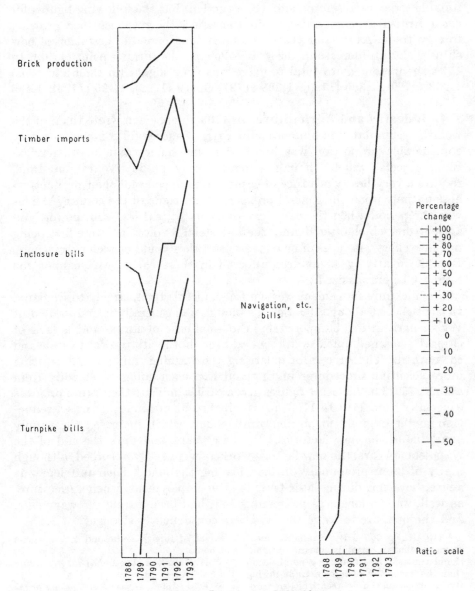

FIG. 4. Investment, 1788-93

The protracted rise in foreign trade in these years led to a considerable increase in the tonnage of British shipping. There is, for this period, no reliable series representing ship construction, but the following figures for total British tonnage indicate, in their rise, the response to a growing foreign trade. As in later years, the fairly long period of gestation of new ships yields an increase in the year following the turning-point (1793). In 1794 the increment to total tonnage was very slight: (in thousand tons) 1,293 (1789), 1,356 (1790), 1,398 (1791), 1,419 (1792), 1,436 (1793), 1,438 (1794).

4. Industry and Agriculture. In 1793 Macpherson wrote that 'of the wealth accumulated in nine peaceful years of successful commerce, a very considerable proportion was invested in machinery and inland naviga- tion; objects, which, though generally very productive in due time, require a very heavy advance of capital, and depend for their productive- ness entirely upon the general prosperity and trade of the country'.[1] This was the period when the new developments in textiles, iron, power, and agriculture, which often define 'the industrial revolution', were first being put into effect. As types of new investment they could be seen everywhere. But the relatively slight area affected in these early years cannot too strongly be emphasized.

The inclosure movement was confined, at this time, largely to England. In Scotland, at about 1790, Small's plough was generally introduced.[2] But Welsh agriculture, hampered by the smallness of farms and a lack of capital, remained much as it long had been, both with respect to scale and to method.[3] The process of enlarging the farming unit and introducing more scientific procedures in England had been going on steadily from about 1760. The inclosure figures given earlier indicate their rapid progress especially from 1791 to 1793. A principal result for industry was a reduc- tion in the demand for agricultural labour, which increased the supply available in the new factories.[4] In these years, and until the end of the Napoleonic Wars, the new factory workers were easily absorbed, although many of them profoundly disliked leaving the land.[5] Their problem was acute, however, during later periods of unemployment, when agriculture, as well, was no longer as prosperous as it had been during the war years, and the pressure to leave the land was consequently stronger.

[1] Op. cit., pp. 265–6. By 'commerce' Mac- pherson almost certainly meant interna- tional trade. It is a familiar generalization that the expansion of foreign trade during the latter part of the eighteenth century pro- vided both the incentive and the capital for increases in the scale of British industry and improvements in technique: the 'commer- cial revolution' is generally held to have preceded and fostered 'the industrial revolu- tion'. This relationship (if it holds as a short- period phenomenon) would also account for the relative lag, noted earlier, between the revival of foreign trade and of enterprise at home.

[2] H. Hamilton, *The Industrial Revolution in Scotland*, p. 53.

[3] E. J. Jones, *Some Contributions to the Economic History of Wales*, p. 16

[4] P. Mantoux, *The Industrial Revolution in the Eighteenth Century*, pp. 186–90. This appears as a relatively lesser increase in the population of agricultural than industrial areas through these years.

[5] Ibid., pp. 187–8.

Although behind in agriculture, Scotland fully shared the industrial advance which began in 1784 :[1]

For ten years after the Treaty of Versailles economic progress was rapid and uninterrupted. Heavy capital expenditure was incurred in the erection of cotton-mills, agricultural improvements, and in finishing the Forth and Clyde and Monkland Canals, which were opened for traffic in 1790.

Machine spinning in the linen industry was introduced in 1787, but did not replace the hand spinners to an appreciable extent until after the turn of the century. In cotton the expansion is symbolized by the opening of David Dale's New Lanark Mills in 1786. There, in 1790, water power was applied to the mule. The extent of the textile industry is roughly indicated by the existence of more than 223,000 spinners and weavers in Scotland in 1790.

Even in Wales, where the textile industry never took root, large cotton-mills were set up in Holywell in 1783 and 1785, and in Mold during 1792. But the movement was not general.[2] In South Wales a lone mill was established in 1786.[3] It survived but sixteen years. In England proper the continued rapid growth of the north country was the major development. In 1788, of a total of 126 spinning-mills, 47 were in Lancashire, 17 in Derbyshire, 11 in Yorkshire. The remaining 51 were scattered among 25 other counties. Not until 1790, when the northern mills had already established their supremacy, did Devonshire and the other counties of the south and west attempt to produce with the new methods.[4] The relatively early stage of steam power is illustrated by the fact that in the decade 1786–95 only 47 engines were installed in cotton-mills.[5] General figures for cotton production are not available. An index of growth, however, are the statistics of cotton imports. For the five years ending 5 January 1787 the annual average import was 16·0 million pounds; for a similar period ending 5 January 1792, 28·9 million pounds.[6] The quantity of raw cotton imports, the official value of cotton goods exports, and the price of raw cotton moved as follows :[7]

	Quantity of raw cotton imports (in million lb.)	Volume of exports of cotton manufactures (in £ millions)	Price of raw cotton including duty (pence per lb.)
1788 .	20	1·3	..
1789 .	33	1·2	..
1790 .	31	1·7	18·5
1791 .	29	1·9	22·9
1792 .	35	2·0	27·1
1793 .	19	1·7	26·1

[1] Hamilton, p. 270.
[2] A. H. Dodd, *The Industrial Revolution in North Wales*, p. 291.
[3] D. J. Davies, *The Economic History of South Wales Prior to 1800*, pp. 111–14.
[4] Mantoux, p. 270.

[5] J. Lord, *Capital and Steam Power*, p. 168. Of these, 13 were in Lancashire, 12 in Nottinghamshire, 5 in Yorkshire.
[6] Macpherson, p. 470.
[7] E. Baines, *History of the Cotton Manufacture*, pp. 347–9.

For the woollen industry there exist the figures from the fulling-mills of the rapidly expanding district of the West Riding :[1]

Woollen Broad and Narrow Cloth Milled in the West Riding

(In million yards)

	Broad	Narrow
1788	4·2	4·2
1789	4·7	4·4
1790	5·2	4·6
1791	5·8	4·8
1792	6·8	5·5
1793	6·1	4·8

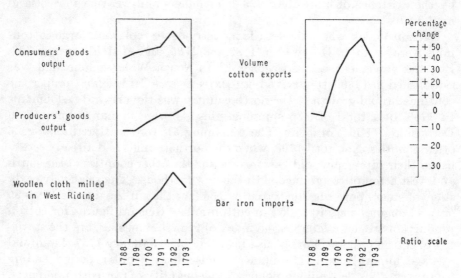

Fig. 5. Industry and Agriculture, 1788–93

These show a steady expansion to 1792, a sharp decline in the following year. The export of woollens, however, reached a peak in 1791; and, in this decade, woollens continued to outrank cottons as Britain's principal export (official values, in £ millions) : 4·4 (1790), 4·6 (1791), 4·0 (1792), 3·2 (1793).

The relation of the canal boom to the development of the heavy industries is well illustrated in Scotland. The Monkland Canal (1790) immediately made profitable the opening of the coalfields in Coatsbridge and Airdrie. These new supplies aided in the expansion of the iron trade.[2] The Clyde Works were lighted in 1787, and in the following year the eight

---

[1] Macpherson, p. 525.

[2] Hamilton, pp. 194–7, describes the fears of the Glasgow coal dealers that the supplies made available by the canal would lower the price of coal. A combine in 1790 was broken in 1793 by the appearance of the output of the new mines (p. 196). Cyclical depression also probably helped to weaken the combine at that time.

furnaces in blast produced 7,000 tons. By 1793 the Carron and Clyde Works together, it was said, consumed as much coal as all the inhabitants of Edinburgh.[1] The great works of John Wilkinson dominated the iron industry of Wales, producing not only pig-iron but armaments, pipes, plates, and other manufactures.[2] Welsh iron was widely used in England and was famous on the Continent.[3] The development in Wales of copper-mines and slate-quarries was on a scale sufficient to warrant the enlarging of the harbour of Port Penrhyn in 1790. In England the pig-iron industry was producing 68,000 tons from 85 furnaces in 1788; in 1796, 126,000 tons from 121 furnaces.[4] The coming of peace in 1783 had 'found the industry with a productive capacity in excess of demand at remunerative prices'.[5] The depression continued at least until 1786. But peace-time uses for iron were increasing, and the industry prospered until the crisis of 1793, with the construction of iron bridges a major stimulus to production.[6]

Although the export markets were of lesser relative importance to the iron than to the textile industries, they reveal a possible cyclical influence on iron output (official values, in £ millions): 0·9 (1790), 1·1 (1791), 1·3 (1792), 1·0 (1793). Bar-iron imports, at this point of considerable significance as a cyclical indicator for the industry, exhibit a typical lag at the peak, declining only in 1794[7] (in thousand tons): 49·2 (1790), 57·2 (1791), 57·7 (1792), 59·0 (1793), 42·5 (1794).

These scattered examples are not meant to be comprehensive. They are designed at best to give some general impression of the stage of Britain's industrial development in the pre-war years, and of the types of advance which were then being effected. The crisis of 1793 may be said to have ended an early and, in some cases, the first phase of the actual application of new industrial techniques to manufacture.

Although Hoffmann's indexes of production are, for this period, by no means inclusive, they move in a way that at least corroborates the previous evidence:

[1] Ibid., p. 164.

[2] Dodd, pp. 131–52.

[3] Ibid., pp. 136 and 139. Wilkinson, both in the American and the French wars, was widely suspected of selling munitions to both sides. Less sinister is the following note from Macpherson, p. 176 (1788): 'It is worthy of observation that orders were sent from Paris to Mr. Wilkinson, a gentleman of great eminence in the iron manufacture, for iron pipes to the extent of no less than *forty miles*, to be used in supplying that capital with water.'

[4] Mantoux, p. 313.

[5] T. S. Ashton, *Iron and Steel in the Industrial Revolution*, p. 139. H. Scrivenor, *A Comprehensive History of the Iron Trade*, p. 87, refers to 'a new era in the history of the manufacture of iron' beginning in 1788 or 1790. For this he holds 'the new double power engine of Mr. Watt' responsible.

[6] Ashton, pp. 140–2. Iron stoves and pipes were also being used increasingly, while Wilkinson produced a cast-iron barge as well as his more famous coffin. Ashton (pp. 198–9) gives figures for the growth of Coalbrookdale, the Darbys' ironworks in Shropshire, which supplement other evidence of the industry's expansion. The parish of Madeley, which included Coalbrookdale and the ironworks, contained:

		Jan. 1782	*Mar. 1793*
Houses	. .	440	754
Families	. .	560	851
Persons	. .	2,690	3,677

[7] Scrivenor, p. 358.

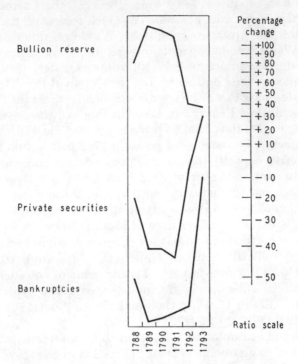

FIG. 6. Finance, 1788–93

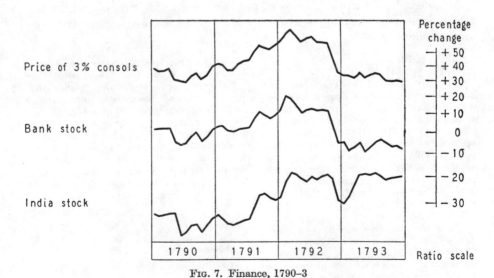

FIG. 7. Finance, 1790–3

	Hoffmann's index of producers' goods production	Hoffmann's index of consumers' goods production	Hoffmann's index of total production
1788 . .	1·9	6·3	3·9
1789 . .	1·9	6·8	4·1
1790 . .	2·0	6·9	4·2
1791 . .	2·1	7·1	4·4
1792 . .	2·1	7·8	4·7
1793 . .	2·2	7·1	4·4

The lag of producers' goods output, it will be found, is a typical phenomenon of the series, probably traceable, in this instance, to the increase in shipbuilding and iron-ore imports in 1793.

5. Finance. Bank of England statistics indicate the monetary pressures that accompanied the increases in production, foreign trade, and prices :[1]

(In £ millions)

	Bullion	Circulation	Private securities
30 Aug. 1788 . .	6·9	10·0	2·7
31 Aug. 1789 . .	8·6	11·1	2·0
31 Aug. 1790 . .	8·4	11·4	2·0
31 Aug. 1791 . .	8·1	11·7	1·9
31 Aug. 1792 . .	5·4	11·0	3·2
31 Aug. 1793 . .	5·3	10·9	4·4

The fall in the bullion held at the Bank may be taken to indicate the usual pressures of prosperity on the reserve. In 1792 there was some gold export, and a weakening in the Hamburg exchange.[2] The rise in private securities in 1792–3 indicates that market rates were rising and borrowers were being forced, at last, to come to the Bank.[3] The fall in the note issue from 1791 to 1793 was associated with the withdrawal of bullion from the Bank.[4]

The financial requirements of these years were met, until their latter stage, outside the Bank and, for the most part, by a rapid extension of

[1] Tooke, ii. 380 (from Appendix, No. 5 of the Report on the Bank Charter).

[2] Ibid. i. 195–6.

[3] Ibid., p. 194, describes the relation between borrowing at the Bank and the tightness of the market in a reference to the period between 1784 and 1789: 'This influx of bullion, and the consequent increase of Bank issues, had the natural effect, as it was in a period of confidence, of reducing the rate of interest; and the fall in the market rate of interest, while the Bank did not lower its rate of discount, enabled the country banks to extend their issues in advances and discounts, which, if the current market rate of interest had been higher, would have been in part, at least, applied for at the Bank.' With respect to 1792–3 Tooke pauses to point out (ibid., p. 196 n.): 'It may here be observed, that a demand for increased discounts at the Bank of England is rarely, if ever, felt in the early stages of a speculative tendency. . . . It is chiefly when a pause takes place in the expected advance, and still more after the commencement of a fall.' For the Bank as the 'dernier resort', see also Sir Francis Baring, *Observations on the Establishment of the Bank of England*, pp. 22 and 47.

[4] Tooke, i. 194. For the connexion between note issue and bullion deposits, see Baring, pp. 10–11.

country banking. Thornton's contemporary statement (1802) was that 'a great increase of country banks took place during the time which intervened between the American and the present war (that is, the French Revolution), and chiefly in the latter part of it; a period during which the trade, the agriculture, and the population of the country had advanced very considerably'.[1] It was estimated that there were 280 country banks in England in 1793.[2]

There is some minor controversy as to the part played by the declaration of war in the crisis of 1793.[3] Sir Francis Baring felt that the crisis could be attributed almost solely to the outbreak of hostilities:[4]

That dreadful calamity is usually preceded by some indication which enables the commercial and monied men to make preparation. On this occasion, the short notice rendered the least degree of general preparation impossible.

Tooke answered:[5]

I am disposed, both from my own recollection and from all that I have been able to collect by research, to doubt whether the war had much influence in the origin of the discredit, although it can hardly have failed of operating in aggravation of the main causes.

These 'main causes' he found in the 'undue extension of the system of credit and paper' both at home and abroad. He notes commercial failures in America and on the Continent in the autumn of 1792, and a fall in the prices of Consols beginning in September. Monthly averages of high and low prices for 3 per cent. reduced Consols and India Stock are as follows in the latter half of 1792:[6]

(In £)

	India Stock	Reduced Consols
July 1790 .	157½	74
July 1791 .	168¾	82
July 1792 .	208½	92½
Aug. 1792 .	205¼	91
Sept. 1792 .	209	90¾
Oct. 1792 .	210¾	89½
Nov. 1792 .	206¾	83¼
Dec. 1792 .	185	78¾

There were, during 1790–2, special influences operating on the price of Consols, connected with the redemption of a part of the National Debt;[7]

[1] *Paper Credit*, pp. 129–30.
[2] Macpherson, p. 266. This figure is from Ellison, before the Committee of 1797 (reprinted, *A.R.*, Chr., 1797, p. 99). Macpherson cites also an estimate of 400 country banks in England and Wales in 1793. Satisfactory statistics of their number or their issues are lacking. But the extraordinary increase up to 1793 is indicated by the fact that their numbers are estimated to have fallen to 1797, and increased only slowly to 1801, despite the growing demand for money.
[3] A. Andréadès, *History of the Bank of*

England, pp. 187–9, holds rather with Baring than with Tooke in this matter.
[4] Op. cit., p. 19.
[5] Op. cit. i. 177.
[6] From the *Annual Register*.
[7] See *A.R.*, Chr., 1790, p. 213; 1791, p. 18; 1792, p. 46: also Macpherson, pp. 235–7 (1792). Over a period of six years the commissioners retired £9,441,850 of the debt. Macpherson states that this process had the effect of keeping the price of Consols 'considerably higher than it could be if such sums were not taken out of the market'.

but the fall in both India Stock and Consols during the latter months of 1792 can probably be taken as an indication of a general weakening of confidence. Bankruptcy statistics, drawn from the *London Gazette* (seasonal trend eliminated), show a low point in April 1792 and an irregular but pronounced rise to a peak in April 1793.[1]

It is clear from the evidence that the boom of the previous four or five years laid the framework of 'extended credit' on which the war crisis operated so drastically. Without the background of a financial system employing its resources close to the limit the panic of 1793 would not have been of the same kind or of the same magnitude. And there is a further case to be made out for 1792–3 as the turning-point in a cyclical movement whose downswing was forestalled by the appearance of war-time expenditure by governments, British and continental.

The outstanding feature of the crisis was the failure of a large number of the country banks :[2] one each in 1791 and 1792, twenty-six in 1793. These failures, and the universal uncertainty which attended the declaration of war in February 1793, shook the entire financial structure :[3]

Houses of great respectability and undoubted solidity, possessing ample funds, which actually did in a short time enable them to pay every shilling of their debts, were obliged to stop payment. . . . Many whom the temporary assistance of even a moderate sum of money would have enabled to surmount their difficulties, could not obtain any accommodation; for in the general distress and dismay, every one looked upon his neighbour with caution, if not with suspicion. It was impossible to raise any money upon the security of machinery or shares of canals; for the value of such property seemed to be annihilated in the gloomy apprehensions of the sinking state of the country, its commerce, and manufactures: and those who had any money, not knowing where they could place it with safety, kept it unemployed, and locked up in their coffers.

On 23 April a meeting was held at the Mansion House 'for putting a

---

[1] Tooke's figures (i. 193) for the annual total of bankruptcies, drawn from the Appendix to the Report of the Lords' Committee on the Resumption of Cash Payments, 1819, are as follows: 769 (1791), 934 (1792), 1956 (1793). Macpherson records (p. 266) the 'unprecedented number of bankruptcies in November, 1792'. His account of the crisis, like Tooke's, places great emphasis on the scale of the previous boom and its precarious position in 1792. The average number of bankruptcies listed in the *London Gazette* shows a less pronounced rise from 1792, although the rise in the latter months supports Tooke's contention: 51 (1791), 53 (1792), 115 (1793).

[2] Tooke, i. 193. Macpherson, p. 267, states that over 100 country banks failed during the crisis: 'whereof there were 12 in Yorkshire, 7 in Northumberland, 7 in Lincoln-

shire, 6 in Sussex, 5 in Lancashire, 4 in Northamptonshire, 4 in Somersetshire, etc.' Tooke suggests that the abundant harvest of 1791, and consequent fall in agricultural prices during 1791–2, may have weakened the position of the country banks (i. 195). Complaints from agricultural interests resulting in a new Corn Law have already been noted. Tooke also mentions an export of bullion and a weakening of the exchanges as possible contributory factors in 1792.

Baring (pp. 17–18) points out that the failure of the banks at Newcastle which began the crisis can be attributed in part to the fact that their notes were payable on demand. The banks in Exeter and in the west of England generally issued notes payable only twenty days after sight, and though less 'opulent', they 'stood their ground'.

[3] Macpherson, p. 266.

stop to this terrible calamity'. The committee proposed 'a Parliamentary
advance of exchequer bills, under proper regulations, to houses of real
capital'.[1] Early in May the plan went into effect, and Macpherson, with the
spirit of another more famous Scotsman hovering over his shoulder, was
able to announce :[2]

This was not one of those officious and ill-concerted interferences, by which
some governments ruin the interests of commerce, while they profess themselves
the protectors of it. The very first intimation of the intervention of the legislature to support the merchants operated all over the country like a charm, and
in a great degree superseded the necessity of the relief by an almost instanta-
neous restoration of mutual confidence.

Only £2·2 million of the bills were actually issued.[3]

The failure of the country banks and the general crisis of confidence
placed great pressure on the reserve at the Bank of England, which
had already fallen by some £2·5 million from 1790 to 1792, as prosperity reduced the resources of the market.[4] The gold reserve moved as
follows[5] (in £ millions): 28 February 1792, 6·5; 31 August 1792, 5·4;
28 February 1793, 4·0; 31 August 1793, 5·3. The holding of private securities
at the Bank increased from £3·19 million on 31 August 1792 to £6·46 million
on 28 February 1793.[6] When the crisis ended, and private credit channels
reopened, the Bank was able to reduce its discounts rapidly. Private
securities held stood at £4·4 million by 31 August. Thus towards the end
of 1793 the Bank's position was relatively strong; but the new problems
of war finance were already presenting themselves.

---

[1] Macpherson, p. 267. An advance of
£5 million in exchequer bills was offered. At
Liverpool, in May, the corporation of the
city was authorized to issue £200,000 in notes
to support 'the credit of the merchants and
traders of that town, whose very extensive
and complicated concerns had involved them
in, perhaps, a greater share of the general
calamity than any other place except London' (ibid., pp. 267–70).

[2] Ibid., p. 269. Macpherson's anti-mercan-
tilist prejudice is a recurring theme in his
Annals.

[3] E. Cannan, *The Paper Pound*, p. ix.

[4] Macpherson, pp. 266–7. The country
banks' failures were accounted 'the chief
cause of the great drain of cash from the
Bank of England, exceeding every demand
of the kind for about ten years back . . . the
failures had begun by a run on those houses
which had issued circulating paper without
sufficient capital, the consequences of which
had affected many houses of great solidity,
possessed of funds in goods and other property much more than sufficient to satisfy
all demands upon them, but unable to con-

vert their funds into cash in due time to
answer the pressure of the moment in the
present general discredit of circulating paper:
the sudden deficiency of so much circulating
paper induced the bankers to retain greater
sums in their hands than were necessary in
the ordinary course of their business, whereby the evil was greatly increased, and bills of
exchange, especially those of a long date,
could not be discounted.' The position of
responsibility in which this situation placed
the central banks is illustrated by the case
of the Royal Bank of Scotland, whose director, Gilbert Innes, stated at the Mansion
House meeting that the demands upon the
two chartered banks in Scotland were so
great that government assistance was immediately required if payment was to be
continued (ibid., p. 268).

[5] N. Silberling, 'British Financial Experience, 1790–1830', *Review of Economic
Statistics*, Preliminary vol. i, 1919, p. 293.

[6] H. James, *The State of the Nation*, p. 16.
For a description of the shift of credit demands to the Bank of England during the
crisis see also Baring, pp. 20–2.

6. Labour. Available statistical evidence, though meagre, seems to indicate that the position of the working classes improved during the years before the war, as shown by the following indexes :

	Tucker's index of		Bowley's index of agricultural money wages[a]
	Money wages of London	Real wages artisans	
1790 .	45·1	46·1	100
1791 .	45·1	47·4	104
1792 .	45·1	48·0	108
1793 .	45·9	46·0	112

[a] Agricultural wages were, in general, lower than industrial wages. In farming areas close to urban industry the agricultural wage scale appears to have been dominated by the prevailing factory wage (Dodd, pp. 335–6).

Mantoux places 1792 as the peak of 'a period of high wages' for weavers.[1] More generally, he traces in many trades a rise in money wages up to the crisis of 1793.[2] A correction for living costs and the new urban social condition of industrial labour, drawn from the land, makes for a somewhat less attractive picture. F. Eden concluded that 'there can be little doubt, that the ten years ending in January 1793, exhibit the most flattering appearances, in every circumstance that has been considered. . . . The demand for employment, and a consequent advance in income, have risen in a progressive ratio'.[3]

The year 1793, however, brought not only a rise in living costs but sudden increases in unemployment. The committee which faced Pitt at the Mansion House emphasized, since even sound banks were refusing to lend, 'that the orders and payments to the manufacturers being thereby interrupted, they were rendered incapable of continuing their regular weekly payments to their workmen, who must be thrown out of employment'.[4] The Scottish representatives reported that manufacturers had 'discharged great numbers of their workmen', with some 160,000 men, women, and children threatened with unemployment in Glasgow and Paisley.[5]

The growth of the Friendly Societies was the most significant development in the direction of labour organization during these years. It is, of course, impossible to establish their total membership; and extremely difficult to establish any connexion between their growth and the cyclical upswing that began in the eighties. The following samples give some

[1] Op. cit., p. 434.
[2] Ibid., pp. 430 ff.
[3] *The State of the Poor*, i. 574–5.
[4] Macpherson, p. 267.
[5] Ibid., p. 268. Macpherson observes that 'many of the discharged workmen enlisted in the army and navy and many emigrated to other countries. It is a melancholy consideration, that the same causes which increase the number of drones, diminish that of the working bees, in the great hive of British industry.'

minor support for a belief that labour's relative prosperity aided in their growth :[1]

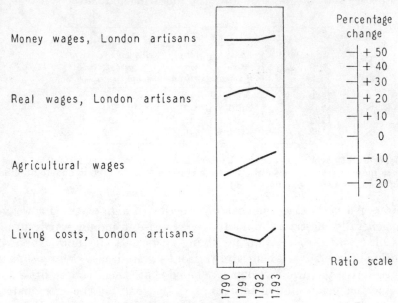

FIG. 8. Labour, 1790–3

	Shoemakers (Newcastle)	Friendly Societies of journeymen shoemakers, tailors, &c. (in a parish near the Tower)		Journeymen, day-labourers (in a parish in Westminster)	
	No. of members	No. of members	Fund	No. of members	Fund
			£		£
1788 . .	135	55	53	97	473
1789 . .	141	56	86	101	481
1790 . .	150	60	104	98	506
1791 . .	152	63	116	100	514
1792 . .	153	63	101[a]	101	539
1793 . .	153	61	112	99	557

[a] The fund was depleted in 1792 by abnormally high funeral expenses.

In 1792 there appeared the London Corresponding Society, 'the first distinctively working-class political body in England'.[2] Influenced by

[1] The fund of the Society of Newcastle Shoemakers was £137 in 1785, £350 in 1796, the only dates available which bear on this period. The funds of both the Newcastle and Tower parish societies fall in 1783, a year of depression: that of the Tower parish falls in 1794 and 1795, possibly under pressure of high food prices and post-crisis depression. But the data are by no means adequate for generalization. The figures are to be found in Eden, i. 617, 621, 622. The membership was in some cases at its limit as set out in the charter, so that the 'state of the fund' is the only available gauge of the society's relative prosperity.

[2] G. D. H. Cole, *A Short History of the British Working Class Movement*, i. 46.

Thomas Paine's version of French revolutionary ideas, it advocated parliamentary reform and adult suffrage.[1] But at this stage, at least, no link can be traced between the Reform movement and the Friendly Societies. They were occupied almost completely with problems of mutual aid, somewhat in the tradition of early guilds.[2] Sick benefits and burial services were the principal uses to which funds were put. But meeting as they did in the local inn, with the publican as treasurer, it was inevitable that broader common interests should be discussed. There was, however, no sense of solidarity among the various societies. They were strictly local in outlook, and, though closely associated with such trade unions as existed, they seem to have dealt with few of the problems that concern a modern labour organization. But the industrial revolution was only beginning to get under way, and food prices were falling.

PART II: 1794–1801

1. **Prices.** The domestic price index remains fairly stable from the post-crisis days of 1793 until the latter months of 1794. Although there was little surplus from the crop of 1793, and that of 1794 was scanty, the price of wheat did not rise until late in the year;[3] moreover, it 'did not rise soon enough to check the consumption; and it was not till the winter and spring following, that the insufficiency of the stock on hand, to meet the average rate of consumption, was discovered'. The price of wheat rose enormously in 1795. A fall occurred in August and September, due to good weather at harvesting time; 'but the original deficiency then manifested itself and prices rose again considerably before the close of the year. . . . The dearth of provisions, and the apprehensions of further scarcity, reached their height in the spring of 1796.'[4] The government had, by this time, taken steps to relieve the shortage: a system of bounties on wheat imports was introduced; government agents in the Baltic ports were attempting to acquire all available grain in eastern Europe; neutral ships bearing grain were seized and their cargo arbitrarily purchased; and inclosures were encouraged within Britain. But it was the abundant harvest of 1796, rather than these palliatives, that made possible a fall in the wheat price which brought the domestic index in the first half of 1797 close to the level of 1793–4. A surplus from the harvest of 1796 counteracted a

[1] Even Thomas Paine's long-range political liberalism was not divorced from the immediate issues confronting the working classes. In 1796 he published the *Decline and Fall of the English System of Finance*, which associated the famine prices of foodstuffs with the inflationary financial programme being pursued by the government. N. Silberling, 'Financial and Monetary Policy of Great Britain during the Napoleonic Wars',

Part II, *Quarterly Journal of Economics*, xxxviii. 400–1.

[2] For an excellent description of their place in the social life of the community, and the fear of the upper classes that they might breed British Jacobins, see E. Halévy, *A History of the English People in 1815*, p. 288.

[3] Tooke, i. 181.

[4] Ibid., pp. 182–3 and 187.

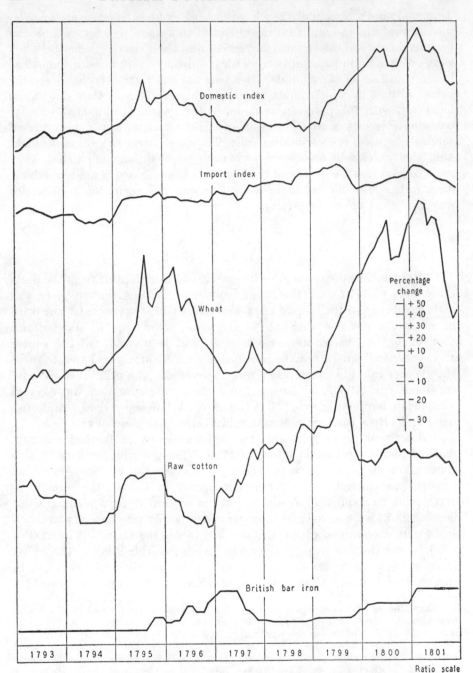

FIG. 9. Prices, 1793–1801

mediocre crop in the following year.[1] The harvest of 1798 was 'moderately productive'; and the domestic index hovers, through this period, at about the same level as in 1792. From the early months of 1799 to the middle of 1800 there is a protracted rise in the domestic index, again to be accounted for by inadequate harvests.[2] Large-scale imports temporarily lowered the prices of foodstuffs in the summer of 1800, but a new peak came in the spring of 1801 to the accompaniment of widespread rioting.[3] In the latter year the price of wheat was affected by the obstructions to imports raised by Russia, Denmark, and Prussia. The Baltic was for a time virtually closed as a source of provisions.

The index of imported commodities shows a more regular movement. Prices fell from a peak in the spring of 1793 to a low point in June 1794. They rose through 1795, fell slightly in the course of 1796, then moved to a peak in July 1799. The forces making for the rise from 1795 to 1799 are itemized as follows by Tooke :[4] competition for Baltic naval stores between Britain and France; the prospect of war with Spain, and the consequences on the prices of Spanish goods of the outbreak of war there; the 'failure of supplies' from St. Domingo, where the natives had been in revolt; the boom in the export and re-export trade with Hamburg; and the failure of harvests on the Continent, which pushed up not only basic grain prices but also silk, wines, linseed and rapeseed, olive-oil, and tallow. The falling prices of 1796 and early 1797 are attributed to a good season on the Continent, although prices did not fall to 'their former level, from the increased cost of production, and in the case of naval stores, from the increasing demand'.[5] In 1799 the fall is traced to commercial failures in Hamburg, where the extensive speculation in West Indian commodities collapsed.[6] The prices of all American and West Indian products were drastically affected.[7] The rise to the early days of 1801 is attributed solely to the operation of the seasons, which explains as well the movement of the domestic index at this point.[8]

The upward movement in import prices was accentuated also by a rise in freight, insurance, and interest rates. The extent of the rise in freight rates is indicated by the table on p. 31, below, referring to the Baltic trade.[9] The relative depressions of 1797 and 1801 seem to have effected a

[1] Tooke, i. 187. There was a sharp, but temporary, rise in the third quarter of 1797 'in consequence of apprehensions entertained of injury from the weather'. The financial crisis of early 1797 is reflected in the fact that the domestic index falls slightly in the first quarter, while the heavily weighted wheat price remains steady.

[2] Ibid., pp. 213–25. [3] Ibid., pp. 217–18.

[4] Ibid., pp. 189 and 233. [5] Ibid., p. 189.

[6] Ibid., pp. 233–4.   [7] Ibid., p. 235.

[8] The rise in the import index, however, was aided by a mild recovery in the price of West Indian and other commodities which had been the object of the previous speculation. Jamaica brown sugar, for example (in bond, exclusive of duty), fell from 64 (s. per cwt.) in March 1799 to 38 in June 1800, but rose to 52 by December of the year. Export figures also reflect the quick revival of foreign trade.

[9] Submitted by John Akenhead, in *Collection of Interesting and Important Reports and Papers on Navigation and Trade*, &c., 1807, p. clxvi. A similar table (submitted by John R. Sherman, p. clxvii) shows a doubling in the freight rates to Portugal in the war years.

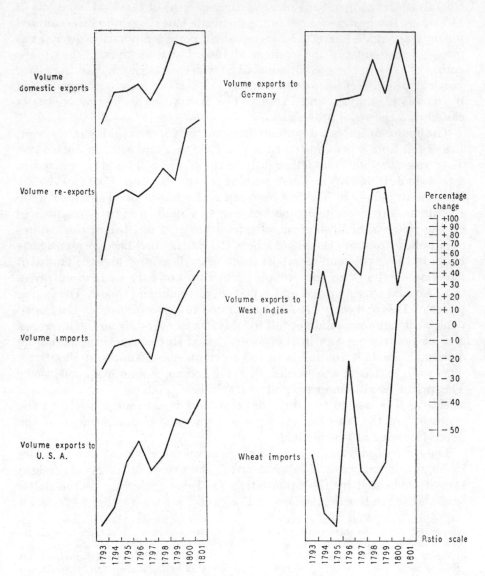

Fig. 10. Foreign Trade, 1793–1801

Freight Rates

| | Petersburg to London | | Riga to London, timber | Memel to London, timber |
| | Hemp and flax | Tallow | | |
	(s. per ton)		(s. per load)	
1792 . .	32	25	18	15–16
1793 . .	65	42–5	32	25–32
1794 . .	65	45	32	25–32
1795 . .	80	50	45	32–6
1796 . .	80–5	50	40	30–5
1797 . .	60	40	25	21
1798 . .	60–75	40–50	25–45	20–35
1799 . .	90–125	60–82	50	44
1800 . .	100	60	55	43
1801 . .	90	55	40	35

lowering of the rates, but the powerful net upward effect on the prices of raw materials from the Baltic area can be clearly seen.

Non-agricultural domestic prices show generally a strong upward tendency broken in some cases during the depressed year 1797, but resumed thereafter :

	Trough 1794	Peak 1796	Trough 1797	Peak 1797–1801
Copper (pence per lb.) .	(throughout) 11·5	(Aug.–Dec.) 12·4	(Feb.–Dec.) 12·1	(June 1801) 15·5
Hides (pence per lb.) . .	(Apr.–May) 12·2	(Sept.–Dec.) 13·2	No trough	(Sept. 1799) 24·5
Iron bars (£ per ton) .	(throughout) 16·9	(Dec.) 20·7	(Nov.–Dec.) 18·0	(Feb.–Dec. 1801) 22·0
Lead pigs (£ per ton) . .	(Oct.–Dec.) 18·0	(Feb.–Aug.) 21·5	(throughout) 19·5	(Dec. 1801) 28·0
Leather butts (pence per lb.)	(Apr.–May) 14·2	(Aug.–Nov.) 16·8	(June–Aug.) 15·8	(Nov. 1799) 27·0
Rape oil (£ per ton) . .	(Feb.) 36·0	(Feb.–Mar.) 62·0	(Sept.) 31·0	(Oct. 1799–Apr. 1800) 63·0
Hard soap (s. per cwt.) .	(Jan.–Aug.) 56·0	(July–Oct.) 79·0	(July–Sept.) 68·0	(Mar. 1801) 84·0
Tin (s. per cwt.) . .	(Aug.–Dec.) 98·0	(Mar.–Dec.) 100·0	No trough	(Nov.–Dec. 1801) 109·0

Wide variations in the behaviour of individual commodities are clearly evident.

2. Foreign Trade. The official total foreign-trade figures move as follows :[1]

[1] The import figures should be considered in conjunction with those for grain imports, which were abnormal in this period:

Wheat and Flour Imports

(In 1,000 quarters)

1793 .	. 475·8	1795 .	. 299·3	
1794 .	. 318·7	1796 .	. 879·2	

1797 .	. 421·2	1800 .	. 1,263·8	
1798 .	. 379·2	1801 .	. 1,424·6	
1799 .	. 447·9			

A part of the fall in the total import figure for 1797, and of the swollen totals for 1800 and 1801, can be traced to the varying requirements for grain imports.

(In £ millions)

	Volume of total imports	Volume of total exports
1793 .	16·9	10·8
1794 .	19·4	14·2
1795 .	20·0	14·5
1796 .	20·3	14·8
1797 .	17·8	14·0
1798 .	25·0	16·0
1799 .	23·9	18·5
1800 .	28·1	20·2
1801 .	31·6	20·8

The figures, broken down by countries, reveal the powerful growth of the German states as purchasers of goods shipped from Britain :[1]

Official Value of Total Exports from England

(In £ millions)

	Germany	U.S.A.	British W. Indies	Russia	France	Prussia
1793 . .	2·4	3·3	2·2	0·3	0·2	0·1
1794 . .	5·9	3·7	3·3	0·5	0·0	0·2
1795 . .	8·0	5·0	2·3	0·8	0·1	0·3
1796 . .	8·1	5·7	3·5	0·7	0·0	0·5
1797 . .	8·3	4·7	3·2	0·5	0·7	0·6
1798 . .	10·5	5·2	5·6	0·7	0·0	0·4
1799 . .	8·4	6·6	5·7	0·7	0·0	0·3
1800 . .	12·0	6·4	3·0	1·0	1·3	0·8
1801 . .	8·7	7·5	4·4	0·8	1·2	0·5

Exports to Asia remain steadily at about £2 million; those to Italy and Holland seem to suffer from the consequences of war, never getting above the figure for 1792.[2] A growth in sales to Portugal and Africa is also notable, the figures in both cases more than doubling in the latter years of the decade, reaching over £1 million in each instance.

Goods of British manufacture constituted 74 per cent. of exports in 1792, only 55 per cent. in 1800. This extraordinary rise in re-exports is illustrated best in figures for exports to Germany, which account largely for the increase in their relative importance (official values, in £ millions):

	Exports of British goods	Per cent.	Re-exports	Per cent.
1792 . .	0·8	38	1·3	62
1793 . .	0·7	29	1·7	71
1794 . .	1·6	27	4·3	73
1795 . .	1·7	21	6·3	79
1796 . .	1·5	19	6·5	81
1797 . .	1·9	23	6·4	77
1798 . .	1·9	19	8·6	81
1799 . .	1·8	22	6·6	78
1800 . .	3·9	32	8·1	68

[1] Figures from Macpherson's *Annals*.   to Holland in 1800 (1792, £1·3 million).
[2] An exception is the total of £3·2 million

This trend was connected with a boom in the 'transatlantic trade'.[1] On the Continent as well as in Britain there was a widespread speculation in commodities. In Hamburg, especially, mercantile houses became heavily involved, with West Indian products the focus of speculation.[2] One effect of the war was 'the almost complete annihilation of the commerce of Amsterdam, formerly the first commercial city of Europe'. Its trade was transferred to Hamburg, which, in turn, became 'the emporium of the middle parts of Europe'.[3] Its merchants as well came to Hamburg. The boom in commodities was partially financed and manipulated by these refugee tradesmen.[4] Through Hamburg much of the trade between belligerent nations took place. Macpherson states, with regard to an account of French trade for the year ending 22 September 1800: 'No imports from Great Britain appear (in the French accounts). But much of the sugar, coffee, cotton goods, etc., imported from Hamburg . . . must have been circuitously obtained from this country.'[5] Hamburg was thus the chief distributing point for West Indian produce and British manufactures.

The United States also used this port extensively, as can be seen from a list of ships which entered there in 1800. Of a total of 2,148 vessels, 198 were from London, 80 from Newcastle, 132 from other British ports, 149 from the United States, 117 from Amsterdam, 71 from Russia, 51 from Bordeaux, 3 from Cadiz, 2 from China. The remainder probably represented Baltic coastwise trade. The United States, like Britain, was serving as an entrepôt for West Indian goods, the French taking advantage of the neutrality enjoyed by her ships.[6] The United States made a good thing of the continental war, in its early stages at least: 'Thus has the war in Europe turned out a mine of gold and silver to the United States of America. . . . This sudden inundation of nominal wealth must introduce a style of living, and a turn of thought, utterly inconsistent with agricultural and mercantile prosperity, and destructive of the simplicity of manners and frugal habits, which, heretofore, rendered America so respectable in the eyes of the discerning part of Europe.'[7]

Of the articles imported into Hamburg, sugar and coffee seem to have been on the largest scale. British dominions and the United States sent the greater part of the 98 million lb. of sugar imported, and of the 46 million lb. of coffee imported; the re-export merchants of Great Britain accounted for about 15 million lb.; the United States, for about 19 million. The obstructions to the French sugar supply from St. Domingo from 1792

[1] Although Tooke dates the boom from 1796 the statistics indicate a movement beginning in 1794. Macpherson (p. 364) in his chronicle for 1795 states that 'the West Indian trade . . . lately increased more than almost any other branch of trade in the port of London'.

[2] Tooke, i. 190–1: 'The demand was chiefly for export to the Continent of Europe, and the principal channel was Hamburg.' A part of these shipments was destined for France (Macpherson, p. 522). British imports from the West Indies (official value) were £3·7 million in 1792, £6·3 million in 1799.

[3] Macpherson, p. 463.

[4] M. Wirth, Geschichte der Handelskrisen, pp. 95–6.

[5] Op. cit., p. 522.

[6] Ibid., p. 387.

[7] Ibid., pp. 387–8.

caused an increase in the output of the British West Indies.[1] The demand for sugar in Britain had been increased by lowering the tax on tea to 12½ per cent. in 1784. And although the tax was raised in the course of the war to 40 per cent., by 1800, 'the increase of price being gradual, and any other articles, which could be used instead of it, being equally increased in price, or unattainable, the people of all ranks found themselves obliged to continue the use of tea, to which they were now accustomed, notwithstanding the advanced price of it, and also of sugar'.[2]

The effect on the prices of colonial commodities in Britain is indicated by Tooke in the following table:[3]

	1793–4	1798–9
Coffee, Jamaica, per cwt.	77s. to 95s.	185s. to 196s.
Sugar, Muscovado, per cwt. . .	32s. to 58s.	62s. to 87s.
Sugar, East Indian, per lb. . .	60s. to 70s.	96s. to 115s.
Cotton, Georgia, per lb. . . .	1s. 1d. to 1s. 4d.	3s. 6d. to 4s. 6d.
Pepper, black, per lb. . . .	13d.	22d.
Logwood, per ton	£6 to £8	£48 to £50
Tobacco, per lb.	3d. to 5d.	11½d. to 16d.

A peak was reached in 1799:[4]

As usual, in such cases, the consumption of the commodities, which had been the objects of speculation, was reduced by the advanced cost, and consequently proved to be much less than had been anticipated, while the supplies were much larger. The prices thenceforward began to fall; and, as the circulation by bills of exchange and other forms of credit had expanded with and promoted the rise of prices, so it was contracted by, and in its turn accelerated the fall of prices until the final adjustment to the metallic standard. This process was attended with very disastrous results in the great commercial towns of Germany and Holland. The number of houses that failed at Hamburg, between August and November, 1799, was eighty-two, and the amount of their engagements upwards of twenty-nine million five hundred thousand banco marks, or about two million five hundred thousand pounds.

'The general and extensive connection' of British merchants with those in Hamburg brought panic to the principal cities. Liverpool, as in 1793, sought government relief for its illiquid traders. Parliament granted a loan of £500,000 in exchequer bills to West Indian merchants there 'in order to avert the evils which hung over their heads from very heavy failures in Hamburg. Security was given for this loan, in property in their ware-

---

[1] Macpherson, p. 232.

[2] Ibid., pp. 523–4.   [3] Op. cit. i. 190.

[4] Ibid. i. 233. Wirth, p. 110, accounts for 136 failures involving nearly 37 million banco marks. He traces the beginning of a pre-crisis piling up of stocks to the cutting off of the markets in Italy and Switzerland upon their occupation, in 1798, by the French armies (ibid., pp. 97–8). Interest

rates, reflecting the crisis, moved as follows in Hamburg (ibid., p. 99) (highest rate per cent. each month):

Jan. 1798	.	4½	Apr. 1799	. 11
July	.	5½	May	. . 12
Dec.	.	9	June	. . 10
Jan. 1799	.	8½	July	. . 6
Feb.	.	5½	Aug.	. . 6½
Mar.	.	7	Sept.	. . 7

houses amounting to upwards of two millions.'[1] The export figures for
1800–1, given above, indicate the quick revival in foreign trade that followed the crisis. Not until 1803 was the increase arrested.

3. Investment. While Britain's foreign trade was expanding in this
extraordinary manner many of the internal developments noted in the
upswing that ended in 1793 seem to have suffered a considerable check.
With grain prices high, and the government making every effort to induce
an increased supply for Britain, inclosures, however, continued to increase.
A revival in all types of enterprise at home can be observed in the last
three years of the period, after a decline from the peak in 1792–3. In part
this sequence can be associated with conditions in the money and capital
markets. Until 1797 all available funds were being drawn, by appeals to
patriotism and high yields, into government stock, while the Bank, occupied with a mass of short-term exchequer bills, was severely restricting its
commercial accommodations. After 1797 the Bank felt itself in a position
to pursue a somewhat easier money policy, while the government's loan-
financed expenditure, although high, remained far below the figures for
1795–6.[2]

In 1799–1800 a new type of capital improvement appeared on a large

	Bills of inclosure (No.)	Production of bricks (in million bricks)	Canal, railway, and navigation bills		Turn-pike bills (No.)	Quantity of fir timber imports (in 1,000 loads of 50 cu. ft.)
			No.	Amount (in £ millions)		
1793 . .	60	848·2	26	3·2	6	200
1794 . .	74	673·4	18	2·6	2	172
1795 . .	77	596·1	11	0·4	2	151
1796 . .	72	575·3	14	1·3	3	204
1797 . .	85	517·2	8	0·2	4	122
1798 . .	48	469·0	5	0·2	2	143
1799 . .	63	482·1	1	0·0	2	151
1800 . .	80	608·8	10	0·5	3	194
1801 . .	122	686·6	11	0·9	4	167

scale. Congestion in the Port of London, which accompanied the boom in
foreign trade, led to the formation of two large dock companies. In 1799
the West India Dock Company was authorized to issue shares to the value
of £500,000, to be increased to £600,000 if necessary; this construction of
wet docks, wharves, quays, and warehouses was 'for the reception and discharge of vessels in the West India trade, whereby greater accommodation
will be given to the other shipping in the river'.[3] In 1800 the London Dock
Company was authorized, with a capital of £1,200,000 and the power to
borrow a further £300,000. Although the strain on shipping facilities
focused in London, it caused an expansion and improvement of harbours
and wharves at many places. Macpherson mentions Margate, Brixham,
Leith, Yarmouth, and Grimsby.[4] The following figures (in thousand tons)

[1] Tooke, i. 234–5.
[2] Cannan, p. xliii.
[3] Macpherson, p. 479.
[4] Ibid., pp. 482, 495, and 501–3.

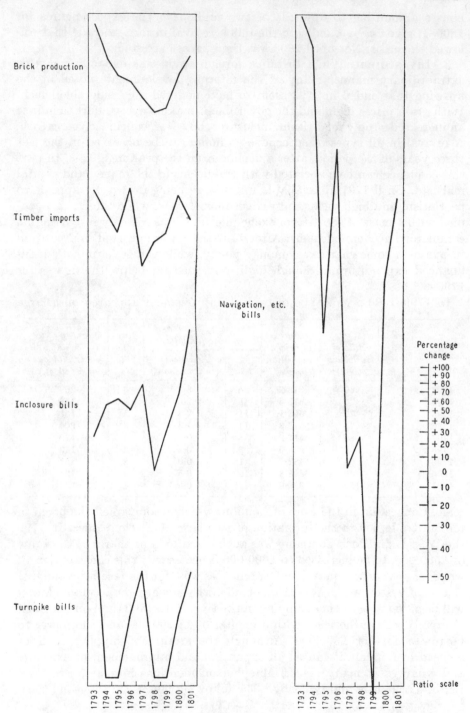

Brick production

Timber imports

Navigation, etc.
bills

Inclosure bills

Turnpike bills

Percentage
change

—— +100
—— + 90
—— + 80
—— + 70
—— + 60
—— + 50
—— + 40
—— + 30
—— + 20
—— + 10
——   0
—— − 10
—— − 20
—— − 30
—— − 40
—— − 50

Ratio scale

1793 1794 1795 1796 1797 1798 1799 1800 1801

1793 1794 1795 1796 1797 1798 1799 1800 1801

FIG. 11. Investment, 1793–1801

permit a quantitative estimate of the growing shipping requirements. The sudden increase in 1799–1801 of the tonnage of shipping belonging to Great Britain and Ireland is especially to be noted, timed, as it is, with increases in other types of new investment :[1]

Tonnage of Shipping

(in thousand tons)

	Entered	Cleared	Tonnage of shipping belonging to United Kingdom
1793 .	1,672	1,427	1,436
1794 .	1,786	1,601	1,438
1795 .	1,632	1,527	1,410
1796 .	1,903	1,631	1,343
1797 .	1,706	1,500	1,438
1798 .	1,709	1,684	1,478
1799 .	1,821	1,716	1,535
1800 .	2,142	2,178	1,683
1801 .	1,702	2,151	1,780

4. Industry and Agriculture. Although several types of large-scale enterprise at home seem to have been under a restrictive influence until about 1799, a further widespread development of industrial technique can be traced.

Inclosure figures indicate the increase in the scale of agriculture during the first nine years of the war. Even in Scotland, where the process of modernization had hitherto been largely confined to the introduction of iron ploughs and harrows, inclosures began to take place under the influence of rising grain prices.[2] Although Welsh agriculture was essentially pastoral, it, too, felt the stimulus towards expansion.[3] There was some inclosure, and the closing years of the century were marked by those other symptoms of the agricultural revolution, the formation of agricultural societies, and the growth of fairs. In England this period was afterwards regarded as a golden age for agriculture. The new large-scale farmers prospered :[4]

Their entertainments are as expensive as they are elegant . . . for it is not an uncommon thing for one of these new created farmers to spend £10 or £12 at

---

[1] While tonnage entered and cleared increased fairly steadily, the boom in shipbuilding seems to have been confined to the latter three years. This may have been merely a natural lag; or it may have been a result of the tight money conditions which existed until after Bank restriction was introduced. It was noted above that, until these latter years, other types of private enterprise were also limited in amount.

[2] Hamilton, pp. 53–4 and 55. In the Highlands the huge tracts of land held by the tacksmen, who had neither the will nor the ability to cultivate them, tended to be broken up, at the same time that the movement towards the consolidation of small farms was developing.

[3] Jones, p. 17; Dodd, p. 41.

[4] A contemporary quoted by Mantoux, p. 186 n.

one entertainment, and, to wash off delicate food, must have the most expensive wines, and those the best of their kind. . . . As to dress, no one that is not personally acquainted with the opulent farmer's daughter can distinguish her from the daughter of a duke by her dress.

Before attempting to describe the development of the textile, iron, and coal trades it is important to emphasize again the consequences for British industry of the canal and road boom which reached a peak in 1792–3, but continued, on a lesser scale, through this period. The development of Lancashire and Birmingham, of Scotland's resources of coal and iron, and of the interior collieries of Wales, all depended on this early 'transportation revolution'.[1]

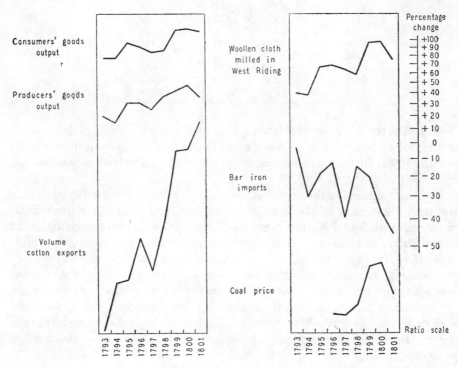

FIG. 12. Industry and Agriculture, 1793–1801

At the end of the eighteenth century, merchandise of every kind, from all parts of the country, could be seen journeying up and down the main waterways, such as the Trent and Mersey Canal: salt from Cheshire, corn from East Anglia, pottery from Staffordshire, coal from Wigan and Newcastle, pig iron from the upper Severn, worked iron and copper from Wolverhampton and Birmingham.

Progress in cotton textiles from 1793 to 1801 was interrupted only

[1] Mantoux, pp. 133–4.

briefly by the crises of 1797 and 1799.[1] A measure of that advance is the following table giving the official value of exports (in £ millions) :[2]

	Manufactured goods	Twist and yarn	Volume of exports of cotton manufactures
1793 .	. .	. .	1·7
1794 .	. .	. .	2·4
1795 .	. .	. .	2·4
1796 .	. .	. .	3·2
1797 .	. .	. .	2·6
1798 .	3·6	0·0	3·6
1799 .	5·6	0·2	5·8
1800 .	5·4	0·4	5·9
1801 .	6·6	0·4	7·1

The two technical trends noted in the decade before 1793 continued even more rapidly afterwards : the relative growth of Lancashire and the north country, and the introduction of steam power. Of the 35 steam-engines installed in cotton mills from the beginning of 1796 to the end of 1800, 29 were in Lancashire.[3] These years were characterized as well by a further development of the water frame and of the mule. Crompton's original invention had 48 spindles. In 1795 the smallest manufactured contained 144, and, by 1799, mules with 408 spindles were being constructed.[4] Although abundant water power in Scotland prevented the widespread use of the Watt–Boulton steam-engine, the technical advance was destroying the domestic system almost as rapidly as in England.[5] But the most striking event of the decade was the invention of the cotton gin in 1793. Its consequences can be seen in the fact that exports of cotton from the United States increased from 487,600 lb. in 1793 to 20,911,201 lb. in 1801.[6] An overwhelming proportion of this total contributed to the supply of British cotton mills. Imports into Britain increased from about 33 million lb. at the peak, in 1792, to 56 million lb. in 1800.[7]

In general the woollen industry did not experience the same rapid mechanization as cotton. The single major exception was the West Riding, close by the new cotton factories.[8] Output of woollen cloths in that district,

---

[1] Baines, pp. 358–9, quotes 'an enlightened merchant and cotton spinner', Mr. Kirkman Finlay, of Glasgow and London: 'I have seen a great many overthrows in the cotton manufacture: in 1788 I thought it was never to recover; in 1793 it got another blow; in 1799 it got a severe blow, and in 1803 again, and in 1810; and at particular periods one would have thought that it was never to extend again; but at every time that it received a blow, the rebound was quite wonderful.'

[2] Ibid., pp. 349–50.

[3] Lord, pp. 170–1.

[4] Hamilton, p. 131.

[5] Ibid., pp. 129–32. Between 1775 and 1800 only eight steam-engines were installed in Scottish cotton mills (Lord, p. 172).

[6] Baines, p. 302.

[7] Macpherson, p. 470; and Baines, p. 215.

[8] Mantoux, pp. 268–9. The factory system, even in the West Riding, came but slowly. In 1803 it was estimated that only one-sixteenth of the pieces of woollen cloth woven there were produced in large factories (ibid., p. 273).

as reflected in the figures from fulling mills, moved as follows, indicating clearly the relative depression of 1797 (in broads alone) and 1801 :[1]

Woollen Broad and Narrow Cloth Milled in the West Riding

(In million yards)

	Broad	Narrow
1793 .	6·0	4·8
1794 .	6·1	4·6
1795 .	7·8	5·2
1796 .	7·8	5·2
1797 .	7·2	5·5
1798 .	7·1	5·2
1799 .	8·8	6·4
1800 .	9·3	6·0
1801 .	8·7	4·8

Wool, unlike cotton, was a long-established industry, with many entrenched interests, slow to adjust themselves to new conditions. In 1794 small manufacturers petitioned Parliament to prohibit wealthy cloth merchants from setting up workshops.[2] In 1792 the introduction of a wool-combing machine also produced petitions to Parliament. Although these were rejected, an Elizabethan statute relating to apprenticeship was relaxed to permit those thrown out of work to seek employment elsewhere, in the woollen or any other trade.[3] The advance in the industry, especially in the Yorkshire area, nevertheless seemed impressive looking backward from 1800 :[4]

This vast manufacture is supposed to give employment to three millions of men, women, boys, and girls, notwithstanding the decrease of the quantity of wool, and the great abridgement of labour by the use of machinery, which, in the various processes previous to the weaving, was stated by one manufacturer to accomplish by the hands of 35 persons the work, which about the year 1785 required the labour of 1,634 persons.

The capital vested in machinery, and buildings appropriated to the woolen manufacture, in various parts of the country, was supposed to be about £6,000,000.

It is evident that the foreign demand for woolen manufactures has lately extended beyond the power of the country to supply it: for many more orders

---

[1] The figures for foreign wool imported were affected not only by fluctuations in output but by a depletion, during the latter years of the decade, of the internal supply of raw wool (Macpherson, pp. 526–7).

Raw Wool Imports (in million lb.)

1792 .	. 4·5	1797 .	. 4·7
1793 .	. 1·9	1798 .	. 2·7
1794 .	. 4·6	1799 .	. 5·2
1795 .	. 5·1	1800 .	. 8·6
1796 .	. 3·5	1801 .	. 7·4

[2] Mantoux, pp. 271–2.

[3] J. Bischoff, A Comprehensive History of the Woolen and Worsted Manufactures, i. 316. A further reminder that these years bordered on a mercantilist age is the government's unsuccessful attempts to prevent the north country manufacturers from stretching their woollen cloth. Only by 1806 had the machinery of control come 'to a standstill' (H. Heaton, The Yorkshire Woollen and Worsted Industries, p. 416). Throughout these years the classic tale of the Yorkshire woollens which shrunk while worn by a parading Russian army was often revived (ibid., pp. 407–8).

[4] Macpherson, pp. 526–7.

have been sent to the manufacturers than they could possibly find wool to execute. The increased demand may be ascribed partly to the failure of some manufactures on the Continent, occasioned by the convulsions of the war, and partly to the augmentation of the military establishments of every country in Europe. The deficiency of wool is pretty certainly owing to the increase of inclosures for the purpose of raising corn for the subsistence of the increased number of people in the country and its foreign dependencies, and the unprecedented number of consumers in the army and navy.

The iron industry felt most directly the results of the war. It remained in a condition of rapid expansion until 1815. The foundries clustered about the coalfields of the midlands, Yorkshire, Derbyshire, and South Wales. These districts accounted for 77 per cent. of the national output in 1788, 80 per cent. in 1796, 87 per cent. in 1806.[1] Output, from 1796 to 1804, rose from 126,000 to 250,000 tons, the number of blast-furnaces from 121 to 221.[2]

Ashton thus describes the relative prosperity of the iron trade from the opening of the war to the Peace of Amiens :[3]

Between the opening of hostilities and 1796 the price of iron had remained fairly steady; for the increased output of British works, combined with the imports from Sweden and Russia, enabled supply to keep pace with accelerating demand.[4] . . . In 1796, however, a rise of about 30 per cent took place in the prices of foreign iron, and a veritable boom in domestic production developed. In every centre of the industry there were indications of abnormal activity; press notices and advertisements for labour show that the casting branch of the industry was developing so rapidly that the existing supply of labor was inadequate to cope with the orders that were pouring in. The successive increases of 1796, 1797, and 1798 in the customs duty on bar iron, amounting in all to 19s. 3d. a ton, brought added gains to the English ironmasters, and not only were existing works extended but the formation of new businesses was again marked. . . . Among the causes which had led to this condition of industry the demand of the Government for ordnance must, perhaps, take first place. Hardly less important, however, in this respect were the relations of Britain with the Northern Powers . . . It might have been anticipated that the conclusion of peace in October, 1801, would have resulted in loss to ironmasters and unemployment to their workers. In this and the following year, it is true, the secondary iron trades suffered. But the impetus derived from recent developments was sufficient to carry iron production across the gulf.[5]

[1] Ashton, pp. 100–1.

[2] Mantoux, p. 313 n. Scrivenor, p. 96, writes: 'The demand for iron articles of all kinds in this country not only continued unabated after the period of 1796, but kept increasing in a greater ratio than formerly, so that, in the short space of five years, situations were occupied for nearly fifty additional furnaces.' In 1800–1 Scrivenor lists within Great Britain some forty-seven new furnaces in blast or building.

[3] Op. cit., pp. 143–6.

[4] Scrivenor, pp. 358 and 420, gives the following figures for the import of bar iron, in tons:

1792	. 57,693	1797	. 36,960
1793	. 58,962	1798	. 51,928
1794	. 42,479	1799	. 48,331
1795	. 49,526	1800	. 38,154
1796	. 53,277	1801	. 33,145

[5] For an account of iron prices in these years which also emphasizes import obstructions, duties, and an increased demand, in part from the government, see Tooke, *High and Low Prices*, Part IV, pp. 36–8.

So rapid was the growth of the iron trade in the last few years of the century that the masters complained of a shortage in the coal supply.[1] With the improved steam-engines making possible deeper mines, and the canals making the supplies available to a growing market, the number of collieries and the output of coal increased.[2] But coal had no Watt or Crompton:[3] expansion had to come rather from scale than technique. Some conception of the extent of the growth can be derived from these figures of coal shipments:[4]

Coal Shipments
(In thousand chaldrons)

	Exports from the Tyne[a]	Exports from the Wear[a]	Imports into London[b]
1789 . .	487	295	811
1793 . .	473	298	801
1800 . .	618	322	1,010

[a] Newcastle chaldrons: 53 cwt.   [b] London chaldrons: 28½ cwt.

It is difficult to weight precisely the direct influence of government demand for military purposes on the expansion in iron, and thus in coal. Tooke places iron among those commodities whose prices were immediately affected by war demand.[5] But this was as well a period when the commercial uses for iron were daily becoming more numerous. As early as 1796 Watt wrote: 'Moulders are still a desideratum with us, and there appears to be a general want of them throughout the country, owing to the vast increases of the consumption of Cast Iron articles.'[6] Ashton emphasizes especially the demand that arose from the increased use of machinery in textiles, and elsewhere. Hamilton, although he states at one point that 'the period of war from 1793 to 1815 acted as a powerful stimulant to the industry',[7] later concludes:[8]

It is usually assumed that a war acts as a vigorous stimulant to the iron industry, and that, unlike other industries, it experiences a period of unexampled prosperity while hostilities last. But this view places undue emphasis on the uses of iron in the wars of the past. During the Napoleonic conflict the demand for

[1] Ashton, p. 101.
[2] For the coal-mine boom in Scotland, following the opening of the Monkland Canal, and lasting through the nineties, see Hamilton, pp. 170–2. For a more general description of the expansion of the coal market, see Ashton and Sykes, *The Coal Industry of the Eighteenth Century*, pp. 226–39. They calculate that from 1770 to 1800 the output of coal increased roughly from 6 to 10 million tons. For the effect of the canals on the development of iron and coal mining in South Wales, see Davies, pp. 94–5.
[3] Ashton and Sykes, p. 12.

[4] Ibid., p. 251.
[5] *History of Prices*, i. 104. He explains movements in its price completely in terms of 'the extent of the government demand', and 'greater or less obstructions to supply', in this case obstructions imposed by Sweden and Russia. Aside from this short-run analysis, Tooke notes the long-run tendency for expanding fixed resources in the iron industry to increase output and lower prices.
[6] Quoted, Ashton, *Iron and Steel*, pp. 101–2.
[7] Op. cit., p. 164.
[8] Ibid., pp. 175–6.

munitions was not sufficient to cause prosperity to all or even most ironworks. A study of the records of the most important concerns in Scotland shows that the main market for the produce of the blast-furnaces was home industry, and we hear very little about the demand for cannon, except in the case of Carron, and Clyde. At this time cast iron was finding fresh uses every day, and it was in the small foundries up and down the country that the ironmasters looked for the sale of most of their pig-iron. . . . It was in these foundries, where they made agricultural implements, machine parts, water-wheels, cisterns, boilers, pipes, domestic utensils, bridge materials, &c., as well as in similar ones within the iron-works themselves, that the bulk of the pig-iron produced in Scotland was used.

High transport costs and, until the invention of the hot blast in 1828, the poor quality of her coals operated against Scotland's iron industry as compared with that of England and Wales.[1] It should, nevertheless, be emphasized that the direct role of government orders was not everywhere of primary importance. Its indirect part in expansion cannot, of course, be traced within a single industry.

From this compressed, and necessarily incomplete account, there emerges the picture of extremely rapid agricultural and industrial development. From 1798 to 1801, especially, the expansion in output is extraordinary. Whether the war influence was direct, indirect, or merely coincidental, there is little question that the first nine years of conflict saw continued the process of Britain's industrialization. Hoffmann's indexes of production roughly reflect this tumultuous advance. They show a recovery in 1794–6, a slump in the crisis year 1797, a strong revival to 1800, and a second set-back in 1801 :[2]

	Hoffmann's index of producers' goods production	Hoffmann's index of consumers' goods production	Hoffmann's index of total production
1793 .	2·2	7·1	4·4
1794 .	2·1	7·1	4·4
1795 .	2·4	7·8	4·8
1796 .	2·4	7·7	4·8
1797 .	2·3	7·3	4·6
1798 .	2·5	7·4	4·8
1799 .	2·6	8·5	5·3
1800 .	2·7	8·6	5·4
1801 .	2·5	8·4	5·2

[1] Ibid., pp. 171–6.

[2] In 1800 the King's speech describes the commerce and resources of the country as flourishing 'beyond all former example' and still 'in a state of progressive augmentation' (A.R., Chr., 1800, p. 246). In February 1801 Pitt, introducing the budget, refers to 'the flourishing state of the finances and of trade' (Smart, *Economic Annals of the Nineteenth Century, 1801–1820*, p. 42). And in June 1802 the King's speech still points to 'our manufactures, commerce, and revenue, which afford the most decisive and gratifying proof of the abundance of our internal resources and the growing prosperity of the country' (ibid., p. 54). 1801 would seem to have been, generally, a worse year than either 1800 or 1802, although the statistical evidence does not tell a very clear story. Tooke (i. 235) quotes the following com-

5. Finance. The crises of neither 1793, 1797, nor 1799 seem to have resulted in prolonged set-backs to home or foreign trade. Although the cost of food created difficulties almost revolutionary in character, there are few complaints of unemployment except for brief periods in 1793 and 1797. To what extent this was due to large loan-financed government expenditure it is difficult to establish. A heavily unbalanced budget characterized all the years under consideration :[1]

Great Britain and Ireland

(In £ millions)

	Expenditure	Revenue	Excess of Expenditure
1793 . .	24·2	19·8	4·4
1794 . .	29·6	20·2	9·4
1795 . .	51·7	19·9	31·8
1796 . .	57·7	21·5	36·2
1797 . .	50·5	23·1	27·4
1798 . .	50·9	31·0	19·9
1799 . .	55·4	35·6	19·8
1800 . .	56·5	34·1	22·4
1801 . .	60·6	34·1	26·5

As a basis for industrial activity, it is possible that government expenditure for supplies partially supplanted the types of new investment which had increased until 1792, but remained on a smaller scale thereafter. Baring's much-quoted statement on the years between 1793 and 1797 is as follows :[2]

The tranquillity, confidence, and general prosperity which succeeded the first six months of the year 1793, and continued for those of 1794, 1795, and part of 1796, was wonderful: during those periods it frequently happened that money could not be employed at an interest of 4 per cent. per annum. . . . Until the close of 1795 money was as plentiful as in time of peace; but some slight appearances began then to arise, which were very much increased in the spring of 1796 . . . money became scarce towards the end of 1796, and the Bank stopped payment in the beginning of 1797 . . . [a] very sudden transition from plenty to scarcity from scarcity to distress, and from distress to bankruptcy.

Government expenditures abroad were at their peak in 1795, and the Bank in that year became frightened by the great increase in its loans to

mercial report, dated 1 April 1801: 'The trade of Birmingham is in a very distressed situation. A large proportion of the workmen are entirely out of employ; and those who still have work have the utmost difficulty to gain a subsistence, from the exorbitant price of all kinds of provisions. The ribbon trade of Coventry is in a most deplorable state; and the woollen trade of Yorkshire, if possible, still worse.' Bankruptcies rose in 1801, fell in 1802, and rose again more sharply in 1803. From the break in the Hamburg trade, in 1799, to the depression of 1803 there is no general, simple cyclical pattern.

[1] Cannan, p. xliii.
[2] Op. cit., pp. 43 and 46.

the government, and, in the latter months, by a fall in the foreign exchanges.[1] On 31 December 1795 the Bank announced that quantitative
control over private discounts would be exercised.[2] Through the early
months of 1793 there appears to have been a shortage of money in the
market. In April a group of merchants, meeting in the London Tavern,
passed the following resolutions :[3]

1. That it is the opinion of this meeting that there has existed, for a considerable time past, . . . an alarming scarcity of money in the city of London.
2. That this scarcity proceeds chiefly, if not entirely, from an increase of the
   commerce of the country, and from the great diminution of mercantile discounts which the Bank of England has thought proper to introduce . . .
   during the last three months.

Although the Bank's statement shows an extremely slight contraction
in private lending, in view of the rise in the volume of trade and prices,
a real credit constriction is indicated :[4]

(In £ millions)

	Notes in circulation	Private securities
Feb. 1793 . .	11·9	6·5
Aug. . .	10·9	4·4
Feb. 1794 . .	10·7	4·6
Aug. . .	10·3	3·6
Feb. 1795 . .	14·0	3·6
Aug. . .	10·9	3·7
Feb. 1796 . .	10·7	4·2
Aug. . .	9·2	6·2
Feb. 1797 . .	9·7	5·1
Aug. . .	11·1	9·5

War financing, especially by exchequer bills, did, then, almost certainly
restrict the short-term credit available to private industry and commerce.[5]
And although existing country banks increased their issues, there was no
increase in the number of such banks like that which supported the expansion which ended in 1792.[6] It is probable that the relative burden carried

[1] For the full correspondence between the
Bank and the government, see Appendix to
Report of Secret Committee, 1797, reprinted
in *A.R.*, Chr., 1797. See also H. Macleod,
The Theory and Practice of Banking, ii. 75-
95, for much of this correspondence, and for
the most complete chronological account of
financial events from 1793 to 1797.

[2] Tooke, i. 200. The notice follows: 'That
in future, whenever bills sent in for discount
shall in any day amount to a larger sum than
it shall be resolved to discount on that day,
a *pro rata* proportion of such bills in each
parcel as are not otherwise objectionable,
will be returned to the person sending in the
same, without regard to the respectability of
the party sending in the bills, or the solidity
of the bills themselves.'

[3] Ibid., pp. 200-1.
[4] Cannan, p. xliv.
[5] The Bank Directors proposed, in 1796,
'as the best remedy for the scarcity of
money, that the floating debt should be
funded' (Tooke, i. 201). It will be recalled
that, except for inclosures, long-term private
investment was also restricted from 1793 to
1797.
[6] Evidence before the Committee of 1797
was unanimous in affirming a decrease in the
issues, and probably in the number of
country banks, from 1793 to 1797. It was
further concluded that, because the country
banks were holding more specie and keeping
lower balances in London, they had contributed to the shortage of money there
(quoted, *A.R.*, Chr., 1797, pp. 99-100). Nor

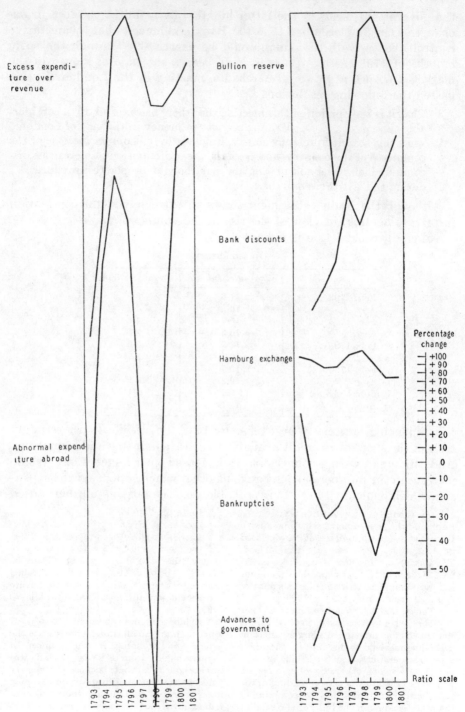

FIG. 13. Finance, 1794–1801

by the London money market and the Bank of England increased from 1793 to 1801.[1]

The effort made to induce private investors to place their funds in government stock forced up, as well, long-term rates.[2] The average yield on 3 per cent. Consols and the price of India Stock, compared with the preceding years of peace, moved as follows:

	India Stock (In £)	Yield on 3 per cent. Consols (per cent.)
1790 . .	166·1	3·90
1791 . .	175·3	3·58
1792 . .	204·2	3·32
1793 . .	204·7	3·95
1794 . .	199·4	4·42
1795 . .	194·6	4·53
1796 . .	193·6	4·83
1797 . .	154·6	5·87

The Committee of 1797 stated in its report :[3] 'During the present war it is worthy of remark that expensive enterprises of a private nature have not diminished, as in all former wars, but even augmented.' As the evidence marshalled above indicates, this generalization, until 1797, applies at best to agriculture and to industrial development, rather than to the building of canals, turnpikes, and, if the brick index and timber imports are a fair indicator, houses and factories.

The central monetary phenomenon of these years is the drain of bullion from the Bank and the consequent suspension of specie payments. Considerable controversy has centred on the part played by the following factors : the unbalancing of the budget and its possible inflationary results; the government's remittances abroad for subsidy and military expenditure; the premium on gold in Paris that accompanied the destruction of the assignats; abnormal imports of grain necessitated by inadequate British harvests; and large imports, at extremely high prices, of naval stores. The forces operating on the reserves and the exchanges can best be evaluated after a fairly strict chronological account.

Silberling has attempted to classify abnormal expenditure abroad under the headings of military expenditure, loans and subsidies, and abnormal

did the country banks increase to an appreciable extent in the years immediately after the suspension. Thornton (p. 129) gives the following figures: 353 (1797), 366 (1799), 386 (1800). He adds his belief that the figure for 1797 somewhat under-estimates the number of country banks. See also Macleod, p. 87.

[1] C. Juglar, *Des Crises Commerciales*, p. 305, holds that the decrease in paper currency caused by the crisis of 1793 created, in the following years, an abnormal demand for guineas at the Bank as a substitute in the ordinary needs of circulation.

[2] Tooke, i. 256, described the situation in a vocabulary surprisingly modern: 'The rate of interest . . . was much higher in consequence of the absorption by the government expenditure of a large part of the savings of individuals.'

[3] Quoted, *A.R.*, Chr., 1797, p. 99.

FIG. 14. Finance, 1794–1801

grain imports. He sets these against the Lisbon exchange and the annual average figures for the Bank's reserves[1] (table, p. 50).

Monthly figures for the Bank of England's holdings of cash, British coin, foreign coin, and bullion show a peak of £9·0 million on 12 April 1794, and a slow decline to £7·4 million on 20 June 1795. At this point the Bank's

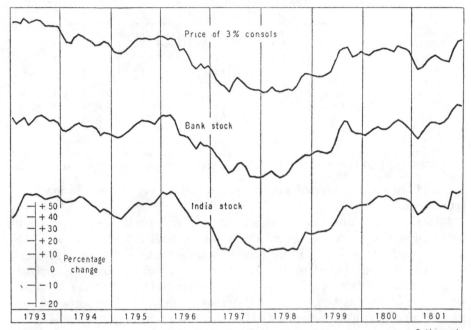

Ratio scale

FIG. 15. Finance, 1793–1801

position was sound, and there was no question of restricting cash payment. There followed, however, a steady fall to the spring of 1796. From May to December 1796 the bullion holdings of the Bank hovered between £3 and £3·5 million; but from 14 January 1797 to 24 March the stock fell from £3·3 to £2·2 million, a low point for the entire period. On 27 February the King had been called from Windsor, and the Privy Council issued a suspension order commanding that 'the directors of the Bank of England should forbear issuing any cash in payment, until the sense of Parliament can be taken on the subject'.[2] The explanation of the Suspension Act reduces, then, to the problem of tracing the two bullion drains on the

---

[1] 'Financial and Monetary Policy of Great Britain during the Napoleonic Wars', Part I, *Quarterly Journal of Economics*, xxxviii. 227.

[2] James, p. 18, quoting from the diary of the Bank's chief cashier. This source also gives the following account of the situation: 'On Friday [24 Feb. 1797], the Committee, composed of the whole Court of Directors, alarmed at the rapid diminution of the cash in their coffers, deputed the Deputy Governor and Mr. Bosanquet, to wait upon Mr. Pitt, to represent to him the *dreadful drain of their cash*, and to ask him how far *he* thought the Bank might continue paying in specie. . . .'

(In £ millions)

	Bills and specie for British armies in Europe (a)	Subsidies and loans (b)	Grain imports over £2 million (c)	Total a, b, c (d)	Deviation from par of Spanish dollar (e)	Bank's reserve (f)
1793 . .	0·6	0·8	—	1·4	−1·0	4·6
1794 . .	2·3	3·0	—	5·3	−1·6	6·7
1795 . .	4·4	5·1	—	9·4	+2·4	5·4
1796 . .	1·0	3·4	2·5	7·0	+4·2	2·3
1797 . .	0·2	1·4	—	1·6	+1·7	3·1
1798 . .	0·2	0·2	—	0·3	−1·0	6·4
1799 . .	1·3	2·1	—	3·4	+5·1	7·0
1800 . .	1·1	3·4	6·8	11·3	+11·2	5·4
1801 . .	1·7	2·2	8·2	12·0	+15·9	4·5

N.B. The failure of column (d) to equal the sum of the previous three columns in 1795, 1796, 1798, and 1801 is due to Silberling's having rounded the figures to the nearest tenth.

Bank: from the summer of 1795 to the spring of 1796; from January to late February 1797.

Silberling's explanation of the loss of bullion depends on a correlation between exchange movements, abnormal expenditure abroad, and the bullion stock at the Bank. Using annual figures, that correlation is impressive over the whole period. Hawtrey, however, has seriously challenged this conception of the course of events, insisting (a) that war-time expenditure abroad was not essentially different from capital exports during peace;[1] and, (b) more particularly that the bullion drain of 1795–6 is to be

---

[1] *Currency and Credit*, pp. 259 ff. Silberling has replied (p. 232 n.) that 'capital flows abroad in peace time because there is a surplus of it seeking a profit; remittances have to be made in the emergency of war irrespective of conditions in the capital market and in the face of existing military and naval obstructions, which affect the rates on insurance and commission'. In the sense that the Bank was redeeming its notes in gold the automatic check of a classically operating gold standard still existed until 1797. Hawtrey is correct, then, to the extent that an adverse exchange should, as under peacetime conditions, have forced a rise in market rates, and a contraction of the credit circulation. And, as noted above, the Bank did attempt to restrict private credit accommodations from the spring of 1796. His statement, however, in no way disproves the possibility that extraordinary remittances at once weakened the exchanges and lowered the bullion reserve. The assumption underlying his argument is that expenditure

abroad came out of a reduction in British incomes from taxation and a contraction in internal credit. If that were, in fact, the case —if there were no net consequences on the reserves of the bullion export—his statement is, by definition, unexceptionable. But Hawtrey does not establish historically the justification for the limiting condition—'so long as there is no inflation' (p. 325 n.). Both Silberling and Hawtrey fail to point out the nice coincidence between the heavy subsidies to Germany and the enormous increase in goods' exports there. Some £6 million were lent to the Emperor of Germany in the period 1794–7 (Silberling, p. 225). Although the Imperial loans were widely cited as an immediate cause of the loss of bullion, and although a part of the remittances may have been made in bullion, as opposed to bills of exchange, the increase in Britain's exports to Hamburg almost certainly made the transfer easier than it would otherwise have been. Evidence before the Committee of 1797 indicated that in remitting the Imperial

traced to the re-establishment of a metallic currency in Paris and a consequent premium there on gold. The period when the French were accumulating bullion most rapidly concurs neatly with the major drain at the Bank.[1] The weight given this factor is increased by other evidence. The Hamburg exchange was rising from the middle of 1795 to the end of 1797, during the most severe bullion drains. Again it is to be noted that the peak in government remittances abroad came in 1795. They fell during 1796–7. Finally, the fairly stable reserve of the last three-quarters of 1796 coincides with the end of the premium at Paris. It coincides as well with the coming of the bountiful harvest of 1796. The wheat price was 100s. in March 1796, 58s. in December. The abnormal expenditure on grain in 1796 must have been concentrated in the early months of the year.[2]

It may be concluded that, up to the early days of 1797, the Bank and the government had managed to find in the market sufficient bills to meet military expenditures, loans, and subsidies; although the additional pressure of a gold premium in Paris and high-price grain and naval stores' imports had, in 1795–6, brought the reserve to a precarious level, despite some contraction of credit within Britain. Nevertheless, without the internal drain which began in January 1797 it is extremely doubtful whether suspension would have occurred at that time. From the end of 1796 to the Act of Suspension the Bank's reserve declined, despite a further contraction in discounts and even in government advances:

(In £ millions)

	Coin and bullion	Bills and notes discounted	Exchequer bills
17 Dec. 1796 . .	2·2	3·7	9·6
14 Jan. 1797 . .	1·8	4·2	9·4
21 Jan. 1797 . .	1·8	4·0	8·3
11 Feb. 1797 . .	1·7	3·3	8·3
25 Feb. 1797 . .	1·1	3·0	8·2
11 Mar. 1797 . .	1·0	4·6	8·2
24 Mar. 1797 . .	0·9	5·5	8·1
8 Apr. 1797 . .	0·9	5·8	8·1

loan, as well as other advances to the Emperor, no British coin was sent out of the country (which could not indeed legally be done); and that foreign coin or bullion only to the amount of about £1,200,000 was exported. The remainder of the loan, and the whole of the advances, were remitted in bills of exchange (quoted from Boyd's testimony, A.R., Chr., 1797, p. 100).

[1] Hawtrey, pp. 326–9.

[2] Tooke places the greatest drain on account of loans and subsidies at the end of 1794 and the beginning of 1795 (i. 198). He emphasizes the influence of grain imports, and the 'enormous prices to which the competition of the French government had raised the prices of naval stores in the Baltic', on the fall of the reserve late in 1795 and early in 1796 (ibid., pp. 199–200). Macpherson (p. 407) also refers to 'the large sums payable for cargoes and freights of neutral ships taken, which the foreign owners required to be paid in bullion'.

The Lords' Committee of Secrecy, 1797, traced the panic as follows:[1]

The alarm of invasion (by the French) which, when an immediate attack was first apprehended in Ireland, had occasioned some extraordinary demand for cash on the Bank of England, in the months of December and January last, began in February to produce similar effects in the North of England. Your committee find, that, in consequence of this apprehension, the farmers suddenly brought the produce of their lands to sale, and carried the notes of the country banks, which they had collected by these and other means, into those banks for payment; that this unusual and sudden demand for cash reduced the several banks at Newcastle to the necessity of suspending their payments in specie, and of availing themselves of all the means in their power of procuring a speedy supply of cash from the metropolis; that the effects of this demand on the Newcastle Banks, and of their suspension of payments in cash, soon spread over various parts of the country, from whence similar applications were consequently made to the metropolis for cash; that the alarm thus diffused, not only occasioned an increased demand for cash in the country, but probably a disposition in many to hoard what was thus obtained: that this call on the metropolis, through whatever channels, directly affected the Bank of England as the great repository of cash, and was in the course of still further operation upon it when stopped by the minute of council of the 26th February.

The Bank's reserve rose quickly throughout 1797 and more slowly in 1798, reaching a peak in February 1799 of £10·5 million. With the return of confidence and the acceptance of the newly issued £1 and £2 notes, gold came quickly out of hiding, while an increasingly favourable foreign exchange brought bullion from abroad.[2]

Tooke believed that suspension could have been avoided.[3] That is an issue open to question; but it is clear that the Bank was quite prepared to resume payment very soon after suspension.[4] The Bank declared itself ready to do so in October 1797, by which time France and Austria had signed the Treaty of Leoben, which seemed to eliminate the need for further British subsidies. The government, however, refused

[1] Quoted, Tooke, i. 203–4. An additional source of uncertainty to the Bank early in 1797 was the possibility of a government loan of £1·5 million to Ireland. Pitt contemplated sending the greater part of this in 'hard cash', which, the directors represented to him, 'would bring ruin upon the bank, and probably compel them to shut their doors' (Macpherson, p. 408; also Macleod, pp. 89–90).

[2] Andréadès, pp. 198–202, cites especially the public support given the Bank by the financial community, in a resolution signed by 4,000 bankers and industrialists.

[3] Op. cit. i. 204–5 n.: 'The reason for this opinion is, that the circulation was already so contracted that the reduced number of notes then outstanding were becoming so much wanted for immediate payments, as to

be less and less likely to be returned to the Bank for gold; while, on the other hand, the tide of the metals was setting in so strongly from abroad as almost to insure a sufficient supply to meet the internal demand.' In this instance Tooke was in agreement with Thornton, who, because the bullion drain of early 1797 was completely internal, held that the Bank should have enlarged rather than contracted its issues in the period of panic (Thornton, pp. 57 ff.). Tooke adds: 'But the doctrine is to be received with great caution, as it may easily be perverted into a justification of a very lax and improvident management' (i. 204 n.).

[4] Third Report, Committee of Secrecy, on the outstanding demands of the Bank, &c., *Reports from Committees of the House of Commons* (1803), xi. 192.

the offer, and the act was renewed year after year until 1803, when it was extended until 'six months after the ratification of a definitive treaty of peace'.[1]

The gold, returning from internal hoards and from abroad, lifted the reserve to a peak early in 1799, from which point it declined steadily until March 1804.[2] The Hamburg exchange shared the decline only during 1799. With money extremely tight during the commercial crisis of that year, traders in Hamburg liquidated whatever holdings on London were in hand, much to the embarrassment of many British merchants; while others in England, apparently without strain, shipped funds 'to support their commercial friends'.[3] The increased financial demands of a booming foreign trade and of general revival at home explains the continuance of the drain at a time when the exchanges were improving.

A rise in the note circulation in 1800 and the substantial increase, at that time, in commercial advances called forth what Tooke calls 'the first important controversy respecting the influence [of the extension of the issues of the Bank] on prices'.[4] Boyd held the increased note issue responsible for the rise in prices, Baring and Thornton opposed his view. Tooke[5] believed that the Bank's enlarged issues at this time were merely 'compensating for the chasm' which the previous 'clandestine export of guineas' had left. Bills and notes discounted at the Bank had hovered between £2 and £4 million from 1794 to 1797. From 1798 to 1801 they moved between £4 and £8 million, increasing, as do the figures for exports, from year to year.[6]

The general recovery in trade and the successful readjustment to the new financial situation are reflected in a rise of both Consols and India Stock, from a low point in the crisis of 1797 to a peak at the end of 1800. This upward movement was broken in the autumn of 1799, due, probably, to the failures in Hamburg and the resumption of war by the coalition. There is a sharp decline from October 1800 to March 1801. But from April

---

[1] For a complete list of the Acts of Parliament relating to the suspension and resumption of payments, see James, pp. 22–3.

[2] For the influx of gold from abroad, see Andréadès, p. 205.

[3] Macpherson, p. 485. This is a reference to the ill-fated Lutine freight. £140,000 were sent: 'The money was put on board a ship of war, which was unfortunately cast away upon the coast of Holland: and the whole loss fell upon the underwriters, who, thinking the risk next to nothing, had taken it at a very low premium.' See also Tooke, i. 234, 240–3. Tooke also lists, as an explanation of the fall in the exchange, the demand for war chests on the Continent, as war was resumed by the coalition in the summer of 1799 (p. 241).

[4] Op. cit. i. 243 n.

[5] Ibid., p. 245.

[6] The total for notes in circulation and private securities (of which 'bills and notes discounted' were a major part) moved as follows:

(In £ millions)

	Notes in circulation	Private securities
Feb. 1798 . .	13·1	5·6
Aug. . . .	12·2	6·4
Feb. 1799 . .	13·0	5·5
Aug. . . .	13·4	7·5
Feb. 1800 . .	16·8	7·4
Aug. . . .	15·0	8·6
Feb. 1801 . .	16·2	10·5
Aug. . . .	14·6	10·3

(Cannan, p. xliv). Annual average commercial discounts were (in £ millions): 4·5 (1798), 5·4 (1799), 6·4 (1800), 7·9 (1801) (ibid., p. xliii).

onward their prices recovered.[1] The recovery was especially pronounced after the signing of the preliminary treaty of peace in October. Its announcement was greeted with a 'frenzy of public delight unequalled since the Restoration. The funds rose 8 per cent. on the news.'[2] The fall in the rate of interest and general financial recovery from the crisis of 1797 to the lesser crisis of early 1801 appear clearly in the annual average price of India Stock and the yield on Consols:

	India Stock (In £)	Yield on 3 per cent. Consols (per cent.)
1797 . .	154·6	5·87
1798 . .	151·9	5·95
1799 . .	181·8	5·10
1800 . .	205·5	4·72
1801 . .	200·4	4·93

6. Labour. The rise in the price of grain and other foodstuffs dominates the story of British labour in the first nine years of the war. Money wages were rising but in 'a very inadequate proportion to the increased price of the necessaries of life'.[3]

	Cost of living[a]	Tucker's index of		Bowley's index of agricultural money wages
		Money wages of London artisans	Real wages	
1793 . .	148	45·9	46·0	112
1794 . .	168	46·7	46·1	115
1795 . .	179	48·6	41·4	127
1796 . .	153	49·4	42·3	138
1797 . .	152	51·0	44·2	142
1798 . .	165	51·1	43·9	148
1799 . .	229	51·1	40·9	152
1800 . .	252	51·1	32·6	156
1801 . .	190	52·6	33·0	160

[a] Gilboy-Boody index (1700 = 100). E. W. Gilboy, 'Cost of Living and Real Wages in Eighteenth Century England', *Review of Economic Statistics*, August 1936, pp. 134–43.

---

[1] Britain's precarious military position at this time probably affected the securities' prices. W. Smart (*Economic Annals of the Nineteenth Century*, i. 42) describes the first three months of 1801 as 'critical and alarming to the last degree', with the war going badly and the food shortage worse than it had been since the war began. It is significant that the peak in the wheat price came in March (154s.). Its price fell and the food crisis eased thereafter, under the influence of good harvest prospects. An even more immediate influence might have been the victory of Nelson in the Battle of the Baltic, which came at this same time. Peace negotiations were secretly opened by the end of March. Whether the City's excellent channels of official gossip operated in this case cannot be established.

[3] Ibid., p. 46.

[2] Tooke, i. 185–6.

Tooke's description of the period substantiates calculations which show a drastic fall in real wages :[1]

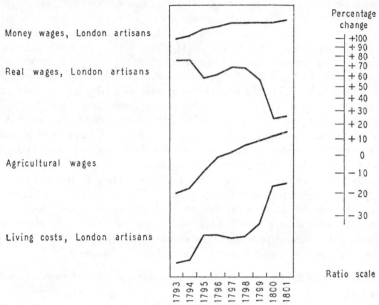

FIG. 16. Labour, 1793–1801

Such and so great being the rise in prices of provisions, and of nearly all consumable commodities, it was quite impossible that the lowest of the working

[1] Ibid., pp. 225–6. The increase in wartime taxation as well as the inadequacy of the harvests is accounted by Tooke 'a major cause' of the price rise. Tooke reprints (p. 228 n.) an estimate of the expenses of housekeeping between 1793 and 1800, by an inhabitant of Bury St. Edmunds, extracted from the Appendix to the *Report of the Committee of the House of Commons*, in 1800.

	1793			1799			1800		
	£	s.	d.	£	s.	d.	£	s.	d.
Coomb of Malt	1	3	0	1	3	0	2	0	0
Chaldron of Coals . . .	2	0	6	2	6	0	2	11	0
Coomb of Oats	0	13	0	0	16	0	1	1	0
Load of Hay	4	10	0	5	5	0	7	0	0
Meat	0	0	5	0	0	7	0	0	9
Butter	0	0	11	0	0	11	0	1	4
Sugar (Loaf)	0	1	0	0	1	3	0	1	4
Soap	0	0	8	0	0	9½	0	0	10
Window Lights (30 windows) .	7	10	0	12	12	0	12	12	0
Candles	0	0	8	0	0	9½	0	0	10½
Poor Rates per Qr. . . .	0	2	6	0	3	0	0	5	0
	16	2	8	22	9	4	25	14	1½

See also Eden, vol. iii, appendix XII, for estimates of earnings and expenditures for agricultural workers in a sample of counties all over England. It is perhaps worth remarking that Eden was induced to undertake his great investigation by 'the difficulties, which the labouring classes experienced, from the high price of grain, and provisions in general . . . during the years 1794 and 1795' (ibid., i. i).

classes could, upon their wages, at the rate of what they were before 1795, obtain a subsistence for themselves and their families, on the lowest scale requisite to sustain human existence ; and the classes above the lowest, including some portion of skilled labourers, could do little, if at all, more than provide themselves with food, clothing, and shelter, without any of the indulgences which habit had rendered necessaries. If under these circumstances there had been no rise of wages, no contributions by parishes and by individuals, in aid of wages, great numbers of the people must have actually perished, and the classes immediately above the lowest would with difficulty have preserved themselves from the same fate. In such case the suffering from dearth would have been correctly designated as a famine, a term which has been somewhat loosely applied to the period under consideration. . . . A rise of wages was imperatively called for by the urgency of the case, and was complied with to some extent in most of the branches of industry, the claims for increase being aided by the resource which workmen and labourers had of enlisting in the army and navy. There had . . . been an advance of wages in 1795 and 1796, and the allowance system had been begun and carried to some extent in those years. A further advance of wages took place in 1800 and 1801 ; but still so inadequate, compared with the prices of provisions, as even with parish allowances and private contributions, to leave a vast mass of privation and misery.

Tea consumption, in its absolute movement, does not indicate a decline in real wages :

(In million lb.)

1790	.	. 16·4	1794	.	. 18·7	1798	.	. 22·5
1791	.	. 17·1	1795	.	. 21·3	1799	.	. 22·8
1792	.	. 17·7	1796	.	. 20·3	1800	.	. 23·3
1793	.	. 17·5	1797	.	. 18·9	1801	.	. 23·7

The relatively slight rise after 1798, however, at a time of rapidly increased employment and output, probably reflects the downward pressure on real wages in these years—accentuated, in the case of tea, by heavy taxation.

The discontent which resulted from the rising prices of provisions constituted a serious political menace, especially under war-time conditions.[1] The government, as noted earlier, took steps towards increasing grain imports, and it encouraged the process of inclosure. But the most striking attempt to deal with the problem was the institution, in 1795, of the Speenhamland system of wage subsidy. These allowances out of local rates were meant to keep labour above the starvation level at least.[2] The system of outdoor relief, designed as a local expedient, spread rapidly throughout the country.[3] Although they probably prevented much actual starvation,[4] the wage subsidies did not keep real wages from falling.[5]

[1] Halévy, pp. 285–7. Also G. D. H. Cole, i. 51, 56, 59, 60.

[2] Tooke mentions the proposal of a Mr. Whitbread in the House of Commons for the regulation of money wages by the price of provisions, with a minimum wage stipulated (i. 227).

[3] Mantoux, pp. 447–8. The situation in Berkshire had been made more acute by the beginnings of the secular decline of the south-west woollen industry.

[4] Tooke, i. 225–6.

[5] For an extended contemporary discussion of their irregular consequences for real wages in the first year of administration see Eden, i. 574–89.

The coincidence of exorbitant living costs, a prosperity demand for labour, the rapid growth of an urban working class, and the presence of liberal ideas, produced widespread riots, strikes, and even some revolutionary activity.[1] The activities of the Corresponding Societies, ruthlessly repressed in 1793–4, had been completely political.[2] But the government, and perhaps the people, did not always distinguish between labour's activities designed to affect wages or to procure cheap food and those aiming to overthrow the monarch. A peasant movement, for example, among Norfolk labourers, which desired to organize a national petition for higher wages, was dealt with by the State in the same manner as the Corresponding Societies.[3] But the typical expression of labour discontent was neither national in scope nor closely linked with clear, long-term political objectives. It was the local strike or bread riot. In the period from the latter months of 1796 to the beginning of 1799, when the wheat price was falling, one can trace few disturbances.

From 1799 to 1801, however, labour made a desperate attempt to maintain its position by forcing higher money wages.[4] Macpherson notes the means employed and the government's response to them:[5]

It being represented in Parliament, that great numbers of journeymen manufacturers and workmen were combining to advance their wages, it was enacted, that such persons entering into written or verbal covenants for the purpose of obtaining higher wages, lessening or altering the hours of work, or deterring others from duly following their business, or refusing to work along with other workingmen, or contributing money for carrying on such combinations, should be committed to prison for not more than three months, or to the house of correction for not more than two months, by order of any justice.

The Combination Acts of 1799 and 1800 made almost every form of collective working-class activity illegal, with the exception of the guild functions of the Friendly Societies. In these years Britain's ruling classes, with the spectre of the French Revolution before them, were seriously frightened: in these years, too, the word 'strike' first came into general usage.[6]

---

[1] For examples see *A.R.*, Chr., 1796, pp. 7–9; 1799, pp. 157–63; 1800, pp. 294, 346.

[2] Cole, i. 48–50.

[3] Ibid., p. 51. Cole traces the failure of liberal ideas to emerge in Britain until after 1815 to the government's active repression. It was unemployment, however, which lay at the roots of post-war discontent and unrest. Except for part of 1803 and 1810–11, unemployment was not a major problem before 1815.

[4] Tooke, i. 225–7.

[5] Op. cit., p. 475. See also p. 500 for parliamentary action with specific reference to disputes in the cotton trade. It is to be noted that the conditions (quoted by Macpherson as constituting the background for the Combination Acts) reflect both the high prices of foodstuffs and a strong, prosperity, bargaining position for labour. The demand for shorter hours represents a situation quite discrete from bad harvests. There might have been strikes in these years even if the supply of grain had been normal.

[6] Halévy, p. 287.

Chapter II

1802–11[1]

INTRODUCTION

THIS chapter covers the decade from 1802 to 1811. It embraces the period from the short Peace of Amiens, through the crisis of 1810, to the beginning of revival, late in 1811. The account is divided again, at the year 1806. The consequences of the Continental System, in full operation, give unity to the years between the Berlin Decree (1806) and the quarrel of Napoleon with the Russian Emperor (1811), which began the dissolution of the Continent's self-blockade. Division in 1806 is also useful in that it permits a continuous account of the immediate background to the cycle from 1808 to 1811, and of the cycle itself.

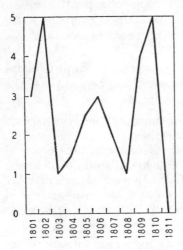

FIG. 17. Business-cycle Pattern, 1801–11

The years 1802 and 1806 are peak years in a mild cyclical movement, with a low point early in 1804. They contain no important financial crises; the years of the upswing, 1804–6, saw only moderate increases in production and prices. This is basically to be attributed to the failure of any important export channels to develop to boom proportions. There was no equivalent to the markets of the United States in 1788–93, or of Hamburg in 1796–1802. Although the blockade was by no means as complete as it was later to become, it was effective enough to keep the export trade hesitant. More concretely, it caused a shift in the routes of British trade, with Norway and Denmark and various Mediterranean ports supplanting the north German cities as major continental entrepôts. In the six years after 1802 trends in almost all indexes of production, foreign trade, and even prices exhibit a slackening in their rate of increase.

The general decline that ran from the latter months of 1802 to the early months of 1804 may be attributed, essentially, to the unsettlement of the export trade, especially after the actual outbreak of war in May 1803. But depression was accentuated by severe agricultural distress, brought on by successive abundant harvests and a drastic fall in grain prices. Bankrupt-

---

[1] Cyclical pattern:

Trough	Peak
1801 (Oct.)	1802 (Dec.)
1804 (Mar.)	1806 (Aug.)
1808 (May)	1810 (Mar.)
1811 (Sept.)	

cies were especially numerous in the agricultural districts, which were of particular significance in this period when the extension of farming acreage constituted a principal outlet for new investment. But war and bad harvests caused, in 1804, a sharp rise in wheat and other farm prices. The Corn Law of 1804, hurriedly put through to protect the stricken farmer, never came into operation.

A more general revival in trade can be traced from 1804 to the latter months of 1806. Exports increased as merchants accommodated themselves to war-time conditions, and all of Britain's industry responded. But advance was at a modest rate. The familiar lines of technical progress proceeded, but not at the pace of the last few years of the eighteenth century.

The fairly even economic tone of these five years was accentuated by a relatively low level of government expenditure abroad. The exchanges were strong, the Bank's reserve fairly high. The Bank, in fact, felt itself able to finance a greater amount of commercial paper than ever before. Although there was in each year a considerable excess of government expenditure over revenue, the barrage of new taxes drew in an increasing proportion of the total annual outlay.

The persistent tendency for money wages to lag behind the cost of living was interrupted somewhat in 1802–6. The fall in grain prices before the inadequate harvest of 1804 eased the pressure on working-class incomes, and although food prices rose thereafter, the 'famine' situation of 1800–1 was not repeated. There was, nevertheless, a considerable ferment of labour organization, with the Combination Acts evaded in many districts. A symptom of the proceeding social change was the passage, in 1802, of an act purporting to establish minimum standards of work and education for pauper children in the textile mills. Without government inspectors, however, the act was merely a gesture towards reform.

Three political situations dominate the story of 1807–11: the mercantile war between Napoleon and Britain; the revolution in, and Britain's military domination of, the Iberian Peninsula; and the necessity for Britain again to export large amounts for subsidy and war expenditure. The first demanded a thorough recasting of the trade with the Continent; the second, by opening the Latin-American colonies to British trade, forestalled Napoleon's plan to 'conquer England by excess' (i.e. to block her exports, drain off her bullion); the third, in conjunction with a prosperity demand for commodity imports and bad harvests, caused a serious weakening in the foreign exchanges.

Trade was relatively stagnant from the close of 1806 to the latter months of 1808. Export channels were quite severely restricted, including those of the United States, where the embargo was operative. A latent spirit of enterprise found outlet only in the floatation of numerous joint-stock companies within Britain and not, as usual, in foreign trade. In the course of 1808, however, Spain revolted successfully from Napoleonic rule, and the Portuguese royal family fled to Brazil. British trade soon followed to

Brazil and then to the whole of Latin America. The Berlin and Milan decrees were effective in reducing slightly the total exports to the Continent and in causing British exporters to employ circuitous routes; but the boom in exports to South and Central American areas more than compensated for the loss. On balance, 1809–10 were years of great prosperity, derived primarily from foreign trade in that direction; the reopening of the trade with the United States in 1810 supplied an important secondary stimulus in that year. Britain was paid, however, in colonial goods which she counted on re-exporting in large part (as in 1796–9) to the Continent. Through most of 1809 that looked feasible. But in the course of 1810 Napoleon prosecuted vigorously his policy of blockade. And in conjunction with indiscretions in the financing of the Latin-American trade, a severe credit crisis developed. Depression followed until the latter months of 1811, marked by heavy unemployment, especially in the cotton textile districts and in the Birmingham area, heavily dependent on exports to the United States. Under these circumstances manufacturers and merchants turned bitterly against the Orders in Council which, it was widely held, were responsible for the stagnation of British foreign trade.

The Bank of England, more than on earlier occasions, appears to have been directly involved in this boom. Private discounts were granted on a record scale, despite a declining reserve, some apparently to finance speculative exports to Latin America. In failing to induce a credit deflation, and thus to cut down the volume of imports, the Bank was partly responsible for the depreciation of the foreign exchanges which called forth, in 1810, the Bullion Committee's hard money report. But a growing number of country banks as well increased their note issue enormously, repeating, in some respects, the situation which occurred before the crisis of 1792–3. In 1810–11 bankruptcies and unemployment increased, and the prices of commodities and securities fell rapidly.

Aside from the direct stimulus of the boom in foreign trade, internal industrial development proceeded, most notably in the latter years of the decade. The coal trade operated under conditions of chronic shortage in supply; iron production, with South Wales leading, continued to increase and to become relatively independent of foreign ores and bar iron; machinery was painfully introduced into woollens; while cottons, most sensitive at this stage to fluctuations in foreign trade, continued to expand, but at a markedly lesser rate than in the previous decade.

After some twenty years of extremely rapid change industrial labour began to assume a more definite character. Trade disputes, especially in textiles, had a distinctly modern tone, with picketing, black-legs, labour spies, and demands for shorter hours and higher wages noted widely, especially in the boom period 1808–10. Labour organization seems to have been on a large scale and relatively efficient in its operation; the Friendly Societies, which had been praised by Frederick Eden in 1797 for their archaic good fellowship, were often now the means of concealing illegal working-class combinations. It is impossible, of course, to gauge the extent to which improved organization forced money wages above the level they would otherwise have attained. But it is clear that the working classes were more successful than in 1796–1801 in preventing rising food costs from lowering real wages. This is, however, to be attributed essentially to the lesser pressure on real wages from the side of living costs rather than to improved organization.

PART I: 1802–6

1. **Prices.** The domestic commodity price index falls from March 1801 until about the middle of 1802. It then remains fairly stable until the early months of 1804, when it dips sharply. In the latter half of 1804 it rises to find a level about which it fluctuates with a slight declining tendency until October 1807.

From March 1801 to March 1804 the price of wheat fell from 154s. to 50s. per quarter. The major part of this decline came within 1801. A good harvest, the coming of peace in October, the opening of the Baltic, and the operation of the import bounty, all assured an immediate large supply;[1] and they also caused expectations of a further fall in price: 'Under these improved prospects of future supply, the markets gave way rapidly.'[2] The harvests of 1802 and 1803, though 'not of superabundant produce', were sufficient, in conjunction with available surpluses, further to depress the price of wheat.[3] The prices of beef, pork, and mutton show no such decline: 'the stock of cattle and sheep, which had been reduced by the previous scarcities, had not time to be restored.'[4] The stability of these prices, as well as the rise in coal, tallow, and butter in 1803 explain the contrary movements of the wheat price and the domestic index in the latter half of the year.[5] The fall in the domestic index early in 1804 is to be attributed not only to the movement of agricultural prices but to others as well,

[1] Tooke, i. 237. A good season, of course, brought forth a supply from the enormously increased area of British farming land. The long-run effect of inclosures had been concealed by the deficient harvests of 1799–1801.

[2] Idem.

[3] Ibid., pp. 238–9. The brief rise from March to June 1803 in all domestic prices may have been due to the political fears which anticipated and accompanied the renewal of war in May. The fall in grain prices produced a situation which foreshadowed post-war agricultural distress. Tooke (ibid., pp. 251–2) points to the rising total of bankruptcies, which he associates directly with the price decline and agrarian distress: 1800, 951; 1801, 1,199; 1802, 1,090; 1803, 1,214.

In 1804 the agricultural interests were aided by a new Corn Bill by which a duty was imposed of 24s. 3d. per quarter when the price was under 63s.; and 2s. 6d. per quarter when at or above that rate and under 66s.; and 6d. when above 66s. But the inadequate harvest of 1804 raised the wheat price over the limit, where it remained until the Corn Law of 1815. The Corn Law of 1804 was thus inoperative.

[4] Ibid., p. 238.

[5] Ibid., pp. 265–6.

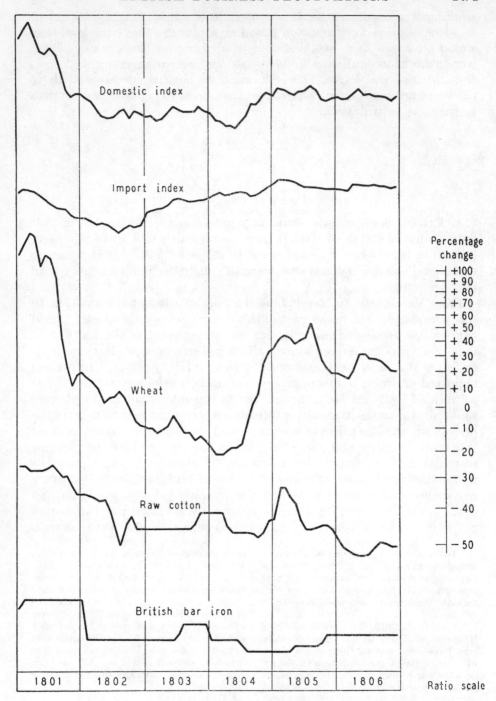

FIG. 18. Prices, 1801–6

affected by the recession, from the outbreak of hostilities to about the spring of 1804.[1]

The harvest of 1804 was 'very deficient',[2] and a sharp rise in agricultural prices resulted. The fall in the domestic index late in 1805 is explained by a somewhat more productive yield in the autumn than had been expected.[3] Early in 1806, however, the continental policy of Napoleon began to take shape and, in fear of possible consequences, prices rose until May.[4] But the harvest was somewhat under-estimated, and the immediate effects of a blockade over-estimated. The domestic index was in December 1806 a shade lower than it had been in January.

The latter half of 1801 brought with it a decline in the import index which continued through the brief interval of peace until August 1802. From that point the index rises to a peak in February 1805, declines slightly, and remains fairly stable until the end of the following year. The index is much influenced by the recovery in the prices of colonial produce which, following the crisis of 1799, had declined, recovered towards the end of 1800, but slumped again badly through most of the ensuing two years :[5] in 1801, due to slackened demands; in 1802, due to peace-time conditions. In the latter months of 1802 and early in 1803 a recovery set in which continued until 1806.[6] The beginnings of the Continental System then caused a depression in prices, as export markets for colonial produce were narrowed.[7] The contrary effect of the system on supplies from the Baltic is indicated in 1806 by the rise in the price of Memel pine timber, from 98s. (per last of 50 cu. ft.) in January to 150s. in December. This upward movement in import prices anticipates a major immediate result of the Continental System when it came into full operation in the ensuing years.

The influence of changes in freight rates in lowering import prices in 1802 and raising them in the following four years is illustrated by the table (p. 64) of Baltic freight rates.[8]

---

[1] Tooke, i. 255.

[2] Ibid., pp. 258–65.

[3] Ibid., pp. 265–6.

[4] Ibid., p. 266. 'The spring, like the preceding one, was backward; and the appearance of the crops was unpromising. This circumstance, combined with political events, namely, the hostile proceedings of Prussia against this country, under the dictation of France, which threatened in their consequences to cut off our supplies of corn from the Baltic, and which had the immediate effect of raising greatly the rates of freight and insurance, occasioned a rally in the average price of wheat to 84s. in June; but thenceforward, notwithstanding that the weather was variable, and rather wet during the harvest, and notwithstanding the apprehension of increased political obstructions, in consequence of the overthrow and

final subjugation of Prussia by the battle of Jena, followed by the Berlin decree, in the autumn of 1806, prices declined slowly, but progressively.'

[5] Ibid., p. 272.

[6] By the end of 1802 war preparations were under way again: 'October 29. The greatest activity prevails at all the different ports in equipping armaments, impressing seamen, and in warlike preparations of every kind' (A.R., Chr., 1802, p. 460). The prices of Baltic products, largely naval stores, rose in the last quarter of 1802.

[7] Tooke, i. 273. From 1804 to 1806 exports were again rising, although colonial produce did not play the dominant role it did in the previous export boom; nor was the expansion in foreign trade as a whole on a comparable scale.

[8] See also above, p. 29, n. 9.

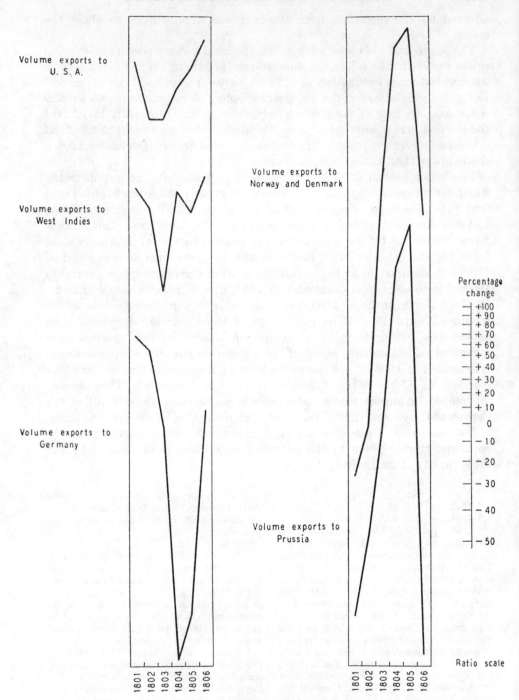

FIG. 19. Foreign Trade, 1801–6

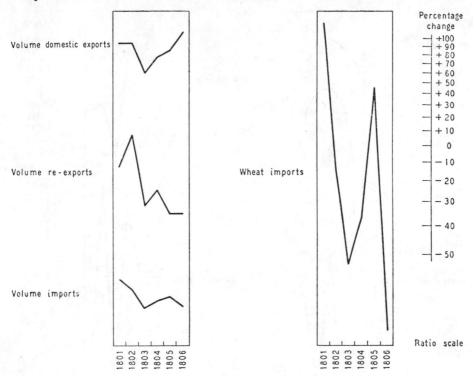

FIG. 19. Foreign Trade, 1801–6

Freight Rates

| | Petersburg to London | | Riga to London, timber | Memel to London, timber |
	Hemp and flax (s. per ton)	Tallow	(s. per load)	
1801 . .	90	55	40	35
1802 . .	45–50	30–5	24	19
1803 . .	90–100	50–5	35–60	30–45
1804 . .	75	50	40	33
1805 . .	75	50	40	33
1806 . .	85	55	38	30

Nor was this influence confined to the Baltic trade :[1]

Jamaica to London

	Sugar	Rum		Sugar	Rum
1792 . .	4s.	6d.	1803 . .	5s.	6d.
			1804 . .	9s.	10d.
1801 . .	10s.	1s. 0d.	1805 . .	9s.	1s. 0d.
1802 . .	6s.	8d.	1806 . .	10s.	1s. 0d.

[1] Akenhead, p. clxv (submitted by John Blacket).

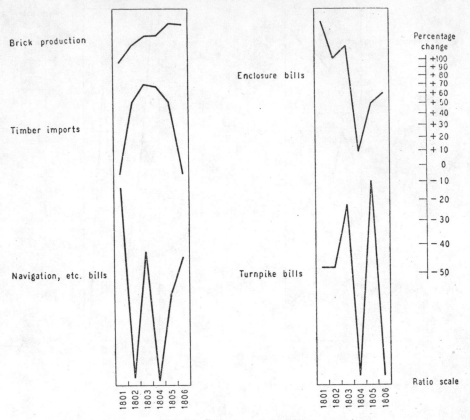

FIG. 20. Investment, 1801–6

Non-agricultural domestic prices exhibit, in most cases, a mild, irregular response to the recovery of 1804–6, with little concordance in the upper turning-points:

	Jan. 1803	Jan. 1804	Jan. 1805	Peak 1805–6
Copper (pence per lb.) . . .	14·3	15·2	17·4	(Jan.–July 1806) 20·0
Hides (pence per lb.) . . .	19·8	23·5	23·5	(Mar.–Apr. 1805) 24·0
Iron bars (£ per ton) . . .	18·0	18·0	17·0	(throughout 1806) 18·5
Leather butts (pence per lb.) . .	22·5	22·5	25·5	(Sept.–Oct. 1806) 27·5
Rape oil (£ per ton) . . .	42·5	46·0	62·0	(Apr. 1805) 67·0
Hard soap (shillings per cwt.) . .	78·0	84·0	78·0	(May 1806) 81·0
Tin (shillings per cwt.) . . .	113·0	113·0	114·0	(Aug.–Dec. 1806) 126·0

2. Foreign Trade. The boom in foreign trade which characterized the period 1798–1802 did not continue in the years up to 1806:[1]

(In £ millions)

	Volume of			Value of domestic exports
	Total imports[a]	Re-exports	Domestic exports	
1801 . .	31·6	7·7	13·1	40·8
1802 . .	29·6	9·4	13·1	46·3
1803 . .	26·5	6·0	10·8	37·1
1804 . .	27·6	6·6	12·0	38·1
1805 . .	28·4	5·7	12·5	38·1
1806 . .	26·7	5·7	14·1	40·9

[a] Imports of wheat and wheat flour were as follows (in 1,000 quarters): 1,424·6 (1801), 538·9 (1802), 312·5 (1803), 391·1 (1804), 836·7 (1805), 208·1 (1806). These figures explain, in part, the fall in total imports in 1802, their rise in 1805.

In British exports a sharp decline is evident in 1803, a gradual recovery until 1806. The decline in the re-export trade is also to be noted. This is at least partially to be attributed to the restoration, by the Peace of Amiens, of Dutch and French colonies, as well as to the attempt of the French to block off the British trade with the northern ports. In June of 1803, shortly after the declaration of war, a decree from Paris laid down an embargo on all British goods and on all goods carried in British ships;[2] while in August an attempt was made to shut off the Elbe and the Weser.[3] This virtually closed Hamburg as a continental entrepôt. The Scandinavian ports, Lubeck and Danzig on the Baltic, and Trieste and Venice in the Mediterranean, partially took its place.[4] But the expansive days of 1793–1802 were over, for the moment at least.

The official value of exports and re-exports to the principal British markets follow:

Official Value of Total Exports from England

(In £ millions)

	Russia	Holland	France	Germany	Prussia	Norway and Denmark	U.S.A.	British West Indies
1801 . .	0·8	3·9	1·2	8·7	0·5	0·3	7·5	4·4
1802 . .	1·3	4·4	2·4	8·0	0·8	0·4	5·3	3·9
1803 . .	1·3	1·7	1·2	5·1	1·5	1·7	5·3	2·4
1804 . .	1·2	2·3	—	1·3	3·9	3·8	6·4	4·3
1805 . .	1·5	0·4	—	1·7	5·0	4·3	7·2	3·8
1806 . .	1·7	1·2	—	5·6	0·4	1·4	8·6	4·7

---

[1] Schlote, pp. 133 and 137.
[2] A.R., Chr., 1803, p. 398. Also E. Heckscher, *The Continental System*, pp. 83–4.
[3] A.R., Chr., 1803, p. 423.
[4] Idem. Also Smart, i. 71.

The chief features revealed in this table are connected with the adjustments of trade to the resumption of hostilities and the early stages of Napoleon's mercantile policy: the fall in the figures for Germany, France, and Holland, after 1802; and the rise in the totals for Prussia, Norway, and Denmark. Exports to the United States and the British West Indies reflect the depression there during the years of peace, and the recovery which came after the war was once more under way.[1] While it is true that

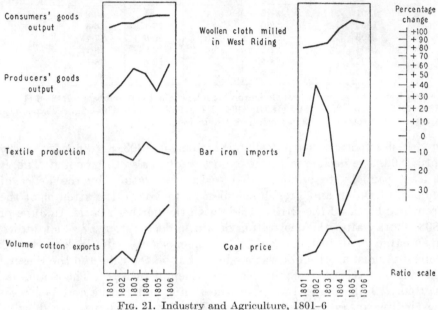

FIG. 21. Industry and Agriculture, 1801–6

expectations of a rupture of the peace, and the actual outbreak of hostilities, had a depressing effect on trade,[2] recovery was under way from the early days of 1804—a recovery heavily dependent on a revival in exports to the United States as well as to those continental ports still open.

The difficulties of the period from the resumption of the war to the opening of the South American markets (1803–8), when the continental trade was intermittently harried by blockade and by the necessity for re-routing, are reflected in a number of publications urging the possibility and even the advisability of Britain's maintaining its prosperity with a lesser dependence on foreign trade; e.g. Oddy's 'European Commerce',[3] 'A Plan of National Improvement'[4] (Anonymous), Spence's 'Britain Independent of Commerce'.[5] These pamphlets reflect the kind of thinking that helped create the Orders in Council a few years later.

[1] See Heckscher, pp. 79–80 and 102–5, for a discussion of the effects of war and peace on the American trade.
[2] See *A.R.*, Chr., 1803, p. 385; Smart, p. 71.
[3] *Edinburgh Review*, viii. 128.
[4] Ibid. v. 1 ff.
[5] Ibid. xi. 429 ff.

3. Investment. No clear cyclical pattern appears in those limited types of home investment that can be traced statistically:

| | Bills of inclosure[a] (No.) | Canal, railway, and navigation bills[b] | | Production of bricks (in million bricks) | Turn-pike bills (No.) | Quantity of fir timber imports (in 1,000 loads of 50 cu. ft.) | Dock bills | |
		No.	Amount (in £ millions)				No.	Amount (in £ millions)
1801	122	11	0·9	686·6	4	167	..	..
1802	96	8	0·3	770·3	4	263	2	0·3
1803	104	6	0·6	818·8	6	297	2	0·3
1804	52	6	0·3	820·6	2	294	1	0·5
1805	71	9	0·5	889·4	7	264	2	—
1806	76	9	0·6	882·2	2	166	2	0·2

[a] The irregular decline in the number of inclosures from 1801 to 1804 is to be connected with the agricultural crisis that followed the fall in grain prices from 1801 to 1803.

[b] In 1801 the first Act of Parliament for the construction of a railway was passed. Until the turn of the century British railways were 'private undertakings, and each was confined to the use of the establishment—generally a colliery—in which it occurred' (Porter, p. 328). The lines listed below were either extensions to canals or lines connecting mining-pits to ports close by. The cars were, of course, horse drawn, but ran on iron rails.

	Name of railway	Terminals	Length in miles	Cost of construction
				£
1801 . .	Surrey	Wandsworth and Croydon	9	60,000
1802 . .	Carmarthenshire	Llanelly and Llanfihangel, Aberbythick	16	53,000
	Sirhowey	Newport and Sirhowey Furnaces (Monmouth-shire)	11	45,000
1803 . .	Croydon, Merstham, and Godstone	Croydon and Reigate—a branch to Godstone	15¾	90,000
1804 . .	Oystermouth	Swansea and Oystermouth —a branch to Morriston	6	12,000

In 1805 an act was passed to extend a line already in existence; in 1806 there were two such acts.

The tonnage of shipping belonging to Great Britain and Ireland had increased from 1,494,000 in 1798 to 1,786,000 in 1801. After 1802 the boom in shipping seems to have slackened.

Tonnage of Shipping belonging to the United Kingdom

(In 1,000 tons)

1801 .	. 1,780	1803 .	. 1,960	1805 .	. 2,066
1802 .	. 1,883	1804 .	. 2,050	1806 .	. 2,054

The failure of foreign trade to increase in this period at its previous rate possibly reduced the incentive and, to some extent, the resources available for capital investment at home. More directly it affected, almost certainly, the construction of new ships. But the recovery, from 1804 to 1806, in the sums authorized for canal, navigation, and railway bills, and the rise of the brick index until 1805–6, indicate that all branches of development at home were not stagnant. That conclusion is supported by the annual average figure for commercial bills under discount at the Bank of England[1] (in £ millions):

1801	.	.	7·9	1804	.	.	10·0
1802	.	.	7·5	1805	.	.	11·4
1803	.	.	10·7	1806	.	.	12·4

The sudden rise in the Bank's discount in 1803 was a result of the pressures accompanying the crisis of that year, which the precarious position of agriculture and the resumption of hostilities had combined to produce. The increase until 1806 reflects a real internal expansion.

4. Industry and Agriculture. Evidence on the progress of the wool, cotton, iron, and coal industries also indicates a pause in 1802–3 and a marked improvement from 1804 to 1806. Lacking the stimulus of a booming export trade, however, the rate of advance appears to slacken somewhat.

The resumption of war affected the textile trades more drastically than any others.[2] The figures for imports of raw cotton and exports of cotton goods and yarn show some recovery, however, in the latter three years of the period under consideration.[3]

	Quantity of raw cotton (in million lb.)		Exports of cotton manufactures (official value in £ millions)		
	Imports	Exports	Manufactured goods	Twist and yarn	Total[a]
1801 . .	56·0	1·9	6·6	0·4	7·1
1802 . .	60·3	3·7	7·2	0·4	7·6
1803 . .	53·8	1·6	6·4	0·6	7·1
1804 . .	61·9	0·5	7·8	0·9	8·7
1805 . .	59·7	0·8	8·6	0·9	9·5
1806 . .	58·2	0·7	9·8	0·7	10·5

[a] These years saw an increase in the relative importance of cotton goods exports (official value, total cotton goods exports, as per cent. of total official value, domestic exports):

1790	.	.	12·2	1801	.	.	28·2	1804	:	.	38·5
1793	.	.	13·7	1802	.	.	29·7	1805	.	.	40·7
1800	.	.	26·6	1803	.	.	34·5	1806	.	.	40·6

Because of the process by which the official value figures are calculated the absolute level of this percentage is not necessarily significant. Changes in the percentage are, however, a fairly reliable index of the altering importance of cotton exports.

[1] Cannan, p. xliii. To the extent that it reduced profits available for home investment, the relatively restricted state of exports was a deflationary force. In shutting off one principal avenue for new investment (i.e. the financing of foreign trade), however, it may have encouraged alternative types of enterprise; in this case building and the construction of canals. There is no evidence on this point for 1804–6. A fairly plausible case, however, can be made out for the joint-stock boom of 1807, as an outlet for enterprise frustrated in foreign markets by the Continental System (see below, pp. 91 ff.).

[2] See Hamilton, pp. 134–5; Baines, pp. 358–9; Baines quotes (p. 338) William Radcliffe, a cotton manufacturer who dates the closing of 'a golden age' in the cotton industry at 1803.

[3] Baines, pp. 347 and 349–50. The decline in raw cotton exported from Great Britain follows the total figure for re-exports.

During the year of peace, following upon a decade of sensational advance, the cotton trade prospered. In the summer of 1802 there were about twenty factories under construction in or near Manchester.[1] But the industry reacted sharply to the resumption of hostilities, with prices falling and bankruptcies increasing. One operator at this time expressed the view that the 'dulness of trade' would continue until 'Bonaparte was settled'.[2] The situation in Ireland and Scotland was even worse than in the Manchester district. Towards the end of 1803, however, trade picked up and remained moderately good until 1806 :[3]

The state of trade in 1804 and 1805 was rather uncertain, as everyone seemed to be in fear as to what might happen. Indeed, from the recommencement of the war, business had been exceedingly risky, and failures in the cotton trade had become increasingly numerous. The position was well summed up by a Glasgow correspondent in the statement that no one could say anything of the state of trade far ahead owing to Continental events. The great demand for yarn from the Continent which had been experienced in the latter months of 1803 continued into 1804, causing a further advance in price. In the latter year, the export of yarn increased by £262,804—a greater increase than had ever been recorded previously. In the following year the increase was little over £12,000 ; then came a decline, as the restrictions imposed by England, France, and the United States came into operation.

It is perhaps worth noting, in the midst of this short-run chronicle, that the long-run tendency in the price of cotton cloth was downward. High labour costs and the other price-raising forces operative during these years were, in net, overcome by the fall in real costs attributable to the increasing mechanization of the industry and to cheaper supplies of raw material :[4]

Price of Cotton Yarn, No. 100

1786	.	.	38s. 0d.	1803	.	.	8s. 4d.
1793	.	.	15s. 1d.	1804	.	.	7s. 10d.
1800	.	.	9s. 5d.	1805	.	.	7s. 10d.
1801	.	.	8s. 9d.	1806	.	.	7s. 2d.
1802	.	.	8s. 4d.	1807	.	.	6s. 9d.

Figures for foreign wool imported and cloth milled in the West Riding district show a somewhat lower level of output in 1801–3 than in 1800, a recovery until 1805 in broads milled and imports, until 1806 in narrows milled and exports :

[1] Daniels, 'The Cotton Trade during the Revolutionary and Napoleonic Wars', *Transactions of the Manchester Statistical Society*, 1915–16, p. 63.

[2] Ibid., p. 64.

[3] Ibid., p. 65.

[4] Baines, p. 357. The fall in price from 1786 to 1793, under conditions of rapidly expanding output—before the cotton gin's invention—mainly reflects technological improvement. The high point for the entire period 1790–1850 in the price of raw cotton was reached in August 1799. After that time the decline in raw material costs was perhaps more powerful an agent in the reduction of the price of manufactured goods than technical improvements. See especially Baines, pp. 352–8.

	Quantity of raw wool imports (in million lb.)	Volume of exports of woollen manufactures (official value in £ millions)	Woollen broad and narrow cloth milled in the West Riding	
			Broad	Narrow
			(in million yds.)	
1800 . .	8·6	6·3	9·3	6·0
1801 . .	7·4	6·7	8·7	4·8
1802 . .	7·7	6·0	8·7	5·0
1803 . .	5·9	4·8	8·9	5·0
1804 . .	7·9	5·2	10·0	5·4
1805 . .	8·1	5·5	10·1	6·2
1806 . .	6·8	5·7	9·6	6·4

The principal institutional development in the woollen industry during these years was the continued slow introduction of machinery. Carding, spinning, and weaving had pretty generally become mechanical operations.[1] But the resistance of the hand operators was strong. A typical example is the following :[2]

The whole of the manufacturing part of the County of Wilts has been, for some months back, in a state of alarming tumult and disorder, occasioned by the general introduction of the shearing machines into the large manufactories, and much valuable property in the cloth racks has been privately cut and destroyed by night.

So serious were the complaints and disorders that in 1806 a parliamentary commission was called upon to investigate the consequences of the factory system on the industry.

The iron trade continued to advance, with only a brief pause in the period of peace.[3] The output in England, Scotland, and Wales was estimated at 170,000 tons in 1802, 250,000 tons in 1806.[4] These years saw also an extremely rapid growth in the scale of operations : a contrast could be drawn between 'the astonishing growth of the iron trade in a large way, and the palsied state of the manufactures of copper and iron in the small way'.[5] There were, in 1801 and 1802, 22 new furnaces in blast and 25 in process of erection; 'and the resumption of the war in May 1803 gave to several of these a guarantee of full employment for many years to come'.[6]

---

[1] Mantoux, pp. 273–4.
[2] A.R., Chr., 1802, p. 440. G. D. H. Cole and R. Postgate (The British Common People, 1746–1938, p. 159) tell of the case of the west of England and Yorkshire weavers who, in 1802, attempted to stem the fall in wages by appealing to the Elizabethan Acts. An attorney was hired to prosecute employers for failing to fulfil the old rules of apprenticeship and wage-fixing. Parliament promptly suspended the acts dealing with that industry, and annually renewed the

suspension—'the instrument broke in their hands'.
    The decline in the position of the hand loom weaver was not confined to the woollen industry. Wages of cotton weavers in Bolton (for weaving a six-quarter 60-reed cambric, 120 picks in one inch) were 33s. 3d. in 1795, 25s. in 1800, 22s. in 1806 (Baines, p. 489).
[3] Ashton, p. 146.
[4] Porter, p. 271.
[5] Quoted by Ashton, p. 146.
[6] Idem.

The increased production was not only for the home market but for an expanding export demand :[1]

Bar- and Pig-Iron Exports

(In tons)

1801 . . 4,584	1803 . . 5,106	1805 . . 9,870
1802 . . 7,274	1804 . . 8,301	1806 . . 6,743

As in the case of other export statistics, the crisis of 1803, and the effects, in 1806, of the restrictions on the continental trade are evident. The number of blast-furnaces in Great Britain was estimated at 121 in 1796, 168 in 1802, and 221 in 1804.[2]

There were two further noteworthy developments in the industry from 1802 until 1806 : a diminishing dependence on foreign iron supplies ; and and extremely rapid growth of iron manufacture in South Wales. The amount of foreign iron retained for home consumption moved as follows (in 1,000 tons) :[3]

1801 . . 33·1	1803 . . 43·4	1805 . . 27·2
1802 . . 52·9	1804 . . 22·3	1806 . . 32·1

In 1803, for the first time, English iron was substituted by the navy and other government services for Russian and Swedish.[4]

The development of the iron-fields of Monmouthshire and Glamorganshire is vividly reflected in the tonnage carried down the Monmouthshire Canal[5] (in thousand tons):

1802 . . 1·1	1804 . . 20·5	1806 . . 24·0
1803 . . 8·7	1805 . . 22·4	

In 1801 a traveller in the district described the feverish activity there, concluding : 'The works are still rapidly increasing in extent and importance, and appear likely to surpass the other iron manufactories throughout the kingdom.'[6] The three largest ironworks in Great Britain in 1806 were located in South Wales.[7] The progress of the iron industry was so striking that the government, searching for new sources of revenue, in 1806 considered placing a duty of £2 per ton on all pig-iron manufactured.[8] The bill, however, was withdrawn, and the import duty raised in its place.[9] Although to contemporaries this advance was impressive, it does not compare with the increase of iron production in the thirties and forties, when railways were being built on a large scale.

A significant consequence of the expansion of the iron industry and its

---

[1] Porter, p. 251.
[2] Mantoux, p. 313 n., and Porter, p. 271. Scrivenor, p. 97, lists 133 works, with 233 furnaces, producing 258,206 tons, in Great Britain, for 1806.
[3] Scrivenor, p. 420.
[4] Ashton, pp. 146–7.
[5] Scrivenor, p. 127.
[6] Ibid., p. 125.

[7] Ibid., pp. 97–8 n. Cyfartha, producing 10,460 tons per annum, was the largest, Blaenavon and Penydarren, with about 7,800 tons each, followed.
[8] Porter, p. 271.
[9] For a full account of the bill, its history, and the arguments mustered on either side, see Scrivenor, pp. 96–108.

diminishing dependence on imports was the beginning, in this period, of the secular decline in the price of iron bars. They exhibit a response to the expansion from 1803 to 1806, but the peak figure is well below that in 1801 (£ per ton):

1801	.	. 21·9	1803	.	. 18·7	1805	.	. 17·5
1802	.	. 18·3	1804	.	. 17·5	1806	.	. 18·5

Manufactured cotton prices, as noted above, also reflect at this early stage the cost-reducing consequences of industrial expansion and improvements in technique.

The slow steady growth of the coal industry is reflected in the figures of coal shipped from Newcastle and Sunderland. The decline in shipments abroad is again due to the restrictive influences which affect most figures of foreign trade during these years :[1]

(In 1,000 tons)

	Shipments from Newcastle			Shipments from Sunderland		
	Coastwise	Exports	Total	Coastwise	Exports	Total
1801 . .	1,198	134	1,332	612	13	625
1802 . .	1,310	117	1,427	808	83	891
1803 . .	1,339	118	1,456	792	27	819
1804 . .	1,537	139	1,676	794	11	805
1805 . .	1,465	131	1,596	830	16	846
1806 . .	1,559	124	1,683	812	7	819

The coal-mines in the Newcastle district were still expanding rapidly at this time. An increased demand for coal in 1804 caused a rise in price.[2] A description of the manner in which new men were drawn to work in the mines to meet the increased requirements forms an interesting commentary on the process of industrialization in this era :[3]

In the year 1804, in consequence of an extraordinary demand for coal having arisen, and the collieries of Sir H. Vane Tempest, at Pensher and Rainton, having become greatly extended under the management of Mr. Arthur Mowbray, a general scramble for hewers and putters took place when the binding time arrived. So great was the fear of not procuring a necessary supply of men, that twelve or fourteen guineas per man were given on the Tyne, and eighteen guineas on the Wear, and likewise exorbitant bounties to putters, drivers, and others. Drink was lavished in the utmost profusion, and every sort of extravagance committed; and a positive increase of wages established to the extent of 30 or 40 per cent.

One reflection of the pressure on existing coal resources is contained in the following quotation from an anonymous pamphlet of 1803, protesting against the monopolistic practices of the Vend :[4]

If it is true . . . that the superior collieries, of the district of the North, are

[1] Porter, p. 278.

[2] Ibid., p. 280, calculates the rise from 10s. 4d. per ton to 11s. 6d.

[3] R. L. Galloway, Annals of Coal Mining

and the Coal Trade, p. 440.

[4] Essay on the Coal Trade with Strictures upon the Various Abuses Now Existing, 1803, p. 22.

unequal to the demand, then new and other resources must be resorted to, or the public good must suffer ; and therefore . . . we should not wait for the actual extinction of the collieries in the Rivers Tyne and Wear, but every encouragement should . . . be given to the providing of new resources.

The response of Parliament in 1804 to complaints by agricultural interests has already been noted. Falling grain prices immediately cut into profits. The recently made investments which accompanied the expansion in the scale of British farming, and the inflexibility of certain of the farmer's costs, made the pressure seem especially severe. An impression of the sort of changes being pursued can be gathered from this famous series of rhetorical questions addressed by Arthur Young to the readers of the *Farmers Magazine* :[1]

Where is the little farmer to be found who will cover his whole farm with marl at the rate of 100 or 150 tons per acre ? Who will drain all his land at the expense of £2 or £3 an acre ? Who will pay a heavy price for the manure of towns, and convey it 30 miles by land carriage ? Who will float his meadows at the expense of £5 per acre ? Who, to improve the breed of his sheep, will give 1,000 guineas for the use of a single ram for a single season ? . . . Who will employ and pay men for residing in provinces where practices are found which they want to introduce into their farms ? At the very mention of such exertions, common in England, what mind can be so perversely framed as to imagine for a single moment that such things are to be effected by little farmers ?

The estimated rise in costs between 1790 and 1803 is given in the following table, along with the average price of British wheat.[2]

Expenses of cultivating 100 Acres of Arable Land in 1790 and 1803

Expense	1790			1803		
	£	s.	d.	£	s.	d.
Rent . . .	88	6	3¼	121	2	7¼
Tithe . .	20	14	1¾	26	3	0¼
Poor rates . .	17	13	10	31	7	7¾
Wear and tear .	15	13	5¼	22	11	10¼
Labour . .	85	5	4¾	118	0	4
Seed . . .	46	4	10¼	49	2	7
Manure . .	48	0	3	68	6	2
Team . .	67	4	10	80	8	0¼
Interest . .	22	11	11½	30	3	8¾
Total . .	£411	15s.	11¾d.	£547	10s.	11½d.

Annual average price of wheat .   .   50s. 6d.   56s. 7d.

[1] Quoted by Lord Ernle, *English Farming Past and Present*, p. 206. Young began the publication of the *Farmers Magazine* in 1800, proclaiming constantly the need and the desirability of the new improvements in farming methods.

[2] L. Adams, *Agricultural Depression and Farm Relief in England, 1813-1852*, p. 35.

This table is from the Report of the Select Committee of the House of Commons appointed to hear petitions on the Corn Laws, *House of Commons Sessional Papers, 1814-15*, Report V, Appendix, pp. 64-5. The data were collected by the Board of Agriculture from circular letters sent out to landlords and tenants.

The pressures evident in 1803–4 reveal briefly the problem that was developing in British agriculture and its potential dangers. The rise in grain prices in 1804, and their maintenance at a high level for almost a decade thereafter, obliterated, for the time, 'the agricultural question'.

Hoffmann's indexes of production are as follows:

	Hoffmann's index of consumers' goods production	Hoffmann's index of producers' goods production	Hoffmann's index of total production
1801 . .	8·4	2·5	5·2
1802 . .	8·7	2·7	5·4
1803 . .	8·7	3·0	5·6
1804 . .	9·1	2·9	5·7
1805 . .	9·2	2·6	5·6
1806 . .	9·2	3·1	5·9

At this stage they fail to reflect adequately the short-run influences playing on British industry, although they are quite possibly a fair measure of secular progress.

5. Finance. The years from 1802 to 1806 fall within the period when the conduct of the Bank and the government has often been described in terms of 'exemplary moderation': 'the rake had suspended his progress'.[1] New taxes yielded an increasing revenue; expenditure, although rising, did so less rapidly than revenue; commercial loans and discounts at the Bank were, compared to what was to come, limited in quantity, 'sound' in character; in 1804–6, when commercial discounts were rising, the reserve was, on the whole, increasing as well; the exchanges, with the exception of a brief period at the end of 1805, showed no marked weakness:[2]

(In £ millions)

	Public finance			Bills and notes discounted at the Bank of England	Bullion in the Bank of England
	Expenditure	Revenue	Excess of expenditure		
1801 . .	60·6	34·1	26·5	7·9	4·5
1802 . .	49·5	36·4	13·1	7·5	4·0
1803 . .	49·0	38·6	10·4	10·7	3·6
1804 . .	58·6	46·2	12·4	10·0	4·8
1805 . .	66·9	50·9	16·0	11·4	6·7
1806 . .	68·5	55·8	12·7	12·4	6·1

[1] Cannan, p. xviii. See also Andréadès, p. 205, for the 'utmost prudence' of the Bank and government.

[2] Ibid., p. xliii. E. B. Schumpeter (*Review of Economic Statistics*, xx, No. 1, 1938) has calculated the following figures for the percentage of the tax revenue to total expenditure:

1801 . . . 56·9 | 1802 . . . 72·2

1803 . . . 81·8 | 1805 . . . 73·7
1804 . . . 76·8 | 1806 . . . 82·4

The average percentage for the period 1794–1801 was 54·1, with the lowest figure for 1797 (34·7). This series differs from calculations based on Cannan's estimates, since Mrs. Schumpeter has taken into account the sums spent each year on debt retirement, through the operation of the Sinking Fund.

The relatively untroubled financial position of Britain, however, was a product of a low level of abnormal expenditure abroad rather than of internal financial orthodoxy: the decline in war-time remittances to foreign countries permitted the moderation of the government and the Bank[1] (in £ millions):

	Bills and specie for British armies in Europe (a)	Subsidies and loans (b)	Grain imports over £2 million (c)	Total a, b, c (d)
1801 .	1·7	2·2	8·2	12·0
1802 .	0·6	0·8	0·2	1·5
1803 .	0·2	0·1	—	0·3
1804 .	0·1	0·6	—	0·7
1805 .	0·8	1·9	1·8	4·5
1806 .	0·7	1·1	—	1·8

N.B. The failure of column (d) to equal the sum of the previous three columns in 1801 and 1802 results from Silberling's having rounded the figures to the nearest tenth.

From July to November 1805 the exchanges weakened. The recurrence of a figure for abnormal grain imports would seem to explain this; but Tooke gives the following account :[2]

There was a fall of the exchange, and an efflux of bullion for a few months in 1805, in consequence of subsidies to Austria and Russia; but after the battle of Austerlitz, which led to a peace between Austria and France, the exchanges rallied, and there was a renewed influx of bullion.

It may be concluded, then, that from 1802 to 1806 the Bank, freed from the automatic check of convertibility, found it possible to finance an increasing amount of private trade as well as extensive war-time government requirements; and to do so without producing a decline in the exchanges. The relatively low level of government payments abroad seems to have been crucial to this successful adjustment.[3]

[1] Silberling, Part I, p. 227.
[2] Loc. cit. i. 281 n.
[3] The ability of the Bank to finance a larger amount of trade, without a proportionate increase in its bullion reserve, was partly attributed by the Bullion Report of 1810 to a variety of institutional developments tending to 'economize the circulating medium' (Cannan, p. 58):

'Your Committee are of the opinion, that the improvements which have taken place of late years in this country, and particularly in the district of London, with regard to the use and economy of money among Bankers, and in the modes of adjusting commercial payments, must have had a much greater effect than has hitherto been ascribed to them, in rendering the same sum adequate to a much greater amount of trade and payments than formerly. Some of those improvements will be found detailed in the Evidence; they consist principally in the increased use of Bankers' drafts in the common payments of London; the contrivance of bringing all such drafts daily to common receptacle, where they are balanced against each other; the intermediate agency of Bill-brokers; and several other changes in the practice of London Bankers, are to the same effect, of rendering it unnecessary for them to keep so large a deposit of money as formerly. Within the London district, it would certainly appear, that a smaller sum of money is required than formerly to perform the same number of exchanges and amount of payments, if the rate of prices

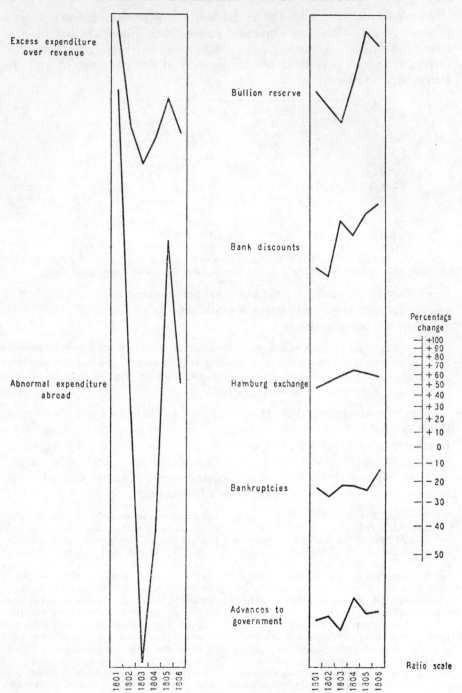

FIG. 22. Finance, 1801-6

The movement of India Stock and Consols conforms to other evidence on the period. After reaching a peak in April 1802 they fall during the latter months of the year, rally briefly from about December 1802 until March 1803, and then fall catastrophically until July of that year, under the first impact of the outbreak of war. A slow and irregular recovery then set in. The peak in the summer of 1806 is well below that in 1802 :[1] India Stock was 226¼ in April 1802, and 189⅝ in August 1806; 3 per cent. Consols were 74³⁄₁₆ and 63³⁄₁₆ respectively. This sequence reflects the war-crisis of 1803, and the restricted, unsensational revival thereafter. The decline in the latter months of 1802 is probably to be connected with the growing tension between the French and British governments; that towards the close of 1806 with the tightening of restrictions on the continental trade, and its attendant effects on the general economic and political outlook.

Although there were no major crises in this period—no sharp fall in the reserves or on the exchanges—an extensive discussion of the relation of Bank restriction to prices and exchange rates was called forth by the acts renewing the legislation of 1797 and by the state of the Irish currency. On 30 April 1802 restriction was extended until 1 March 1803; on 28 February 1803 it was extended until six weeks after the meeting of the next session of Parliament; on 15 December 1803 it was extended to six months after the ratification of a definitive treaty of peace.[2] Addington, Chancellor of the Exchequer, justified renewal on the grounds that there was still some incentive to export guineas to the Continent.[3] Fox pointed out that the profit on the export of gold coin might be due to the fact of restriction.[4] The argument of the Bullion Committee of 1810 was even more clearly anticipated in the report of 1804 on the Irish currency. In what Andréadès calls 'a mania for uniformity' the Suspension Act of 1797 had been imme-

---

had remained the same. It is material also to observe, that both the policy of the Bank of England itself, and the competition of the Country bank paper, have tended to compress the paper of the Bank of England, more and more, within London and the adjacent district. All these circumstances must have co-operated to render a smaller augmentation of Bank of England paper necessary to supply the demands of our increased trade than might otherwise have been required.'

[1] These figures are the mean of the highest and lowest quotation for the month. The movement of Bank of England stock is an exception in that its price in 1806 was far above the figure for 1802. From 1802 to 1806 the dividend on Bank Stock was 7 per cent. It rose, in 1807, to 10 per cent., where it remained until 1822, a period when the government was converting its stock at lower rates. Eight per cent. was then established; and, in 1839, 7 per cent., which con-

tinued until 1852 (H. Ayres, *Financial Register*, Appendix, p. 461). The basis for the sharp rise in the price of Bank Stock may have been the steady increase in profits and surplus—'The Rest' (in £ millions):

Feb. 1802	.	4·1	Feb. 1805	.	4·6
Aug. .	.	4·2	Aug. .	.	5·0
Feb. 1803	.	4·3	Feb. 1806	.	4·9
Aug. .	.	4·7	Aug. .	.	5·0
Feb. 1804	.	4·6			
Aug. .	.	4·8			

Until 1800 the figure had ranged between £2·7 and £3·5 million (Cannan, p. xliv).

[2] James, p. 22; Cannan, p. 58.

[3] Macleod, pp. 110–11.

[4] Ibid., pp. 112–13. See also the statement of Lord King (p. 114), who stated: 'A very strict attention to the price of bullion, and the state of the foreign exchanges, was alone capable of affording a just criterion by which the quantity (of Bank loans) could be truly ascertained.'

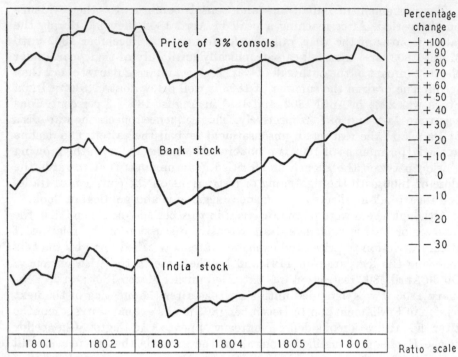

FIG. 23. Finance, 1801-6

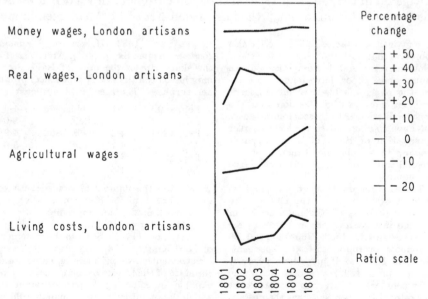

FIG. 24. Labour, 1801-6

diately extended to the Bank of Ireland, which, at the time, was under no extraordinary pressures.[1] Up to that point the exchange on London at Dublin had been unfavourable to England. But paralleling a tremendous increase in Bank of England notes, and the appearance of a substantial premium on gold, the exchange reversed itself and prices in Ireland rose rapidly.[2] The directors of the Bank of Ireland raised the eternal cries of the banker during inflation. They claimed to have supplied merely the just needs of trade; they blamed an adverse balance of payments for the fluctuations in the exchange; they talked of the increasing demands for gold as a cause of its rise in price.[3] But the fact that a very small premium on gold existed at Belfast, where paper money was banned, and that the exchange on London in Belfast was favourable,[4] proved to the committee's satisfaction that the depreciation of the Irish currency could be traced to banking policy. They urged that the Irish and English currencies be assimilated. But this recommendation was not heeded; nor was the line of argument that lay behind it.[5]

6. Labour. The fall in the price of foodstuffs reversed the declining tendency of real wages in 1802; and, although the downward trend was resumed, real wages were higher in 1806 than in 1801:

| | Tucker's index of | | Bowley's index of agricultural money wages |
	Money wages of London	Real wages artisans	
1801 . .	52·6	33·0	160
1802 . .	53·1	39·2	162
1803 . .	53·3	38·1	164
1804 . .	53·7	38·0	177
1805 . .	54·8	35·2	188
1806 . .	54·8	36·2	198

The relative stagnation of money wages in 1802–3 is appropriate both to the slackening of trade in those years and to the fall in grain prices. The slight rise in money wages in 1804–6 probably represents the effect of increasing prosperity as well as an adjustment to the higher prices of foodstuffs. It is virtually impossible to weight the relative force of each influence.

The positive action of working-class combinations designed to raise wages also point to a strong demand in the labour market. Despite the

[1] Andréadès, p. 214.
[2] Idem. Testimony of Lord Archibald Hamilton stated that in 1797 the note issue was £600,000; in 1804, £2,700,000. Numerous small private banks also arose in these years. One estimate of the total currency in circulation indicated an increase from £4 million in 1797 to £320 million in 1804. The

premium on gold was calculated at 2s. 6d. in 1804.
[3] For a fairly complete restatement of the testimony see Andréadès, pp. 215–17; Macleod, pp. 115–32; C. Conant, *A History of Modern Banks of Issue*, pp. 172–3.
[4] Smart, p. 83.
[5] Macleod, pp. 131–2.

Combination Acts there is evidence not only of action by local groups in a single craft but of co-operation among workers in widely different occupations.[1] It is difficult to gauge the scale of the underground warfare of labour. But in the textile trade, especially, the power of the clandestine organizations appears to have been extensive.[2] The violent reaction in some quarters against them indicates a considerable power, in certain areas at least. A Mr. Cookson, in 1806, urging a strengthening of the Combination Acts, contended that great evils would follow if :[3]

'The working people were allowed to feel and make known the extent of their power.' He wished to 'repress if not extirpate the Combination system. . . . Indeed the evils call aloud for a Cure, or would soon extend beyond computation,—perquisites, privileges, Time, Mode of Labour, Rate, who shall be employed, etc. etc., all are now dependent on the Fiat of our Workmen . . . it is now a Confirmed thing that a Bricklayer, Mason, Carpenter, Wheelwright, etc., shall have 3s. per week higher Wages in Leeds or in Manchester, than at Wakefield, York, Hull, Rochdale and adjacent Towns, it is in orders too that Bricklayers and Masons Labourers at Leeds shall have 2s. per week extra—no Workman will or dare deviate from these Terms, no Matter from whence he comes, and there arrived here last week on their way to Manchester Two Delegates from Carlisle summoned by the Lancashire Cotton printers, to agree upon certain advances in their Wages, who made no secret of their mission.'

These were days when labour spies appeared, when the term 'scab' came into usage, when a man carrying a letter to striking weavers in Knaresborough (1805) could be sent to prison for three months.[4] At this time, too, the Friendly Societies were quickly losing their strictly guild character and becoming identical in some cases with the new trade unions.[5]

Although many instances of trade disputes can be found in the period 1802–6, organized strikes were more numerous during the high prices of the boom years 1809–10 and the depression immediately following. But much of the foundation for later militancy seems to have been laid in the years immediately after the turn of the century.

Another symptom of the process of industrialization was the passage, in 1802, of the first Factory Act. Pauper children were being drawn from all over the country to do minor tasks in the factories. The conditions under which they worked were incredibly unhealthy, causing chronic epidemics, as well as less flagrant social injury.[6] Peel, whose income was

---

[1] See J. L. and B. Hammond, *The Town Labourer*, pp. 262–3, on the case of the Shearmen's Society. Ibid., pp. 247–67, for other instances of collective action in these years.

[2] Ibid., p. 253, for the Spinners' Union which extended on all sides of Manchester, to Stockport and Macclesfield in the south, Staleybridge, Ashton, and Hyde in the east, and Oldham, Bolton, and Preston in the north. Business was conducted by a general congress of fifty deputies.

[3] Ibid., pp. 263–4.

[4] Ibid., pp. 259, 264–5.

[5] Ibid., p. 253. In 1825 the report of the Committee on Friendly Societies said that 'most alliances to raise wages cloaked themselves under the rules of Friendly Societies'.

[6] Ibid., p. 150. Smart, pp. 80–1; and see also Halevy, pp. 244–6, for some of the more famous ugly details of working conditions in the early factories.

derived from the cotton mills, led the fight for the bill.[1] From its title it would appear to have been designed 'for the better preservation of the Health and Morals of Apprentices and others employed' in the cotton and woollen mills. In fact its terms covered only the pauper apprentices, amounting at most to about 20,000 children.[2] A twelve-hour day and certain minimum conditions for work and education were stipulated; but enforcement was left in the hands of local magistrates or parsons. Until the coming of government inspectors factory regulation was virtually non-existent. Nevertheless the bill called forth protests from many of the large mill centres.[3] A cry went up often to be heard again from British industry upon the institution of reforms: the reduction in hours 'would amount to a surrender of all the profits of the establishment'.

PART II: 1807–11

1. Prices. The domestic price index sags slightly from the close of 1806 until October 1807, then rises steadily to a peak in March 1809. It breaks sharply to June, then rises to a second, higher peak in October. After falling off until February 1810, it rises to September. From October 1810 to September 1811 it remains fairly steady, well below the level of the three peaks (March and October 1809 and September 1810). The autumn of 1811 saw the beginnings of an increase that was to carry the index, in July 1812, to its highest point since 1801. A broader view of the index shows a rise from the end of 1807 to a new higher level in 1809, about which it fluctuates until the end of 1811.

The major movements are to be explained largely in terms of the British harvests. Despite ominous political developments throughout 1807, which threatened to cut off the whole Baltic grain trade, the wheat price declined until November. The English crop of 1807 was about average.[4] The fall in price would almost certainly have been greater had not 'the increasing gloom of the political horizon' led to fears of future scarcity and to the holding of large stocks by farmers.[5] An early winter in 1807–8, and a poor

---

[1] J. L. and B. Hammond, pp. 150–1. The elder Peel thus describes his reaction to the condition of children working in his own factories: 'Having other pursuits, it was not often in my power to visit the factories, but whenever such visits were made, I was struck with the uniform appearance of bad health, and, in many cases, stunted growth of the children; the hours of labour were regulated by the interest of the overseer, whose remuneration depending on the quantity of work done, he was often induced to make the poor children work excessive hours, and to stop their complaints by trifling bribes.'

[2] Ibid., p. 155.

[3] Ibid., p. 152. Protests came from Manchester, Glasgow, Preston, Leeds, Keighley, Tutbury, and Holywell.

[4] Tooke, i. 267.

[5] Ibid., pp. 267–8: 'Under these circumstances (the closing of the Baltic), the farmers were naturally induced, as by their increased capital from their great gains of late years they were enabled, to hold large stocks. There is, therefore, every reason to suppose that if political appearances had been less threatening, and the crops less scanty, the subsidence in 1807, to the level from whence the rise in 1804 took place, would have been complete.'

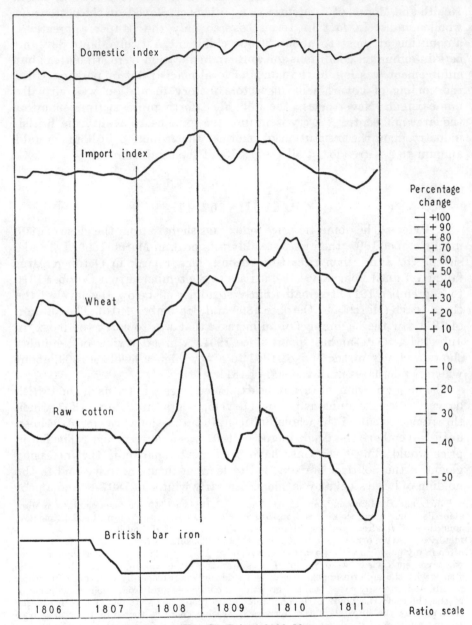

FIG. 25. Prices, 1806–11

harvest in the following year, caused an almost steady rise in the wheat price: 'the high price . . . was a necessary condition for eking out a reduced supply of our own growth, when the obstructions to importation had become great, and were thought in that year (1808) to be insurmountable.'[1] The price of beef and pork did not share in this rise.[2]

The short supply of 1808, and the fear that no foreign grain could be obtained, kept the price of wheat rising until March 1809:[3] 'But it then became apparent that the stock on hand was not so much reduced as had been apprehended, and that it was likely to suffice for the consumption, restricted as that was by the high price, and by the prohibition of distillation from grain.' The price fell, but rose again as the harvest of 1809 proved insufficient. The second decline, in the last quarter of 1809, is to be attributed largely to the import of grain from France and the Netherlands, to the amount of about 400,000 quarters.[4] The continental harvest had been abundant, and mercantilism was not dead in Napoleon's councils.[5] Harvest prospects early in 1810 were 'ominous, and the wheat price again rose':[6]

A great turn, however, took place in prices after the middle of August, 1810. The weather, thenceforward, cleared up, and continued uninterruptedly propitious. . . . The wheats, although considered to be deficient in quantity, were, by their good condition, all available for early use; and from this circumstance, combined with the very large foreign supply,[7] the markets declined thenceforth.

A deficient harvest sent up the prices of grain again from the middle of 1811.[8] The rise was accentuated by the fact that Napoleon had tightened the restrictions on grain exports from July 1810 onwards.[9] Fewer than 5,000 quarters were exported in England in 1811 and 1812.[10]

Non-agricultural domestic prices and the import index reflect the boom of 1808–10 and the sharp deflation until the middle of 1811. From December 1807 to January 1809 there is an uninterrupted rise in the import index. A fall followed until July, then an upward surge to a second, lesser peak in March 1810. The decline until August 1811, when a slow general recovery in trade began, is without a serious break.[11] The speculative boom in prices had two quite separate sources: the blocking off of trade with the

---

[1] Tooke, i. 269–70. The government at this time prohibited distillation of spirits from grain, because of the 'apprehended deficiency of grain and of potatoes'. Tooke notes that the measure was also designed 'to afford some relief to the West India planters, by the substitution of sugar in the distilleries'.

[2] Ibid., p. 271.

[3] Ibid., p. 293.

[4] Ibid., p. 295.

[5] For an extensive discussion of the licensing system which permitted these imports from the Continent, see W. F. Galpin, *The Grain Supply of England during the* *Napoleonic Period*, pp. 168–88; for the economic theory which justified them as a means of draining Britain's bullion, see Heckscher, pp. 71–3.

[6] Tooke, i. 297–8.

[7] See also Galpin, pp. 170–1.

[8] Tooke, i. 319–20.

[9] Galpin, p. 171. Napoleon's mercantilist leanings, in the matter of grain exports to Britain, were restrained by an inferior harvest of 1810.

[10] Ibid., p. 173.

[11] See Tooke, i. 316–17, for the recovery in commerce as well as prices that began in the summer of 1811.

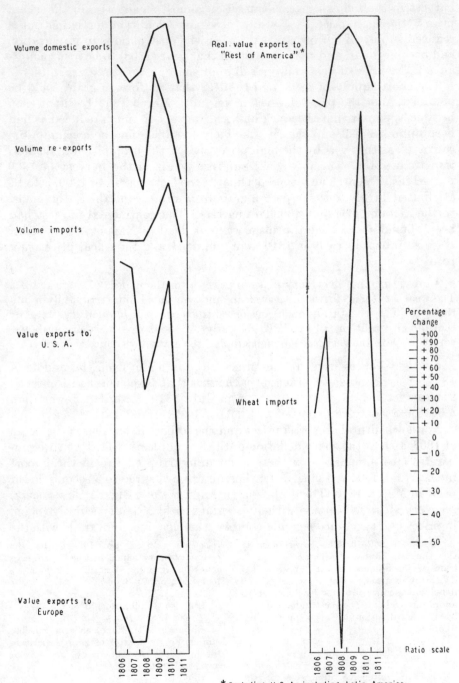

FIG. 26. Foreign Trade, 1806–11

Baltic that accompanied the Continental System, and the general prosperity which resulted from the opening of the South American markets and from an investment boom at home.[1] The break in import prices from January to July 1809 was due principally to a temporary relaxation of vigilance in the continental ports, relieving some of the tension that had aided the speculative rise up to that time. In July 1809, however, the Rees-Bremen Barrier was created, ending smuggling on its previous large scale.[2] The collapse of the South American boom adequately accounts for the fall in the index from the early months of 1810 to July 1811.[3]

Non-agricultural domestic prices responded in varying degrees to the expansion and subsequent depression:

	Jan. 1807	Jan. 1808	Jan. 1809	Peak 1809–10	Trough 1811
Copper (pence per lb.).	16·6	14·9	14·5	(May 1809) 16·6	(Oct.) 14·1
Iron bars (£ per ton) .	18·5	15·5	16·5	(Jan. 1809) 16·5	(Jan.) 16·5
Lead pigs (£ per ton) .	39·5	30·0	42·0	(Jan.–Apr. 1809) 42·0	(Nov.–Dec.) 27·5
Leather butts (pence per lb.)	25·5	25·2	25·0	(Oct.–Dec. 1809) 25·5	(May) 22·0
Rape oil (£ per ton) .	36·0	33·8	56·0	(Mar. 1809) 70·0	(Aug.) 49·2
Hard soap (shillings per cwt.)	73·0	88·0	112·0	(Feb. 1809) 116·0	(June) 76·0
Block tin (shillings per cwt.)	126·0	126·0	118·0	(Aug.–Dec. 1810) 171·0	(Sept.–Dec.) 137·0

The monopolistic control of prices in the iron industry probably explains the failure of the price of bar iron to decline in 1811. The force of the depression is reflected, although not uniformly, in all other cases.

2. Foreign Trade. The figures for British foreign trade clearly show the stagnation which immediately followed the beginning of the Continental System, and the successful outcome of the search for compensating markets:[4]

(In £ millions)

	Volume of			Value of domestic exports
	Total imports	Re-exports	Domestic exports	
1806 . .	26·7	5·7	14·1	40·9
1807 . .	26·6	5·7	12·5	37·2
1808 . .	26·6	4·3	13·6	37·3
1809 . .	31·5	9·5	17·7	47·4
1810 . .	39·0	7·0	18·6	48·4
1811 . .	26·3	4·6	12·4	32·9

[1] Tooke, i. 276–9, 300–16.
[2] Heckscher, pp. 183–5.
[3] Tooke, i. 309–16.
[4] Wheat and wheat flour imports were

(in 1,000 quarters): 208·1 (1806), 360·0 (1807), 41·4 (1808), 389·0 (1809), 1440·7 (1810), 188·9 (1811).

The battle of Jena was fought on 14 October 1806. The control of Prussia which this gave Napoleon was 'the natural antecedent to the execution of the Continental System, inasmuch as that battle placed into his hands the control of the Weser, Elbe, Trave, Oder, and all the coast-line as far as the Vistula'.[1] The Berlin Decree, issued 21 November 1806, laid down four fundamental regulations : the British Isles were formally declared in a state of blockade ; British subjects in territory occupied by the French were declared prisoners of war, and their property fair prize ; all trade in British goods was prohibited ; all vessels coming directly from British ports or colonies were forbidden entry to the Continent. Inasmuch as Britain controlled the seas the blockade of Britain was meaningless. The measure, in fact, was merely a symbol of Napoleon's making the com-mercial war 'the central point in the entire internal and external policy of France, around which everything else had to turn in an ever-increasing degree'.[2]

The British replied with a series of Orders in Council beginning as early as 7 January 1807. The most important of them came in November 1807. In some measure these were political, a bravado counter-statement of strength. And to the extent that they prohibited British trade with the Continent they were either ineffective or harmful in their consequences.[3] But the order of November struck at a vital point : it prohibited direct intercourse between the enemy colonies and their mother countries. And further, it prohibited all direct intercourse between the enemy countries and other ports, except when the 'other ports' were either European British ports or ports in the vessel's own country :[4] 'The principal thing in all respects was the obligatory call at a British port.' The intention of this regulation was, above all, to raise the prices of the products of the enemy colonies and of the enemy-controlled parts of the European main-land, in all ports where they might compete with goods of Great Britain or her colonies.[5] The Milan Decree of November and December 1807, in angry response to the November Order in Council, merely strengthened and amplified the Berlin measures.

France, then, was determined to cut off Britain's export trade with the Continent, drain off her bullion supply, and bring her financial system to a state of collapse ; Britain, though nominally refusing to trade with the

---

[1] Heckscher, p. 88. The following account of the Continental System is drawn, unless otherwise indicated, from Heckscher's work.

[2] Ibid., p. 92.

[3] The burden of the Orders in Council was especially felt during the depressed interval from the latter months of 1810 to the early months of 1812. When the South American markets were booming, and, in 1810, those of the United States, complaint against them from British manufacturers and merchants was less frequently heard.

[4] Ibid., p. 117.

[5] The re-export trade, for a decade a sub-stantial source of profit to the United States, was thus obstructed, unless American vessels were willing to put in at a British port. Two concessions, however, were made to the American trade. Commerce between the United States and the French colonies was permitted ; and certain American articles of export (grain, flour, and other manufactured articles brought direct from the producing countries) were not required to be discharged on arrival at a British port.

Continent, was devoting herself to impeding the flow of colonial produce there, or diverting its trade into British hands.[1]

Figures for the chief channels of British exports reveal the adjustments made to the new situation :[2]

Official Value of Total Exports from England
(in £ millions)

	Spain and Canaries	Russia	Sweden	Norway, Denmark	Germany	Gibraltar, Malta, Ionian Isles
1806 . .	0·1	1·7	0·2	1·4	5·6	0·8
1807 . .	0·1	1·7	0·7	4·9	0·4	1·6
1808 . .	0·9	0·4	2·4	0·0	1·5	4·3
1809 . .	2·4	0·9	3·5	0·3	6·0	5·8
1810 . .	1·4	0·9	4·9	0·2	2·2	4·0
1811 . .	1·2	0·7	0·5	0·7	0·1	5·4

	Prussia	U.S.A.	British W. Indies	Foreign W. Indies	British America	Portugal, Madeira, and Azores
1806 . .	0·5	8·6	4·7	1·8	1·0	1·4
1807 . .	0·2	7·9	4·6	1·3	1·1	1·0
1808 . .	0·1	4·0	5·9	4·8	1·1	1·1
1809 . .	0·6	5·2	6·0	6·4	1·7	1·4
1810 . .	2·6	7·8	4·8	6·0	1·8	2·0
1811 . .	0·1	1·4	4·1	3·0	1·9	5·1

The following movements are especially to be noted :

1. The growth of Sweden, Gibraltar, Malta, and the Ionian Isles, as substitute entrepôt ports in the continental trade.[3]

[1] The British Minister at Washington, Foster, in 1811 thus explained the central purpose of the Orders in Council: 'You will perceive that the object of our system was not to crush the trade with the Continent, but to counteract an attempt to crush the British trade. Thus we have endeavoured to permit the Continent to receive as large a portion of commerce as might be practicable through Great Britain' (Heckscher, p. 208).

[2] Heckscher, p. 245, sets out the following table of real or declared values, which become available from 1805 (in £ millions):

	North of Europe, including France	Spain	Portugal	Gibraltar, Malta, Sicily, the Levant, &c.	Ireland, Guernsey, &c.	Asia	Africa	U.S.A.	Rest of America
1805 . .	10·3	0·0	1·8	1·4	5·0	2·9	0·8	11·0	7·8
1806 . .	7·6	0·0	1·7	3·0	4·5	2·9	1·2	12·4	10·9
1807 . .	5·1	0·0	1·0	2·9	5·1	3·4	0·8	11·8	10·4
1808 . .	2·2	0·9	0·4	5·6	5·9	3·5	0·6	5·2	16·6
1809 . .	5·7	2·4	0·8	7·0	5·4	2·9	0·8	7·3	18·0
1810 . .	7·7	1·4	1·3	5·2	4·2	3·0	0·6	10·9	15·6
1811 . .	1·5	1·2	4·6	5·4	5·0	2·9	0·3	1·8	11·9

The inverse movements of the figures for the 'North of Europe' and the 'Rest of America' (including South America) vividly indicate the manner in which new markets for the obstructed continental trade were found.

[3] Tooke, i. 273: 'The close of the year 1807 found us, by the events of the war, excluded from direct commercial intercourse with every country in (northern) Europe, Sweden excepted.' See Heckscher, pp. 178–80, for the role of Sweden and Heligoland; p. 244, for the manner in which the

2. The relative success of the blockade in impeding direct trade with Russia, Prussia, Norway, Denmark, and, sporadically, Germany.[1]

3. The restricted trade with the United States, as a result of British and French obstruction, and the self-imposed American blockade.[2]

4. The extraordinary increase in exports to Spain and the 'Foreign West Indies' (including Mexico and South America). These two outlets constituted the main source of new trade in these years, as opposed merely to a successful adjustment to the continental blockade. The Spanish revolution of 1808 was responsible for the opening up of markets both on the Iberian Peninsula and in the Spanish colonies.[3]

5. The sharpness of the decline in the trade with the Baltic and the American continent in 1811; the relative maintenance in that year of the Mediterranean trade.[4]

The general results of this shift in the direction of British exports (real values) are given in the following tables[5] (percentage distribution, by countries of destination):

	A. Domestic goods			B. Foreign and colonial goods		
	Europe	United States	Rest of World	Europe	United States	Rest of World
1805	37·8	30·5	31·7	78·7	5·1	16·2
1806	30·9	31·3	37·8	72·9	5·7	21·4
1807	25·5	33·4	41·1	80·0	3·1	16·9
1808	25·7	15·0	59·3	71·1	0·9	28·0
1809	35·4	16·2	48·4	83·1	1·4	15·5
1810	34·1	23·9	42·0	76·9	2·7	20·4
1811	42·9	6·2	50·9	83·6	0·4	16·0

Mediterranean trade was maintained, with the Balkan peninsula a 'port of penetration' for a new trade route to Vienna.

[1] The large figure for the exports to Germany in 1809 represents a relaxation of the vigilance at the Baltic ports, which was corrected by an 'intensified blockade' in 1810 (Heckscher, p. 243).

[2] For a complete statement of the position of the United States, see Heckscher, pp. 127–49, especially figures for imports and exports and the discussion of them, pp. 146–9. The virtually free trade enjoyed between Britain and the United States in 1810 is apparent in the British export figures for that year. This sudden opening of the market, and consequent speculative exports, played a minor role in the crisis of that year (ibid., p. 241). See also Henry Adams, *A History of the United States, 1801–17*, iv. 165 ff., for the Embargo and its effects; v.

289, for the renewal of trade in 1810.

[3] Henry Adams, v. 174–6.

[4] It is probable that monthly export figures would reveal a peak in 1810 and a decline in the latter months. It is clear that in the course of 1810 prices were falling, stocks were piling up and bankruptcies already increasing (see Heckscher, pp. 243–4; Tooke, i. 303–9). The increase in the figures for exports to Portugal and Spain in 1811 'constituted the first sign of the limitation of the crisis in the sphere of foreign trade' (Heckscher, p. 244). Tooke (i. 317) in analysing the recovery of 1811 cites, as a primary 'favourable circumstance', 'the complete expulsion of the French from Portugal, and the progress of the British army in Spain, which opened nearly the whole Peninsula to a commercial intercourse with this country'.

[5] Heckscher, pp. 324–5.

The relative increase in exports to the 'Rest of World' represents largely the South American boom : in a real sense the freeing of the Spanish colonies had 'called the New World into existence to redress the balance of the Old'.

The progressive tightening of the continental blockade in 1807 caused serious repercussions in Britain. Exports appear to have fallen only slightly ;[1] but the prices of goods from the Baltic, Spain, Italy, and, later, the United States became the objects of a sharp speculative rise, which continued throughout 1808.[2] Until that point the relative stagnation of trade had caused a price decline.[3] Typical import price movements are as follows (without duties) :

	Jan. 1807	Apr. 1807	July 1807	Oct. 1807	Jan. 1808	Apr. 1808	July 1808	Oct. 1808	Jan. 1809
Flax (£ per ton) .	72·0	67·0	67·0	70·0	76·0	86·0	116·0	110·0	138·0
Cotton, Berbice, or Demerera (pence per lb.)	22·0	22·0	21·8	20·4	19·5	21·2	23·0	33·5	33·8
Hemp, Petersburg, clean (£ per ton) .	69·0	65·0	66·0	66·0	75·0	90·0	107·0	100·0	125·0
Spanish quicksilver (pence per lb.) .	40·0	35·5	29·5	30·0	29·0	35·0	37·0	35·0	36·5
Piedmont thrown silk (s. per lb.) .	47·0	47·8	46·5	46·9	53·0	67·0	73·0	62·0	72·0
Jamaica sugar (s. per cwt.) .	31·0	30·0	29·0	28·0	28·0	33·0	35·0	35·0	50·0
Stockholm tar (s. per barrel) .	30·5	29·5	31·2	28·5	36·8	43·5	43·6	41·6	52·0
Memel pine (s. per last)	166·0	157·0	142·0	155·0	162·0	162·0	195·0	207·0	237·0

The speculation in commodities was accompanied by a surge of joint-stock company formation,[4] and, after the Spanish Revolution of 1808,

[1] Ibid., pp. 171–2.
[2] Tooke, i. 275, gives the following example 'of the falling off in supply, which gave occasion to this great advance in prices'.

Imports into Great Britain

	Sheep and lamb's wool	Raw and thrown silk (in 1,000 lb.)	Cotton	Tallow (in cwt.)	Hemp
1806 .	7,334	1,318	58,176	536,652	729,786
1807 .	11,769	1,124	74,925	367,398	756,824
1808 .	2,354	776	43,606	148,282	259,687

[3] Ibid., pp. 272–3.
[4] Tooke (i. 277–8) thus cites the relation between the speculation in commodities and the joint-stock company floatations: 'The encouragement thus offered for speculative exports coinciding with the inducements held out by actual, and still more by prospective scarcity, to speculation in so many articles of general consumption, combined, in 1807 and 1808, to produce an almost universal excitement, leading, as usual on such occasions, to hazardous adventure, and extending itself to new projects of various kinds, such as canals, bridges, fire offices,

and the freeing of the Spanish colonies, a great boom in the trade with
Brazil, Cuba, Mexico, Puerto Rico, and other South and Central American
areas.[1] The famous description of this boom, first uncovered by McCulloch,
is worth quoting again :[2]

The exportations consequent on the first opening of the trade to Buenos
Ayres, Brazil, and the Caraccas were most extraordinary. Speculation was then
carried beyond the boundaries within which even gambling is usually confined,
and was pushed to an extent and into channels that could hardly have been
deemed practicable. We are informed by Mr. Mawe, an intelligent traveller,
resident at Rio Janeiro, at the period in question, that more Manchester goods
were sent out in the course of a few weeks, than had been consumed in the
twenty years preceding; and the quantity of English goods of all sorts poured
into the city was so very great, that warehouses could not be provided sufficient
to contain them; and that the most valuable merchandise was actually exposed
for weeks on the beach to the weather, and to every sort of depredation. Elegant
services of cut-glass and china were offered to persons whose most splendid
drinking-vessels consisted of a horn, or the shell of a cocoa nut; tools were sent
out, having a hammer on the one side and a hatchet on the other, as if the
inhabitants had had nothing more to do than to break the first stone that they
met with, and then cut the gold and diamonds from it; and some speculators
actually went so far as to send out *skates* to Rio Janeiro.

The crisis of 1809–10 had two separate causes: a reaction from the
speculation in South America, and a loosening and then tightening of the
continental blockade. Until July 1809, while Napoleon was engaged in the
Austrian campaign, the Baltic trade had been active, as indicated by a
figure of £6·0 million for exports to Germany in that year. Import prices
began to fall early in 1809, as the northern channels opened.[3] The increase
in British imports thus made possible is indicated in the following table :[4]

| | | Silk | | | | | |
| | Wool | Raw | Thrown | Tallow | Hemp | Flax | Linseed |
		(in 1,000 lb.)			(in cwt.)		(bushels)
1808 . .	2,354	637	139	148,282	259,687	257,722	506,332
1809 . .	6,846	698	502	353,177	858,875	533,367	1,119,763
1810 . .	10,936	1,341	451	479,440	955,799	511,970	1,645,598

This flow of imports was not only in articles for consumption within

breweries, distilleries, and many other descriptions of joint-stock companies.'

[1] Heckscher, pp. 173–8. In 1806 Sir Home
Popham had sailed to Buenos Aires, and, of
his own initiative, attacked and captured
the town. He sent home eight wagon-loads
of silver and a most promising prospectus.
His expedition ended disastrously, but the
prospectus was not forgotten (ibid., p. 176;
Tooke, i. 276; *A.R.*, Chr., pp. 236 ff.).

[2] Tooke, i. 276–7.

[3] Ibid., p. 303: 'As in the short importations in 1808, combined with the apprehension of failure of future supply, there was
substantial cause for a great advance of
price, so, in the superabundant supplies of
the two following years, there was a sufficient cause for the great fall which, in many
instances, left to the importer, after paying
for the enormous charges of importation,
nothing whatever for the prime cost.'

[4] Ibid., p. 301.

Britain but also in colonial products (used as a means of payment for British exports to Latin America) designed for re-export to the Continent.[1] But the situation there changed quite suddenly. Napoleon, from the middle of 1809 and more especially in the summer of 1810, tightened his blockade; and the possibility of a re-export boom like that of 1795–6 disappeared. The flow of colonial commodities to Britain, however, continued on an even larger scale in 1810 than in 1809, as the process of repayment in kind went on. Stocks piled up in the warehouses of British merchants:[2] 'a total stop was put to our exports to the Baltic, by the extensive confiscations which had occurred in the summer of 1810 in the ports of Germany and Prussia. The returns, too, from South America were now coming round; and these left a ruinous loss to the exporters, many of whom had bought the goods on credits maintained by the circulation of accommodation paper.'

Prices fell sharply, bankruptcies increased, and in the manufacturing districts unemployment appeared on a large scale.[3] The decline accelerated in the latter months of 1810; but a revival had begun by the end of 1811, led by recovery in certain of the export markets.[4] Bankruptcy statistics

[1] Heckscher, p. 241.

[2] Tooke, i. 303. For the interrelation of the colonial and continental trade see Heckscher, pp. 241–3. Perhaps the best contemporary account is the following report from Liverpool, dated 22 November 1810 (Tooke, i. 308): 'The effects of a vast import of colonial and American produce, far above the scale of our consumption at the most prosperous periods of our commerce, and attaining a magnitude hitherto unknown to us, have, in the present cramped state of our intercourse with the Continent, developed themselves in numerous bankruptcies, widely spreading in their influence, and unprecedented in extent of embarrassment. It is but fair, however, to ascribe a portion of these evils to the consequences of a sanguine indulgence of enterprise, in extensive shipments of our manufactures to South America, which so confidently followed the expedition to La Plata, and the removal of the government of Portugal to Brazil, they are further aided by the speculations which prevailed during the various stages of the American non-intercourse, and which, unfortunately, were not confined to the duration of the circumstances which excited them. In the struggle to support themselves, the speculators have had recourse to new and extensive engagements, in the face of probabilities and facts too incontrovertible to have been slighted, until the united action of the accumulating imports, and the want of an adequate vent, have

overwhelmed them. The event only can enable us fully to appreciate the effects of this imprudence, which, more than any preceding defalcations, have involved the mercantile character of our country, and destroyed confidence in a degree that will require a long period of prosperous circumstances to retrieve.'

[3] Ibid., pp. 306–7. Tooke quotes from the speech of the Chancellor of the Exchequer, in the debate on the Commercial Credit Bill of 1811 commenting on a report on the crisis: 'All the principal manufacturers had been compelled to contract, and some wholly to suspend, their works. It appeared by the report that there was scarcely a cotton manufacturer in the kingdom who had not diminished, by one half, the number of persons employed in his mills; and that many of the smaller manufacturers had discharged their people altogether.'

[4] Ibid., pp. 316–18. The government advance of £6 million in exchequer bills, 'to distressed merchants and manufacturers by way of loan on adequate security' helped set the stage for revival, although Tooke believed 'that it did not come into operation at all till circumstances had occurred favourable . . . to a removal of the causes of the then existing distress'. The final freeing of the Spanish peninsula, noted above, was perhaps the principal positive impulse. But, as well, 'the glut of our exports to South America, and the West Indies had been carried off by low prices, and a brisk demand

and the import price index clearly reflect the improved situation in the course of the latter months of 1811:

	Number of bankruptcies	Import price index
Jan. 1809 .	83	173·9
Apr. . .	104	158·8
July . .	68	144·8
Oct. . .	92	155·9
Jan. 1810 .	96	162·6
Apr. . .	87	160·0
July . .	192	149·3
Oct. · .	166	143·5
Jan. 1811 .	239	137·8
Apr. . .	155	135·2
July . .	171	128·2
Oct. . .	132	131·4
Jan. 1812 .	143	140·1

The limitations imposed by the Orders in Council and the growing diffi-culties with the United States limited recovery strictly until the latter months of 1812 at least.[1]

3. **Investment.** As early as 1807 a considerable speculation in the formation of joint-stock companies was under way in Britain. Tooke quotes a letter, dated 12 January 1808, which lists some forty-two 'public companies proposed to be established by subscription' in 1807.[2] They include principally bridges and banks, insurance, breweries, coal, cloth, paper, and mining companies. This boom accompanied the early specula-tion in commodities (based on restrictions in the American and continental trade) and apparently reached a peak in 1808.[3] After that time it is likely that available speculative funds were diverted into the expanding export trade.

The usual measures of internal enterprise broadly reflect the revival from 1808. The high figures in 1811 for the brick index, inclosures, and navigation, canal, and railway bills probably represent the usual lag at the peak of investment series in this period. Although a strictly cyclical sequence can be traced only in the number of turnpike bills authorized and in timber imports, the rise in each series in this period is evidence

had succeeded. The intention of Russia to resist the French was becoming manifest; and an anticipation was confidently enter-tained of a relaxation of the prohibitions against imports into the Russian ports.'

[1] See Evidence against the Orders in Council, 1812, pp. 1–3 (Birmingham iron manufacturers), pp. 13–14 (potteries), pp. 14 ff. (textiles).

[2] Ibid., pp. 278–80 n. This was probably the most extensive boom of its kind since the South Sea Bubble of 1719–20. For a fairly full account of these speculations see B. C. Hunt, *The Development of the Business Corporation in England, 1800–1867*, pp. 14–20.

[3] Tooke, i. 278.

that the 'spirit of speculation was on the alert' at home as well as in foreign trade :

| | Bills of inclosure[a] (No.) | Canal, railway, and navigation bills[b] | | Production of bricks (in million bricks) | Turn-pike bills (No.) | Quantity of fir timber imports (in 1,000 loads of 50 cu. ft.) | Dock bills | |
		No.	Amount (in £ millions)				No.	Amount (in £ millions)
1806	76	9	0·6	882·2	2	166	2	0·2
1807	91	8	0·2	836·4	4	267	1	..
1808	92	7	0·3	810·4	4	86	..	..
1809	122	13	0·6	826·8	13	156	2	0·1
1810	107	7	0·4	912·5	12	277	2	0·9
1811	133	14	2·0	945·1	9	320	1	0·1

[a] Inclosures were, of course, stimulated by the high prices caused by the blocking off of grain imports and bad harvests. One contemporary, writing in 1810, stated: 'Never have agricultural improvements advanced with such rapid strides, as within the last two years. This has naturally arisen; first, from the increased price of domestic produce, in consequence of that of the Continent being withheld; and secondly, from the employment in agriculture of much of that accumulating capital, which otherwise might probably have been employed in the extension of the commerce by which it was produced' (*Effects of the Continental Blockade*, 1810, by F. D'Ivernois, p. 59).

[b] Railway acts in 1806–11 were:

	For new lines	For extension of existing lines			For new lines	For extension of existing lines
1806 . .	—	2		1809 . .	3	—
1807 . .	—	—		1810 . .	1	1
1808 . .	1	—		1811 . .	3	1

The following railway lines are listed as completed:

	Name of railway	Terminals	Length in miles	Cost of construction
				£
1808	Kilmarnock	Kilmarnock and Troon	9¾	95,000
1809	Forest of Dean	Newnham and Churchway Engine	7½	125,000
	Severn and Wye	Lidbrook and Newern, and branches	26	115,000
1810	Monmouth	Howler, Slade, and Monmouth	—	28,000
1811	Hay	Brecon and Parton Cross	24	65,000
	Llanfihangel	Abergavenny and Llanfihangel Crucorney	6½	35,000

Porter, p. 329. For the growth of railways, and their place in the coal industry in the first decade of the century, see Galloway, pp. 366–70.

The revival in foreign trade brought about, moreover, a sharp increase in the tonnage of British shipping, which had stagnated from 1804 to 1807 (tonnage belonging to the United Kingdom, in thousand tons) :

1806 .	. 2,054	1809 .	. 2,142
1807 .	. 2,071	1810 .	. 2,187
1808 .	. 2,105	1811 .	. 2,222

The movement of the prices of India Stock, Bank Stock, and Consols,

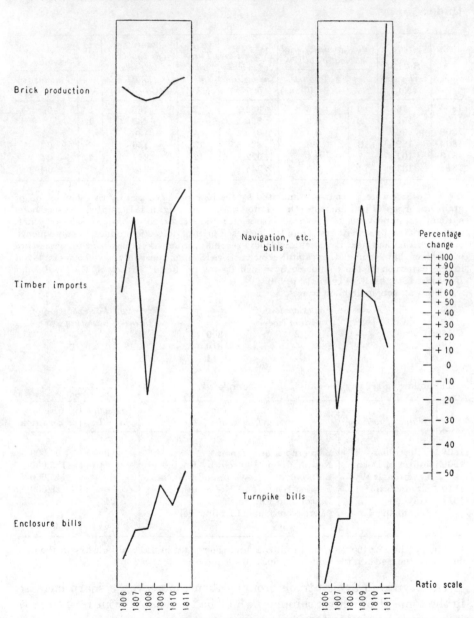

FIG. 27. Investment, 1806–11

as shown in the table below, reflects a sharp speculative advance, losing momentum by early 1810, giving way to decline until late 1811.[1] Unlike

	Bank stock	India stock (In £)	Three per cent. Consols
Jan. 1807 . .	212¾	182¼	60⅝
Apr. . . .	234¾	185	62 7/16
July . . .	230½	177½	62⅜
Oct. . . .	226	173¾	62½
Jan. 1808 . .	225⅜	172⅜	63 9/16
Apr. . . .	232⅛	177¾	65⅝
July . . .	242¼	185⅝	69 7/16
Oct. . . .	234	178½	66⅜
Jan. 1809 . .	239¼	183⅛	66⅛
Apr. . . .	244	185	68
July . . .	260¾	191⅜	68 7/16
Oct. . . .	266	191	68 11/16
Jan. 1810 . .	275¼	181⅞	69⅜
Apr. . . .	272½	186⅛	69 3/16
July . . .	259⅜	181	69¾
Oct. . . .	252½	178	65¼[a]
Jan. 1811 . .	241	177⅜	66 13/16
Apr. . . .	239¼	180⅜	64 7/16
July . . .	236⅞	175¼	62
Oct. . . .	230¾	181¾	63½
Jan. 1812 . .	230⅞	182¼	63 1/16

[a] The relatively marked fall of Consols in the third quarter of 1810 may have been due to the suicide of the banker Goldsmid who had been joint-contractor, with the Barings, for the latest government loan of £14 million. Losses on the Stock Exchange were accounted the cause of his action: 'the Funds immediately felt the effect' (*A.R.*, Chr., 1810, pp. 279–80).

debentures at a later date, these securities represent fairly accurately the state of general expectations; a rise in price does not carry the connotations of 'a fall in the rate of interest'.

4. Industry and Agriculture. It is difficult to trace in detail the course of the iron industry from 1807 to 1811. The usual import series, iron shipments down the Monmouthshire Canal, and a specially calculated figure for exports, however, are available (see p. 99).[2]

[1] There is also available, from 1806, the dividends paid by the West India Dock Company (Silberling, *Review of Economic Statistics*, 1919, p. 290):

	Actual dividends (in £ thousands)	Average prices (in £s)
1806 . .	108·6	144·7
1807 . .	111·2	146·8
1808 . .	115·4	153·5
1809 . .	120·0	177·6
1810 . .	108·0	172·0
1811 . .	108·0	161·1

These figures roughly support the conclusions, as to the timing of security price movements, derived from the monthly data.

[2] Scrivenor, p. 127, for Monmouthshire Canal shipments, and p. 420 for imports. The official value of iron exports has been calculated by E. B. Schumpeter, 'Trade Statistics and Cycles in England' (unpublished dissertation in Radcliffe College Library), p. 411.

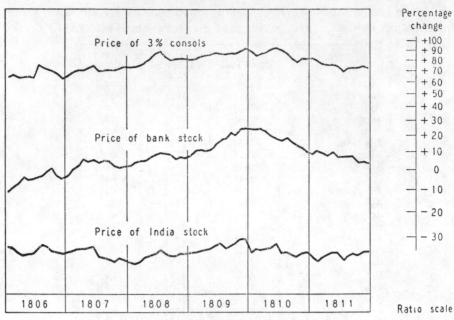

FIG. 28. Investment, 1806–11

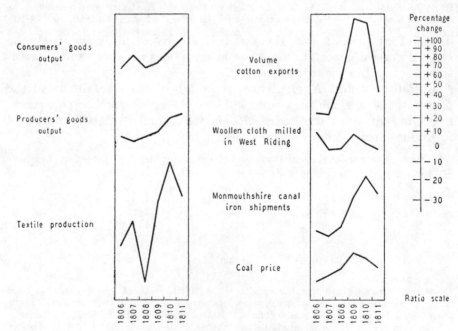

FIG. 29. Industry and Agriculture, 1806–11

	Monmouth-shire Canal iron shipments (in 1,000 tons)	Iron imports	Official value of exports of iron, steel, and their manufactures (in £ millions)
1806 . .	24·0	32·1	1·5
1807 . .	23·0	23·7	1·4
1808 . .	24·6	21·0	1·2
1809 . .	29·7	24·5	1·4
1810 . .	34·1	20·2	1·6
1811 . .	30·5	28·0	1·2

The import series reflects the varying success of the northern blockade as well as the secular decline in the use of foreign iron. The fall in exports in 1808 is probably a result of the first impact of the Continental System : the movement in 1809–11 measures the boom and slump as it affected the export branches of the trade. The Welsh series, representing an area undergoing rapid development, is a useful if somewhat optimistic indicator of the state of the trade as a whole. It shows the relative stagnation until 1808, the booming rise until 1810, and the relapse of 1811. Ashton cites the adverse effects of the blockade on the industry, and traces in detail the circuitous routes, via Malta and Heligoland, by which continental trade was partially maintained.[1] Exports of hardware, especially, were injured by the difficulties with the United States.[2]

There is evidence, nevertheless, that until 1810 the industry enjoyed a 'quiet prosperity' with signs of a labour shortage in some districts during 1809–10.[3] But it suffered fully the effects of the crisis of 1810 and the subsequent depression. Through 1811 and 1812 complaints of unemployment were frequent, the iron industry being consistently slower to reflect general recovery than the textile trades. Attwood thus described the state of the iron industry in April 1812 :[4]

The stock of iron has increased ; every manufacturer is overloaded with stock, and if he sells his iron he . . . sells at his own loss. . . . Great numbers of labourers have been dismissed within the last twelve months ; labourers that twelve months ago could obtain in the ironworks 20s. a week, cannot now obtain more than 10s. or 12s. ; and hundreds of them are to be had at 12s.

The Coalbrookdale partners, who, as late as June 1810, found their orders greater than available stocks, in November 1812 were still ordering furnaces to be blown out.[5]

---

[1] Op. cit., pp. 147–50

[2] The distribution of the products of Birmingham, already specializing in manufactured iron, indicates the relative dependence of that branch of the industry, at least, on the export markets. At this time Thomas Attwood roughly estimated the annual total produce of Birmingham at £2 million, of which £1 million was for the home market, £800,000 for America, £200,000 for the Continent. The consequences in Birmingham of the American Embargo and Non-Intercourse Acts were probably considerable (ibid., p. 150). But in general the iron trade was less dependent than textiles on foreign orders.

[3] Idem.

[4] Ibid., p. 151. See also Evidence against Orders in Council (1812), pp. 1–11.

[5] Ashton, pp. 147 and 151.

Statistics from Newcastle and Sunderland on the coal industry similarly reflect the difficulties suffered in the export trade. The general internal expansion of 1808–10 also affected these figures, although the recession of 1811 can be traced only in shipments from Sunderland. These series do not contain coal used in the manufacture of iron, which was probably the most sensitive of the demands facing the industry. In 1808–10 the growth of the iron industry placed the resources of the British coal-mines under chronic pressure.[1] In 1811, if our view of the iron trade is correct, such demands must have fallen off severely. Coal shipped from Newcastle and Sunderland moved as follows:

(In 1,000 tons)

	Shipments from Newcastle			Shipments from Sunderland		
	Coastwise	Exports	Total	Coastwise	Exports	Total
1806	1,559	124	1,683	812	7	819
1807	1,404	77	1,481	776	11	787
1808	1,641	42	1,683	924	5	929
1809	1,429	36	1,465	859	3	862
1810	1,644	46	1,690	982	5	987
1811	1,678	48	1,726	877	5	882

Although the meagre output figures available show no very distinct cyclical pattern the price of coal does. Sunderland coal rose from a low point of 40·5s. per chaldron in August 1807 to a peak of 66·0s. in November 1809, and declined irregularly thereafter, with a low point of 42·3s. in July 1812:

	1807	1808	1809	1810	1811	1812
Jan.	45·8	51·0	51·0	57·0	56·0	49·4
Apr.	46·0	44·0	45·5	52·0	45·2	43·8
July	46·1	43·2	53·0	48·0	48·8	42·3
Oct.	40·8	46·0	58·0	49·1	45·4	42·6

With a considerably greater part of their output dependent on the export market, the textile trades show more marked fluctuations than either iron or coal.[2] Foreign trade in raw cotton and cotton goods moved as follows:[3]

[1] Porter, p. 278. In 1809 a new coal-mining concern was greeted with the hope that the new supply would bring down the price of coal, raised by this chronic shortage (A.R., Chr., 1809, p. 320).

[2] Comparing the iron and textile trades, Ashton concludes (p. 151): 'Never during the war were the smelters, forgemen, and rollers in a plight similar to that of the cotton or lace operatives. . . . The fact is that the iron industry still found its principal market in England; foreign trade was not of immediate importance to more than a minority of the ironmasters.'

[3] Baines, pp. 347 and 350.

	Quantity of raw cotton (in million lb.)		Exports of cotton manufactures (official value in £ millions)		
	Imports	Exports	Manufactured goods	Twist and yarn	Total
1806 . .	58·2	0·7	9·8	0·7	10·5
1807 . .	74·9	2·2	9·7	0·6	10·3
1808 . .	43·6	1·6	12·5	0·5	13·0
1809 . .	92·8	4·4	18·4	1·0	19·4
1810 . .	132·5	8·8	17·9	1·1	19·0
1811 . .	91·6	1·3	11·5	0·5	12·0

Daniels traces the game of hide-and-seek with the Continent and the role played by the opportunities in South America.[1] The tightening of the Continental System in 1810 hit the textile centres with especial severity.[2] A good summary is that of a contemporary Paisley muslin manufacturer, whose description conforms to evidence bearing on cottons :[3]

In 1808 trade revived considerably; a great quantity of our goods, and of English merchandise, was introduced into the Continent through Heligoland; considerable exports were made to the Baltic; the trade in the Mediterranean increased very considerably; a very great trade was open to this country in consequence of the Royal Family of Portugal removing to the Brazils, which likewise made an opening to Spanish South America. . . . The trade of this country in the years 1808, 1809, until the spring of 1810, increased very considerably. . . . We attribute the depression which took place in 1810 to the effect of the Berlin and Milan Decrees. After the spring of 1810, the whole of the northern coast from Holland to the Elbe was completely shut against us. It was the same with all the lower part of the Baltic; in fact, I may say, up as high as Stettin. Immense exportations took place to the Baltic that year; but from some unfortunate circumstance . . . they could not get forward to their port of destination. They at last got forward, but at that period the King of Prussia had become, I may say, a vassal of France. He had adopted the French system, and all the vessels belonging to this country . . . were seized and confiscated. . . . This occasioned at the end of 1810 . . . joined to some other causes . . . a depression from which the country has not yet absolutely recovered. (1812.)

A further reflection of the course of the cotton industry is the movement in the price of cotton twist (in pence per lb.), given here in annual and semi-annual averages :[4]

1807 . . .	36·70	July–Dec. 1810 . .	38·51
1808 . . .	38·00	Jan.–June 1811 . .	34·40
Jan.–June 1809 .	41·91	July–Dec. 1811 . .	28·71
July–Dec. 1809 .	37·01	Jan.–June 1812 . .	29·72
Jan.–June 1810 .	40·79		

[1] Op. cit., pp. 66–80.
[2] Ibid., p. 79. The records of McConnel and Kennedy graphically indicate the turning-point in the spring of 1810. 'In May prices commenced to fall a little; in July the hurricane of bankruptcies which swept over England and Scotland . . . had arrived, and things were very depressed. In October it was useless to quote prices.'

[3] Quoted, ibid., pp. 78–9.
[4] Porter, p. 185. These figures, collected from the reports of the Factory Commis-

The sharp movements of cotton output in these years produced grave labour difficulties. These called forth from the government the most severe and often brutal repression. Through the early months of 1810 labour was forcing a higher wage on the basis of the expanding market; in the latter months of 1810 and 1811, despite living costs which did not fall, workers faced unemployment and lower wage rates. Although these matters belong in the main to the later discussion of labour's position, it is worth indicating the phenomenon here, since much of the difficulty in the labour market centred in the cotton textile areas.[1] It provides additional testimony to the extent of the swift advance and collapse of trade there.

The woollen trade was subject to somewhat less violent fluctuations than cotton, although raw wool imports and the West Riding production statistics clearly reflect the general movements as already established in other areas within the system:

	Quantity of raw wool imports (in million lb.)	Volume of exports of woollen manufactures (official value in £ millions)	Woollen broad and narrow cloth milled in the West Riding	
			Broad (in million yards)	Narrow (in million yards)
1806 . .	6·8	5·7	9·6	6·4
1807 . .	11·5	4·9	8·4	5·9
1808 . .	2·3	4·4	9·1	5·3
1809 . .	6·8	4·9	9·8	6·0
1810 . .	10·9	5·3	8·7	6·2
1811 . .	4·7	4·0	8·5	5·7

The sharp drop, then gradual increase, in the import and export figures show the first results of the blockade, and the opening up of markets from 1808, their collapse in 1811.[2] An increase in production during 1809 is noted in the *Annual Register*, despite 'the prohibitory decrees of the enemy'.[3] The stocks which had been piled up during 1807 (in anticipation of a cutting off of supplies) were being quickly worked off. But South America was a better market for cotton than for woollen goods, although the renewed trade with the United States in 1810 yielded a considerable net increase in the volume of exports.

The Kondratieff index of textile production and the Hoffmann indexes moved as follows:

sioners, run from 31 December in the annual averages; from 31 December to 30 June in the semi-annual averages.

[1] See Tooke, i. 328–30; Daniels, pp. 75–88; Ashton, p. 151.

[2] There is available for this period the rather remarkable diary of Joseph Rogerson, a Leeds wool manufacturer (W. B. Crump, *The Leeds Woollen Industry*, pp. 77–166). From January to about May 1808 trade is described as 'flat' (pp. 77–84); through 1809 the predominant note is 'plenty of work at the mill', with evidences of tight money conditions in the latter months of the year (pp. 91–109); the diary, unfortunately, is not available for 1810; 1811 was an exceedingly bad year, with money tight and work scarce (pp. 110–32).

[3] Chronicle, 1809, p. 270.

	Kondratieff's index of textile production	Hoffmann's index of consumers' goods production	Hoffmann's index of producers' goods production	Hoffmann's index of total production
1806 . .	5·7	9·2	3·1	5·9
1807 . .	6·7	10·0	3·0	6·2
1808 . .	4·5	9·2	3·1	5·9
1809 . .	7·6	9·5	3·2	6·1
1810 . .	9·9	10·3	3·5	6·6
1811 . .	7·9	11·2	3·6	7·0

The textile index conforms to other information on those industries; but the depression of 1811 fails to appear in Hoffmann's computations. It is possible, but not likely, that technological advance permitted severe unemployment in that year without a decline in total output. But the increased figures for 1811, especially in the consumers' goods index, more probably indicate a defect in the data. The continued increase in the producers' goods index can be traced to the rise in coal shipments, iron imports, and in ship construction in 1811, the latter, perhaps, a bona-fide lag.

5. Finance. Abnormal expenditure abroad moved to a high level in 1809–11; but despite war-time needs, the excess of government expenditure over revenue never approached the enormous figures of 1795–1801[1] (all figures in £ millions):

	Bills and specie for British armies in Europe (a)	Subsidies and loans (b)	Grain imports over £2 million (c)	Total a, b, c (d)	Excess expenditure over revenue (e)
1806 . .	0·7	1·1	—	1·8	12·7
1807 . .	1·7	0·9	—	2·6	8·0
1808 . .	3·9	2·8	—	6·6	10·0
1809 . .	5·6	2·7	0·7	9·1	12·8
1810 . .	6·8	2·3	5·1	14·1	9·7
1811 . .	11·6	2·2	—	13·8	18·4

Although exports increased in 1809–10, the foreign exchanges weakened drastically. That problem, which called forth the Bullion Report of 1810, will be examined shortly.

But it is necessary first to trace the manner in which the commercial and industrial boom was financed. The Bank's note circulation, coin and bullion holdings, and private securities held, moved as follows:

[1] Silberling, p. 227, and Cannan, p. xliii. The diminished excess of expenditure over revenue was due to an increase in the yield of taxation rather than to lower annual expenditure (in £ millions):

	Expenditure	Revenue
1806 . . .	68·5	55·8
1807 . . .	67·3	59·3
1808 . . .	73·0	63·0

	Expenditure	Revenue
1809 . . .	76·5	63·7
1810 . . .	76·8	67·1
1811 . . .	83·6	65·2

The largest excess of expenditure over revenue (36·2) came in 1796, when the figures were 57·7 and 21·5, respectively. The decline in revenue in 1811, it is to be noted, reflects the depression of that year.

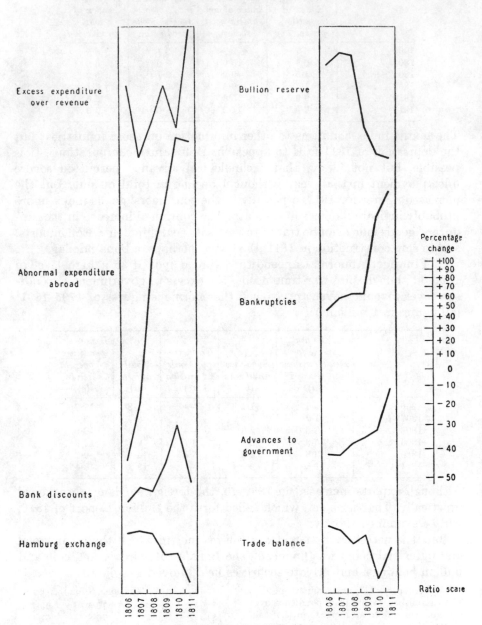

Fig. 30. Finance, 1806–11

(in £ millions)

	Notes in circulation	Coin and bullion	Private securities
Feb. 1806 . .	17·7	6·0	11·8
Aug. . . .	21·0	6·2	15·3
Feb. 1807 . .	17·0	6·1	14·0
Aug. . . .	19·7	6·5	16·5
Feb. 1808 . .	18·2	7·9	13·2
Aug. . . .	17·1	6·0	14·3
Feb. 1809 . .	18·5	4·5	14·4
Aug. . . .	19·6	3·7	18·1
Feb. 1810 . .	21·0	3·5	21·1
Aug. . . .	24·8	3·2	23·8
Feb. 1811 . .	23·4	3·4	19·9
Aug. . . .	23·3	3·2	15·2

From the end of 1808 onwards there appears to have been an enormous increase in the Bank's accommodation to private borrowers, against a declining reserve: a real 'inflationary' movement. The Bank, freed of the necessity for watching the exchanges, played an active role in the 'phrenzy of speculation'.[1] Sir Francis Baring, in testimony before the Bullion Committee, stated that 'he knew of . . . instances of clerks not worth £100, who had started as merchants, and had been allowed to have discounts of £5,000 to £10,000, which demand was caused by the Bank, and not by the regular demands of trade, and which could not exist if the restriction were removed'.[2] Whether, in fact, the quality of the Bank's discounts seriously deteriorated is an open question. It is clear that the Bank felt itself free to pursue quantitatively an easy-money policy despite a falling reserve and weakening foreign exchanges.

The boom was characterized as well by an increase in the number of country banks:[3]

Along with this extravagant speculation, partly caused by it, and partly fanning it, a multitude of country banks started up in all directions, and inundated the country with their notes, exactly as had happened before 1793.

The number of country banks was 270 in 1797, 600 in 1808, and 721 in 1810, when the Bullion Committee sat. It was estimated in 1810 that there were fully £30 million country bank notes in circulation, a figure considerably above that for the Bank of England note circulation.[4]

But the phenomenon which most struck contemporaries was the depreciation of the British currency as measured by the price of the precious metals and the foreign exchanges:[5]

[1] Macleod, p. 137.
[2] Quoted ibid. Macleod was a stern hard-money advocate, and evidence on which he seizes is not necessarily to be taken as a reflection of typical profligacy on the part of the Bank's directors.
[3] Macleod, p. 137.
[4] Ibid., p. 138.
[5] A. W. Acworth (Financial Reconstruc-

tion in England, 1815–1822, Appendix D, p. 141) gives index numbers for the price of silver and the Hamburg exchange, par = 100. A continuous series for the gold price is not available until 1811, when Acworth's figure (par = 100) is 123·9. Macleod (p. 221) lists the following quotations, which were published only when sales of some magnitude took place (par = £3. 17s. 10½d.)

	Price of silver (par = 100)	Hamburg exchange
1807 . .	110·2	104
1808 . .	107·1	106
1809 . .	110·4	121
1810 . .	113·9	120
1811 . .	120·7	144

The abnormal British war expenditure abroad was certainly a large factor in this movement. But accentuating forces were the need for grain imports

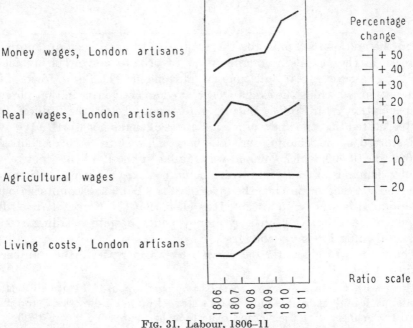

FIG. 31. Labour, 1806–11

and the prosperity demand for foreign goods, on the one hand; the clamping down of the Continental System on British exports, in 1810, on the other. Britain bought too much and sold too little.

The Hamburg exchange began to fall in the latter months of 1808 and remained stable at a low level from the middle of 1809 to about March 1810; it recovered somewhat until about September 1810, as the deflation began. But the cutting off of continental exports caused a further sharp fall to March 1811, the low point in the Hamburg exchange for the entire period. By the end of the year the exchange, although well below par, had recovered considerably.

In February 1810 the depreciation of the exchanges commanded parliamentary attention, and the Bullion Committee was appointed. The conclu-

£4. 0s. 0d. (1805–10), £4. 5s. 0d. (9 October 1810), £4. 12s. 0d. (12 February 1811), £4. 16s. 0d. (26 March 1811), £4. 18s. 0d. (25 October 1811).

sion of its famous report was that the Bank of England had permitted credit expansion to continue, despite the fact that the British balance of payments was yielding an increasingly adverse exchange; and that this was due to the fact that a fall in the exchange no longer could cause the Bank to lose bullion. In short it held that restriction had removed an automatic check, through the exchanges, on internal credit. It proposed that the check should be restored.[1] The report was rejected not so much because of disagreement over the causes of depreciation as because, depreciation or not, the war had to be carried on. A successful return to the gold standard in 1810 would have involved a sharp contraction in the advances of the Bank, not only to the public, but to the government. For it was the government's abnormal expenditure abroad, as much as the boom in imports and the grain shortage, that must be held responsible for the depreciation. Deflation might have cut down imports; but it could not increase exports, nor, without the co-operation of the government, limit the flow of war-time payments abroad.[2]

[1] Both in analysis and conclusions the report of the Bullion Committee was 'absolutely identical' with that of 1804, on the Irish currency question; although the former 'is written in a more methodical and scientific form, and is superior as a literary performance' (Macleod, p. 139).

[2] The following passage from Tooke (i. 354–6) admirably pierces the veil of the quantity theory abstractions as applied to this problem. It is worth quoting fully:

'If, seeing the enormous speculations which were on foot between the close of 1807 and the summer of 1808, and becoming aware of the political circumstances which inevitably led to a very large government expenditure abroad; feeling, indeed, the effect of those circumstances by the demand for bullion, of which the stock in the Bank was rapidly decreasing; and seeing, moreover, the strong tendency which, early in the autumn of 1808 was manifested to a fall of the exchanges, the Bank had contracted its issues, it is fairly to be presumed that a contraction so timed would, although carried only to a moderate extent, have had a considerable influence upon the amount of the imports in the following season. If the merchants had become apprized, by a notice similar to that which the Bank had given in December, 1795, of a limitation somewhat below the usual or the expected amount of accommodation by discount, and by a generally diminished facility in the money market, which would have followed from such a limitation by the Bank, in the autumn of 1808, that they were not to rely, in entering into further engagements, upon the accustomed facilities, there is every reason to believe that their orders would have been under lower limits of price; or, if they sought consignments, they would not, indeed, they could not, have offered such large advances upon them. The consequence of such lower limits, or, of lower offers of advance, or, in other words, of greater prudence in mercantile engagements for importation, would have been most important in its influence on the exchanges. The whole of the imports in 1809 and 1810 would have been less, and the cost of the smaller quantity would have been less, not only in the ratio of the lesser quantity, but also of the lower price. But if the whole quantity imported had been less, there would have been a considerable reduction of the sums to be paid to foreigners for freight, not only by the diminished quantity, but by a lower rate, in consequence of the less demand for foreign shiproom. From the difference under these two heads alone, there would have been a great abatement of the pressure for foreign payment; and, considering the very circumscribed sphere of exchange operations which then existed, it can hardly be doubted that this saving of the sums to be transmitted from hence or drawn for from abroad, would have had a sensible effect on the exchanges. And in whatever degree the exchanges had been higher, their improved state would have caused a further saving of the sums to be transmitted for our government expenditure abroad, inasmuch as it would have diminished the amount to be paid by the government here for a given amount of foreign currency required.

6. Labour. General indexes of labour's position show that the rise of money wages was a more adequate counter-weight to the rise in living costs than in the boom of 1797–1802:

	Tucker's index of the cost of living of London artisans	Tucker's index of		Bowley's index of agricultural money wages[a]
		Money wages	Real wages	
		of London artisans		
1806 . .	151·4	54·8	36·2	198
1807 . .	151·0	60·8	40·3	198
1808 . .	158·9	63·0	39·6	198
1809 . .	174·2	64·2	36·9	198
1810 . .	174·4	66·5	38·2	198
1811 . .	173·0	69·5	40·2	198

[a] Kondratieff gives the following series for the annual wages of agricultural labour for these years: 97 (1806), 94 (1807), 91 (1808), 89 (1809), 89 (1810), 84 (1811). They reveal a strong secular decline, beginning in 1806, with wages merely held steady by the boom and rising wheat prices of 1809–10. This secular decline does not begin in the Bowley index until 1813.

Their general import is substantiated in a statement by Tooke, who also cites the severe unemployment of 1811–12 as a major feature of the period :[1]

The wages of agricultural labourers and artisans had been doubled, or nearly so. Salaries from the lowest clerks up to the highest functionaries, as well as professional fees, had been considerably raised on the plea of the greatly increased expenses of living ; the expense of living having been increased, not only by the increased price of necessaries, but by a higher scale of general expenditure, or style of living, incidental to the progress of wealth and civilisation. Thus, upon the recurrence of the seasons of dearth between 1808 and 1812, there was more of an adjustment, although still inadequate, of the pecuniary means of a large part of the different classes, which prevented so great a degree of the pressure of distress as had been observable in the previous scarcity.

But while the wages of agricultural labourers and of artisans had been raised in a considerable, although still inadequate proportion to the increased price of necessaries, this was not the case, or only partially so, as regarded the wages of the working people in manufactories. Considerable numbers of these had no advance of wages ; or if they had, the advance was more than compensated by reduced hours of work. In the branches of trade which were affected by the state of stagnation and discredit in 1810 and 1811, and in those which depended upon a demand for export, many workmen were thrown wholly out of employ. The distress accordingly among these classes was very severe, and was the cause of considerable disturbances in the manufacturing districts.

These years saw some of the most brutal industrial conflict in British labour history. Early in 1808 a plea for a minimum wage was again rejected in Parliament and a wave of cotton strikes and riots broke out in Manchester.[2] The militia were called out, and at least three persons were

---

[1] Op. cit., i. 329–30.   [2] A.R., Chr., 1808, pp. 47–8.

killed. At that point the cotton industry was beginning to recover from the stagnation which followed the first application of the Berlin Decree. A 10 per cent. wage increase was granted; but the workmen felt it an inadequate adjustment.[1] Throughout the cotton districts there were riots: at Rochdale, Manchester, Oldham. Looms were destroyed and soldiers came 'pouring into Manchester from all quarters';[2] but the 'refractory spirit amongst the weavers continued'.[3]

They not only stopped all the looms they found at work, but intercepted every weaver coming in with finished pieces, and going out with fresh work. . . . Some pieces are said to have been actually cut out, or destroyed in the looms. . . . Guards here patrolled the streets in the day. . . . Many pieces of different goods have been maliciously destroyed by means of spirit of vitriol and aqua fortis. . . . The women are, if possible, more turbulent and mischievous than the men. . . . Written papers were this day (June 22, 1808) stuck upon the walls . . . threatening destruction to the houses of all weavers who shall attempt to throw a shuttle, until every manufacturer agrees to an advance of wages.

Combination Acts or no, such strong action indicates a considerable militancy and even a high degree of organization.[4] Nor were such strikes confined to the cotton trade.[5]

The strikes of 1808–10, of which the above are typical, were the joint products of prosperity and rising food prices. The disturbances of the latter months of 1810 and 1811 were characteristic of depression. Severe unemployment was reported from Nottingham, Manchester, the West Riding.[6] The 'curtailment of hands', in Nottingham, as well as the introduction of new machinery, caused riots which again brought forth the militia.[7] There had been some unemployment in 1793, 1797, 1803, and 1807–8; but that of 1811 was, so far as one can judge from the qualitative evidence available, on a much larger scale than on previous occasions within our period.

[1] Ibid., p. 51.
[2] Ibid., p. 54.
[3] Ibid., pp. 58 and 63–4.
[4] For an attempt to form a 'General Union' in Manchester, in 1810, see J. L. and B. Hammond, *The Skilled Labourer*, pp. 92–3.
[5] See, for example, the coal strike of 1810, which resulted in the imprisonment of many of the miners (Galloway, p. 441). Also J. L. and B. Hammond, p. 78, for an account of the cotton strikes.
[6] *A.R.*, Chr., 1811, pp. 47, 50, 129.
[7] Ibid., p. 129. See also J. L. and B. Hammond, *The Town Labourer, 1760–1832*, p. 101, for an account of the effects on textile areas of the depression of 1811: 'The distress of Lancashire was such that Sir Robert Peel declared that English labourers had never known such misery.'

Chapter III

1812–21[1]

INTRODUCTION

THE decade from 1812 to 1821 includes, roughly, two full cycles. In 1812 recovery from the relapse of 1810–11 was under way. It reached its peak early in 1815, although the large exports of 1815 were dumped, in many cases, on unreceptive markets at falling prices. The low point in this downswing came late in 1816. 1817–18 were years of recovery, with the peak in the latter year. By the end of 1818, however, crises had occurred both on the Continent and in the United States; and an international depression began which affected all of British industry. 1819 marks the low point, after which a slow and partial recovery can be traced in 1820–1. Agriculture suffered chronic and severe depression from 1813 to 1823, when a rise in the wheat price heralded a decade of relative agricultural peace. But in the period under examination here the farmer found relief from falling prices only in the year running from about the middle of 1816 to June 1817.

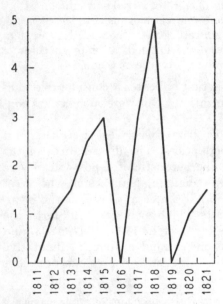

FIG. 32. Business-cycle Pattern, 1811–21

More broadly, this chapter of the *History* includes the latter years of the Napoleonic Wars and the first six years of peace. The Continental System, however, was dead by 1812, as well as the British Orders in Council. But loan-financed government expenditure—the other great war influence on the British economy—continued on a considerable scale until 1816. The year 1821 has been chosen as a terminal date because the return to a gold standard symbolizes, in a limited sense, a final adjustment to the conditions of peace. By that time British industry, commerce, agriculture, and labour had undergone the immediate difficulties of the transition and were being confronted by a new set of situations, some of which were to prevail through the following three decades.

[1] Cyclical pattern:

Trough	Peak
1811 (Sept.)	1815 (Mar.)
1816 (Sept.)	1818 (Sept.)
1819 (Sept.)	1825 (May)

The boom of 1811–15, especially in its latter speculative stages, was based largely on the expected opening of foreign markets, calculated to follow the conclusion of a final peace. A speculative rise in prices resulted, which collapsed in the spring of 1814. Exports to the Continent fell sharply in 1815, as markets there proved incapable of absorbing the stocks of goods (including large amounts of imported colonial produce) which had been accumulated in the previous few years. The end of the war with the United States (at the close of 1814) caused a tremendous increase in exports there in 1815; but again hopes were disappointed. Prices fell, bankruptcies increased. Foreign trade decreased sharply in 1816. Stocks of commodities were permitted to run down, laying the groundwork for the succeeding expansion (1817–18).

Foreign trade and government war expenditure were the only major bases of recovery in 1812–15. The building of canals, houses, and factories seems to have been on a relatively small scale, while inclosures began to decline with the fall in agricultural prices, from 1813. Internal enterprise was at a surprisingly low level in view of the speculative spirit in the markets concerned with foreign trade.

The depression of 1815–16, and the cessation of government expenditure abroad, brought the exchanges back to par in 1816. But revival, accompanied by an abnormal boom in imports, and the floatation of foreign loans in London, weakened the exchanges in 1817–18. The Act of 1819 came at a time when deflation was already operating to make possible a resumption of specie payments. In May 1821, two years before the date scheduled, Britain returned to a bullion standard. An analysis of the forces operating on the exchanges in each period leads to the conclusion that the rise in the exchanges (1814–21) was little influenced by conscious Bank of England policy. The fact that the Bank maintained its traditional passive position, that its policy was directed essentially on the principles of a private bank, had, in itself, important consequences. But major criticism of the directors can properly be couched only in terms of what they did not do; and, even so, only from standards of policy alien to nineteenth-century bankers.

The period contains three years of extremely bitter labour unrest—1812, 1816, and 1819. The first was the high point of Luddite riots, in one sense the final large-scale protest of the handicraft worker against the machine. Much was to be heard of the hand-loom weaver before the middle of the century; but his protest was never more vigorous than in 1812. Severe unemployment in 1816, coupled with a rise in food prices in the latter half of the year, made for innumerable strikes and riots, which subsided towards the end of 1817. Although in 1819 the working classes were probably in less economic distress than in 1816, the Peterloo Massacre and the political character of labour's protests cause the disturbances of 1819 to overshadow the post-war period. In 1818 (a year of prosperity) the large-scale strikes of spinners and weavers for higher wages, and a wage minimum, indicate the extent to which labour organization had developed despite the

Combination Acts. In terms of real wage calculations the position of labour shows a decided improvement, dating from the fall in agricultural prices in 1813, to 1821. But money wages fluctuated with the state of trade, and there were periods of extremely severe unemployment.

Evidence on the position of the major British industries shows cotton still the most sensitive to cyclical fluctuation. It was no accident that Manchester was the centre of labour difficulties and of the movement towards parliamentary reform, as well as the fount of free-trade agitation: in respect of politics as well as of industrial technique it was true that 'what Lancashire does today England does tomorrow'. The woollen trade, in the post-war years, was much injured by the depression in the United States, its largest foreign market. The agricultural depression also affected the wool manufacturers, in that it led to successful appeals to Parliament (1819) for a tax on foreign wool. This was later repealed (1824); but British wool-growers were, at the same time, rewarded with the abolition of the historic restriction on the export of British wool.

The iron trade, which had benefited more directly than any other from the government's war-time orders, suffered severely in 1816. But in 1817–18, and again in 1820–1, some recovery took place on the basis of an expanding home demand. Birmingham, however, remained, even until 1821, a partially distressed area, due to its previous dependence on the manufacture of small arms and, like the woollen industry, its extensive markets in the United States. Estimates of coal output show no clear cyclical fluctuation. This may have been due in part to the monopolistic controls still exercised in the northern coalfields; but the lack of a continuous estimate of coal used in iron production makes the calculation of a total output series impossible.

Perhaps the most significant of the trends that appeared in the post-war years is the scarcity of outlets for new investment. In 1816–17 and 1819–21 the prices of existing securities were bid up and the interest rate fell. The government, in the latter years, was actually reducing its debt. Canals and inclosures no longer held their former attractiveness. Under these circumstances the investing public seized eagerly (in 1817–18) on four foreign government loans that were partially floated in London. In 1822–5 this situation was to be repeated on a grander scale.

Idle savings in the capital market (1819–21) found their industrial counterpart in the paradox of falling prices and increased output. The prices of many of the principal raw materials had fallen; and plant, expanded during the previous decades, was capable of a higher level of production than that called forth by the current state of demand. With the continental and American markets depressed, and their governments flirting with protection, British merchants began to search for new outlets and to look kindly on free trade; for they held Britain's Corn Laws and her high tariff schedules partially responsible for protectionist sentiment abroad.

A brief summary cannot indicate adequately the full extent of the adjustments that necessarily followed the termination of the war. In public finance it involved the end of government loan-financing; in the capital markets, the closing of a principal channel of new investment; in the money market, the return to a gold standard; in foreign markets, the loss of a monopoly of the carrying and re-export trades, and the appearance of competitors that the limitation on international trade during the wars had bred; for home industry, the loss of government orders; in the labour markets, the appearance of some 400,000 men discharged from the army and navy; in agriculture (from 1813 rather than the end of the wars), a violent fall in grain prices which caused distress so severe that it has coloured the view of the following three decades. The resultant situation was such that Professor Clapham was led to designate the years between 1815 and 1820 as 'economically probably the most wretched, difficult, and dangerous in modern English history': a judgement which must, however, be tempered by an awareness of the quite powerful expansion of 1817–18.

Part I: 1812–16

1. Prices. The domestic index moves upward from April 1811 to August 1812, with a set-back only in the opening months of the latter year. Although the period coincides with the beginnings of general recovery, the movement is to be attributed to a deficient supply of agricultural produce rather than to a revived demand for commodities in general. The harvest of 1811 left inadequate stocks, and that of 1812 was bad.[1] In the spring of 1812 anticipations of a short supply produced—[2]

a great excitement and spirit of speculation among all persons in the corn trade; and as the range of high prices (with an interval of depression between the harvests of 1810 and 1811, so short as not to have been felt at all by the landlord, and very little by the farmer) had been of an unusually long continuance, it was hastily concluded . . . that the causes of that high range were permanent. This accordingly was the period in which rents experienced their greatest rise, and speculations in land became most general. And there is reason to believe that, under these circumstances, the country circulation must . . . have acquired a renewed extension. . . . The deficiency of our own crops in 1811 and 1812 does not appear to have been so great as it had been in 1794 and 1795; or, again in 1799 and 1800. It is clear, therefore, that the prices of 1811 and 1812 would not have been so high if there had not been a virtual exclusion of foreign supply, which rendered it necessary to eke out our own produce by economy; and this could only be effected through the medium of a relatively high range of prices.[3]

[1] Tooke, i. 322–3.
[2] Ibid., pp. 323 and 325.
[3] Tooke is probably correct in attributing a part of the 'relatively high range of prices' to obstructions in the foreign wheat supply. But he fails at this point to take account of the long-run forces operating to increase both the demand and the supply of agricultural produce between the years to which he refers: the rapid growth of the population, and the increase in the scale and the improvement in the technique of British farming. The state of the weather and the quality of the crop are not sufficient criteria

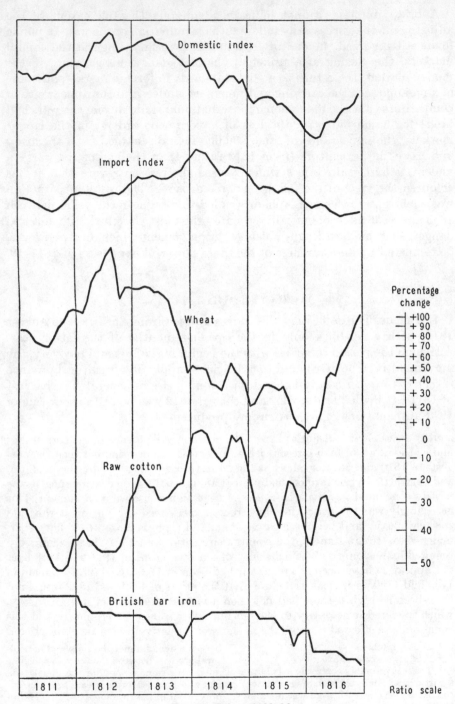

Fig. 33. Prices, 1811–16

The domestic index begins to decline in the latter half of 1812, and continues irregularly to a low point in March 1816. The harvest of 1813 was especially abundant and the wheat price fell from 152s. (per quarter) in August 1812 to 75s. in December 1813. This catastrophic decline was confined largely to wheat and oats. The prices of almost all other domestic commodities were rising sharply. But farmers felt the full effects of the previous extension and intensification of cultivation: a Committee on the Corn Laws sat in 1814.[1]

The harvest of 1814 was inferior, but a large surplus from the previous year supported the supply and kept the wheat price from any very marked recovery. The freedom enjoyed by the foreign trade in corn also impeded an advance in price, except for a brief speculative spurt in the third quarter of 1814.[2] Another brief upward movement occurred early in 1815, due to expectations engendered by Napoleon's return from Elba, and by the passage of the Corn Bill which prohibited the importation of foreign grain unless the wheat price was 80s. per quarter.[3] But a handsome harvest in 1815 drove agricultural prices and the domestic index to a low point, in March 1816.[4] This decline was shared by other commodities in the index, for general depression was under way by the close of 1815.

For the remainder of 1816 the domestic index rises steeply, reaching a peak in June 1817. Poor harvests on the Continent, as well as in Britain, drove the wheat price up sharply: there was actually some export of wheat in the early months of the year, before the 'lamentable deficiency in quantity and miserable inferiority of quality' in the British crop became evident.[5] Most other domestic prices continued to decline throughout 1816, which marks the low point in the post-war deflation.[6]

As in the periods hitherto examined, the index of imported commodities shows a decidedly more regular movement than the domestic index. A

---

for establishing what the appropriate price should be, even assuming, as he does, uniform competitive conditions.

[1] Tooke, i. 341–3. The committee thus described the agricultural revolution that had proceeded since the beginning of the wars: 'It appears to your committee to be established by all the evidence, that, within the last twenty years, a very rapid and extensive progress has been made in the agriculture of the United Kingdom: that great additional capitals have been skilfully and successfully applied, not only to the improved management of lands already in tillage, but also to the converting of large tracts of inferior pasture into productive arable, and the reclaiming and inclosing of fens, commons, and wastes, which have been brought into a state of regular cultivation.'

[2] Ibid., ii. 2–3: 'The harvest being very late, and attended in its progress by variable, and, upon the whole, inclement weather,

some speculation arose, and the prices experienced a momentary advance before the completion of the harvest, of nearly 10s. the quarter. The apprehensions that had been entertained of injury to the crops were, to a considerable extent, confirmed; for it turned out that the wheat generally had been much affected with blight and mildew, and was considered, upon the whole, inferior in quality, and much below the former year in quantity. But the increased breadth of cultivation, the large surplus from the superabundance of the produce of 1813, and an unexpectedly large importation of foreign corn (about 800,000 quarters of wheat, and a like quantity of oats), overpowered the markets, and the prices thenceforward declined again to the close of the year.'

[3] Ibid., p. 3.

[4] Ibid., pp. 3–4.

[5] Ibid., p. 14.

[6] Ibid., pp. 23–4.

clearly marked cycle proceeds from a low point in August 1811 to a peak in February 1814 and again to a low point in August 1816.[1] The upswing is accounted for by speculation in commodities for re-export, based upon the break-up of the Continental System, the unsuccessful Russian campaign of Napoleon, and the anticipations of peace :[2]

By the retreat of the French from Moscow, not only the ports of Russia were secured from the danger of being again shut against us, but daily tidings were received of other ports in the north of Europe being opened to a trade with this country ; and sanguine expectations were beginning to be entertained that the ports of France itself would at no remote period be open to us. The new markets —for such they might then be called—which were thus presented, and the prospect of more, gave rise to a speculative demand for all the articles really wanted, and for many others which it was anticipated would probably be wanted, by the countries with which we had then suddenly come into communication. Colonial produce, as it had been most depressed by our previous exclusion from those markets, experienced the greatest and most rapid advance, but many other articles of export participated in the demand, which prevailed thenceforward till the close of 1813, and the early part of 1814, with greater or less intensity according as the events of the war seemed to hasten or retard a general peace. The conclusion of the war was then hailed as holding out the prospect of an unlimited demand on the part of the inhabitants of the Continent, for the articles from the use of which they had been so long debarred.

But speculators seriously over-estimated the consequences of peace :[3]

The shippers found to their cost, when it was too late, that the effective demand on the Continent for colonial produce and British manufactures had been greatly over-rated ; for whatever might be the desire of the foreign consumers to possess articles so long out of their reach, they were limited in their means of purchase ; and accordingly the bulk of the commodities exported brought very inadequate returns. The low prices, which alone the consumers abroad were able to pay, were still further reduced in value by the advance in our exchanges, which was accelerated by the very extent of those shipments.[4]

---

[1] Although no great significance is to be attached to this fact, the two low points are quite close to one another: August 1811— 127·2; August 1816—123·4.

[2] Tooke, i. 345. Articles for export to the United States were an exception to the general movement. These were depressed by the War of 1812; and they spurted upward in 1815 when most other markets were already depressed.

[3] Ibid., ii. 8–9 and 24. The fall in prices was accentuated by a sharp lowering in freight and insurance rates. Tooke (pp. 10– 12) accounts this reduction in costs a major consequence for prices of the 'transition from war to peace': 'Of that great and memorable fall of prices (1814–16), the principal part beyond that which was the effect of the seasons, and a recoil from the extravagant speculations in exportable commodities, is clearly attributable to the transition from war to peace; not from war, as having caused extra demand, but as having obstructed supply and increased the cost of production; nor to peace, as having been attended with diminished consumption, but as having extended the sources of supply, and reduced the cost of production.'

[4] See James, pp. 39–43, for an extended discussion of the effect of exchange movements on the fortunes of the British exporter in the period when the pound was appreciating: 'After the goods were shipped and the exchange rose, a merchant selling his goods at the rate of 17 francs, when the exchange was at 17 francs the pound sterling, this sum would have given a pound, or would have purchased a bill upon England for a pound to pay for the same goods; but if in the interval, between the sale of the goods

And it is a well known fact, that the losses upon a large proportion of the goods shipped to the Continent, in the spring and summer of 1814, were very great; not less, I have reason to believe, from what I heard at that time of the result of many of them, than 50 per cent. . . . The disastrous effects of these ill-judged and extravagantly extensive speculations began to manifest themselves in the numerous failures which took place towards the close of 1814; these continued increasing in number, as the several losses were ascertained, through 1815 and the early part of 1816. . . . It was not till towards the close of 1816 that many important articles of consumption, which had been greatly depressed, experienced an improved demand with an evident tendency to higher prices. The very low prices of 1815 and 1816 had induced a greatly increased consumption. The stocks of importers, dealers, and manufacturers had become greatly reduced; and a general confidence began to prevail among the best informed persons in the several branches of trade, that prices had, for that period, seen their lowest, inasmuch as the stock in hand of most of the leading articles had become manifestly below the average rate of consumption.

As in 1792–3, 1799–1800, and 1810–11, we have here a crisis the basis of which was prior investment in consumption goods for export and re-export: a relatively brief cessation in the flow of commodities was sufficient to work off the over-supply. And prices immediately reflect a general commercial recovery, although their general level does not again return to the pre-1814 level within our period.

The following are typical movements of non-agricultural domestic prices. Unlike the domestic price index, dominated by wheat, most of these prices reached a high point, like import prices, in 1814:

	Jan. 1812	Jan. 1813	Peak 1814–15	Trough 1816
Copper (pence per lb.) . .	14·1	13·6	(Jan.–June 1814) 16·2	(Nov.–Dec.) 11·2
Iron bars (£ per ton) . .	16·5	14·8	(May 1814–Feb. 1815) 15·0	(Dec.) 11·1
Lead pigs (£ per ton) . .	27·9	29·0	(Apr.–June 1814) 34·0	(Nov.) 17·2
Leather butts (pence per lb.) .	25·0	25·5	(Sept.–Oct. 1814) ·27·5	(Aug.–Dec.) 24·5
Rape oil (£ per ton) . .	66·0	76·0	(Jan. 1814) 54·0	(Jan.) 35·0
Hard soap (s. per cwt.) . .	92·0	97·0	(Jan.–Apr. 1814) 112·0	(Apr. and Sept.) 78·0
Block tin (s. per cwt.) . .	137·0	137·0	(Apr.–July 1814) 176·0	(Dec.) 94·0

On the whole these prices rose less than those of imported commodities, for activity during expansion was concentrated overwhelmingly in foreign trade. Several important prices, in fact, declined from 1812 to the highest

and making the returns, the exchange rose to 25½ francs for the pound sterling, then the 17 francs would only produce 13s. 4d. to remit to England, and the exporter would lose the third of the price of the goods shipped (in British money), although the price in foreign money on the Continent had remained the same, and this was the case in a majority of instances.'

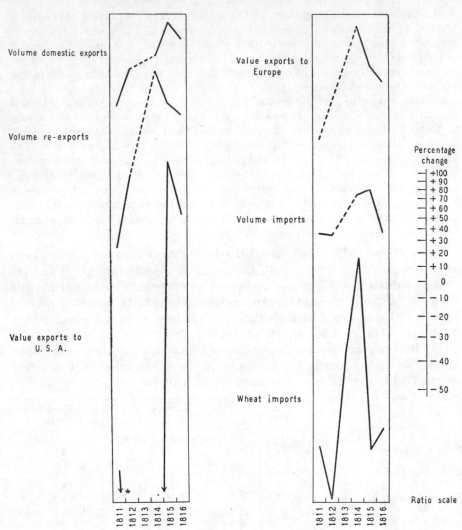

Volume domestic exports

Volume re-exports

Value exports to
U. S. A.

Value exports to
Europe

Percentage
change
+100
+ 90
+ 80
+ 70
+ 60
+ 50
+ 40
+ 30
+ 20
+ 10
0
- 10
- 20
- 30
- 40
- 50

Volume imports

Wheat imports

Ratio scale

1811 1812 1813 1814 1815 1816

1811 1812 1813 1814 1815 1816

* Negligible for 1812, 1813, and 1814

Fig. 34. Foreign Trade, 1811–16

point in 1814–15, notably iron and copper. They share, however, the sharp
decline in 1815–16, which, in all cases, brings prices below their level at
the opening of 1812.

2. **Foreign Trade.** The official records of foreign trade in 1813 were
destroyed by a fire at the London Custom House in February 1814. Existing figures show a tremendous rise in exports from 1812 to 1815, a sharp
decline in 1816. This decline is more severe in the real than in the official
values, indicating the relative importance of the fall in prices to the
movement of the former :

(In £ millions)

	Volume of			Value of domestic exports
	Total imports[a]	Re-exports	Domestic exports	
1811 . .	26·3	4·6	12·4	32·9
1812 . .	26·0	7·2	15·8	41·7
1814 . .	33·5	14·3	17·2	45·5
1815 . .	34·8	11·6	21·5	51·6
1816 . .	26·4	10·8	19·2	41·7

[a] Fluctuations in wheat and wheat flour net imports were on a relatively small scale (in 1,000 quarters): 188·9 (1811), 132·4 (1812), 341·8 (1813), 627·1 (1814), 194·9 (1815), 210·9 (1816).

Exports, viewed by countries, reveal that an increase in the continental trade explains the boom almost completely from 1812 to 1814:

Official Value of Total Exports from England

(In £ millions)

	Spain and Canaries	Germany	Gibraltar, Malta, and Ionian Isles	Prussia	U.S.A.	Italy	British America	British W. Indies
1811	1·2	0·1	5·4	0·1	1·4	0·3	1·9	4·1
1812	1·1	0·2	8·7	0·1	4·1	0·4	1·4	4·8
1814	2·7	9·8	2·5	1·6	0·0	2·3	4·1	6·3
1815	0·8	8·1	2·6	1·1	11·9	1·9	3·1	6·9
1816	0·8	8·7	2·5	0·9	7·8	1·8	2·2	4·6

The total figure for 1815 would have been considerably lower than that for 1814 but for the tremendous rise in exports to the United States upon the cessation of hostilities (24 December 1814). As noted above, the export boom based on expectations of peace on the Continent reached its peak in 1814. But British exporters over-estimated the powers of absorption of the American as well as of the continental markets. The growth of exports to British North America during the War of 1812 probably represents a considerable indirect trade with the United States.

Another obvious feature of the table is the break-up of the Continental System. It emerges not only in the increased exports to Germany, but in the decline in the figures for Gibraltar and the other Mediterranean ports, which had served as smuggling entrepôts. From the time that Napoleon fell out with the Russians the system was doomed. There is evidence as well that early in 1812 Napoleon was seriously revising his concept of commercial warfare.[1] In any case the Russian campaign brought its

---

[1] Heckscher, pp. 248–54. The 'epitaph of the system' was a memorandum (22 December 1812) in which Napoleon informed his minister of commerce that some additional 150 million francs in customs revenues were needed: 'undoubtedly it is necessary to harm our foes, but above all we must live'.

end.[1] In 1812, reacting to bitter complaint from merchants and manufacturers, the British government abandoned the Orders in Council,
serving further to free foreign trade.

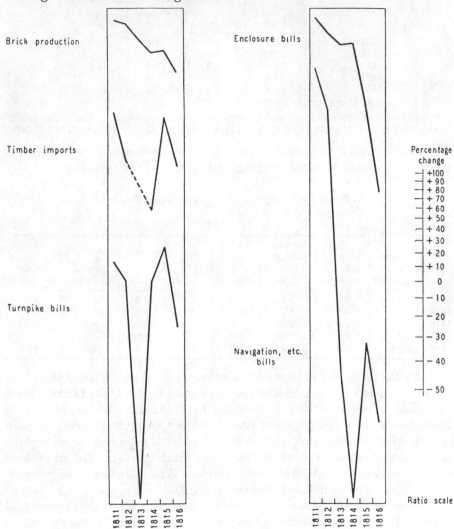

FIG. 35. Investment, 1811–16

In the markets not listed here, exports to Portugal decline steadily;
those to Turkey and the Levant show a peak in 1812, a low point in 1814,
and a rise thereafter that culminates in 1818; those to China and the East
begin a recovery in 1812 that runs steadily to the same year: those to the
foreign West Indies (including Central and South America) recover to
1814, but never reach the peak of 1809 in the subsequent decade.

[1] Heckscher, p. 252. In 1813 there were   shipped from Britain; but they did not pre-
still sporadic confiscations of colonial goods   vent a general disintegration of the blockade.

The severe depression in the export trade in 1815–16 was long and bitterly remembered by contemporaries.[1] It was accompanied by a great increase in bankruptcies (annual totals, from *London Gazette*): 2,112 (1811), 1,813 (1812), 1,583 (1813), 1,258 (1814), 1,759 (1815), 2,145 (1816). And it was accentuated by an extreme contraction of both country bank and Bank of England credit.[2] British exporters and the banking system had counted on ready markets with the coming of peace; they found instead universal 'exhaustion'.[3]

3. Investment. The available indicators of large-scale private enterprise reveal a clear cyclical pattern only in the case of turnpike bills (1813–16). The increase in foreign trade seems, moreover, to have stimulated the construction of some docks in 1814–15. Inclosures, however, fall drastically with the beginnings of agricultural distress; canal, railway, and navigation bills remain on an extremely small scale; the brick production and timber imports (except for 1815) decline from 1811 on.

	Bills of inclosure (No.)	Canal, railway, and navigation bills[a]		Production of bricks (in million bricks)	Turn-pike bills (No.)	Quantity of fir timber imports (in 1,000 loads of 50 cu. ft.)	Dock bills	
		No.	Amount (in £ million)				No.	Amount (in £ millions)
1811	133	14	2·0	945·1	9	320	1	0·1
1812	119	9	1·5	925·8	8	235	1	..
1813	111	5	0·3	835·1	2	..	..	..
1814	112	6	0·1	768·3	8	172	2	0·1
1815	75	7	0·3	778·0	10	311	1	0·3
1816	43	2	0·2	673·0	6	229	..	..

a There were two railway acts for new lines in 1812, and one in 1814, 1816; one act extending lines in 1812, 1814, 1815. Porter (p. 329) lists the following railways completed:

Date of Act	Name of railway	Terminals	Length in miles	Cost of construction
				£
1812 . .	Grosmont	Llanfihangel Crucorney and Llangua Bridge	7	20,000
1815 . .	Gloucester and Cheltenham	Gloucester and Cheltenham	9	50,000

[1] For a dramatic description of the consequences of depression see *Hansard*, xxxiii. 1060 ff., especially the speeches of C. Grant and Lord Brougham. The latter pictures 'clerks, labourers, and menial servants' as having been tempted into investment in commodities for export to the Continent. By 1816 these 'poorer dupes of the delusion had lost their little hoards, and went upon the parish'. See also Smart, pp. 461–508; A.R., 1816, pp. 92–3, Chr., pp. 110, 155, 157.

[2] The financial reflection of the boom and slump will be examined below.

[3] The coming of peace not only revealed the continental markets unprepared to take British goods on the expected scale, at existing prices; but so long a period of enforced protection had caused a growth of manufacturing there which undermined, to some extent, the monopoly position on which British manufacturers and merchants had counted: 'there is reason to apprehend a powerful rivalry to our manufactures in the improved skill and much lighter expense of workmanship by which those of our neighbourers are favoured' (A.R., 1814, quoted by Daniels, 'The Cotton Trade at the Close of the Napoleonic War', *Transactions of the Manchester Statistical Society*, 1917–18, p. 21).

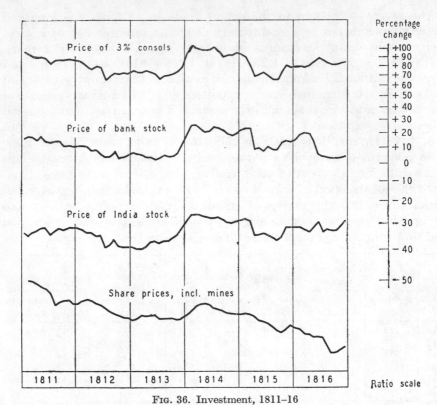

FIG. 36. Investment, 1811–16

It is evident that, even more than in the other cases thus far examined, the sources of this cycle lay strictly in foreign trade.

As one would expect in such circumstances, the tonnage of shipping belonging to Great Britain and Ireland continued the increase begun in 1808[1] (in thousand tons) :

1811	.	.	2,222
1812	.	.	2,239
1813	.	.	2,324
1814	.	.	2,392
1815	.	.	2,454
1816	.	.	2,479

The total for 1816 was not surpassed until 1839.

Consols, Bank Stock, and India Stock, as well as our index of security prices, show roughly similar movements in 1812–16.[2] After a slight revival in the closing months of 1811, they decline throughout 1812. They strengthen slightly early in 1813, but continue at a low level until the middle of that year. Consols, Bank Stock, and India Stock begin a sharp

[1] It is worth noting that the steamship was already in existence at this time. In 1815 five were plying the Thames (Smart, p. 508).

[2] The security price index begins in 1811. For a description of its construction, and the area of investment it reflects, see pp. 359 ff., below.

upswing in the third quarter of 1813, the security index in December. A peak in the latter was reached in February–March 1814, the height, too, of the speculation in commodities. The individual securities show two other high points, at the middle and close of 1814, each successively lower than that in the first quarter; the total index remains steady until July, and then declines, to level off in November and December. There is a precipitate drop in all security prices in 1815, accompanying Napoleon's hundred days' return. The recovery in the latter months did not regain completely the earlier losses. India Stock and Consols, strengthened by the end of military operations, fluctuate irregularly about a constant level in 1816; Bank Stock and the security index fall to a new low point in October. All securities, following the lines of general recovery, then begin a strong revival which extends throughout 1817.

In general, then, one can trace a cycle which conforms fairly closely to that in non-agricultural commodities: a peak early in 1814, a low point late in 1816. Government securities, however, decline in the early stages of revival (1812–13) and show, due to political influences, a somewhat less regular movement to depression (1814–16). The brief mercurial rise in the first quarter of 1814 emphasizes the limited and speculative nature of the upward phase of this cycle. There was little to sustain it beyond the hope of export markets that peace was expected to bring.

4. **Industry and Agriculture.** The cyclical pattern emerges clearly in the figures for the export of cotton manufactures; but raw cotton imports were kept at an abnormally low level until the end of the war with the United States:[1]

	Exports of cotton manufactures						
	Manufactured goods		Twist and yarn		Total cotton exports		
	Official value	Declared value	Official value	Declared value (in £ millions)	Official value	Declared value	Quantity of raw cotton imports (in million lb.)
1811 .	11·5	..	0·5	..	12·0	..	91·6
1812 .	15·7	..	0·8	..	16·5	..	63·0
1813 .	..	..	..	..	..	..	51·0
1814 .	16·5	17·2	1·1	2·8	17·7	20·0	60·1
1815 .	21·5	18·9	0·8	1·7	22·3	20·6	99·3
1816 .	16·2	13·0	1·4	2·6	17·6	15·6	93·9

The declared values become available only in 1814. Their movement, as compared to that of the official values, reveals clearly the situation in 1815, when large-scale shipments to the United States were dumped for whatever they might bring, with prices declining rapidly after the continental débâcle of the previous year. The quantities shipped in 1815 are far above those of the previous year; the declared values only very slightly so. It is difficult to estimate the generality of the following figures (average prices in Manchester, 2nd quality), but they probably indicate fairly well the typical movement of the prices of manufactured cotton goods in the

[1] Baines, pp. 347 and 350.

years for which the declared value of exports is available :[1] £1. 4*s*. 7*d*.
(1814), 19*s*. 8¾*d*. (1815), 16*s*. 8½*d*. (1816).

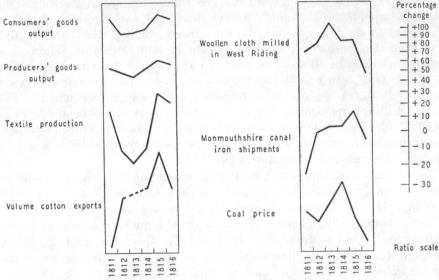

FIG. 37. Industry and Agriculture, 1811–16

Daniels, from the correspondence of his Manchester firm (McConnel and
Kennedy), traces a revival from the end of 1812, continuing slowly through
1813.[2] In the course of the latter year trading relations with the Continent
were re-established and exports there boomed; but the war with the
United States 'immensely complicated the situation'. As early as June
1814 reports came in that, 'contrary to expectation, the demand at the
Leipzig and Frankfort Fairs had been very limited, and that the anticipated orders from Switzerland had not materialized'.[3] By the end of 1814
weavers in some districts were already being laid off. The news of peace
with the United States in December brought some encouragement, and
there was a measure of recovery based on shipments there.[4] But prices
were falling and the tone of gloomy disappointment continued. 1816 was

[1] Baines, p. 356. These figures are from the
firm of James Grimshaw, spinner and manufacturer, of Barrowford, near Colne. Bankruptcies in the cotton trade were: 8 (1814),
12 (1815), 16 (1816) (Tooke, *High and Low
Prices*, Appendix).

[2] Op. cit., pp. 14 ff.

[3] Ibid., p. 15.

[4] Ibid., pp. 16–17 and 22. The embargo
and, later, the war with Great Britain had
seen a considerable growth in the American
cotton manufacture. It was estimated that
there were 2 cotton mills, consuming 500
bales, in 1800; 165, consuming 90,000 bales,
in 1815. The consequences of peace on the

budding industry are thus described by E. J.
Donnell (*History of Cotton*, p. 69): 'The
recommencement of the importation of goods
at the close of the war with England, in this
year (1815), and the sudden reduction of
prices consequent thereon was very destructive to manufacturing operations; business
was prostrated and many establishments
that had been built at extravagant rates
became almost if not quite worthless. For
the purpose of protecting this interest,
which was supposed to have some claim
upon the country on account of the aid
afforded during the war, a tariff was passed.'

universally a bad year with heavy unemployment, bankruptcies, and riots. A report from Glasgow in December 1816 states that 'the general misery . . . was said never to have been equalled, and general subscriptions were being raised to relieve the distress'.[1] On the Continent British goods were sold at prices 'so low as to defy all profitable competition'.[2]

The woollen industry seems to have been affected by the same forces, although probably not so drastically, because of its somewhat lesser dependence on exports.[3] With the repeal of the Orders in Council in 1812, wool exports began to revive, as the tabulation below indicates, and the whole industry felt the consequences.[4] The reports of 1812 were full of

	Quantity of raw wool imports (in million lb.)	Volume of exports of woollen manufactures (official value in £ millions)	Woollen broad and narrow cloth milled in the West Riding	
			Broad	Narrow
			(in million yards)	
1811 . .	4·7	4·0	8·5	5·7
1812 . .	7·0	4·6	9·9	5·1
1813 . .	..	..	11·7	5·6
1814 . .	15·5	4·9	9·3	6·0
1815 . .	13·6	7·1	8·8	6·6
1816 . .	7·5	5·6	8·6	3·7

Luddite riots in the woollen districts; 1813 was a year of 'internal public tranquillity'.[5] The peak in raw wool imports comes in 1814; the peak in broadcloth milled in the West Riding came in 1813, in narrow cloth in 1815; but even in the latter case, the increase from 1814 to 1815 is not comparable to that in exports. It would appear that manufacturers produced, to some extent, for stocks, which were held by the exporters until the foreign markets appeared favourable.

Kondratieff's index of textile production, because of the considerable weight given to raw cotton imports, fails to show any increase in 1812–13. Its movement in 1814–16, however, conforms to the evidence of the various textile foreign trade series: 7·9 (1811), 6·1 (1812), 5·6 (1813), 6·2 (1814), 8·9 (1815), 8·4 (1816).

Like other agricultural interests, the British wool growers, in 1815–16, looked to the government for protection. The prices of home-grown wool and mutton moved as follows (in pence per lb.) :

[1] Daniels, p. 24.

[2] A.R., Chr., 1816, p. 74.

[3] From 1815 the declared value of woollen manufactures exported becomes available. It declines from 1815 to 1816, from £9·4 to £7·8 million (Porter, p. 168).

[4] A.R., Chr., 1812, p. 87.

[5] A.R., 1813, p. 98. Rogerson's diary (Crump, pp. 133–66) is available from January until June 1814. His business appeared to pick up about May 1812 (pp. 137–9); despite the set-back of the war with the

United States, 1813 was a good year (p. 159): 'This year taking it altogether has been a very lucky one for us (tho' it has been in the midst of Wars) and I think I may say it has been a very good one for the Country at large—Thank God for it—I am sure we have great reason to be thankful in regard to the things of this world; our property keeps increasing more and more every year'; the early months of 1814 were rather 'flat', but there was no decisive downturn (pp. 160–6).

	Southdown wool	Kent long wool	Smithfield mutton (March price)
1811 . .	20·4	13	7
1812 . .	18·6	13½	8
1813 . .	20·6	15	9¾
1814 . .	24·8	21	10¾
1815 . .	24·0	22	7¾
1816 . .	17·6	14	6

A petition was presented to Parliament urging a tax on foreign wool and free export of the British growth; and a Select Committee was appointed to investigate the case of the wool grower.The manufacturers and merchants of Leeds, Wakefield, Huddersfield, and Rochdale immediately protested that Britain's export trade in woollens would be ruined; and that manufacturers were purchasing the current home supply at 'fair' prices. To the relief of the manufacturers the Select Committee concluded (29 April 1816) that 'no part of the present agricultural distress arises from the inadequacy of the prices [of British wool], and therefore that it is not expedient to make any alterations in the laws relating to woollen goods and the trade in wool'.[1] The agitation of the wool growers, however, continued, keeping 'the manufacturers in a constant state of alarm and anxiety, prejudicial to their . . . interests'.[2]

Next to cotton, the iron industry was probably hardest hit in 1815–16. Although it depended relatively little on its export orders, it had probably been affected more directly than any other branch of British trade by the government's military expenditure.[3] The excess of expenditure over revenue declined from £35·2 to £2·5 million between 1814 and 1816. The war was over, and the iron industry suffered severely. Iron exports and shipments on the Monmouthshire Canal moved as follows:

	Monmouthshire Canal iron shipments (in 1,000 tons)	Official value of exports of iron, steel, and their manufactures (in £ millions)
1811 . .	30·5	1·2
1812 . .	40·0	1·4
1813 . .	41·8	..
1814 . .	41·8	1·4
1815 . .	46·2	2·0
1816 . .	38·4	1·9

[1] Quoted, Bischoff, i. 409.

[2] Ibid., p. 425.

[3] Ashton, p. 152, makes the following comment on the position of the iron industry during the war: 'Secure in the home market, and not yet feeling the necessity for other outlets, the English ironmasters could give their energies to the production of munitions and of iron for structural purposes at home, without the perpetual dread which must have haunted other industrialists, that some new turn in politics might sever their supplies of raw material or block their access to a foreign market.'

The tonnage in 1815 on the Monmouthshire Canal, which shows a strong secular increase, was not surpassed until 1821. In comparison with the export figure (which declines only slightly) it would seem to indicate that the depression in 1816 was, almost completely, the result of a fall in the home demand for iron.

Ashton has amassed striking evidence as to the seriousness of the decline :[1]

At the end of the war the English iron industry again found itself with a capacity for production in excess of the immediate peace-time needs of the country. In spite of attempts made by the associated ironmasters to maintain prices, a general fall in values took place and such sales as were effected were at figures below those recorded in the books of the various 'Meetings,' which are the chief source from which information has generally been drawn. But with the prices of their product falling, the ironmasters found further production impossible; for rents and royalties were generally subject to long-period contracts which had, for the most part, been drawn up in the profitable years when war-prices prevailed. In these circumstances ironworks everywhere were being shut down: many works were sold at a sixth or a seventh of their original cost; the plant of others was broken up and sold for whatever it would fetch; and in some cases whole ironworks were abandoned and allowed to revert to the land-owner. 'It appears that in Shropshire at this moment (August, 1816) there are 24 iron furnaces out of blast, and only 10 in blast. It also appears that the works of Mr. Reynolds (the oldest family in the trade in the Shropshire district) have totally ceased; and that out of 34 furnaces (each casting 50 tons of pig iron per week, and each employing about 300 men) only 10 are at present in work; and of these the Colebrookdale company has given orders for the discontinuance of two; and others must inevitably do the same, for it is estimated that the company at Lilleshall has 5,000 tons of iron on hand, and the one at Madeley-Wood not less than 3,000. These extinguished works consumed not less than 8,000 tons of coal per week, so that a corresponding number of colliers are also destitute.' After a few months Joseph Reynolds dismantled the Ketley works and sold the machinery—with results disastrous to the social life of the Wellington district. In Staffordshire the story was the same; and a visitor to Bradley speaks

---

[1] Ashton, pp. 153–4. He traces in detail the fortunes of a single firm, Messrs. Newton, Chambers and Co., of the Thorncliffe Iron-Works. Founded in 1793, with a capital of £2,270, the firm grew steadily until 1811, when it was capitalized at £46,481. One of the partners then withdrew, and the capital was reduced to £27,720; but it continued its increase thereafter. Profit figures from 1813 to 1817 support more general evidence on fluctuation in the iron trade (ibid., p. 160):

Period	Capital at beginning of period	Net profits or losses (−)	Profits or losses (−) per cent.
	£	£	
1813–14 . .	34,576	6,501	18·8
1814–15 . .	39,527	6,000	16·7
1815–16 . .	49,672	nil	nil
1816–17 . .	50,031	−3,856	−7·7

of the 'silence of unmingled desolation' of the great ironworks which John Wilkinson had brought into being there. The miseries of the workers have often been detailed; their savings spent and their household furniture sold, many wandered about the district literally starving. In Bilston alone there were 2,000 unemployed, and the death-rate increased fifteen per cent. In Walsall, Wednesbury, Tipton, Dudley, and Wolverhampton at least 12,000 were out of work. At Merthyr Tydfil, where rioting took place, military had to be called in to preserve order, but elsewhere the poverty and dejection were too intense for the spirit of revolt to assert itself.

The price of iron bars (£ per ton) fell from 15·0 in February 1815 to 11·1 in December 1816. A low point was reached (9·5) in February 1817.[1] The period from 'the latter end of 1815 to about 1817' was accounted one of 'very extensive ruin' by a contemporary iron master.[2] And when revival came it was in the form of orders for waterpipes, bridges, and castings, not for cannon.[3]

With the iron industry thus affected, the coal trade must have been severely hit as well.[4] The figures for coal shipments, however, do not decline in 1815–16. This, of course, proves little, since the iron-foundries were located, in most cases, close to the pit-heads :[5]

[1] The following are annual average prices for pig iron, at the forge, in the midlands (Ashton, p. 156):

	£	s.	d.
1811	6	5	0
1812	5	10	0
1813	5	2	6
1814	6	0	0
1815	5	0	0
1816	3	15	0

Ashton considers prices, rather than output, the better measure of prosperity in the iron trade at this point: 'The fluctuations of the iron trade during the early part of the nineteenth century are not easily represented in statistics of output; for the volume of iron produced is no criterion of profit. In periods of good trade there was, needless to say, a tendency for production to increase, but it required a very serious depression to bring about a large diminution in the output of pig and bar iron. One ironmaster, indeed, even went so far as to assert that when trade was bad ironmasters increased the volume of their product—partly because of the need to sell more iron when prices were low, to cover the instalments of the purchase price of minerals in the soil, and of the works themselves. Although this statement need not be accepted in its entirety, there was certainly an inelasticity in iron-production that renders crude statistics of output somewhat delusive. Prices are a better index of the prosperity of the ironmasters.'

[2] Quoted by Ashton (p. 155 n.) from *Report on Manufactures* (1833), evidence of William Matthews, 9639.

[3] Ibid., pp. 154–5.

[4] Galloway (p. 444) indicates the following distribution of the consumption of coal, exclusive of waste, in 1815:

	Tons
In the iron and other manufactories in the coal countries, about	4,000,000
Coals paying coast duty; about 3,600,000 ch. Winchester or	5,040,000
Coals consumed for culinary and other purposes in the counties not paying duty, about	4,000,000
Total	13,040,000

One would expect the first of these three outlets to show the greatest cyclical fluctuation; continuous estimates, however, are not available for this period.

[5] Porter, p. 278.

(In 1,000 tons)

	Shipments from Newcastle			Shipments from Sunderland		
	Coastwise	Exports	Total	Coastwise	Exports	Total
1811 . .	1,678	48	1,726	877	5	882
1812 . .	1,671	66	1,737	898	8	906
1813 . .	1,548	39	1,587	920	5	925
1814 . .	1,720	85	1,805	989	29	1,018
1815 . .	1,723	113	1,836	895	45	940
1816 . .	1,797	116	1,913	1,027	42	1,070

The price of coal (Sunderland, s. per chaldron), however, does indicate the existence of depression: as in the case of iron, a peak was reached in March 1814, of 80·0s.; in June 1816 the price was 35·7s.[1] These coal and iron prices reveal roughly the cyclical movement in output and employment that has been generally established. The upswing, however, in each case begins somewhat later than other evidence would indicate; and the fall in prices in 1816 was unquestionably more severe than in output, despite the monopolistic controls that existed in both industries.

At various stages of this *History* the extension of farming land, the improvement of methods, and the rise in agricultural costs have been described. The abundant harvest of 1813 and the low grain prices that followed precipitated severe agricultural depression. In 1790, with an average wheat price of 50·5 (s. per quarter), the cost of cultivating 100 acres of arable land was estimated at £411. 15s. 11¾d.; in 1813, similar costs were £711. 16s. 4½d.[2] But in the course of 1813 the wheat price fell from 122 (s. per quarter) in March to 75 in December.[3] The average wheat price was, in 1816, 75·7.

The story of the resultant agricultural distress is familiar.[4] A large part

[1] The annual average price of Sunderland coal moved as follows (s. per chaldron): 47·4 (1811), 44·3 (1812), 50·3 (1813), 57·5 (1814), 45·4 (1815), 39·1 (1816).

[2] Adams, p. 35.

[3] Towards the close of 1813 and early in 1814 foreign grain as well was pouring into England. The *Farmers Magazine* (1814) complained that 'it will soon be indifferent to all but the farmers whether the Corse of Gowrie be sown in wheat or planted with Scots fir'. See also Halévy, p. 179 n.

[4] The following quotation (Lord Ernle, pp. 322–4) makes vivid the consequences of the depression:

'In the period 1814–16 the agricultural industry passed suddenly from prosperity to extreme depression. At first farmers met their engagements out of capital. When that was exhausted, their only resource was to sell their corn as soon as it was threshed, or their stock, for what it would fetch. The great quantity of grain thus thrown on the market in a limited time lowered prices for producers, and the subsequent advance, which benefited only the dealers, suggested to landlords that no reductions of rent were necessary. Farms were thrown up; notices to quit poured in; numbers of tenants absconded. Large tracts of land were untenanted and often uncultivated. In 1815 three thousand acres in a small district of Huntingdonshire were abandoned, and nineteen farms in the Isle of Ely were without tenants. Bankers pressed for their advances, landlords for their rents, tithe-owners for their tithe, tax-collectors for their taxes, tradesmen for their bills. Insolvencies, compositions, executions, seizures, arrests and imprisonments for debt multiplied. . . . Many large farmers lost everything, and became applicants for pauper allowances. . . . Agricultural improvements were at a standstill. Live-stock was reduced to a minimum.

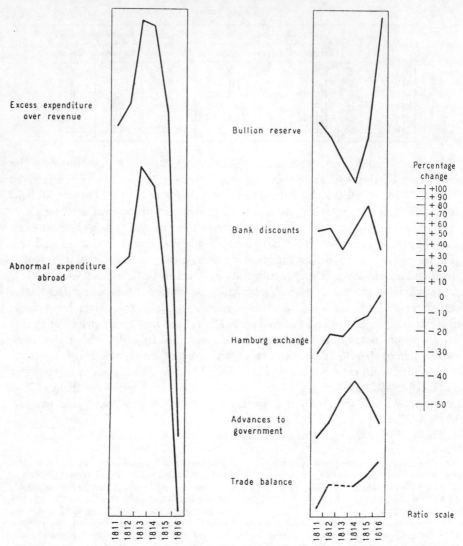

FIG. 38. Finance, 1811–16

Limekilns ceased to burn; less manure was used on the land; the least possible amount of labour was employed. The tradesmen, innkeepers, and shopkeepers of country towns suffered heavily by the loss of custom.

'Blacksmiths, wheelwrights, collar makers, harness makers, carpenters, found no work. At first the depression had been chiefly felt in corn-growing districts, especially on heavy land. But by 1816 it had spread to . . . grass farms. In that year, bad seasons created a temporary scarcity; the rise of wheat to the old prices aggravated rural distress without helping any person except dealers, and the wealthier farmers who could afford to wait; the potato crop, which had recently become important in England, failed; perpetual floods in the spring and summer were succeeded by a winter of such unusual severity, that the loss of sheep in the North was enormous. Landlords, whose land was thrown upon their hands, or who had laid charges on their estates, found themselves confronted with ruin. The alternative was hard.'

of the population of Great Britain was affected : the census returns of 1811 show 6,129,142 persons employed in agriculture and mining, 7,071,989 in commerce, navigation, and manufacture. And the landowners in the former group were not only extremely articulate, but they had, in these pre-Reform Bill days, political connexions quite out of proportion to their numbers. The Corn Bill of 1815 (with an import restriction limit at 80s.) was widely unpopular ;[1] but Parliament felt that 'something must be done for agriculture'. Even protection on this scale, however, failed to prevent the long-run forces from operating :[2]

Between 1813 and the accession of Queen Victoria falls one of the blackest periods of English farming. Prosperity no longer stimulated progress. Except in a few districts, falling prices, dwindling rents, vanishing profits did not even rouse the energy of despair. . . . The men who survived the struggle were rarely the old owners or the old occupiers. They were rather their fortunate successors who entered on the business of land-cultivation on more favourable terms.

5. **Finance.** The final stages of the war were marked by government expenditure abroad to a larger amount than at any other period ; but peace brought loan-financed expenditure virtually to an end in 1816 (in £ millions) :[3]

---

[1] It is significant that the opposition arose not only from the working classes (whose political interests at this stage were rarely represented in the House of Commons) but from manufacturers, who were later to campaign successfully for Corn Law repeal (*A.R.*, 1814, p. 219).

[2] Ernle, p. 319. This general picture of unrelieved agricultural depression has been somewhat modified by a recent article (*Economic History*, February 1939), 'Agricultural Adjustments after the Napoleonic Wars', by G. E. Fussell and M. Compton. The authors, surveying Britain district by district, find that the expansion of the home market, the continued improvement of agricultural technique, and a shift from arable to grazing and dairy farming, permitted a fairly easy adjustment to the new conditions, in some cases. Their evidence serves to alter the picture of long-run,

universal depression, extending uninterrupted through the twenties and thirties: it does not challenge 'the uniform story of disaster' in 1816.

[3] Silberling, p. 227 and (for excess expenditure over revenue) Cannan, p. xliii. The conclusion of the final peace, coming at a time of falling prices and accelerating depression, brought great pressure to bear on the government to reduce its taxation. The income tax, introduced as a war-time expedient, was singled out for special attack. Expenditure decreased as follows from its peak in 1814 (in £ millions): 106·3 (1814), 92·1 (1815), 64·8 (1816). Acworth (p. 24) gives the following comparison of expenditure in 1792 and 1817. Even when corrected for changes in population and prices, these figures represent a great increase in the scope and magnitude of government responsibilities (in £ millions):

	1792 (U.K. net)		1817 (U.K. gross)	
	Amount	Percentage	Amount	Percentage
Debt charges . . .	9·4	51	31·4	54
Civil government . .	2·7	15	9·6	16
Fighting services . .	6·2	34	17·7	30
	18·3	100	58·7	100

	Bills and specie for British armies in Europe (a)	Subsidies and loans (b)	Grain imports over £2 million (c)	Total a, b, c (d)	Bank's reserve (e)	Excess expenditure over revenue (f)
1811 . .	11·6	2·2	—	13·8	3·3	18·4
1812 . .	13·0	1·8	—	14·8	3·0	21·2
1813 . .	17·9	8·2	0·2	26·3	2·6	36·7
1814 . .	15·5	6·8	0·8	23·1	2·2	35·2
1815 . .	7·0	4·9	—	11·9	3·0	19·9
1816 . .	1·3	1·6	—	2·9	6·6	2·5

Until 1816 the Bank's reserve did not recover from the drains of 1808–10. An almost steady fall can be traced from February 1808 to February 1815. Nevertheless, against this low and declining base, commercial discounts, as shown in the following table, were expanded, in 1808–10 and 1813–15.[1] It is apparent, however, that the Bank was not involved in

Average Commercial Bills under Discount

(In £ millions)

1810	.	. 20·1	1814	.	. 13·3
1811	.	. 14·4	1815	.	. 14·9
1812	.	. 14·3	1816	.	. 11·4
1813	.	. 12·3			

financing the boom in 1813–15 to the same extent as in 1808–10. The country banks supported the major part of the expansion, increasing in number from 728 in 1811 to 940 in 1813.[2] The collapse of the speculation in commodities in 1814–15 and the disastrous fall in agricultural prices produced a tremendous contraction of credit. The Bank, on 10 January 1816, had £19·1 million in bills and notes under discount, on 24 December £6·5 million. As for the country banks, Macleod concludes that the reduction in their issues was such that in 1816 they amounted to 'little more than half' their total in 1814.[3] A part of the Bank of England's contraction was certainly due to a conscious effort to prepare for a resumption of specie payments.[4] But it represents as well the low state of demand for money in that year. The contraction of country bank notes was intimately connected

[1] Cannan, p. xliii. The rise in 1815, as in the other years of crisis examined, represents the increased demands on the Bank that followed any weakening of the private banking structure.

[2] Macleod, p. 181; also Tooke, ii. 36–8.

[3] Macleod, p. 182.

[4] Ibid., p. 183: 'In 1815, when peace was finally restored, they (the Bank Directors) prepared in good faith to be ready to do so as soon as they should be required, and, during that year and 1816, they . . . gave notice of their intention to pay all their Notes dated previously to the 1st January 1812, and in April 1817, all their Notes dated before 1st January 1816. When this was done, there was found to be scarcely any demand on them for gold. The nation had got so accustomed to a Paper Currency that they were most unwilling to receive gold for it. Mr. Stuckey, one of the largest bankers in the West of England, said, that during this partial resumption of cash payments it cost him nearly £100 to remit the surplus coin which accumulated upon him to London, as he could not get rid of it in the country, his customers all preferring his Notes; many persons who had hoarded guineas requested as a favour to have Notes in exchange.' See also G. Browning, *The Domestic and Financial Condition of Great Britain*, p. 452.

with the tremendous decline in agricultural prices and the consequent general distress.[1] In 1814–16 there were some ninety-two bank failures.[2]

The role played by banking policy in this credit contraction much engaged the attention of contemporaries. The fall in agricultural prices (1813–16) and the commercial depression (1815–16) were held by some to be the result of a contraction of credit, consciously executed by the Bank of England. It may be concluded, however, that on the whole the monetary deflation was caused by forces outside the Bank's parlour : the cessation in government spending, the collapse of the export boom, the depression in agriculture, and finally the all-round fall in prices which partly caused, and partly was caused by these factors. In the case of agriculture a sudden increase in supply caused the price decline which virtually defines the agricultural distress. In the case of the export trade the initiating factor was the failure of expected demands to materialize. The decline of fully £17 million in the government's loan-financed expenditure must have had wide consequences, in its primary and secondary results, for the home industrial demand. As deflation proceeded, however, the fact of falling prices certainly accentuated the basic depression tendencies.

Peace was first proclaimed with France on 20 June 1814. Restriction at the Bank would then have lapsed (according to the Act of 1803) six months later. But shortly after Napoleon returned from Elba[3] it was extended to 5 July 1816, and again on 21 May 1816 until 28 May 1818.[4]

As noted earlier, the Bank's reserve fell fairly steadily from 1811 to

---

[1] See Tooke, ii. 34–8, for a full discussion of the manner in which the fall in agricultural prices initiated the contraction of country bank issues: 'It is quite clear that so great a fall of prices as took place between 1813 and 1816 could not fail of producing failures and general discredit, and a great reduction of the credit part of the circulation. But it is a fact susceptible of the fullest proofs, that prices fell before any reduction of the circulation of the country banks had taken place. The reduction of that part of the circulating medium was an inevitable consequence, and not the cause of the fall of prices ; as the previous growth of it had been the consequence of the tendency of markets from causes distinctly affecting the supply and demand to a rise of prices, so a contraction necessarily followed the fall of prices.'

Tooke (ibid., p. 37 n.) also quotes Horner (Chairman of the Bullion Committee of 1810), who stated in the House of Commons (1 May 1816) that 'The reduction of the currency had originated in the previous fall of the prices of agricultural produce. This fall has produced a destruction of the country bank paper to an extent which

would not have been thought possible without more ruin than had ensued.'

[2] Ibid., p. 38.

[3] Macleod, p. 183, states that this extension of the Act was passed before the news of Napoleon's return had reached London. The position of the Bank's reserve and the foreign exchanges would have permitted a painless resumption of the gold standard in 1816. As early as April 1816 this was urged by Grenfell in Parliament (Smart, p. 477). But when the government concluded a new credit arrangement with the Bank, restriction was renewed for a further two years. Grenfell led an attack in Commons on the Government's relations with the Bank, contending that the former had not driven hard enough bargains, and that abnormal profits had thereby accrued to the Bank. He even implied collusion between the Vansittart government and the directors. Collusion or not, there seems to be evidence of a considerable incompetence. (See the eloquent diatribe of Clapham on this point, 'Europe after the Great Wars', Economic Journal, 1920, p. 430.)

[4] James, pp. 22–3.

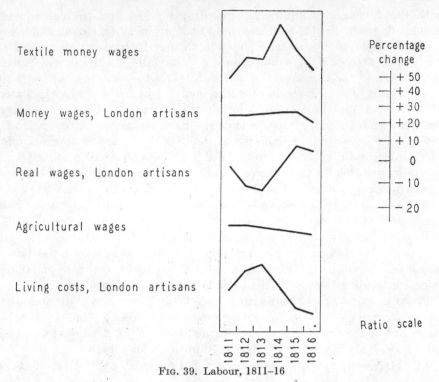

FIG. 39. Labour, 1811–16

February 1815. At that time it began an enormous rise which continued throughout 1816 to a peak in September 1817.[1] In this phase the Bank was certainly pursuing a policy of bullion accumulation. In fact its actions probably prevented the pound from falling to its old parity (£3. 17s. 10½d.); for the Bank was offering £3. 18s. 6d. for gold.[2] In November 1816 the Bank, embarrassed by its hoard, made a first gesture towards resumption. It offered to pay in gold £1 and £2 notes dated prior to 1 January 1812. But in almost twenty years of restriction the nation had become accustomed to bank-notes; and there was virtually no demand for coin.[3]

A commercial deflation of the kind that occurred after the break of the continental markets in the early months of 1814 would be expected to improve the position of the pound on the foreign exchanges, especially since it involved an end to the speculation in imported commodities and a drastic fall in their prices. It was accompanied in this case by a sharp decline in government expenditure abroad, which had constituted the principal abnormal influence on the exchanges. A strengthening of the pound did, in fact, occur; but it accentuated a trend (interrupted in 1813) under way from 1811 :[4]

[1] On 31 February 1815 coin and bullion at the Bank amounted to £2·0 million; on 31 August 1817, £11·7 million (Cannan, p. xlv).

[2] Report on the Resumption of Cash Payments, i, pp. 3–4.
[3] Acworth, p. 73.
[4] Ibid., p. 141.

	Total extraordinary expenditure abroad (in £ millions)	Price of gold	Price of silver (par = 100)	Hamburg exchange
1811 . .	13·8	123·9	120·7	144
1812 . .	14·8	130·2	126·5	128
1813 . .	26·3	136·4	136·7	130
1814 . .	23·1	124·4	124·3	119
1815 . .	11·9	118·7	117·5	114
1816 . .	2·9	102·9	100·9	100

The low level of exports and heavy government expenditure of 1811 had brought the Hamburg exchange to an extremely low point in March–April 1811. Except for a decline in the second quarter of 1813 (attributable to expenditures abroad) its movement is generally upward; for the rise in imports did not fully match that in exports, and the trade balance became increasingly favourable. In 1814 the decline in prices and the end of speculation in imported commodities (designed for re-export) accentuated this tendency towards appreciation. The shock of Napoleon's return from Elba is clearly reflected in a temporary decline; but from May 1815 to October 1816 the rise in the exchange is virtually uninterrupted. At its peak (15 October 1816) the Hamburg exchange, at 38 bancos per pound, was over par (36).

As in the case of the fall in prices, Bank policy was relatively unimportant in this movement. It countenanced a contraction of both government and private credit, and perhaps, in 1816, accentuated that contraction to some extent. But the real forces at work (i.e. agricultural depression, the collapse of foreign trade, and the end of government spending) constitute a sufficient explanation of the return of the pound to par.

6. Labour. Labour statistics show clearly the effects of the boom and slump, as well as the decline in food prices after 1812:

	Kondratieff's index of money wages in the textile industry	Bowley's index of agricultural money wages	Tucker's index of		Gilboy-Boody index of the cost of living in London
			money wages of London	real wages artisans	
1811 . .	55·1	198	69·5	40·2	266
1812 . .	60·9	198	69·5	37·6	270
1813 . .	60·4	196	70·0	36·0	224
1814 . .	71·5	194	70·6	40·2	198
1815 . .	63·3	192	70·6	44·5	183
1816 . .	57·5	190	67·3	43·6	—

In 1811 and the early months of 1812 there was a serious outbreak of Luddite (frame-breaking) riots in Nottingham, Lancashire, Cheshire, and the West Riding.[1] They were severely repressed by the government.[2] The

---

[1] A.R., 1812, p. 131; see Chr., pp. 11–149, for numerous specific references to phases of

[2] A.R., 1812, pp. 35–6. Frame-breaking

the rioting and its suppression.

relative peace of 1813–14, however, is almost certainly to be accounted a result of the revival of trade and the fall in food prices, not of a more successful repression. But, while money wages for London artisans and textile workers were rising,[1] those of agricultural labourers were already on the decline, reflecting immediately the fall in grain prices and general agrarian distress.

1814 was a year of disappointment for British manufacturers. It marks the turning-point in industrial activity, if not in foreign trade.[2] The end of the American war revived the export trade for a time in 1815; but, on the whole, 1815–16 was a period of increasing depression. In any case prices had reached their peak in 1814; and wages (especially in the cyclically sensitive textile industries) fell even during 1815.[3] By 1816 money wages were at or below the depression level of 1811; although it should be recalled that the cost of living, too, had fallen considerably between those years.

The coincidence of agriculture and industrial depression made 1815–16 one of the most difficult periods in the history of the British economy. As the account of specific industries indicated, unemployment can be shown to have existed in every branch of manufactures on which there is evidence.[4]

was made a capital offence, and a system of deputy constables was created. The legislation enacted was emergency in character, running only until 1 March 1814. Various members of Parliament regarded the riots as an outgrowth of the 'decay of trade' and high food prices. Wilberforce, however, treated them as manifestations of political unrest. See also J. L. and B. Hammond, *The Town Labourer, 1760–1832*, pp. 82–3 and 278; and, for a more complete account, *The Skilled Labourer, 1760–1832*, chaps. ix, x, and xi, where the Luddite movement in Nottingham, Lancashire, and Yorkshire is described in detail.

[1] *A.R.*, 1813, p. 104: 'The increased de-

mand for the manufactures of the country, in consequence of the subversion of the French system of their exclusion from the Continent, has given full scope for industry and raised wages to their former rates.'

[2] *A.R.*, 1814, p. 219: 'On the whole the close of the year has not gratified the country with those anticipations of increased prosperity which a state of general peace might have been hoped to justify.'

[3] See Baines (pp. 488–90) for specific wage-rate movements which support the evidence of the Kondratieff index, given above. Typical is the wage paid for weaving the second quality of 74's calico in the neighbourhood of Bumley and Skipton:

	s.	d.		s.	d.
1811 .	. 3	9	1814 .	. 5	10
1812 .	. 4	7	1815 .	. 4	1
1813 .	. 5	7	1816 .	. 2	10

[4] The problem of unemployment was made more acute by the unceremonious disbanding of a large part of the army and navy. Some 400,000 men were returned to

civil life in 1814–16, almost three-quarters of whom appeared on the labour market between the middle of 1815 and the end of 1816, when the depression was most severe:

	Soldiers and ordnance voted	Sailors and marines voted	Total
1814 . .	394,351	140,000	534,351
1815 . .	275,392	90,000	365,392
1816 . .	145,724	33,000	178,724
1817 . .	102,168	19,000	121,168

(Acworth, p. 23.)

The *Annual Register* for 1816 is cluttered with accounts of riots, strikes, and arrests under the Combination Acts.[1] The fall in the prices of foodstuffs in 1814 and 1815 had eased the position of labour somewhat;[2] but the rise, in 1816, with heavy unemployment and falling money wages, was severely oppressive, as the rioters' anger against bakers and millers indicates.

The spirit of unrest lent itself to sentiment for political reform.[3] The seeds of the movement which culminated in 1832 can be traced in the orderly mass meetings of 1816.[4] It is extremely doubtful, however, if the trade unions received any impetus at all from the distress, whatever its broad consequences for reform and class consciousness. Their position almost certainly weakened under the pressure of falling wages and heavy unemployment.

7. A Note on the Yield of the Income Tax, 1806-15. A recent and rather elegant monograph has made available the first-fruits of the discovery of the county by county returns on the war-time income tax.[5] The data given embrace the period from 1806 to 1815, during which time the tax remained steadily at 2s. in the pound.[6] The income tax was administered under five schedules:[7] 'Schedule A was a tax on the rent of land and real property; Schedule B was a tax on the produce of the land; Schedule C taxed the interest received by the holders of Government funds; Schedule D was a tax on the profits from trade and commerce, manufactures, professional earnings and salaries; Schedule E was a levy on certain "offices, pensions, and stipends".'

[1] *A.R.*, Chr., p. 13, miners assemble to resist wage reductions; p. 51, outbreak among journeymen tanners in Bermondsey; p. 60, bread riots in Bridport; p. 66, agricultural workers destroy machinery, burn barns in Suffolk; p. 68, mob at Bidford prevents shipment abroad of potato cargo; p. 70, mob at Bury demands that hosier give up machinery; p. 72, riots at Settleport and Ely, in Suffolk, Essex, and among the unemployed coal-miners on the Wear; p. 75, five weavers convicted of unlawful combination, and for persuading other weavers to give up their employment without the master's consent; p. 76, mob in Halsted frees prisoners convicted for destroying machinery; p. 115, riot at a Glasgow soup-kitchen; p. 127, strike at Preston, cotton machinery broken to prevent the continuance of work; p. 131, 24 of 34 iron furnaces out of blast in Shropshire; p. 161, Luddite activity in Nottingham; p. 165, riots over wage reductions at Newport ironworks; p. 173, 'tumult'among colliers at Calder ironworks, as wages are withheld because of arrests for combinations; p. 174, destruction of bakers' homes and flour-mills in Staffordshire and Wiltshire; p. 192, bread riots at Dundee, in response to a rise in prices. See also Cole and Postgate, pp. 194–5.

[2] Tooke, ii. 13: 'It is to be observed, that the labouring classes were, in 1814 and 1815, and until the renewed rise in the price of provisions, in a comparatively satisfactory state; as the price of labour had not fallen in anything like the proportion of the fall of the prices of necessaries. There were indeed complaints of workmen thrown out of employ, in consequence of the depressed state of so many branches of industry; and the reduction of the number of men in the army and navy created further a temporary surplus; but, notwithstanding these drawbacks, there is every reason to believe—indeed all the evidence of which the subject is susceptible, proves—that the great bulk of the working population were in an improved state, compared with that which they experienced in 1811 and 1812.'

[3] *A.R.*, 1816, p. 93.

[4] Ibid. See also Halévy, pp. 132–4, and Cole and Postgate, pp. 194 and 200.

[5] Arthur Hope-Jones, *Income Tax in the Napoleonic Wars*.

[6] Ibid., p. 29. In 1806 the rate was raised to that level, from 1s. 3d. in the pound.

[7] Ibid., p. 6.

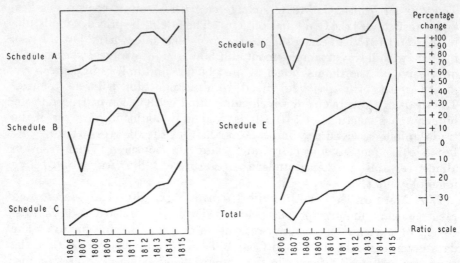

FIG. 40. Total Yield from Income Tax, by Schedules, 1806–15

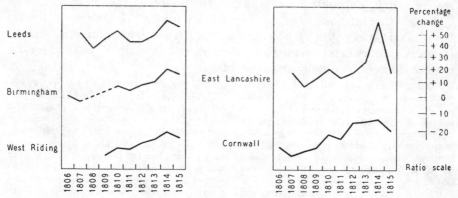

FIG. 41. Yield of Income Tax, by Areas, 1806–15

If the efficiency of collection were uniform these series might be expected to be sensitive to fluctuations in the money income of the various groups. It would appear, however, that the yield was as much a function of the assiduity of the collectors as of income changes.[1] Nevertheless, some reflection of cyclical movements can be discerned.

The accompanying table reveals the yield for the country as a whole under each of the schedules, as well as the total. The years are dated from 5 April; e.g. 1806 represents the tax-payments made during the interval from 5 April 1806 to 5 April 1807.[2]

[1] Hope–Jones, pp. 72 ff.
[2] Reports from Commissioners (9), 20,1870, p. 184. Hope-Jones has unfortunately perpetuated in the chart for the total yield (p.

77) an error in addition made in the official returns. The figure given officially and charted by Hope-Jones for 1814 is £14·2 million whereas the proper total of the five

Income or 'Property' Tax
'Account of Amount of Duty Assessed on Property and Income in Great Britain'

	Schedules (in £ millions)					
	A	B	C	D	E	Total
1806 . .	4·4	2·0	2·2	3·5	0·6	12·7
1807 . .	4·4	1·6	2·4	2·7	0·8	11·9
1808 . .	4·7	2·2	2·5	3·3	0·7	13·5
1809 . .	4·7	2·2	2·4	3·3	1·0	13·6
1810 . .	5·1	2·4	2·5	3·4	1·1	14·5
1811 . .	5·1	2·3	2·5	3·3	1·1	14·5
1812 . .	5·6	2·6	2·7	3·4	1·2	15·5
1813 . .	5·7	2·6	2·9	3·5	1·2	15·8
1814 . .	5·3	2·0	2·9	3·9	1·1	15·2
1815 . .	5·9	2·2	3·3	2·8	1·4	15·6

Since the tax was levied on different types of income and property, the movement of the yields under the different schedules might be expected to differ, even if the conditions of collection were uniform. Hope-Jones comments as follows :[1]

The yield of the Income Tax, between 1806 and April 1816, was, on the whole, a matter for official satisfaction. The yield of Schedule A was steadily increasing in amount throughout with the exception of the year 1813. The amount collected from farmer tenants and 'owner cultivators' under Schedule B fluctuated more, as they would be the first to feel changes in the price level. The yield from the taxation of fundholders under Schedule C naturally increased steadily from 1806 to 1816 as new loans were floated. The yield of Schedule D is more unsatisfactory. There is a fall in 1807, possibly reflecting the first effects of the Continental system. But in 1811, a year of bad trade and general depression, there is practically no drop in the amount collected. The Administration, the Tax Office and Surveyors must have made a great effort. In 1812 and 1813 there is an increase in the amount collected, and a striking advance for 1814. During the last year the tax was in force, 5 April 1815 to 5 April 1816, there was a big fall in the yield under Schedule D. This can only be explained by disappointment with the renewed European trade and by public resistance to the payment of the tax, most easily made effective in Schedule D. The progressive nature of the Income Tax returns, and the steady advance in the amount collected, was largely the result of the increasing efficiency of the organization under the control of the Commissioners for the Affairs of the Taxes.

The principal contribution of the volume, however, are the returns by counties. That from east Lancashire, for example, which included

schedules as given officially is £15·2 million. There is a further, but lesser, error in the figures for 1806. The total of the five schedules is £12,722,056: the total is given in the parliamentary returns as £12,822,056. The total figure presented here is the sum of the sub-totals as given officially. The errors, however, may have occurred in printing rather than addition, and may exist in any one or more of the schedules, although that is somewhat less plausible than our assumption that they were made in calculating the total.

[1] Ibid., pp. 76–8.

Manchester and the centre of the cotton textile area, exhibits a clearly marked cyclical pattern, with troughs in 1808 and 1811, peaks in 1810 and 1814.[1] A similar sequence appears in the returns from the West Riding and Leeds.[2] Returns from Birmingham and from Cornwall differ, so far as the direction of movement is concerned, only in that a trough comes in 1807 rather than 1808.[3] The consequence of business fluctuations can thus be traced in several important areas, despite the relative insensitivity of the total returns.

PART II: 1817–21

1. Prices. The domestic price index rises from March 1816 to a peak in April 1818, after which it falls irregularly to September 1822. The high point, in 1818, is well below that of 1813; the low point, in 1822, below that of 1816. Except for the upward movement in 1816–18, the domestic index declines from May 1813 to September 1822.

Grain prices rose in 1816–17 due to an extraordinary demand from France. The harvest of 1816 there was so deficient as to be regarded by contemporaries as 'actual famine'.[4] In the spring of 1817 nearly 300,000 quarters of wheat were shipped from England to French ports.[5] During the early months of 1817 a bad harvest had been anticipated in Britain; but—[6]

'Immediately after the middle of June, 1817, the weather, both in France and in this country, became fine and favourable in the highest degree to the growing crops, so that, from having a backward and sickly appearance, they became luxuriant and promising. Prices consequently declined in both countries; but in France more rapidly than here, because the French government, as soon as it was relieved from its apprehensions for the coming harvest, let out its stores of warehoused corn, and thus added to the natural causes of depression of the markets. Accordingly, the fall in the Paris markets, between June and September, 1817, was nearly 50 per cent.: viz. from 92fs. the septier (137s. the quarter) on the 11th of June, to 48fs. (71s. 9d.) on the 17th of September. While the markets of this country, as they had followed the rise in France, so they likewise followed the fall.'

The repercussions of this movement on the domestic index are evident. The decline in the latter half of 1817 would have been more severe but for the fact that other domestic prices were then rising:

[1] Reports from Commissioners (9), 20, 1870, p. 81.

[2] Ibid., pp. 84 and 85.

[3] Ibid., pp. 89 and 100.

[4] Tooke, ii. 16.

[5] Ibid., pp. 17–18. It was estimated that the French government spent in excess of 70 million francs (£2·8 million) in the attempt to ensure an adequate grain supply. It is to be noted that Britain's wheat was paid for chiefly in gold, a factor accentuating the already abnormal bullion accumulation at the Bank of England (ibid., p. 18).

[6] Ibid., pp. 19–20.

	June 1817	Dec. 1817
Wheat (s. per quarter)	113·0	84·0
Oats (s. per quarter)	39·3	28·0
Iron pigs (£ per ton)	7·2	8·5
Lead pigs (£ per ton)	19·0	25·0
Sunderland coal (s. per chaldron) . .	38·6	42·3
Linseed oil (£ per ton)	45·0	48·5
Irish pork (s. per barrel). . . .	98·0	102·0
Soap (mottled, s. per cwt.) . . .	94·0	104·0
Tallow (unmelted, s. per cwt.). . .	54·0	77·0

A general revival was already under way, and non-agricultural domestic commodities were affected, although imported commodities were the principal objects of speculative advance.[1]

Fears of a bad harvest brought on by a few months' drought arrested the fall in agricultural prices during most of 1818.[2] Wheat was up to 90s. in April, largely explaining the sharp rise in the domestic index from December 1817 to that date. But by the end of 1818 the commercial boom was at an end, and the supply of grain, supplemented by imports, was larger than had been expected.[3] A second long fall in prices had begun: agricultural and non-agricultural, import and domestic.

The harvest of 1819–21 was about average in quantity, those of 1820 and 1821 abundant.[4] The poor quality of the wheat in 1820 and 1821 contributed to the fairly steady price fall. The minor interruptions in this fall are attributed by Tooke to optimism on the part of the farmers as to the effects of the Corn Law of 1815, and to the recurrent expectations of a deficient crop :[5]

There was still a lingering of opinion among farmers, and persons generally in the corn trade, that upon the shutting of the ports, although the prices might decline somewhat below the import rate, they could not fall very much, nor continue for any considerable length of time much lower. And the grounds for this opinion seem to have been, that it was, in the first place, taken for granted, that in ordinary seasons we did not grow enough for our own consumption; and, in the next place, there was a strong impression, founded upon the experience of the preceding thirty years, that no long interval was likely to elapse without the occurrence of a season of decided deficiency. There was, on the whole therefore, under the influence of these opinions, a considerable degree of buoyancy in the corn markets upon every occasion of adverse weather, or of unfavourable appearances of the coming crops.

Non-agricultural domestic prices, affected by the depression which extended from the latter months of 1818, also decline. The following

---

[1] Ibid., pp. 24–5.
[2] Ibid., pp. 21–3.
[3] Ibid., pp. 22–3 and 27.

[4] Ibid., pp. 79–86.
[5] Ibid., pp. 80–1.

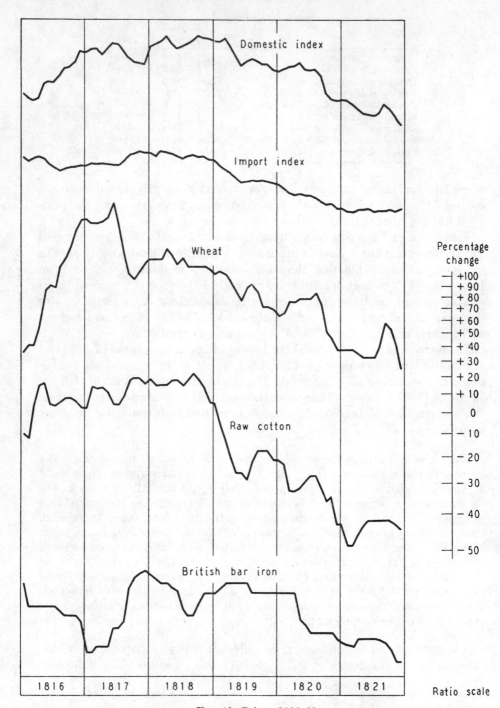

FIG. 42. Prices, 1816–21

examples indicate the kind of individual price movements which the
domestic index summarizes :[1]

	Apr. 1818	Dec. 1821	Sept. 1822
Wheat (s. per quarter)	90·0	49·0	39·7
Oats (s. per quarter)	31·8	18·0	17·8
Iron pigs (£ per ton)	8·5	6·0	6·5
Lead pigs (£ per ton) . . .	25·5	22·5	22·8
Sunderland coal (s. per chaldron) .	37·9	41·4	37·8
Linseed oil (£ per ton) . . .	50·5	29·0	30·5
Irish pork (s. per barrel) . . .	111·0	63·0	54·0
Soap (mottled, s. per cwt.) . . .	111·0	82·0	76·0
Tallow (unmelted, s. per cwt.) . .	82·0	46·8	39·2
Leather butts (pence per lb.) . . .	25·5	23·0	25·0
Sal-ammoniac (s. per cwt.) . . .	152·0	138·0	122·0

It is evident that iron, lead, coal, and leather did not fully share the general
decline, and that the turning-point in non-agricultural prices comes earlier
than that in the index, following more nearly the course of general business
recovery.

The import price index rises from August 1816 to March 1818. It then
falls steadily to March 1821. At that point it recovers and remains stable at
a level near the low point until about May 1822.

There had been, in 1816, a tremendous fall in the quantity of all imported commodities.[2] In 1817 the low level of stocks induced 'that sort of
excitement which characterizes periods of speculation'.[3] The third quarter
of 1817 marked the most intense speculative advance in import prices;
they sag from the spring of 1818 and then fall sharply from February 1819.
A tremendous increase in the quantity of imports occurred in 1818, removing, by the close of the year, the principal cause of the previous price
rise.[4] Tooke offers the following explanation for the state of the markets
until the close of 1818 and the fall in prices thereafter :[5]

Here is a doubling of the whole quantities of imported colonial and foreign
produce, after deducting the quantities exported. Now, can anyone acquainted
with the course of markets hesitate for a moment to pronounce what must be
the effects of such an excess of supply ? And what, indeed, can be more legitimate or simple than the inference, that if the scantiness of supply in 1816 and
1817 was a sufficient ground for a considerable advance, the restoration of
abundance would fully account for the fall ?

It is well known, however, that the resistance to a change, whether from a low
to a high, or from a high to a low range of prices, is at first very considerable,
and that there is generally a pause of greater or less duration before the turn
becomes manifest; in the interval, while sales are difficult or impracticable,

[1] Although the date falls outside the
period under immediate consideration, the
prices for September 1822 have been included, in that the domestic index is then at
its low point.

[2] Tooke, ii. 23–5.
[3] Ibid., p. 26.
[4] Ibid., pp. 60–2.
[5] Ibid., pp. 62–3.

unless at a difference in price, which the buyer, in the one case, and the seller, in the other, are not yet prepared to submit to, the quotations are regulated by the last transactions, but are said to be, and are, in fact, nominal. A struggle of this kind prevailed more or less, according as the articles were in greater or less

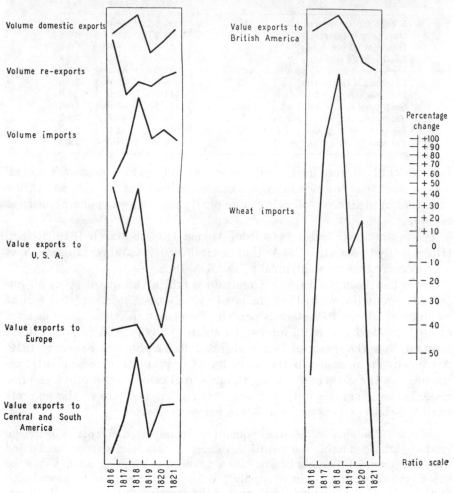

Fig. 43. Foreign Trade, 1816–21

abundance, through the autumn, and into the winter of 1818–19, when many articles which had become unsaleable from excess were still quoted at nearly as high prices as they had attained at any time in 1818.

The early months of 1819 saw the markets suddenly weaken. A sharp fall in import prices occurred from February to June 1819, accompanied by the liquidation of credits used to finance the previous advance. But prices continued to fall :[1]

Before the autumn of 1819, however, every vestige of discredit had dis-

[1] Tooke, ii. 78–9.

appeared; and it was not, as the consequence of either discredit or distress, that the prices of most commodities continued to decline, with few exceptions, to the close of 1822. The sources of supply of all the raw materials of our principal manufactures were experiencing a progressive extension, at a diminished cost of production; and, although there had been in the two or three years immediately following 1818, a slight falling off in the amount of imports of some of the articles, from the great excess of that particular year, there was a progressive increase on the average of three years, compared with the average of any preceding three years.

Tooke here is, of course, contending against any explanation of the fall in price—import and domestic—in terms of a general monetary deflation. His hypothesis must obviously be examined in greater detail before it can be accepted. It involves a full consideration of the state of British industry, commerce, and finance. The limited view of the commodity markets taken in this section is patently inadequate. But it is worth noting, with Tooke, that 'among the few articles of which there was not an excessive supply, the prices in 1819 were higher than they had been in 1817'.[1]

2. Foreign Trade. Exports show a marked recovery in 1817–18, a low point in 1819, a mild recovery in 1820–1. The great increase in imports during 1818 is especially to be noted, as well as their unsustained recovery in 1820:[2]

(In £ millions)

	Volume of			Value of domestic exports
	Total imports	Re-exports	Domestic exports	
1816 . .	26·4	10·8	19·2	41·7
1817 . .	31·2	7·5	20·4	41·8
1818 . .	44·5	8·2	21·5	46·6
1819 . .	34·2	8·0	16·9	35·2
1820 . .	36·3	8·4	18·1	36·4
1821 . .	33·8	8·7	19·7	36·7

The figures for the principal export channels are given on p. 146.[3] The fall in exports to the United States in 1819 is the most decisive movement revealed by this table. Beyond that, perhaps its most important characteristic is the lack of substantial increase in any direction. The recovery in 1817–18 and the depression in 1819 appear in most cases; but there is no very regular movement from 1819 to 1821. In five cases exports were lower in 1821 than in 1820; in five cases a consecutive increase can be traced from 1819 to 1821. But in every instance, excepting Prussia, Holland, and British North America, the figure for 1821 is above that for 1819.

---

[1] Ibid., p. 78 n. Tooke mentions lead and iron. The annual average price of British iron pigs was 7·5 (£ per ton) in 1817, 8·8 in 1819; of lead pigs (£ per ton) 19·4 and 24·6.

[2] The total value of imports was affected by the large imports of wheat and wheat flour (in 1,000 quarters) in 1817–18: 210·9 (1816), 1,034·4 (1817), 1,589·1 (1818), 471·8 (1819), 593·1 (1820), 137·7 (1821).

[3] For note [3] see p. 146.

Official Value of Total Exports from England

(In £ millions)

	Russia	Holland	France	Prussia	Germany	Portugal, Madiera, and Azores	Gibraltar, Malta, and Ionian Isles
1816	1·7	6·6	1·6	0·9	8·7	1·8	2·5
1817	2·8	4·4	1·6	1·1	8·2	1·6	2·1
1818	2·8	4·0	1·2	1·1	8·7	1·4	1·6
1819	2·0	4·1	1·0	1·0	8·4	1·5	1·7
1820	3·7	3·6	1·2	1·3	9·9	1·8	2·3
1821	2·1	3·9	1·4	0·9	8·6	2·6	2·2

	Italy	Foreign W. Indies	British W. Indies	U.S.A.	British America	E. Indies and China
1816	1·8	3·3	4·6	7·8	2·2	2·2
1817	2·9	4·8	6·8	6·4	1·4	2·8
1818	4·3	5·5	5·8	8·4	1·8	3·2
1819	3·8	3·5	4·5	4·3	2·0	2·4
1820	3·8	4·4	4·4	3·9	1·7	3·3
1821	4·0	4·9	5·1	6·6	1·4	4·3

In examining price movements it was noted that, by the end of 1816, stocks of imported goods were low; while exporters were acting—[1]

with great forbearance and prudence, because almost every class of merchants was at that time suffering from the effects of the too great eagerness of adventure of the two preceding years: this general forbearance was, of course, attended by a large profit to those who adventured; and the consequence of the favourable result of shipments on a small scale was, as usual on such occasions, not only that the houses regularly in the trade extended their shipments, but that fresh adventurers embarked in them to a considerable extent. Under these circumstances, all indicating revived confidence, there arose inevitably a tendency to speculation.

[3] Real values broken down under somewhat broader categories, follow (in £ millions):

						Value of Domestic Exports to		
	Northern Europe	Southern Europe	Africa	Asia	U.S.A.	British North American colonies and W. Indies	Foreign W. Indies	Central and S. America (including Brazil)
1816	11·4	7·3	0·4	3·1	9·6	7·0	0·9	2·1
1817	11·4	7·7	0·4	3·7	6·9	7·4	1·3	2·7
1818	11·8	7·6	0·4	3·9	9·5	7·8	1·2	4·0
1819	9·9	6·9	0·3	2·7	4·9	6·9	0·9	2·4
1820	11·3	7·1	0·4	3·8	3·9	5·8	0·9	2·9
1821	9·0	6·9	0·5	4·3	6·2	5·5	1·1	2·9

(Porter, p. 261.) The real value of exports to Central and South America, to Asia, and to Africa, above, were higher in 1821 than in 1817. This increase in the importance of un- developed areas as customers for British industry marks, of course, the beginning of an important secular trend.

[1] Tooke, ii. 26.

Imports increased sharply, especially of the commodities which were the objects of price speculation :[1]

| | Silk | Wool | Cotton | Hemp | Tallow | Linseed |
	(in 1,000 lb.)			(in tons)		(in qrs.)
1816 .	1,138	8,118	93,920	18,473	20,858	70,892
1817 .	1,178	14,716	124,913	22,863	19,298	162,759
1818 .	2,102	26,405	177,282	33,020	27,149	237,141

Exports increased under the same impulses :[2]

The result of overtrading on so large a scale, was experienced in numerous and extensive failures, which began in the latter part of 1818, and continued more or less through the earlier part of 1819. Importers, speculators, and manufacturers were successively ruined by having embarked too largely upon the anticipation of the maintenance of the former range of high prices.

With the arrival of the 'second period of distress' in 1819[3] bankruptcies increased[4] (London Gazette figures):

1816	.	.	2,145	1819	.	.	1,582
1817	.	.	1,578	1820	.	.	1,385
1818	.	.	1,012	1821	.	.	1,268

In the following two years there was some recovery and the quantity of exports was above the figure for 1819. But to the merchant engaged in foreign trade, falling prices gave to this period a decidedly gloomy character.

3. Investment. Of the data on large-scale home investment, brick production and timber imports (the only series available beyond 1818) show a clear cyclical pattern:

| | Bills of inclosure (No.) | Canal, railway, and navigation bills[a] | | Production of bricks (in million bricks) | Turn-pike bills (No.) | Quantity of fir timber imports (in 1,000 loads of 50 cu. ft.) |
		No.	Amount (in £ millions)			
1816 .	43	2	0·2	673·0	6	229
1817 .	30	6	0·5	701·7	6	240
1818 .	38	5	0·2	952·1	7	378
1819 .	—	—	—	1,101·6	—	415
1820 .	—	—	—	949·2	—	341
1821 .	—	—	—	899·2	—	392

a For note a see p. 148.

[1] Ibid., p. 61.
[2] Ibid., pp. 77–8.
[3] J. Lowe, The Present State of England, p. 263.
[4] Although industry complained bitterly in 1819–21, it is to be noted that bankruptcies were at no time on the scale of 1816.

Bischoff (vol. ii, appendix, table X) gives a bankruptcy series which shows an even more pronounced decline: 2,284 (1815), 2,731 (1816), 1,927 (1817), 1,245 (1818), 1,499 (1819), 1,381 (1820), 1,238 (1821). A similar cyclical movement appears in both series.

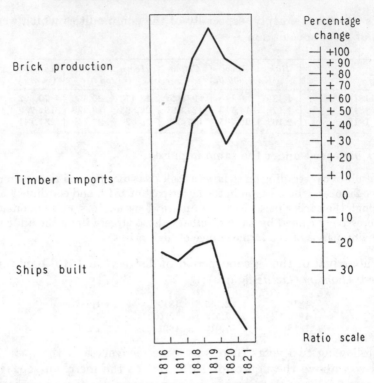

FIG. 44. Investment, 1816–21

The peaks in brick production and timber imports, evident in 1819, do not contravene evidence on the depressed state of the country in that year. They reflect, almost certainly, the normal lag that might be expected to accompany a type of investment with a fairly long period of gestation. It is to be noted that the figure for brick production in 1819 marks a new high point for this series. Neither the real nor the official value of exports was as high in 1818 as in 1815. In the other figures available there is no clear reflection of the upswing from 1816 to 1818. Enclosures, of course, could not, under the generally depressed conditions of agriculture, be expected

ᵃ Porter (p. 329) lists one Act for new railway lines in each of the years 1816–19, 2 in 1821. In 1820 there was one bill extending or enlarging the power of an existing railway line. Railways completed follow:

Date of Act	Name of railway	Terminals	Length in miles	Cost of construction
				£
1817 .	Mansfield and Pinxton	Mansfield and Alfreton	8¼	32,800
1818 .	Kington	Parton Cross and Kington	14	23,000
1819 .	Plymouth and Dartmoor	Plymouth and Lydford	25½	44,983
1821 .	Stratford and Moreton	Stratford-upon-Avon and Moreton-in-Marsh	18½	77,449

to increase; while the day of the canal and the turnpike was almost at an end. In 1817–21, 66½ miles of railways, at a cost of £178,232, were constructed. These totals are greater than for the period 1811–16; but they are dwarfed by those of 1823–4 alone. Nevertheless, the persistence of railway building in 1817–21, even on this modest scale, at a time of general stagnation, is significant of the new secular forces gathering strength.

With Waterloo, Britain lost the monopoly of the carrying trade that war had given. Shipbuilding in the following two decades was notoriously depressed.[1] Tonnage belonging to Great Britain and Ireland, after a long increase, actually declined, while the tonnage of new ships built and registered exhibits only a very mild increase in the course of general expansion:

(In 1,000 tons)

	Tonnage of shipping belonging to the United Kingdom	Tonnage of ships built and registered in the United Kingdom
1793 . .	1,436	—
1802 . .	1,883	—
1816 . .	2,479	84·7
1817 . .	2,398	81·3
1818 . .	2,427	86·7
1819 . .	2,426	89·1
1820 . .	2,413	66·7
1821 . .	2,330	58·1

It will be noted that, like brick production, the series representing new tonnage lags at the peak, and fails to respond immediately to revival in 1820–1.

The prices of Bank Stock, India Stock, and 3 per cent. Consols roughly agree in their general movement with the security index. A cycle can be dated from the last quarter of 1816, when revival begins, to a second low point at about the beginning of 1820.[2] The peaks, however diverge. The share index rises slowly through 1818, while the other securities decline drastically from January 1818 onwards. This lag is probably to be explained by the relatively small amount of trading carried on in the shares included in the index. This fact also accounts, in all probability, for the lack of any fluctuation as violent, for instance, as that in Consols, which were still a primary outlet for savings and the object of considerable speculative dealing.

Two features of the cycle are especially to be noted: the fall in Consols, Bank Stock, and India Stock (from January 1818) precedes the turning-point in commodity markets, where prices did not begin to fall until much

---

[1] Porter, pp. 397–401; Smart, i. 755–6; also Acworth, p. 116, on the 'ruinous state' of the shipbuilding industry in these years.

[2] Although Consols slump towards the end of 1819, and are rising, with the other series, by the end of 1820, their lowest point comes rather early—in June 1819.

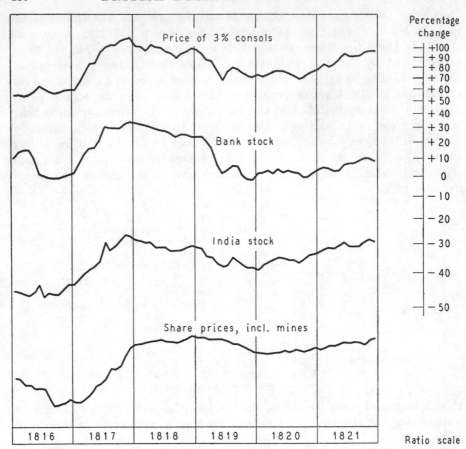

FIG. 45. Investment, 1816–21

later in the year; the low point, at the end of 1819, is, in each case, except for Bank Stock, above that of 1816.[1] This bidding up of security prices may have been a result of the cessation of government loans, the lack of speculative activity (after 1818) in foreign trade, and the decline of canals, turn-

---

[1] The Bank in these years was limiting its discounts and purchasing bullion on a large scale. Profits declined. 'The Rest', which was £8·6 million at the end of February 1816, was down to £3·2 million five years later. The stock of the West India Dock Company, however, follows the more general pattern: its average annual price was 145·8 in 1816, 170·7 in 1820 (the second low point when measured in annual averages). The calculated yield in these two years was 6·8 and 5·9 per cent., respectively; the yield on 3 per cent. Consols moved from 4·8 to 4·4 per cent. in the same period (Silberling,

'British Financial Experience 1790–1830', Review of Economic Statistics, 1919, pp. 289–90.) See also (Letters of Ricardo to Trower, edited by J. Bonar and J. H. Hollander, pp. 75–7) Ricardo's letter to Trower (1 June 1819) in which he states his belief that Bank Stock was overvalued. The Bank's statement did not seem to justify the 10 per cent. dividend, which had been paid since 1807. Ricardo predicted that the contraction accompanying a return to specie payments would necessitate a reduction in the dividend to 8 per cent. In 1823 the dividend was lowered from 10 to 8 per cent. (Ayres, p. 461).

pikes, and inclosures as investment outlets.[1] The position of the investor whose savings commanded a declining yield, and who therefore was driven to seek out new channels of enterprise, was to become even more clear in the period 1822–5. But in 1817–18 the possibility of at least one alternative emerged in the form of foreign government loans. France, Prussia, Austria, and Russia floated fully £10 million of their current new issues in London during these two years.[2]

4. Industry and Agriculture. Iron shipments on the Monmouthshire Canal and iron exports move as follows :[3]

	Monmouth-shire Canal iron shipments	Iron and steel exports excl. of hardware (in 1,000 tons)	British hardware and cutlery exports	Exports of iron, hardware, and cutlery	
				Volume	Value
				(in £ millions)	
1816	38·4	51·6	13·1	1·7	2·8
1817	43·4	67·1	7·4	1·5	2·1
1818	42·0	78·3	9·9	1·9	2·8
1819	37·7	52·6	7·5	1·4	2·1
1820	45·5	67·1	5·7	1·4	1·7
1821	57·3	66·6	7·9	1·5	1·9

The boom (1817–18), slump (1819), and mild recovery (1820–1) are reflected in these figures. The irregular movement of hardware and cutlery exports (in their failure to revive until 1821) follows the total figure for exports to the United States, a principal market for the products of Birmingham and Sheffield.[4] The iron trade, as in the previous period examined, was only moderately influenced by fluctuations in foreign trade. The strong secular increase in the use of iron within Britain probably explains the fact that Monmouthshire's shipments were higher in 1821 than in 1818, while quantities exported were lower.

Iron prices, although less violent in their fluctuations than most others, show not only a cyclical movement but the beginnings of a secular decline :[5]

[1] For 'lack of profitable outlets for capital', as early as 1820, see A.R., 1820, p. 4.

[2] Acworth, p. 80. The extent, purpose, and consequences of these loans are discussed below, under *Finance*.

[3] Scrivenor, pp. 127–8, for Monmouthshire Canal shipments.

[4] The consequences, in part, of the decline in exports of hardware and cutlery (1816–17) can be seen in the famous petition of the Distressed Mechanics of Birmingham (28 April 1817), reprinted by Acworth (Appendix F, pp. 149–51). Birmingham also suffered directly from the cessation of the demand for small arms which it had supplied during the wars (A.R., 1817, p. 46). Birmingham remained distressed into 1821, when most other manufacturing districts already were enjoying revival (Smart, ii. 20–1).

[5] The annual average price of forge iron in the midlands reveals a similar movement, although the price in 1821 is not yet below the depressed level of 1816 (Ashton, p. 156):

	£	s.	d.			£	s.	d.
1816	3	15	0	1819		6	2	6
1817	4	5	0	1820		4	10	0
1818	5	10	0	1821		4	0	0

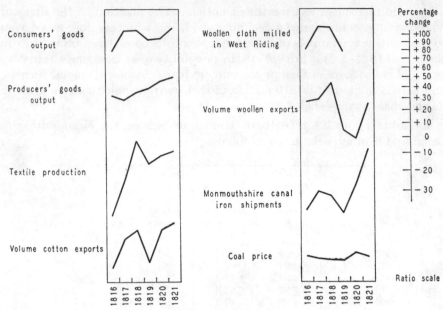

FIG. 46. Industry and Agriculture, 1816–21

	Price of British bar-iron	Price of British pig-iron
	(£ per ton)	
January 1816 . .	13·5	8·0
,,　　1817 . .	9·5	7·4
,,　　1818 . .	14·0	8·5
,,　　1819 . .	12·8	8·5
,,　　1820 . .	12·8	8·8
,,　　1821 . .	10·0	7·0
December 1821 . .	9·1	6·0

At the end of 1821 the price of iron bars was at its lowest point for the whole period 1790–1821; of iron pigs, at its lowest point since July 1790. It is to be noted that in 1820–1 prices fell while output (judging from the limited available estimates) increased: this phenomenon was to become painfully familiar to the manufacturer in the following three decades.

Ashton's brief summary of the period follows:[1]

In 1818 the cloud appeared to be lifting and there were a few months of brightening trade extending into the following year;[2] but gloom once more settled on the industry; and though between 1819 and 1822 conditions were

[1] Op. cit., p. 155.

[2] 'The iron trade is so much revived in most of its branches that the present works are not able to supply the demands' (*The Cambrian*, 19 December 1818). The high level of activity at the close of 1818 and during part of 1819 (witness the price of forge iron) may represent, in part, the usual lag of the iron industry, in this instance supported by an abnormal and temporary demand for iron from France (Tooke, *High and Low Prices*, Part IV, p. 38).

never as bad as in 1816, works were still being closed, plant was being sold, and new construction was practically at a standstill.[1]

The gloom of the latter years is to be traced in prices rather than in output statistics; although it is clear that these were not years of full employment in the iron industry.[2]

The quantities of coal shipped coastwise, from Newcastle and Sunderland, show no very significant movement; coal exports, however, reveal, from 1816 to 1821, a revival, a slump, and the beginnings of a second recovery :[3]

(In 1,000 tons)

	Shipments from Newcastle			Shipments from Sunderland		
	Coastwise	Exports	Total	Coastwise	Exports	Total
1817	1,651	137	1,788	964	31	995
1818	1,780	127	1,907	1,038	42	1,080
1819	1,696	105	1,801	1,003	41	1,044
1820	2,005	119	2,124	1,102	38	1,141
1821	1,835	127	1,962	1,050	39	1,089

The average price of coal is perhaps most significant in its lack of important fluctuation (Sunderland, s. per chaldron) :

1816	.	. 39·1	1819	.	. 38·0
1817	.	. 38·4	1820	.	. 39·8
1818	.	. 38·1	1821	.	. 38·9

Although any analysis of the price of coal must take into account the powerful monopoly controls affecting it, it is probable that from 1817 onwards the industry was not operating very much below capacity.[4] The revival in iron output sustained the home demand; exports were a minor outlet, while there was no equivalent to the harvests in agriculture, or speculation in imports, to alter supply conditions for coal.

The cycle 1816–19 appears clearly in the foreign trade statistics for the cotton trade. Its position in 1819–21 emphasizes, as in the case of iron, the beginnings of the secular association of falling prices with increased output :[5]

Quantity of Raw Cotton Imports
(In million lb.)

1816	.	. 93·9	1819	.	. 149·7
1817	.	. 124·9	1820	.	. 151·7
1818	.	. 177·3	1821	.	. 132·5

[1] 'There are two periods of very extensive ruin: one was from the latter end of 1815 to about 1817, and the other in 1820, 1821, and 1822.' Report on Manufactures (1833), Evidence of William Matthews, 9639. For a similar view of the iron industry in Scotland, see Hamilton, p. 178. Profits from July 1818 to December 1820, in the Thorncliffe Ironworks, were 14·7 per cent.; from July 1820 to December 1821, 4·8 per cent. In 1817 they had been 5·7 per cent.; in 1816 losses of 7·7 per cent. were suffered.

[2] See complaints from iron districts (especially Birmingham) in 1821 (A.R., 1821, p. 69).

[3] Porter, p. 278.

[4] 1819 was an exception. Newport coal merchants and proprietors of collieries met, in May, to discuss 'the sorry condition of the trade', with severe unemployment reported (A.R., Chr., p. 36).

[5] Baines, pp. 347 and 350.

Exports of Cotton Manufactures

(In £ millions)

	Manufactured goods		Twist and yarn		Total	
	Official value	Declared value	Official value	Declared value	Official value	Declared value
1816 . .	16·2	13·0	1·4	2·6	17·6	15·6
1817 . .	20·1	14·0	1·1	2·0	21·3	16·0
1818 . .	21·3	16·4	1·3	2·4	22·6	18·8
1819 . .	16·7	12·2	1·6	2·5	18·3	14·7
1820 . .	20·5	13·7	2·0	2·8	22·5	16·5
1821 . .	21·6	13·8	1·9	2·3	23·5	16·1

The official value of exports (reflecting quantities) was in 1821 rather higher than that for the peak year 1818 : declared values were substantially lower. Typical price movements are the following :[1]

	Average selling price of 30-hanks water-twist of common quality (per lb.)	Average selling price of 40-hanks cop weft (per lb.)	Price of 18 oz. of cotton wool required to make 1 lb. of the twist	Average selling price of a four-cut warp	Price of raw cotton including duty (Berbice or Demerara)
	s. d.	s. d.	s. d.	s. d.	(pence per lb.)
1815	— —	3 0½	1 10	28 11¼	21·0
1816	— —	2 7½	1 8¾	26 1½	19·2
1817	— —	2 6	1 10½	25 0¾	20·6
1818	2 9	2 6	1 10½	25 9¾	21·2
1819	2 1	1 10½	1 3¼	20 9	15·4
1820	1 10½	1 7¼	1 1¼	18 0½	12·9
1821	1 6½	1 5¼	0 10¾	15 10½	10·4

The boom of 1818 merely halted the price fall from 1815, or produced but slight increases.

Contemporary reports indicate a revival in 1817–18, renewed depression in 1819, and a modest recovery in the latter two years.[2] In 1821 an improvement, begun in the previous year, was reported as giving the working classes of Yorkshire and Lancashire 'regular employment at liberal remuneration'.[3]

The figures presented above have shown that the price of both raw

[1] Baines, p. 355. This table of prices of manufactured cotton was submitted by George Smith of the firm of James Massey and Son, spinners, manufacturers, and commission agents, of Manchester, to the Commons' Committee on Manufactures (1833).

[2] For the continued but easing distress of 1817, see Smart, i. 539, 595; for the boom of 1818, pp. 610, 654; for the depression of 1819, pp. 671, 688–9, 725; for improvement in 1820 and 1821, pp. 740–2, and ibid. ii. 20–1. See also W. Page, Commerce and Industry, i. 37, for the recovery in the latter part of 1817, stemming from the 'foreign markets gradually becoming available to us'.

[3] The clearest statement of the industrial position in 1821 is the following: 'The improvement which had begun, in the course of the preceding year, to show itself in the state of our manufactures, still continued. In Yorkshire and Lancashire, the seats of the woollen and cotton manufactures, the working classes found regular employment, and received a liberal remuneration for their services. Other branches of industry were not equally prosperous. The iron trade was still in a very depressed state; and petitions setting forth the decay of the principal branches of industry in Birmingham, were, at an early period, introduced.' (A.R., 1821, p. 69.)

cotton and cotton manufactures fell in these years. The complaints of the manufacturers would also seem to indicate a fall in profit margins. The difference between the prices of raw cotton and cotton twist may perhaps be used as a rough indicator of profits. Between 1803 and 1815 the average difference was 14·3d. It then moved as follows :[1]

July to Dec. 1816 .	. 13·07	Jan. to June 1819 .	. 16·36
Jan. to June 1817 .	. 12·35	July to Dec. 1819 .	. 13·88
July to Dec. 1817 .	. 13·16	Jan. to June 1820 .	. 11·59
Jan. to June 1818 .	. 14·09	July to Dec. 1820 .	. 9·78
July to Dec. 1818 .	. 11·82	Jan. to June 1821 .	. 10·29

This was not a short-run movement, but the beginning of a secular trend. By 1832 the margin was 5·37d.

The cycle in the woollen industry is somewhat less clearly marked than in the cotton, although it follows roughly the same course :

	Quantity of raw wool imports (in million lb.)	Exports of woollen manufactures		Woollen broad and narrow cloth milled in the West Riding	
		Official value	Declared value	Broad	Narrow
		(in £ millions)		(in million yards)	
1816 . .	7·5	5·6	7·8	8·6	3·6
1817 . .	14·1	5·7	7·2	9·1	5·2
1818 . .	24·7	6·3	8·1	8·5	5·7
1819 . .	16·1	4·6	6·0	7·2	4·9
1820 . .	9·8	4·4	5·6	..	..
1821 . .	16·6	5·5	6·5	..	..

As in 1814–15 the peak in the production of broad cloth comes earlier (1817) than that in narrows (1818). The quantity of wool exports, like the other exports series, is at a peak in 1818, but they show no revival until 1821. A comparison of real and official values indicates a fall in prices from 1818 to 1821. Raw wool prices moved as follows (in pence per lb.) :

	Southdown wool	Kent long wool
1816 . .	17·6	14
1817 . .	19·5	15
1818 . .	25·2	24
1819 . .	22·2	15
1820 . .	17·0	16
1821 . .	15·1	13

The most striking movement, however, among the figures presented above is the extraordinary peak in wool imports in 1818 and their decline

[1] Porter, pp. 185–6. The large margin of profit in the first half of 1819 is indicative of a general characteristic of this table. The price of raw cotton was set in a wider and more sensitive market than cotton twist. A sharp downward movement in prices would appear there before it affected the market for manufactures. A similar leap in the 'difference' occurred in the latter half of 1810 and the first half of 1816, periods analogous in their cyclical position to the first half of 1819—an early phase of depression.

until 1820. This is explained by the agitation which preceded the imposition of a tax (6d. per lb.) on the import of foreign wool in 1819.[1] As the government's support swung to the agricultural interests, manufacturers hurriedly purchased a large future supply. Wool imports in 1818 were greater than in any previous year. The manufacturers, however, continued to agitate against the tax; and it was reduced, in 1824, to a nominal 1d. per lb.[2]

A full arsenal of free-trade arguments was brought to bear on the government in this campaign. The virtual repeal of the tax marks an important turning-point in the direction of free trade. It is to be noted that the manufacturers were forced to accept the extension of their general argument to wool exports, which they had previously opposed. Combining political compromise with theoretical consistency, Parliament lifted the historic ban on wool exports at the same time that the import tax was virtually eliminated.[3]

The Kondratieff index of textile production supports the evidence on cottons and woollens. It shows low points in 1816 and 1819, with recovery to 1821 failing to bring the index to the peak figure of 1818. This is true of raw cotton imports, and of the volume of wool exports; cotton exports, however, are at a higher point in 1821 than in 1818.

Kondratieff's Index of Textile Production

1816	.	. 8·4	1819	.	. 11·8
1817	.	. 10·6	1820	.	. 12·5
1818	.	. 13·7	1821	.	. 12·8

From June 1817 to December 1821 the wheat price fell (with an interruption in 1818), from 113s. to 49s. per quarter.[4] Although rents and wages also declined, the farmer was in a difficult position in 1819–21.[5] Parliament

---

[1] Bischoff, i. 450–2. For a full account of the efforts on behalf of and in opposition to the tax, see chap. xi, pp. 426–52. Although the manufacturing interests flooded Parliament with petitions against the tax, and although the price of domestic wool in 1818 was, in every case, above the peak in 1814, the government met the desires of the agricultural groups. Bischoff contends that the 'landed autocracy in Parliament' blackmailed the government by refusing to pass the important tax on malt unless a tax on foreign wool was also imposed (i. 451).

[2] Ibid. ii. 67.

[3] The famous petition of the London Merchants (reprinted in full, Smart, i. 744–7) came, of course, four years earlier, in May 1820. This petition (drawn up by Thomas Tooke), and similar ones from Manchester and Glasgow, mark more properly the formal beginnings of the free-trade movement. The London petition points to the need of

Britain's taking steps against 'the restrictive or protective system' as a means of forestalling the growth of economic nationalism abroad. As peace brought falling prices and unemployment to both the Continent and the United States, tariffs, aimed chiefly at Britain, were imposed: 'The merchants and manufacturers in foreign states have assailed their respective governments with applications for further protective or prohibitory duties and regulations, urging the example and authority of this country, against which they are almost exclusively directed, as a sanction for the policy of such measures.'

[4] The price of British wheat in Dec. 1821 was at its lowest point since Dec. 1798 (48·4s. per quarter).

[5] For agricultural distress, see A.R., 1820, p. 1; A.R., 1821, p. 66. This wave of difficulty did not pass until the rise in the wheat price early in 1823. From April 1823 to December 1833 it remained above 50s. In

was flooded with petitions :[1] Select Committees on Agriculture sat in 1820, 1821, and 1822.[2] The obvious plea would have been that the import limit be raised from 80*s*. But grain imports from February 1819 to the close of 1821 were on so slight a scale that further protection patently offered no solution.[3] The report of 1821 confined itself largely to an almost academic analysis of the agricultural problem ;[4] although a series of possible remedies was hesitantly considered—a bounty on exports, a subsidy to farmers, a scheme for government storage of grain in times of over-abundance, and government subsidies to private companies and individuals for the warehousing of grain, in order to produce a more even supply.[5] Commons, however, contented itself with lowering the import limit to 70*s*., and a provision for preventing warehoused grain from being dumped on the market when the ports opened. The Corn Law of 1828 was passed before these modifications in the Act of 1815 came into effect: 'the act was virtually a dead letter'.[6] Some form of restriction on output and/or subsidy to income would have been required to remedy the farmer's short-run position ; and the British government in 1821 was unprepared for intervention of that type :[7] 'So far as the present depression in the markets of agricultural produce is the effect of abundance from our own growth, the inconvenience arises from a cause which no legislative provision can alleviate.'

Hoffmann's indexes of production, unlike several of the specific series examined, show an increase in 1820–1 that brings his figures in the latter year above those for the cyclical peak in 1818 :

	Hoffmann's index of consumers' goods production	Hoffmann's index of producers' goods production	Hoffmann's index of total production
1816 . .	11·2	3·7	7·1
1817 . .	12·8	3·6	7·8
1818 . .	12·8	3·8	7·9
1819 . .	12·1	3·9	7·6
1820 . .	12·2	4·1	7·8
1821 . .	13·1	4·2	8·2

1834, 1835, and most of 1836 it was below that level. Select Committees on Agriculture were again convened in 1833 and 1836. There were none between 1823 and 1833.

[1] Smart, i. 672–4 (1819), 741–2 (1820); ii. 1 and 6–19 (1821).

[2] Ernle, p. 324.   [3] Adams, p. 105.

[4] In its clear-eyed free-trade bias the report excited admiration among the antirestrictionists (Smart, ii. 15). The *Farmers Magazine*, however, regarded it as a 'very ominous document' (idem), although 'more like a chapter in a work on political economy than a report of the Committee of the House of Commons' (Adams, p. 102). The attitude of the committee is well illustrated by the following general reservation: 'Your Committee may entertain a doubt (a doubt,

however, which they wish to state with that diffidence which a subject so extensive naturally imposes upon their judgment) whether the only solid foundation of the flourishing state of agriculture is not laid in abstaining as much as possible from interference, either by protection or prohibition, with the application of capital in any branch of industry.' (Smart, ii. 14.)

[5] Adams, pp. 109–10.

[6] Ibid., p. 112.

[7] Quoted, Smart, ii. 14–15. The committee added: 'so far as it (the fall in agricultural prices) is the result of the increased value of our money, it is one not peculiar to the farmer, but which has been, and still is, experienced by many other classes of society.'

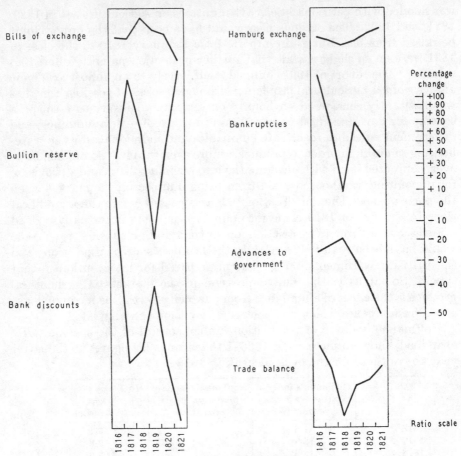

FIG. 47. Finance, 1816–21

The index for producers' goods, in its failure to show a decline in output in 1819, probably reflects the shipbuilding component, which exhibits, in this cycle, its usual lag. Whether output was greater in 1821 than in 1818 is open to question. It does seem clear, however, that output was increasing in 1820–1. Accompanied as it was by a continued fall in prices, this movement yielded widespread dissatisfaction, of which the free-trade agitation was but one reflection. Lords' and Commons' Committees on Foreign Trade reported in 1820 on 'means of extending and securing the foreign trade of the country'. Their recommendations supported free trade, in principle.[1] But there was more general controversy, too, on the nature of the depression from which Britain was suffering. Lord Lansdowne argued that a decrease in consumption lay behind the general distress; to which Lord Liverpool was able to reply by pointing to an increase in the imports of the major articles of consumption, concluding that whatever local distress

[1] Smart, i. 749–55.

there might be, the general wealth of Britain had not declined.[1] Others advocated a search for new export markets as a means of reviving a foreign trade that had lost its buoyancy;[2] while there is even evidence of an 'encourage home industries' sentiment.[3] Meanwhile the government was confronted with the continuous complaints of agriculture, with the problem of returning to a gold standard, and (in 1819) with almost revolutionary working-class dissatisfaction. These were indeed difficult days for Britain.

5. Finance. The Bank's discounts and the total value of inland bills of exchange created give some rough indication of the extent to which credit instruments were called upon in the financing of trade from 1817 to 1821 :

(In £ millions)

	Commercial discounts at Bank of England	Total bills of exchange created		Commercial discounts at Bank of England	Total bills of exchange created
1816 .	11·4	232·4	1819 .	6·5	242·8
1817 .	4·0	230·7	1820 .	3·9	236·5
1818 .	4·3	264·1	1821 .	2·7	199·2

The Bank's discounts in 1819 show the usual increase in the demands upon Threadneedle Street at a time of crisis. The peak in bills and notes discounted came on 13 January 1819 (£10·27 million). In the first half of 1818 they had fluctuated around £3 million. In the latter months they increased, and by 23 December 1818, £8·8 million in bills and notes were under discount. This was the period when the speculation in commodities and securities reached its peak, and collapsed. After the middle of 1819 the demands on the Bank relaxed; commercial credit granted there was down to £5·8 million on 22 December 1819, £3·7 million a year later :[4] 'It was the early part chiefly of 1819 that was marked by a considerable degree of commercial discredit and distress, originating clearly in great previous overtrading. . . . Before the autumn of 1819, however, every vestige of discredit had disappeared.' In 1822 and 1823 there were minor sporadic increases; but not until 1824 did the Bank's discounts exhibit a powerful, sustained advance. Bills of exchange, a more normal type of financing, rise in 1818, but fail to reflect revival in 1817 and 1820–1.

Two facts probably explain this insensitivity to the cyclical pattern : inland bills tended to be called upon in the latter rather than the earlier stages of general expansion, when cash and book credit transactions were the more usual means of exchange; through part of 1817 and during 1820–1 prices were falling, tending to reduce the volume of credit necessary to finance even an increasing volume of business.

Although the figures are notoriously unreliable, all estimates of country bank note issues exhibit the decline to be expected at a time of falling

[1] Ibid. i. 749–52; also *A.R.*, 1821, pp. 71–3.
[2] Ibid. ii. 21. Smart cites (1821) an article in Blackwood's urging that British exporters turn to Africa—to the vast territories opened up by the great river Niger.
[3] Ibid. i. 742–3.
[4] Tooke, ii. 78.

agricultural prices. There had been, in 1814–16, an enormous contraction of country bank issues,[1] and a considerable number of country bank failures.[2] The boom in foreign trade (1817–18) and the temporary recovery of agricultural prices (1818) called forth an increase in their note issues; but the persistent fall in prices and the lack of any important advance in foreign trade during 1819–21 yielded a decline thereafter.[3]

In the case of both the Bank of England and the country banks, however, the fall after 1818–19 seems abnormally severe. During 1819 final arrangements were made for a return to a gold standard at the pre-war mint price, £3. 17s. 10½d. per ounce. In these years, and in the whole period up to about 1850, there were groups within Britain who held that the decline in prices and an allegedly chronic state of restricted commercial and industrial activity were a direct result of the return to gold. No account of this period (1819–21) would be complete without an effort to judge the extent to which the contraction of credit in 1819–21 was due to inelasticity on the supply side of the markets for short-term funds.

The average annual Bank reserve and the usual measures of the position of the pound on the foreign exchanges follow :[4]

[1] Sedgwick's estimate of total country bank note issues were (in £ millions): 22·7 (1814), 15·1 (1816). As noted earlier, this decline was initiated from the side of the agricultural markets, not from the banks. Tooke (ii. 112 n.) quotes the answer of Hudson Gurney (a private banker) to the committee's question (1819), 'What determines, in your opinion, the fluctuations in the amount of country bank paper ?' He answered: 'The price at which the staple commodity of each district is selling: for example, I consider that our circulation would increase with a high price of corn, and would decrease with a low price of corn: corn being the staple of Norfolk.'

[2] Tooke (ii. 38 and 113) states that 92 country banks failed in the three years 1814–16, only 27 in 1819–21. The following are the number of country banks licensed to issue promissory notes (Resumption II, Appendix F. 9, pp. 416–17):

1812 to 1813	.	761	1816 to 1817 .	585
1813 to 1814	.	733	1817 to 1818 .	576
1814 to 1815	.	699	1818 to 1819 .	587
1815 to 1816	.	643		

There was a slight increase in the number of country banks in 1819; but the total is still far below that which preceded the fall in agricultural prices in 1813.

[3] The two principal estimates of the country bank note issue for this period are the following:

(In £ millions)

	£1 and £5 country bank notes (Silberling)	Total country bank notes (Sedgwick)
1816 . .	4·2	15·1
1817 . .	6·8	15·9
1818 . .	7·3	20·5
1819 . .	3·0	17·4
1820 . .	2·7	11·8
1821 . .	3·4	8·4

These estimates are to be used with the greatest reserve, since they are derived from the number of government tax stamps issued and, in fact, supply no true criterion for judging the number of notes actually in circulation.

[4] Acworth, p. 141, for index numbers of gold and silver prices, and the Hamburg exchange; the annual average reserve of the Bank of England, 1816–20, from Silberling

	Annual average Bank reserve (in £ millions)	Price of gold	Price of silver (par = 100)	Hamburg exchange
1816 . .	6·6	102·9	100·9	100
1817 . .	10·8	102·2	104·3	102
1818 . .	7·8	104·6	106·5	105
1819 . .	3·9	101·7	104·3	102
1820 . .	7·3	100·0	99·3	97
1821 . .	11·6	100·0	97·0	94

From its position close to par in 1816–17, the pound depreciated somewhat in 1818, then proceeded quickly back to par in terms of gold, above par in terms of silver and the Hamburg exchange. This movement was accompanied by a decline and recovery in the gold reserve, an expansion and contraction in Bank of England discounts and other forms of credit. The Hamburg exchange began to decline in November 1816, reached its low point in February 1819, recovered until June 1821, and then sagged to March 1822. The Bank's reserve reached its peak in September 1817, fell slightly until February 1818, and then declined sharply until April 1819. Its low point came in September 1819, after which it recovered strongly to June 1821, declining somewhat to May 1822. The movement of the exchange followed closely the course of the boom and collapse in the export trade, beginning its recovery at the same time that prices began to fall. The reserve lagged somewhat in its fall, and recovery did not come until the panic had been liquidated in the third quarter of 1819. The slight weakening of both series in 1821–2 coincides.

The character of the boom in foreign trade (1817–18) supplies an obvious explanation for the fall in the exchange in that period. It was notably a boom in imported commodities, stocks of which had fallen low in 1816. Britain's 'adverse' trade balance almost certainly increased.[1] But two other forces operated to affect the exchanges. Grain imports were abnormally high in 1817 and 1818, negligible from 1819 to 1821.[2] Perhaps more

(*Quarterly Journal of Economics*, xxxviii. 227), 1821, calculated from bi-monthly Bank statement.

[1] Schlote (p. 124) and E. V. Morgan ('Some Aspects of the Bank Restriction Period', *Economic History*, February 1939, p. 213) have made estimates of the movement of the trade balance (in £ millions):

	Morgan	Schlote
1816 . .	− 7·7	+14·7
1817 . .	−20·5	− 1·0
1818 . .	−35·1	−26·4
1819 . .	−21·8	−10·9
1820 . .	− 1·1	− 7·8
1821 . .	+ 6·3	+ 1·0

Morgan has calculated from a sample of Silberling's price data an import index by which he has corrected the official value of total imports. Although his figures probably over-estimate the movement in the trade balance, and although it would appear that he has included 'abnormal' (above £2 million) grain imports twice, the direction of their movement is probably correct. His estimates conform, in most cases, so far as the direction of movement is concerned, to Schlote's figures.

[2] Acworth (p. 83) concludes: 'so far as increased imports were concerned with the outflow of gold, our attention should be directed to importation in general, rather than to that of corn only.'

important were the international capital movements of the period. With Amsterdam in decline, London emerged from the wars occupying the position she was to hold for the next century as Europe's chief financial centre.[1] Following the pattern begun in the war-time loans and subsidies, France, Russia, Prussia, and Austria came to London to float a part of their new issues. Except for the French loan[2] these were designed to rehabilitate the respective currencies by the acquisition of bullion stocks from the proceeds. Some £10 million were raised in England in 1817–18.[3] In addition about £5 million were withdrawn by foreign holders of British government stocks, who had sought security in London during the wars.[4] There were, then, ample reasons for a decline in the foreign exchanges during 1817 and 1818. Tooke summarizes them as follows :[5]

Foremost among these causes doubtless were the large loans negotiated for the French and Russian governments, the high rate of interest granted by them, and the comparatively low rate in this country, holding out a great inducement for the transmission of British capital to the Continent. The importations of corn in the latter part of 1817, and through the whole of 1818, were on a large scale, and at high prices, our ports being then open without duty. And there was at the same time, as has before been noticed, a very great increase of our general imports ; while a great part of the exports of 1817 and 1818 were speculative, and on long credits, the returns for which therefore would not be forthcoming till 1819

---

[1] C. K. Hobson, *The Export of Capital*, pp. 80, 96–7, 106.

[2] See Tooke, ii. 94–5, for the purpose of and difficulties experienced with the French loan, which contributed to the crisis of 1819: 'It is well known, that soon after the negotiation of the loan, which was raised in 1818, by the French government, for the purpose of enabling it to fulfil its engagements with the allied powers, as a condition of their army of occupation quitting the territories of France, and upon the approach of the period for the departure of the allied troops, a sudden and great fall of the French funds occurred. The contractors for the loan applied for and obtained an extension of the time, for the fulfilment of their engagements; but many individuals and firms, who had speculated largely in the same view in the French funds, were ruined by the very great fall which those funds had experienced. In consequence of this great fall in the French funds, combined with the great and sudden fall of the prices of grain on the Continent, extensive failures occurred in Paris, Marseilles, and other parts of France, as also in Holland, and in Hamburg, in 1818, before an indication had appeared of discredit, or of any material pressure on the money market in this country. Those failures on the Continent entailed heavy losses on their connections here, and contributed to the commercial dis-

credit which soon after began to manifest itself on this side, in aggravation of the reaction from the overtrading in this country, as also in the United States of America.' See also Conant, pp. 618–19; and L. Jenks, *The Migration of British Capital to 1875*, 'Financing the French Indemnity', pp. 31–40.

[3] Report of the Committee on Resumption II (Appendix G.I), pp. 423–4. The totals raised in London and in other centres were as follows (in £ millions): France, 27·7 ; Russia, 4·5; Austria, 3·6; Prussia, 2·8. There were also small loans for Holland, Naples, and Denmark 'in which British subjects are supposed to have little or no interest'.

[4] Acworth, p. 80. Foreign investments in British government stocks fell from £17·3 in February 1816 to £12·7 million in February 1818 (Resumption I, Appendix 43, p. 354). In the same report Tooke (pp. 125–32) and N. Rothschild (pp. 157–63) testified that the low rate of interest prevailing in London (1816–17) provided an incentive for foreign holders to withdraw their funds, for British investors to send capital abroad. For a discussion of gold movements between London, Paris, Vienna, and St. Petersburg as a consequence of these capital movements see Rothschild's testimony, pp. 161–3. See also A. Baring's testimony on the adverse effects of the foreign loans on the exchanges, pp. 185–6.   [5] Op. cit. ii. 53.

and 1820. Under these circumstances it is rather matter of surprise that the exchanges were not more depressed, than that they were so much depressed in 1818.

From 1819 to 1821 there were no important foreign loans[1] and no grain imports, while commodity imports, after the over-stocking in 1818, were relatively low. The pound sterling in the latter two years was at par, payment in gold coin having been fully resumed in May 1821. As Tooke notes, the large export shipments of 1818 were made on long-term credits. In 1820–1 the returns on these swelled the flow of funds to Britain.[2] No manipulation on the part of the Bank is required to explain the broad movement of the exchanges either from 1816 to 1818 or from 1819 to 1821.

Even playing a passive role, however, the Bank obviously had a part in the course of financial events.[3] The offer of the Bank, in November 1816, to pay in gold £1 and £2 notes dated prior to 1 January 1812 was received with little interest. In 1817 further steps towards resumption were taken when gold was offered on notes dated prior to 1 January 1816, and, in September, on notes dated prior to 1 January 1817.[4] But in the course of 1817 the Hamburg exchange was already weakening and it was profitable to export gold from July 1817 on.[5] The Bank's limited redemption policy made such exports easy.[6]

The Bank, further, permitted an expansion in its commercial loans, and thus allowed the speculation in prices and securities to continue through 1818. It was from Paris rather than Threadneedle Street that the monetary

[1] In 1821 the Spanish government floated a loan of £840,000 in London, the only foreign issue between 1818 and 1822 (I. Bowen, 'Banking Controversies in 1825', *Economic History*, February 1938). This loan may explain the mild weakening in the Hamburg exchange in the latter half of 1821.

[2] Tooke, ii. 107–8.

[3] Acworth (pp. 76–8) puts great emphasis on an increase in the accommodations of the Bank to the government in 1817, as an inflationary force tending to weaken the exchanges. Some £12 million were borrowed to balance payments made into the Sinking Fund for debt retirement. The net excess of government expenditure over revenue was as follows (Cannan, p. xliii), in £ millions:

1816 .	. +2·5	1819 .	. −0·4
1817 .	. +1·5	1820 .	. −1·9
1818 .	. −2·0	1821 .	. −2·8

In 1816–17 the government's financial operations as a whole were only very slightly inflationary; in 1818–21 they were faintly deflationary. It is doubtful if the government's policy played any important part in the reversal of the exchanges in 1817–18. The Bank's gold stock and public securities moved as follows (in £ millions):

	Coin and bullion	Public securities
Feb. 1816 . .	4·6	19·4
Aug. . . .	7·6	26·1
Feb. 1817 . .	9·7	25·5
Aug. . . .	11·7	27·1
Feb. 1818 . .	10·1	26·9
Aug. . . .	6·4	27·3
Feb. 1819 . .	4·2	22·4
Aug. . . .	3·6	25·4
Feb. 1820 . .	4·9	21·7
Aug. . . .	8·2	19·2
Feb. 1821 . .	11·9	16·0
Aug. . . .	11·2	15·8

The period when the government increased its borrowings at the Bank coincides with an increase in the reserve; the government was already decreasing its loans when the great drains appeared. The borrowings were made necessary by the elimination of the income tax. It can, of course, be maintained that to some minor extent the inflationary movement of 1817–18 was aided by this reduction in taxation.

[4] Acworth, p. 73.

[5] Ibid., pp. 73–4.

[6] Ibid., pp. 74–5. The Committee on

phase of the collapse was finally initiated.[1] If, then, the Bank had contracted credit in 1817 the volume and prices of imports would not have been so great; and, moreover, the foreign loans which further shifted the balance of payments against Britain could not, probably, have been floated in London.[2] In thus countenancing the credit expansion the Bank may be held partially responsible for the fall in the exchanges.

Early in 1819 committees were appointed to investigate the existing depreciation and to examine the means and the advisability of returning to gold. Resumption (by an Act of May 1818) was scheduled for 5 July 1819; but the price of gold was £4. 3s. 0d. (6 per cent. above the mint price) and the exchanges were even more heavily unfavourable.[3] Under these circumstances the committees urged a gradual return to gold. The Act of Resumption, introduced by Robert Peel, contained the provisions:

I.—The Acts restraining cash payments were continued until May 1st, 1823, at which date they were to cease.

> 1. Between February 1st and October 1st, 1820, the Bank was bound to pay all notes presented to it at the rate of £4 1s. an ounce. 2. Between October 1st, 1820, and May 1st, 1821, the rate was to be £3 19s. 6d. 3. Between May 1st, 1821, and May 1st, 1823, the rate was to be £3 17s. 10½d.

II.—The trade in bullion and coin was declared free.

III.—Moreover, a law of July 6th, 1819 (statute 1819, c. 76), forbade the Bank to make any advance to Government without the authority of Parliament.

But by July 1819 the price of gold was falling, the exchanges appreciating. The turning-point in prices and securities had come several months earlier; the speculative boom was over. The bullion reserve at the Bank began to rise towards the end of September, by which time the financial effects of the liquidation had passed. Early in 1821 the Bank held almost £12 million in coin and bullion, which had come to Threadneedle Street 'in the ordinary routine' of the Bank's business.[4] The directors, embarrassed by

Resumption (1819) concluded: 'Whatever might be the policy, and however laudable the intentions of the Bank, in engaging to make partial issues of coin in payment of their notes, yet when the exchanges became unfavourable, and the price of gold rose above the mint-price, the only mode by which they could have retained the coin in circulation would have been a contraction of their issues; and unless the Bank at that period possessed such a control over the amount of those issues, as would have enabled them to effect that object, your Committee must consider it to have been inexpedient, in the then state of the exchanges, to undertake an extensive though partial issue of coin, which subjected the Bank to considerable loss, and a great drain of treasure.'

[1] Tooke, ii. 94–5; Acworth, pp. 83–4; Hawtrey, pp. 340–1.

[2] N. Rothschild (Resumption I, p. 158) stated flatly that if restriction had been ended in 1816, the loans could not have been financed in London during the following two years.

[3] Acworth, p. 74. On 6 April 1819 restriction was continued indefinitely, pending the reports of the committees and the action of Parliament on them. The bill making provision for a return to gold was passed on 2 July 1819.

[4] Ricardo and others have implied that the Bank pursued a conscious policy of bullion accumulation. This Tooke denies (ii. 108 n.): 'Mr. Ricardo does not appear to me to have sufficiently appreciated the state of things, when he charged the Bank directors with mismanagement, in having prematurely and unnecessarily enhanced the value of the currency by their large purchases of gold after the passing of Mr. Peel's

this hoard, petitioned to resume full cash payments, early in 1821, and from 1 May the last vestige of restriction had passed.

During these years (1819–21) and in the following three decades, there was much controversy on the allegedly deflationary consequences of the Act of 1819. These speculations (along with those of 1810) evoked perhaps the most fruitful monetary discussion of the nineteenth century. From the limited view of this chronicle, however, the only question immediately relevant is the extent to which Bank policy contributed actively to the fall in prices and the relatively stagnant state of industry and commerce from 1819 to 1821 : the extent, in other words, to which there was an 'abnormally' inelastic supply of money.

The account of foreign trade, given above, showed (1819–21) no activity on a large scale in any foreign markets of which British exporters could take advantage; in the capital market there was a lack of outlets for new investment, and the long-term rate of interest was bid down. The complaints from home industry indicated an inadequate demand for products, cheapened supplies of factors, and falling prices. Agriculture suffered from good harvests. Once the financial crisis had ended (third quarter of 1819) there was no evidence of activity limited by a restrictive Bank policy : there is no reason to believe that the Bank would not have been willing to lend if borrowers had come to it. Bank discounts, further, were not the normal means of financing in the early phase of recovery : its rate still was rigid at 5 per cent. It should be remembered that, despite an enormous gold reserve, the Bank's private discounts did not increase until 1824–5, almost four years after resumption. If their low level in 1819–21 is to be taken as evidence of an induced deflation, it did not end with a return to specie payments. But when commercial demands increased, in 1824–5, the Bank was found quite willing and able to meet them. Tooke's conclusions on this point follow :[2]

During the period of advancing prices, and of speculation and general excitement, which prevailed from 1816 to 1818, there must accordingly have been, as there is the strongest presumptive evidence that there was, a considerable enlargement of the country circulation. But at the time immediately preceding the passing of Peel's Bill, there was a cessation, from causes totally independent of that measure, of obvious grounds for speculation of any kind. The excess of supply of nearly all imported commodities in 1819, which continued more or less through the two following years, was calculated to discourage all anticipation of a speedy advance of prices, at the same time that the fall of prices and commercial failures narrowed the range, within which accommodation from the

bill. His mode of expression conveys the idea that the directors made an effort to buy gold; that they created a demand for it by a designed reduction of their issues for that specific purpose. Now, the truth is, that they were perfectly passive, and moved only in the ordinary routine of their business: they bought gold simply as it was brought to them at or below the Mint price; and it was a matter of indifference, as concerned the amount of the currency, whether the gold were taken by the importers to the Mint, and thence brought directly into circulation as coin, or were taken in the shape of bullion to the Bank in return for its notes.'

[2] Op. cit. ii. 111–12.

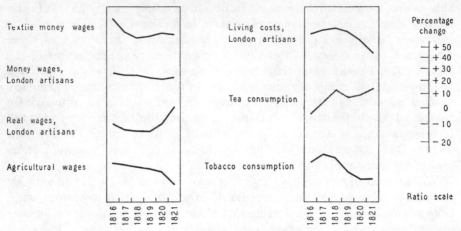

FIG. 48. Labour, 1816–21

bankers could be sought or granted; and after the summer of 1820, when the extraordinary productiveness of that harvest began to be appreciated, there was not only no reasonable ground for speculating on an advance of the price of corn, but a well-founded apprehension of a fall. There was accordingly a greatly diminished inducement to farmers and to cattle dealers, and corn dealers, and millers, with a view of being enabled to keep up or increase their stock to seek advances from the country banks. And what was of still more importance, where the inducement to borrow existed, the credit necessary for the purpose was impaired. Whether in the trading and manufacturing towns, therefore, or in the agricultural districts, there did not exist the inducement, or the means of putting out or keeping out the same quantity of paper: a reduction of the amount was consequently inevitable, even if the Bank of England had coincidently made a forced enlargement of its issues.

At this period convention denied the Bank the power to lower its discount rate. Even that means for 'a forced enlargement of its issues' did not exist. Moreover, it regarded itself as a private bank; the conception of a central bank's responsibility at a time of depression was foreign to the directors, and it was to be so for the next century. Neither the tools nor the attitude necessary for a successful compensatory banking policy existed, and the propriety of such a policy is what most criticisms of the Bank of England in these years imply.

The Act of 1819, however, did have a powerful psychological effect. So completely had the quantity theory carried the day that it was widely believed that a return to gold must inevitably involve a general deflation. Even Ricardo, who most bitterly condemned the conduct of the directors, stated in Parliament (*Hansard*, xl. 743–4):

The measure of 1819 was chiefly pernicious to the country on account of the unfounded alarms which it created in some men's minds and the vague fears that other people felt lest something should occur, the nature of which they could not themselves define.

This uncertainty emerged in actions which indicated that a further fall in prices was expected. Even before the Act of 1819 Tooke noted the manner in which expectations affected prices :[1]

. . . An impression upon the public mind that the Bank would shortly resume its payments in cash . . . induced a greater disposition among sellers to come forward, and among buyers to hold back.

The tendency for prices to fall would have, in itself, caused this kind of market relationship. The public's fears as to the consequences of resumption accentuated it.

It may be concluded, then, that in not obstructing the boom of 1817–18 and in not attempting to alleviate the deflation of 1819–21 the Bank contributed to the movement of the exchanges and of general prices. The basic causal forces, however, lay well outside the terrain of Bank policy as it was then defined.

6. Labour. The most striking movement in the available statistics on labour is the rise in real wages, as shown in the tabulation below, between 1816 and 1821.[2] Even agricultural workers appear to have enjoyed an improvement in their net position, despite a drastic decline in money wages :[3]

	Tucker's index of		Bowley's index of agricultural money wages	Kondratieff's index of money wages in the textile industry
	money wages of London	real wages artisans		
1816 . .	67·3	43·6	190	57·5
1817 . .	66·4	41·9	188	52·7
1818 . .	66·4	41·5	185	50·7
1819 . .	65·1	41·4	183	51·2
1820 . .	64·7	43·7	179	52·2
1821 . .	65·4	48·7	165	51·7

There is no fact which admits of being more fully proved, if the notoriety of it were not such as to render detailed proofs superfluous, than that the wages of artisan labour are in most cases as high as they were before 1819, in some instances higher, and in none so much lower as the difference in the prices of provisions and other necessaries. But a much more important consideration, inasmuch as it is one that affects the great bulk of the community, is, that wages, not of artisans only, but of labour generally, have not fallen in proportion to the

[1] Resumption I, p. 126.
[2] Baines (p. 438) gives the following annual average prices of various food staples in Manchester. They indicate concretely the extent to which falling prices eased the position of labour in these years:

	1816		1821	
	s.	d.	s.	d.
Flour (per 12 lb.) . .	3	0	1	11
Butcher's meat (per lb.)	0	7½	0	5½
Bacon (per lb.) . .	0	8	0	5
Potatoes (per 20 lb.) .	0	8–14	0	6

[3] Tooke, ii. 70–1.

reduced prices of necessaries. . . . Even in the case of the agricultural labourers, whose wages have fallen in a greater proportion than those of other classes, the hand-loom weavers, perhaps, only excepted, there is concurrent testimony of the most unexceptionable description . . . that the condition of the agricultural labourer has been greatly improved, compared with the period of high prices.

Tea retained for home consumption moved as follows (in million lb.):

1816	.	.	22·69	1819	.	.	25·24
1817	.	.	24·61	1820	.	.	25·71
1818	.	.	26·53	1821	.	.	26·75

This series follows the general business cycle, with low points in 1816 and 1819, a peak in 1818, a recovery to 1821. It is significant of the state of real wages that tea consumption was greater in 1821 than in 1818 or the previous peak, 1815 (25·92). The 'state of the working classes' in 1821, unlike that of their employers, could be described as 'contented'.[1] But 1817 and 1819 were two of the most disturbed years in British labour history. Both were marked by severe unemployment. Not until 1818, and even the early months of 1819, did money wages reflect the upswing.[2]

There were riots, especially in the early months of 1817.[3] In June, however, the Edinburgh relief works were closed because of a falling off in applicants;[4] by September the country was so 'tranquil' that it was considered unnecessary to bring rioters in Manchester and Derby to trial;[5] in November all was 'cheerful' in the Leeds woollen trade, and the cotton workers at Spitalfields were 'in full employment'.[6]

The major difficulties in 1818 were inspired by the desire for wage increases. A clear picture of the labour market in that year emerges from the address of the cotton spinners to the public in the course of a ten weeks' strike in Manchester:[7]

Two years ago (1816), when our employers demanded a reduction of ten hanks, they affirmed, that the state of the market imperiously called for such reduction; but when the markets would admit of an advance, they would willingly give it. We depended on their honour, and continued to labour for more than 12 months at the reduction proposed. About 10 months since, on comparing the price of cotton and yarn, we found that the markets would allow our employers to fulfill their promise; we therefore solicited them to that purpose, and only wished to be reinstated in the same prices we worked at previously to that reduction. Some declared they could not give it; others they

[1] Tooke, ii. 74.
[2] See Baines's tables of individual wages in the cotton industry, pp. 438, 488, 489, and 490. There are many cases, however, where no wage changes took place during the years 1816–20 (ibid., p. 438; also A. Bowley, *Wages in the United Kingdom*, table facing p. 119).
[3] *A.R.*, Chr., pp. 7, 15, 19; Smart, i. 539, 541, 542, 546, and 548.
[4] Ibid., p. 563. At the end of Apr. 1817 the government issued exchequer bills

amounting to £500,000 for public works projects designed to relieve unemployment. But they came at a time when revival had already begun in most manufacturing districts (*A.R.*, 1817, p. 45; Smart, ii. 543 and 563).
[5] Ibid., i. 554.
[6] Ibid., p. 564.
[7] *A.R.*, Chr. 1818, pp. 100–3. For a full account of the strikes of 1818 see J. L. and B. Hammond, *The Skilled Labourer*, pp. 94–120.

would not; but the greater part, that they would, if others did, but they should not like to be the first. Thus we continued working and soliciting for the last eight months, though the demand for yarn has been unprecedented, and the consequent rise in twist great; they have still refused our just request; and in order to cause a belief that trade was in a declining state, gave notice, that their mills should only work three days in the week, which appeared so extremely ridiculous, that the very children employed in factories laughed at it.

Some advance in wages was granted, but the men were reported as dissatisfied.[1] It should be remembered that the boom of 1818 was accompanied, at best, by very slight increases in the price of manufactured cotton goods. The position of the employer, faced by demands for wage increases, was not as simple as in the years when high costs could be easily passed along. Even in 1818 British merchants at the Leipzig Fair were forced to dump their goods at unexpectedly low prices.[2] But on the side of the workers, the slight rise in living costs (1817–18), as well as the obvious increases in output, made the advance in wages seem inadequate.

Despite the strikes in Lancashire, 1818 was a year of relative content for the working classes. The year 1819, however, saw perhaps the most serious labour disturbances of the entire period 1790–1850.[3] Wages in many districts were reduced, and unemployment again was severe.[4] A peculiar character was imparted to the discontent of 1819 by its distinct political overtones. Meetings begun over wage decreases ended with petitions for parliamentary reform. The movement had its centre in Manchester, and reached its climax with the meeting at St. Peter's Field on 16 August.[5] Somewhere between 50,000 and 80,000 persons gathered. A deputy constabulary, frightened by the mob, lost its head and charged. Eleven persons were killed, about 400 injured. The government, feeling revolution in the air, overrode a distinguished opposition to pass the famous Six Acts, which virtually suppressed freedom of speech, of the press, of free assembly.[6] But

[1] *A.R.*, Chr., pp. 121, 123, and 128. Following the lead of the spinners, the Burnley weavers struck in September. Troops were called to quell the resulting riots.

[2] Ibid., p. 72.

[3] Largely on the basis of the scale of the meeting at St. Peter's Field, and a few isolated plots on the life of the Regent, historians have often implied that Great Britain was 'close to revolution' in 1819. There is no question that in that year, as in 1816, sections of the working classes were desperate. But a chronological view emphasizes the part cyclical depression played in the riots. In the latter months of 1817 and 1820, and throughout 1818 and 1821, there is little evidence of acute and general unrest. Although the Tory government, by later standards, was severely repressive in its policies, peaceful channels for political agitation were not completely

closed: with economic recovery after 1819, 'it became easier to conceive of reform as something different than revolution' (see Cole, i. 79–86).

[4] See Smart, i. 724, for an account of wage reductions in Manchester, Glasgow, and Paisley. In a spirit like that of the NRA, a group of the large cotton manufacturers proposed a minimum wage, in 1819, to defeat the men 'of little capital and less feeling', who paid starvation wages, and were able to underbid them in the market (J. L. and B. Hammond, *The Skilled Labourer*, pp. 121–6). In many of the strikes a minimum wage was included in the workers' demands (ibid., pp. 121–2).

[5] Smart, i. 720–2. See also Cole, i. 72–3, and J. L. and B. Hammond, *The Town Labourer*, pp. 89–94.

[6] Smart, i. 723–4. The tone of the government's fears is illustrated by the speech of

most significant were the banners carried at the Peterloo meeting: they forecast the direction of reform agitation during the following years—'No Corn Laws', 'Vote by Ballot', 'Equal Representation or Death'. The British working classes had travelled a considerable distance from the bread riots of twenty-five years before.

Like 1817, 1820 saw a turning-point in the fortunes of both industry and labour. A further sharp fall in living costs aided the working classes, as did the mild trade revival which set in during the year.[1] The repressive acts of the previous year, combined with these factors, caused a virtual cessation of rioting and strikes: 'the country was comparatively tranquil'.[2] In 1821 there were again few industrial disputes. Unemployment and food prices were falling.[3]

During these years the chief legislative measure on labour's behalf was the Factory Act of 1819. It was similar to a bill considered, but set aside, in 1815 which had dealt with the problem of child workers in the cotton mills. Peel presented the bill in Commons, where it was passed in 1818, but defeated in Lords. The diluted measures of 1819 prohibited the employment of children under nine; for children from nine to sixteen, limited the working day to twelve hours,[4] and forbade night work in the factories.[5] Perhaps most important was the failure to provide for government inspectors. The lack of centralized control had made the Act of 1802 (regulating pauper apprentices) virtually a dead letter. Continued supervision by magistrates and clergymen destroyed 'the whole efficacy' of the Act of 1819.[6]

the Regent to Parliament when it was convened in November (ibid., p. 722): 'They have led to proceedings incompatible with the public tranquillity and with the peaceful habits of the industrious classes of the community; and a spirit is now fully manifested utterly hostile to the constitution of this kingdom, and aiming not only at the change of those political institutions which have hitherto constituted the pride and security of this country, but at the subversion of the right of property and of all order in society.'

Sydney Smith's letter to Lord Grey is typical of the opposition (ibid., p. 723): 'Force alone, without some attempts at conciliation will not do. . . . The worst of it all is that a considerable portion of what these rascals say is so very true. Their remedies are worse than the evils; but, when they state to the people how they are bought and sold, and the abuses entailed upon the country by so corrupted a Parliament, it is not easy to answer them, or to hang them. What I want to see the State do, is, to listen in these sad times to some of its most numerous enemies—anything that would show the Government to the people in some other attitude than that of taxing, punishing, and restraining.'

[1] A.R., 1820, pp. 1–4.
[2] Smart, i. 727.
[3] Ibid., ii. 20–1 and 23.
[4] One and a half hours were set aside for meals, making the total time spent at the mills 13½ hours.
[5] Smart, i. 659–60. The attacks on the bill were varied; but most common was that the Act interfered with the liberty of the parent to control the destiny of his children (ibid., pp. 665, 667–9). Peel's defence of the measure was set forth completely in humanitarian terms. It is probable that, in part, it was designed to appease the discontent of the cotton workers, already clamouring for higher wages (February 1818). The bill was introduced as a result of a petition from cotton spinners in Manchester, describing in lurid terms the conditions under which children were working 14 and 15 hours a day (ibid., pp. 658–9). Robert Owen, then a successful manufacturer with no radical connexions in the public mind, played an important role in publicizing the question, and in bringing pressure to bear on Peel (Halévy, pp. 251–2).
[6] J. L. and B. Hammond, The Town Labourer, p. 169.

Chapter IV

1822–32[1]

INTRODUCTION

THE two periods included in this chapter of the *History* offer sharp contrast. From 1822 to the end of 1824 the economic system gradually recovered. Security and commodity prices then rose in a spectacular inflationary movement, industry moved to unstable full employment. In the spring of 1825 a turning-point came, and in December there was severe financial panic. The depression deepened until the closing months of 1826, when a mild revival began. A clearly marked cycle, then, can be traced from 1820, when recovery was already under way, to 1826, the bottom of the succeeding depression. The period from 1827 to 1832, however, saw no such straightforward conventional movement. There was some recovery in 1827–8, but depression through most of 1829. In 1830 textiles revived, and the export branches of the iron industry. But a second discouraging relapse came early in 1831. Only in 1832, after the Reform Bill had passed, did confidence begin to return, and the money market become steadily easy.

Chronic unemployment of men and materials distinguished this second period, and under such circumstances the secular decline in prices and profits (accompanied by an increase in productivity and output) emerge as its principal feature. The downward trend in prices had been evident from 1820 through the first half of 1824. The final stages of the boom temporarily obliterated it; but the expansion of plant and the improvement of methods undertaken in 1824–5 accentuated the trend in the six years that followed.

The prosperity that reached its climax in 1825 has often been referred to as the first truly modern cyclical boom in British economic history. The basis for that conception is the enlarged role played by capital market floatations. From 1822, but more particularly in 1824–5, docks, railways, gas and water companies, and, above all, foreign governments and mining companies came for funds to London on an unprecedented scale. After the preceding years of revival (based largely on expanding exports), savings were abundant in 1824, and the view taken of the future highly optimistic. The mining shares, particularly, moved to extravagant heights, diverting funds from other sections of the capital market. The price of mining shares broke early in 1825; other securities had begun to decline some months

[1] Cyclical pattern:

Trough	Peak
1819 (Sept.)	1825 (May)
1826 (Sept.)	1829 (Jan.)
1829 (Dec.)	1831 (Mar.)
1832 (July)	

before, in the face of the competition offered by the florid mining prospectuses.

Coinciding in time with the stock market boom was a considerable speculation in imports. Commodity stocks were found to be low towards the end of 1824; and with cotton leading, import prices rose, and enormous quantities of the staple commodities were contracted for. Exports, too, paid for in part by the new South American loans, were shipped in large quantities. A boom at the same period in the United States also brought increased orders to the textile and iron industries.

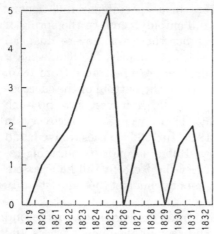

FIG. 49. Business-cycle Pattern, 1819–32

These demands, coming when the system was already close to full employment, pushed capacity to the limit and induced investment in new plant and machinery. In cotton, wool, iron, and even the monopolistic coal industry, the same pressures can be traced in 1824–5, and the same sorts of expansion.

Non-agricultural prices, after sagging in 1822–4, rose sharply in this final phase of prosperity. They turned downward, however, in the spring of 1825, and rose again only at the close of 1826. By that time the financial aspects of the panic had been liquidated, and excess stocks had, largely, been worked off.

The early years of prosperity saw a general fall in interest rates. The Bank rate fell to 4 per cent., and the government reduced the interest on two of its bond issues. By freeing the funds of those who did not accept the new rate and by making current holders 'restless' for a higher return on their funds, the conversion operations contributed somewhat to the floatation and Stock-Exchange boom. The government further aided the inflationary movement by meeting its pension obligations by borrowing at the Bank. Some of these payments fell due in January 1825, and, it is believed, swelled the flow of funds into the new securities promiscuously floated at that time.

In general the Bank of England did little to finance the boom. Funds were drawn from current income, by shifting from less to more speculative securities, from the private banks in London, and, above all, from the country banks. The latter doubled their issues from 1822 to 1825. During the crisis, however, the Bank disregarded its reserve proportion and lent freely, when other agencies found themselves unable or unwilling to maintain their advances.

Small country bank notes were singled out as a source of the inflation in

1826, and their further issue outlawed (from 1829). Post-crisis legislation also made possible the development of joint-stock banking outside the metropolitan area.

Labour, naturally, fared well in the final years of the boom. There was a shortage of hands, and money wages rose rapidly in 1824–5, to the accompaniment of many bitter strikes. Efforts at organization were aided by the repeal, in 1824, of the Combination Acts. A part of the new freedom was withdrawn in the revised Act of 1825; but labour's organization at least was no longer illegal. In 1826, however, money wages fell sharply, retail prices considerably less: it was a year of widespread and severe distress.

There was in 1827–8 some modest recovery in output and employment, but an upward price movement could not be sustained. In 1829, due largely to gold withdrawals and consequent monetary stringency as well as a decline in exports to the United States, a sudden relapse into deep depression occurred. None of Britain's export markets were enjoying very full prosperity, and internal enterprise was at a low ebb, still suffering from the defaults on interest and the many bankruptcies that followed the collapse of 1825. The revival of 1827–8 lacked any solid basis. In 1830 a second mild recovery got under way, with the American markets especially strong. But a second group of financial pressures, and the insecurity which accompanied the agitation for the Reform Bill, again brought revival to a quick halt early in 1831. This slight upward movement was largely in textiles. The iron and coal trades from 1828 suffered a chronic depression in the home markets.

Both commodity and security prices declined, from 1826 to 1832, while real wages and output, in net, increased. Despite the lack of any concentration of new investment, secular technical progress continued. Evidence before the Committee on Manufactures (1833) indicates, however, that in each of Britain's major industries, these were difficult years for the industrialist. Overhead costs weighed heavily. The value of fixed capital had steadily to be revalued downward. This situation, in itself, encouraged the introduction of new labour-saving devices in an effort to widen the margin between costs and prices; but this latter development did not, apparently, induce a volume of investment sufficiently great to prevent chronic over-capacity in the capital goods industries.

From about 1824 to 1832 the agricultural situation was generally better than it had been in the previous decade. There were no very abundant harvests, and several abnormally small ones. The price of grain was high enough to relieve the chronic pressure that had existed since 1813. In the years of low profits (1826–32), the farmer fared somewhat better than the rest of the community, despite large grain imports. The Corn Laws were revised in 1828, introducing a sliding scale of imports that varied with the domestic wheat price. On the whole this was a movement towards freer trade; although, in absolute terms, considerable protection was still afforded to agriculture.

The years after 1825, with profits falling, unemployment chronic, and food prices relatively high because of poor harvests (1829–31), witnessed great unrest among the middle and working classes. The former looked to free trade, an inflationary 'reform' of the currency, and to increased representation in Parliament. The latter joined in the movement for parliamentary reform ; and, led by Robert Owen and John Doherty, the working classes expanded their unions and accepted, in part at least, the immediate implications of co-operative socialism : in textiles and coal-mining there were impressive strikes on a remarkably broad scale. Labour's unrest, at a time when France and Belgium were suffering revolution, helped to force the hand of the Parliament and create the Reform Bill of 1832. Though labour received no direct or substantial benefits from the Reform Bill, its fight for representation lapsed in the ensuing years of prosperity, to be taken up again by the Chartists with the return of severe unemployment in 1837.

Part I: 1822–6

1. **Prices.** The index of domestic prices reaches a trough (in the decline from 1818) in May 1822. It remains at this low level through the rest of 1822, but moves up rapidly from January to June 1823. After breaking sharply to October, it rises, by February 1824, to about the level of the previous June. Until September it sags slightly, only to rise steadily through the last quarter of 1824 to a cyclical peak in May 1825. From that date the domestic index falls away to a low point in July 1826, which is, however, some 30 per cent. higher than the low point in 1822.

The principal movements of the index are to be related chiefly to the conditions of supply for agricultural commodities. The rise in the early months of 1823 and the fall and recovery in the latter half of the year are clearly connected with fluctuations in the grain markets :[1]

The rise which is observable in the average price of wheat in [the early months of] 1823 . . . was mainly the effect of the necessarily increasing proportion of the superior new to the very inferior old coming to market. And a part of the further advance was ascribed in the contemporary accounts, and with great probability, to the circumstance of purchases by persons who had previously sold their old wheat, with a view to reinvestment in the new. Some speculative purchases were also made at that time, in pursuance of an opinion which had become prevalent, that prices had seen their lowest ; and the excellent quality and condition of the wheat of 1822, afforded additional inducements to act upon that opinion. The winter of 1822–23, although not memorable for

---

[1] Tooke, ii. 121–2. The inferiority of the wheat crop of 1823 is illustrated by the fact that, in January 1824, new wheat (harvest of 1823) ranged between 48s. and 63s., old wheat (harvest of 1822) between 55s. and 78s. (ibid., p. 132 n.). It was estimated, as well, that the crop of 1823 was only 10 million quarters or 2 million under the 'average' (i.e. 12 million).

severity and duration of frost, was rather a rigorous one, and the spring of 1823 was very backward, with a prevalence of cold dry weather till the latter end of June. . . . [From January to June the price of wheat rose from 40·4s. per quarter to 61·0.] The weather, however, afterwards improved, and as the recent rise had induced large supplies from the farmers, the old stock being found to be more considerable than had been supposed, the markets gave way. Although the weather at harvest was unsettled, with a considerable proportion of wet, accompanied, with reports of injury to the crops, prices still continued to decline.

[In October the price of wheat was 48·2s. per quarter.] But as it had been found on threshing, that the produce of the crops was really deficient, while the old stock had been materially reduced, there was a rally of the markets at the close of the year.

In 1824 there is, again, a brief rise in the early months (limited, in fact, to January and February), a decline to the autumn, and the beginnings of a second upward movement :[1]

In the commencement of 1824, a considerable advance took place in the price of corn, wheat especially, of which the crop of 1823, having been found to be deficient in quality and in quantity, in a degree beyond the previous estimates, rose rapidly. [From 52·0s. per quarter in December 1823, to 66s., in February 1824.] . . . After the rise of . . . wheat in the early part of 1824, it was discovered, by the large supplies from the farmers, that, although the crops of 1823 had on all hands been allowed to be deficient, yet, with the old stock from previous years, it was adequate to supply the consumption at its ordinary rate till after the ensuing harvest. A conviction of this kind, when there is no ground for speculation upon the coming crops, is always attended with dull and drooping markets; and there was, as we have seen, a progressive fall of upwards of 10s. per quarter in the six months following. [The wheat price was down to 55s. in September.]

The weather, however, during the harvest of 1824, was unsettled; and the latter part of it, in the more northern districts especially, was remarkably wet. The produce was, according to all reports, again deficient. The stock on hand had in the interval been further reduced, there being no longer, as heretofore, samples of wheat of three or four years old at market. Under these circumstances, an advance of price, after the harvest of 1824, proceeded upon perfectly reasonable and adequate grounds.

The rise was sustained until May 1825 in both the wheat price and the domestic index :[2]

The agitation of the question of the corn laws, in the spring of 1825, contributed probably among other causes to preserve the corn market from the effects of the spirit of speculation which then prevailed in other branches of trade. But such was the general impression of the progressive reduction of the old stock of grain, and of our consequent increasing dependence on the produce of the forthcoming harvest, that, notwithstanding the admission in April of 525,231 quarters of foreign wheat for home consumption, at a duty of 10s. the quarter, the price did not fall below 68s. the quarter till the commencement of an unusually early and a promising harvest. It was not till after the crops in the

[1] Ibid., pp. 132–4.   [2] Ibid., pp. 134–5.

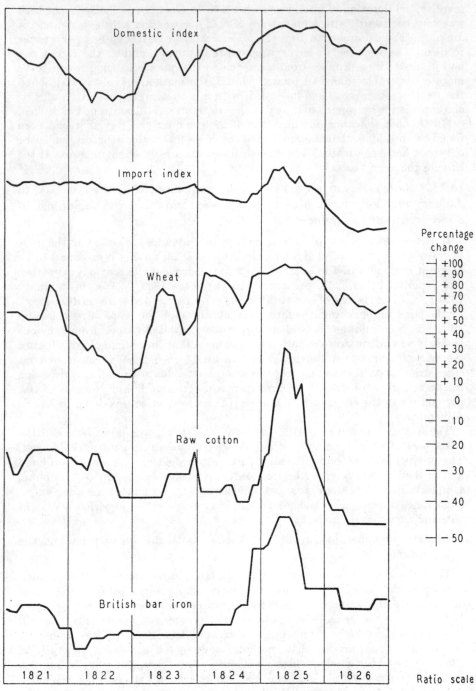

FIG. 50. Prices, 1821–6

great corn districts were secured in good condition, and found to be productive, that the price gave way at all, and then very slowly.

The fall in the wheat price during 1826 (to a low point of 54s. in October) was aided by the government's decision to release a maximum of 500,000 quarters of wheat from bond. The relatively high range of food prices, in the face of severe unemployment, was causing considerable unrest, and the government was frightened as well by anticipations of an indifferent harvest. The crop, however, turned out 'somewhat above an average in quantity', and the lower level of prices was maintained throughout 1826.[1]

The low point in the domestic index comes in May 1822, in grain prices in October. The movement of non-agricultural domestic commodities determines the lower turning-point. They tended to recover slightly in the spring of 1822, from the long downward movement begun in 1818. A few domestic commodities reflect a further brief spurt about December 1822 to February 1823, in response to fears of a general European war.[2] The major rise was in colonial products, whose supply, it was feared, would again be obstructed. But some domestic commodities as well were affected. After this short rise, they sagged again until 1824. There was, in the latter half of that year, a substantial rise, which ended in the middle of 1825. This movement coincides with the final phase of the upswing in general business activity. The collapse of non-agricultural domestic prices, after the turning-point in 1825, brought them, in the following year, to a substantially lower level. The abortive and irregular movement in the first two months of 1823, and the rise and fall in 1824–6, are represented in the following cases:

	May 1822	Feb. 1823	June 1824	June 1825	Dec. 1826
Sunderland coal (s. per chaldron) . . .	35·7	47·0	37·6	34·3a	32·1
Iron bars (£ per ton)	8·6	8·8	9·2	15·8	10·5
Iron pigs (£ per ton)b	6·0	6·2	6·8	12·5	8·0
Linseed oil (£ per ton)	30·0	29·5	25·0	27·0	24·0
Unmelted tallow (s. per cwt.) . . .	38·0	44·5	37·0	40·0	38·0c
Block tin (s. per cwt.)	77·0d	112·0	88·0	104·0	82·0
Lead pigs (£ per ton)	22·5	23·0	23·0e	29·0	22·0

a The highest price for coal in the first half of 1825 came in Jan. (37·7s. per chaldron). The coal price fluctuated not only in response to changing supply and demand conditions but with the varying effectiveness of monopoly arrangements within the industry. The fall from 1823 to 1826 is probably to be connected with the failure of the control provisions to operate (see P. M. Sweezy, *Monopoly and Competition in the English Coal Trade, 1550–1850*, p. 41).

b The price of iron bars was at its low point, for 1822, in Feb.–Apr. (£8·2 per ton); for iron pigs, in Apr. (£5·6 per ton). The upward tendency in iron prices seems fairly continuous from 1822 to 1825.

c Low point for 1826 (Apr.–July).   d Low point for 1822 (Jan.–Apr.).

e The price of lead pigs fell in the next month (July 1824) to £22·8 per ton.

[1] Tooke, ii. 134–5.

[2] Ibid., pp. 79 n. and 140–1. These fears were engendered by the 'movements of the French armies on the frontiers of Spain, and the measures of the French government with reference to Spain, which were thought to endanger the peace of Europe. . . . But upon its being found that a general war, which had been apprehended, did not ensue, the markets relapsed to their former state.'

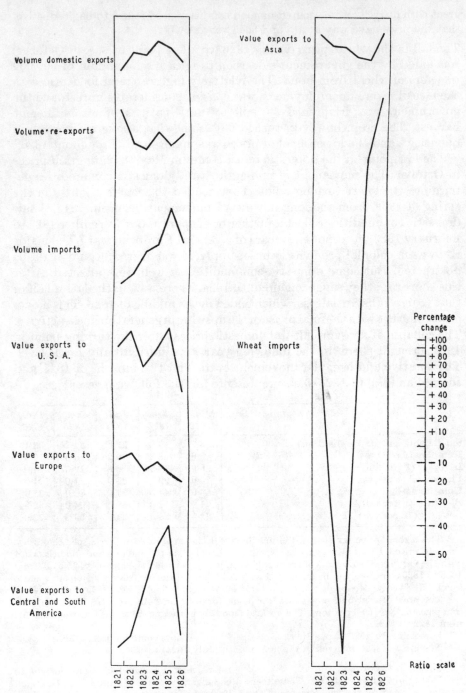

Fig. 51. Foreign Trade, 1821–6

These, and other individual domestic prices, differ considerably in their movement. From February 1823 to June 1824 some remain constant, others fall or rise slightly. They agree, however, in the decisive rise and fall in 1825–6; although, even there, the amplitudes vary, and the relative positions as between 1822 and 1826.

Except for the rise in the prices of colonial produce in the early months of 1823, and of cotton, in the latter months of the year, import prices tended to fall steadily from the beginning of 1822 to October 1824:[1]

In the early part of 1823 the entrance of the armies of France into Spain, giving rise to the apprehension of a general war in Europe, caused a speculative advance in the prices of colonial produce, and of some other commodities of which the cost of production was likely to be raised, or the supplies obstructed, by such an event. Coffee and sugar, and several other articles, were supposed to be likely to be so affected, and experienced therefore a considerable rise of price in the three first months of 1823. But, when it was found that the government of this country did not interfere to prevent the occupation of Spain by the armies of France, and that consequently there was no longer any ground for apprehension of a general war, the markets for those articles relapsed to their former state.

Later in the season, a speculation in cotton, and consequent advance of prices, occurred, on the ground that the reduced stock on hand, with the computed probable importation, was likely, according to the estimates then formed, to fall short of the rate of consumption. But the importations proved to be beyond the estimated quantity, while the consumption appeared to have been checked, and prices soon subsided to the state from which they had been speculatively raised.

With these exceptions, and other isolated speculations of less note, attended by the same result, the prices of goods generally were either stationary or dull and drooping through the first six months, and in some cases (the important article of coffee for instance), till the close of 1824.

At that time, however, an apparent deficiency of commodity stocks, combined with the fever of speculative optimism which pervaded the stock exchange and industry, caused a commodity import boom. This reached its peak in May 1825, when a severe decline set in, which persisted to July 1826. The import index then arrived at a level about which it fluctuated, with a slight drooping tendency, until May 1833:[2]

The speculations both in purchases of goods on the spot, and in overtrading in imports and exports, which had their origin mostly at the close of 1824, and continued through the greater part of the spring of 1825, terminated, in the course of the summer and autumn of that year, as such speculations commonly do terminate. The usual effects of prices driven up beyond the occasion soon manifested themselves in diminished demand, and in advices of forthcoming supplies, large beyond the utmost previous computations.

Thus, to small stocks of goods had succeeded overwhelming importations, some of them from unusual sources; and a consequent accumulation beyond the

---

[1] Tooke, ii. 140–1.   [2] Ibid., pp. 154–6

utmost computed rate of consumption. At the same time there was a diminished export, most articles having risen beyond the price which the foreign consumer could or would afford to pay for them. But, as has been remarked, with reference to former instances of a recoil of markets, from speculation and overtrading, there was a pause, and a resistance, of greater or less duration, to the fall; the

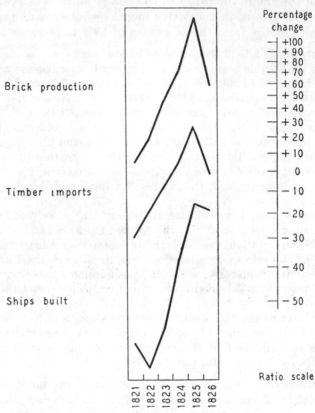

Fig. 52. Investment, 1821–6

greater or less resistance depending upon the nature of the articles, and the time in which the engagements for payment fell due.

The tendency downwards of most articles was manifest before the summer of 1825. The principal overtrading in goods, combining the extent of engagements with advance of prices, had occurred in the article of cotton, which is the most important of all others, as regards the magnitude of the capital embarked, and the interests involved in it. And in this article the reaction was first felt. Considerable failures, connected with the cotton trade, occurred in the United States, in the latter end of 1825. These were felt chiefly in Liverpool, where the commercial discredit preceded that of the metropolis. But the full effect of the depressing causes was not experienced till the spring of 1826; and it was not till then that failures and discredit of mercantile establishments became extensive and important.

The whole of the great fluctuations of the prices of goods were confined to the interval from the last few weeks of 1824 to June, 1826.

The magnitude of the price movements is revealed in these individual import prices (inclusive of duty) :[1]

	Nov. 1824	June 1825	June 1826
Yellow American pine timber (s. per load) . .	91·0	96·0	80·0
Cotton (pence per lb.)	9·0	16·5	7·4
East India indigo (s. per lb.) . . .	13·6	16·2	12·6
Jamaica rum (pence per gallon) . . .	152·4	157·9	121·0
Sugar (s. per cwt.)	56·0	62·0	51·0
Tar (s. per barrel)	36·5	38·5	29·0

The decline of import prices in 1825–6 brings the index to its lowest point since 1791.

2. Foreign Trade. With the exception of 1823, there was a steady increase in the volume of exports, from 1821 to 1824, followed by a minor decline in 1825, a drastic fall in 1826. The rise in prices in 1824–5, however, makes 1825 a peak year in the annual figures for the real value of exports. It is probable that the turning-point, in the export markets, occurred towards the end of the first half of 1825. The official values of imports also are at their peak in 1825.[2]

(In £ millions)

	Volume of			Value of domestic exports
	Total imports[a]	Re-exports	Domestic exports	
1821 . .	33·8	8·7	19·7	36·7
1822 . .	36·0	7·0	22·2	37·0
1823 . .	41·5	6·7	21·9	35·5
1824 . .	43·4	7·6	23·9	38·4
1825 . .	54·8	6·9	22·9	38·9
1826 . .	43·8	7·4	20·9	31·5

[a] The quantities of wheat and wheat flour imported moved as follows (net imports, 1,000 quarters):

1821 . . 137·7	1824 . . 85·2
1822 . . 47·6	1825 . . 391·6
1823 . . 24·0	1826 . . 582·3

The sharp rise in total imports, in 1825, is explained partially by the suddenly increased grain requirements. The large quantity needed as well, in 1826, helped cushion the decline in total imports in that year.

A breakdown of the real value of exports in 1823 shows the fairly large declines in shipments to southern Europe and the United States. There does not appear to have been any very general recession in that year, the period from 1821–4 being, generally, one of fairly universal, moderate

---

[1] See also Tooke, ii. 157.   [2] Schlote, pp. 133 and 137.

prosperity. Smart suggests that the decline was due merely to an over-stocking by foreign merchants in British exports in the previous year, when the official value of exports rose (1821 to 1822) by about £3·5 million.[1] Real values of domestic exports follow:[2]

(In £ millions)

| | | | | | | British North American colonies and W. Indies | Foreign W. Indies | Central and S. America (including Brazil) |
	Northern Europe	Southern Europe	Africa	Asia	U.S.A.			
1821	9·0	6·9	0·5	4·3	6·2	5·5	1·1	2·9
1822	8·3	8·3	0·4	4·0	6·9	4·8	0·9	3·2
1823	9·1	6·8	0·5	3·9	5·5	5·3	1·1	4·2
1824	7·7	8·0	0·4	3·7	6·1	5·8	1·2	5·6
1825	8·5	6·1	0·4	3·6	7·0	5·8	0·9	6·4
1826	7·8	6·1	0·3	4·3	4·7	4·6	0·6	3·2

Value of Domestic Exports to

The most important increase (1821–5) and the sharpest decline (1825–6) appear in the export figures for Central and South America. This movement was a fairly direct outcome of the large-scale capital exports undertaken to that area in this period and their virtual cessation after the crises of 1825.[3] The substantial decline in shipments to the United States, in 1826, reflects clearly the consequence of the panic (1825) and depression there.[4] While the sales of British merchants to the Continent still constituted the largest single category of their business, they play a relatively minor role in the fluctuations of total exports.[5] The stability of exports to Europe explains as well the steady level of re-exports, of which over 80 per cent. were shipped to the Continent.

The speculative boom in foreign trade, from the closing months of 1824 to about April 1825, has been described in its impact on prices. The magni-

[1] Op. cit. ii. 148. It is possible that the war fears, of the early months of 1823, affecting France and Spain, especially, were a factor in reducing trade with the Continent. In so far as exports were financed on credit, uncertainty might reduce shipments. See Levi (p. 184) for such an explanation of the 'slight check experienced in 1823'. The tariff and trade agreement manœuvres of these years had, probably, little net effect on the short run movement of British exports (Smart, ii. 260–3).

[2] Porter, pp. 361–2.

[3] See below, *Investment*. Also Tooke, ii. 145: 'The remittances to South America of the very capital for the mining projects then afloat, as also for the loans raised in the country for those states, were made, in large part, in manufactures, besides mere stores and machinery; thus forming a great temporary increase of demand for manufac-

tures.' Also Jenks, pp. 58–64, 'What the Money Accomplished'.

[4] Tooke, ii. 156 and 171. See especially quotations from New York and Boston newspapers, pp. 171–3 n.

[5] The even character of the continental demand for British goods and the extent to which North and South America constituted the 'dynamic' area in British exports is revealed as well by the following figures (official value, in £ million):

| | Totals for | | | |
	Europe	Asia	Africa	America
1821	18·8	3·8	0·5	16·9
1825	19·0	3·6	0·4	23·2
1826	20·1	4·4	0·3	15·2

(Macgregor's *Commercial Statistics*, v, Supplement, p. 98.)

tude of the shipments which came to Britain as a result of current expectations is indicated in the following table :[1]

| | Silk | Wool | Cotton | Flax | Tallow | Linseed |
		(in 1,000 lb.)		(in cwt.)		(in bushels)
1822 . .	2,060	19,058	142,838	610,106	805,238	1,413,450
1823 . .	2,453	19,367	191,403	553,937	830,271	1,662,456
1824 . .	3,052	22,564	149,380	742,531	680,382	2,195,093
1825 . .	2,856	43,817	228,005	1,055,233	1,164,037	2,888,247

Many of the contracts had been made when prices and interest rates were low, and the general prospects for trade highly optimistic.[2] The rise in prices, however, discouraged purchases abroad, while producers at home found that their import requirements were more than fully met. A money market experiencing severe stringency—partly in consequence of the increased credit demands for foreign trade financing—helped reverse the upward trend :[3]

The increase of commodities which speculation had caused, could no longer be kept from being realised, prices fell as rapidly as they had risen. The obligations

[1] Ibid., p. 155. The boom in cotton had, as one consequence, a great increase in the supply from Egypt: 'the quantity which previously to 1824 had been imported from Egypt into this country was perfectly insignificant, reached in 1825 to 20 million lbs. And the effect on opinion of the sudden increase from this source, was greater than the mere quantity relatively to the total supply, inasmuch as it operated on the minds of buyers, as opening a great and indefinite source of supply at a reduced cost.' Tooke notes, more generally that, 'in the instance of several descriptions of produce, not only was the importation larger than on any former occasion, but supplies came in considerable quantities from new sources; or comparatively insignificant sources were greatly enlarged'. Donnell (p. 103) gives the following account of the speculation in cotton: 'The immediate or ostensible cause of the great speculation in cotton during this season was the delay in shipments from this country. On the 1st January, 1825, it was found that the stock of American cotton in Liverpool was reduced to about 100,000 bales, whereas the trade had counted on twice that quantity. Without steam or telegraph to convey information, Liverpool was in the dark, and at once became alarmed for her supply. This excited the speculators in this country. The speculation in cotton was only a part of the general movement, which extended to nearly all departments of business.'

[2] Ibid., p. 147. Tooke clearly describes the manner in which, due to necessary lags, an accumulation of individual decisions, based on a prevailing set of conditions, altered those conditions, and produced the setting, at least, for commercial crisis: 'Not only was this exaggeration of demand, compared with the supply, at high prices, the cause of increased importations, but it also operated temporarily in inducing increased exports. The reduced stocks of raw materials in this country, and the speculations thereupon, would, in most cases, be attended, in the first instance, with improved markets abroad for the manufactured goods into which those raw materials extend; and the improved markets abroad would give an impulse both to orders from thence, and to speculative shipments thither, beyond what would be found to be eventually carried off by consumption at the advanced prices. The transactions hence arising, and the engagements consequent upon them, might be, as, in fact, they were, entered into to a vast extent, long before any effect of them could be felt in the exchanges, or in the rate of interest, or in prices, or in the state of credit.' With stocks redundant, prices high, money dear, and the banks attempting to make their position liquid, the principal inducement to speculation in foreign trade no longer existed.

[3] Macleod, ii. 244–5.

of the speculators now became due, and the sale of the commodities had to be forced to meet them. Universal discredit now succeeded, goods became unsaleable, so that stocks which are usually held in anticipation of demand, were wholly unavailable to meet the pecuniary engagements of the holders. Merchants who had accepted bills for only half the value of the goods consigned to

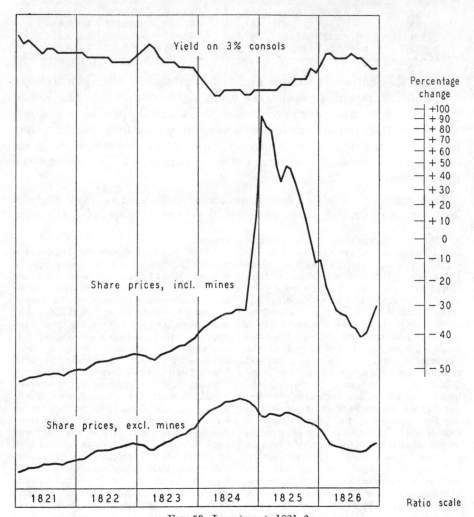

FIG. 53. Investment, 1821–6

them, were unable to realize even that half, or even obtain advances, on security of the bills of lading, and even the advances already made were peremptorily called in. The usury laws which limited interest to 5 percent. greatly aggravated the distress; nobody would lend money at 5 percent. when its real value was so much greater; hence, numbers who would gladly have paid 8 or 10 percent. interest, were obliged to sell goods at a difference of 30 percent. for cash, compared with the price for time.

But, as in the other cases of 'inventory' cycles, recovery came fairly soon. Import prices were rising slightly in the second half of 1826; and in 1827 the official values of both imports and exports were at a new high level.

3. Investment. The movement of foreign trade (1824–5) differs little, in essentials, from that of 1792–3, 1798–9, 1809–10, 1814–15, 1817–18. The character of this cycle as a whole, however, can be distinguished from earlier cycles by the scale and the scope of new private investment. There was an increase in railway construction, new docks were built, and what appears to be the greatest building boom until the forties took place.[1] Gas-light, insurance, building, trading, investment, provision companies, in addition to many others, were formed on a large scale. These, the floatations of foreign government and mining issues, and the fabulous Stock Exchange boom and crash (1824–5) impart to these years their unique character.[2]

The framework for the boom in the new investment was laid in the period of easy money which began in the latter months of 1819. On the demand side of the money market there were no extraordinary requirements to be met. The continued fall in prices reduced the money required for a given turnover of goods. The modest increases in the volume of foreign trade were easily financed. While on the Stock Exchange the lack of new investment outlets resulted in a rise in the price of bonds, a fall in the rate of interest. The situation was accentuated by the government's extension (April 1822) of the privilege of circulating small country bank notes (under £5). It had been expected that this privilege would be revoked, and the Bank had, apparently, been accumulating bullion for the purpose of substituting coin for them. The government's action put the Bank in a position of embarrassing ease.[3] On 20 June 1822 it lowered its rate for the first time to 4 per cent.[4] Towards the close of 1823 the government converted £135 million of its 5 per cent. bonds to 4 per cent., and early in 1824, £80 million 4 per cent. to 3½ per cent.[5] Partly reflecting, partly accentuating the downward tendency in the long-term rate of interest, the conversions had the immediate effect of exciting 'among persons whose incomes were in consequence diminished, a restless feeling, and a disposition to hazardous investment'.[6] Even in that day 'John Bull could not stand two per cent.' Holding profits accumulated in the previous four years of expanding output, investors were receptive, by 1824, to virtually anything that came on the market.

Fifteen new railways, covering 256 miles and costing £3·64 million,

---

[1] *A.R.*, 1825, stated 'On all sides new buildings were in the progress of erection' (quoted, Tooke, ii. 153 n.).

[2] Hunt, pp. 30–55.

[3] Bowen, pp. 69–70. Also Levi, p. 184; Tooke, ii. 114–16 and 191.

[4] R. Hawtrey, *A Century of the Bank Rate*, p. 14.

[5] Bowen, p. 73; Andréadès, p. 249; Tooke, ii. 149.

[6] Ibid., pp. 191.

were completed from 1823 to 1826.[1] In 1824–5 two large dock companies and the West India and General Steam Navigation companies were formed, the latter two involving £4 million.[2] Brick production and the quantity of timber imports moved as follows:

	Production of bricks (in million bricks)	Quantity of fir timber imports (in 1,000 loads of 50 cu. ft.)
1821	899·2	392
1822	1,019·5	451
1823	1,244·7	512
1824	1,463·2	582
1825	1,948·8	709
1826	1,350·2	556

Before the middle of the century the figure for brick production in 1825 was surpassed only in 1846 and 1847. Among the types of investment traced in the previous cycles, railway building and general construction would appear to have been on a new high level in this boom and several large new docks were built; inclosures, canals, and turnpikes, however,

[1] Porter, pp. 329–30.

Date of Act	Name of railway	Terminals	Length in miles	Cost of construction
				£
1823	Stockton and Darlington	Stockton and Wilton Park Colliery	54	450,000
1824	Redruth and Chaswater	Redruth and Point Quay, and branches	14½	32,500
	Monkland and Kirkintilloch	Palace Craig and Kirkintilloch	10¾	204,000
1825	Rumney	Abertyswg and Sirhowey Railway	21¾	67,100
	Cromford and High Peak	Cromford and Whaley Bridge	34	197,280
	Nanttle	Nanttle Pool and Caernarvon	9¼	40,000
	Portland	Portland Stone Quarries and Portland Castle	2	7,000
	Duffryn Llynvi	Llangoneyd and Perth Cawl	16¾	110,000
1826	Ballochney	Airdrie and Ballochney	5¾	93,333
	Hereford	Monmouth and Hereford	12¼	35,000
	Dundee and Newtyle	Dundee and Newtyle	10½	170,000
	Edinburgh and Dalkeith	Edinburgh and Newbattle Abbey	17¼	208,753
	Garnkirk and Glasgow	Gartsberrie Bridge and Glasgow	8¼	169,195
	Heck and Wentbridge	Heckbridge and Wentbridge	7½	21,700
	Liverpool and Manchester	Liverpool and Manchester	31	1,832,375

In the same period 20 parliamentary acts for new lines were passed; 5 extending or amending the powers for existing lines.

[2] Henry English, *A Complete View of the Joint Stock Companies Formed During the Years 1824 and 1825*, p. 8. See also pp. 422 ff. below, for further discussion of dock companies.

largely drop from view.[1] There was, also, a substantial increase in the building of new ships, although the movement of the total for ships belonging to the United Kingdom would seem to suggest that they were largely for replacement.

(In 1,000 tons)

	Tonnage of shipping belonging to the United Kingdom	Tonnage of ships built and registered in the United Kingdom
1821 . .	2,330	58·1
1822 . .	2,289	50·9
1823 . .	2,277	63·2
1824 . .	2,322	91·1
1825 . .	2,300	122·5
1826 . .	2,382	118·4
1827 . .	2,150	93·1

In its delayed response to recovery (trough, 1822) new tonnage built displays what appears to have been a general characteristic of the cyclical behaviour of new investment.

An enormous number of joint stock companies went through at least the preliminary stages of organization in 1824–5. There are records of 624 companies, seeking £372 million, desiring to dispose of almost 6 million shares. Most of these were either abandoned or merely 'projected'.[2] In 1827 Henry English, a London broker, made the following classification of the fortunes of these companies.[3]

	Capital required	Amount actually paid	Number of shares
	£	£	
127 companies now (1827) existing . .	102,781,600	15,185,950	1,618,340
118 companies abandoned . . .	56,606,500	2,419,675	848,600
379 companies projected . . .	212,785,000	. .	3,494,380
	£372,173,100	£17,605,625	5,961,320

The scale of this promotional boom can be gauged from the figures which

---

[1] A considerable number of new canal companies were planned, but they were all, apparently, either abandoned, or never got beyond the stage of issuing prospectuses. No important canal building took place (English, pp. 29–30).

[2] The companies classed by English as 'projected' 'include those which published prospectuses, or announced their projection through the medium of the public press, but of the actual formation of which, by issue of their Shares, no precise information can be obtained. In some instances they may have existed, or even do now (1827) exist, but certainly are of an unimportant nature, no publicity having been given to warrant their being classed in the preceding list' (i.e. of existing companies).

[3] Op. cit., p. 30.

compare the number and capital of the companies formed in 1824–5 which weathered the crisis (until 1827), with all those existing before 1824 :[1]

	No. of Companies	Capital	Amount advanced	No. of shares
		£	£	
Existing in 1824 . . .	156	47,936,487	34,065,937	764,534
Founded in 1824–25, existing in 1827	127	102,781,600	15,185,960	1,618,340

The following classification is given of the latter group :[2]

	Capital	Amount paid	Present value	Amount liable to be called	No. of shares
	£	£	£	£	
44 Min. Co. . .	26,776,000	5,455,100	2,927,350	21,320,900	358,700
20 Gas. Co. . .	9,061,000	2,162,000	1,504,625	6,899,000	152,140
14 Ins. Co. . .	28,120,000	2,247,000	1,606,000	25,873,000	545,000
49 Miscell. . .	38,824,600	5,321,850	3,265,975	33,502,750	562,500
127	£102,781,600	£15,185,950	£9,303,950	£87,595,650	1,618,340

The 'miscellaneous' group includes salt, silk, lard, bridge, emigration, glass, distilling, brick, bank, and agricultural companies, among many others.[3]

The boom in Mexican and South American mining shares was the most sensational of the developments in the capital market in these years. The attitude of the investing public was made optimistic by the government's formal recognition of these states in 1824 ;[4] and the 'restlessness' of those suffering from a declining yield made for any easy acceptance of both government and mining prospectuses.[5] More than half of the forty-four

[1] English, p. 31.

[2] Ibid., p. 30. For special accounts of mining companies see pp. 433–5; of gas companies, pp. 429–33; of insurance companies, pp. 451–6.

[3] Ibid., p. 8.

[4] Macleod, ii. 241: 'the long struggle for independence had inspired the British people with much sympathy for the juvenile republics, and when they wanted to borrow money to support their public credit, the British were only too eager to lend it. It is alleged that £150,000,000 of British capital was sunk in different ways in Mexico and South America.' In 1823 the South American markets seemed so important to the Lancashire cotton trade that the Manchester chamber of commerce persuaded the government to appoint consuls in the chief commercial cities. Pressure, during the next few years, for the recognition of these states

came from the same body. See, A. Redford, *Manchester Merchants and Foreign Trade*, pp. 99–101.

[5] See Tooke (ii. 149) for the tone of the market on the appearance of the South American issues: 'It was a restlessness of feeling of this kind, combined with the facilities of the money market, or, in other words, with the fall in the general rate of interest, and with the too highly-coloured accounts of the resources and good faith of the states of South America, which gave occasion to the projects for loans to those states, and, at the same time, enabled the contractors to fill their lists. A considerable impulse to those projects, and to the eagerness with which they were entered into by the public, was given by the steps announced on the part of the government of this country, as preliminary to the formal recognition of the independence of the South American

mining companies which appeared in 1824–5, and survived until 1827, were operating in Latin America.[1]

Finally, the public from 1821 to 1825, was induced to export enormous amounts of capital in government bonds. In 1817–18 they had been confined to European states. In these years the new republics of South America were the largest borrowers :[2]

Year	Destination	Nominal capital (in £1000)	Contract price (£)	Actual amount (in £1000)
1821 . .	Spanish 5%	1,500	56	840
1822 . .	Chile 6%	1,000	70	700
	Colombia 6%	2,000	84	1,680
	Prussian 5%	3,500	84	2,940
	Russian 5%	3,500	82	2,870
	Peruvian 6%	450	88	396
		10,450	..	8,586
1823 . .	Austrian 5%	2,500	82	2,050
	Portuguese 5%	1,500	87	1,305
	Spanish 5%	1,500	30¼	454
		5,500	..	3,809
1824 . .	Brazilian 5%	3,200	75	2,400
	Buenos Ayres 6%	1,000	85	850
	Colombian 6%	4,750	88¼	4,204
	Greek 5%	800	59	472
	Mexican 5%	3,200	58	1,856
	Neopolitan 5%	2,500	92½	2,312
	Peruvian 6%	750	82	615
		16,200	..	12,709
1825 . .	Brazilian 5%	2,000	85	1,700
	Danish 3%	5,500	75	4,125
	Greek 5%	2,000	56½	1,130
	Guatamala 6%	1,429	73	1,043
	Guadaljara 5%	600	60	360
	Mexican 6%	3,200	89¾	2,872
	Peruvian 6%	616	78	480
		15,345	..	11,710

These bonds, in the amounts actually paid up, constituted the largest single category of new investment which can be estimated for the period.

states. Specious statements were held forth of the great resources and capabilities of revenue of those states ; and assurances were held out, and believed, of the good faith and power of the several governments to raise and appropriate the sums requisite for the payment of the dividends. The most sanguine expectations were entertained of the unbounded resources of those states, now that, being relieved from the trammels of the old Spanish government, those resources were about to be developed by a free commercial intercourse with this country.'

[1] See English's list, pp. 4–6.

[2] This is an estimate made by the committee of 1831–2. It differs slightly from figures given by English (P.P. 1831–2, vi, App. 95, p. 98).

The Stock Exchange boom, that accompanied these floatations in their latter stages, collapsed early in 1825 :[1]

As regarded the majority of the loans and schemes . . . it was soon discovered, that while the calls for payments were immediate and pressing, the prospect of returns was become more remote and uncertain; doubts too began soon to arise as to their being sufficient security for *any* income. Accordingly, after the greatest elevation in January and February, 1825, there was a pause in the first instance, then a slight decline, and, after a few weeks, namely, in the May and June following, a rapid decline. . . . The process by which the fall took place is simple and obvious:—As regarded the schemes, a more accurate appreciation of a greater outlay, and of smaller returns, than had been before anticipated; and a limitation of the demand for investment in them, to such persons only as could afford to depend upon remote contingencies for an income, where any income was to be expected; above all, a general deficiency of means among the subscribers to pay up the succeeding instalments, as they had relied for the most part upon a continued rise, to enable them to realise a profit before another instalment should be called for, or upon the same facility as had before existed, or raising money for the purpose at a low rate of interest;—and, as applied to foreign loans, the absence of security for some of them, and the rise of the rate of interest in this country, which had the same depressing effect upon all of them. It is to be considered that the greater part of the transfers of the original shares in the foreign loans, and in the new schemes, while the payments on them were light, . . . were carried on by a medium engendered in a great degree by those very transactions; and that the profits realised or anticipated by the successive shareholders, afforded a fund of additional credit, as well as of nominal capital, with which they might and did appear as purchasers of other objects of exchange. But as new loans and schemes were successively brought forward on grounds more or less specious, all tending to the additional absorption of capital, while the increasing calls, with the high premium payable on the former loans and schemes, were beginning to press upon the shareholders, the weakest, in the first instance, would endeavour to realise without any longer finding ready buyers. A pause naturally ensued: and, under such circumstances, a pause is generally fatal to projects that do not proceed on solid grounds.

The course of this extraordinary cycle in new investment can be traced in the security indexes as well as in the price of Consols, Bank Stock, and India Stock. The security index, inclusive of mining shares, moves up gradually throughout 1822. From December to April 1823 it declines, in response to the war fears, which, as was noted earlier, caused a temporary rise in import prices, a decline in foreign trade. This movement appears in all security prices. From the spring of 1823 the upward movement is resumed at an accelerated pace, until June 1824. From June to October the index tapers in its rise. In October the wild speculation in mining shares broke out. It is to be noted that it came after a steady rise of four and a half years in other security prices, and when the advance seemed about to end. From October to January the index inclusive of mines rises extravagantly.

---

[1] Tooke, ii. 158–9.

It falls slightly in February–March, sharply to May, recovers in June, and then begins a disastrous drop to September 1826, when a brief revival took place, until December.

The index exclusive of mines, after rising through 1822–3, begins gradually to decline in October 1824, after a very minor advance in the previous quarter. The decline was checked in the first half of 1825. This interim stability was probably due to a shift from mining shares, on their first decline, into other securities, before the credit structure supporting the whole market collapsed.[1] From September 1826 the index falls without interruption, the major decline ending, however, by March 1826. The mild general recovery in the last quarter of 1826 then appears, as in the index inclusive of mines.

The prices of Consols, India Stock, and Bank Stock, although there are marked dissimilarities in their movement, all show turning-points in 1824. Consols, until October 1822, continue the steady rise begun exactly two years before. The sharp break at that time (running from November 1822 to March 1823) is possibly to be associated not only with the fears of war, which affected other securities, but with the conversion operations of the government. The rise is, however, resumed in April 1823, and proceeds to April of the following year. There is a break and recovery to October 1824, and then a severe decline begins that finds its trough as early as February 1826; by that time the worst of the panic was over, and Consols began again to look attractive to investors who still had any funds available for investment. The early phases of the weakening and decline, however, represent the competitive force of the securities which promised a higher return. The steady fall in Consols—a 'rise in the rate of interest'—indicates, then, the operation of different forces on each side of the turning-point (roughly May 1825): a fall in price due to more attractive alternatives; and then a fall due to a panic for liquidity.[2]

The price of India Stock moves similarly. From March 1823 to April 1824 there is a sharp rise; from April to October an irregular decline, and in the following months of panic a continuous severe drop. By February 1826, as in the case of Consols, a bottom was reached. Bank Stock, however, followed a less regular course. The decline in the latter months of 1822 and early 1823 is more severe than in the other cases; for the yield on Bank Stock was reduced, in 1823, from 10 to 8 per cent.[3] On the new basis,

---

[1] During these months Tooke (ii. 155–6) notes a similar 'pause' in the commodity markets, before the catastrophic decline began.

[2] At the height of the panic (Dec. 1825) money could not even be borrowed on, nor purchasers found for Consols (Macleod, ii. 248–9): 'It was impossible to convert into money to any extent the best securities of the government. Persons could not sell Exchequer bills nor Bank stock, nor East India stock, nor the public funds. Mr. Baring said that men would not part with their money on any terms, nor for any security. The extent to which the distress had reached was melancholy to the last degree. Persons of undoubted wealth and real capital were seen walking about the streets of London not knowing whether they should be able to meet their engagements for the next day.'

[3] Ayres, p. 461.

however, a recovery took place until May 1825. The decline thereafter, interrupted briefly in January 1826, continues irregularly to March 1826, when the rising trend begun in January 1820 is resumed.

4. Industry and Agriculture. Iron shipments on the Monmouthshire Canal show a steady recovery from 1822 to 1825, a decline in 1826. It is to

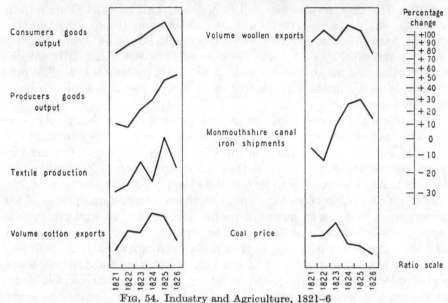

FIG. 54. Industry and Agriculture, 1821–6

be noted that this decline leaves the figure well above the level for the prosperous year 1823.[1]

The export figures, however, are less regular:

| | Monmouth-shire Canal iron shipments | Iron and steel exports excl. of hardware | British hardware and cutlery exports | Exports of iron, hardware, and cutlery | |
| | | (in 1,000 tons) | | Volume | Value |
				(in £ millions)	
1821 . .	57·3	66·6	7·9	1·5	1·9
1822 . .	52·4	70·1	9·3	1·7	2·0
1823 . .	66·6	74·0	9·1	1·7	1·95
1824 . .	76·3	59·3	10·6	1·7	2·1
1825 . .	78·8	58·8	11·0	2·4	2·4
1826 . .	69·8	76·4	9·6	1·9	2·3

Cutlery, and hardware exports, depending largely on the American markets, show a slight weakening in 1823, a steady recovery to 1825, and the expected decline in 1826. Due to the rise in prices the declared value of total iron and steel exports (including manufactured goods) moves similarly. The Continent, however, constituted the largest market for the

[1] Scrivenor, p. 127.

semi-manufactured materials; and there a peak was reached in 1823, after which export to Germany, Italy, France, and the Netherlands declined.[1] Recovery on the Continent seems to come in 1826, when iron and total exports there are at a new high level.

The figures for shipments on the Monmouthshire Canal (as well as the movement of prices) are probably a more reliable index of the position of the iron industry than those of foreign trade. There exist, as well, contemporary estimates of total pig-iron production in England, Wales, and Scotland for 1823 and 1825. They show, like the Monmouthshire figures, but unlike exports of semi-manufactured iron, a strong increase from 1823 to 1825:[2]

			Tons
1823	.	.	452,066
1825	.	.	581,367

It may be concluded that, although there was a minor slackening in some branches during 1823 and that the continental markets remained weak from 1824 until 1826, iron output, as a whole, increased to 1825, declined somewhat in 1826.

The movement of iron prices also places a peak in 1825:

Price of British Bar-iron

(£ per ton)

	Annual average	Jan.	Apr.	July	Oct.
1821 . .	9·9	10·0	10·2	10·2	9·6
1822 . .	8·6	9·1	8·2	8·6	8·8
1823 . .	8·8	8·8	8·8	8·8	8·8
1824 . .	10·1	8·8	9·2	9·2	10·2
1825 . .	13·4	13·5	15·8	14·8	11·0
1826 . .	10·4	11·0	10·0	10·0	10·5

The downward trend in prices began in July 1825. Until August 1824 (when the price moved from £9·2 to £10·0 per ton) output had increased against a steady slightly declining or slightly rising level of iron prices. In the last quarter of 1824 and the first half of 1825 the industry, however, moved to 'full employment', with every slight expansion in demand calling forth large price increases.[3]

Along with other types of new investment the floatations of 1824–5, in their repercussions on the demand for industrial products, help account for this final stage of the upswing:[4]

[1] Ibid., p. 424.

[2] Ibid., pp. 135–6. The size of the figure, when set against the volume of exports, indicates the minor dependence of the iron industry on foreign markets. There exists another estimate of total iron production for these two years, given in evidence before the Committee on Manufactures · (1833), by Samuel Walker (p. 574): 1823, 441,000; 1825, 613,000.

[3] Ashton, from his records of individual iron companies, concludes that: 'During the frenzy of 1825 . . . the supply of iron for purposes of all kinds was far below the demand at customary prices' (p. 181): this being precisely the way the economist's 'full employment' appears to the individual entrepreneur.

[4] From Annual Register, 1825 (quoted by Tooke, ii. 153 n.), describing the early months of 1825.

The various departments of the iron trade were flourishing. . . . This substantial and solid prosperity was stimulated to an additional extent, and was, in appearance, still further magnified, by the operation of the many joint-stock companies which had sprung into sudden existence in the former year. Some of these had put in motion a considerable quantity of industry, and increased the demand for various articles; and all of them, at their commencement, and for some time afterwards, tended to throw a certain sum of money into more active circulation, and to multiply the transfers of property from one hand to another. As these speculations still retained their popularity, the apparent prosperity arising from their artificial stimulus presented an imposing aspect.

Between 1821 and 1824 Tooke states that 'the trade and manufactures of the country had never before been in a more regular, sound, and satisfactory state'. That picture conforms to available non-statistical evidence on the iron industry. In 1822 the Staffordshire iron trade was reported 'in the fullest state of activity', while hardware and cutlery manufacturers boasted their wares 'were beyond the danger of rivalry'.[1] A similarly cheerful view of 1823 emerges from the reports.[2]

Even in Birmingham, which had suffered most directly from a cessation of war-time orders after 1815, 'the whole body of the working classes were well employed, and a great number of new houses had been built'.[3] 1824 was, of course, a year of 'great prosperity everywhere'[4] with the rising prices of the latter months extending profits and causing strikes.[5] As a result of the new investments, orders for rail iron, water-mains, lamp-posts, and mining machinery were coming to the foundries on a larger scale than ever before.[6] And, as noted above, the iron industry, in the early months of 1825, exhibits all the characteristics of an industry operating at strained full capacity: consumers eager to buy; manufacturers raising prices in

---

[1] Smart, ii. 123.

[2] Examining the position of individual firms in England and Scotland respectively, Ashton and Hamilton date 1823 as the first year that business was definitely prosperous (Ashton, p. 155; Hamilton, p. 178). Also Dodd, p. 146, and *A.R.*, 1823, p. 1.

[3] Smart, ii. 145. A Birmingham manufacturer of iron lamps (T. C. Salt) stated before the Committee on Manufactures (1833) p. 280: 'During the whole of 1824 and 1825 the stock went off so rapidly into consumption that we could hardly keep the shopkeepers supplied fast enough, and when the trade began to fall off then they got an accumulation.'

[4] Smart, ii. 183.

[5] Ibid., pp. 231–3.

[6] Ashton, pp. 157, 181, 183; Jones, p. 54: 'In 1825 the introduction of the steam locomotive and the consequent demand for iron rails gave yet another stimulus to the iron industry. Such a heavy demand was made

on some of the works in South Wales that the proprietors had special mills built to cope with the requirements of the new trade.' When the news of the spurt of gas company formations reached the northern foundries early in 1824, the masters met at Sheffield and pledged 'themselves not to sell pipes in London or elsewhere for less than £9 per ton, Money'. The flood of rail-iron orders induced the masters further to exploit the natural possibilities of the market with monopolistic agreements. A writer in 1825 stated: 'A great consumption for the iron rail-ways is anticipated, and the consumers of iron have no doubt displayed a considerable eagerness to purchase. Of this anxiety the iron masters have not failed to take due advantage, and the consequence is that the price of English iron had advanced from £9 to £15. . . . It is to this combination that we must, in a great measure, attribute the present enormous price of English iron.' (Ashton, p. 183.)

natural response to the inelastic demand as well as by monopoly agreement; rising wages and strikes.

In the latter months of 1825 and during most of 1826 the situation deteriorated. There is less evidence on the iron industry than on textiles; but unemployment certainly increased. The rise in continental exports, however, cushioned the depression of 1826 for the iron manufacturers :[1]

Total Iron Exports

(In tons)

	Germany	Portugal	France	The Netherlands	Italy	Gibraltar
1825 . .	1,804	3,859	3,273	2,441	6,805	1,233
1826 . .	2,615	6,067	7,911	4,760	9,435	1,601

Nevertheless iron prices declined until the last quarter of 1826 and the monopoly agreements were broken.[2] The boom of 1825 was followed 'by collapse and stagnation',[3] despite the secular increase in the demand for iron. And it left the industry with a heritage of enlarged plant.[4]

Total coal shipments and the annual average price of Sunderland coal moved as follows (in thousand tons) :[5]

	Price of Sunderland coal (s. per chaldron)	Total exports	Total coastwise coal shipments (in 1,000 tons)
1821 . .	38·8	171	3,732
1822 . .	39·2	173	3,810
1823 . .	42·5	164	4,373
1824 . .	36·9	180	4,309
1825 . .	36·5	197	4,384
1826 . .	34·7	223	4,730

As in the previous periods examined, a clear cyclical pattern cannot be traced easily in those limited statistics available on the coal industry. The price of coal, moreover, failed to respond to the general price rise of 1824–5. There is a rise in the price of coal from 35·3 to 37·7 (s. per chaldron) from July 1824 to January 1825; but by the end of 1825 it stood at 38·8s. In 1826, however, there was a fall from 40·2 in January to 32·1 in December. Sweezy suggests that, from August 1824 to July 1825, monopoly price regulation was off; that it was maintained briefly in the latter months of 1825; that it lapsed in 1826.[6] This would explain the failure of the sharp rise in general prices in the first months of 1825 to find a counterpart in

---

[1] Scrivenor, p. 424. It should be remembered as well that much of the actual construction of railways, gas, and water lines, bridges, &c., which had been promoted in 1824–5, took place in 1826. The decline in iron output was probably very much less, proportionately, than the decline in iron prices. On rail orders after the panic, see, for example, Jones, p. 54.

[2] Ashton, pp. 181–2.

[3] Ibid., p. 155.

[4] See, for example, Hamilton, p. 178; Dodd, p. 146.

[5] Porter, pp. 278 and 281.

[6] Op. cit., pp. 155–6.

coal prices ;[1] it would explain as well the strange rise in the latter half of 1825, the fall in 1826. A further influence on the price of coal was a reduction, in April 1824, of the duty (3s. 4d.) on coal imported into London.[2] This appears in the decline, from March to April, from 38·5 to 35·1 (s. per chaldron).

The figures for coal shipments, as noted in earlier sections, do not include the centrally important output sold to the iron industry. There is some little evidence, in 1826, of a decline in activity in the coal pits, and that decline must represent decreased orders from the nearby foundries. There were wage reductions for the colliers, complaints of unemployment, and at least two strikes are recorded.[3] Some of the symptoms of depression can be traced then in the coal industry in 1826, despite the ambiguity of the statistics. But the depression must have been relatively mild.

As in other branches of British industry, the expectations engendered in the latter stages of the boom caused an expansion of 'plant'—in this case an extension of old pits and the sinking of new ones. Galloway lists about six such projects begun in 1824–5.[4] These years saw also an improvement in the pumping machinery in several of the collieries, making possible the exploitation of deeper veins.[5]

The course of the cotton industry exhibits a clearer cyclical pattern than that of the heavy industries :[6]

Quantity of Raw Cotton Imports

(In million lb.)

| 1821 | . | . | 132·5 | 1823 | . | . | 191·4 | 1825 | . | . | 228·0 |
| 1822 | . | . | 142·8 | 1824 | . | . | 149·4 | 1826 | . | . | 177·6 |

Exports of Cotton Manufactures

(In £ millions)

	Manufactured goods		Twist and yarn		Total	
	Official value	Declared value	Official value	Declared value	Official value	Declared value
1821 . .	21·6	13·8	1·9	2·3	23·5	16·1
1822 . .	24·6	14·5	2·4	2·7	26·9	17·2
1823 . .	24·1	13·7	2·4	2·6	26·5	16·3
1824 . .	27·2	15·2	3·0	3·1	30·2	18·4
1825 . .	26·6	15·0	2·9	3·2	29·5	18·3
1826 . .	21·4	10·5	3·7	3·5	25·2	14·0

The export figures show an increase in 1822, the minor relapse of 1823, a peak in 1824, a slight decline in 1825, a major decline in 1826. Although these annual figures place 1824 as a turning-point, it is likely that the direction of foreign trade changed, in fact, some time in the first half of

[1] Sweezy, p. 156.

[2] Porter, pp. 155–6. There had been an extra duty of 3s. 4d. in London. The reduction equalized the duty at all coastal ports at 6s. (Galloway, p. 458, gives the residual duty at 6s. 6d.).

[3] Galloway, pp. 464–5; A.R., Chr., 1826,

p. 115. The position of the coal-mines, as well as the owners, was made difficult in the Tyne area by the secular decline in the importance of the mines there (Galloway, pp. 458–9 and 464).

[4] Op. cit., pp. 446–51.   [5] Ibid., p. 446.

[6] Baines, pp. 347 and 350.

1825. The decline in cotton imports in 1824, as stocks were permitted to run down, suggests the setting for the speculative boom in cotton which affected both British and American markets so severely in the latter months of 1824 and 1825.

The price of raw cotton and various types of manufactured goods moved as follows :[1]

	Average selling price of 30-hanks water-twist of common quality (per lb.)	Average selling price of 40-hanks cop weft (per lb.)	Average selling price of a four-cut warp	Price of raw cotton including duty (Berbice)
	s. d.	s. d.	s. d.	(pence per lb.)
1821 .	1 6½	1 5¼	15 10½	10·4
1822 .	1 5½	1 4¾	15 2	9·6
1823 .	1 6¾	1 4¾	15 2½	9·1
1824 .	1 7¼	1 3½	14 10¼	8·7
1825 .	1 7¼	1 5½	16 3	12·7
1826 .	1 1	1 1	11 2½	7·6

With the exception of a brief rise in the early months of 1822, the price of raw cotton sagged until October 1824, when it stood at 8·3d. per lb. The large importations of 1823 kept the price down until that point, despite considerable increases in output. But by May 1825, under pressure from the commodity speculation, the price stood at 18·0d.; by December, however, it was 9·0d.; and in 1826 it found a new low level. Although only annual figures are available, the prices of manufactured goods would appear to have moved similarly, with the upward tendency in 1824 anticipating that in raw cotton.[2]

Industrial reports, rare for iron and coal, are abundant for the textile trades. From these it would appear that 1822 and 1823 were years of increasing output, relatively low profits; and that towards the end of 1824 the cotton industry moved into a brief, excited phase of 'full employment'.[3] This period saw strikes for higher wages, and apparently some slackening of effort and efficiency on the part of workers, who preferred to take some of their enlarged earnings in leisure.[4] The riots and distress of 1826 make

[1] Ibid., pp. 355-6.

[2] As in the other years of crisis, however, the latter price fell more precipitately, giving an abnormal margin of profit in 1825 to the manufacturer of the finished product—a profit, however, more apparent than real, in the declining state of the markets during the latter months:

Average profit per piece of
calico (Manchester)

	d.		d.
1821	−2¼	1824	+0½
1822	+4½	1825	+4¾
1823	+3	1826	+0½

Ibid., p. 356. These figures represent the difference between the average cost and selling price of one piece of 3d. quality of 74's. The wide margin of 1822 is, like that of 1825, due to a greater decline in costs than in the selling price.

[3] Smart, ii. 122 (1823), 145-6 (1823), 186-7 (1824). Early in 1825 the Annual Register reports 'the persons employed in the cotton and woollen manufactures were in full employment' (quoted, Tooke, ii. 153 n.).

[4] Smart, ii. 231-2. See also testimony of John Dixon before the Committee on Manufactures (1833), p. 272, who describes in

clear the great decline in employment which followed the crisis.[1] Tooke states that the decline was even more severe than in 1793, when the end of a boom and the outbreak of war brought industry, for a few months, to a standstill.[2]

It is significant that the riots of 1826 were characterized by the destruction of many of the new power-looms.[3] In 1824–5 there had been an enormous expansion of plant in the cotton industry, and power-looms were installed on a large scale.[4] In Manchester, for example, there were 44 cotton mills in 1820, 49 in 1823, 63 in 1826, and only 68 in 1832.[5] From a sample drawn from the whole Manchester district it appears that fully two-thirds of the increase in the number of mills between 1820 and 1832 came in 1823–6 ;[6] and it is probable that most of the construction can be allocated to 1824–5.[7] The number of power-looms in England and Scotland was estimated by contemporaries as follows, in 1820 and 1829 :[8]

	1820	1829
England　.　.	12,150	45,500
Scotland　.　.	2,000	10,000
	14,150	55,500

'In England, the great increase took place during the years of speculation, 1824 and 1825 ; and comparatively few power-loom mills were built betwixt that time and 1832.'

Wool imports and exports, in their sharp peak, and decline in 1826, conform roughly to the movement of the foreign trade series on cotton :

	Quantity of raw wool imports (in million lb.)	Exports of woollen manufactures	
		Official value	Declared value
		(in £ millions)	
1821　.　.	16·6	5·5	6·5
1822　.　.	19·1	5·9	6·5
1823　.　.	19·4	5·5	5·6
1824　.　.	22·6	6·2	6·0
1825　.　.	43·8	5·9	6·2
1826　.　.	16·0	5·0	5·0

The West Riding figures for cloth milled unfortunately end in 1820, so that

detail the reaction of the working classes to boom conditions in Wolverhampton—'working less for more pay'. He estimates that the men averaged only four days a week for a brief period at the height of prosperity.

[1] Smart, ii. 330–4.　　[2] Op. cit. ii. 166–8.

[3] A.R., Chr., 1826, pp. 10, 63, 67, 109–12. It was estimated that 865 power-looms were destroyed in the riots during the early months of 1826.

[4] Evidence before Committee on Manufactures (1833), Kirkman Finlay, p. 72; also George Smith, p. 565.

[5] Baines, p. 395.　　　　[6] Idem.

[7] Finlay, in the testimony noted above, comments on the fact that the crisis of 1825 caused some of the construction to be abandoned, half-complete. It is unlikely that much new building was undertaken in 1826.　　　　[8] Baines, p. 235.

no index of wool production is available after that date. This is especially unfortunate since the woollen industry depended, less than cottons, on the export markets. The movement of wool prices, however, shows a clear upward tendency from 1823, a sharp peak and decline in 1825-6.

Price of Raw Wool
(Pence per lb.)

	Southdown	Kent long
1821 .	15·1	13
1822 .	14·0	11
1823 .	15·0	12
1824 .	13·0	13
1825 .	15·5	16
1826 .	10·4	11

Although the general movements of trade certainly affected the woollen industry in these years, the reports are dominated by controversy leading up to and following the government's action in 1824. Compromising the interests of wool growers and manufacturers, wool export was permitted, and foreign wool was admitted at a nominal duty (1*d*. per lb.).[1] The partially consequent decline in the price of foreign wool proved highly gratifying to the manufacturer (*d*. per lb.):

	Annual average	Jan.	Apr.	July	Oct.
1822 .	99	105	105	93	93
1823 .	94	93	93	93	96
1824 .	95	96	96	96	93
1825 .	91	91	91	91	91
1826 .	74	85	81	67	67

The boom of 1825 merely held the price stationary. With the exception of the minor increase in 1824, the decline is continuous, on an annual basis, from 1822 to 1826. The woollen trade as a whole was reported increasingly prosperous in 1822, 1823, and 1824;[2] it shared, however, from the latter months of 1825, in the 'universal depression of manufactures'.[3]

The Kondratieff index of textile production and the Hoffmann indexes move as follows:

---

[1] Smart, ii. 162-3, 196-7, 204-5. For a fully documented account of the new legislation, Bischoff, ii. 30-92. It is significant of the future course of the free-trade movement that the wool manufacturers emphasized repeatedly the competition they faced because of cheap labour abroad. Implicit in their arguments was the faith that the repeal of the Corn Laws would bring lower money wages in Britain. See especially Bischoff (ii. 69-71), who, in a letter to Huskisson, describes the low standards under which British competitors existed, urging that 'the gradual but total repeal of the Corn Laws, must be looked to as the only means of preserving to this country the most important branches of our national industry'.

[2] *A.R.*, 1822, p. 1; 1823, p. 1; 1824, p. 2.

[3] Ibid., 1826, p. 57.

	Kondratieff's index of textile production	Hoffmann's index of consumers' goods production	Hoffmann's index of producers' goods production	Hoffmann's index of total production
1821 . .	12·8	13·1	4·2	8·2
1822 . .	13·4	13·9	4·1	8·6
1823 . .	15·6	14·4	4·6	9·1
1824 . .	13·7	15·4	4·9	9·7
1825 . .	18·3	16·2	5·6	10·4
1826 . .	15·0	13·8	5·8	9·5

The decline in the textile index, in 1824, probably results from the decline in the import of raw cotton in that year; and this, as noted above, represents a movement of inventories rather than of output. The Hoffmann consumers' goods index, more heavily weighted with steadily rising exports, fails to show that decline. Both series, however, clearly reveal a movement to the peak in 1825, the decline in 1826. The somewhat slower recovery (beginning in 1823) in the capital goods index conforms to information on the manufacturing branches of the iron industry, where 1823 was noted as the first really prosperous year since the coming of peace. It is difficult to estimate whether the failure of that index to decline in 1826 is justified or not. Evidence on the coal and iron trades indicates some unemployment in 1826, but an increase in the coastal shipments in the former case, in exports in the latter. In view of the expansion of fixed capital in both industries during 1824–5, it is possible that the unemployment of 1826 was accompanied by a minor increase in output, although the statistics available are certainly an inadequate basis for final judgement.

This period was distinguished by a temporary respite for the farmer from falling agricultural prices. The price of wheat moved from January to December 1823, from 40·4 to 52·0s. per quarter.[1] In May 1825 it stood at 69s., and the decline thereafter kept it well above 50s. throughout 1826. This relief from chronic distress was a factor in the general optimism which pervaded Britain in 1823–5.

The rise in price of wheat in 1825 would probably have been greater had not agitation arisen for a lowering of the duty on foreign corn.[2] Rising food costs and a prosperity demand for labour made the working classes militant. Their demand for higher wages had to be met. For a time the industrialist was able to pass along the consequent increase in costs. But in the latter half of 1825 and 1826, in the face of falling prices and severe unemployment, he combined with the working man to urge on the govern-

[1] This rise came in the midst of impassioned pleas from the farmers for further protection (Smart, ii. 135–43). The inadequate harvest of 1823 and the fears that Britain would become involved in a Franco-Spanish war forced the price of wheat quickly upwards. The consequent agricultural optimism is reflected in statements such as this:

'Something like a new era has begun in agriculture; rents have been reduced and leases renewed; things, in short, are getting into something like their old train—the effects of the revulsion from war to peace are beginning to disappear.'

[2] Tooke, ii. 134.

mont a freer trade in grain. As a result the Corn Laws were altered in
1827–8.

In 1823–5, however, important steps were taken in the direction of free
trade. Tariffs, with the exception of those on grain, were generally lowered,
and their administration simplified. The old rates ranged between 18 and
40 per cent., Huskisson's new tariffs between 10 and 30 per cent.[1] These
alterations did not necessarily require for their support an acceptance of

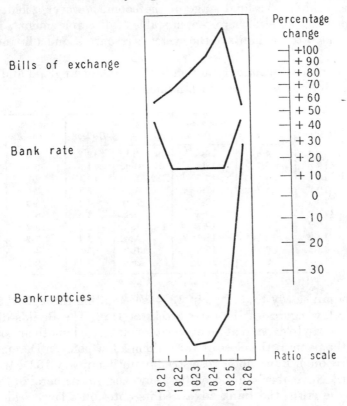

Fig. 55. Finance, 1821–6

pure free-trade doctrine;[2] but the assumption that unrestricted international competition would best serve the interests of the British manufacturer and consumer crept into the debates and public consciousness.

From the perspective of political trends Huskisson's tariff reforms are
to be regarded as an important incident in the secular progress of free
trade. In another sense, however, they were strictly a product of the
boom of 1822–5. In 1825 manufacturers were less concerned with foreign

---

[1] Smart, ii. 192–226, 264–90.

[2] Aside from the benefits to the consumer
of increased competition it was pointed out
that the new duties would discourage smuggling, increase price stability, and encourage
reciprocity from foreign countries (ibid.,
pp. 285–6).

competition than with cheaper supplies of raw materials.[1] They could afford, under conditions of relatively full employment, to be liberal in their trade policy. In short, the timing of the tariff reductions is intimately connected with Britain's economic position in the early twenties; although they represent, as well, the growing persuasiveness of the new ideas.

5. Finance. From 1822 to the latter months of 1824 the general industrial recovery was easily financed. Money was still cheap, the Bank's gold reserve high. The final stage of the boom, however, yielded, in the money markets as elsewhere, an unstable 'full employment', i.e. loans were expanded to the limits of the system's resources, and a financial crisis resulted.

Bills and notes discounted, bullion in the Bank of England and the note circulation moved as follows (in £ millions):

	Bullion	Discounts	Notes in circulation		Bullion	Discounts	Notes in circulation
1822 Jan.	11·4	4·6	19·4	1824 July	12·7	3·3	21·7
Apr.	10·5	3·7	18·2	Oct.	11·5	2·4	20·4
July	10·1	4·8	19·5	1825 Jan.	10·1	2·8	21·8
Oct.	10·2	3·7	17·6	Apr.	7·3	3·2	20·7
1823 Jan.	10·4	5·5	19·1	July	4·4	6·3	20·9
Apr.	11·3	3·5	18·6	Oct.	3·3	6·6	18·8
July	12·2	3·8	19·7	1826 Jan.	1·9	13·4	24·9
Oct.	13·2	2·5	18·7	Apr.	3·4	7·2	24·9
1824 Jan.	13·8	2·7	19·8	July	5·5	4·0	22·5
Apr.	13·7	2·5	20·6	Oct.	8·1	2·1	20·5

Bullion began slowly to decline in 1824, accelerating through 1825 to the incredibly low figures of the early weeks of 1826. The Bank's discounts, however, began to expand at an even later point, reaching their peak in the midst of the panic at the close of 1825. From a low point in December 1822 the circulation of Bank notes rose steadily until January 1825. It declined then, until November. In December, however, in an heroic attempt to alleviate the crisis, the Bank advanced its notes on a large scale, in substitution for discredited country bank paper currency. From April 1826 to the end of the year, as panic subsided, the Bank's note issues declined to about the level of the early months of 1824. The rise from 1822 to 1824 in the note issue might seem prima-facie evidence of the Bank's participation in the credit expansion, despite the almost inverse movement of bills and notes discounted. But the increase during 1823 represents, almost surely, the increase in bullion holdings at the bank; while that during 1824 is to be associated with payments on the 'dead-weight' for which the Bank had

---

[1] The same spirit produced a repeal of the Spitalfields Acts in 1824. These had provided for the regulation of wages in the silk industry. Smart (ii. 235–6) notes the connexion between the repeal and the current prosperity: 'We no longer dreaded the rivalry of the foreigner in our market, and were able to contend with him in the markets of the continent.'

contracted in 1823.[1] Tooke speaks especially of the payments made in January 1825 as 'endangering an excess of the circulation'.[2] But from January to November 1825 the note issue was contracted. The Bank sharply reduced its holdings of public securities, at the same time that it was expanding its private discounts to meet the deepening crisis. It may be concluded, then, that the note circulation in this case measures neither the volume of credit as a whole nor even the extent of the Bank's accommodations to private borrowers; and that, until the turning-point in the spring of 1825, the Bank's only important inflationary action was its assumption of the 'dead-weight'.

The exchange on Paris, after strengthening at the time of the war fear, early in 1823, declined slowly thereafter. From a peak (25·90) in May 1823 it fell, by October 1824, to 25·28. In the period of greatest speculative activity it declined further, to 25·15, in March 1825. As prices broke and imports were checked the exchanges turned favourable. There was no crisis in Paris; and Britain's position was made easier, during the second half of 1825, by the rising exchange and the cessation of gold flows abroad.

It is evident that the Bank again served as last resort in crisis. During the period of industrial and commercial expansion its discounts were not enlarged. Only in June 1825, when the commodity and security markets had already reached their turning-points, did the Bank increase its private loans; and it continued to do so, against a rapidly declining reserve, until January 1826.[3] The Bank of England did not, then, initiate the crisis by a restriction of public credit, but, in fact, pursued an extraordinary easy-money policy throughout its duration. The Bank rate was not raised to 5 per cent. until the end of 1825, although the market rate moved from $3\frac{1}{2}$ to 4 per cent. as early as May.

This passivity characterized as well the action of the Bank in the years preceding the crisis. In 1823–4 it was embarrassed by the size of the bullion reserve in relation to its holdings. The Bank, it is true, had lowered its discount rate to 4 per cent.; it offered to advance money on mortgages;[4] and it extended the currency of eligible bills from 65 to 95 days.[5] But borrowers were finding funds elsewhere. The debt redemption policy of the government accentuated the low level of the bank's liabilities. As late as October 1824 its position was uncommonly liquid, with the proportion of reserves to liabilities more than one-third.[6] The exchanges had been weakened by the floatation of the new foreign loans, and some bullion had flowed abroad; but the Bank's resources had not yet been seriously tapped.

---

[1] For the connexion between the note issue and the Bank's holdings of public securities, see Tooke, ii. 177–84. Also, more generally, N. Silberling, 'British Financial Experience, 1790–1830', *Review of Economic Statistics*, 1919, p. 292.

[2] Ibid., ii. 179.

[3] Macleod, pp. 243–4.

[4] For a full description of the Bank's dilemma, see Tooke, ii. 172–7. The 'offer to advance sums by way of mortgages' was 'a departure from its former practice' (ibid., p. 174).

[5] W. T. C. King, *History of the London Discount Market*, p. 35.

[6] Tooke, ii. 177.

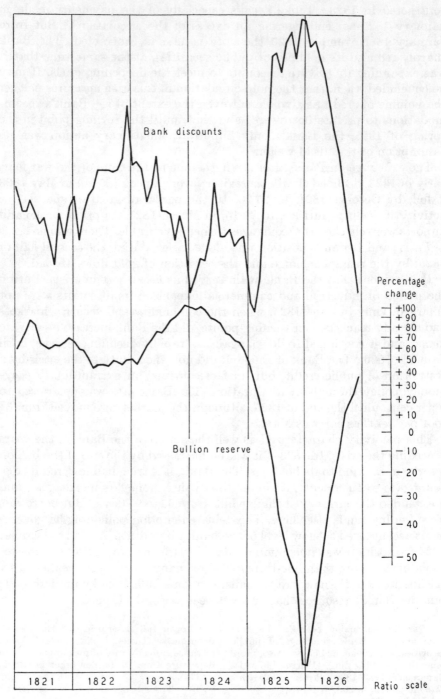

FIG. 56. Finance, 1821–6

The withdrawal of bullion continued, on foreign account, until the spring of 1825. At that time the foreign exchanges turned favourable, and the pressure from abroad virtually ended. The reduction in the Bank's holdings from that point on was in support of the country banks, which were experiencing extensive demands for the redemption of their notes.[1]

The commercial and banking panic of December 1825–January 1826 caused further bullion withdrawals from Threadneedle Street as well as an increased demand for discounts. The boom in foreign trade and the speculation in new issues had depended on Britain's private banking facilities. The obligations, contracted early in 1825, came due in the latter months, when prices were declining; and many merchants and bankers found their position illiquid. Bankruptcies increased as follows :[2]

1825 Sept.	.	. 52	1826 Jan.	.	. 270	1826 May	.	. 271
Oct.	.	. 95	Feb.	.	. 300	June	.	. 232
Nov.	.	. 161	Mar.	.	. 254	July	.	. 111
Dec.	.	. 206	Apr.	.	. 321	Aug.	.	. 134

Private bankers, in the general catastrophe, could not support the burden even of legitimate demands made upon them. They rushed to rediscount at the Bank; and several large London banking firms were among the failures.[3] It was under these circumstances that the Bank made its greatest credit advances, issuing fully £5 million in notes during the worst week of the crisis (from Monday the 12th to Saturday the 17th of December 1825).[4] On the 19th any danger of restriction of cash payments at the Bank was averted by bullion shipment to the amount of £400,000, sent from Paris.[5] The banking aspect of the crisis was over, although the total of bankruptcies mounted to a peak in February 1826; and the Bank's discounts remained abnormally high until the summer of that year.

Thus the Bank of England financed merely the crisis : the private bankers of London and the provinces financed the boom. A rough measure of the expansion is the following estimate of the value of country bank notes stamped (in £ millions) :[6]

[1] Tooke, ii. 184–5.

[2] Annual bankruptcies were:

1822	.	. 1,132	1825	.	. 1,141
1823	.	. 988	1826	.	. 2,590
1824	.	. 999			

[3] Macleod, pp. 247–50. It was stated in evidence before the Committee of 1832 on the Bank Charter that 'At Norwich, when the Gurneys shewed upon their counter so many feet of Bank notes of such a thickness, it stopped the run in that part of the country.' The action of the Bank was thus described, more generally, by one of the directors: 'We lent by every possible means, and in modes we had never adopted before; we took in stock as security, we purchased exchequer

bills, we made advances on exchequer bills, we not only discounted outright, but we made advances on deposit of bills of exchange to an immense amount; in short, by every possible means consistent with the safety of the Bank, and we were not on some occasions over-nice; seeing the dreadful state in which the public were, we rendered every assistance in our power.'

[4] Macleod p. 247 and Tooke, ii. 185 n.

[5] Macleod, p. 248. On the 16th the directors of the Bank discovered a forgotten box containing a million pounds in bank notes. These were sent off to the country to meet the crisis demands (Bowen, p. 80).

[6] P.P. 1826–7 (125), xvii. Bowen (p. 80) reprints an index number based on a survey

1822	.	. 4·3	1825	.	. 8·8
1823	.	. 4·5	1826	.	. 1·5
1824	.	. 6·7			

The first action of the government, in response to the crisis, was its decision to forbid the further issue of £1 and £2 notes. Those printed before
5 February 1826 were permitted to be issued, reissued, and circulated until
April 1829, but no longer.[1] A large part of the drain on the Bank had come
from the threatened country banks; and their small notes were made the
scapegoat of the crisis.[2]

Like previous financial crises, that of 1825 aroused controversy which
attempted to allocate responsibility for the débâcle to specific institutions.
The government's action against country bank notes is, of course, a reflection of this attitude. But the policy of the Bank of England, and of the
government itself, was critically examined. It was widely held that the
Bank, by complying with the government's desire to dispose of its 'dead-
weight' securities, had contributed to the over-supply of money in 1825.[3]
The net economic effect of this procedure was to increase the Bank's holdings of public securities: to some extent, an act of inflationary public
finance.[4] Londonderry, in proposing the sale of the annuities (1823), noted
that it would 'stimulate circulation and help to restore economic activity'.[5]
In 1823 there was no danger implicit in such action; but the payments
made early in 1825 may have contributed somewhat to the speculations
then under way.[6] Tooke suggests that, at the height of the boom, the
proper Bank action would have been to sell some of its 'dead weight' in
the open market.[7] More generally he contends that the Bank, from the
latter months of 1824, should have pursued a strict deflationary policy:[8]

A reduction of the circulation at the close of 1824, to the extent of one or two
millions, would inevitably have tended to prevent some part of the extravagance of speculation which prevailed during some months following, and would
in so far likewise have obviated a great part of the pressure on the exchanges.
The transmission of capital abroad, in payment of the foreign loans and the
mining projects, would not have been on so large a scale; nor would the engagements for importations, to be forthcoming in 1825, have been of such magnitude
as they proved to be; nor would there, consequently, have been the same pressure on the exchanges, and a good deal of the subsequent mischief might have
been averted. The difference on such occasions, of the effects of an increase,
however apparently moderate, when the indications, more especially that of a

of 122 country banks made by Henry Burgess, secretary of the Country Bankers'
Committee (1818 = 100): 1821, 93·05; 1822,
88·34; 1823, 88·10; 1824, 95·41; 1825, 102·28.
This sample includes about one-third of the
total number of principal (not branch)
country banks, but 'much more than one-
third' of the total note issue.
    [1] Macleod, pp. 255–6.
    [2] Bowen, p. 80.
    [3] The dead weight consisted of the naval

and military pensions converted into an
annuity of £585,740 per annum, for forty-
four years, which the Bank purchased in
March 1823 for the sum of £13,089,424, payable by instalments up to April 1828 (Tooke,
ii. 179 n.).
    [4] Bowen, pp. 76–7.
    [5] Ibid., p. 77.
    [6] Tooke, ii. 179.
    [7] Ibid., pp. 179–80.
    [8] Ibid., pp. 180–1.

drain of bullion for export, point clearly to a reduction, is very much greater than might be inferred from the mere sums.

This criticism applied only until the turning-point, in the spring of 1825. With the exchanges favourable Tooke, and most other commentators, agree that the Bank acted justly and courageously in placing its resources at the services of the banking system during the period of private credit collapse. Without its open-handed action Britain would have come even closer than 'within twenty-four hours of barter'.[1]

Easy money in 1822–3,[2] and the failure to institute credit restriction late in 1824 certainly contributed to the crisis of 1825. For these the passivity of the Bank is partially responsible. But it must again be emphasized that ex-post criticism of the Bank for its part in the credit expansion not only implies foresight and initiative on the part of the directors to a degree to which few twentieth-century central bankers could lay claim, but also a theory and technique of central banking which is not to be associated with Britain in the first half of the nineteenth century.[3]

'The year 1825', writes King, 'is one of the few key-dates in Bill Market history, for the great crisis of that year wrought changes in the banking structure which were responsible for every major influence upon market evolution in the succeeding twenty years.' These changes involved the be-ginnings of joint-stock banking; the establishment of Bank of England branches;[4] the cessation of rediscounting of the London private banks; and the assumption of certain central banking functions by the Bank of England. Each constitutes an important development in the institutional structure of British banking; but none, of course, seriously altered the character of trade fluctuations.

[1] King, p. 38.

[2] See above, *Investment*, for the stimulus given by the period of easy money to the boom in issues, 1824–5.

[3] The theory associated with the Bullion Report, of course, would have called for Bank restriction throughout 1824 to stem the flow of bullion abroad and to correct the exchanges. The Bank, however, consistently held less than £2·5 million in private dis-counts until April 1825. Not only did its bullion reserve justify that level of liabilities, but their amount was so small as to give the directors little direct leverage on the market. A raising of the discount rate and some gestures in the direction of restriction might have had a psychological effect, although, in view of the strength of the speculative mania, it seems doubtful. The Bullion Re-port theory implies that the Bank, having financed the expansion, was in a position opportunely to check it. As we have seen, the Bank had played an amazingly small role in the expansion of credit, and could, in 1825, merely serve as a 'dernier ressort'

when the rest of the system collapsed. As for a consciousness on the part of the directors of the public function of a central bank, King notes a series of scattered references which indicate at least a verbal appreciation of the connexion between Bank policy and general business activity. He concludes: 'even before 1825 the Bank had some con-ception of the functions of a central bank, on whom there was a duty imposed to pro-tect and assist the public. But although this principle was becoming dimly recognized by the Bank board, its application was crude in the extreme. The central theory which governed the Bank's credit policy was a conviction that it was impossible to over-issue notes so long as the issues were made by commercial discounts, and for legitimate business only. The working-rule was, "Let the public act upon the circulation"' (King, p. 73).

[4] On the early history of joint-stock banks and the Bank of England branches, see p. 441, below.

6. Labour. Available wage-statistics show, for industrial labour, a rise in 1824–5, a decline in 1826.

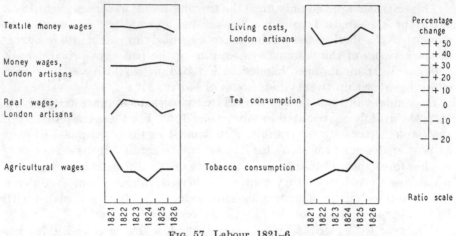

FIG. 57. Labour, 1821–6

| | Tucker's index of | | Bowley's index of agricultural money wages | Kondratieff's index of money wages in the textile industry |
	Money wages of London	Real wages artisans		
1821 . .	65·4	48·7	165	51·7
1822 . .	65·4	53·5	144	51·7
1823 . .	65·4	52·7	144	51·2
1824 . .	66·1	52·4	136[a]	51·7
1825 . .	66·9	48·8	146	51·7
1826 . .	66·1	50·2	146	49·8

[a] There is no evidence available on the reasons for the strange decline of agricultural wages in 1824, when, in fact, the farmers were enjoying their first year of prosperity after a depression extending back to 1818, or even 1813. The decline also appears in the Kondratieff agricultural wage index: 1822, 75; 1823, 75; 1824, 71; 1825, 76; 1826, 76.

Three factors aided in the rise of money wages in 1824. First, of course, the demand for labour was high. Industry was approaching full employment in the latter months of the year. Second, in 1824 the Combination Acts were repealed. Although this action holds an important place in working-class history, it is to be regarded as part of the same movement towards *laissez-faire* as the lowering of tariffs by Huskisson.[1] The third factor, which goaded a working class, free to organize, to take advantage of its natural prosperity bargaining position, was the rise in food prices which began in 1823.

[1] J. L. and B. Hammond, *The Town Labourer*, pp. 134–5. Francis Place and his associate Joseph Hume were both essentially liberals. They regarded the Combina-tion Acts as an artificial irritant and believed that their repeal would result in the disappearance of the trade unions.

In 1822–3 labour was relatively peaceful. The fears engendered among the silk workers by agitation for the repeal of the Spitalfields Acts resulted in the only serious unrest to be discovered.[1] In the early months of the year there were still meetings of protesting farmers;[2] but rising prices soon brought them to an unaccustomed state of contentment. During 1824 the demand for labour was reported as having secured for the working classes 'steady employment and good wages':[3]

We should then, in any case, expect to find 1824 marked by labour disturbances. But the repeal of the Combination Laws, for the moment at least, aggravated the tendency. Trade societies sprang into existence on all sides; for the next six months the newspapers are full of strikes and rumours of strikes. In the month of September alone, there were serious stoppages among the dyers, the cloth-lappers, the journeymen shoemakers, and the colliers in and around Glasgow, accompanied by rioting, picketing, and intimidation. But the most prominent was in the cotton trade, where from the end of August till the following January, cotton spinners and powerloom weavers struck work almost in a body. They formed themselves into associations, held public meetings—the Weavers' Association sent weekly reports of their proceedings to the newspapers—sent delegates to Ireland to promote combination on the same principles, established a regular system of organisation, fixed the terms on which they were willing to negotiate with their employers, dictated the rules by which the conduct of the workmen was to be regulated—and all in a peaceable and orderly way. The masters, on the other hand, took joint action in their own defence.

The same phenomena happened up and down the country. So serious was the reaction towards Combination that Hume, on 14th September, wrote to the operative weavers of Glasgow: 'I still do expect that great benefit will be derived from the Repeal if the imprudent conduct of the operatives does not urge the masters to obtain a renewal of the power they formerly had to oppress,' and, more distinctly in December, to the Manchester Cotton Spinners: 'I should be very uncandid if I did not inform you that, unless the operatives act in a manner more moderate and prudent than they have done in some parts of the country, I fear that many members of the House of Commons may be disposed to re-enact the laws that have been repealed—I allude particularly to the secret unions in Stockport and Dublin, the association and declaration of the colliers of Lanark, Dumbarton and Renfrewshire, which are estranging their best friends, and gradually raising the community against them.'

Strikes for higher wages continued into 1825, and with them grew the conviction that the repeal had gone too far. The result was a new Combination Act which permitted the existence of trade unions, but strictly limited their ability to strike.[4] Although the industrial turning-point came probably in the second quarter of 1825, strikes for higher wages continued until the end of the year:[5] 'But, by December, combination, it was broadly

---

[1] *A.R.*, Chr., 1823, p. 71.
[2] Ibid., p. 8.
[3] Smart, ii. 232–3.
[4] Ibid., pp. 306–12; also Cole, i. 88–93. The chief benefit of the Act of 1825, as com-

pared with the situation before 1824, was that the act of combination itself was no longer grounds for prosecution.
[5] Smart, ii. 312–13.

asserted, was knocked on the head. Bradford weavers and combers went back to work at the old wages after five months of a strike. So did the Renfrewshire colliers, of whom it was said that, six times in the year, they had demanded an advance of wages, each advance being accompanied by a corresponding diminution of the hours of labour and of the output.'

The year 1826 ranks with 1811, 1816, and 1819 as a year of the most serious distress: 'The demand for the labour of the artisan had not yet revived; and want of employment, and its concomitant misery, were the results.'[1] There were violent riots, especially in the cotton textile districts, where the operatives—'in unparalleled distress and famishing state'[2]— took out their resentment on the newly installed power-looms. 'Very inflammatory addresses' were heard at Manchester meetings;[3] a strike of colliers against lower wages called out special constables;[4] there were riots in Tyldesley, Oldham, and London;[5] in the metropolis bands of unemployed gathered in an open field—and 'on the brick-kilns in this field they cook whatever meat and potatoes they plunder from the various shops in the neighbourhood'.[6]

The relatively high range of living costs at a time of wage cuts and severe unemployment caused the government to release from bond large stocks of grain. By the end of the year retail prices were lower; but, on the whole, the difficulties had been accentuated by their failure to fall more rapidly.[7] The rise in real wages of London artisans in 1826 probably over-estimates the net fall in living costs.

The course of labour during the period 1822–6 thus conforms closely to a normal cyclical pattern. The early stages were perhaps made less eventful than usual by the low level of retail prices. But the strikes of 1824–5 closely fit the industrial picture of 'full employment'; the difficulties of 1826 are clearly part of the general stagnation. The repeal of the Combination Acts and the high level of foodstuffs prices in 1826—factors distinctive to the period—tended to accentuate unrest on either side of the turning-point.

---

[1] *A.R.*, 1826, p. 1.
[2] Ibid., Chr., p. 67.
[3] Ibid., pp. 109–12.
[4] Ibid., p. 115.
[5] Ibid., pp. 141, 149, 151.
[6] Ibid., p. 141.

[7] Baines (p. 438) gives the following examples, from Manchester, which, in some cases, show a rise from 1825 to 1826.

	1825		1826	
	s.	*d.*	*s.*	*d.*
Beef (best: per lb.) . .	0	7½	0	6½
Beef (coarse: per lb.) .	0	4½	0	4¾
Cheese (per lb.) . .	0	7	0	7½
Bacon (per lb.) . .	0	8	0	7½
Bread flour (per 12 lb.) .	2	2	2	5

See also Tooke, ii. 136, on food prices relatively high 'in the distressed state of the manufacturing population'.

PART II: 1827–32

1. Prices. The domestic price index is, from 1827 to 1832, remarkably steady. Its movement reveals neither a sustained cycle nor a pronounced secular trend, although its predominant tendency is downward.

From its low point, in July 1826, the index recovers mildly to April 1827, declining then to June 1828. Although non-agricultural prices, for the most part, either ceased to decline or rose slightly in the last quarter of 1826 and the early months of 1827, the movement of the index is to be associated with fluctuations in the grain supply. It had been believed that the harvest of 1826 would be inadequate; and the government released considerable quantities of stored grain. Fully 5 million quarters of foreign grain, moreover, were admitted in 1826–7.[1] Thus, when the crop of 1827 appeared promising, the grain markets broke: the wheat price was 60s. per quarter in August 1827, 52s. in December. The domestic index, however, turns downward earlier in the year (April). At about that time non-agricultural commodities (hides, iron bars, camphor, rape oil, tin, &c.) resumed their slow decline, as did the more heavily weighted price of oats. These prices determine the turning-point in the index, although the principal fluctuation was in wheat.

A second upward movement in the index runs from June 1828 to January 1829. Even more completely, that rise represents a fluctuation in the price of wheat and associated commodities: wheat was 56s. per quarter in July 1828, 75s. six months later. An extremely wet summer in 1828 inaugurated the rise.[2] The quality of the wheat was poor, its quantity inadequate. But the corn market pushed the price above the import limit, and somewhat underestimated the available supply of old wheat. Foreign wheat poured in, the warehouses were opened, and farmers, anxious to take advantage of the high range of prices, rushed their crops to the markets.[3] By November 1829 the wheat price was down to 56s. There were once again agricultural petitions for relief.[4] The downward trend in the index is broken by brief revivals with peaks in August 1830 and March 1831. These movements were again connected primarily with fluctuations in the price of wheat. In 1830 and 1831 the harvests were inadequate and large-scale imports were required.[5] In 1832, however, 'the harvest was well secured, and the yield was reported, upon the whole, to be abundant. As, therefore, the previous prices had been those of deficiency, so, upon the restoration of abundance, they naturally fell.'[6] In February 1831 wheat was at 74s. per quarter, in November 1832, at 53s.

There was, in 1828 and the first months of 1829, some measure of general recovery, which is reflected in minor increases in non-agricultural domestic prices. In the following year, however, they continued their decline. The

---

[1] Tooke, ii. 139 n.
[2] Ibid., p. 194.
[3] Ibid., pp. 195–6.
[4] Ibid., pp. 197–8.
[5] Ibid., p. 205 n.
[6] Ibid., pp. 203–4.

extent of the fall from the peak in 1825, to the low point in 1832 (November), as well as the brief recovery in 1828–9 are revealed in the following table:

	Apr. 1825	Dec.[a] 1826	July 1828	High point 1828–9	Nov. 1832
Sunderland coal (s. per chaldron) . .	34·4	32·1	33·8	(Jan. 1829) 37·9	29·8
Iron bars (£ per ton)	15·8	10·5	8·4	(Feb. 1829) 8·5	6·0
Iron pigs (£ per ton)	12·5	8·0	5·0	(Jan. 1829) 5·0	4·4
Lead pigs (£ per ton)	28·0	22·0	18·0	(Dec. 1828) 19·0	13·0
Leather butts (pence per lb.). . .	23·5	22·5	22·5	(Feb. 1829) 23·7	19·0
Linseed oil (£ per ton)	25·0	24·0	22·2	(Feb. 1829) 26·5	32·0
Sal-ammoniac (s. per cwt.) . . .	95·0	92·0	89·0	(Jan. 1829) 83·0	61·0
Unmelted tallow (s. per cwt.) . .	45·3	50·2	40·0	(Jan. 1829) 45·0	47·0
Block tin (s. per cwt.)	104·0	82·0	74·0	(May 1829) 80·0	72·0
Alum (£ per ton)	14·5	15·5	15·2	(Jan. 1829) 15·2	9·5

[a] The figure for Dec. 1826 is included because the decline from the peak in 1825 to the end of the following year may be attributed largely to a reaction from the previous speculative advance. It does not, properly, constitute a part of the secular fall.

The movements are by no means uniform. In most cases, however, a substantial fall is recorded, from 1825 to 1832. This fall is shared by manufactured textiles. Typical is the price of calico, which sold in Manchester during 1825 (average) at 8s. 5¼d. per piece; in 1832, at 5s. 8d.[1] The prevailing downward trend in the prices of manufactured domestic goods is a major feature of these years. The following sections of the *History* will attempt more fully to account for this persistent decline. The forces at work may be summarized briefly as follows :[2]

1. The tremendous expansion of plant in 1824–5.
2. The introduction of new machinery, even after 1825.
3. The steady fall in the prices of imported raw materials which accompanied the progressive opening of new sources of supply, and a reduction in freight rates.
4. A decline in money wages and interest rates.
5. The absence of any concentrated large-scale new investment; the lack, in short, of any equivalent for the new floatations and other types of investment of 1824–5.

[1] Baines, p. 356.
[2] See Tooke, ii. 209–14, for an account of the price fall in this period in terms of 'increased powers of supply' due to the introduction of machinery and new, cheaper sources for raw materials: 'In the case of every one of the articles that fell in price, there was actual or prospective abundance, or increase of quantity compared with the previous ordinary rate of supply, and actual or supposed diminution of the cost of production to account for such fall.' (Ibid., p. 212.)

From 1827 to 1832 the import index, like non-agricultural domestic commodities, shows a persistent tendency to fall. There are slight increases in the third quarter of 1827, the fourth quarter of 1828, and the early months of 1831, the peaks of which are successively lower. In the case of cotton, silk, flax, indigo, coffee, sugar, and other colonial produce Tooke accounts for the decline by reference to the large stocks accumulated in the period 1827–30; in the case of lead, tin, and copper, the expanded mining resources, not only within Britain, but also in Spain, Russia, South America, and Cuba.

The outstanding feature of the index, aside from its decline, is the relative steadiness of the movement. Although foreign trade increased, there was no boom. Occasional apprehensions of a shortage of supply were quickly disappointed :[1]

There had, at different times during the fall, been a rally of markets from the influence of opinion that they had seen their lowest. Under the influence of this opinion, the importers and manufacturers were occasionally induced to extend their stocks; but fresh supplies, at a reduced cost, repeatedly disappointed their expectations, and entailed losses upon their previous purchases. The repetition of disappointments naturally abated confidence in the maintenance of markets, and the usual buyers became discouraged from embarking freely, even at the reduced prices, by a feeling of distrust, from having been before mistaken as to the probable sources of supply, and the lowest possible cost of production.

This picture of the large commodity markets describes as well the tone of British industry as a whole: a general atmosphere of disappointment, unrelieved by the promise of rising prices and profits.

2. Foreign Trade. The quantity of Britain's foreign trade shows a remarkable rise in 1827, to a level sustained and even increased in the following years (in £ millions):

	Volume of			Value of
	Total imports[a]	Re-exports	Domestic exports	domestic exports
1826	43·8	7·4	20·9	31·5
1827	53·2	7·6	25·8	37·2
1828	53·1	7·5	26·6	36·8
1829	51·3	7·7	27·8	35·8
1830	54·1	7·1	29·7	38·3
1831	58·4	8·2	30·3	37·2
1832	50·6	8·4	32·5	36·5

[a] Wheat and wheat flour imports moved as follows (in 1,000 quarters):

1826	582·3	1829	1,671·1	1831	2,310·4
1827	306·6	1830	1,676·0	1832	464·1
1828	757·7				

A substantial part of the rise in the official value of imports to 1831, their sharp decline in 1832, can be related to these figures, and the chronically inadequate British harvests.

[1] Ibid., pp. 213–14.

The real value of exports, however, indicates the extent to which the fall in prices affected the gross income of British exporters. In 1827 the official value was well above the peak in 1824; the real value does not surpass the figure for its previous high point (1825) until 1833.

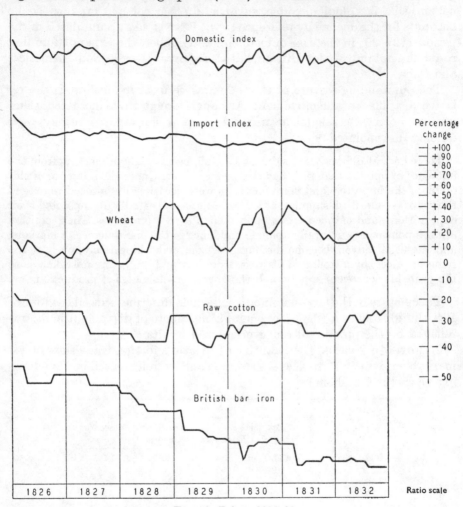

FIG. 58. Prices, 1826–32

These movements are to be explained by reference to the position of specific British markets (in £ millions): see table opposite. In 1827 each of these sub-groups, with the exception of southern Europe, shows an increase, that of the United States being much the most important. In 1828 the substantial decline in the real value of exports to the United States (where the new tariff went into effect), the lesser decline in the European markets, outweigh the increase in shipments to Latin America. The official value increases by less than £1 million. In 1829 the

					British North American colonies and W. Indies	Foreign W. Indies	Central and S. America (including Brazil)
	Northern Europe	Southern Europe	Africa	Asia	U.S.A.			

Value of Domestic Exports to

	Northern Europe	Southern Europe	Africa	Asia	U.S.A.	British North American colonies and W. Indies	Foreign W. Indies	Central and S. America (including Brazil)
1826	7·8	6·1	0·3	4·3	4·7	4·6	0·6	3·2
1827	8·5	5·9	0·7	4·8	7·0	5·0	0·9	4·0
1828	8·2	5·5	0·7	4·9	5·8	5·0	0·8	5·5
1829	8·3	6·2	0·8	4·2	4·8	5·2	1·0	4·9
1830	8·4	7·2	0·9	4·5	6·1	4·7	0·9	5·2
1831	7·3	6·2	0·8	4·1	9·1	4·7	1·0	3·6
1832	9·9	5·7	0·9	4·2	5·5	4·5	1·2	4·3

rise of over £3·5 million in the official value is explained largely by increased sales to Europe, Africa, and the colonial areas in America, although the effect of the fall in prices was further to reduce the total real value. All markets, with the exception of the American colonial areas, show a recovery in 1830, which caused an increase of about £2 million in real value, £5 million in the official figures. If one were to attempt to delineate a cyclical pattern in the foreign trade statistics, 1830 would appear as the peak in a movement, the trough of which lies in 1826. The sales to the United States and the foreign West Indies, alone, increase in 1831; a decline is recorded in every other instance. A sharp recovery in the real value of shipments to northern Europe, in 1832, is set off against a decisive fall in the purchases of the United States. The South American markets also recover somewhat in that year. But again the real value declines, although the official figure is at a new high level.

There is no simple sequence to be discerned in this complex tale. The figures for the United States alone show a clear cyclical pattern with troughs in 1826 and 1829, peaks 1827 and 1831.[1] There are important fluctuations, as well, in exports to Latin America and the Continent; but they do not represent a major movement of any kind. In Britain's foreign trade these years were an interim of irregular progress in the face of declining prices and profits.

3. **Investment.** British investment, from 1827 to 1832, presents a strange contrast to the optimistic development which preceded 1825. Foreign loans and mining ventures virtually disappear from the market; railways and joint-stock companies were put forward on a much reduced scale; statistics of brick production, from 1827, fluctuate irregularly about a level well below the peak of 1824–5. The long term interest rate tended to fall. A *Circular to Bankers*, in 1832, commented as follows:[2] 'The general absence of speculation in the commercial affairs of England is, from the

[1] This fluctuation conforms to the description of the state of American prosperity given in Willard Thorp's *Business Annals*, p. 120. It fits as well the movement of the industrial price index constructed by W. B. Smith and A. H. Cole, *Fluctuations in Ameri-* *can Business, 1790–1860*, p. 65. That index recovers slightly in 1827, sags in 1828, falls sharply in 1829. It revives towards the close of 1830, continuing upward to the end of 1831, when it again falls away.

[2] Quoted, Hunt, p. 56.

extraordinary length in which it has been manifest, the most remarkable
feature in the history of commerce of the present time.'

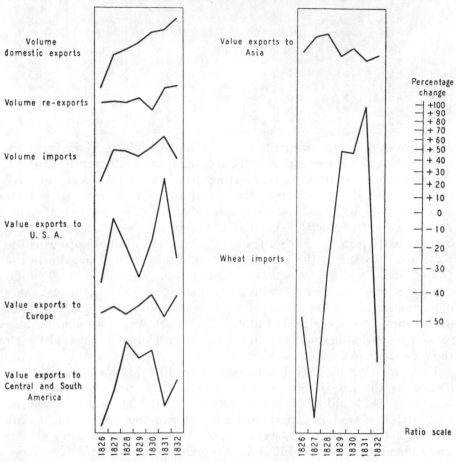

FIG. 59. Foreign Trade, 1826–32

The gains of 1824–5, however, were not completely lost. Railway construction and brick production were on a larger scale than in the years
before 1825. In the period 1827–32, 12 new lines were completed, 188 miles
in length, costing over £2 million.[1] The number of railway bills passed
through Parliament is impressive :[2]

	For new lines	For extension or enlarging powers of existing lines		For new lines	For extension or enlarging powers of existing lines
1827	1	5	1830	5	3
1828	5	5	1831	5	4
1829	5	4	1832	5	4

[1] Porter, p. 330.   [2] Ibid., p. 329.

The total of such bills in 1827–32 equals that for the period 1806–26, although it is dwarfed by the later figures. Similar, but less marked, is the movement of series reflecting the volume of construction. Brick production and timber imports, after the collapse in 1826, hover about the level of 1822–3. They do not return to the previous low point (1821):

	Production of bricks (in million bricks)	Quantity of fir timber imports (in 1,000 loads of 50 cu. ft.)
1826 . .	1,350·2	556
1827 . .	1,103·3	467
1828 . .	1,078·8	470
1829 . .	1,109·6	493
1830 . .	1,091·3	457
1831 . .	1,125·4	512
1832 . .	971·9	494

With the exception of 1828, these series move in the same direction, with 1829 and 1831 as minor peak years.[1]

Relative stagnation also appears in the figures for shipping tonnage belonging to the United Kingdom. The figure for total tonnage is consistently below the average of 1822–5:

(In 1,000 tons)

	Tonnage of shipping belonging to the United Kingdom	Tonnage of ships built and registered in the United Kingdom
1826 . .	2,382	118·4
1827 . .	2,150	93·1
1828 . .	2,161	88·7
1829 . .	2,168	76·6
1830 . .	2,169	75·5
1831 . .	2,191	83·9
1832 . .	2,225	90·2

New tonnage built, ignoring the minor expansion in general business activity of 1827–8, declines from 1826 to a trough in 1830, and then rises slightly in the two succeeding years. The figure for 1832, however, is slightly less than that for 1827 and far below the totals for 1825–6. The shipping industry remained, as chronically from 1815, a source of bitter complaint. In 1822, 1823, and 1825, under Huskisson's influence, the Navigation Acts had been relaxed.[2] In 1827 behind a barrage of petitions, the shipowners made an unsuccessful bid for a re-establishment of protection.[3] It was clear

[1] As in several other cases, the brick index here lags the movements of general business. Turning points came early in 1829 and 1831 for home trade generally (January and March, respectively).
[2] Smart, ii. 101–6.
[3] Ibid., pp. 423–4; also A.R., 1827, p. 161.

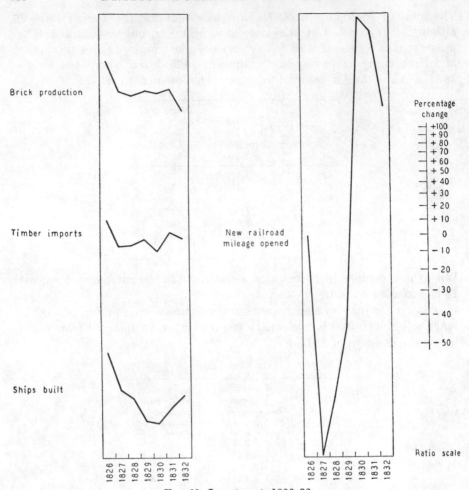

FIG. 60. Investment, 1826–32

that profits in shipping had fallen, and there was some excess capacity.[1] But that situation was virtually universal to British industry in these years.

[1] See Committee on Manufactures (1833), testimony of Edward Gibson, shipowner and builder, pp. 456 ff., for an account of the industry's over-expansion in 1824–6, the new competition it faced (1827–33), and the unprofitable level of shipping rates. The relative inferiority of new British to foreign ships and the adverse effects of the relaxation of the Navigation Acts were particularly emphasized. For similar testimony see Thomas Young (p. 476) and Robert Anderson (pp. 452–6). Anderson presented the following figures for the profits of two ships:

	Percival	Wellington
	£	£
Total profit	(1816–23) 4,557	(1818–24) 2,582*
,, ,,	(1824–31) 1,695†	(1825–31) 1,270‡

* including loss of £90 in 1819.   ‡ including loss of £342 in 1829.
† including loss of £119 in 1827.

The building of steamships, however, continued, like building and railway construction, as a modest outlet for new investment, at a higher level
than in the early twenties:

Steamships Built and Registered in the United Kingdom

	No.	Tons		No.	Tons
1820 .	8	655	1827 .	28	3,376
1821 .	22	3,008	1828 .	30	2,039
1822 .	27	2,449	1829 .	16	1,751
1823 .	19	2,469	1830 .	18	1,745
1824 .	17	2,234	1831 .	31	2,749
1825 .	24	3,003	1832 .	33	2,851
1826 .	72	8,638			

After 1825 the first foreign loans to be floated in London came in 1829 :[1]

	Country	Amount
		£
1829 .	Brazil	800,000
1830 .	Prussia	3,800,000
1831 .	Holland	500,000
1831 .	Portugal	2,000,000
1832 .	Belgium	—
1832 .	Portugal	600,000

Aside from Brazil, the South American borrowers drop from view.[2] It is
probable that Britain's holding of foreign securities actually declined in
1827–32. The abnormal grain imports necessitated by poor harvests (1828–
31) were financed in part by the sale of newly acquired international
securities.[3] But while Britain was recovering from her indiscretions in
Latin America, her investors were gradually increasing their interest and
holdings in securities of federal and state governments, canals, and banks
in the United States. The success of the Erie Canal (1826) had stirred promotional activity there, and the new issues were beginning to find their way
to London.[4] Although this process had, by 1832, not gone far, it foreshadowed a major characteristic of the ensuing boom (1832–6).

Joint-stock floatations also decreased drastically after 1825. The legislation of 1826, however, opened the field of joint-stock banking :[5]

Number of Banks Established

1826 .	. 3	1830 .	. 1
1827 .	. 3	1831 .	. 7
1828 .	. –	1832 .	. 7
1829 .	. 7		

[1] Spackman, *Statistical Illustrations of the British Empire*, p. 111.

[2] Brazil alone, among the large borrowers of 1824–5, was not in default of interest in 1826 (Jenks, p. 58).

[3] Ibid., pp. 61–2.

[4] Ibid., pp. 73–7.

[5] See below, pp. 441 ff., for an account of new enterprise in joint-stock banking after the legislation of 1826.

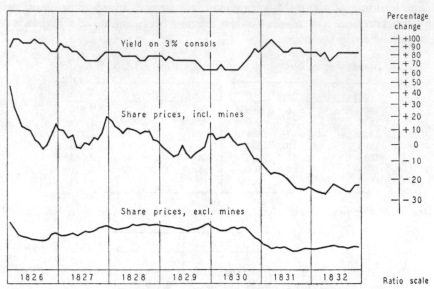

FIG. 61. Investment, 1826–32

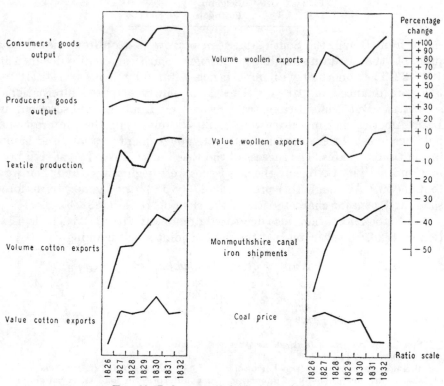

FIG. 62. Industry and Agriculture, 1826–32

In public utilities and within each industry there is further evidence of a continued increase in fixed capital; but the movement was sporadic. There was no general promotional boom.

The course of security prices presents a similar picture of somewhat stagnant stability. From the low point to which prices fell in the third quarter of 1826 a mild recovery begins, which continued irregularly throughout 1827–8. Our index of security prices (exclusive of mines) and the prices of Bank Stock and Consols concur in this mild upward trend. India Stock, however, after recovering until August 1827, declines sharply to October 1829. Bank Stock, Consols, and the security index continue to rise, the latter two reaching a peak in December 1829, the former, two months later.[1] In the last quarter of 1829 and the first quarter of 1830, India Stock revived as well. Until the latter months of 1830, security prices sagged slightly. But with the growth of agitation for political reform,[2] all prices fell quickly, remaining at new low levels throughout 1831–2.[3] The revolution of 1830, in France and Belgium, as well as the Russo-Polish war, contributed to the pessimism reflected in the decline.[4]

The prevailing trend in the long-term rate of interest was downward, until the break of the security markets late in 1830, as shown by the annual average per cent. yield on Consols:

1826	.	. 3·78	1830	.	. 3·35
1827	.	. 3·56	1831	.	. 3·69
1828	.	. 3·50	1832	.	. 3·56
1829	.	. 3·38			

In 1828–9 and 1831–2, however, the London money market was prevented, by a variety of external factors, from attaining the ease and confidence precedent to a boom in new floatations.[5]

4. Industry and Agriculture. Although evidence on the state of British industry suggests that there was no major cyclical movement from 1827 to 1832, the character of these years can be clearly defined. Evidence before the Committee of 1833—on cotton, wool, iron, and shipping—is remarkably unanimous in designating the period as one of falling prices and

---

[1] The rise, from the middle of 1828 to the middle of 1829, is in all cases very slight. This is probably to be associated with the tightness of the money market, caused by gold drains to Russia (at war with Turkey), to the United States (in reaction from 'over-trading' in 1827), to Ireland (because of a run on the Provincial Bank) and, generally, in payment for the large grain imports then necessary (Tooke, ii. 216–18).

[2] Ibid., p. 219, refers to 'the political disquiet and distrust which prevailed in this country from the first agitation of the reform question in November, 1830, to the final passing of the bill in the spring of 1832'.

[3] Typical of the effect of the reform agita-

tion on security prices is the following dispatch in the City article of the *London Times*, 4 March 1831: 'It would appear from the further decline in the funds which has taken place to-day, that the alarmists, who endeavour to work on the fears of the timid and ignorant stockholder in regard to the great question of reform, are making a greater impression than most people here were at first disposed to anticipate. The sales to-day have been extremely heavy, and prices of all descriptions of stock are lower.'

[4] Tooke, ii. 219; also Browning, pp. 459–60.

[5] See below, *Finance*.

profits, increasingly severe competition, rising output.[1] Fixed plant had been expanded in all directions in the boom which ended in 1825; and, even in the following years, there was a strong cost-reducing incentive to take advantage of new technical possibilities. The cost of machinery and construction, moreover, was falling, and long-established firms faced the competition of new plants, better equipped and more cheaply constructed.[2] For many manufacturers they were extremely difficult years.[3] A falling value for fixed capital had steadily to be accepted.

These were the underlying trends from 1815, and perhaps earlier. They lie at the heart of the secular process called the Industrial Revolution. An extraordinarily inflated state of demand was required in the middle twenties, thirties, and forties to yield, and then only briefly, rising prices and profit margins.

The strong secular forces operating to increase output and to reduce prices are strikingly revealed in the foreign trade figures for cotton :[4]

Quantity of Raw Cotton Imports
(In million lb.)

1826	.	.	177·6	1830	.	.	264·0
1827	.	.	272·4	1831	.	.	288·7
1828	.	.	227·8	1832	.	.	286·8
1829	.	.	222·8				

Exports of Cotton Manufactures
(In £ millions)

	Manufactured goods		Twist and yarn		Total	
	Official value	Declared value	Official value	Declared value	Official value	Declared value
1826 . .	21·4	10·5	3·7	3·5	25·2	14·0
1827 . .	29·2	14·0	4·0	3·5	33·2	17·5
1828 . .	29·0	13·5	4·5	3·6	33·5	17·1
1829 . .	31·8	13·4	5·5	4·0	37·3	17·4
1830 . .	35·4	15·2	5·7	4·1	41·1	19·3
1831 . .	33·7	13·2	5·7	4·0	39·4	17·2
1832 . .	37·1	12·6	6·7	4·7	43·8	17·3

[1] There is an obvious analogy between the state of British industry in these years and that which prevailed chronically in the two decades after 1873. Testimony before the Committee of 1833 is remarkably similar to that before the Committee on the Depression of 1886. See H. L. Beales, 'The "Great Depression" in Trade and Industry', *Economic History Review*, 1934, and W. W.

1826	.	.	2,590	1820	.	.	1,385
1827	.	.	1,372	1821	.	.	1,268
1828	.	.	1,214	1822	.	.	1,132
1829	.	.	1,656	1823	.	.	988
1830	.	.	1,308	1824	.	.	999
1831	.	.	1,433				
1832	.	.	1,365				

[4] Baines, pp. 347 and 350.

Rostow 'Investment and the Great Depression', *Economic History Review*, 1938.

[2] See especially testimony of John Brooke, wool cloth manufacturer, pp. 115–18.

[3] The heavy burden of overhead costs under these circumstances produced a level of bankruptcies chronically above that typical of years of greater profitability (annual totals: *London Gazette*):

1833	.	.	1,020
1834	.	.	1,101
1835	.	.	1,032

The quantity of exports declined only in 1831, although there was but a slight increase in 1828. The official value of exports in 1832 is far above that in 1824–5;[1] the real value about £1 million lower.

Prices of cotton, raw and manufactured, moved as follows:[2]

	Average selling price of 30-hanks water-twist of common quality (per lb.)	*Average selling price of a 40-hanks cop weft (per lb.)*	*Average selling price of a four-cut warp*	*Price of raw cotton including duty (Berbice)*	*Average selling price of 3rd 74's calico*
	s. d.	*s. d.*	*s. d.*	*(pence per lb.)*	*s. d.*
1826	1 1	1 1	11 2½	7·6	6 3¼
1827	1 0½	1 0½	10 3¼	6·8	6 6
1828	1 0⅛	0 11¾	10 0½	6·3	6 5¼
1829	1 0½	0 11¾	9 9¼	6·5	5 8
1830	1 0¼	1 0¼	10 1½	6·8	6 3¼
1831	0 10½	0 11¼	9 1½	6·7	6 2¼
1832	0 11¾	0 11¼	9 8¾	7·2	5 8

An increase in productivity, as well as a decline in raw-material prices, helped produce this fall. It is roughly indicated in the following table, which compares spinning costs in 1812 and 1830. The wage rate has been estimated as the same in both years, 20*d.* a day for every person employed, man, woman, or child:[3]

Spinning Costs of English Cotton Yarn

Description of yarn	*Hanks per day per spindle*		*Price of cotton and waste per lb.*		*Labour per lb.*		*Cost per lb.*	
	1812	*1830*	*1812*	*1830*	*1812*	*1830*	*1812*	*1830*
No.			*s. d.*	*s. d.*	*s. d.*	*s. d.*	*s. d.*	*s. d.*
40	2·00	2·75	1 6	0 7	1 0	0 7½	2 6	1 2½
60	1·75	2·50	2 0	0 10	1 6	1 0½	3 6	1 10½
80	1·50	2·00	2 2	0 11¼	2 2	1 7½	4 4	2 6¾
100	1·40	1·80	2 4	1 1¾	2 10	2 2½	5 2	3 4¼
120	1·25	1·65	2 6	1 4	3 6	2 8	6 0	4 0
150	1·00	1·33	2 10	1 8	6 6	4 11	9 4	6 7
200	0·75	0·90	3 4	3 0	16 8	11 6	20 0	14 6
250	0·05	0·06	4 0	3 8	31 0	24 6	35 0	28 2

The reduction in costs resulted both from the fall in imported raw-material prices, upon the development of new cotton lands, and from the enlarged use of machinery; and, it was believed, 'still greater improvements have

[1] The increase in official value from the peak in 1824 to 1832 was 45 per cent.: the increase from the peak in 1815 to 1824, 35 per cent.

[2] Baines, pp. 355–6. The average price of twist was estimated at 16·5*d.* per lb. in the first half of 1826, 12·6 in the latter half of 1832 (ibid., p. 405).

[3] Quoted by Baines, p. 353. The table was furnished by a Mr. Kennedy, of Manchester, to a Parliamentary Committee on East India affairs, to illustrate relative production costs in England and in India.

been made in weaving, by which more goods are produced with the same expenditure of labour'.[1]

The low state of profits constituted a major subject of inquiry before the Committee of 1833. Speaking of the cotton industry, Kirkman Finlay attributed their decline 'certainly not to any want of demand, if we compare the demand now with the demand in any former period; but to an extremely extensive production with reference to the demand, arising out of a great competition, doubtless caused by the high rate of profit in former times, which, by attracting a large amount of capital to the business, has necessarily led to the low rate of profit we now see. . . . I think its character (i.e., that of the cotton industry) is one of great extension, of a rapid sale and activity, but making very moderate returns of profit.'[2] This view of the cotton trade was substantiated by other witnesses, many of whom were unable to view the decline from Finlay's handsome social perspective.[3]

The building of new textile factories, of course, declined considerably after 1825. The number of cotton mills in Manchester was 49 in 1823, 63 in 1826. By 1832 only five more mills were added to the total.[4] It is probable, however, that the introduction of machinery continued at a less retarded rate. The stickiness of the wages of factory workers provided an incentive to the extension of mechanical processes.[5]

Although exports increased in volume to successively higher levels, British manufacturers felt the pressure of increased competition abroad as well as at home: 'Now (1833) there is not a single country in which there is not a great manufacture of cotton carried on.'[6] France, Austria, Switzerland, and the United States (especially in 1824–5) had substantially increased the number and output of their mills.[7] The protectionist spirit bred under these conditions is typified by this quotation from the *Leeds Intelligencer*.[8] The writer was pleased by the American 'Tariff of Abomination'

[1] Idem.

[2] Evidence before Committee on Manufactures (1833), p. 35. An estimate of profit margins per piece (in pence) is the difference between the cost and selling price of calico in Manchester (Baines, p. 356):

1826 .	. 0½	1830 .	. −2¼
1827 .	. 2½	1831 .	. 1½
1828 .	. 0¾	1832 .	. −0¾
1829 .	. −3		

The average margin for the seven years previous to 1826 was 4¾d.

[3] Finlay's optimism, and the more reserved expressions of hope of some of the other witnesses, were partly due to a rise in prices and business prospects in the early months of 1833. Trade was clearly in a state of revival when the evidence was heard (pp. 65–6, 1072–3). Also Redford, p. 80: 'By 1833 there were some indications that trade (in

Manchester) had once more turned the corner.'

[4] Baines, p. 395.

[5] Report on Manufactures (1833), testimony of George Smith, p. 565. Also Porter, p. 188; and, on the use of machinery in Scottish weaving mills, Hamilton, p. 141. Hardly a year passed without some new improvement in textile machinery: Donnell, pp. 137, 146, 147, 167; Redford, p. 78.

[6] Kirkman Finlay, quoted by Hamilton, p. 148.

[7] In 1810 there were 102 cotton mills in the United States, in 1831, 795 (Donnell, pp. 65 and 157). The American tariff of 1828 was, of course, viewed as a blow to British industry, although its effects were probably slight (Smart, ii. 455 and 461–3).

[8] Smart, ii. 463 n. Also on protectionist agitation in 1829, ibid., pp. 457–65 and 493–5.

because he felt it once and for all had destroyed free trade and reciprocity :
'it absolutely knocks on the head—it turns into dust and ashes—it holds
up to the scorn of mankind, as a vile delusion and quackery, that accursed
cant of the present generation, that pest of nations, corrupter of the
human heart and bane of the human understanding—called Political
Economy'.

The persistent downward trend in prices and profits dominated the industrial reports for these years: nevertheless, minor fluctuations in the
position of the cotton industry can be traced. The year 1827 was clearly
one of general revival :[1] 'The different monied and manufacturing interests
of the kingdom, likewise, were rallying from the confusion of the preceding
eighteen months, by a progress, which, though slow, was sensible and sure.
. . . Employment was now furnished to the artizan in his ordinary calling,
so generally as to be almost universal.' In May 1827 the *Manchester Mer-
cury* described the market for manufactured goods as 'the briskest which
there has been for a very long time . . . and some further advance has, in
particular instances, been made to the wages of the weavers'; in August
the same journal reported the manufacturers of the West Riding as having
'attained to a steady and prosperous condition on the woollen cloth,
worsted stuff, linen and cotton branches . . . while prospects from abroad,
particularly in North and South America, are of the most favourable kind'.[2]
The year 1828 is chiefly distinguished, in British economic history, as the
year during which nothing happened. But among the 'scraps of information' Smart was able to glean is the fact that in February the cotton trade
was very active.[3] From the available statistical evidence it may be concluded that activity was on about the same or at a slightly higher level
than in the previous year.[4]

It was noted earlier that non-agricultural domestic prices and import
prices rose through the last quarter of 1828. The peak of the minor wave of
prosperity which began towards the close of 1826 seems to come in the
early months of 1829. Smart titles the year 'Sudden Relapse into Deep
Distress';[5] the *Annual Register* refers to 'the depression in every branch of
trade'.[6] Although a principal source of unrest appear to have been a rise in
foodstuff prices, industrial reports indicate a brief recession, with evidence
of recovery towards the close of the year.[7] By March 1830 all the principal
textile districts agreed 'in affirming that trade was improving and that
wages were rising. In some places there was a scarcity of weavers. . . . In
moving the Address on November 2nd, the Marquis of Bute said that every
day brought fresh proof of increasing activity in the manufacturing districts . . . there was not a man who did not now find full employment. . . .

[1] *A.R.*, 1827, pp. 1-2.
[2] Redford, p. 78.
[3] Op. cit. ii. 455.
[4] Smart calls 1827 a year of 'revival',
1828, of 'steady progression'.

[5] Op. cit. ii. 466. See below, *Finance*, for
the part played by monetary stringency in
this 'sudden relapse'.
[6] 1829, p. 131.
[7] Smart, ii. 471-2.

By the end of the Year (1830), the improvement, at least in everything outside of agriculture, was beyond question.'[1]

Cotton export statistics show a clearly defined slump in 1831. The turning-point came in the early months of the year (March).[2] This can be attributed largely to political difficulties on the Continent and within Britain. The agitation for the Reform Bill, and pressure on the money market caused by the withdrawal of funds to Paris and other centres, placed serious restraints on both home and foreign markets.[3] There was as well a minor financial crisis in the American markets, followed by a decline in exports there. In 1832, however, a general recovery movement slowly got under way, with prices tending to rise in the latter months. A new wave of cotton-factory building can be dated from that year.[4]

As the statistical evidence has shown, the fluctuations described here were not of very great amplitude. For cotton textiles, and industry in general,[5] there was mild recovery in 1827–8, a slump in 1829, a recovery in 1830 and the first few months of 1831, a second slump in 1831–2, with the first signs of recovery appearing as the period ends.[6] It should be remembered, however, that, in cotton, these were fluctuations about a steadily rising upward trend in output.

Falling prices, increased output, and minor fluctuations also distinguish the woollen industry from 1827 to 1832.

	Quantity of raw wool imports (in million lb.)	Exports of woollen manufactures	
		Official value	Declared value
		(in £ millions)	
1826 . .	16·0	5·0	5·0
1827 . .	29·1	6·0	5·2
1828 . .	30·2	5·7	5·1
1829 . .	21·5	5·4	4·6
1830 . .	32·3	5·6	4·7
1831 . .	31·7	6·2	5·4
1832 . .	28·1	6·7	5·5

The increase in output achieved during these years of relative stagnation

[1] Smart, ii. 511–12. But even in the recovery of 1830 there was still sufficient unemployment and 'distress', because of the high prices of foodstuffs, to warrant reference in the King's speech (Tooke, ii. 197–8).

[2] At the beginning of 1831 the *Westminster Review* was still able to speak of the general prosperity of industry (Jan. 1831, xiv. 244); in December the King's speech lamented 'the distress which prevails in many parts of my dominions' as well as the 'lack of employment' (*A.R.*, 1832, p. 2).

[3] Tooke, ii. 218–19. Also *A.R.*, 1832, pp. 2 and 182–3, for an account of debates on distress in the closing months of 1831. An

additional cause of relative depression in 1831–2 was the failure of a number of trading houses in Calcutta (Tooke, ii. 213 n.).

[4] Porter, p. 188.

[5] The recovery of 1830 was only slightly shared by the iron and associated trades. They were seriously depressed from 1828 to 1832. See below, pp. 231–4.

[6] It is to be noted that this description conforms almost exactly to the movement of the bankruptcy series. Bankruptcies declined in 1827–8, rose sharply in 1829, declined in 1830, rose again, moderately, in 1831, declined in 1832.

was probably less than in cotton manufactures. It is roughly indicated by
the following figures, which compare the quantity of various types of exports in 1831–2 with the previous major peak, in 1824.[1]

	1824	1831–2
Cloth of all sorts (pieces)	407,720	436,143 (1831)
Stuffs, woollen or worsted (pieces) . .	1,242,403	1,800,714 (1832)
Hosiery (dozens)	113,123	152,810 (1832)

This increase was not shared by all branches of the export trade. Several
declined considerably, but, in net, as the official value figures show, more
woollens were being shipped abroad in 1831–2 than at the peak in 1824
(£6·2 million).

Domestic raw wool prices moved, generally, slightly upward from 1827
to 1832, although the price of imported (Saxon) wool declined :[2]

(Pence per lb.)

	Saxon imported	South-down	Kent long		Saxon imported	South-down	Kent long
1826 . .	73·8	10·4	11·0	1830 . .	73·0	10·5	10·5
1827 . .	70·0	9·1	10·5	1831 . .	70·0	12·2	10·5
1828 . .	73·0	9·0	12·0	1832 . .	59·2	12·8	12·5
1829 . .	73·0	7·4	9·0				

In every case, however, raw wool prices were, in 1832, well below the peak
in 1825. The decline in manufactured woollen prices was, probably, fairly
continuous until the close of 1832.[3]

The most substantial evidence on the character of the woollen trade in
these years is again the testimony before the Committee of 1833 :[4]

[Henry Hughes] 1303. Then do the present prices of wool indicate an unfavourable state of trade for the manufacturers ?—Although the present price of
wool is much higher than it has been for many years, still the manufacturers
are certainly in as healthy a condition, and more so than they have been for
many years past; there is less distress among the master manufacturers. 1304.
Will you explain what you mean by a healthy state ?—I mean by the factories
being well employed, and their cloths sold almost as soon as they are brought
to market. 1305. Do you mean that they make more profit than they did at any
time within the last few years ?—I think their profit is generally small. 1306. Did
you ever know it so small as it is at present ?—I have no knowledge of their
real profit; but it is generally understood that they are working at less profit
than they have been for many years, from the great competition there is in the

---

[1] Porter, p. 168.

[2] The rise in the price of domestic wool
(1829–32) is attributed by Tooke (ii. 200–1)
to the effects of 'a rot which had prevailed
among the sheep, as a consequence of the
preceding wet seasons'.

[3] Committee on Manufactures (1833),

testimony of Henry Hughes, wool broker,
p. 82: '1315. Has the price of cloth decreased
within the last three or four years ?—It has
till recently, when it is on the increase
again'; also John Brooke, woollen cloth
manufacturer, ibid., p. 152.

[4] Ibid., pp. 82, 117, 118, 152.

woollen trade. 1307. Then the healthy state you speak of does not arise from the profits the manufacturers are getting, but from the extent of the business ?— The extent of the business, and the ready demand for goods. 1895. Do you think the annual profit attending the employment of capital in those mills (woollen) is sufficient to keep up the value of the capital sunk in the buildings and machinery ?—Decidedly so ; but it depends upon what time the mill was built ; we must take everything at the present value. Some machinery is now bought at a cheaper rate than formerly, it is merely owing to the fall in the market, just the same as any other commodity ; there is a great fall in the value of some machinery ; for example, a patent may have run out, and in consequence, it will be much cheaper. 1905. Has any change taken place of late years with respect to the extent of the domestic manufacture in Yorkshire ?—I should think it has rather increased. 1906. To what do you attribute that ?—I can hardly tell ; there is of course an increased demand for clothing in consequence of increased population. 2317. And therefore, when you say that profits remain much the same as usual, you allude to the last seven years ?—I mean to say that profits are at present smaller than what I have known them to be, which I entirely attribute to competition, and to no other cause.

In 1827–9 the chronic battle between British wool growers and manufacturers continued.[1] The former complained of the rising quantity of foreign wool imported, and the consequently low price of the British growth : the latter held that even with raw wool prices at a low level, their margin of profit was inadequate ; and that an increase in the import duty would involve the loss of substantial foreign markets. The government refused to raise the duty.

Such cyclical movement in the woollen industry as can be discerned differs somewhat from that in cotton. It would appear that the gains of 1827 were not fully maintained in 1828. This minor decline in the quantity of exports probably resulted from the passage of the American tariff, which was designed especially to protect the budding woollen industry against British goods ;[2] and to a reaction from the over-stocking of the American market in an effort to sell as much as possible there before the tariff went into effect. The passage of the Act 'cast a gloomy shadow over the woollen trade'.[3] There is little doubt that the industry shared the general decline of 1829 and the recovery towards the end of the year.[4] Export statistics show a steady recovery from 1829 to 1832. It would appear that the generally depressing political and financial forces which operated in 1831–2 did not affect wool to the same extent as cotton manufactures ; although the American trade, a principal source of revival in 1830, was somewhat less profitable in 1831.[5] By the early months of 1833 an increase in prices added a touch of optimism to reports on the trade,

[1] Smart, ii. 422–3, 458–9.
[2] Ibid., p. 461.
[3] Ibid., p. 455.
[4] Ibid., pp. 466–73.
[5] Committee on Manufactures (1833), testimony of Joshua Bates, p. 48, '787. Was

not the export trade from this country in woollens to America, in the year 1830, a very lucrative trade ?—I think it was. 788. Was 1831 equally so ?—I should think not ; one of those years was profitable, and the following one not very profitable.'

an optimism which was previously lacking even when sales were being expanded.[1]

The indexes of textiles and consumers' goods production move as follows:

	Kondratieff's index of textile production	Hoffmann's index of consumers' goods production			Kondratieff's index of textile production	Hoffmann's index of consumers' goods production
1826 .	15·0	13·8	1830 .		21·9	19·4
1827 .	20·5	16·7	1831 .		22·3	19·6
1828 .	18·5	18·2	1832 .		22·1	19·4
1829 .	18·3	17·3				

Their fluctuation conforms, in general, to the account of the cotton and woollen industries presented above, with the exception of the decline in 1832. The quantity of exports of both commodities increased in that year, although imports of foreign wool and the consumption of raw cotton declined. This explains the slight fall in the textile production figure for 1832. A similar decline appears in the Hoffmann index of consumers' goods production, which differs from the Kondratieff index principally in its rise in 1828. The heavy weight given to the quantity of cotton exports (which rose in 1828) is, almost certainly, responsible for this divergence. The two series share the low point in 1829, and show a similar net increase from 1827 to 1832.

Data on the iron industry in these years also tell a story of a generally higher level of output accompanied by falling prices and profits:

	Estimates of total production[a] (in tons)	Price of British pig-iron (£ per ton)	Monmouth-shire Canal iron shipments (in 1,000 tons)	Exports of iron, hardware, and cutlery[b]	
				Volume	Value
				(in £ millions)	
1826 . .	581,367 (1825)	8·1	69·8	1·9	2·3
1827 . .	690,000	6·9	91·6	2·3	2·6
1828 . .	703,184	5·2	110·9	2·4	2·6
1829 . .	—	4·8	116·5	2·5	2·5
1830 . .	678,417	5·1	112·6	2·7	2·5
1831 . .	(590,000)	4·9	119·2	3·0	2·7
1832 . .	(500,000)	4·6	124·2	3·3	2·6

[a] Estimates of total iron production are thoroughly confusing in this period. The figures given here for 1825, 1828, and 1830 are Scrivenor's (p. 136). Porter (p. 271) presents estimates for the same years: that for 1825 coincides with Scrivenor's, those for 1828 and 1830 are slightly less (702,584 and 653,417 tons, respectively). In testimony before the Committee on Manufactures (p. 574) Samuel Walker, iron proprietor in Staffordshire, quoted roughly the same figures as Porter's for 1828 and 1830, but 613,000 tons for 1825. He added the estimates for 1831 and 1832 which are decidedly suspect in their drastic decline. Walker may have been led to use them by his desire to impress the committee with the extent of the depression in the iron industry.

[1] Ibid., pp. 49 (Joshua Bates), 82 (Henry Hughes), 152 (John Brooke).

b The growing importance of exports to the iron industry may be roughly calculated by comparing the tonnage of exports to the estimates of total output:

		Per cent.
1825 . .	$\dfrac{69,828}{581,367}$	12
1828 . .	$\dfrac{112,365}{703,184}$	16
1830 . .	$\dfrac{130,417}{678,417}$	19

(Scrivenor, facing p. 424.)

Shipments on the Monmouthshire Canal and the quantity of exports increase steadily.[1] It is, nevertheless, probable that the home demand fell off to some extent, but hardly on the scale indicated by the estimates of output for 1831–2.

That conclusion is suggested as well by the following table, which gives the number of blast-furnaces erected in 1824–30 :[2]

	Blast-furnaces erected in						
	South Wales	Stafford-shire	Shrop-shire	York-shire	Derby-shire	North-umber-land and Durham	Totals
1824 . .	12	3	3	..	..	..	18
1825 . .	7	12	..	1	2	..	22
1826 . .	14	5	1	..	..	..	20
1827 . .	2	6	4	..	..	..	12
1828 . .	4	10	2	..	1	..	17
1829 . .	..	3	..	..	..	2	5
1830 . .	2	..	..	..	..	..	2

	South Wales	Stafford-shire	Shrop-shire	York-shire	Derby-shire	North-umber-land and Durham	Totals
1823							
No. of furnaces . . .	72	84	38	26	15	2	237
Pig-iron produced (in 1,000 tons)	182	134	58	27	14	2	418
1830							
No. of furnaces . . .	113	123	48	27	18	4	333
Pig-iron produced (in 1,000 tons)	278	213	73	29	18	5	616

The increase in the quantity made in the year 1830 over the quantity made in the year 1823 is 47½ per cent.

[1] Scrivenor (pp. 123 and 293) also gives figures for shipments on the Glamorganshire Canal, which, like the estimates for total production, decline from 1828 to 1831 (in 1,000 tons):

| 1826 . | . 60·1 | 1828 . | . 89·8 |
| 1827 . | . 84·9 | 1829 . | . 83·9 |

| 1830 . | . 81·5 | 1832 . | . 83·7 |
| 1831 . | . 70·3 | | |

[2] Ibid., p. 134. On the extension of iron-works after 1826, see also Evidence before Committee on Manufactures (1833), William Mathews, p. 576.

The impulse towards expansion would appear to have waned rapidly after 1828. From that year, it was stated, the iron industry ceased 'to make a fair return . . . wages have been reduced, but not in proportion to the reduction of the price of iron'.[1] The iron manufacturers, under pressure from the burden of fixed costs, incurred in previous expansion of plant, entered monopoly agreements to restrict output;[2] and they adopted, almost unanimously, a monetary explanation of the fall in prices which beset them.[3] The preamble to a statement submitted (4 October 1831) by the Staffordshire iron manufacturers to Earl Grey, First Lord of the Treasury, indicates the sources of this inflationary bias :[4]

1. That for the last five years, ever since what is called the Panic of 1825, we have found, with very slight intermissions, a continually increasing depression in the prices of the products of industry, and more particularly in those of pig-iron and bar-iron, which have fallen respectively from upwards of £8 per ton to under £3 per ton, and from £15 per ton to under £5 per ton.

2. Against this alarming and long continued depression, we have used . . . every possible improvement in the working of our mines and manufactories. Our workmen's wages have, in many instances, been greatly reduced, and such reduction has been attended with, and effected by, very great suffering and distress; but the royalties, rents, contracts and other engagements under which we hold our respective works and mines, have scarcely been reduced at all, nor can we get them effectually reduced, because the law enforces their payment in full.

3. The prices of the products of our industry having thus fallen within the range of the fixed charges and expenses which the law compels us to discharge, the just and necessary profits of our respective trades have ceased to exist; and in many cases a positive loss attends them.

4. If we should abandon our respective trades, our large and expensive outlays in machinery and erections must be sacrificed, at an enormous loss to ourselves, and our honest and meritorious workmen must be thrown in thousands upon parishes already too much impoverished by their present burdens to

---

[1] Evidence before Committee on Manufactures (1833), Samuel Walker, Staffordshire manufacturer, p. 571. Also, Anthony Hill of South Wales, p. 611; and William Sparrow of Stafford, p. 635, who described the state of the trade (1829–32) as 'dreadfully bad'.

[2] Ibid., pp. 581 and 609 (William Mathews and Anthony Hill). Such agreements were made in South Wales, Shropshire, and Staffordshire.

[3] Ibid., pp. 572 and 592–3 (Samuel Walker and William Mathews). The political unrest of 1830–2 also seems to have affected general confidence in the iron industry. (Anthony Hill, 10479): 'I think, in the first place, that the restoration of confidence through the country generally would have a material effect on the iron trade; I mean that confidence in the stability of the establishments and institu-

tions of the country which would assure security to property; capital would soon exhibit itself abundantly, and would as soon find useful employment' (p. 619).

[4] This statement was introduced into the evidence by Mathews (ibid., pp. 594–5). It blames the price deflation on an inadequate supply of money, which was traced to the Act of 1819 and the elimination of £1 and £2 notes. The analysis consisted largely in a statement of faith that monetary forces were responsible for the fall in prices. When confronted by the committee with the fact that money rates of interest were exceedingly low (ibid., pp. 592–3), Mathews could not resolve the inconsistency of his position. See also A.R., 1830, p. 68, for an account of the controversy over 'the state of the currency'.

support them ; and if we should continue our respective trades, we see nothing
but the prospect of increasing distress, and certain ruin to all around us.

In the face of the industry's expanded resources, the domestic demand
for iron was insufficient to maintain prices or full employment. The new
uses to which iron was being put—in railways, building, ships, gas and
waterworks—were still in evidence.[1] But in the state of general political
uncertainty and tight money which prevailed from 1830 to 1832, new
enterprise was virtually at a standstill, and the iron industry suffered in
consequence.

It is worth noting that during this period the hotblast was invented and
passed through its early experimental stages. Nielson's new method made
possible the extensive use of blackband ironstone deposits in Scotland,
and, in effect, created the modern Scottish iron industry.[2] That type of ore
had previously been regarded as worthless. It served as the basis for an
enormous relative expansion of output in Scotland during the years which
followed. The 'new era' in the Scottish iron industry began in 1828, with
the founding of the Gartsherrie Works by William Baird.[3]

Coastwise shipments from Newcastle and Sunderland, total exports,
and the annual average price of Sunderland coal follow :[4]

	Price of Sunderland coal (s. per chaldron)	Coastwise shipments		
		Total exports	Newcastle (in 1,000 tons)	Sunderland
1826 . .	34·7	223	2,100	1,456
1827 . .	35·5	244	1,812	1,387
1828 . .	34·5	228	1,921	1,350
1829 . .	33·4	241	1,957	(1,497)
1830 . .	34·0	357	2,167	(1,387)
1831 . .	29·3	356	2,098	(1,256)
1832 . .	29·2	415	1,809	(1,201)

It is probable that, like the iron industry, the coal industry was relatively
depressed, from about 1828.[5] In that year the owners reduced the guaranteed minimum wage from 15s. to 14s. per week ;[6] and in 1830 the guarantee
was withdrawn altogether 'by a section of the coalowners, with the result

---

[1] Evidence before Committee on Manufactures (1833), p. 576.

[2] Hamilton, pp. 179–83.

[3] Ibid., p. 183.

[4] Porter, pp. 278 and 281. There is no
figure available for total coal shipments to
ports in England, 1830-2, because of the
repeal of the coastwise duty on coals. The
custom-houses ceased to record the entrance
of coal shipments. From 1829 to 1833 the
exports from Sunderland are not divided
into coastwise and foreign shipments. The
figures in parentheses represent total shipments from Sunderland. Since exports to

foreign countries rose steadily, it is probable
that the decline in those figures (as in the
case of Newcastle) represents a decline in
coastwise shipments.

[5] It was estimated in 1829 that the Tyne
collieries were capable of producing as much
again and the Wear half as much again as
their current output (Sweezy, p. 112).

[6] Galloway, p. 465. It is interesting to
note that this guarantee of a minimum
wage appeared in an industry which was
dominated by monopoly arrangements limiting output and maintaining prices.

that in many collieries wages fell very low, as low as 8s. and 10s. per week, owing to want of work':[1] in 1831 and 1832 the miners, complaining of inadequate work and wages, staged major strikes.[2] The breakdown of monopolistic practices in the labour market due to unemployment may, then, properly be taken as evidence of a falling off in the home demand for coal.

It is even more significant that 1827 was afterwards regarded in the industry as the last year in the 'golden era' of successful monopoly regulation.[3] In 1828 the mine-owners on the Tyne and the Wear quarrelled, the former group, led by Lord Londonderry, having exceeded their allotted output. This friction was resolved; but, until the latter months of 1829, the mine-owners could not come to any agreement as to an appropriate basis for regulation. As a result the price of coal fell sharply, remaining at an abnormally low level from March to September.[4]

The public's fight against the coal monopoly brought the mine-owners together in 1830. A pamphleteer, hired by the Committee of Coal Operators, put their case, urging that there was no monopoly, that the coal owners were scarcely making any money, and that the root of the evil lay in taxes and government interference.[5] The government left the internal organization of the industry untouched, but eliminated the tax on coastwise shipments of coal.[6]

The successful colliers' strike of 1831 dominated the industry in that year. The union, which had been founded immediately after the repeal of the Combination Acts, forced a 30 per cent. rise in wages and a reduction in hours from 14, or even at times 16, to 12 per day.[7] In the latter months of the year the mines were busily employed completing orders obstructed by the strike. In 1832, having learned their lesson, the owners sent out recruiting agents to bring in 'strangers' to take the place of strikers. The disputes of that year resulted in clean-cut victory for the operators, 'as it appears certain that more strangers are inclined to offer their services than the trade can possibly employ'.[8] But, as we shall see, the turmoil of 1831–2 did a great deal to disrupt the functioning of the industry's internal regulation in the following two years.

Hoffmann's indexes of capital goods and total production for these years move as shown on p. 234. The figures for total production show adequately the net increase in output from 1827 to 1832, the slump in 1829, but an irregular recovery after that date. From the limited evidence

---

[1] Idem. (Quoted from *Report on the Coal Trade*, 1830, p. 274.)

[2] Ibid., pp. 464–70; Sweezy, pp. 96–101;

[4] The price of Sunderland coal moved as follows in 1829 (s. per chaldron):

Jan.	. 37·9	Apr.	. 30·7	July	. 31·5	Oct.	. 36·9
Feb.	. 34·1	May	. 31·5	Aug.	. 30·1	Nov.	. 33·6
Mar.	. 30·6	June	. 32·9	Sept.	. 33·2	Dec.	. 38·1

[5] Sweezy, p. 96 n.

[6] Smart, ii. 547–8 and 551.

[7] Sweezy, pp. 96–8; Galloway, pp. 464–7.

A.R., Chr., 1831, pp. 38–47.

[3] Sweezy, pp. 85–9.

[8] Quoted from the report of a recruiting agent to the Tyne Committee, 19 June 1832 (Sweezy, p. 100).

available on the coal and iron trades it would seem that the index of capital goods production (relying heavily on export statistics) presents too opti-

	Hoffmann's index of producers' goods production	Hoffmann's index of total production
1826 . .	5·8	9·5
1827 . .	6·0	10·9
1828 . .	6·1	11·6
1829 . .	6·0	11·2
1830 . .	6·0	12·1
1831 . .	6·2	12·2
1832 . .	6·3	12·2

mistic a view of the net movement of output in 1831–2. The rise in that index from 1830 to 1832 is partially determined, as well, by the slight recovery in shipbuilding.

The generally high range of agricultural prices from 1827 to 1832 relieved the farmer from the chronic pressure he had experienced since 1813.[1] The revision of the Corn Laws in 1828 (which instituted a sliding scale of duties) indicated that the farmer, in fact, was viewed as in a somewhat better position than other members of the community.[2] The working classes were restive, with food prices high and wages falling; the crash of 1825 had left the farmer relatively untouched;[3] and free-trade sentiment was growing. But until the sharp decline in wheat prices in 1832, the farmers' position was relatively good.[4]

5. Finance. With prices falling rapidly, new floatations at a low level, and output, at best, rising slowly, it was to be expected that the financial requirements of the economy should be on a relatively modest scale. This, in fact, was the case, despite the substitution of gold coin for small bank notes:[5]

[1] An exception noted above was the decline in the latter months of 1829, when the price of wheat fell to 56s. See above, *Prices*.

[2] Smart, ii. 408, 412–17, 437–9, 443, 492. Adams, pp. 122–4. The duty as established in the 1828 measure follows:

When the home price was	the 1828 Duty was		Duty proposed in the 1827 bill	
s.	s.	d.	s.	d.
52	34	8	40	8
53	33	8	38	8
54	32	8	36	8
55	31	8	34	8
56	30	8	32	8
57	29	8	30	8
58	28	8	28	8
59	27	8	26	8
60	26	8	24	8
61	25	8	22	8
62	24	8	20	8
63	23	8	18	8

When the home price was	the 1828 Duty was		Duty proposed in the 1827 bill	
s.	s.	d.	s.	d.
64	22	8	16	8
65	21	8	14	8
66	20	8	12	8
67	18	8	10	8
68	16	8	6	8
69	13	8	4	8
70	10	8	2	8
71	6	8	1	0
72	2	8	1	0
73	1	0	..	

[3] In 1826 it was reported that 'the agricultural interest had met with no material check by the recent difficulties' (Smart, ii. 435).

[4] For distress in 1832–3, see Macleod, p. 268.

[5] Tooke, ii. 214–15.

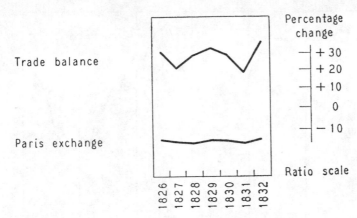

FIG. 63. Finance, 1826–32

The circulation, as far as related to the regulation by the Bank of its issues, was, in the interval now under consideration, in a more equable state than in any of the preceding epochs (with the exception of that between 1803 and 1808), notwithstanding that in this interval the suppression of the small note country circulation had been accomplished. And it should seem therefore that the substitution of the metals for those small notes had served only to absorb the gold which had flowed into the country by the balance of trade, and which would otherwise have created an incumbrance of treasure in the Bank of England in 1828, such as it experienced between 1821 and 1824.

The following figures afford a rough view of Britain's financial state during these years (in £ millions) :[1]

	Bullion in the Bank of England	Bills and notes discounted by the Bank of England	Bank of England notes in circulation	Total bills of exchange created	Market-rate of discount (per cent.)[a]
1826	5·4	5·5	22·3	196·0	4·50
1827	10·1	1·4	21·6	204·9	3·25
1828	9·7	1·3	21·0	211·0	3·04
1829	6·4	2·4	19·6	211·3	3·38
1830	9·5	1·6	20·5	198·2	2·81
1831	7·0	2·3	18·6	207·3	3·69
1832	6·8	2·2	18·1	194·1	3·15

[a] This is the rate on first-class bills of exchange discounted by Overend Gurney. The Bank-rate, in July 1827, was lowered to 4 per cent., where it remained until July 1836.

In the last quarter of 1828 and through most of 1829 the bullion stock at

[1] Tooke abstracted from the financial picture of these years, as its central feature, the fact that reserve fluctuations were on a much larger scale than fluctuations in discounts or notes. He praises the Bank for the elasticity of its policy with respect to its reserve proportion, emphasizing that the Bank should not, and in fact did not, govern its lending policy solely with regard to its bullion stock or exchange movements (ibid., pp. 216–24).

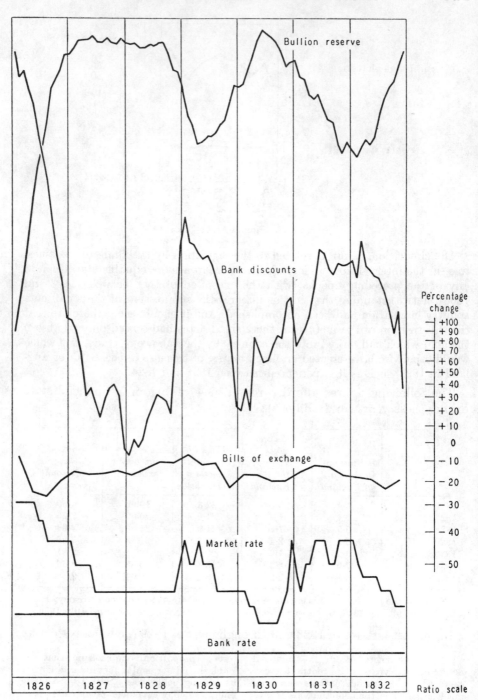

FIG. 64. Finance, 1826–32

the Bank fell off sharply, and the market-rate of interest rose. The pressures represented by these movements were the following :[1]

1. The completion of the substitution of metal coins for the small note country circulation.[2]
2. The withdrawal of about £1 million by Russia for expenditure in connexion with the war against Turkey.
3. Withdrawals in connexion with the liquidation of over-trading in the American markets.[3]
4. Payment for large grain imports.
5. A drain to Ireland of about £1 million in connexion with a run on the Provincial Bank.

The exchange on Paris began to weaken late in 1827, remained low throughout most of 1828, and recovered only with the period of tight money in London early in 1829. As the market-rate rose, from the latter months of 1828, an increasing number of borrowers came to the Bank of England. Discounts there increased from £0·85 million on 8 October 1828 to £4·8 million on 7 January 1829.[4] Pressure then gradually subsided, and the market-rate and the Bank's discounts fell. But this period of stringency almost certainly contributed to the sudden industrial relapse of 1829.

By the middle of 1830, however, the position of the Bank was strong, with bullion holdings of over £10 million, on 21 June. From that time until the spring of 1832, the Bank's reserve and the money-market were again strained. Revolution on the Continent, renewed drains to Ireland, large grain imports, and, above all, the 'political disquiet and distrust which prevailed in this country from the first agitation of the reform question' (November 1830), were responsible for the renewed stringency.[5] This

---

[1] Tooke, ii. 216–17. In the course of these drains Tooke notes (ibid., p. 218) that the Bank was advised that it would be impossible to maintain a gold standard and that some form of bimetallism should be adopted. The recovery in the reserve during the early months of 1830 eliminated discussion along those lines, although less concrete forms of the inflationist spirit persisted.

[2] This was of relatively little importance by 1829. The greater part of the job was completed by August 1828.

[3] See especially Tooke, ii. 216–17 n.

[4] Ibid., pp. 220–1.

[5] Ibid., p. 219. Typical of the pressures on the money-market due to the political unrest of this period is the situation described as follows in the City articles of the *London Times*, 3 and 10 October 1831:

'The pressure for money continues to be felt very generally in the city, and loans on the best securities are hardly obtainable at the highest rate of interest allowed by law.

Business suffers from this in every way, and no relief can be looked for before the payment of the dividends. It is this general distress for money which continues to depress the market for Government securities; and this depression every day gives rise to a variety of sinister rumours and predictions, which the small number of anti-reformers of which the city has to boast seem glad enough to give the utmost currency to, forgetting that if the price of public securities is really to be affected by any prospect of the rejection by the Lords of the Reform Bill, it would be because the dealers in them anticipate disasters from such an event (October 3). . . .

'There has occurred to-day a very unusual demand for gold at the Bank, many persons, connexions of provincial banks, having thought it prudent to send off a supply to those parts where the greatest degree of popular excitement is expected, in order to guard against the consequences of a run (October 10).'

'distrust' expressed itself in a considerable hoarding of cash, which helped deplete the reserve.[1] After the passage of the Reform Bill, however, the Bank's reserve rose, the Paris exchange strengthened, and the market-rate of interest fell.[2] The easy-money framework for the coming boom had at last been prepared.

Fluctuations in total inland bills of exchange follow, broadly, the movements of general business, as nearly as they can be ascertained.[3] The only exceptions are 1829, when inland bills were slightly greater in amount than in the previous year, although business conditions almost certainly deteriorated; and 1831, when inland bills rise while other evidence indicates relative depression in the latter months, at least. This is to be explained partly by the tendency of inland bills to lag behind other indexes of trade;[4] partly by the fact that the figures are given here in annual form. Quarterly statistics show a decline from the third quarter of 1831 to the fourth quarter of 1832.[5] This movement conforms somewhat better to other evidence on trade fluctuations than the annual figures when taken alone.

To some extent the lack of protracted ease in the money-market accounts for the relative industrial stagnation of these years. But the American stringencies of 1828–9 and 1831, the continental difficulties, and the agitation for political reform had direct consequences on the orders coming into British industry and on its general confidence, as well as indirect repercussions through the money-market. In short they affected the demand as well as the supply side of the markets for loanable funds.

6. Labour. A slight fall in money wages, with real wages fairly well maintained, is indicated by available statistics on the position of labour from 1827 to 1832:

	Tucker's index of		Bowley's index of agricultural money wages	Kondratieff's index of money wages in the textile industry
	Money wages of London artisans	Real wages		
1826 . .	66·1	50·2	146	49·8
1827 . .	66·2	51·2	146	49·3
1828 . .	65·9	52·6	146	48·3
1829 . .	64·3	52·4	146	47·8
1830 . .	65·3	56·2	142	44·4
1831 . .	63·3	51·5	146	43·5
1832 . .	63·2	52·2	150	44·0

[1] Shannon (p. 312) states that there was, as well as hoarding within Britain, a considerable flight of capital to the United States: 'in the troubled days preceding the Reform Bill, the sharp fall in price and rise in yield (of Consols) tell in figures the panic of British aristocrats yearning for the safer protection of the American constitution.'

[2] The large harvest of 1832, and consequently diminished imports, helped, of course, to relieve pressure on the bullion reserve, although it was probably not a factor of first importance.

[3] See above, pp. 171–4.

[4] Silberling, Review of Economic Statistics, 1923, 'British Prices and Business Cycles, 1779–1850', p. 246.

[5] Ibid., pp. 259–60.

The money wages of London artisans move broadly with general trade fluctuations, rising in 1827–8, falling in 1829, recovering somewhat in 1830, falling away in the course of 1831–2. The textile wage index, however, shows an unrelieved decline until 1832. This is to be explained by reference to the position of hand-loom weavers. The rapid introduction of the power-loom in 1824–5 and in the following years congested the market with men, who, even when work was to be had, were at the mercy of their employers.[1] Factory workers suffered no equivalent decline in money wages, although, after bitter strikes, wage reductions were accepted in 1829–30.[2]

The rise in agricultural wages in 1831–2 is difficult to explain, except, possibly, as a belated reaction to the rising grain prices of the previous two years. The violent unrest among agricultural workers, in 1830, producing riots, the destruction of machinery, and widespread rick-burning, may be partly accountable as well.[3]

The real wages of London artisans show the effects of a rise in living costs in 1831, and of their failure to decline sufficiently in 1829 to offset the fall in money wages.[4] As noted earlier, prices of foodstuffs dependent on the British grain supply were made artificially high in 1830–1 by inadequate harvests, only partially tempered by large imports.[5] In its trend,

---

[1] Baines, pp. 493–500. Baines enumerates the forces making for a fall in the wages of hand-loom weavers as follows:

1. The easy nature of the employment.
2. The more agreeable character of work at home than in the factories.
3. The surplus of hands, caused in part by an influx of Irish workers (see also Smart, ii. 435, for Irish agricultural workers).
4. The power-loom.

Typical hand-loom weavers' wages are the following, paid in the neighbourhood of Burnley and Skipton, for weaving 2nd quality of 74's calico:

	s.	d.			s.	d.
1825	. 2	2½		1829	. 1	1
1826	. 1	3		1830	. 1	5
1827	. 1	5		1831	. 1	7
1828	. 1	8		1832	. 1	3½

(Ibid., p. 490.) It is to be noted that this series conforms to the textile production index, with low points in 1826, 1829, 1832, high points in 1828, 1831.

[2] J. L. and B. Hammond, *The Skilled Labourer*, pp. 128–36. For wages of factory workers see Baines, pp. 444–5. Typical are the following, paid by Thomas Ashton, cotton manufacturer of Hyde (weekly averages):

	1826			1831			1832		
	£	s.	d.	£	s.	d.	£	s.	d.
Spinners, 1st class	1	15	0	1	14	9	1	15	0
Spinners, 2nd class	1	7	0	1	8	0	1	8	2
Dressers	1	10	0	1	10	6	1	10	6
Weavers	0	13	0	0	12	0	0	12	0

Also G. H. Wood, *The History of Wages in the Cotton Trade*, pp. 42–3.

[3] Smart, ii. 514–16. It was as a result of his defence of these riots that Cobbett was tried, but acquitted, of sedition (July 1831). Also G. D. H. Cole, i. 108–11; and *A.R.*, 1830, p. 149; 1831, Chr., pp. 1–5.

[4] The fall in 1830 appears also in foodstuff prices in Manchester (Baines, p. 439).

[5] Silberling's cost-of-living index, calculated from raw materials' prices (1790 = 100), clearly shows this upward movement (1830–1) in basic consumption commodities:

1826	. 111	1830	. 108
1827	. 110	1831	. 111
1828	. 108	1832	. 109
1829	. 106		

and in specific movements, except those in 1827–8, the amounts retained
for tea consumption conform roughly to the real wage estimate (in million
lb.):

1826	.	.	29·05	1830	.	.	30·05
1827	.	.	29·93	1831	.	.	30·00
1828	.	.	29·31	1832	.	.	31·55
1829	.	.	29·50				

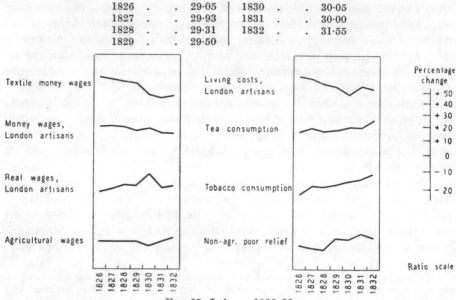

FIG. 65. Labour, 1826–32

It is clear that the support given the Reform movement came from the
proletariat as well as its chief beneficiaries, the urban middle classes.[1]
William Mathews was asked in 1833:

9991. Do you conceive that the depression in trade in late years has had any
effect in producing . . . discontent ?—Very great. 9992. Do you think the working
classes of Staffordshire ever show political discontent so long as they are doing
well in their particular trade ?—Not at all; you cannot get them to talk of
politics so long as they are well employed. 9993. Do you think any man could
create discontent among them so long as they were doing well ?—It is utterly
impossible.

In some measure, the unemployment of 1830–2, and the high price of
foodstuffs until the latter year, contributed to the dissatisfaction which
found partial expression in agitation for parliamentary reform.[2]

But there was a more general development under way. From the repeal
of the Combination Acts the trade-union movement grew rapidly despite
the weakened bargaining position of labour, due to depression; and in
Robert Owen and his followers the movement found articulate leadership
which viewed the trade unions from a broader perspective than that of the

---

[1] G. D. H. Cole, i. 94–101: 'The Reform
Act was carried chiefly by working-class
agitation, and by the threat of revolution in
which the workers would have played the
leading part.'

[2] The rejection of the Reform Bill by the
House of Lords in 1831 called forth especially
severe rioting (A.R., 1831, pp. 1, 78, 296;
and, Chr., p. 161).

labour market.[1] Their energy was channelled into the Reform movement, the propagation of the co-operative ideal, and the fighting of numerous large-scale labour disputes. The history of labour during the ensuing prosperity (1832–6) and the course of the later Chartist agitation would seem to suggest that to some extent labour turned towards political reform only when its market position made efforts to raise money wages fruitless.

The conception of working-class co-operation found concrete expression in the tendency to amalgamation among the trade unions. In December 1829 a Grand General Union of All the Operative Spinners of the United Kingdom was founded at a conference on the Isle of Man, attended by delegates from England, Scotland, and Ireland.[2] In 1830 the new union was already involved in a series of strikes for higher wages. There was a mild business recovery in that year, especially in textiles, and the spinners for a time were successful in gaining wage increases.[3] The owners, however, frightened by the new union, united in a counter-movement for lower wages.[4] Towards the close of 1830, 23,000 men were out of work. The union attempted to bring about a general strike in the industry; and even tried to induce the colliers to co-operate.[5] But by March 1831 the spinners were all back at work, at reduced wages.

Among the miners, too, there was an attempt at a general union. In South Wales a Friendly Society of Coal Mining was founded in 1831. Like the spinners, the colliers at first were successful (1831), but met defeat in the following year (1832).[6] There were also Doherty's National Association for the Protection of Labour and his new journal, the *Poor Man's Advocate*. A Metropolitan Trades Union was founded in London in 1831, and associated itself with the N.A.P.L., as did unions of potters, builders, millwrights, blacksmiths, mechanics, and clothiers.[7]

This powerful trend, of course, had roots deeper than the relative industrial stagnation of these years. But the break in working-class political agitation that occurred during the prosperity of the middle thirties, and the joint appearance of Chartism and unemployment, at the end of the decade, would suggest that William Mathews was, on the whole, correct: 'You cannot get them to talk of politics so long as they are well employed.'

[1] G. D. H. Cole, i. 105–19.

[2] Ibid., p. 105.

[3] J. L. and B. Hammond, *The Skilled Labourer*, pp. 128–35.

[4] Ibid., p. 132. The mill owners resolved upon this action in the belief that 'if the men are reduced to accept their terms "the power of the Union and the Union itself will be at an end"' (ibid., p. 132 n., quoted from Home Office reports, 40.26, 8 December 1830).

[5] Ibid., p. 135.

[6] G. D. H. Cole, i. 107–8. See above, *Industry and Agriculture*, p. 234.

[7] Ibid., pp. 106–7.

Chapter V

1833–42[1]

INTRODUCTION

THE period 1833–42 offers a quite remarkable parallel to that from 1820 to 1832. It contains two cycles, with peaks in 1836 and 1839, low points in 1837 and 1842. The first cycle was climaxed by a period of full employment (1835–6), with rising security and commodity prices, large new floatations, and expansion of plant; it saw enormous exports of British goods largely financed by British capital, in this instance to the United States, as opposed to Latin America; it ended in financial crisis. The second cycle (1837–42), like those from 1826 to 1832, never reached full employment and was marked by chronic financial stringency, falling prices, working-class discontent. Inadequate harvests in both cases contributed to financial stringency and political unrest.

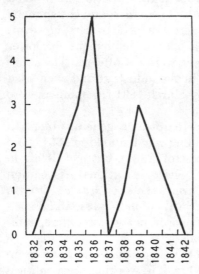

FIG. 66. Business-cycle Pattern, 1832–42

A principal distinction between the two intervals is that the crisis of 1839, and the preceding recovery from 1837, were on a larger scale than the crisis of 1829 and the preceding two years of relative prosperity. This difference can be traced largely to the partial nature of the liquidation of the Anglo-American credit structure in 1836–7 and the greater support given the economy by railway construction, inaugurated in 1835–6 but completed, in some cases, in subsequent years. In 1825 South American loans ended suddenly and with finality; while railway construction was a minor element in the boom.

Recovery from 1832 was based on a revival in exports and on internal investment. Railway construction played a much more important part in the years before 1836 than it had a decade before. Joint-stock floatations were less diffused than in the boom of 1824–5, with joint-stock banks commanding a major share of the home market's interest. Loans to foreign governments were, relatively, unimportant, except those to the United

[1] Cyclical pattern:

Trough	Peak
1832 (July)	1836 (May)
1837 (Aug.)	1839 (Mar.)
1842 (Nov.)	

States. These appeared on a large scale relatively late, serving as a means of converting enormous short-term commercial advances in the American trade to a more stable basis. On the Stock Exchange domestic securities commanded a major share of the speculator's attention, and this fact explains the conventional generalization that this was a 'domestic', as opposed to the 'foreign' boom in 1824–5. In fact the short- and long-period loans to the United States were quite as important to British industry and to the balance of payments as the loans to Latin America in the early twenties. They financed a major source of new orders to British industry.

From 1832 to 1836 industrial output increased steadily. Prices rose sharply only in the latter stages of prosperity, from the last quarter of 1835; but, on the whole, they show a greater response to prosperity conditions than in the previous decade. Iron and cotton prices, for example, rise from 1832 on. The iron and coal industries, because of considerably increased railway construction, showed more rapid advance than in the previous decade, with iron output in Scotland of special importance. New coal pits were dug, old ones extended to new depths; smelters were erected in Wales, the north country, and Scotland; and in cotton textiles, as well, a wave of capital development can be traced. The industrial revolution lurched forward much as it had in 1824–5, with somewhat greater relative emphasis on coal and iron. The woollen industry, while it shared generally in the prosperity, showed fewer signs of technical advance than the more dynamic areas of the economy.

The prices of securities, like commodities, rose most considerably in the latter months of 1835 and the first quarter of 1836. Rail shares were the centre of this speculative movement, and, as in 1824–5, their advance was accompanied by a decline in Consols and other debentures. Only in this stage was the secular decline in the long-term rate of interest checked.

The crisis of 1836 climaxed a period of gradually increasing stringency. The annual average market-rate of interest rose steadily from 1833. In the spring of 1835 a minor monetary crisis occurred, stemming from gold exports on loans floated by Spain and Portugal. The Bank, however, continued an easy money policy thereafter, despite growing evidences of pressure on its reserve, both internally and externally. The bullion demands of the United States in 1836 precipitated a more severe crisis. The American land and public works boom had come, for the moment, to an end, and stringency in New York was communicated to the provinces and to London through the banks that were involved in financing the American trade. Although the Bank of England was called upon as 'dernier ressort' from April 1836, its rate was not raised until August. Many of the new joint-stock banks required assistance, and those in Ireland were especially under strain. There were, nevertheless, relatively few bank failures, in large part because the import of long-term American securities kept the credit structure between the two countries from complete and immediate collapse. In the spring of 1837 the money-market again became easy.

In the years 1832–6 labour enjoyed increased employment and, until the close of 1835, falling food prices. From the destruction of Owen's Grand National Union in 1834 to the coming of severe unemployment and bad harvests in 1837, the British working classes were relatively peaceful. In 1837, however, the Chartists appeared on the scene, and their protest was heard, with varying intensity, during the five following years. In this latter period (1837, 1839–42) the pinch of the Poor Law of 1834 was, for the first time, seriously felt. Prosperity had largely concealed its rigours until 1837.

The financial crisis of 1839 is much more clearly marked than that of 1829, although both events helped prematurely to reverse incipient recovery. 1838 was clearly a year of general revival. Both the American and continental markets revived, and, due to the arrangements made by Nicholas Biddle, there was a further import into Britain of American securities. Although there were few new floatations of railway issues, railway construction continued, completing lines begun in 1836, extending older lines. In late 1839, however, the London money-market was tightened by the necessity of grain imports and by banking difficulties on the Continent which drew bullion there. The import of American securities, too, was weakening the reserve. A severe crisis resulted, which necessitated large borrowings in Paris and Hamburg to avoid a suspension of specie payments. Large grain imports and internal and external political difficulties kept the market from a return to easy money until 1842.

Industry generally was depressed from 1839 to 1842, especially in the latter two years of the period. Exports to the United States fell off drastically, while other markets showed little advance. Non-agricultural prices were falling, profits were reduced, the severity of competition increased. The unrest of the working classes, stimulated by unemployment and high food prices, channelled by the Chartist and to some extent the Anti-Corn Law agitation, helped to prevent any real return of industrial confidence. The Scottish iron industry and shipbuilding alone exhibited consistent advance. Output, nevertheless, continued to show a secular increase, with total production probably greater in 1842 than at the peaks, 1836 and 1839.

Agriculture suffered a period of abundant harvests and distress, from 1833 through 1835, but from 1836 to the summer of 1842, agricultural prices were abnormally high. Grain imports on a large scale were required in the years 1838–42, contributing to the chronic stringency of the money-market. Both the middle and working classes were largely converted to the necessity of the repeal of the Corn Laws. In 1842 tariffs generally were considerably reduced, with the duties on many articles, of little importance to the revenue, completely removed. Politically, then, the farmer was on the defensive; but an important positive response to the pressures upon him was an increase of interest in scientific farming, which, during the next three decades, was to alter considerably British agricultural methods.

PART I: 1833–7

1. Prices. The domestic price index falls irregularly from January 1833 to October 1835. This movement conceals a divergence between agricultural and non-agricultural commodities. The wheat price fell, imparting its trend to the index as a whole. Non-agricultural commodities rose through 1833, continuing generally upward until about the middle of 1834. They declined somewhat until the last quarter of 1835, when a sharp, decisive rise in all commodity prices got under way. In most cases the decline of 1834–5 left prices above their level at the beginning of 1833.

Abundant harvests are clearly responsible for the fall in the wheat price from 1833 to 1835.[1] It will be recalled that 1828–31 were years of relative deficiency, and that, in 1832, a good wheat crop caused a decline from 63*s.* per quarter in July to 54*s.* in December. At the close of 1833 the wheat price was 49·4*s.*; 1834, 41·1*s.*; 1835, 36·5*s.* The consequent agricultural distress called forth parliamentary committees of investigation. The evidence before these bodies indicates overwhelmingly 'that the four seasons ending in 1835, were, as a series, extraordinary in their produce of wheat'.[2] A typical case was that of Mr. Robert Hope who, in 1836, said that his average wheat crop in 1832–6 was 657 quarters, in 1828–31, 385 quarters. And this he attributed to 'the favourable seasons'.[3]

These seasons were, however, not equally favourable to all agricultural products. The prices of barley, oats, beans, and peas rose somewhat from the spring of 1833 to August 1835; but at the close of 1835 they were at about the same level as December 1832:[4] 'the spring crops were more or less deficient'. The price of oats, for example, moved as follows:[5]

		s. per *quarter*			*s. per* *quarter*
Dec. 1832	.	18·6	July 1834	.	24·1
Mar. 1833	.	16·7	Jan. 1835	.	21·9
Nov. 1833	.	19·9	Aug. 1835	.	24·1
Mar. 1834	.	18·0	Dec. 1835	.	18·7

These irregular fluctuations were countered, however, by other forces operating on the domestic index from 1833 to 1835. Its decline over these years is the result, almost exclusively, of influences operating on the supply

---

[1] Tooke, ii. 226–40. The fall in agricultural prices (and the domestic index) was arrested in 1833 by a slight speculative upward movement based largely on conclusions reached in the Report of the Agricultural Committee of 1833 (ibid., pp. 228–9). The committee held that a diminishing amount of labour and capital was being devoted to agriculture, and that the domestic yield could be expected chronically to be inadequate for the home consumption.

[2] Ibid., p. 236.

[3] Quoted, ibid., p. 237.

[4] Ibid., pp. 230, 232, 239. Tooke (p. 239) states that the prices of these commodities would have been even higher 'had it not been for the superabundance of wheat, which was so largely substituted in consumption for them. . . . As, on the other hand, had it not been for the deficiency of the spring crops, the price of wheat, low as it was, would have been still lower.'

[5] The figures given are the turning-points in the movement of the price of oats; i.e. it fell from Dec. 1832 to Mar. 1833, rose to Nov. 1833, fell to Mar. 1834, &c.

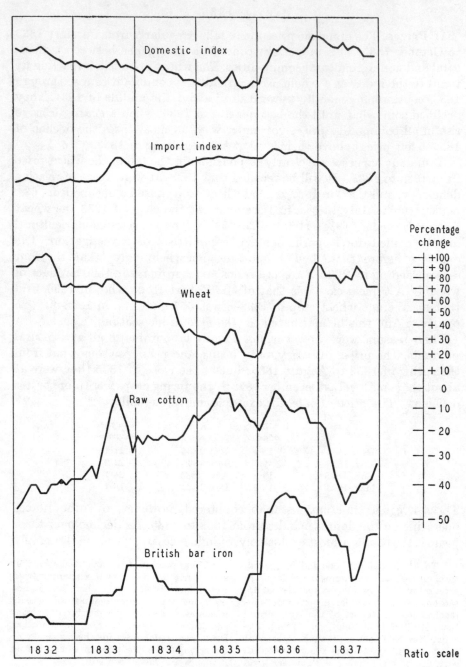

FIG. 67. Prices, 1832–7

of British wheat :[1] 'an excess of supply, relatively to a greatly increased consumption'.

In the years 1833–5 industrial output was steadily increasing. Significant non-agricultural domestic price movements are the following:

	Jan. 1833	Apr. 1834	Sept. 1835	Dec. 1835
Alum (£ per ton)	9·5	12·0	12·0	12·0
Sunderland coal (s. per chaldron) .	26·9	27·4	29·2	31·8
Copper (pence per lb.) . . .	11·0	12·0	10·5	11·0
Iron bars (£ per ton)	6·0	8·2	6·8	7·8
Lead pigs (£ per ton)	13·0	18·0	18·0	19·0
Leather butts (pence per lb.) . .	19·0	20·0	18·7	18·7
Rape oil (£ per ton)	32·0	42·0	49·0	51·0
Tallow (s. per cwt.)	52·0	46·0	46·5	51·0
Block tin (s. per cwt.) . . .	72·0	76·0	88·0	94·0

These movements are by no means uniform. They agree (except leather butts) only in their rise during the last quarter of 1835. But there would appear to have been in 1833–4 (as in 1822–3) a price rise, stemming from a decline in inventories and a general reversal of market expectations. This minor speculative wave lasted until about the spring of 1834. As the supply of most goods appeared sufficient,[2] prices remained steady or sagged until about September 1835, when a sharp inflationary rise developed (as in the last quarter of 1824).[3] But on the whole, for the first three years of recovery domestic prices were remarkably steady.

From the close of 1835, however, Britain again moved into a situation of relatively full employment :[4]

This state of things led naturally to the inference that the causes of the extension of demand were in such progressively increasing operation, that the ordinary sources of production, at the existing cost, would be inadequate to keep up the required supply. The lamentations about over-production, which had

[1] Tooke, ii. 239–40.

[2] See ibid., pp. 251–2, for the chronic relative shortage of certain commodities (especially lead and tin) in the manufacturing districts where the demand sharply increased: 'Among the greater number of the manufacturers, the orders on hand exceeded what could be executed within the time prescribed. New mills were in the course of being constructed, but could not come into operation fast enough to meet the great and increasing demand for wrought goods.'

[3] Tooke notes the parallel between price movements 1822–5 and 1833–6, ibid., pp. 250–1: 'In the early part of 1833, there was, as there had been in the spring of 1823, a speculative advance in the prices of colonial produce, which advance not having been responded to by the state of markets abroad, was not maintained. That partial rise of

prices, had, in each case, the effect of restoring the balance of supply, and was followed by a further interval of low prices; the consequence of which was, that the consumption again was extended, so as to produce a still more marked reduction of stocks in the course of the two following years. It is not to be supposed that the process was strictly analogous at the two periods. All that is to be observed is, that there was some resemblance of the general circumstances of manufactures and commerce, each of the great leading articles being of course more under the influence of its own peculiarities. It is only however as regards trade and manufactures, that the resemblance holds at all. In the prices of provisions the difference between the two periods is great and striking.'

[4] Ibid., p. 252.

prevailed in the epoch last under notice (1828–32), had now been replaced by apprehensions of insufficient production.

Non-agricultural domestic prices rose until about the end of the third quarter of 1836, declined to the close of 1837:

	Dec. 1835	Aug. 1836	Dec. 1837
Alum (£ per ton)	12·0	12·0	11·0
Sunderland coal (s. per chaldron) . .	31·8	29·1	32·3
Copper (pence per lb.)	11·0	13·5	11·0
Iron bars (£ per ton)	7·8	11·6	9·6
Lead pigs (£ per ton)	19·0	27·5	19·5
Leather butts (pence per lb.) . . .	18·7	19·0	18·5
Rape oil (£ per ton)	51·0	47·0	35·0
Tallow (s. per cwt.)	51·0	46·0	49·5
Block tin (s. per cwt.)	94·0	130·0	90·0

Metals show a neat cyclical movement, with prices in December 1835 and those two years later at about the same level. Other prices (except coal)[1] moved less regularly, but share the decline of 1837.

The domestic price index would show a lesser rise and an even greater decline in 1837, but for the movement of the wheat price, which rose from 37·3s. per quarter in January 1836 to 60·0 in December, falling by the end of 1837 to 53·0. The low wheat prices of 1835 caused from one-fifth to one-fourth less wheat to be sown in the autumn of that year.[2] And when the crop turned out to be deficient, the price rose rapidly, reaching a peak in December 1836. It fell away somewhat in the course of 1837: foreign wheat was coming in, the deficiency of the crop of 1836 was somewhat over-estimated, and the surpluses accumulated in the preceding years were larger than had been anticipated.

The domestic index thus had its turning-point in December 1836, although the prices of goods connected with the demands of home industry begin their decline in September, or even earlier. The index shows a minor relapse from July to October 1836. This, too, reflects a movement of the wheat price (July 49·8: October 47·8), as well as the decline in other domestic prices, begun about September.[3]

The import price index, like the prices of many domestic industrial raw materials, moves upward in two phases. A sharp rise occurs from May to October 1833. After a brief decline, the index rises slightly but steadily until February 1836. A second sharp rise then takes place until April. From October 1836 until July 1837 the index falls rapidly to a new low point for the period 1790–1837. Import prices, however recover in the latter months of the year.

[1] The upward movement of the coal price from 1834 to 1837 was almost certainly the result of successful regulation of output and prices by the industry itself as well as (and made possible by) an increased industrial demand (Sweezy, pp. 78 and 157).

[2] Tooke, ii. 257.

[3] Ibid., p. 258, for an account of the weakening of the grain market in the summer of 1836 due to favourable weather and a somewhat better outlook for the harvest.

The first increase in import prices was a speculative advance based on a feeling that stocks of goods were unduly low. Speculative hopes were, for the moment, disappointed, but[1]—'that partial rise of prices had, in each case, the effect of restoring the balance of supply, and was followed by a further interval of low prices; the consequence of which was, that the consumption again was extended, so as to produce a still more marked reduction of stocks in the course of the two following years'.

The second boom and slump in the commodity markets during 1836-7 is thus clearly described by Tooke:[2]

In the early part of 1836, it having appeared, by the usual returns at the close of the year, that the stocks of some articles had been reduced below the ordinary rate of consumption, a tendency to a speculative demand for them became perceptible, but not in any very marked degree. The articles that came more immediately under this description were cotton, indigo, sugars, and silks; and an advance, greater or less, took place in each of these at different times till the summer of 1836. But, although in each of these articles there was a brisk demand, and consequent rise of markets, it was remarked at the time, that as the demand was chiefly by the trade, and for immediate manufacture or export, and that as the advance did not appear to be greater than according to fair reasoning on mercantile grounds was perfectly legitimate, it could not with propriety be characterised as speculation or overtrading. And it must be admitted, that there was nothing of the extravagance of purchases, by persons out of the trade, which had marked some former memorable periods of speculations in goods.

It was not till nearly the close of 1836 that there was any serious fall in the prices of those articles which had experienced the greatest advance in the early part of the year; and, although there were sufficient causes in the state of supply relatively to the consumption for the tendency to dulness and decline in the case of most of the articles, there cannot be a doubt but that the notoriety of the growing difficulties of the American houses, combined with some recent failures in the silk trade, and in the East India trade, and the increasing pressure on the money market, operated greatly in adding to the depression which might otherwise have prevailed. The greatest degree of depression occurred in the interval between December, 1836, and the commencement of June, 1837, when three of the principal houses in the American trade suspended their payments, besides three or four other firms of less note, but of great respectability. The state of markets, at that precise period, for those articles which were more or less connected with the branches of trade in which those houses were engaged, would naturally be most affected. In the instance of cotton more especially, there was an unusually large importation at hand, under circumstances which rendered it certain that a considerable proportion of it must be immediately forced upon the market.

It is evident that the speculative movement was not carried as far as it was in 1824-5 and in some of the earlier booms. (See p. 250.) It is true that sugar, silk, and cotton fluctuated sharply; and in response to the high prices increased amounts were imported, causing a 'cessation of scarcity'.[3]

---

[1] Ibid., p. 250.
[2] Ibid., pp. 264 and 270-1. Also A.R.,
1837, p. 181.
[3] Tooke, ii. 268.

	Jan. 1836	May 1836	Dec. 1836	June 1837	Dec. 1837
Cotton (pence per lb.)	9·3	11·2	9·7	6·4	7·9
Ginger (s. per cwt.)	107·0	109·0	91·0	73·0	58·5
Hides (pence per lb.)	6·3	6·5	7·3	7·0	6·3
Piedmont silk (s. per lb.)	35·0	44·5	42·5	31·5	33·0
Sugar (s. per cwt.)	62·0	63·0	54·0	52·0	61·0
Tar (s. per barrel)	25·5	27·0	27·3	28·5	28·0
Tea (pence per lb.)	43·5	44·8	40·2	40·0	44·0
Pine timber (s. per last)	85·0	78·0	88·0	85·0	85·0

But even in the case of cotton and silk the manufacturers 'seem to have been particularly on their guard, and so distrustful of the high prices that they bought only what was strictly necessary to keep their mills from an absolute stand '.[1] In many cases the upward price movement was moderate and the fall, if any, was very slight. The recovery in the latter half of 1837 was quite general:[2]

After the clearance which was effected of the excessive and unsound part of the circulation by the consequences of the great failures, chiefly in the American trade, which occurred in the first week of June, 1837, and when the prices of those articles which had been raised by an exaggerated demand had fallen as much below their due level as they had before been raised above it, the confidence of buyers was restored: there was consequently a considerable revival of demand in the latter part of 1837, and the trade and manufactures of the country, reduced, as they necessarily have been, from the swollen dimensions which they had attained by exaggerated anticipations and an undue extension of credit, appear to be in a sound, although necessarily (as following a period of overtrading) in a comparatively stagnant and dull state.

2. Foreign Trade. Import and export statistics indicate a massive boom, with a peak in 1836, a sharp decline in 1837:

(In £ millions)

	Volume of			Value of domestic exports
	Total imports[a]	Re-exports	Domestic exports	
1832	50·6	8·4	32·5	36·5
1833	52·7	8·2	33·9	39·7
1834	58·0	9·4	34·4	41·6
1835	54·6	9·2	38·7	47·4
1836	65·1	8·3	40·2	53·3
1837	62·6	9·7	35·3	42·1

[a] Wheat and wheat flour imports were as follows (in 1,000 quarters):

1832	464·1	1835	89·0
1833	322·2	1836	262·4
1834	202·0	1837	575·0

To some minor extent the rise in grain imports necessitated by the bad harvests of 1836–7 helped to sustain total imports in the latter year.

[1] Ibid., p. 272.   [2] Ibid., pp. 272–3.

The figures of 1836 are far greater than any others thus far recorded. Despite the secular fall in prices, even the declared value of exports is above their previous high point in 1815 (£51·6 million). The large volume of imports in 1834 shows the response to the reversal of price movements in the previous year, as well as the increased requirements of the early phase of prosperity. Their decline in 1835 indicates the basis for the boom in import commodities of 1836. Re-exports, dependent on the continental markets, do not share the general cyclical movement.

The substantial part played in Britain's export trade by the boom and slump in the United States is revealed in the following figures of declared value (in £ millions) :[1]

	Value of Domestic Exports to						
	Northern Europe	Southern Europe	Africa	Asia	U.S.A.	British North American colonies and W. Indies	Foreign W. Indies	Central and S. America (including Brazil)
1832	9·9	5·7	0·9	4·2	5·5	4·5	1·2	4·3
1833	9·3	6·3	0·9	4·7	7·6	4·7	1·0	4·8
1834	9·5	8·5	1·0	4·6	6·8	4·4	1·3	5·2
1835	10·3	8·2	1·1	5·5	10·6	5·3	1·2	4·9
1836	10·0	9·0	1·5	6·8	12·4	6·5	1·2	6·0
1837	11·5	7·9	1·4	5·6	4·7	5·6	1·1	4·3

Perhaps more important, as a long-run feature of British foreign trade, are the considerable increases in shipments to Asia and Africa, as well as the colonial areas in the western hemisphere. Total exports to Europe were still large, but the sources of fluctuation were, principally, elsewhere.

The boom in the United States had begun with the alteration of the status of the United States Bank in 1832 (July). It was accompanied by the spread of innumerable land banks,[2] by a considerable investment in railways,[3] and enterprise in many other directions, partly financed from London.[4] British exporters extended commercial credits to American traders on an unprecedented scale;[5] and it was these credits (combined with substantial new investment at home) which lay at the basis of the British financial panic of 1836–7. The impulse which led to the final collapse of the boom generally, and the Anglo-American trade specifically, came, in July

---

[1] Porter, p. 362.

[2] The sale of the public lands in the United States began to increase in 1824, after declining from a peak in 1818 to a low point in 1823. From 1824 to 1828, sales remained steady; they rose moderately to 1832, and very rapidly in 1833–6, reaching a peak in the latter year. They fell catastrophically in 1837. The suppression of the Second United States Bank would seem to have accelerated a trend already under way (Smith and Cole, p. 53).

[3] Tooke, ii. 254.

[4] Jenks, chap. iii, 'A Cycle of Anglo-American Finance'; also Smith and Cole, pp. 41–3.

[5] Page, *Commerce and Industry*, i. 99–100; also C. J. Bullock, J. H. Williams, and R. S. Tucker, 'The Balance of Trade of the United States', *Review of Economic Statistics*, 1919, p. 218. Mercantile credits to the United States were estimated as £20 million at the peak in 1836.

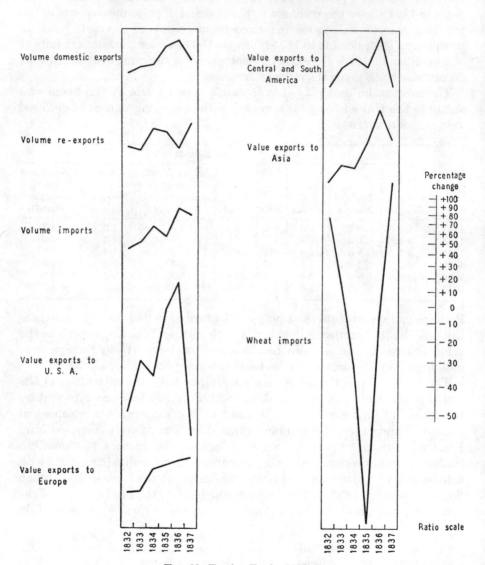

FIG. 68. Foreign Trade, 1832–7

1836, with the issue by President Jackson of the Specie Circular.[1] The demand for bullion was immediately felt in the Eastern banking centres and this communicated itself to London. The movement of British exports and re-exports to the Continent, which rise in 1837, would seem to indicate that no equivalent expansion and contraction took place there.

3. Investment. Although capital exports, especially to the United States, played a considerable part in the boom of 1833-6, the principal channels of new investment were internal. As in the case of 1822-5, the construction of new factories, railways, and industrial equipment increased moderately from the first years of recovery. The period from 1829 to 1832, when exports were increasing, but when new investment was at a standstill,

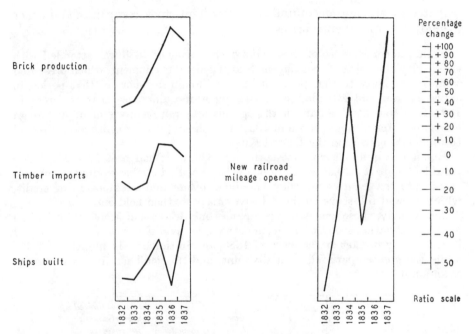

FIG. 69. Investment, 1832-7

may be viewed as bearing the same relation to the period of industrial expansion (in fixed equipment) of 1833-6 as the period of 1819-22 to 1823-5. The preceding interval (1829-32) of expanding exports probably explains the fact that new cotton factories were under construction as early as 1833, and that other symptoms of full employment (e.g. rising prices and interest rates) appear somewhat earlier, relative to the previous cyclical trough (1832), than in the cycle 1819-26. But the final phase of the boom was

[1] Commodity and security prices, however, had begun to turn downwards somewhat earlier, in April-May 1836. The Anglo- American credit structure showed signs of weakening well before July.

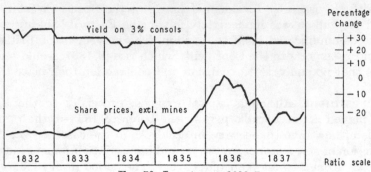

FIG. 70. Investment, 1832–7

featured by an enormous number of new joint-stock companies and other formally organized enterprises :[1]

From the concurrence of these causes, the spring of 1836 was attended with the display of a spirit of speculation, and of general excitement, which presented some resemblance to the spring of 1825, although far short of that period in extravagance, and attended with the important difference that, whereas in 1824–25 a considerable part of the speculations ran on investment in foreign loans and foreign mines, those of 1836 were chiefly, if not exclusively, directed to undertakings within the United Kingdom.

But it was quite clear in the spring of 1836, as it had been in 1825, that a considerable part of the speculations in shares could only have admitted of proceeding to the length that they had done by an undue extension of credit, which allowed full scope to the delusive prospects then held out.

Accordingly, those joint-stock companies only which had been established on a solid foundation stood their ground through the difficulties which prevailed in the money market at the close of 1836, and in the first six months of 1837, while the greater part fell to a discount, and no small number were finally abandoned.

	No.	Railways cost (in £ millions)	Completed mileage	Sums authorized by Parliament for railways (in £ millions)
1832 . .	—	—	26	0·6
1833 . .	4	10·1	42	5·5
1834 . .	7	3·9	90	2·3
1835 . .	10	10·7	40	4·8
1836 . .	26	28·4	66	22·9
1837 . .	11	11·1	137	13·5
1838 . .	—	—	202	—
1839 . .	—	—	227	—
1840 . .	—	—	528	—

[1] Tooke, ii. 278–9. See also *Edinburgh Review*, July 1836, pp. 419–41, 'Joint-Stock Banks and Companies'. This is probably the best contemporary account of the spirit, the direction, and the mechanics of the joint-stock boom.

The importance of railway building in 1833–6 is shown in the figures on p. 254.[1] The totals, of course, overshadow those of any previous period. Mileage opened is shown here down to its peak, for this decade, in 1840, because of the lag between enterprise and completion.

Joint-stock banks were a second important branch of internal enterprise, serving as the focus of much speculation,[2] and supplying, when established, the needs of an expanding trade. At the same time a considerable amount of capital was attracted into insurance companies:

	Number established	
	Joint-stock banks	Insurance companies
1832 . .	7	—
1833 . .	10	1
1834 . .	11	4
1835 . .	9	5
1836 . .	59	7
1837 . .	5	4

Again the figures for 1836 mark a clear peak.

Brick production increases gradually and its decline, in 1837, is moderate.

	Production of bricks (in million bricks)	Quantity of fir timber imports (in 1,000 loads of 50 cu. ft.)
1832 . .	972	494
1833 . .	1,011	467
1834 . .	1,152	489
1835 . .	1,349	627
1836 . .	1,606	623
1837 . .	1,478	580

It is probable that the construction of new fixed capital, generally, follows the more easy pattern of the brick index rather than the data of new flotations or even railway construction, which are concentrated in 1836.

The construction of new ships increased from 1833 to 1835, declined in 1836, but rose in the following year as a more imposing wave of ship construction began:

[1] Porter, pp. 329–32, and H. G. Lewin, *Early British Railways*, p. 186. The great boom in railway construction was set in motion when the success of the Liverpool and Manchester lines became generally known (Tooke, ii. 275–6). Liverpool and Manchester, rather than London, were the great centres of speculation in rail shares: 'The press supported the mania; the government sanctioned it; the people paid for it. Railways were at once a fashion and a frenzy. England was mapped out for iron roads. The profits and percentage of the Liverpool and Manchester were largely quoted. The prospects and power of the London and Birmingham were as freely prophesied' (Francis, *A History of the English Railway*, i. 290). Also Clapham, pp. 386–8; and p. 436, below.

[2] *A.R.*, 1837, p. 171. Also Hunt, pp. 61–73.

	Tonnage of shipping belonging to the United Kingdom	Tonnage of ships built and registered in the United Kingdom	Steamships built and registered in United Kingdom	
	(in 1,000 tons)		No.	Tons
1832 . .	2,225	90·2	33	2,851
1833 . .	2,234	89·2	33	2,928
1834 . .	2,274	100·4	36	5,128
1835 . .	2,321	116·6	86	10,924
1836 . .	2,313	86·5	63	8,758
1837 . .	2,296	131·2	78	11,669

The amount and direction of new joint-stock company formation in 1834–6 is indicated in the following table :[1]

	Nominal capital (in £ millions)
Railways	69·7
Mining companies	7·0
Packet and navigation companies . .	3·5
Banking companies	23·8
Conveyance companies	0·5
Insurance companies	7·6
Investment companies	1·7
Newspaper companies	0·3
Canal companies	3·7
Gas companies	0·9
Cemetery companies	0·4
Miscellaneous companies . . .	16·1
	£135·2

The best known description of the state of new floatations is that of Poulett Thompson, President of the Board of Trade, made in the House of Commons, 6 May 1836 :[2]

It is impossible not to be struck with the spirit of speculation which now exists in the country, but I believe that there is a great difference in the state of things, and what took place in 1825. The spirit of speculation was then turned to foreign adventure of the most extraordinary description ; but now speculation is directed to home objects, which if pushed too far may be very mischievous, though the consequences may not be quite so mischievous as in 1825. But really, on turning to any newspapers, or any price current, and observing the advertisements of joint-stock companies upon every possible subject, however unfit to be carried on in the present state of society, every man must be struck with

[1] Levi, p. 220. These years saw some extension of joint-stock company organization to industrial firms, most successfully in the woollen trade of the West Riding, but also in the manufacture of locomotives, nails, metal rolling, iron and coal mining (Hunt, pp. 76–8).

[2] Quoted, Macleod, pp. 274–5, also, more fully Tooke, ii. 276–8 n.; and Hunt, pp. 60–1. Thompson in the course of his speech gave many examples of the type of new company then coming onto the market, among them shipping, trading, whale fishery, beet-sugar, and joint-stock bank companies.

astonishment at the fever which rages at this moment for these speculations. I felt it my duty, some time ago, to direct a register to be kept, taking the names merely from the London and a few country newspapers, of the different joint-stock companies, and of the nominal amount of capital proposed to be embarked in them. The nominal capital to be raised by subscriptions amounts to nearly £200,000,000, and the number of companies to between 300 and 400. . . . The greater part of these companies are got up by speculators, for the purpose of selling their shares. They bring up their shares to a premium, and then sell them, leaving the unfortunate purchasers, who are foolish enough to vest their money in them, to shift for themselves. I have seen, also, with great regret, the extent to which joint-stock banks have sprung up in different parts of the country. I believe, indeed, that great good has arisen from joint-stock banks, but the observations I have made with regard to other companies are equally applicable to many of the joint-stock banks that are springing up in different parts of the country, and the existence of which can only be attended with mischief.

Some new foreign issues were launched in London, despite the greater relative importance of internal floatation (in £000):

	Country	Amount
1833 . .	Greece	2,344
	Portugal	2,000
	Russia	3,000
	Portugal	1,000
1834 . .	Spain, Cuba	450
	,,	4,000
1835 . .	Portugal	6,000
1836 . .	Belgium	1,200
	Florida	200
	Portugal	900
1837 . .	,,	1,000
	Spain, Cuba	113

The absence of South American borrowers and the amounts granted to Portugal and Spain are notable.[1] These loans were the last 'political sympathy' borrowing in London for many years.[2]

But of Britain's new foreign investments, those in the United States were of the greatest importance. The purchase of American securities was the means by which short-term mercantile balances were stabilized.

[1] The declared value of British exports to Portugal tripled from 1832 to 1835 (£0·5 million and £1·5 million, respectively); but a relatively small amount of the loans would appear to have been spent directly in Britain during these years. The boom in Portuguese and Spanish securities came to an end in the spring of 1835. The first loan, in 1833, helped Don Pedro to overthrow Don Miguel. When London's debtor came to power a 'specula-tive mania' followed until May 1835, 'when a panic seized the dealers in foreign securities' (J. Horsley Palmer, *The Causes and Consequences of the Pressure Upon the Money Market* (1837), pp. 27–9). See also the City article of the *London Times* (22 May 1835) for an account of the Stock Exchange panic in Spanish securities.

[2] Jenks, p. 83.

Without such loans the American balance of payments would have been seriously deranged.[1] Although the flow of British capital to the United States was interrupted in 1837, the process was not brought to a full halt until 1839. Estimates as to the extent of long-term borrowing vary. The amount of new capital that came to the United States from abroad in 1821–30 (largely 1830–9) has been calculated by Bullock, Williams, and Tucker as somewhat over $125 million;[2] Jenks, however, sets a larger figure:[3] 'It will not be far wrong to estimate the total quantity of British capital invested in the United States during the thirties as approximately equal to the indebtedness incurred by the several states. By 1835 this amounted to $66,000,000. In the three following years, $108,000,000 were added to this amount.'

In terms of the British balance of payments these securities played a role, in 1833–6, equivalent to that of the Latin American issues of 1822–5; i.e. they financed a major line of expansion in Britain's export trade. There was one important difference; they were the object of no extravagant speculative Stock-Exchange boom in 1835–6. Rail shares, not American bonds, dominated the security market. The disillusion of British investors with American securities in the early forties, however, easily matched that which followed the repudiation of the Latin American investments after 1825.[4]

The relatively conservative character of the boom of 1833–6 appears in the movement of security prices. From 1833 to June 1835 the security index (exclusive of mines) remains extremely steady, with a slight rise in 1833 giving the movement an upward trend for the two-and-a-half year interval. Mining shares showed some recovery throughout 1833, but fell away thereafter, with a slight revival in the early months of 1835, during a minor speculative surge at that time.

In 1833–4 Consols rose slightly, but weakened in the next two years under competition from the more speculative investments available. The secular tendency of the long-term interest rate to fall asserted itself, however, in 1837. India Stock, after a sensational rise in 1833–4, fell slightly like Consols in 1835–6, rose in 1837. Bank Stock too, conformed to this typical cyclical pattern for debentures: rising in the early stages of recovery, falling as more promising securities came on to the market, falling still at the height of financial panic (fourth quarter, 1836), rising again as panic ended and the monetary situation eased.

Dominated by railway shares the security index rises sharply from June 1835 to May 1836. The rise of bank shares (the other major outlet for

---

[1] Bullock, Williams, and Tucker, p. 218. The larger number of immigrants (550,000) who came to the United States in the twenties and thirties helped to counteract the adverse trade balance, as did considerable sales of American ships to foreigners; but this latter factor was almost nullified from the early twenties by a relative decline in income from the carrying trade (Jenks, pp. 69–70).

[2] Op. cit., p. 218.

[3] Op. cit., p. 85.

[4] Ibid., pp. 99–106.

speculative investment included in the index) was gradual, from about April 1833. Rail shares, however, after remaining stable in 1831–5, boomed suddenly from June 1835 to May 1836, imparting to the index its special character. With two slight interruptions the index then falls to April 1837. A recovery occurred before the year-end. Although the rise and fall in railway shares was considerable, the movement of their prices was not comparable to that of their Stock-Exchange equivalent in 1824–5—the shares of Latin American mining companies; nor was the British investor to face a similar 'harvest of insolvency'.

Despite the appearance of highly speculative securities in the latter stages of the boom, and the consequent fall in the price of Consols, their yield, following the secular tendency, was lower in 1837 than in the preceding five years:

Yield on 3 per cent. Consols

(Per cent).

1832	.	. 3·56	1835	.	. 3·29
1833	.	. 3·40	1836	.	. 3·32
1834	.	. 3·31	1837	.	. 3·28

4. Industry and Agriculture. Estimates of pig-iron output show a rise from about 500,000 tons in 1832 to 1,000,000 in 1835; 1,200,000 in 1836.[1] On the side of demand railways were being built on an unprecedented scale;[2] on that of supply, the Scottish iron producers were beginning to assume an important place in the industry.[3] In 1830 there were only twenty-seven furnaces in Scotland. They turned out about 37,500 tons of pig-iron. In 1838 forty-one furnaces in blast made 147,500 tons.[4]

Iron shipments on the Monmouthshire and Glamorganshire canals and iron exports moved as follows:

| | Monmouth-shire[a] canal iron shipments (in 1,000 tons) | Glamorgan-shire[b] | Exports of iron, hardware, and cutlery | |
			Quantity (in 100 tons)	Declared value (in £ millions)
1832 . .	124·2	83·7	162·8	2·6
1833 . .	118·9	112·3	179·3	2·9
1834 . .	127·6	110·0	174·4	2·9
1835 . .	155·3	119·9	219·2	3·5
1836 . .	151·4	123·1	213·4	4·6
1837 . .	144·3	124·8	207·7	3·5

    a Scrivenor, pp. 294–5.   b Ibid., p. 293.

[1] Porter, p. 271; J. Clapham, *An Economic History of Modern Britain*, i. 425. The estimate for 1832 is that given by Samuel Walker before the Committee on Manufactures (1833). A more widely accepted figure is that for 1830: 653,417. Although iron output probably declined somewhat between 1830 and 1832, Walker's figure, almost certainly, overestimates that decline. See also Tooke, ii. 254.

[2] 'The railway demand, direct and indirect, dominated the home market' (Clapham, p. 427, in reference to the iron industry during the whole period, 1830–47).

[3] Hamilton, pp. 179–84.

[4] Clapham, pp. 425–6.

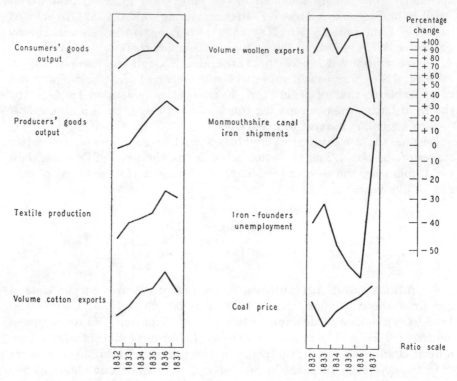

Fig. 71. Industry and Agriculture, 1832–7

The quantity of iron exports declined sharply in the second half of 1836, making the total for the year somewhat less than in 1835. The high range of iron prices, however, makes 1836 clearly a peak year in the declared value of exports.

As in 1824–5, the iron industry was pushed to full employment in the final stages of the boom :[1]

. . . there is reason to suppose that there had been a considerable number of furnaces put out of blast between 1828 and 1833; and while the supply had thus been diminished, the consumption was increased, more especially by the extension of railway undertakings which were then in progress in America as well as in this country. There was, in consequence, a steady demand, at gradually improving prices, coincidently with an increasing supply by the restoration of the furnaces that had been put out of blast, and by the erection of new ones, with the application of improved machinery. The increase of supply was, however, insufficient to meet the great increase of demand; and the price, which had improved very slowly till nearly the close of 1835, thenceforward, and for many months after, experienced a very considerable further advance.

[1] Tooke, ii. 254–5.

British iron bar and pig prices moved as follows:

| | Iron bars | Iron pigs | | Iron bars | Iron pigs |
	(£ per ton)			(£ per ton)	
Jan. 1833 . .	6·0	4·4	Apr. 1836 . .	11·5	7·9
Jan. 1834 . .	8·2	6·2	May 1836 . .	11·8	8·0
Jan. 1835 . .	7·2	5·5	June 1836 . .	11·9	8·0
Sept. 1835 . .	6·8	5·0	July 1836 . .	11·6	8·0
Oct. 1835 . .	7·3	5·3	Aug. 1836 . .	11·6	8·0
Nov. 1835 . .	7·8	5·6	Sept. 1836 . .	11·1	7·6
Dec. 1835 . .	7·8	5·6	Oct. 1836 . .	11·0	7·4
Jan. 1836 . .	7·8	5·6	Nov. 1836 . .	10·5	7·0
Feb. 1836 . .	10·8	7·8	Dec. 1836 . .	10·5	6·8
Mar. 1836 . .	10·8	7·8	Dec. 1837 . .	9·6	6·0

Like iron exports and canal shipments, prices in 1837 did not fall to the level from which the upward movement had begun.[1]

There is evidence, at the end of 1836 and in 1837, of a 'temporary cessation of demand'.[2] In December 1836 the ironmasters of South Wales called a meeting at Newport and agreed to the following resolutions:

'That the make of pig-iron be reduced 20 per cent.
'That the reduced make be persevered in till the 31st March, 1837.
'That the price of iron be continued at £10 per ton.'

The iron-masters present agreed to blow out twenty-two furnaces, and to meet, by a reduction of make in their remaining furnaces, the specified quantity required of them of the one-fifth proposed to be reduced—to be calculated on the make of the previous twelve months.

The Staffordshire, Shropshire, North Wales, and Scotch ironmasters were requested to join in this arrangement, to which they acceded.

Again, in 1840, there was an agreed reduction in the make, of 20 per cent, to remain in force from 22d Feb. to 1st July.[3]

The depression in the iron industry, though severe, was not prolonged.[4] In 1838 output again increased. Iron prices were rising and the monopoly agreement lapsed.

---

[1] There is available, from 1831, the unemployment percentage in the Friendly Society of Iron-founders. These figures show revival setting in during 1834, a peak in 1836, an extremely sharp decline in employment in 1837 (per cent.):

1831 .	. 5·8	1835 .	. 5·4
1832 .	. 7·1	1836 .	. 5·0
1833 .	. 8·1	1837 .	. 12·4
1834 .	. 6·2		

'Unemployed' here includes all those on superannuation, sick, and donation benefit; those out on labour disputes are not on benefits.

[2] Scrivenor, p. 314.
[3] Ibid., p. 314 n.
[4] Birmingham, centre of the trade in manufactured iron, and other areas dependent on exports to the United States, were especially hard hit in 1837. In June a large meeting was held there 'to consider what measures should be adopted, calculated to relieve the appalling state of commercial distress' (Levi, p. 223). See also 3rd Annual Report of Poor Law Commissioners, P.P. 1837, xxxi. 136. The cessation of the American demand for rail iron was particularly felt (Tooke, ii. 322).

The average annual price of Sunderland coal and total coastwise and foreign coal shipments follow:

	Price of Sunderland coal (s. per chaldron)	Total coastwise shipments	Exports to		Total shipments
			British colonies	Foreign countries	
			(in 1,000 tons)		
1832 . .	29·2	—	174	415	—
1833 . .	24·8	5,859	192	442	6,494
1834 . .	27·5	5,823	190	425	6,438
1835 . .	29·1	6,118	190	546	6,854
1836 . .	30·4	6,472	198	719	7,389
1837 . .	32·6	7,091	247	866	8,204

General depression and the severe strikes of 1831–2 succeeded in disrupting briefly the monopoly structure of the coal trade.[1] Through 1833 and part of 1834 the controls lapsed, competition was severe, coal prices remained low. In March 1834, however, new agreements went into effect. Demand was beginning to increase, excess capacity to decrease;[2] the period of 'fighting' trade, for the time, was over.[3] Coal shipments and price increased steadily, failing to show any decline in 1837.[4]

Total coal-production estimates show an increase from 21 million tons in 1826 to 30 million tons in 1836.[5] It may properly be assumed that—as in the case of iron production—the greater part of this increase came in the years from 1832 to 1836. The magnitude of these estimates, when set against the figures for coal shipments, emphasizes once again the relatively small part of the trade for which continuous evidence is available. As noted earlier, the type of demand reflected in these shipments was fairly insensitive to cyclical fluctuations. There probably was, in fact, a considerable decline in coal output in 1837, resulting from a lesser industrial demand.

The boom, as in 1824–5, caused a wave of expansion in the chief mining areas:[6]

. . . in the great northern coal field the local records teem with notices of existing collieries being extended, new pits being sunk, and old ones reopened, not only as in former times for household coal chiefly, but for cooking, gas-making, manufacturing, and steam purposes. Large joint-stock companies were also entering into competition with individuals and private companies.

[1] Sweezy, pp. 101–8.
[2] For the role of excess capacity in the willingness of producers to co-operate in control agreements, ibid., pp. 39 and 112–13.
[3] Sweezy considers 1833 a year which illustrates 'perfectly' the expected pattern in a year of open (i.e. competitive or 'fighting' trade)—the 'actual consumption of coal was greater than in any of the three preceding years or the next succeeding year. The low price obviously acted as a deterrent to new supply and as a stimulant to demand.

At the same time the absence of regulations stimulated production and the search for new markets' (ibid., p. 165).
[4] Although the annual average price of coal is higher in 1837 than in 1836, there was a sharp decline in 1837 (from 36·6s. per chaldron in February to 30·3s. in June) which may reflect a fall—actual or expected —in the industrial demand.
[5] Clapham, p. 431.
[6] Quoted, Sweezy, p. 122.

In South Wales, for the first time, coal mining was undertaken by independent operators, unconnected with the iron industry—in the Rhondda, Aberdare, and Merthyr valleys.[1] Elsewhere pits were sunk to new depths.[2] As the railways brought coal within the range of an increasing number of persons, and as the requirements of the railways themselves and the iron industry increased, the rate of growth of coal output rose.[3] This acceleration can be traced roughly to the early thirties, although it became more pronounced in the following decades.[4]

Cotton imports and exports, and stocks of raw material in hand, moved as follows:

	Quantity of raw cotton imports	Stocks of raw cotton	Exports of cotton manufactures	
	(in million lb.)		Official value	Declared value
			(in £ millions)	
1832 . .	287	104	43·8	17·3
1833 . .	304	94	46·3	18·5
1834 . .	327	82	51·1	20·5
1835 . .	364	90	52·3	22·1
1836 . .	407	116	58·6	24·6
1837 . .	407	116	51·1	20·6

It is clear that the cotton industry fully shared the boom of 1833–6. The decline in the volume of exports during 1837, as in the case of iron, was mild, although there is evidence of severe unemployment.

The pressure of increased output on stocks of raw cotton (1833–5) is also apparent. The annual average price of cotton and of its manufactures rose steadily:

	Price of raw cotton including duty (pence per lb.)	Selling price of 72⅞[a] calicoes		Price of raw cotton including duty (pence per lb.)	Selling price of 72⅞[a] calicoes
		s. d.			s, d.
1832 . .	7·2	8 0	1835 . .	10·5	9 9
1833 . .	8·9	8 6	1836 . .	10·3[b]	10 0
1834 . .	9·1	9 0	1837 . .	7·6	8 3

[a] Porter, p. 187.

[b] The cotton price reached a peak (11·5d. per lb.) in Apr. 1836, and by Dec. it had fallen to 9·7.

[1] Jones, pp. 67–8.

[2] Galloway, pp. 471–7. Until 1830 shafts deeper than 1,200 feet were considered unprofitable. In the early thirties, however, a shaft was sunk to 1,590 feet at the Monkwearmouth Colliery, and by the end of the decade such shafts were fairly common.

[3] The introduction of the hot-blast, however, worked in the other direction, reducing somewhat the amount of coal necessary per ton of iron produced (Clapham, pp. 430–2). The average figure for Britain in these years was about 4 tons of coal for the smelting of 1 ton of iron. The least efficient cold blast-furnaces required as much as 8 or 9 tons, the new hot-blast smelters in Scotland less than 3 tons (Porter, p. 282 n.).

[4] Clapham, pp. 430–2.

The fall in prices in 1837 was much more pronounced than the decline in the volume of exports.

The low level of stocks in 1834 produced a sharp rise in cotton imports and prices in the following year. The cotton price in May 1835 (11·4d. per lb.) reached a peak only slightly below that of April 1836 (11·5d.). The increased volume of imports then permitted a decline in price until a relative shortage in the cotton supply again developed, early in 1836.[1]

The years 1833–6 saw considerable expansion in the scale and technology of cotton manufacture, similar to that in 1824–5 :[2] 'the trade has been rapidly extending ; many mills have been built, and many spinners have added power-loom factories to their spinning mills'. From 1829 to 1835 the number of power-looms in Great Britain was estimated to have increased from 56,000 to 110,000 :[3] 'At the present time (1835) the machine-makers of Lancashire are making power-looms with the greatest rapidity, and they cannot be made sufficiently fast to meet the demands of the manufacturers.' This expansion partially explains the fact that the fall in prices in 1837 is disproportionate to the fall in output, as reflected in exports.

Redford's account of the industry during these years conforms to the statistical evidence already presented ; it emphasizes as well that, despite the secular increase in output, 1837 was a severely depressed year in the cotton as in the iron trade :[4]

By 1833 there were some indications that trade had once more turned the corner, and it was hoped that the business world had learned enough wisdom from the bitter experience of the preceding years to check any recurrence of reckless speculation. The trade of Manchester was reported to be particularly sound and to be increasing in volume, though profits and wages remained low. This healthy condition was thought likely to continue ; there were signs, indeed, that the foreign demand would increase, especially the demand from America for manufactured goods. . . . British trade and industry was remarkably prosperous during the years 1834 and 1835, and remained healthy. Early in 1836, however, it became evident that the supplies of such raw materials as cotton and silk were again running short ; speculative interest was therefore aroused, and prices began to rise sharply. From this and other causes a serious financial crisis occurred before the end of the year, comparable with the crisis of 1825, and a most disastrous depression of trade developed during 1837. Many business firms went bankrupt, thousands of workers were suddenly thrown out of

---

[1] Tooke, ii. 264 n.: 'The stocks in the ports at the close of 1835 being barely equal to three months' consumption, and prices moderate, the markets opened at the commencement of the year with a good demand, and a great deal of fluctuation was experienced, which continued until April, when prices attained their highest' (quoted from contemporary trade circular).

[2] Baines, p. 236.

[3] Ibid., p. 237. Although the position of the handloom weavers almost certainly de-teriorated between 1820 and 1834, their number was estimated to have remained about constant or even increased slightly (ibid., pp. 237–8). The industry was by no means completely mechanized (Clapham, pp. 143–8).

[4] Op. cit., pp. 80–1. See also *A.R.*, Chr., 1837, pp. 55–6, and 3rd Annual Report of Poor Law Commissioners, *P.P.* 1837, xxxi. 136–7, 141, 157–8, for unemployment in the cotton textile districts.

employment, and severe distress was reported from all the manufacturing districts.

The Lancashire cotton trade experienced the full force of this renewed commercial depression, and the Liverpool merchants were obliged to seek special assistance from the Government and the Bank of England.

Bankruptcies snow a similar pattern for industry and commerce as a whole (*London Gazette*):

Computed Monthly Average

1832	.	.	114	1835	.	.	86
1833	.	.	85	1836	.	.	77
1834	.	.	92	1837	.	.	139

As in most other series, a sharp peak appears in the foreign trade figures of the wool trade in 1836:

	Quantity of raw wool imports (*in million lb.*)	Exports of woollen manufactures	
		Official value	Declared value
		(*in £ millions*)	
1832 . .	28·1	6·7	5·5
1833 . .	38·0	7·9	6·5
1834 . .	46·5	6·6	6·0
1835 . .	42·2	7·5	7·2
1836 . .	64·2	7·7	8·0
1837 . .	48·4	4·8	5·0

Recovery was, however, less continuous than in cotton, with a marked setback in 1834, probably due to overstocking in the previous year.[1]

Wool prices were not subject to the same speculative demands that affected cotton, silk, and various other commodities:[2]

(Pence per lb.)

	Saxon imported	South-down	Kent long
1832 . .	59	12·6	12·5
1833 . .	59	16·7	10·5
1834 . .	65	16·9	19·5
1835 . .	64	17·6	18·0
1836 . .	62	17·3	20·5
1837 . .	55	14·8	15·0

The woollen industry broadly shared the relative prosperity to 1836 and the depression that immediately followed. But the secular forces of expansion operating on it were less strong than in either cotton or iron.

[1] Tooke, ii. 251.   [2] Ibid. p. 271.

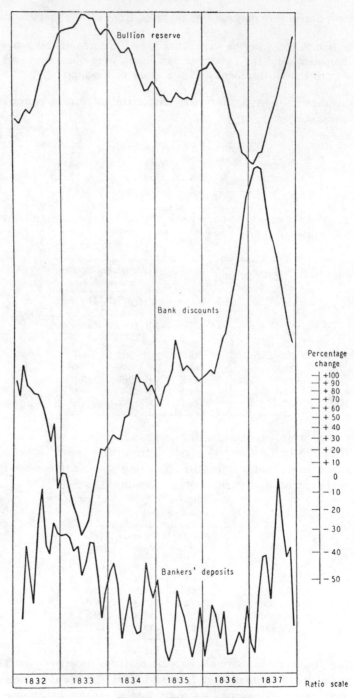

FIG. 72 a. Finance, 1832–7

Production estimates for these years moved as follows:

	Kondratieff's index of textile production	Hoffmann's index of consumers' goods production	Hoffmann's index of producer's goods production	Hoffmann's index of total production
1832 .	22·1	19·4	6·3	12·2
1833 .	24·5	21·0	6·5	13·0
1834 .	25·2	21·8	7·3	13·8
1835 .	26·2	22·0	8·1	14·4
1836 .	30·3	24·7	8·7	15·9
1837 .	29·0	23·2	8·2	15·0

They reveal the expected cyclical pattern as well as the secular increase which distinguishes the period.

The position of agriculture from 1833 to 1837 was dominated by variations in the harvests.[1] The falling prices of 1832–5 bred the usual complaints and parliamentary investigations;[2] the rise in the latter two years (1836–7) relieved somewhat the burden of fixed rents. No important action was taken by the government, whose attitude was that any adjustment of rents to the new price range was strictly a private matter. This relative insensitivity to the farmer's pleas may be viewed as a partial result of Parliament's new, and more urban, constitution under the Reform Bill of 1832.

5. Finance. Financial statistics from 1833 to 1837 show a conventional cyclical pattern of recovery, prosperity, and crisis.

	Bullion in the Bank of England	Bills and notes discounted by the Bank of England	Bank of England notes in circulation	Total[a] bills of exchange created	Bank-rate of discount	Market-rate of discount
			(in £ millions)		(per cent.)	
1832 .	6·8	2·2	18·1	194·1	4·00	3·15
1833 .	10·4	1·3	19·1	204·9	4·00	2·73
1834 .	8·1	2·2	18·8	211·6	4·00	3·38
1835 .	6·4	2·8	18·1	229·6	4·00	3·71
1836 .	6·3	4·5	17·8	280·3	4·39	4·25
1837 .	6·0	7·6	18·3	258·7	5·00	4·44

[a] A corollary to the internal credit expansion (reflected by the rise of inland bills of exchange) is the decline in London bankers' deposits at the Bank of England (in £ millions):

1832 .	. 1·4		1835 .	. 0·9	
1833 .	. 1·4		1836 .	. 0·8	
1834 .	. 1·1		1837 .	. 1·3	

The rise in 1837 began in March, at about the same time as the Bank's discounts started to decline; when, in fact, the crisis was over.

Inland bills of exchange and the market-rate rise steadily; the Bank's discounts rise moderately in the early stages of expansion, sharply during the crisis. The Bank-rate moved to 5 per cent. relatively late (August 1836),

[1] See above, *Prices.*   [2] Adams, pp. 135–6.

although the Bank's bullion holdings began to decline in July 1833. The note issue conforms roughly to movements in the bullion reserve. The crisis came in the latter part of 1836 and the early months of 1837. The annual figures fail to reveal the fall in discounts and interest rates, the sharp rise in the reserve which took place in the course of 1837. By the end of the year confidence was largely restored, the money market was easy.

The steady decline of the annual average of the Bank's bullion stock conceals a break in its movement from May 1835 to March 1836. The Bank's holdings began to decline in July 1833; they fell with only minor

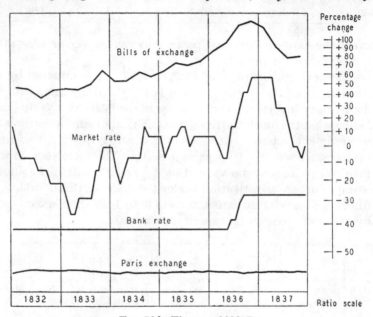

FIG. 72 b. Finance, 1832–7.

interruption to May 1835, and increased considerably in the last quarter of 1835 and the first quarter of 1836. Renewed pressures then reduced the reserve steadily until February 1837, after which the bullion hoard rose rapidly until February 1838. There are thus two separate drains to be analysed. In a famous pamphlet J. Horsley Palmer (a director of the Bank of England) ascribed the loss of bullion in 1833–5 to payments on the Portuguese and other foreign loans.[1] In a competent reply Samson Ricardo

[1] *The Causes and Consequences of the Pressure upon the Money Market from 1st October, 1833, to 27th December, 1836*, pp. 24, 27–9: 'Allusion has already been made to the effect upon the currency from a deranged state of commercial prices between this and foreign countries. It must be evident to every one reflecting upon the subject, that similar effects may be produced by employing capital in speculative loans to foreign powers or investing it abroad at a higher rate of interest than the securities of this country may afford. This, it is obvious, may occasion large and sudden foreign payments without any reference to the exchanges. And it is to payments of that character that we may attribute the loss of bullion which took place from October 1833, to April 1835 . . . until the spring of 1835 hardly a packet arrived from the continent which did not come

(a London stock-broker) claimed that no gold was exported on the Portuguese loans until July 1834 ;[1] and that, in net, the demand for bullion in consequence of these loans was too small to explain the great decline in the reserve. In any case, he believed the boom in foreign securities itself to have been a result of an unjustified easy-money policy on the part of the Bank.

He ascribed the depletion of the reserve to a general disequilibrium in the balance of payments, to which capital exports only partially contributed.[2] The exact nature of the other factors is difficult to establish. Neither Ricardo nor Tooke (who was in agreement with him)[3] is specific. Their contention was simply that the Bank had permitted a general overexpansion of credit, and that the minor crisis of May 1835 was required as a corrective.[4] They held that the stock speculation of 1835 and the other influences on the balance of payments were not factors independent of the Bank's policy, as Palmer considered them.

The market-rate of interest rose sharply from February to June 1835, declining thereafter in a period of easy money which laid the framework for the more extravagant commodity and stock speculations of 1836. Similar criticism was levelled at the Bank for its failure to prevent the boom of 1836 from going as far as it did. Not only did the Bank not intervene

---

loaded with every sort of foreign securities for realization upon our Foreign Stock-Exchange. During that period, and through the means here referred to, the bullion and coin held by the Bank in October, 1833, was reduced by the sum of £5,100,000, effected by £2,900,000 silver sold, and £2,200,000 sovereigns exported.' There were at least two replies to Palmer's explanation of the monetary events of the period—those of Samuel Jones Loyd and Samson Ricardo. Palmer, in turn, published a second pamphlet in specific rebuttal to Loyd.

[1] *Observations on the Recent Pamphlet of J. Horsley Palmer, etc.*, p. 6. The floatation of the Portuguese loan in London was handled through Ricardo & Co.

[2] Ricardo dismisses Palmer's insistence that the exchange on Paris was not unfavourable, and thus that exchange disequilibrium could not exist: '. . . with an exchange apparently not unfavourable it may not be practicable to obtain bills, without creating a depression which renders it equally advantageous to export the precious metals. It may also happen that, in the engagements attendant on a foreign loan, when payments are fixed at stated periods, shipments of bullion may be made to particular places upon which bills cannot be obtained, without the exchanges generally being below par' (op. cit., pp. 7–8). The

exchanges did, in fact, weaken from April 1833 to January 1835, although not sufficiently to make profitable the export of gold.

[3] Op. cit. ii. 282–3.

[4] The immediate point at issue in this pamphlet was whether the Bank's policy had been conducted properly. Ricardo, Tooke, and other critics maintained that the Bank's advances should have been contracted immediately upon the appearance of the drain, not, as they were, from July to Sept. 1835. See Ricardo, pp. 11–12:

'The abundance of money, created by excessive issues, has not been gradually lessened by a progressive reduction of paper —the evil has been allowed to prevail, till the exhausted coffers of the Bank required to be replenished. Then have come a sudden contraction of the circulation ; a rise in the rate of interest ; the necessity of refusing accommodation when it is most required ; a violent depreciation of prices ; and the serious injury inflicted by these causes on the commercial interests of the country.

'From almost the earliest period of the Bank's incorporation, great variations in the amount of bullion held are observable. This establishment seems to have been occupied in endeavouring alternately to amass and to divest itself of treasure ; and the same system appears more or less to have prevailed since the return to cash payments.'

positively to check the expansion, but, the critics alleged, it ignored a tool that was opportunely placed in its hands. The Bank received considerable 'extra deposits' arising out of a loan for the West India compensation in the autumn of 1835 and from money borrowed by the Bank from the East India Company.[1] Tooke and Ricardo believed that these funds should have been largely held idle at the Bank, since the bullion stock was decreasing and signs of excessive activity were evident :[2]

The mere retention of a part, if not of the whole, of these sums . . . would have constituted the most simple and easy means conceivable of reducing its (i.e., the Bank's) securities, of somewhat contracting the circulation, of moderately raising the rate of interest, and of replenishing the coffers of the Bank to an amount that might have made its position at once satisfactory and safe.

Palmer's reply to this line of argument was that when the West India funds were temporarily lent out—[3]

. . . the foreign exchanges were high, increasing the quantity of gold in the coffers of the Bank to a considerable extent—a circumstance which would have rendered it quite unjustifiable for the Bank to have permitted a contraction of the currency . . . and an advance in the rate of interest . . . to the detriment of the commerce of the country.

As for the timing of the events, Palmer seems to be correct. In the autumn of 1835 the bullion in the Bank was rising, the Bank's discounts and commodity prices were low, the speculation in railway and bank securities was only beginning to get under way. Nevertheless, in the light of subsequent events, Tooke is able to maintain that a deflationary rise in the interest rate at that time would have had salutary consequences.[4]

Palmer, however, admits implicitly that the second loan—that of the East India Company—may have had unfortunate inflationary consequences; but he contends that the Bank could do nothing about it. The East India Company asked the Bank if it would take its idle funds at a given rate of interest :[5]

if declined, the Company were prepared to lend it themselves, having received offers from some of the principal money-dealers for it. The question, therefore, simply was, whether the notes should be paid away by the East India Company or the Bank ? It never could be expected that the Bank should be required to pay a rate of interest for notes or bullion belonging to others, merely for the sake of keeping them unemployed.

This final sentence indicates the difference in attitude which separated the Bank directors from their critics. The latter, impressed with the per-

[1] Tooke, ii. 289; Palmer, pp. 12–15; Ricardo, pp. 27–8.
[2] Tooke, ii. 289.
[3] Op. cit., p. 13.
[4] Op. cit. ii. 295–7. The most substantial evidence in support of Tooke's view is the

fact that the market rate of interest fell from 4 per cent. in July 1835 to 3¼ per cent. as late as May 1836, due presumably to the funds flowing to the market from the Bank.
[5] Op. cit., p. 14.

vasive consequences of Bank policy, felt that its primary function was to protect the reserve and to avoid any over-expansion of credit, even if it involved 'paying interest merely for the sake of keeping notes and bullion unemployed'. The directors, although they were, abstractly, more or less aware of the implications of the Bank's position, still operated essentially from the perspective of a private bank, with primary responsibility to the stockholders. Throughout Palmer's pamphlet it is implied that the forces making for credit expansion and contraction lay outside the influence of Bank policy.[1] Tooke and Ricardo emphasized constantly the importance of the Bank's action even when it appeared to be negative,[2] and the potential power of its action, properly directed, to alter and smooth the course of events. They wished, in short, the perspective of the central rather than the private bankers to control from Threadneedle Street. It is significant of this attitude that Ricardo suggests a national bank as the only proper solution.[3]

The role of 'extra deposits' in bringing about the general credit expansion of 1836 is, like the manipulation of the 'dead weight' in 1823-5,[4] a matter open to controversy. On the drains which affected the reserve in the

---

[1] Palmer, for example, considered the credit expansion of the new joint-stock banks and the provincial banks generally a factor outside the Bank's control and influence (pp. 43–50). Tooke points out (ii. 287–8) that the Bank had the power to cause a restriction in their advances if it wished to do so: 'It is possible that for a short time during a small rise in the rate of interest, while confidence was entire, and trade and manufactures flourishing, and opinions in favour of joint-stock companies sanguine, the diminished accommodation granted by the Bank of England might be compensated by an enlargement of that afforded by the country banks. But such counteraction on the part of the country banks could not proceed far, nor last long, under a resolute reduction of its securities by the Bank of England. The reserves of the country banks must be in gold or Bank of England notes: these they would have an increasing difficulty to possess themselves of, the resource of re-discounting in London being greatly curtailed, so that the means of making advances, as well by discounts and by book credits, as by the issue of notes, would be abridged, and the whole of the country circulation would thus be more or less restrained, with consequently a less eventual tendency to an efflux of bullion.' Palmer, and the directors generally, did not consider such preventative action a proper function of the Bank of England.

[2] 'The Bank of England, by enlarging its securities in the autumn of 1835, in violation of the principle of management announced by the directors in 1832, and by thus forcibly reducing or keeping down the rate of interest, promoted the formation and extension of joint-stock banks, and encouraged and facilitated the system of discounts and re-discounts, and advances on personal securities, which was carried on by those banks to a mischievous extent. That measure, namely, of re-issuing its extra deposits, also greatly favoured the overtrading in America, and in the American branch of trade in this country.' (Tooke, ii. 344.)

[3] Op. cit., pp. 37–43. 'As directors of a Joint Stock Company, they have to obtain the greatest possible advantages for their proprietors. As regulators of the currency they have to protect the interests of the community . . . during the continuance, therefore, of the Bank Charter, this question should be carefully considered with the view of establishing a NATIONAL BANK at the period of its expiration; the subject should constantly be brought before the attention of the public that it may be fairly and fully discussed, and when the merits of the case are perfectly understood, no party who is not personally interested will be content to continue subject to the evils of an ill-regulated currency when a better system can be adopted, combining at the same time a sound and wholesome circulation, with a great pecuniary saving to the nation.'

[4] See above, p. 206.

course of 1836–7, however, there seems to be general agreement. There was an enormous demand for bullion from the United States,[1] and the internal pressures on the Bank that usually accompanied a period when the private banking system was under suspicion.[2] The crisis in the United States, under way even before the appearance of the Specie Circular, became more severe with its issue. Monetary pressure communicated itself to Britain through the commercial and financial connexions which had grown up in the previous few years. American traders liquidated much of their available holdings on London, and cut down their imports.[3] American securities were dumped in the British markets and 'the cash remitted to America'.[4]

In March 1836 the Bank's bullion began to decline; in April discounts began to rise. The Bank raised its rate to 5 per cent. in August. In the autumn internal evidences of movement from mere stringency to crisis appeared.[5] Many of the newly formed joint-stock banks required assistance, and from Ireland, especially, there were demands for British bullion.[6] From November to January many banks in London, Manchester, and Liverpool, which had advanced heavily to houses engaged in the American trade, were supplied by the Bank of England with necessary funds.[7] There were relatively few banking failures,[8] although, until April

[1] Bullion exports to the United States were a feature of the money market as early as 1834 (see City articles of the *London Times*, 25 Jan., 21 Feb., 8 Mar., 6 Aug., 15 Nov.— of 1834). In May 1836, however, the situation became serious with the United States Bank attempting to borrow 'in the very select monied circles of the City' some £1·5 million, to be taken in bullion (ibid., 16 May 1836). On 20 May it was reported: 'From the turn which the exchanges between New York and London have taken, it has become clearly a profitable operation for individuals to ship gold to the United States. No inquiry need be made therefore whether that is actually the case or not, for British merchants are too quick and intelligent not to avail themselves promptly of any opening of the kind that presents itself. . . . There can be no doubt, however, that shipments of bullion to a considerable extent are already in progress, and as the turn in the exchanges must have been foreseen by many persons, it is probable that they have been going on for some time, though they have not till now attracted general notice.'

[2] Subsidiary to the American drain, but present in 1836 and the early months of 1837, were pressures deriving from payments on continental loans, for increasing grain imports, and bullion withdrawals to support the tottering Irish banks (Tooke, iii. 73).

[3] See King, pp. 94–5 for the manner in which provincial banks took the paper of firms in the Anglo-American trade and, after endorsement, unloaded it on the London discount market.

[4] Macleod, p. 277.

[5] King states (p. 96) that in the autumn 'the Bank of England belatedly refused to take the paper of the Anglo-American houses as collateral from the bill brokers, and thereby at once rendered all such paper virtually undiscountable'. The dangers of wholesale commercial and financial bankruptcy then became so serious that the Bank was forced to reverse its policy and support the Anglo-American credit structure in the following months. See also *A.R.*, 1837, p. 181.

[6] Tooke, ii. 314–17; iii. 73.

[7] Macleod, pp. 279–80.

[8] Tooke, ii. 316: 'It is an important fact, with reference to the vast mass of bills of exchange which were the subject of discount and re-discount, with the endorsements of the joint-stock banks, that, in the collapse of credit which had followed the late excessive expansion, there has been so little of failure or discredit, excepting among houses connected with the American trade, and excepting, of course, the two flagrant instances of the Agricultural and Commercial Bank in Ireland, and the Northern and Central Bank in Manchester. It is very probable that, in other instances less flagrant, there may have been much mismanagement,

1837, the Bank of England was called upon to bear a substantial burden of temporary advances.

By the end of 1837 the money market was easy, commodity and security prices were showing some tendency to rise. The market rate of interest had begun to fall in May from its peak figure, $5\frac{1}{2}$ per cent. In December it was $3\frac{1}{2}$ per cent. The Bank rate, which had ruled at 5 per cent. since September 1836, was reduced to 4 per cent. in February 1838. The deposits of London bankers at the Bank of England, which had been £1·1 million in April 1836, £0·7 million in December, were up to £2·5 million in August 1837. The financial basis for recovery was fully prepared. But the United States was still enormously in debt to Great Britain. The short- and long-term loans made in the previous years had by no means been fully liquidated.[1]

6. Labour. Statistics on money wages do not conform to the expected cyclical pattern. In all cases a peak is reached in 1834. Textile and agricultural wages rose again in 1836–7, but there is a clearly marked decline in 1835.

	Tucker's index of		Bowley's index of agricultural money wages	Kondratieff's index of money wages in the textile industry	Tea consumption in the United Kingdom (in million lb.)
	Money wages of London	Real wages artisans			
1832 . .	63·2	52·2	150	44·0	31·5
1833 . .	63·4	55·0	152	44·9	31·8
1834 . .	63·5	57·3	148	48·3	35·0
1835 . .	62·3	57·2	142	46·4	36·6
1836 . .	61·3	53·5	144	47·3	49·1
1837 . .	61·2	50·4	146	47·8	30·6

The quantity of tea retained for home consumption, however, shows a continuous increase to 1836. Although its level in 1836 is abnormal, its rise in that year is probably a more accurate reflection of the direction of movement of real wages as a whole than the calculated figure for London artisans.[2]

There seems to be no question that real wages rose from 1833 to 1835. The increase in general activity made for—[3]

and much loss to the proprietors by bad debts, from the improvidence with which the credits must, in some instances, have been granted. But still there is no doubt of the fact, that no derangement whatever, analogous in kind, or approaching in degree, to that which occurred in 1792–93, 1796, 1810 to 1812, 1814 to 1816, and, lastly, in 1825–26, is chargeable upon the country circulation in 1836–37. And I must here confess that this is a result different from that which I had anticipated in the spring and summer of 1836, when I heard, on all sides, of the immense magnitude of the operations of joint-stock banks.'

[1] King, p. 97.

[2] The imports for 1836 are unnaturally large due to the fact that tea was one of the group of commodities subject to extreme speculation (Tooke, ii. 267–8; iii. 62–3). The decline in 1837 was thus a consequence of the previous over-importation as well as the decline in money wages, and the rise in living costs.   [3] Tooke, ii. 255.

a very extensive and general employment of the working population at full wages. At the same time, the extensive works upon the lines of the great railways which were in progress, served to employ considerable numbers of agricultural labourers, and the earnings, even in money, by the operative classes, were, in some instances, greater than in the periods of the highest prices of provisions. But, while the working classes were thus extensively employed at full wages, the prices of food and other necessaries had been progressively falling, and were, at the close of 1835, lower than they had been since the middle of last century. The increased means of expenditure, thus enjoyed by the bulk of the population, were shown in the progressive increase of the revenue.

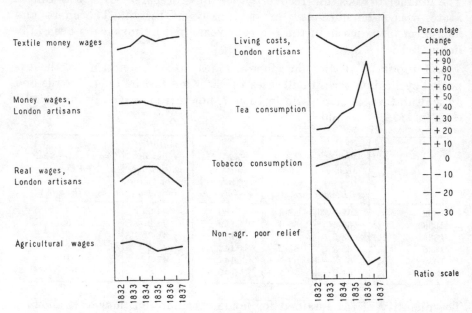

FIG. 73. Labour, 1832–7

There were three factors operating in 1835 which might explain the decline in money wages. The fall in food prices might have permitted, in certain cases, a lowering of wage rates without precipitating any violent response from labour. The minor monetary crisis of early 1835 may have had some slight repercussions on the demand for labour, possibly inducing manufacturers to take advantage of the fall in living costs; for throughout most of 1835 the general tendency of domestic non-agricultural prices was slightly downward. Finally the destruction of Owen's Grand National Consolidated Trades Union, in 1834, may have opened the way for wage reductions in the following year.[1] By the close of 1833 it was estimated that trade-union membership in Britain was over a million.[2] But a lock-out in Derby, lost by the men after a costly four months' fight, and the action of

---

[1] G. D. H. Cole, i. 121–30.   [2] Ibid., p. 124.

the Whig government in transporting the Tolpuddle agricultural unionists broke confidence in the Grand National. There were many strikes in 1834, conducted independently of the central organization ;[1] but the dream of co-operative socialism perished with the dissolution of the Grand National in August. And to some extent it is possible that the defeats suffered by the trade unions in that year left the men in a somewhat weakened bargaining position in 1835. Nine important strikes are listed by Bowley in 1833–4, only one in 1835. This relative industrial peace, however, like the failure of the grandiose union itself, can be attributed partially to the fact that, on the whole, 1835 was a year of increasing industrial prosperity, with falling food prices.

Despite the evidence on London artisans and the textile wage index, in many cases money wages were, as one would prima facie expect, higher in 1836 than in 1834.[2] Although rising living costs cut into real wages in 1836, the position of labour generally was affected favourably by the prevailing state of full employment. Despite the rise in food prices, poor-rate expenditure in non-agricultural counties fell considerably in 1836 (in £ millions):

1832	.	. 4·0	1835	.	. 2·8
1833	.	. 3·7	1836	.	. 2·5
1834	.	. 3·2	1837	.	. 2·6

Like tea imports these figures show a continuous cyclical movement with a peak indicated in 1836.

In 1837, however, there is ample evidence of severe unemployment, especially in those branches of industry dependent on the American trade.[3] In Staffordshire, Notts., and Leicestershire—

the interruption of the American trade produced a cessation in the demand for labour, more sudden in its approach and more extensive in its operation than has been known on any former occasion.

In Nottingham men were rapidly being discharged in the spring of 1837.[4] From March onward Birmingham suffered a depression 'almost unexampled in extent and duration'.[5] Similar reports came from Manchester, Wigan, the West Riding, and Scotland.[6] So severe was unemployment that the Poor Law Commissioners were forced to discontinue their previous policy of promoting the migration from the southern agricultural counties to the manufacturing districts of the north.[7]

---

[1] Ibid., p. 127. For a more complete list of strikes at this time see Bowley, pp. 135–6. In an article in the *Journal of the Royal Statistical Society*, i. (1839), 37–45, John Boyle gives an excellent account of two strikes in the Potteries. The first, in 1834, was won by the men; the second, late in 1836, after the cyclical turning-point, resulted in their defeat.

[2] See Bowley, chart facing p. 119 (cotton workers). Also Clapham, p. 559 (coal miners).

[3] 3rd Annual Report of Poor Law Commissioners, *P.P.* 1837, xxxi. 136.

[4] Ibid., p. 137. A subscription was raised in Nottingham 'to alleviate the great distress'.

[5] *P.P.* 1837–8, xxviii. 175.

[6] *A.R.*, Chr., 1837, pp. 55–6.

[7] *P.P.* 1837–8, xxviii. 183.

Out of this severe unemployment, accelerated by high foodstuff prices, arose the first Chartist agitation.[1] Discontent was especially strong in the north, where the Poor Law Commissioners attempted to apply the new act of 1834 for the first time. The restrictions on poor relief had not been seriously felt in the prosperous years, 1834–6; but in 1837 they furnished the basis for 'a great mass movement of unrest'.[2] Currency reformers, hand-loom weavers, idealistic Tories, Owenites, and the mass of urban unemployed began to group themselves and their various and specific economic discontents about the six-point programme for parliamentary reform.

Aside from the Poor Law of 1834 the principal legislation affecting labour was the Factory Act of 1833. It prohibited employment in textile factories (except silk mills) at less than nine years of age, fixed a maximum working day of nine hours for children under thirteen (from 1835), prohibited night work by young persons, and, most important of all, established a system of factory inspection.[3] The introduction of government inspectors was, of course, a major improvement over the previous acts of 1803 and 1819. They had been very loosely enforced. Effective factory regulation can be dated from 1833.

PART II: 1838–42

1. Prices. The domestic price index, which, despite general depression, fell only slightly in 1837, due to a second consecutive bad harvest, rises again sharply in 1838. It then falls away slowly and irregularly to July 1842, precipitately to a low point in May 1843. Only at its nadir in 1843 does it return to the level of late 1835, before the speculative stage of the previous boom and the coming of inadequate crops.

The movement of the wheat price again controls the character of the index. The season of 1838 was bad, and the wheat price rose from 53s. per quarter in January to 74s. in August.[4] Sudden large imports at the end of August and September caused a considerable fall in the latter month, clearly reflected in the index.[5] The rising trend was, however, resumed, and a peak was reached in the wheat price (and the index) in January 1839, of 81s. per quarter, the highest price since December 1818. By December 1839 the price was down to 66s., falling with only slight interruption. The high prices of 1838 had caused an increase in acreage sufficient to yield about one million additional quarters;[6] and thus, although the weather conditions and the harvest of 1839 were little better than in the previous year, the total supply available of home-grown wheat was somewhat greater, and it was augmented by an increased grain import.[7]

[1] Cole, i. 139–40.
[2] Ibid., p. 139.
[3] Ibid., p. 133.
[4] Tooke, iii. 8–10. The wheat crop of 1838 was 'proved to be the most deficient crop . . .
since 1816'.
[5] Ibid., pp. 10–11.
[6] Ibid., pp. 16–17.
[7] Ibid., pp. 17–18.

Until August 1840 the wheat price again rose. July was 'cold and wet. This unfavourable weather, combined with a general impression that the stocks of old wheat were low, and that the growing crop would not prove to be a large one, favoured the speculations for a rise of price.'[1] The weather, however, cleared in August, and 1,500,000 quarters of foreign wheat were released from bond;[2] the wheat price fell from 72s. per quarter in August to 66s. in September, 59s. in December. The harvest and wheat price of 1841 followed a similar pattern, with a rise to August (73s.), a re-lease of foreign stocks, a decline to the end of the year (63s.).[3] The yield, however, was somewhat greater than in the previous years, although the quality of the wheat was inferior.[4] Large imports were again required.

Early in 1842 the wheat price declined, 'in some degree attributable to the change in the corn law, which was announced by Sir Robert Peel, in his speech on the budget, on March 1. Some relaxation, however, had been anticipated.'[5] Nevertheless, from April to June a speculative movement again set in, due to the 'cold and ungenial weather'.[6] But the good weather of June and the summer suddenly broke the spell of the previous four years of 'dearth'.[7] Harvest prospects turned favourable, and from June to December the price of wheat fell from 64s. to 47s. per quarter.

The average net import of wheat and flour, from 1821 to 1837, had been 582,641 quarters. The extraordinary imports of the following years were (in thousand quarters):

1838	.	. 1,380·8		1841	.	. 2,681·4
1839	.	. 2,852·4		1842	.	. 2,939·6
1840	.	. 2,352·2				

Non-agricultural domestic prices tended generally to recover from their low levels of 1837 in the following two years and to fall fairly steadily from about the spring of 1839 to the end of 1842. In many important cases prices at the end of 1842 had reached new low levels for the entire period. There were, however, numerous exceptions to this pattern :[8]

[1] In May and June the brief appearance of 'seasonable weather' caused expectations of a better harvest and a slight fall in the wheat price (ibid. iv. 4).

[2] Ibid., p. 5.   [3] Ibid., pp. 7–10.
[4] Ibid., p. 8.   [5] Ibid., p. 10.
[6] Ibid., p. 11.

[7] Ibid., pp. 10–14. The years of 'dearth' are measured by Tooke from the summer of 1838 to that of 1842.

[8] The table, giving low points for 1838, 1840–2, and the high point for 1839, empha-sizes somewhat unfairly the general pattern. The most important movement obscured is the minor rise in prices which took place in the last quarter of 1840, the first half of 1841: 'In the first months of 1841 . . . there was a somewhat general feeling of hope pre-valent that a revival of trade was about to take place. The raw materials of our manu-facturers, generally, were observed to be low in price ; the manufacturers on the con-tinent were known to be even more depressed, and more crippled in their resources, there-fore less capable of meeting efficiently any revival of the usual demand in markets open to both, than our own ; and the demand for manufactured produce, both at home and abroad, had been so long below an average level, that its increase, at no distant period, was deemed almost certain. Commercial credit had everywhere been brought within narrow limits ; and there seemed to be no longer any sufficient ground for the prevail-ing want of confidence in the results of commercial transactions conducted with ordinary prudence. . . . But as the summer advanced it became evident that the con-tinued high price of corn and cattle together with the general scarcity of employment for

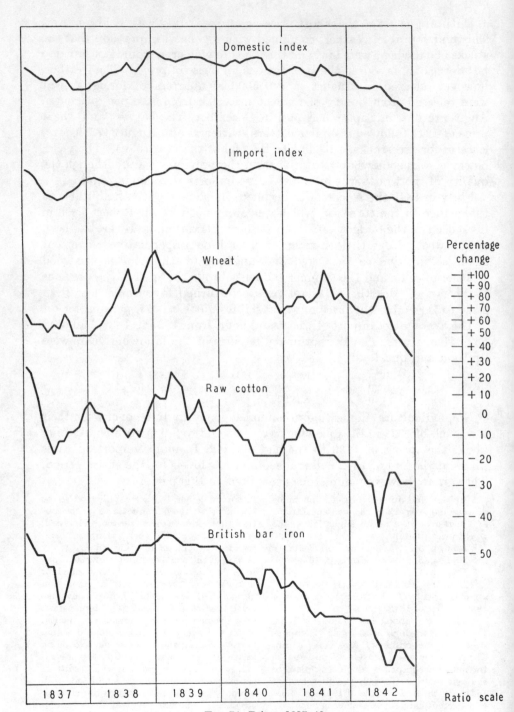

FIG. 74. Prices, 1837–42

	Low point 1838	High point 1839	Low point 1840	Low point 1841	Low point 1842
Iron bars (£ per ton) . . .	(Sept.) 9·5	(Mar.) 10·5	(Aug.) 7·8	(Dec.) 6·9	(Dec.) 5·5
Iron pigs (£ per ton) . . .	(Aug.) 5·5	(May) 6·2	(Aug.) 4·8	(Dec.) 4·8	(Dec.) 3·5
Block tin (s. per cwt.) . . .	(Dec.) 84·0	(Feb.) 90·0	(June) 78·0	(Dec.) 78·0	(Dec.) 64·0
Lead pigs (£ per ton) . . .	(Sept.) 19·0	(Feb.) 20·5	(June) 17·0	(Apr.) 19·8	(Dec.) 17·0
Copper (pence per lb.) . . .	(Sept.) 10·5	(Apr.) 11·5	(Aug.) 11·0	(Dec.) 11·5	(Dec.) 9·5
Unmelted tallow (s. per cwt.) . .	(June) 48·0	(Jan.) 59·0	(May) 50·0	(June) 48·0	(May) 48·0
Mottled soap (s. per cwt.) . .	(Aug.) 58·0	(July) 62·0	(Dec.) 57·0	(Dec.) 52·0	(July) 50·0
Rape oil (£ per ton) . . .	(May) 37·0	(Jan.) 44·8	(Jan.) 36·0	(July) 44·5	(Dec.) 42·0
Sunderland coal (s. per chaldron) .	(July) 29·8	(Dec.) 32·7	(June) 29·2	(Sept.) 26·4	(Aug.) 25·7
Leather butts (pence per lb.) . .	(Oct.) 18·5	(Dec.) 19·4	(July) 19·0	(Dec.) 19·4	(Dec.) 18·7

The prices of metals conform best to the general movement. But, as in the period 1827–32, there is considerable diversity in amplitude, and, in some cases, direction. In most cases, however, unlike the domestic index, individual non-agricultural prices were lower in 1842 than in 1832. The secular trend operative from 1814 (even earlier in some instances) again appeared.

From a low point in July 1837 the import price index rises irregularly to a peak in September 1840, declining steadily thereafter, without important interruption, to the end of 1842, when it is at a new low point for the period 1790–1842. In 1838–9 the fluctuations in import prices can be traced largely to inventory demands :[1]

As the markets were advancing at the close of 1838, in consequence of the stocks (of which comparative statements, at that time of the year, are usually made) being found to be rather below expectation, so, in December, 1839, the markets in some instances, have declined upon its being found that stocks were larger than they had been at the corresponding period of 1838.

In cotton especially there was a sharp rise from the autumn of 1838 (6·9d. per lb., in October) to the spring of 1839 (9·5d. per lb. in April), due to a deficient American crop.[2]

Although the import index reaches a peak in September 1840, prices

the labouring population, precluded any material improvement for the present; and the reports from the manufacturing districts grew gradually more gloomy than ever. Towards the close of the summer, it was ascertained that the consumption of raw materials in our principal manufactures was proceed- ing at a rate considerably lower even than that of the previous year. During the latter half of 1841 the general depression rather increased than diminished.' (Tooke, iv. 45–6.)

[1] Ibid. iii. 64–5.
[2] Ibid., pp. 63–4.

generally sagged from April 1839. The more general trend is, however, distorted by the speculations in tea and in sugar, caused by obstructions in

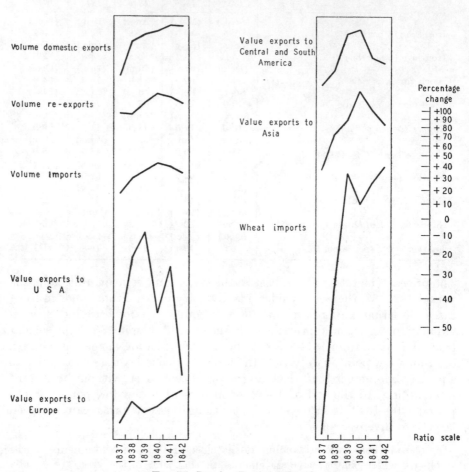

FIG. 75. Foreign Trade, 1837–42

the supply from China and the West Indies, respectively. On the whole, in 1840, 'the markets for produce were dull, and prices, generally, declining, under a diminished demand, during the whole year'.[1] Expectations of revival in 1841 were quickly disappointed and prices fell steadily to the end of 1842.[2] Although easy money and a return of confidence can be discerned in 1842, no revival of demand took place sufficient to halt the down-

[1] Tooke, iv. 44.
[2] Ibid., pp. 45–9. 'Excepting a few weeks at the end of 1842 the markets for produce other than corn may be said to have retained during the whole of the year, the quiet and drooping character observed in those of the previous year. The only striking exception was seen in the article of indigo, the price of which, in consequence of reports from India of a deficient crop, rose considerably during the autumn.' Indigo rose from 7·3s. per lb. in March to 7·9s. in December.

ward movement of prices.[1] The basis for general revival was, however, well established by the close of the year.[2]

Significant individual import prices (inclusive of duty) moved as follows :

	Aug. 1838	Aug. 1839	Sept. 1840	Dec. 1841	Dec. 1842
Coffee (s. per cwt.) . . .	143·0	152·0	135·0	113·0	99·0
Cotton (pence per lb.) . .	6·9	7·8	6·3	6·1	5·5
Ginger (s. per cwt.) . . .	53·0	58·0	57·5	54·5	46·5
Hemp (£ per ton) . . .	30·3	36·1	39·6	36·9	32·0
Indigo (s. per lb.) . .	8·1	9·7	9·2	8·5	7·9
China silk (s. per cwt.) . .	26·1	23·6	24·6	21·1	20·3
Sugar (s. per cwt.) . . .	50·0	63·0	81·0	58·0	56·0
Tea (pence per lb.) . . .	44·0	42·5	54·6	47·6	43·7
Timber (s. per load) . .	90·0	90·0	88·5	80·5	71·0

In most cases a decline can be dated from the spring or summer of 1839. The delayed peaks (1840) in the prices of sugar, Chinese silk and tea, and hemp appear clearly. In most instances, however, the movement is fairly regular ; and, like non-agricultural domestic prices, the level of 1842 is below that of 1838.

With many exceptions, then, prices other than domestic grain rose in 1838 to a peak early in 1839, and fell away to the end of 1842, finding, on the whole, new low levels at the latter point. As in the period 1827–32, there are several instances of minor inventory booms, none of which resulted in protracted price rises.

[1] The import price index does, in fact, rise slightly from June to August 1842; but this is a movement confined almost exclusively to cotton, which moved from 4·5d. per lb. in June 1842 to 5·8d. in September. It then fell away, more or less regularly, to April 1846.

[2] Tooke, iv. 47–8.

'During the first months of the year (1842) several important branches of our foreign trade were held in suspense by the uncertainty attending the fate of the tariff proposed by Sir R. Peel at the opening of the session.

'Towards the close of the spring some signs of returning prosperity became distinctly visible. It was evident that commercial operations were again being extended— slowly, and for some time with but little effect on the apparent condition of the community—but the movement was observable in several directions; and especially in a gradually increasing demand for capital. And when, as the summer advanced, it became generally known that the harvest was likely to prove better than any that had been gathered in this country for several years, the improvement was perceptibly though slightly accelerated. . . . This con-

fidence was checked and diminished for a time by the disturbances in the manufacturing districts which, beginning in the midland counties in June, had spread, before the first week in August, to Lancashire, Yorkshire, and the west of Scotland. But these were not of long continuance, and were suppressed with little if any violence. And when tranquillity was restored in the disturbed districts, the work-people—their means being entirely exhausted by want of employment, and the long previous high prices of food, and other necessaries—readily met the renewed offers of employment which the manufacturers, finding their stocks materially reduced by the increasing demand and the long cessation from work, were enabled to offer.

'These circumstances, if taken in combination with the assurance of abundant grain crops, the news of the Chinese Treaty, the settlement of the corn laws and the tariff, and a great fall in the prices of cattle, may be regarded as having opened, in the last quarter of 1842, the prospect of revived prosperity which was realised in the spring of the following year.'

2. Foreign Trade. The volume of British exports increased steadily from 1838 to 1841, then fell slightly to a low point in 1842; due to a declining price level, however, the real value of exports is at its peak in 1839. The quantities of imports, swollen with large grain purchases, and of re-exports reach a peak in 1840, and then decline to 1842:

(In £ millions)

	Volume of			Value of domestic exports
	Total imports	Re-exports	Domestic exports	
1837 . .	62·6	9·7	35·3	42·1
1838 . .	69·0	9·6	44·0	50·1
1839 . .	72·2	10·4	46·3	53·2
1840 . .	76·0	11·0	47·2	51·4
1841 . .	74·2	10·8	49·1	51·6
1842 . .	71·3	10·3	48·8	47·4

As in the years 1827–32 the real value of the sales in Britain's chief markets varied irregularly, with no sustained upward movement in any direction (in £ millions):

	Value of Domestic Exports to							
	Northern Europe	Southern Europe	Africa	Asia	U.S.A.	British North American colonies and W. Indies	Foreign W. Indies	Central and S. America (including Brazil)
1837	11·5	7·9	1·4	5·6	4·7	5·6	1·1	4·3
1838	12·1	10·1	1·8	7·0	7·6	5·4	1·3	4·7
1839	12·3	8·5	1·6	7·6	8·8	7·0	1·3	6·0
1840	12·3	9·2	1·6	9·3	5·3	6·4	1·1	6·2
1841	13·2	9·7	1·9	8·2	7·1	5·5	1·1	5·1
1842	14·0	9·9	1·7	7·5	3·5	4·9	0·9	5·0

In all but the instance of the British American colonies, there was an increase in sales in 1838. A further rise followed in 1839, except for southern Europe and Africa. In 1840 a decline in the real value of exports to the United States, Canada, and the West Indies more than offset a considerable increase in Asiatic sales, minor increases elsewhere. The official value of exports, however, increased considerably in 1840.[1] Severe depression was confined to the markets of the United States.[2]

---

[1] Evidence before the Select Committee on Import Duties (1840) indicates the following caution in interpreting the increase in the quantity of exports in 1840 (p. 81): 'The increased amount of exports must not always be considered as showing . . . an increased demand for them in foreign markets; the great bulk of that increase of exports which appeared during the last year consisted of goods that have been manufactured for home consumption, and which were sent to foreign countries for the purpose of finding a market, and not from their having been ordered or prepared according to order.'

[2] The domestic and foreign trade indexes,

An increase in exports to the United States, and a fairly general revival in the early months of 1841, account for the increase in both the value and quantity of total exports in 1841. By the end of the year, however, both home and foreign markets were depressed :[1]

During the latter half of 1841 the general depression rather increased than diminished; and at its close, though the pressure upon commerce had not then reached its maximum, the distress experienced by almost every class of producers, and more particularly by the operatives in the manufacturing districts, was probably greater than at any other period, as being yet wholly unrelieved by any definite prospect of improvement.

Led by the United States, there was, in 1842, a decline in the real value of sales to all markets except those of northern Europe. The total volume of exports declines as well, although less drastically, the difference in the declines measuring, roughly, the extent of the fall in prices of the articles of British export. By the end of 1842 signs of general recovery in foreign as well as in home markets were evident; but on the whole it was a severely depressed year, the low point in the cyclical movement dating from 1837.

A number of non-economic factors affected the course of foreign trade in these years. In the summer of 1840 'the prospect of hostilities with the United States, and, somewhat later, the threatening aspect of our relations with France, tended strongly to increase the prevailing disposition of mercantile men to contract their engagements'.[2] In 1840–1 the China trade, freed from the East India monopoly in 1833, was obstructed by the Opium War.[3] The real value of exports there fell from £1·2 million in 1838 to £0·5 million in 1840. In April 1841, however, preliminary arrangements for peace were negotiated.[4] At about the same time the danger of an American war passed, as both Harrison and Tyler spoke pacifically.[5]

In the early months of 1842 'important branches of our foreign trade were held in suspense by . . . the fate of the tariff proposed by Sir R. Peel at the opening of the session'.[6] The new tariff schedules ranged from 5 to 20 per cent.[7] Although an unpopular income tax was imposed at the same time, merchants, as a whole, were pleased. The free trade movement, with the onset of unemployment and bad harvests, had grown impressively after 1837.

compiled for the United States by Smith and Cole (p. 73), move as follows:

	Domestic trade	Foreign trade	Combined
1837 .	100	110	103
1838 .	96	100	97
1839 .	103	122	109
1840 .	92	102	95
1841 .	95	104	98
1842 .	91	86	89

[1] Tooke, iv. 46.
[2] Ibid., pp. 43–4.

[3] A definite peace was not signed until 1842. The Treaty of Nanking ensured peace in the China trade for about the next ten years. For an account of the somewhat ruthless development after the end of the East India monopoly, see Redford, pp. 118–21; also more fully, Levi, pp. 238–43, and Clapham, pp. 486–9.
[4] Tooke, iv. 45–6. From 1841 to 1845 exports to China rose steadily, to a peak of £2·4 million.
[5] Ibid., p. 46.
[6] Ibid., p. 47.
[7] For a full account of the tariff reforms of 1842, see Levi, pp. 259–71.

The official value of exports in 1842 is far above the peak figure for 1836; the real value is considerably below. Again the secular character of the period emerges, with falling prices reducing, at a time of relative stagnation, the gross income of British exporters, despite a substantially increased

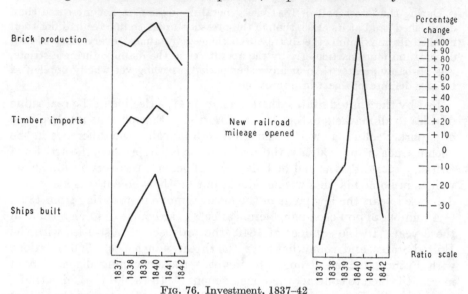

FIG. 76. Investment, 1837–42

volume of sales. A more specific feature of these years is the sharp decline in the value of shipments to the United States. The credit structure which financed the swollen figures of 1835–6 was largely liquidated by 1842. In 1836 the real value of exports to the United States constituted the largest category of British trade; in 1842 it stood sixth in relative importance.

3. Investment. Although the crisis of 1836 had been, in the first instance, associated primarily with the American trade, it brought about a stagnation in new investment generally. There was some revival in 1838 and the early months of 1839, but from the financial crisis of 1839 to the return of monetary ease and general confidence in 1842 enterprise was at a fairly low level.

The sums authorized by Parliament for railway construction moved as follows (in £ millions):[1]

---

[1] Porter, p. 332. The decline in the expected dividends of the railway lines led to a relative growth in the floatation of preference shares in the late thirties and early forties (in per cent.):

Preference shares as percentage of all shares

1836 .	. ..	1840 .	. 31
1837 .	. 3	1841 .	. 27
1838 .	. 7	1842 .	. 28
1839 .	. 15		

At the peak in 1845 only 4 per cent. of the shares were preferred. Speaking in 1839, the president of the Birmingham, Bristol, and Thames Junction line stated: 'The present scarcity of money, and the temporary depreciation of railway property in all parts of the Kingdom preclude the expectation of raising the . . . funds by any other means' (Evans, *British Corporation Finance*, pp. 84 and 89).

1837	.	.	13·5	1840	.	.	2·5
1838	.	.	2·1	1841	.	.	3·4
1839	.	.	6·5	1842	.	.	5·3

Between 1839 and 1843 no new railway lines were opened. Funds raised, for the most part, were for the extension and improvement of existing lines.[1] Although new enterprise fell off drastically, the decline in railway building was not proportionate.

Brick production and timber imports move as follows:

	Production of bricks (in million bricks)	Quantity of fir timber imports (in 1,000 loads of 50 cu. ft.)
1837 . .	1,478	580
1838 . .	1,427	647
1839 . .	1,569	623
1840 . .	1,678	692
1841 . .	1,424	654
1842 . .	1,272	—

The peak in 1840 is at a higher level than that in 1836. The continuance of railway building, inaugurated in the previous years, as well as the more general revival of 1838 and the early months of 1839, probably accounts for the rise.[2]

The most striking form of new investment activity in these years was, however, the construction of new ships. The industry had been chronically

[1] New railway lines completed in these years were:

Date of Act	Name of railway	Terminals	Length in miles	Cost of construction
1838	Edinburgh and Glasgow	Edinburgh and Glasgow	46	£1,200,000
1839	Bristol and Gloucester Extension	Westerleigh and Standish	22	£533,000
	Newcastle and Darlington	Newcastle and Darlington	57¼	..
	Gravesend and Rochester	Gravesend and Rochester	6½	..

Railway acts passed by Parliament were:

	For new lines	For extension of existing lines and for giving amended and enlarged powers	Total
1838 . .	2	17	19
1839 . .	3	24	27
1840 . .	..	24	24
1841 . .	1	18	19
1842 . .	4	18	22

(Porter, pp. 329 and 331.)

[2] Shannon, p. 309. Another factor was the demand for new houses consequent on the shift of labour from agricultural to industrial areas (*A.R.*, 1842, p. 16).

depressed since the end of the Napoleonic War. In 1837, however, a ship-building boom got under way which reached its peak in 1840 :[1]

(In 1,000 tons)

	Tonnage of shipping belonging to the United Kingdom	Tonnage of ships built and registered in the United Kingdom
1837 . .	2,296	131·2
1838 . .	2,384	157·3
1839 . .	2,531	181·3
1840 . .	2,724	211·3
1841 . .	2,887	159·6
1842 . .	2,991	129·9

In 1839 the total tonnage in the United Kingdom, for the first time, surpassed the figure for 1816 (2,479). The tonnage built in 1840 constituted a new record total, and even the figure for 1842 is above that for the peaks in 1825 and 1835 (122·5 and 116·6, respectively).

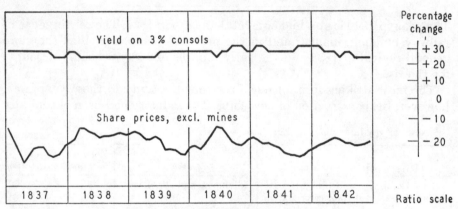

FIG. 77. Investment, 1837–42

A growing percentage of new ships were equipped with steam power. The tonnage of new steamships built and registered increased as follows (in 1,000 tons) :[2]

1837 .	. 11·7	1840 .	. 10·3
1838 .	. 9·5	1841 .	. 11·4
1839 .	. 6·1	1842 .	. 13·7

New steamships built were 11 per cent. of all new ship construction in 1842: total steamships, however, were but 4 per cent. of total shipping registered at that time.

---

[1] Shipping companies were one of the subsidiary 'objects of the speculative mania' of 1835–6. The increase in new shipping in the following years was probably connected directly with these new building firms, al-though 'in many cases the whole of the capital has been lost, and the companies dissolved' (Matthias Dunn, *A View of the Coal Trade*, p. 204).

[2] Porter, p. 318.

Joint-stock floatations and foreign loans attracted little new capital.
The numerous joint-stock failures in 1836–7, the believed irresponsibility
of their promoters, the lack of any effective regulation produced a 'stern
opposition to joint-stock enterprise which continued from even the commercial community'.[1] A considerable number of insurance companies,
however, continued to be formed, as well as a few joint-stock banks (the
latter, on the whole, had weathered the crisis of 1836–7 well):

	Number established	
	Joint-stock banks	Insurance companies
1837 . .	5	4
1838 . .	1	2
1839 . .	6	8
1840 . .	6	4
1841 . .	2	2
1842 . .	2	3

From 1837 to 1842 there were few new foreign government loans issued,[2]
and, in 1839, the credit of the United States in the London market collapsed. That it was maintained until then is testimony largely to the
ingenuity of Nicholas Biddle. Jenks thus describes the process whereby
British bankers were persuaded to extend American credit from 1837 to
1839:[3]

The Bank of the United States (Biddle's institution), with other banks along
the coast, was caught between the demand for gold in the interior and the
rapidly maturing indebtedness to London. Ultimately it joined in the general
suspension of specie payments. However this action could only defer liquidation
which must be effected in commodities and securities whose prices were falling
rapidly. It appeared to Biddle that the country could only be rescued, in the
first place, by persuading the London money market to absorb more American
securities in liquidation of the most pressing obligations, and secondly, by extending sufficient credit to American planters and cotton factors to enable them
to hold their stocks for a rise in the price of raw cotton. As it developed the two
policies were but aspects of a single grandiose operation.

How was London to be captivated by new securities when she was paying
heavily for possession of the old? Some short-term paper with something of
the prestige of a Treasury note, which the Bank of England could not reasonably
refuse to discount, seemed to be required. A conference of leading bankers of
New York and Philadelphia took place in the former city on the evening of

---

[1] Hunt, p. 86. A typical view is that expressed in the *Circular to Bankers* (1838):
'Nothing should be done by the legislature
to weaken the motives for personal industry,
economy and thrift. The moral effect of all
joint stock associations for mercantile objects which are properly within the compass
of individual exertion is bad; they introduce
in the place of patient labour and moderate
expectations, ambitious hopes and habit of
gambling in shares.' (Idem.)

[2] In 1839 Brazil issued in London a loan
of £313,000, and in 1842 Chile drew £757,000.
In addition, calls on previously contracted
loans occasionally affected the market.

[3] Op. cit., pp. 89–90. See also Andréadès,
pp. 267–8.

March 29, at which Biddle disclosed his plan and enlisted support. On the morrow he announced the readiness of the Bank of the United States to sell 'post-notes'—interest-bearing bonds to bearer, maturing within ten to eighteen months—up to $5,000,000. The Manhattan Banking Co., the Bank of America, the Girard Bank, and the Morris Canal and Banking Company issued similar notes for smaller amounts. In New York these six percent notes commanded an immediate premium of 12½ percent, but even this was less than the premium demanded for gold. The correspondents of British firms bought them in with avidity for shipment to London in place of bullion or bills. The arrival of the 'post-notes' on Lombard Street at the end of April created great excitement and surprise. Journalists became sensational as they considered the momentousness of the event. No one ventured to doubt their intrinsic security. Not even the Bank of England would decline to honor them. And it began to appear that that venerable institution was being outwitted by the clever Mr. Biddle. Its policy during the crisis had turned upon manipulating the discount rate and circulation to recover gold from the United States. Instead of gold, its net was gathering more securities.

The domestic bills acquired by the Biddle syndicate represented loans in anticipation of the cotton crop.[1] Their value depended on the success of the harvest and the maintenance of a high cotton price. The syndicate extended credit freely throughout 1838. The cotton price in Britain rose from 7·1*d*. per lb. in May 1838 to 9·5*d*. in April 1839.

A general recovery in the United States and, partially in Britain, led to further purchases of American state securities. Capital exports to the United States, in fact, substantially increased. Until the spring of 1839 optimism in London was almost as whole-hearted as it had been in 1835–6. The temporary resuscitation of the Anglo-American financial structure ended in the financial crisis of 1839.[2] The cotton price, moreover, fell to 7·1*d*. per lb. by December as Manchester manufacturers cut down output and went on short time. The American banking system, holders of great quantities of paper dependent on a high cotton price, suffered severe panic.

---

[1] Jenks, pp. 90–5.

[2] Jenks lists the forces which produced the panic in London as follows (pp. 95–6): 'The resources of the London money market were, in the first place, imperilled by the crop failure of 1838 which necessitated the expenditure in that year and the one succeeding of ten million pounds for foreign grain. At the same time the new textile industries of Belgium, Prussia, and Saxony reached a crisis in their development which curtailed their demand for English yarn. The consequent strain upon the resources of the Bank of England was only partly relieved by large gold borrowings from the Bank of France. The stoppage of the Bank of Belgium in December, 1838, was an early symptom of acute financial malaise throughout western Europe. The political news from all parts of the world was of the most unsettling nature. In the Near East a major European crisis was brewing over the pretensions of Mehemet Ali. In Asia the Afghan border seethed with intrigue and unrest. In China the dispute over the opium traffic was sundering a highly important link in the foreign trade system both of Great Britain and of the United States. There was a French blockade at Buenos Ayres, destroying trade to protect the merchants. At home the Chartist movement was alarming to fund-holders, while the periodic flare-ups over the Maine boundary were causing private investors to turn a deaf ear to the blandishments of American securities.'

In the course of 1841 and 1842 nine states stopped payment on their bonds.[1] In the summer of 1842 agents of the United States Treasury were coldly turned away from the London market. *The Times* wrote:

The people of the United States may be fully persuaded that there is a certain class of securities to which no abundance of money, however great, can give value; and that in this class their own securities stand pre-eminent.[2]

In this atmosphere of outraged innocence 'it was highly embarrassing for an American to be in London in the winter of 1842–3'. It is little wonder that diplomatic relations were under serious strain, and that British investors placed their funds fairly close to home in the ensuing boom.

On the whole, then, there was some revival of investment activity in 1838–9, which extended, for building and ship-construction, into 1840. The financial crisis of the spring of 1839 appeared to have destroyed confidence finally in American securities and induced a general pessimism and caution.

Security prices, however, after recovering throughout 1837, had turned downward during the first half of 1838: the security index had its peak in March, India Stock in May, Consols in June of that year. They share a revival in the early months of 1840, but then continue to fall. In every case, however, a strong recovery set in during 1842, anticipating somewhat the up-turn in general business activity. The decline of these prices in 1838 was probably a result of the revival of speculative activity in American securities at that time. Bank Stock sagged until February 1838, then fell to the end of 1840, more sharply than either India Stock or Consols; it shared the revival of the first quarter of 1841, but moved up strongly only from October 1842. The dividend on Bank Stock was lowered in 1839 to 7 per cent.[3] The abnormal decline in its price during 1839–40 almost certainly is to be explained as a consequence of this reduction in yield.

The yield on Consols reflects the financial ease and recovery of 1838, the stringency of 1839, the political uncertainties and difficulties of 1840–1, the coming of monetary ease and the framework of general recovery in 1842:

Yield on 3 per cent. Consols

(Per cent.)

1837	.	. 3·28	1840	.	. 3·32
1838	.	. 3·20	1841	.	. 3·36
1839	.	. 3·26	1842	.	. 3·26

In 1843–4 the yield on Consols reached new low levels, continuing the secular downward tendency of the long-term interest rate, which the artificial stringency of 1840–2 served only briefly to interrupt.

4. Industry and Agriculture. Pig-iron production had been estimated at 1·2 million tons in 1836. Other fairly reliable figures for 1838–42 are the following:

[1] Ibid., pp. 102–4.
[2] Quoted, ibid., p. 106.
[3] Ayres, p. 461.

Tons

1838	. .	—
1839	. .	1,248,780
1840	. .	1,396,400
1841	. .	1,500,000
1842	. .	1,099,138

Iron output recovered from the depression of 1837 until 1841, then declined in 1842. Unemployment among iron-founders, however, would indicate a peak in 1838 rather than 1840, and some recovery in 1842.

1837	. .	12·4 per cent.	1840	. .	14·8 per cent.
1838	. .	10·5 ,,	1841	. .	18·5 ,,
1839	. .	11·1 ,,	1842	. .	11·0 ,,

The unemployment figures, however, do not include Scottish workers; and it was in Scotland that output was increasing most rapidly in these years. Even at the height of the depression, in 1841, new furnaces were being erected there.[1] But in England and Wales the entire period 1838–42 was relatively depressed, especially the latter three years.

Until 1841, however, the quantity of iron exports continued to increase :[2]

Exports of Iron, Hardware, and Cutlery
(In £ millions)

		Volume	*Value*
1837	. .	3·5	3·5
1838	. .	4·5	4·0
1839	. .	5·2	4·5
1840	. .	5·2	3·9
1841	. .	6·2	4·5
1842	. .	6·1	3·9

[1] Hamilton, p. 184. In 1838 'the Carnbroe Works was established by Merry and Cunningham, in the same district, while westwards the Shotts Iron Company was building additional furnaces at Castlehill. In the parish of Govan, Dixon, proprietor of Calder, was establishing eight furnaces besides his coal mine, four of which were in blast by 1840. In May 1841 there were no less than sixty-four furnaces in blast in Lanarkshire and eight new ones were in process of erection. Most of these works were in the parishes of Old and New Monkland, and the rapid expansion of the coal and iron industries is seen in the very marked increase in population. Between 1831 and 1841 the former had increased by 105 per cent. and the latter by 108 per cent. Before 1821 Airdrie had been a weaving town, now it was predominantly a coal and metallurgical population. The weavers, it was said, were deserting the looms for the coal-mines and iron-works.

'Meantime the industry was making headway in Ayrshire, the other main centre of it. By 1840 the Blair Works near Dalry had two furnaces in blast, and at Galston there were two others, while at Kilbirnie one was being built in 1841. But this was only the beginning.' 'In 1839 the make of iron was 1,248,780 tons, with a depressed trade. With a view to its improvement it was agreed by the iron-masters, that there should be a reduction in the make of 20 per cent., to remain in force from the 22nd February to 1st July, 1840. . . . Notwithstanding the agreed reduction of make, there was a considerable increase in the year 1840, attributable principally to Scotland, the quantity made being 1,396,400 tons.' (Scrivenor, edition of 1854, p. 290.)

[2] Iron shipments on the Monmouthshire and Glamorganshire canals are available only to 1840. The latter declined in 1840, the former rose steadily from 1837 to 1840 (in 1,000 tons):

		Glamorganshire	*Monmouthshire*
1837	. .	124·8	144·3
1838	. .	130·6	169·4
1839	. .	132·8	176·3
1840	. .	132·0	194·7

(Scrivenor (1854), pp. 257–8.)

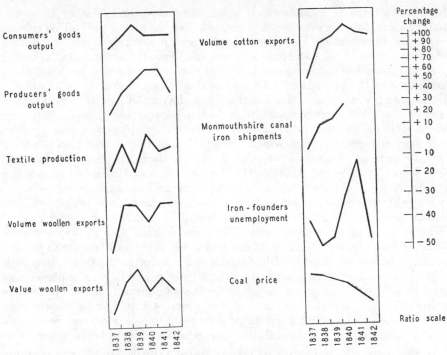

FIG. 78. Industry and Agriculture, 1837-42

Iron prices fell from the spring of 1839 to new low levels in 1842. Increased sales abroad yielded British iron exporters a lesser gross return in 1842 than in 1838. The annual average price of pig-iron, for example, moved as follows (£ per ton):

1837	.	. 5·5	1840	.	. 5·2
1838	.	. 5·9	1841	.	. 5·0
1839	.	. 6·0	1842	.	. 4·6

The distress of the iron industry in the few years preceding 1842 was explained at the time by reference to competition from Scotland and a diminished demand from the railways :[1]

Fourteen years ago (1828) the whole of Scotland scarcely produced 35,000 tons of iron per annum, the greater portion of which being absorbed at home, its influence on the English market was unknown. Last year Scotland, stimulated and encouraged by the large advances and paper issues of her banks, produced an enormous quantity of iron, with which she has deluged every part of England without the least regard to the important fact, that the demand all the time was decreasing in the same ratio that their supply increased; and what is the result ? Prices have been forced down, even in Scotland, below the cost of production, the workmen in the meantime being ground to the earth to enable

---

[1] Quoted by Scrivenor (1854) from *The Times* (5 December 1842) and the *Circular to Bankers* (18 November 1842), pp. 284-6 and 290-1.

the masters there to continue their insane conflict with each other as to who shall produce the greatest quantity, and sell it at the lowest price! This ruinous system of over-trading has reacted with fearful severity upon the mining interests of Staffordshire and South Wales, and hence the outbreak in the month of August last, which was to be attributed entirely to the pressure upon those districts from the excessive production of the Scotch works, which has placed the English ironmasters in this position—that having to pay their workmen in hard money, while their competitors in Scotland are paying in paper, they were undersold in the market, and had no alternative but to stop their works altogether, or to reduce wages to a point which threw their men into almost open rebellion. This, be assured, is the true solution of the riots in the mining districts of August last; for whatever may be said to the contrary, neither Chartists nor corn-law agitators would have been listened to for a moment, had not distress (mainly to be traced to the immense production in Scotland) made the workmen ripe for disturbance. . . . The production of iron has of late years been in excess of all probable demand for consumption. This new demand (for railways) cannot continue with the same force as in the period which elapsed from 1833 to 1841 inclusive, because of the diminished operations in constructing railways in England, the reluctance of capitalists to embark their money in such undertakings, since proof of their inadequate returns for it was obtained, and the protective tariffs of foreign countries. The annual production of iron in Great Britain must be diminished considerably from the highest point to afford any chance of a sale for it at prices which will remunerate the capitalists engaged in the trade.

In the boom which reached its climax in 1836 the iron industry expanded rapidly, much as it had in 1824–5. When the demand for rail iron declined and the application of the hot-blast in Scotland reduced costs there, the British and Welsh works were in the same difficult position they had faced from 1826 to 1832. Monopoly attempts were made to limit output and maintain prices;[1] and, as in the testimony before the Committee on Manufactures (1833), the iron masters stated their belief that 'the depression . . . their trade was suffering, as well as that affecting most other branches of productive industry, was attributable to the great falling off in the demand, occasioned by the vicious operation of our present money laws'.[2] Peel's reply to this explanation was that—

the production of iron had been forced, by the requirements for railroads and other causes, so much beyond the ordinary demand that, now that these sources of consumption had been supplied, he could hold out no prospect of immediate improvement from any measures within the power of the Government.

Whatever the cause, it is clear that in 1842, and if the figures for unemployment are at all trustworthy, in the five years previous, the iron industry, its fixed resources expanded, was suffering severely a lack of new orders.

The disintegration of monopolistic controls in the coal industry 'turned around one great central fact, namely, the continuous and unexampled expansion in productive capacity'.[3] The crucial period of that expansion

[1] Scrivenor (1854), pp. 290–2.
[2] Ibid., p. 293, quoted from the statement   of the deputation which visited Sir Robert Peel.   [3] Sweezy, p. 109.

was 1836-43, when various estimates indicate an increase in productive capacity of between 60 and 70 per cent.[1] The sale of coal, in this interval, increased by only 30 per cent.—'the conclusion to be drawn from the evidence submitted seems to be the obvious one that productive capacity was running ahead of sales and to a greater degree after 1836 than before'.[2] Even when the new collieries fell within the regulation, the older collieries suffered from the need of giving up part of their quotas to the new-comers. This movement is illustrated by the following figures which give the annual quota per 1,000 chaldrons of basis (i.e. roughly, full capacity):[3]

1835	.	. 768	1840	.	. 555
1838	.	. 695	1842	.	. 500

The cyclical decline in general business conditions in 1839-42 undoubtedly accentuated the regulative problems of the coal industry. 1837-8 were 'two relatively untroubled years', with the contracts in 1838 showing evidences of real prosperity.[4] But the difficulties of regulation then became progressively worse, with the number of collieries outside the control increasing, those within (as in 1829-32) violating the restrictive rules of the organization.[5]

The annual average price of Sunderland coal and coal shipments follow :[6]

	Price of Sunderland coal (s. per chaldron)	Total coastwise shipments	Exports to		Total shipments
			British colonies	Foreign countries	
			(in 1,000 tons)		
1837 . .	32·6	7,091	247	866	8,204
1838 . .	32·3	7,190	261	1,053	8,504
1839 . .	31·4	7,223	254	1,195	8,672
1840 . .	30·7	7,476	300	1,307	9,082
1841 . .	28·8	7,650	351	1,497	9,498
1842 . .	27·2	7,649	352	1,647	9,649

Coal shipments reveal little about the state of the industry in these years. The steady decline in price, however, indicates the chronic state of relative depression after 1838—this despite the fact that total coal output was probably increasing. The Hoffmann index of capital goods' production, like coal shipments, shows an increase from 1837 to 1841, but declines in 1842:

1837	.	. 8·2	1840	.	. 11·0
1838	.	. 9·4	1841	.	. 11·0
1839	.	. 10·2	1842	.	. 9·4

[1] Ibid., pp. 111-12.

[2] Ibid., p. 112. See also Dunn, p. 203: 'The disproportionate increase of consumption to the inordinate supply of coal has so reduced the proportionate vend from each colliery, that, generally speaking, the quantities and consequent depressed prices have gradually become inadequate to effect a remunerative trade.'

[3] Sweezy, p. 119.

[4] Sweezy, p. 123: 'The clauses guaranteeing 10 days' work and 30s. wages per fortnight were restored, having been out ever since the strike of 1832; while the owners were exhorted not to hire men away from each other. There are no surer signs than these that the labor market was tight and wages in danger of going up.'

[5] Ibid., pp. 125-7.

[6] Porter, p. 281.

The divergent secular trends for prices and output appear clearly in statistics in the cotton industry. Prices, except in 1839, fell steadily; the volume of exports, however, increased sharply to 1840, declining only slightly even in the depressed two years that followed.

	Price of cotton		Consump- tion of raw cotton	Stocks of raw cotton	Exports of cotton manufactures	
	Raw cotton including duty (pence per lb.)	Yarn exports			Official value	Declared value
			(in million lb.)		(in £ millions)	
1837 . .	7·6	16·1	368	116	51·1	20·6
1838 . .	7·4	15·6	455	161	64·8	24·2
1839 . .	8·2	15·6	352	126	67·9	24·6
1840 . .	6·7	14·4	528	207	73·1	24·7
1841 . .	6·6	14·2	437	217	69·8	23·5
1842 . .	5·6	13·6	474	242	68·7	21·7

The piling up of cotton stocks (1840–2) is a familiar depression symptom, although partially a result of the abnormally large imports of 1840. As in the coal and iron industries, there is evidence of general depression from the latter months of 1839 through 1842.[1] Writing of the Manchester cotton trade Redford says:[2] 'During the early part of 1838 trade showed some signs of recovery, both at Manchester and in other parts of the country; but before the end of the year the financial situation was once more critical. . . . After this renewed shock, business confidence could not be expected to recover quickly; and gradually the depressed 'thirties merged into the hungry 'forties.' The cotton textile districts were the centre of the Chartist agitation which accompanied the period of unemployment and high food prices.[3] The manufacturers, at the same time, became much concerned with the growth of foreign competition, and agitated for Corn Law repeal as a means of lowering wages and reducing the threat it seemed to offer.[4]

Foreign trade figures for the woollen industry present a similar picture of recovery and irregular stagnation against a background of sagging prices:

	Quantity of raw wool imports (in million lb.)	Price of Saxon im- ported wool (pence per lb.)	Exports of woollen manufactures	
			Official value	Declared value
			(in £ millions)	
1837 . .	48·4	55	4·8	5·0
1838 . .	52·6	55	6·6	6·2
1839 . .	57·4	55	6·6	6·7
1840 . .	49·4	52	5·9	5·8
1841 . .	56·2	49	6·6	6·3
1842 . .	45·9	49	6·6	5·8

[1] For the worsening position after 1839, see *Evidence before Committee on Import Duties* (1840), p. 171.   [2] Op. cit., p. 83.
[3] For evidence of unemployment in the textile areas:—1839: *P.P.* 1840, xvii. 401–5;
1840: *P.P.* 1841, xi. 319; 1841: *P.P.* 1842, xix. 10–11, and Tooke, iv. 46; 1842: *P.P.* 1843, xxi. 5, and *A.R.*, 1842, pp. 135–9.
[4] *Evidence before Committee on Import Duties* (1840), pp. 160 ff.

The peak in the export branches of the trade seems to have come in **1838–9,** with the decline thereafter broken by a revival in 1841 (related, probably, to the mild American recovery of that year). The divergence in the movement of official and declared values indicates a rise in the average price of woollen exports in 1839, a steady decline thereafter. The home market, on which the industry was largely dependent, was severely depressed in 1840–2, and unemployment was high in the woollen manufacturing districts.[1]

The Hoffmann indexes of consumers' goods and total production and the Kondratieff index of textile production move as follows:

	Kondratieff's index of textile production	Hoffmann's index of consumers' goods production	Hoffmann's index of total production
1837 . .	29·0	23·2	15·0
1838 . .	34·5	25·0	16·4
1839 . .	28·7	27·2	17·9
1840 . .	36·7	25·3	17·5
1841 . .	32·9	25·3	17·4
1842 . .	33·7	25·3	16·6

The index of textile production follows the movement of raw cotton consumption. The index of consumers' goods production shows a turning-point in 1839, following the export figure for wool rather than cotton goods. A strong secular increase in output is indicated by the net rise from the low point in 1837 to that in 1842.

From 1838 to the summer of 1842 the farmer steadily enjoyed high prices for his products. Although b'ad harvests caused a reduction in the amounts available for sale in the market, in net there was little complaint from agricultural areas. The farmer was on the defence in Parliament, and perhaps the major consequence for him of this series of inadequate crops was the growth of free-trade sentiment. Of almost equal importance, however, was the interest, developed by the same situation, in the application of scientific principles to British agriculture. The natural conservatism of the farmer had been accentuated, on the one hand, by the persistence of falling prices and redundant acreage; but, on the other, the more enterprising farmers had also been stimulated to seek reductions in unit costs. From about 1837 there can be dated a movement towards the modernization of agricultural methods.[2] In 1840 the Royal Agricultural Society was founded; and despite the depressing psychological effects of the Corn Law repeal (1846) an era of profitable agricultural development got under way, which ended only with the coming of the Great Depression in 1873. To this mid-century profitability, however, not only did new British methods

---

[1] Ibid., pp. 247 ff.
[2] Ernle, pp. 355–9; also Adams, pp. 135–9, and Clapham, pp. 454–65.

contribute but also, of course, an altered world market position for agricultural produce.

5. Finance. Financial statistics reveal the crisis of 1839 and the failure of the money market to attain easy money thereafter until 1842 (in £ millions):

	Bullion in the Bank of England	Bills and notes discounted by the Bank of England	Number of bankruptcies (monthly average)	Total bills of exchange created	London bankers' deposits in the Bank of England	Bank-rate of discount (per cent.)	Market-rate of discount (per cent.)
1837 . .	6·0	7·6	139	258·7	1·4	5·00	4·44
1838 . .	9·7	3·3	82	266·4	1·3	4·13	3·00
1839 . .	4·4	5·9	108	303·6	0·7	5·10	5·12
1840 . .	4·2	4·6	156	300·4	0·8	5·00	4·98
1841 . .	4·7	4·7	149	286·4	0·7	5·00	4·90
1842 . .	8·3	4·2	160	249·4	1·1	4·27	3·33

The money market recovered in 1838 from the previous crisis: bullion holdings at the Bank rose, interest rates fell, bankruptcies decreased, and

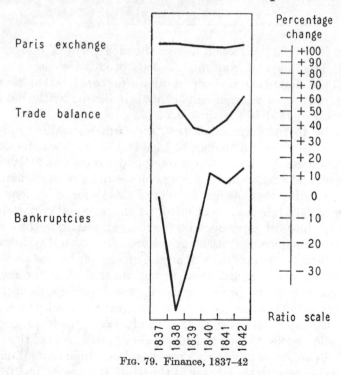

FIG. 79. Finance, 1837–42

business generally revived. Bullion reached its peak in March 1838, but declined only slightly until December; the market-rate of interest, however, showed a pronounced tendency to rise from April on, and in the last quarter especially the tightening of the market was pronounced.[1] From January to August 1839 the bullion reserve fell catastrophically and the market-rate rose to a peak in September (6½ per cent.). The Bank, however, did not raise its rate to 5 per cent. until May; and even the 5½ per cent. rate, instituted on 20 June, proved to be considerably below the market in the latter months of the year.[2] Aside from raising its rate the Bank attempted to improve its position in the following ways:

   a. By limiting the currency of bills discounted from 95 to 60 days.[3]
   b. By refusing advances except on exchequer bills.[4]
   c. By selling £760,000 of public securities in the open market.[5]
   d. By borrowing £2,000,000 in Paris, £900,000 in Hamburg.[6]

These measures succeeded in raising the reserve steadily throughout the latter months of 1839.

The major cause of this panic was the drain of bullion to the United States in payment for the large quantity of American securities then being imported.[7] But there was, as well, a banking crisis on the Continent, which centred around the newly founded joint-stock banks of France and Belgium. A part of the increase in bullion in the Bank of England for May 1837 to May 1838 can be attributed to their inflationary operations:[8]

But in the autumn of 1838, the Bank of Belgium failed, and there was a severe run upon Lafitte's bank in France, accompanied by a considerable revulsion of commercial credit, the extent and degree of which are attested by the number of bankruptcies in those countries in 1838 to 1839, and by a much more severe pressure on the trade and manufactures in those countries than has been experienced here.

The inevitable effect of the derangement of commercial credit in France and Belgium was an increased value of the precious metals; which, through the

---

[1] Tooke, iii. 83–4.
[2] Ibid., p. 86. In August the Bank rate was further raised to 6 per cent., still under the market.
[3] King, p. 82.
[4] Tooke, iii. 86–7.
[5] Macleod, p. 284.
[6] Ibid. 'Messrs. Baring entered into an agreement with twelve of the leading bankers in Paris, to draw bills upon them to the amount of upwards of £2,000,000; and as each of them had only a fixed credit at the Bank of France, that bank agreed to honour their acceptances in case they should be presented there and exceed their usual limits. An operation of a similar nature to the amount of £900,000 was organized with Hamburg. As soon as any bill was drawn on account of one of these operations, the Bank transferred an equal amount of the annuities it had offered for sale in July, to two trustees, one for the drawers and the other for the

acceptor. Out of this second credit, the bills which fell due from the creation of the first credit were paid. This measure had the effect of gradually arresting the drain of bullion, which reached its lowest point in the week ending the 2nd September, 1839, when it was reduced to £2,406,000. From that time it began slowly to increase; and in the last week of the year it stood at £4,532,000, the liabilities being £23,864,000, and the securities £22,098,000. The operations ensuing from this foreign credit extended over nine months, from July, 1839, to April, 1840, and the highest amount operated upon was in November, 1839, when it was £2,900,000.'
[7] See above, *Investment*. Also Tooke, iii. 73–4.
[8] Ibid., p. 75. The drain to the Continent in 1839 was accentuated by fears there that the Bank of England would be forced to suspend payment in specie (King, pp. 96–7).

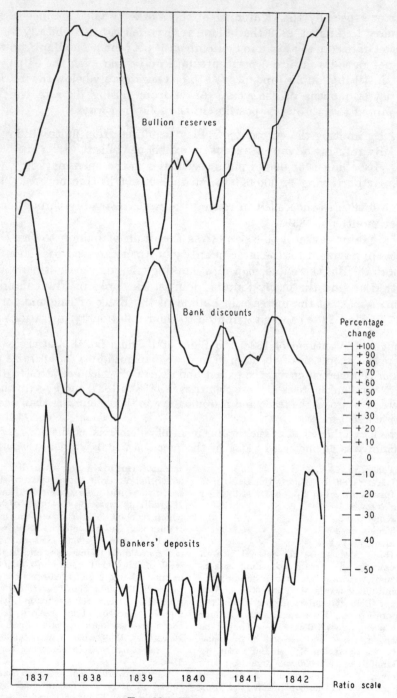

Percentage
change

+100
+ 90
+ 80
+ 70
+ 60
+ 50
+ 40
+ 30
+ 20
+ 10
0
− 10
− 20
− 30
− 40
− 50

Bullion reserves

Bank discounts

Bankers' deposits

1837   1838   1839   1840   1841   1842

Ratio scale

Fig. 80 a. Finance, 1837–42

medium of their foreign exchanges, would therefore be re-imported, and in part, if not chiefly, from this country.

A third drain on the British reserves was the large import of foreign grain required in 1839.

The first half of 1840 was a period of relatively easy money. The market rate of interest fell, the stock of bullion increased until July, the Bank rate, from 10 January, was down to 5 per cent. From July to October 1840, however, a second period of stringency occurred, by no means as severe as in the previous year but sufficient to help induce a general relapse.[1] In October the Bank again reduced the currency of bills for discount as an alternative to raising its rate ;[2] and in the last quarter of 1840 the market again became easy, with interest rates falling from November.

The pattern of the previous year was repeated in 1841 with a period of stringency occurring in the third quarter, after the earlier months had seen a continued rise in the reserve, a fall in interest rates, and some revival in the commodity markets.[3] The decline of the reserve, from July to October, was less than in 1840, as was the rise in interest rates. Large grain imports appear to have been the most important single factor operating on the bullion reserve, although, as in 1830–1, there may have been some hoarding in the interior due to political unrest, stemming from the activities of the Chartists and the more rabid Anti-Corn Law Leaguers.

From October 1841 to December 1842 the Bank's bullion holdings rose almost without interruption. The coming of an abundant harvest lifted one pressure which had been chronically operative in the previous year. The continued fall in prices and output also eased the market's position. Interest rates in the market fell close to 2 per cent., the Bank-rate went to 4 per cent., London bankers' deposits rose sharply :[4]

[1] Tooke, iv. 43–4: 'This expansion of the currency, as it was called, gave a temporary animation to the markets for manufactures and other produce, under the influence of the common opinion of the connection of the money market with the prices of commodities. But it turned out, as usual, that there was no ground for that opinion; and as the spring advanced the aspect of affairs was materially altered.

'Early in the summer the prospect of hostilities with the United States, and, somewhat later, the threatening aspect of our relations with France, tended strongly to increase the prevailing disposition of mercantile men to contract their engagements. This disposition was probably further increased by the circumstance that on the 15th of October the Bank of England, not finding the reflux of bullion to be so great as had been expected, reduced the date of bills admissible for discount from ninety-five to sixty-five days. And a review of the year at

its close exhibits, on the whole, throughout its course, a decided increase of the depression observed during the two previous years.'

[2] Ibid., p. 44; also Hawtrey, *A Century of the Bank Rate*, p. 19: 'That meant applying an absolute refusal to those who brought longer bills to be discounted, but it caused far less embarrassment than a more general refusal, because most people who had any bills probably had some shorter ones, and even those who had none but long bills might get accommodation from those who had short ones, so long as these latter could get money from the Bank. In fact the discount market as a whole held enough short bills to raise the money it required from the Bank.' The restriction was withdrawn in Jan. 1841.

[3] Tooke, iv. 45–7.

[4] Ibid., p. 47. On 28 Apr. 1842 *The Times* reported: 'The ill effects of the Bank of England lowering the rate of discount to 4 per cent. are now universally felt and

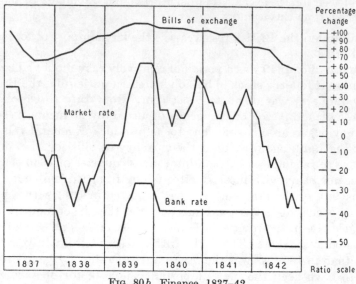

FIG. 80*b*. Finance, 1837–42

The supply of floating capital became . . . unusually large. . . . And there was a general feeling of confidence in an approaching termination of the period of general depression.

The Bank's failure to raise its rate until the spring of 1839, and, more generally, its apparent blindness to symptoms of the approaching crisis called forth much bitter criticism of the directors:[1] 'Of all acts of mismanagement in the whole history of the Bank this is probably the most astounding.' The Bank Act of 1844 was forged largely from the monetary experiences of these years, and the judgement of contemporaries on them.

6. Labour. Despite severe unemployment money wages were slightly raised from 1838 to 1842, but probably not to an extent sufficient to counteract the rise in living costs:

acknowledged. Money is so very abundant that dealers in it have literally no employment for it, apart from the public securities and shares, which in some branches of business would not be a fitting employment of capital.'

By 26 July, the first signs of recovery were evident: 'The intelligence from the manufacturing towns is such to show that at least a hope of increased activity in trade generally prevails. From Leeds we have descriptions of animation in the Cloth Halls, and of Manchester it is said that there is more

healthy feeling than has been known for some time past. There the effect of the new tariff has been to set free a quantity of capital which had been previously locked up, and a disposition to purchase cotton manufactures for the foreign market is arising from the impression that these goods have already reached their lowest price. From Sheffield there is a corresponding mention of symptoms of a revival of trade.'

[1] Quoted from Macleod, Andréadès, p. 267.

	Tucker's index of		Kondratieff's index of money wages in the textile industry	Bowley's index of agricultural money wages	Poor relief expenditures in non-agricultural counties of England and Wales[a] (in £ millions)
	Money wages of London	Real wages artisans			
1837 . .	61·2	50·4	47·8	146	2·6
1838 . .	61·2	50·3	48·3	150	2·7
1839 . .	61·2	46·7	47·8	154	2·8
1840 . .	61·2	49·2	48·3	154	3·0
1841 . .	61·6	47·9	49·3	154	3·1
1842 . .	61·6	54·7	49·8	154	3·4

[a] As one would expect, a relatively lesser rise occurred in poor relief expenditure in predominantly agricultural counties (in £ millions):

1837 . .	1·5
1838 . .	1·7
1839 . .	1·7
1840 . .	1·8
1841 . .	1·8
1842 . .	1·8

The decline in the calculated figure for real wages is partially substantiated by the amounts of tea, tobacco, and wine retained for home consumption and rum charged with duty:[1]

Consumption in the United Kingdom

	Tea	Tobacco	Wine	Rum
	(in million lb.)		(in million gallons)	
1837 . .	30·6	22·6	63·9	3·2
1838 . .	32·4	23·5	69·9	3·1
1839 . .	35·1	23·2	70·0	2·8
1840 . .	32·3	23·1	65·5	2·5
1841 . .	36·7	22·1	61·9	2·3
1842 . .	37·4	22·2	48·2	2·1

Except for the consumption of tea, which rose in 1840–2, these figures all show a pronounced decline from 1838, a year of general revival, to 1842. The impression of relative depression is borne out by all other evidence on labour's position in the period 1839–42.[1]

Centring in the Chartist movement there were, in 1839, disturbances and political agitation on an unprecedented scale. Unemployment was increasing rapidly in the latter months and food prices were high.[2] From June

[1] For a clear picture of increasing unemployment, falling money and real wages, in 1840, see *Evidence before Committee on Import Duties* (1840): cotton, p. 166; wool, p. 247; silk, p. 184; iron, p. 131; ship-building, p. 231.

[2] The Poor Law Commissioners reported that, from 1 May 1839, 'in the manufacturing districts, and especially those in the Midland parts of England, there has been continued and severe distress among the manufacturing population' (*P.P.* 1840, xvii. 401). Describing the situation at the close of 1839, Tooke wrote (iii. 52–3): 'In a few instances the wages of agricultural labourers have been raised, but in a very trifling proportion to the rise of necessaries; and in cases where an advance of wages has been granted, it has been rather from motives of fear or humanity on the part of the employers, than as a legitimate consequence, on principles of business, of an improved

FIG. 81. Labour, 1837–42

onwards there were spectacular meetings—in Birmingham, Manchester, Newcastle, Sheffield, Bolton, London, and Wales.[1] The hand-loom weavers and the unemployed in the mining and manufacturing areas rallied around the programme with a parliamentary platform, a revolutionary spirit.[2] The failure of the Chartist convention to produce effective action or leadership weakened the position of the movement in 1839, and, as well, many of the leaders went to prison:[3] 'By the middle of 1840 the Chartist Movement was wholly leaderless, broken, and disorganized.' Unemployment and bad harvests, however, kept 'the uneasy spirit in the manufacturing counties' alive during the following two years.[4]

The trade unions, too, reflected the profound unrest, but strikes had little chance of success in the depressed state of the demand for labour. There was again resort to sabotage tactics, the most famous action being

demand relatively to the supply of labour. While in the manufacturing districts there is not only no increase of money wages, but there is a falling off of employment, so that while the prices of provisions are in some instances nearly doubled, and while several other necessaries, and more especially the secondary necessaries, such as tea, sugar, and tobacco, are at a considerable advance, the earnings of the work-people are reduced; they are thus suffering cruelly under the twofold evil of having their little income less, and of finding that reduced income going a much less way in the supply of their most urgent wants.' See also 'Statistics of the Labouring Classes and Paupers in Nottingham' (*Journal of the Royal Statistical Society*, ii, 1839, pp. 457–9) for an account of the 'dreadful operation upon a manufacturing population' of the panic of 1836–7.

[1] *A.R.*, 1839, pp. 49–50, 66, 304–6; Chr., pp. 73–5, 132–3.

[2] For a brief discussion of the forces behind the movement, its form and objectives see G. D. H. Cole, i. 137–8.

[3] Ibid., p. 153. The desperate state of the labouring classes in 1840 is illustrated by a petition of 20 M.P.s to save the life of the leaders of the Newport Riots: 'That the death punishment . . . would raise a strong sympathy for the convicts on the part of a great body of the working classes, who would regard those unfortunate men . . . in the light rather of martyrs than of criminals; . . . that this body of the working classes would be still further alienated than they now are from the other classes of her majesty's subjects.' (*A.R.*, 1840, Chr., p. 10.)

[4] Cole, i. 161–4 and *A.R.*, 1840, p. 310.

that of the 'Plug Plot':[1] 'Bodies of strikers went round Lancashire and parts of Yorkshire stopping the mills where work was still proceeding, and removing the plugs from the boilers in order to cut off the source of power.' In 1842 especially, the strikes were severe, and a brief and violent revival of Chartist activity occurred, climaxed by the presentation of the second great petition, purporting to carry three million names.[2] The Chartist spirit was inextricably connected with the north-country strikes, which probably explained their vitality after some four years of increasing unemployment and the drain on workers' incomes of high food prices.

The movement, fostered by the same pressures, which enjoyed more immediate success, was, of course, the Anti-Corn Law League. The merchants of Manchester could appeal not only to the unemployed and the dispossessed hand-loom weavers, but to the working classes as a whole, all of whom felt the pressure of high food prices. With Peel's major reform of the whole tariff schedule (1842) the movement won an important victory, although not until 1846 was the triumph sealed. The important part played by short-run factors—depression and bad harvests—in this surge of free-trade activity is indicated by the bitter struggle waged between the Chartists and the Anti-Corn Law League for the patronage of the disaffected working classes. As often in British political history the movement with the more concrete and immediately applicable programme won the day.

[1] Cole, i. 164. See also *A.R.*, 1842, Chr., pp. 76–7, 107, 132, 163, and Tooke, iv. 48.

[2] *A.R.*, 1842, p. 152.

Chapter VI

1843–50[1]

INTRODUCTION

FROM the low point in 1842 a cycle can be traced with a peak in 1845, a second trough in 1848. The cyclical peak in the United States in 1847, and consequently large British exports there in that year, as well as the persistence of railway construction in Britain to that time, make for some slight symptoms of a double peak (like 1825–8, 1836–9). The movement is, however, much less clearly defined than in the other cases and, indeed, can hardly be detected at all in annual statistical data. Such data yield merely a single cycle with troughs in 1842 and 1848, a peak in 1845.

The boom of the forties is properly identified with the rapid expansion of British railways. Railways played the same role as capital exports to Latin America and joint-stock floatations in 1824–5, and as capital exports to the United States and joint-stock bank and railway floatations in 1835–6: some 4,500 miles of new railway line constituted, as it were, Britain's permanent fruits of the boom. It is chiefly distinguished from its predecessors of the previous two decades by the extraordinary concentration of the investor's interest in railways; and by the relatively lesser importance of capital exports.

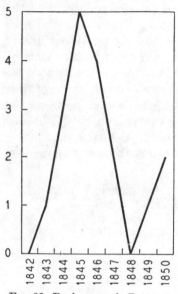

FIG. 82. Business-cycle Pattern, 1842–50

As in other cases, however, the floatation boom came after several years of mounting prosperity, based largely on increased export orders—in this instance, to the United States, India, and China. The latter market, particularly, made temporarily secure by the Treaty of Nanking, in 1842, attracted considerable speculative enterprise. When the money market tightened (1845–7) only the Eastern trade appeared to have large credit advances outstanding. Other branches of commerce had been 'soundly' financed.

In the third quarter of 1844 the capital market was still enjoying abnormally easy money conditions. Commodity prices, on the whole, had fallen, despite two years of increasing output and falling unemployment;

[1] Cyclical pattern:

	Trough	Peak
	1842 (Nov.)	1845 (Sept.)
	1846 (Sept.)	1847 (Apr.)
	1848 (Sept.)	

the commercial demand for funds put no strain on the money market; in the long-term capital market the price of Consols was at a new high point, the short-term rate was under 2 per cent. In the year following the autumn of 1844 a tremendous boom in railway floatations occurred, dwarfing, in scale, all that had gone before. In August 1845 railway securities began to decline and there was a minor crisis in the last quarter; but the time required to receive parliamentary sanction placed the peak for sums authorized in 1846.

The financial difficulties attendant upon railway financing were delayed by the fact that payments on shares purchased were called up gradually. Purchase involved only a small initial outlay. Financial stringency was precipitated by the government's provision that a certain portion of the funds raised be placed on deposit with its agents. The calling up of these required sums progressively impoverished the market, serving largely as the immediate cause of the crises of 1845 and 1847.

Further strain was placed on Britain's financial resources by the necessity for abnormally large grain imports in 1846–7, especially in the latter year. In 1847 parallel financial crises in the United States and on the Continent accentuated the deflationary pressures; while the revolutions and counter-revolutions early in 1848 further delayed financial readjustment. Only in the latter half of 1848 did Britain emerge into a protracted period of easy money, accompanied, late in the year, by the first symptoms of commercial recovery.

As one might expect in a railway boom, the iron industry experienced great expansion. The effects of rail orders can be clearly traced in both the English and Scottish iron industries. Although railway building continued on a large scale at least until 1847, unemployment in the iron industry was at a high level after 1845, despite a continued rise (until 1847) in the quantity of iron exports. Total iron-output estimates, nevertheless, show a large net increase for the decade as a whole, due to expansion of plant, especially in Scotland. The coal industry, too, felt pressures towards expansion, which were responsible, fairly directly, for the destruction of the Vend, in 1845. Limitation of output meant a steadily decreasing allotment for each firm, as the number of firms increased. The textile industries, somewhat less sensationally, shared in the industrial expansion. With the coming of Australian wool and the spread of mixed cotton and woollens, the woollen industry, after several decades of relative stagnation, showed marked secular expansion. Wool exports, largely to the United States, exhibit clearly the second peak in 1847. The enlarged markets, of course, benefited Manchester and the cotton interests. Cotton manufactures increased to 1845, declined in 1846–7, but led general recovery in 1848.

With the exception of the iron industry, where prices rose sharply in 1844–5, the tendency of non-agricultural prices was downward. No protracted upward movement in either imported or domestic prices developed. The relatively full employment of the latter stages of the boom did not produce any extended speculation in the commodity markets. Security prices, however, followed a conventional cyclical pattern, with Consols and other non-speculative issues declining in the final stages of expansion as railway shares dominated the market; the decline continued through the periods of financial crisis, when, in the struggle for liquidity, acceptable securities were unceremoniously dumped in an effort to meet previous commitments on railway shares.

Until 1846 labour enjoyed increasing employment and real wages. In 1847–8 high food prices and unemployment produced a period of intense suffering and unrest. The Chartist movement flared again briefly in 1848, and there were the usual strikes in the year after the turning-point in general business activity (1846); employers sought to cut costs, as demand fell off and prices declined, while the strengthened union organizations were willing to risk conflict. After 1842, only part of 1846 and 1847 were 'hungry', in the forties, although, due to unemployment, 1848 was an extremely depressed and difficult year for the British working classes.

Three important acts of legislation fall within these years. In 1844 the Bank Act went into effect, a somewhat misguided attempt to enforce a strict relationship between the note issue and the Bank of England's bullion holdings. It failed, of course, to prevent general credit expansion, and its chief consequence was the widespread belief, during the panic of 1847, that it would, of necessity, involve an extremely severe deflationary policy on the part of the Bank. The suspension of the Act served largely to restore confidence, without any substantial increase in advances at the Bank. The second act was, of course, the repeal, in 1846, of the Corn Laws, motivated partly by the apparent success of the tariff reforms of 1842, partly by the failure of the Irish potato crop, as well as by the long-run arguments mustered with special vigour by the Anti-Corn Law League from 1837. Finally, in 1847, the Ten-Hour Bill was passed, limiting the working hours in the cotton textile factories. The parliamentary supporters of this bill were largely Tories, some of whom were acting in retaliation against the Corn Law repeal of the previous year. The widespread existence of short-time in the cotton districts, in removing an important argument of the opposition, facilitated its passage.

Part I: 1843–8

1. **Prices.** The domestic price index, after falling through the first quarter of 1843, moves up fairly steadily to a peak in November 1845. A decline then follows to August 1846. At that point an enormous rise in the wheat price brings the index to a second peak in June 1847, after which it falls until the early months of 1850.

In the years 1843–8 there were three periods of relatively high grain prices: July 1843 to June 1844, August 1845 to April 1846, August 1846 to July 1847. Only in this latter period did the price of wheat reach or surpass the chronically high level of 1838–42. In the summer of 1843 there was a brief, rapid rise in the wheat price due to unusually wet weather, 'apprehensions having been generally entertained of consequent damage to the harvest'.[1] From August on, however, the weather turned fair, the price fell, and, except for the southern counties, a fairly abundant harvest was gathered in good condition. In 1844 the wheat crop 'was computed to be in bulk and yield the largest of all since the harvest of 1834'.[2] In the third quarter the wheat price fell, remaining under 50s. until August 1845. The harvest of 1845 was inadequate, but a considerable surplus remained from that of 1844, which checked, at the close of 1845, a rise in the wheat price. In August 1846 it stood at 46s.[3] In June 1847 the price stood at 93s., the movement between these dates being one of the sharpest in the entire period 1790–1850. A second failure of the potato crop, an inadequate British wheat harvest, and similar conditions on the Continent account largely for this movement.[4] In July 1847 the price broke with the coming of clear weather, and from September an irregular decline is evident which reached its low point in February 1850, when wheat was at 37·8s. The annual average price of wheat and grain imports were as follows:

	'Gazette' price of wheat (s. per quarter)	Wheat and wheat flour imports (net) (in 1,000 quarters)		'Gazette' price of wheat (s. per quarter)	Wheat and wheat flour imports (net) (in 1,000 quarters)
1842	57·2	2,939·6	1847	69·3	4,366·4
1843	50·2	1,030·1	1848	50·5	2,986·6
1844	51·1	1,338·6	1849	44·2	4,660·1
1845	50·9	1,109·7	1850	41·8	4,691·8
1846	54·6	2,291·1			

[1] Tooke, iv. 15.

[2] Ibid., p. 17.

[3] The virtual repeal of the Corn Laws was in effect from 26 June 1846. Some 2 million quarters of wheat were immediately released from bond and the price fell (ibid., p. 26). The act provided for a sliding scale of duties until 1 Feb. 1849, when a flat 1s. per quarter duty came into effect. But in Jan. 1847, with the wheat price rising rapidly, the Corn Laws were suspended and remained so until 1 March 1848. Eleven months later the 1s. duty became operative (Clapham, pp. 497–8).

[4] Tooke, iv. 26–8:

'On the 1st of August, 1846, London, and its immediate vicinity, were visited with the most violent and long-continued and destructive storm of hail and rain, of which there is any record. The weather in the remainder of the month was favourable to the ripening and securing of the crops of grain in the southern division of the kingdom. But during the first three weeks of August the weather in Yorkshire and to the northward of that county was wet and close, and there were, in consequence, complaints,

in those districts, of the sprouting of the wheats.

'Early in August the failure of the potato crop was again apprehended; and as the season advanced the worst apprehensions were more than realized. This circumstance was of itself calculated to enhance the value of wheat.

'The comparative deficiency of the stock on hand, the prospect of a large extra demand, to supply the deficiency of the potato crop, and the improved quality of the grain, combined to raise the price, till, in the week ending the 7th of November, the weekly average reached 62s. 3d. But though the failure of the potato crop, to a very great extent, was, by that time, placed beyond doubt, this advance was not quite sustained; and the price declined during the next few weeks, and afterwards ranged at about 60s. down to the close of the year, when it was 61s. 6d.

'The state of the markets for grain in the ensuing year leads to the conclusion that the actual deficiency of the supply of wheat in the autumn of 1846 was much greater than was generally supposed at the time.'

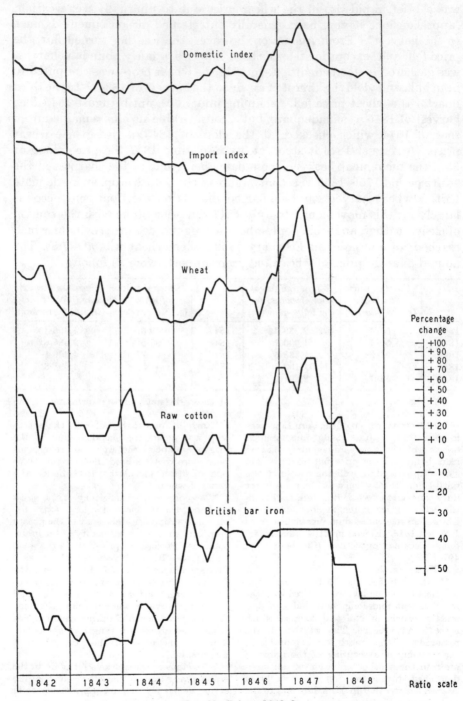

Fig. 83. Prices, 1842–8

Relatively free access to the world's grain markets, and consequently large imports, could not prevent the rise of price in 1847, although the record level of imports in 1849–50 aided significantly in maintaining the low prices of those years.

With a few significant exceptions non-agricultural domestic prices at no time rose steadily or to any great extent. The boom was, primarily, based on railway construction, and as one might expect, iron prices responded to the increased demand in the latter stages of the expansion.

	May 1843	May 1844	May 1845	May 1846	May 1847	May 1848	Dec. 1850
Alum (£ per ton)	9·2	10·8	10·2	9·2	9·1	8·5	8·4
Sunderland coal (s. per chaldron)a .	25·2	29·7	25·4	23·7	26·1	21·9	22·8
Copper (pence per lb.) . . .	9·2	9·2	9·5	10·5	11·0	10·0	9·5
Iron pigs (£ per ton) . . .	3·5	4·1	6·8	5·6	5·0	5·0	3·4
Iron bars (£ per ton) . . .	5·0	6·4	10·2	9·1	10·0	8·0	6·0
Lead pigs (£ per ton) . . .	16·6	17·0	17·6	19·4	19·0	17·0	17·1
Leather butts (pence per lb.) . .	18·7	17·5	17·8	17·2	17·5	16·2	15·2
Rape oil (£ per ton)	38·0	39·0	37·0	35·0	37·0	36·5	37·8
Tallow (s. per cwt.)	45·0	42·0	41·0	41·5	47·0	48·0	37·0
Block tin (s. per cwt.) . . .	62·0	75·0	85·0	91·0	95·0	77·0	80·0

a The self-regulation of the coal industry ended early in 1845. The coal price fell immediately (Sweezy, pp. 127–9). Sunderland coal stood at 32·9 (s. per chaldron) in Jan. 1845, 24·2 in Dec.

Iron prices reach a clearly marked peak in 1845, while the price of iron bars shares with various other commodities (e.g. copper, coal, leather, tin) a second high point in 1847. As in the booms of the twenties and thirties, there are two peaks—in 1845 and 1847.[1] In the early months of 1847 there was a considerable recovery from the crisis of 1845 :[2]

During the first four months of the year (1847) the markets for produce (excepting the districts of the cotton manufacture, in which business was checked by the high price of the raw material) were, generally, in an active and prosperous condition, the demand for home consumption being, throughout, well maintained.

A severe financial crisis then followed, which brought this brief phase of revival to a premature end.

The average declared values of cotton yarn and piece goods' exports also exhibit a second phase of upward movement in 1847 (see table, p. 310).

The import price index, viewed broadly, falls from September 1840 to September 1846. After recovering to February 1847 it declines again to September 1848, when a steady upward movement sets in, running to the end of 1850. There is, then, no cyclical peak in 1845, although that of 1847 emerges clearly. Examined closely, however, the index reveals a number of significant minor movements.

[1] These parallel, very roughly, the peaks of 1825 and 1829, 1836 and 1839.   [2] Tooke, iv. 74.

(pence per lb.)

	Price of cotton yarn exports	Price of cotton piece goods exports
1842 .	13·6	3·6
1843 .	12·3	3·4
1844 .	12·1	3·5
1845 .	12·4	3·4
1846 .	11·7	3·2
1847 .	11·9	3·6
1848[a] .	10·5	2·9

[a] For the sharp fall in textile prices in 1848 see *The Economist*, 1848, p. 1045.

After strengthening somewhat in the latter months of 1842, import prices fell to a stable lower level from March to September 1843:[1]

The hopes of renewed prosperity commonly indulged during the last months of 1842 having, as is usual in such cases, been pitched rather too high, were followed by some degree of disappointment—not so much at any reversal of, or even check to, the progress of the improvement, as with its slow advance, as experienced in the first months of 1843.

It has already been stated that the general tendency of prices down to near the close of 1842 was a declining one. And if the price-currents of July 1843 be compared with those of the same period in 1842, it will be observed that, with few exceptions, and those of little importance, prices were even lower in July 1843 than they had been a year before.

From the summer of 1843, forward, the general aspect of commercial affairs was one of decided prosperity.

Until May 1844 the import index has an upward tendency. A gentle decline then follows to February 1845:[2]

The only movement observable in the markets for produce during the earlier months of the year (1844) was a tendency to advance in the prices of those articles the consumption of which had been materially augmented in the latter months of 1843. The renewed activity of our manufacturers, and the consequent increase of the amount of capital currently devoted to the payment of wages, and thence conveyed through the hands of the retail dealers in payment for increased supplies of food, clothing, household furniture, &c., the demand for which had been reduced much below the ordinary level during the previous years of depression, may be distinguished as the most general of the causes of this movement. The consequent rise of prices in this direction, however, was but slight, and was anything but universal. It was in the markets for colonial produce, where in the first months of 1844, deficiency of supply, actual or prospective, combined, in several prominent instances, with the increasing demand, to cause an advance, that the upward tendency of prices was most remarkable, and attracted most attention.

With some exceptions, already referred to, and of minor importance in a general review of the principal markets for produce, prices were in most in-

[1] Tooke, iv. 49 and 51–2.   [2] Ibid., pp. 55, 58, and 64.

stances even lower at the end of the first six or eight months of 1844, than at its commencement: the supply of the more important articles of consumption being found to be very generally beyond the demand; although the latter had materially increased.

In the last months of 1844, and for some time afterwards, frequent complaints were heard of losses incurred upon importations from abroad. The commodities imported in that and the previous year, in exchange for the increased quantity of goods exported, were found, with one or two exceptions (among which were timber and sheep's wool), so far to exceed the demand for them, home and foreign, that in very many instances the prices obtainable not only left no profit to, but entailed a loss upon, the importer; and hence, notwithstanding an increased rate of consumption, prices at the opening of 1845 ranged, generally, quite as low as, or even lower than, at the beginning of the previous year.

From March to April 1845 import prices fell sharply, recovered slightly to October, and then declined again to September 1846 :[1]

The markets for produce in 1845 did not share, in the slightest degree, the speculative spirit so prominently displayed in the markets for railway shares, and also, though in a minor degree, in some other and similar fields of enterprise. . . . There was a slight general tendency, during the latter half of 1845, to an advance of the prices of some of the raw materials of our manufactures the consumption of which had most rapidly increased, and also in the prices of some of the principal articles of colonial produce, more particularly sugar and coffee, the quantities of which entered for consumption in 1845 greatly exceeded those of any former year. . . . The markets for produce were, during the winter and spring, remarkably quiet: buyers and sellers being alike unwilling to act upon the future, and prices varying but slightly and only in accordance with immediate and tolerably well founded anticipations. . . . The markets for produce were, during the spring and summer of 1846, in a remarkably quiet and uniform condition, the consumption of nearly all articles of common use being fully sustained at the high level reached in the previous year. In the autumn of 1846 circumstances arose which in a few weeks materially changed the aspect of commercial affairs at home and abroad.

The import index rises from September 1846 to February 1847, remains relatively high until September, and then falls away rapidly in the course of the following year, to its low point for the entire period 1790–1850, in September 1848 :[2]

As the demand in the home market (1846) for articles of general consumption was found not to be nearly so much affected as the high prices of food had led importers and producers to expect, the markets assumed a more animated appearance as the opening of the new year approached.

The prospective scarcity of cotton led, in December 1846, to some considerable purchases being made on speculation; but an advance of price commensurate with the estimated deficiency of the supply having been established, and the rate of consumption proportionately checked, the movement quietly subsided. One or two other articles of importance, as tallow and hemp, of which the supply, already short, was deemed likely to fall much below the current demand

[1] Ibid., pp. 68–70.					[2] Ibid., pp. 71–2, 74, 76–7, 78–9.

in the ensuing year, also rose considerably in price during the last months of the year; but in no instance did the advance exhibit any symptoms of what is usually termed speculation. In every instance it was gradual; and in most of it was amply justified by the event. . . . In January 1847 a variety of circumstances combined to induce a pressure upon the money market. Railway calls upon British lines, and on foreign lines, shares in which were extensively held in this country, were becoming immediately due to an amount estimated, in the aggregate, at not less than 6,000,000£. The exchanges with the continent, and especially with Russia, again showed a decidedly adverse tendency. Difficulties which had for some time previously beset the Bank of France had now come to a crisis; and the measures found requisite to sustain the credit of that establishment began to operate upon this country. And at the same time the prospect of still higher prices for corn, and of very large importations before the next harvest, with the ascertained deficiency of the supply of cotton, and the expectation, at this time becoming general, that the drain of floating capital for railway construction would eventually prove too heavy for the diminished resources of the country, tended strongly to produce among the mercantile classes a vague feeling of apprehension.

During the first four months of the year the markets for produce (excepting the districts of the cotton manufacture, in which business was checked by the high price of raw material) were, generally, in an active and prosperous condition, the demand for home consumption being, throughout, well maintained. . . .[1] Before the end of August the high rate of interest was very severely felt by all whose current business required the aid of credit; and as it became evident that no relief was to be expected even from the assurance of an abundant harvest, complaints became general as to the large amount of capital being sunk in the construction of new railways; and various propositions were made and discussed for reducing the demand in this direction; but without any practical result. The markets for produce remained undisturbed from the beginning of the year down to the month of September: the demand for home consumption continuing rather active than otherwise, and the deficiency of the foreign demand in Europe for articles of export from this country being largely made up by increased orders from America and the Mediterranean. . . . From the second week of September, to near the close of November, the ordinary course of commercial transactions in this country was so much deranged by the violent contraction of credit, that the state of prices during that period cannot be regarded as otherwise than exceptional.

If the price-currents of November be compared with those of June or July, it will be observed that the price of nearly every article of any importance had fallen in the interval, though in various degrees. If particular attention be given to the instances in which the fall was greatest, it will be observed that they are all comprised in one or both of two classes: that they were either articles, the prices of which had been declining for some time previously, from an excess of supply, as compared with the current demand, (and therefore could not but continue to fall, when the general demand was still further diminished,) or such as, having been largely held upon credit, were forced upon the market, in considerable quantities, under the monetary pressure. The instances of lower

[1] The slight decline in the index from February to May 1847 can be connected with the minor financial crisis of the spring (Tooke, iv. 74–5).

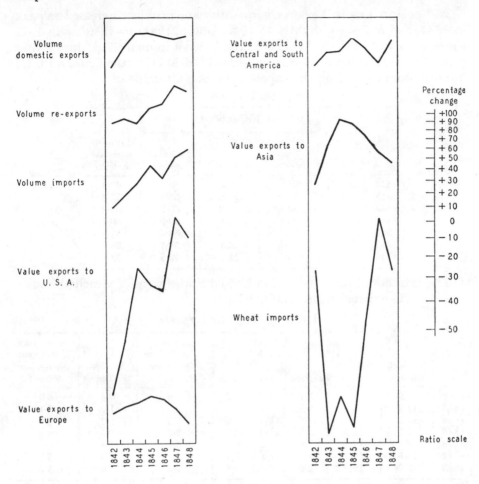

FIG. 84. Foreign Trade, 1842–8

prices not obviously comprised in either of these classes are less remarkable; and they are clearly traceable either to a corresponding change in the relation of supply to demand, or to the necessity to raise money by extraordinary methods for immediate purposes which has lately been felt by wholesale dealers of every denomination.

As in the markets for non-agricultural domestic commodities, there were no sustained upward movements on a large scale in these years. Speculative sentiment was checked in every instance before it could develop to boom proportions :[1] and the supply of commodities was sufficient to yield, in net, chronically falling prices, despite an enormous increase in demand and output in the years 1843–5.

[1] See especially testimony before Committee on Distress (1848), p. 69 (Turner), on the failure of any speculative movement to develop in the large commodity markets.

2. Foreign Trade. Exports, in quantity and in value, increase to a peak in 1845, and fall away slightly to 1848. Due to the price increase in 1847 there was a rise in the value of exports, but not in quantities, during that year. The large volume of grain imports (1846–8) keeps the figure for total imports from exhibiting the expected decline after 1845:

(In £ millions)

	Volume of			Value of domestic exports
	Total imports	Re-exports	Domestic exports	
1842 . .	71·3	10·3	48·8	47·4
1843 . .	77·0	10·6	55·6	52·3
1844 . .	83·8	10·3	60·7	58·6
1845 . .	93·4	11·4	60·9	60·1
1846 . .	86·4	11·6	59·6	57·8
1847 . .	98·6	13·1	58·7	58·8
1848 . .	103·7	12·7	59·8	52·8

The markets of Asia and of the United States were of principal importance in the expansion (in £ millions):

Value of Domestic Exports

	Northern Europe	Southern Europe	Africa	Asia	U.S.A.	British N. American colonies and W. Indies	Foreign W. Indies	Central and S. America (including Brazil)
1842	14·0	9·9	1·7	7·5	3·5	4·9	0·9	5·0
1843	14·0	10·9	1·7	9·5	5·0	4·6	1·0	5·4
1844	14·3	11·3	1·6	11·3	7·9	5·5	1·2	5·4
1845	15·1	11·2	1·9	11·0	7·1	6·3	1·5	6·0
1846	14·7	11·4	1·8	10·2	6·8	5·8	1·4	5·6
1847	13·9	10·7	2·0	9·1	11·0	5·5	1·5	5·1
1848	12·0[a]	10·4	2·0	8·5	9·6	3·5	1·0	5·8

[a] Exports to northern Europe were, of course, adversely affected by the revolutions of 1848.

The cyclical pattern centring about 1845 appears in every important case but that of the United States, which shows a second major peak in 1847.[1]

The treaty with China, late in 1842, set the stage for a strong revival in the Eastern trade, in which India shared.[2] Four new ports in China were

---

[1] The Smith and Cole trade indexes for the United States move as follows (p. 104):

	Domestic trade	Foreign trade	Combined trade
1843 . .	98	111	102
1844 . .	104	108	105
1845 . .	102	98	101
1846 . .	104	99	102
1847 . .	108	100	105
1848 . .	102	90	98

American prices, too, show a clearly defined peak in 1847 (ibid., pp. 93–101).

[2] The Eastern trade was the one branch of British foreign commerce where there was any considerable speculation in commodities (Tooke, iv. 56): 'With a single exception, that of the China trade, there was no appearance of speculation in the markets for produce in 1844. Nor was the exception referred to palpable at the time, otherwise than as a disposition to rely somewhat confidently upon an immediate extension of the

opened, and from 1842 to 1844 exports increased from £0·97 to £2·3 million. In the same period exports to India rose from £5·2 to £7·7 million. Although capital exports to the United States were relatively slight during the forties,[1] British trade in that direction revived, as did exports to Brazil.[2] Tooke's summary of the state of foreign trade in 1844 follows :[3]

Abroad, the trade opened with the four new Chinese ports, the renewal of commercial intercourse with the United States upon a sounder basis of credit, and an increase of British exports to Brazil, in view of the expiration of our commercial treaty with that country in November, together with the improved state of our commerce with the continental countries of Europe, (resulting from their having experienced a renewal of internal prosperity in many respects similar to, and nearly simultaneous with, our own,) produced a rapid and steady growth of every branch of the export trade.

In Britain's export markets, with the exception of the United States, 1845 was a turning-point. The value of exports to Europe and (from 1844) to Asia fell off, those to the United States, after increasing from 1842 to 1844, declined until 1847; while all other American markets weakened steadily after 1845. Falling prices, of course, lower the real value of exports, except in 1847.

3. Investment. Railways virtually monopolized the attention of investors in the boom of the forties. The borrowing of foreign states was on a small scale, while joint-stock companies other than railways were relatively unimportant.[4] This channelling of new enterprise along a single

China trade greater than, to the few persons in this country well informed as to the probabilities of the subject, seemed likely. So little to the purpose, however, was really known in the commercial world, with any degree of certainty, that those who embarked at once and largely in the export trade to the new ports, could scarcely have been said to hope too much, until the experience and better information of the two following years proved that they had done so. This exception should therefore, perhaps, be referred to rather as an illustration of the prevailing soundness and legitimacy of the commercial transactions of the period, than as indicating anything of a contrary character.' For 'over-trading' in the trade to both India and China, see also *Evidence before Committee on Commercial Distress* (1848), p. 51 (Turner).

[1] Bullock, Williams, and Tucker, p. 220. It is estimated that between 1838 and 1849 not more than $40 million in new foreign investment came to the United States. The structure of the American balance of payments and of relative price levels reflects this relative cessation of capital imports.

[2] The British trade with Latin America was seriously disrupted throughout the forties, especially after 1845: in 1842 the

Mexican government doubled its customs duties, and further altered them in 1845; in 1846 the war between the United States and Mexico broke out; in 1845 the French and British fleets were required to keep open the trade to the River Plate; in 1846 intervention was necessary to prevent revolution in Ecuador; in 1845, and after, there was difficulty with Brazil over the slave traffic (Redford, pp. 104–7).

[3] Op. cit. iv. 55.

[4] There is, nevertheless, some evidence of general promotional activity. Hunt (p. 112) states: 'For a time during the boom railway shares had rendered others unfashionable. Nevertheless, promotions in the other fields rode in on the tide of railway speculation and continued apace over the decade after it had receded.' Hunt quotes *The Times* (5 Nov. 1845) referring to the rail boom as having 'begotten others of an ephemeral character' and (leading article, 31 Oct. 1845), in commenting on an official return: 'The Registrar must find his office no sinecure. Stationed to catch and note down the bubbles as they rise and soar into mid-air, he must feel almost stifled in the froth of a thousand schemes.'

path proceeded to a greater extent than in either 1824–5 or 1835–6, when, although certain avenues of investment predominated, there was a considerably greater dispersion of joint-stock promotion.

The overwhelming importance of railway floatation is indicated by the following figures of capital authorized for their construction, the previous high having been in 1836, when £22·9 million were authorized (in £ millions) :[1]

1842	.	5·3	1847	.	39·5
1843	.	3·9	1848	.	15·3a
1844	.	20·5	1849	.	3·9
1845	.	59·5	1850	.	4·1
1846	.	132·6			

[a] The sober retrospective view of the railway problem in 1848 is exemplified by the following comments in *The Economist* of 21 Oct. (pp. 1186–8): 'There is no question which at this moment so much demands from all who either influence or lead the public mind, and from the public themselves, so calm and grave a consideration as the present conditions and prospects of the railways and railway property of this country. It would now be of little utility to refer to the mad scenes of 1845 and 1846, and to prove to demonstration that the present prostration and dejection is but a necessary retribution for the folly, the avarice, the insufferable arrogance, the headlong, desperate, and unprincipled gambling and jobbing, which disgraced nobility and aristocracy, polluted senators and senate houses, contaminated merchants, manufacturers, and traders of all kinds.'

The number of railway acts passed in Parliament follows :[2]

	For new lines	For extension and completion of existing lines	Total
1842 . .	4	18	22
1843 . .	5	19	24
1844 . .	26	22	48
1845 . .	76	44	120
1846 . .	225a	45	270
1847 . .	115a	75	190
1848 . .	28a	57	85
1849 . .	—	34	34

[a] These figures include new lines and some acts of extension.

[1] See D. Morier Evans, *The Commercial Crisis of 1847–1848*, pp. 1–52, 'The Railway Mania and its Effects'; Hunt, pp. 102–12, and Jenks, pp. 126–34. Hunt quotes a contemporary *Circular to Bankers* (pp. 102–3): In various earlier periods, 'when confidence was restored, enterprise had taken the direction of Joint Stock companies. It did so in 1824; and in 1834–36; . . . again in 1844–45, recovery takes exactly the same direction. . . . At the first of these epochs associations were for mining enterprises in South America; at the second they were for banks both here and in the United States; (now), they are railways. It would seem from this view of the subject, that individual enterprise is as active in the minds of our country-

men as ever, but having been so frequently checked, thwarted, and mortified in its exercise individually, it seeks the support and strength of numbers in association for large undertakings. This is a curious and novel feature in our national character, and the cause which produces it will produce similar effects in other and new channels. . . . All public enterprise at this epoch takes the direction of Railways.'

[2] Porter, p. 329 and (edition of 1851) p. 327. The previous high figures came in 1836 when 29 new lines were authorized and 6 acts of extension; and in 1837, when the total was even higher, with 15 new acts but 27 acts of extension: the totals for the two years being, respectively, 35 and 42.

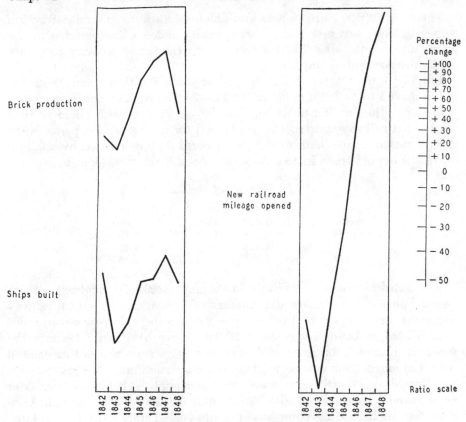

Fig. 85. Investment, 1842–8

The importance of this boom is perhaps most dramatically indicated by the fact that, in December 1843, 1,952 miles of railway were open in Britain; seven years later, 6,621 miles were open, an increase of well over 200 per cent.

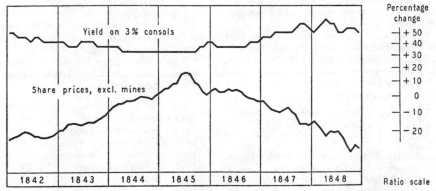

Fig. 86. Investment, 1842–8

The peak in new railway acts and amounts authorized for construction comes in 1846, but new enterprise virtually ended with the crisis in the latter months of 1845.[1] The lag was due to the time necessary to secure parliamentary authorization.

Largely in direct response to the railway construction boom, the brick index moved to a new high figure in 1846–7.[2] The peak comes in 1847, two years after the turning-point for the system as a whole.[3] There is little doubt that railway construction continued for a considerable period after the floatation bubble had burst.[4] The general decline induced by a falling off in the export trade in 1845 was thus considerably cushioned:

Production of Bricks
(In million bricks)

1842	. . 1,272		1846	. . 2,040
1843	. . 1,159		1847	. . 2,194
1844	. . 1,421		1848	. . 1,461
1845	. . 1,821		1849	. . 1,463

The attractiveness of railway investment seriously blighted foreign issues;[5] although a considerable amount of foreign and American railway securities were acquired.[6] In the period 1843–8 the only new government loan floated in London was the £732,000 drawn by Brazil.[7] Perhaps the most significant trend in capital exports at this time was not associated with the market for new securities—the construction of foreign railways by English contractors, workers, and materials. This tendency, later accompanied by the large-scale flotation of foreign railway issues in London, became increasingly important in the years before 1873. It was, however, of minor importance in the forties.[8]

The wave of shipbuilding which took place between 1836 and 1840 was not maintained in the following decade. New tonnage registered decreased

---

[1] The high point in the railway share index comes in August 1845.

[2] See Shannon, pp. 304 and 309, for the connexion between railway building and brick production.

[3] It should be remembered, as well, that the brick index shows throughout a tendency to lag in its decline; e.g. 1793, 1811, 1819, 1829, 1840.

[4] This is indicated by the miles of new railway lines opened:

1845 .	. 293		1848 .	. 1,182
1846 .	. 595		1849 .	. 904
1847 .	. 909			

Shannon (p. 304) notes that in 1849, on most of the new lines the stations were incomplete, and that the depots and other permanent buildings had not been begun. He concludes that, after 1847, 'whatever the

railways were spending on, they were not spending on bricks'.

[5] Jenks, p. 127.

[6] Clapham, pp. 492–5.

[7] H. Clarke, 'On the Debts of Sovereign and Quasi-Sovereign States', *Journal of the Royal Statistical Society*, xli, 1878, p. 314.

[8] The following are the foreign railway contracts undertaken by Thomas Brassey, 1841–9 (Jenks, p. 419):

Year	Contract	Mileage
1841	Paris and Rouen	82
1842	Orleans and Bordeaux	294
1843	Rouen and Havre	58
1844	Amiens and Boulogne	53
1847	Rouen and Dieppe	31
1848	Barcelona and Mataro	18
1850	Prato and Pistoja	10

See also Clapham, pp. 493–5.

to 1843, rose again to 1847; but the peak in the latter year was far below that in 1840:[1]

Tonnage of Ships built and registered in the United Kingdom

(in 1,000 tons)

1842	129·9	1846	125·4
1843	83·1	1847	145·8
1844	95·0[a]	1848	122·6
1845	123·2		

[a] As late as 23 Mar. 1844 the shipowners were complaining that ships 'were selling for half the sums they cost three years ago. . . . It was high time that something was done, or they would all go down together' (minutes of meeting of Sunderland Shipowners' Society, quoted in *The Economist*, 1844, pp. 610–11). The shipowners, as perennially, blamed the depression on the repeal of the Navigation Acts in its customary broad free-trade terms. The *Annual Register* (Chr., 1848, p. 22) reported 'a demonstration in favour of protection to the shipping interest, by nearly three thousand persons, masters, mates, and seamen of the mercantile marine' in Feb. 1848.

The security index and the prices of India Stock, Bank Stock, and Consols show a familiar cyclical pattern. Dominated at this stage by the movement of railway securities, the index (exclusive of mines) moves up steadily from January 1843 to July 1845.[2] The index then falls off in the second half of the year, rallies slightly until July 1846, and then falls to a low point in October 1849. The upper turning-point in Consols, Bank Stock, and India Stock, as in the Canal, Gas Light, and Dock sub-indexes, comes earlier than for the index as a whole (controlled by rail shares). India Stock turned downward, after a two-year rise, in May 1844, Consols in January 1845, Bank Stock in February. The attention of an optimistic market was almost completely devoted to the railways in the first half of 1845;[3] and the prices of other types of securities suffered. The interest rate

[1] The tonnage of steamships built and registered, however, reached a new peak in 1847. 1842 was the previous high figure (in 1,000 tons):

1842	13·7	1846	16·0
1843	6·1	1847	16·2
1844	6·1	1848	15·3
1845	10·9		

There was, as well, a growth in the relative importance of iron ships at this time (*The Economist*, 1845, p. 310); also Hamilton, pp. 219–20, and Scrivenor (1854), pp. 310–12.

[2] The speculative boom broke in Aug. (Tooke, iv. 65–6): 'In August, after the fate of the bills before Parliament had been decided for the session, the speculation assumed all the apparent characteristics of a mania. Symptoms of an approaching revulsion were, however, then clearly discernible. It was remarked by the least observant, that the lapse of a few months had introduced among the speculators a great number of persons who acted without reference to any hope of profit on the completion of the undertakings in question, or, indeed, to anything whatever but the speculative opinions concerning them most current, for the moment, in the share market. Thus shares were commonly, indeed almost invariably, bought, not for permanent investment, but with a view to a speedy sale at an inordinate profit. And there is reason to believe that almost the only real buyers of shares after the middle of August, and during the few weeks in which the speculation rose to its climax, were persons of limited means, and of still more limited information on the subject, who were tempted to speculate by instances of enormous gain apparently realised by the fortunate adventurers who had been earlier in the field.' See also Evans, p. 19 n.

[3] See Tooke, iv. 65–8. As early as 5 Apr. *The Economist*, 1845, p. 310, predicted a Stock Exchange collapse: 'When we deliberately express our opinion that there

rose. On the other hand, recovery came earlier to the less speculative investments than to railway securities. Consols, Bank Stock, and India Stock began to rise again in 1847 or 1848, while railway shares declined until October 1849.

The annual average yield on 3 per cent. Consols moved as follows (per cent.):

1842	.	. 3·26	1847	.	. 3·43
1843	.	. 3·14	1848	.	. 3·50
1844	.	. 3·02	1849	.	. 3·24
1845	.	. 3·04	1850	.	. 3·10
1846	.	. 3·14			

The interest rate, thus measured, continued to fall until late in the upswing, until, in fact, its final speculative stage. It rose most rapidly during the two periods of financial crisis, in 1845 and 1847. In its effect on all interest rates, the crisis of 1847 was relatively more severe than the panics of 1836–7 and 1839. This is possibly to be associated with the fact that railway securities were more widely held in this boom than the securities which dominated the major speculations of the twenties and thirties;[1] although the drains on the money market caused by abnormal grain imports probably contributed, as well. By the latter months of 1848, however, both short- and long-term rates were falling, and the framework for recovery was being laid.

4. **Industry and Agriculture.** The concentration of investment activity in railways in 1844–5 'gave a great stimulus to the iron trade'.[2] Pig-iron production was estimated at 1·2 million tons in 1843, 2·0 million tons in 1847.[3] Although output continued to rise, until 1846, at least, prices and employment reached peaks in 1845 (see table, p. 321). Railway building continued on a large scale after 1845, but the industry was far

does not exist at this time any apparent cause why a sudden reaction should occur in this property . . . we would specially guard against being understood in any way to express an opinion that the present prices of railway shares, and particularly of the new lines, are justified by any value which they can possibly possess as a permanent investment. . . . It is our opinion that there is not a single new line . . . which, before it is finished, and in a condition to pay a dividend will not be at a large discount. . . . We see much . . . to lead us to anticipate enormous losses and intense suffering . . . through these undertakings, whether we look upon them as objects of speculation or investment.'

[1] See Jenks (pp. 130–4) on the 'democratization' of the investment market.

[2] Scrivenor (1854), p. 286. Although unemployment in the iron industry falls sharply, from 1842 on, the Poor Law Com-

missioners (*P.P.* 1845, xxvii. 258–9) noted it as the last major trade to recover from the general depression. This was also the case in the major booms of the twenties and thirties.

[3] Estimates of pig-iron production available for this period are the following:

1842	.	. 1,099,138
1843	.	. 1,215,350
1844	.	. 1,400,000
1845	.	. 1,512,500
1847	.	. 1,999,608
1848	.	. 2,093,736
1850	.	. 2,249,000

Although no estimate is available for 1846, Scrivenor places the peak in iron production in that year (1854, p. 295). Unemployment statistics would almost certainly indicate a fall in output in 1848. The estimate for 1848 given here is almost certainly incorrect.

from full employment. Since iron output increased from 1845 to 1847, this may be regarded as evidence of the expansion in the fixed facilities for iron production.

| | Prices | | Percentage of iron-founders unemployed |
	Iron pigs (£ per ton)	Railway iron[a] (£ per ton)	
1842 . .	4·6	—	11·0
1843 . .	3·7	6·5	7·4
1844 . .	3·7	6·7	5·1
1845 . .	5·6	10·8	3·9
1846 . .	5·7[b]	10·3	19·3
1847 . .	5·0	9·0	15·7
1848 . .	4·6	6·1	33·4

[a] Scrivenor, pp. 296 and 298. This price is for railway iron in Cardiff and Newport.

[b] Although the average price of iron pigs is higher in 1846 than in 1845, the peak price (£5·9 per ton) appears in both years. The price declines from December 1845 to Apr. 1846 (£5·2) and then rises again to October (£5·9), falling away thereafter in a fairly steady movement. The peak price for iron bars comes in Apr. 1845 (£11·5 per ton). The price of iron bars, too, reflects slightly the recovery which appears in the employment and foreign trade statistics for 1847.

This conclusion is reinforced by the export statistics, which show the quantity of iron exports at a clearly marked peak in 1847:

Exports of Iron, Hardware, and Cutlery

(In £ millions)

	Volume	Value
1842 . .	6·1	3·9
1843 . .	7·0	4·3
1844 . .	7·8	5·4
1845 . .	7·2	5·7
1846 . .	7·8	6·4
1847 . .	9·5	7·6
1848 . .	8·9	6·6

A comparison of the real and official values indicates a high point in average iron prices in 1845. Increased sales, to 1847, were, as so often in the years after 1815, made in the face of falling average receipts.

The iron industry in 1843 presented a picture of profound depression :[1]

The present state of the iron trade annihilates hope—we see nothing but ruin before us and behind us. The kingdom for a few years past has been making iron in enormous quantities. Capital, accumulated annually from extensive

[1] Quoted by Scrivenor (1854, pp. 293–4) from the *Monmouthshire Merlin*. This article urged that some sort of monopoly agreement be set up to limit output and maintain prices: 'The trade must retire within its proper limits.' Two years later a condition of virtually full employment existed in the industry. The parallel between this statement and those made before the Committee of 1833 is obvious (see above, pp. 229–32).

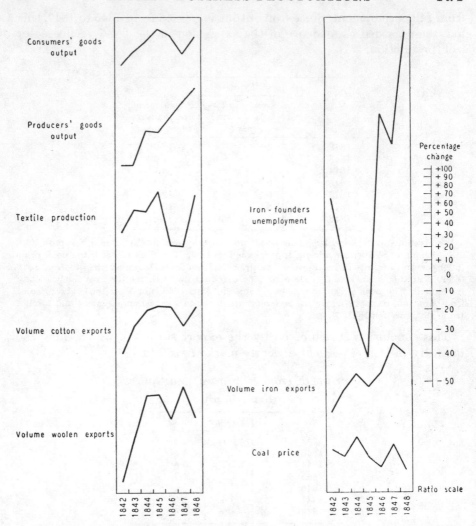

FIG. 87. Industry and Agriculture, 1842–8

orders and large sales, was laid out in building new furnaces, opening fresh mines, exploring mineral districts hitherto untouched. The large fortunes already secured in times when the foreign markets were all our own, and the produce at home scarcely sufficient for the demand, arrested the eager eyes of small capitalists, and induced the formation of companies, into which the whole livings of professional men and private individuals of comfortable means were recklessly cast—each member of every company so formed expecting to be at least a Bailey, a Guest, or a Crawshay, if not eventually a Peel or an Arkwright. . . . The result is a collapse of the whole trade—a fatal reaction—doubt and dismay.

In the following year, however, the effects of railway building were first felt, and to this 'the great increase in the manufacture is mainly attributable'.[1] In 1845 the markets reached a peak and broke;[2] complaints of unemployment and 'over production' were heard, especially after 1846.[3]

The English and Welsh firms still felt the competition of the rapidly expanding Scottish industry. In 1828 Scotland made only 5 per cent. of the pig-iron of Great Britain; by 1840 it had increased to 17 per cent., and in 1848 to 26 per cent. At the latter date only South Wales produced more.[4] New furnaces and rolling mills were again being set up; and the average scale of the individual firm, especially in Scotland but elsewhere as well, tended to grow.[5]

The accelerated expansion of the iron industry in response to the demand for rail iron, was shared, in the forties, by coal. Clapham estimates that total output (30 million tons in 1836) had reached 44 million tons in 1846, and that by 1856 the total output of coal in Great Britain was 65 million tons.[6]

The annual average price of coal and coal shipments follow:

| | Price of Sunderland coal (s. per chaldron) | Total coastwise shipments | Exports to | | Total shipments |
			British colonies (in 1,000 tons)	Foreign countries	
1842 . .	27·2	7,650	352	1,647	9,649
1843 . .	26·0	7,447	319	1,547	9,313
1844 . .	29·5	7,378	324	1,430	9,132
1845 . .	25·8	..	..	..	..
1846 . .	24·2	..	..	..	..
1847 . .	28·1	..	..	..	..
1848 . .	23·8	..	..	..	..

Shipments for which statistics are available amounted to about only one-fifth of the total coal output in these years; and, moreover, they fail to include those branches of the industry where the most rapid advance was being made.

The central institutional feature of the period is the final breakdown of the Limitation of the Vend. In 1842, after serious difficulties in the preceding few years, regulation was tentatively re-established.[7] It could not, however, prevent a decline in price in 1843.[8] In the following year,

[1] Scrivenor, p. 295. For the beginnings, in 1844, of railway construction, see Tooke, iv. 63-4; also A.R., 1844, p. 10.

[2] Early in 1845 (8 Mar.) the iron industry was described as being in a state of 'great excitement': 'No trade has experienced a greater change in the last twelve months' (The Economist, 1845, p. 228).

[3] The Economist noted (28 Mar. 1846, p. 401) that the iron industry, up to that point, was spared the 'depression in the usual demand' evident in 'the most important seats of manufactures and commerce'.

[4] Hamilton, pp. 185-6.

[5] Clapham, pp. 425-30.

[6] Ibid., p. 431.

[7] Sweezy, pp. 123-6.

[8] Dunn (p. 220) notes that, 'So disproportionate has been the augmentation of power of production to the demand, that the basis of 1843 only allowed of a real vend of 44 per cent.; or, in other words, a colliery standing upon a basis of 50,000 chaldrons, realized a vend of 22,000 chaldrons; whereas the basis of 1838 allowed of a vend of 80 per cent., or 40,000 chaldrons.' For an account of the depressed state of the coal trade in 1843, see Westminster Review, 1843, 'The

however, the industry was faced with a major strike.[1] Although the mine-owners won, the possibility of further regulation was made unfeasible by the fact that those producers unaffected by the strike had gone far above their allotments. Lord Londonderry's mines alone were nearly 40,000 tons over their vend and he 'defended himself by saying that they were all doing it and that he would not be "faithful among the faithless" '.[2]

The Vend came formally to an end on 3 May 1845,[3] near the peak in general industrial activity :[4]

Immediately following the breakdown of the regulation, quantities were greatly extended and prices brought so low as to bring losses even to the best collieries. Instead of 9s. 6d., which some thought open trade would produce, the owners could scarcely get 7s. on board ship. At the same time 'came the stoppage, in succession, of the Newcastle, the North of England and the Union Banks; and these banks, being greatly in advance to many of the colliery proprietors, forwarded, in no small degree, the progress of a deplorable crisis. In consequence, many collieries fell into the hands of their securities, at a very great loss, and were either sold at very reduced prices, or laid up altogether. Others again changed hands from the inducements held out to new men, for entering upon ready made collieries, with stock, etc., at a nominal value.'

The depression was probably as much a result of a declining industrial demand for coal as of the demise of monopoly. The coal price responded to the general revival in 1847. Although its high point for the year came in January (35·2s. per chaldron), it remained throughout above the figures for the same months in 1846. In June and July 1850 the price of Sunderland coal stood at 20·8s. per chaldron, the lowest price in the entire period 1790–1850. To this movement the industry's new competitive conditions partially contributed; but cyclical depression in demand and expanded facilities for supply were probably more significant factors.

Hoffmann's index of capital goods' production fails to reveal the general cyclical pattern :[5]

Coal Trade'. The situation is there ascribed to a reduced industrial demand, increased competition at home, a tax on exports, and the beginnings of competition abroad.

[1] See also Dunn, pp. 224–8 and Sweezy, pp. 126–7.

[2] Ibid., p. 127.

[3] *The Economist*, 1845, p. 455: 'The combination of the coalowners of the Great Durham and Northumberland fields, which has subsisted with but a short interval for many years now, and the object of which was to limit the vend, or sale, and therefore to raise the price of the important article in which they deal, was suddenly broken up on Tuesday in Newcastle-upon-Tyne. . . . It will now be settled by fair and honorable competition, instead of, as heretofore, arbitrarily, and with only a vague reference to

the great laws of supply and demand. The coalowners will no longer be obliged to keep their machinery idle ten days out of every other fortnight, and their pitmen . . . will never think of striking if they get abundant employment, and even *moderate* wages. It is idleness, whether enforced or voluntary, which is the great father of mischief. We are glad, therefore, to find that for the present there is to be an end of it in the coal trade.'

[4] Sweezy, pp. 127–8, quoting from M. Dunn, *Treatise on the Winning and Working of Collieries.*

[5] Since Hoffmann does not give the figures from which his indexes are composed it is impossible to trace the reasons either for the decline in 1845 or the continued increase in 1849. A probable explanation of the abnormal increase in 1844 and the failure of

1842	.	.	9·4	1847	.	.	14·3
1843	.	.	9·4	1848	.	.	15·7
1844	.	.	11·8	1849	.	.	15·6
1845	.	.	11·7	1850	.	.	16·3
1846	.	.	12·9				

Data on the cotton industry show a peak in 1845, a decline until 1848 :

	Consumption of raw cotton (in million lb.)	Stocks of raw cotton	Exports of cotton manufactures	
			Official value (in £ millions)	Declared value
1842 . .	474	242	68·7	21·7
1843 . .	581	342	82·2	23·4
1844 . .	554	390	91·0	25·8
1845 . .	607	454	93·7	26·1
1846 . .	614	245	93·4	25·6
1847 . .	441	184	82·2	23·3
1848 . .	577	220	93·1	22·7

Recovery came earlier to the cotton than to either the woollen, iron, or coal industries.[1] Revival can be dated at least from the early months of 1843, and continued strongly throughout the following year.[2] The cotton industry, unlike coal and iron, was not directly cushioned, in the years after 1845, by the continued construction of railways. There were clear evidences of growing depression in the course of 1845.[3] Manchester's merchants, too, had been deeply involved in the agitation for Corn Law repeal. During the parliamentary debates which ended in their victory, confidence, already weakened by the crisis of 1845, was further shaken.[4] During 1847 a shortage of the American supply led to a sharp rise in raw cotton prices, which, at a time of relative depression in the foreign markets, weighed heavily on the manufacturers.[5] In 1848, however, the quantity of exports

the index to rise in the following year is the existence of a figure for iron production of 2·0 million tons, which, though calculated for 1847, has occasionally been assigned to 1844. That figure is well above the estimate for 1845 (1·5), and, if used by Hoffmann, would explain the irregularity. In the years after 1845 it is, of course, possible that total capital goods' production increased, due to expansion of fixed plant, despite rising unemployment. But the index probably over-estimates the extent to which this occurred.

[1] P.P. 1843, xxi. 15; also Tooke, iv. 50.

[2] Hansard, 1844, lxxii. 57–9 (Cardwell); also Donnell, p. 316: 'All the mills of England were working full time (1844–45), with orders in advance of production, and new machinery was being put in rapid operation, the manufacturing trade appearing to be in

a more healthy and prosperous state than at any former period . . . in its history.'

[3] The Economist, 1846, p. 401 (28 Mar.) and P.P. 1847, xxviii. 10.

[4] The Economist, 1846, p. 402: 'We will not deny that the suspense and uncertainty as to the final result of the present discussions upon the Corn Bill, and the great political considerations which are involved in its fate, are calculated to lessen that confidence so necessary to commercial credit.' See also ibid., p. 1081.

[5] Donnell, pp. 339–40. This shortage is reflected in the low level of cotton imports and consumption in 1847, and the unexpected revival in the following year. The American shortage led to considerable discussion of the possibilities of an increased growth in India (The Economist, 1847, pp. 89 and 174).

increased, although the continued fall of prices caused, for the third consecutive year, a decline in real values. This tendency for prices to fall probably explains the low level of stocks in 1846–8; the expectation of a continued decline made the manufacturers cautious.[1]

The export of British woollens exhibits peaks in 1845 and, due largely to the American demand, in 1847:

	Quantity of raw wool imports (in million lb.)	Price of Saxon imported wool (pence per lb.)	Exports of woollen manufactures	
			Official value	Declared value
			(in £ millions)	
1842 . .	45·9	49	6·6	5·8
1843 . .	49·2	49	8·8	7·5
1844 . .	65·7	46	11·6	9·2
1845 . .	76·8	48	11·6	8·8
1846 . .	65·3	39	10·0	7·2
1847 . .	62·6	35	12·3	7·9
1848 . .	70·9	35	10·0	6·5

The fall in the price of woollens conceals, in the figures for real value, an enormous expansion in the quantities exported.[2] Woollen exports (in yards) were lower in 1842 than in 1815 (12·17 million yards).[3] In the ensuing boom they almost quadrupled:

1842 .	. 10·7	1845 .	. 29·7	1847 .	. 39·3
1843 .	. 15·4	1846 .	. 26·9	1848 .	. 32·2
1844 .	. 26·9				

Both 1844 and 1845 were extremely prosperous years, with the more substantial increase in the former.[4] The relapse in 1846 and the second recovery of 1847 appear clearly in the export figures.[5] After a severe decline, increased sales and improved prospects appeared once again in the second

[1] Donnell, pp. 351–2: 'During the past year the stocks in Great Britain, at least for the greater portion of the period, have been unusually low; but so great have been the derangements of trade, that the manufacturers could not work with profit, even upon a lower cost of the raw material than was ever before known; and many mills were stopped, while many others were compelled to resort to short-time working. Speculation has been comparatively unknown, as will readily be seen by the fact that, during the first six months of the present year, the quantity taken by speculators at Liverpool was only 27,800 bales, against 228,400 bales for the same period in 1847.'

[2] In June 1844 the 1d. import tax on foreign wool was removed (The Economist, 1845, p. 107). See also Page, i. 148–9.

[3] This and the following figures include British flannels, blankets, carpets, and mixed woollens exported, expressed in yards. The largest expansion came in the export of mixed cottons and woollens, of which the United States took over half the total output, the Eastern markets constituting the other principal source of increased orders. For a discussion of this expansion see Clapham, pp. 481–2.

[4] Signs of recovery in the woollen trade were evident as early as May 1843 (Page, i. 147 and Tooke, iv. 50). For the improvement of 1844 over 1843 see The Economist, 1844, p. 1237, and 1845, p. 107; for the industry's prosperous condition early in 1845, P.P. 1846, xix. 109 (Appendix B. 3).

[5] Recovery in 1847 was largely confined to the early months. Average employment around Bradford in November was two and a half days a week.

half of 1848.[1] The woollen industry, now enjoying an upward spurt from its relatively stagnant secular level of the previous several decades, was among the first industries to show recovery. By 1850, 63·7 million yards of woollens were exported, the official value of exports stood at £19·5 million.

Textile and consumers' goods production indexes and bankruptcies show a peak in 1845, a decline in 1846-7, and (except bankruptcies) some recovery in 1848.[2] The index of total production, reflecting the (probably incorrect) figure for capital goods production in 1846, has its peak in that year.

	Kondratieff's index of textile production	*Hoffmann's index of consumers' goods production*	*Hoffmann's index of total production*	*Number of bankruptcies (monthly average)*
1842 . .	33·7	25·3	16·6	160
1843 . .	39·0	27·5	17·6	131
1844 . .	38·6	29·5	19·8	109
1845 . .	44·0	32·1	20·9	105
1846 . .	30·9	30·8	21·0	144
1847 . .	30·7	27·3	20·2	186
1848 . .	43·0ᵃ	30·6	22·4	198

ᵃ The abnormally sharp rise in this index in 1848 follows the movement of cotton imports rather than textile exports, and, probably, textile production.

The history of agriculture in the period 1843-8 is dominated, of course, by the repeal of the Corn Laws. So far as the price of British wheat was concerned, there was considerably less reason for repeal in 1846 than in the period 1839-42.[3] The strongest influence from the side of the supply of food was, of course, the fears engendered by the Irish potato famine. But the arguments mustered on both sides were couched in long-run terms. Contemporaries were sensitive to the political and social symbolism of Corn Law repeal. Peel's full conversion to the cause of free trade, however, was probably much aided by the fact that four relatively prosperous years had followed the tariff revisions of 1842.[4]

The short-period consequence for agriculture of Corn Law repeal was

[1] *The Economist*, 1848, p. 1044. The continental revolutions temporarily arrested incipient recovery early in 1848 (Tooke, v. 236).

[2] In 1848 bankruptcies, with seasonal movement eliminated, and compared with the same months in 1847, declined sharply in the course of the year. They were 279 in January 1848, 176 in December; corrected for seasonal, 260 and 172, respectively. They thus bear out the picture of a lower turning-point in the course of 1848.

[3] The annual average price of wheat moved as follows (*s.* per quarter):

1839 .	. 70·6	1843 .	. 50·2
1840 .	. 66·2	1844 .	. 51·1
1841 .	. 64·3	1845 .	. 50·9
1842 .	. 57·2	1846 .	. 54·6

[4] In presenting his case in January 1846, Peel said that the experience of the last three years had shown him that reduced protection meant 'increased productiveness in the revenue, an increased demand for labour, increased commerce, increased comfort, contentment and peace in the country' (quoted, Page, i. 161). These years of relatively low agricultural prices were, however, a period of considerable agricultural distress. As late

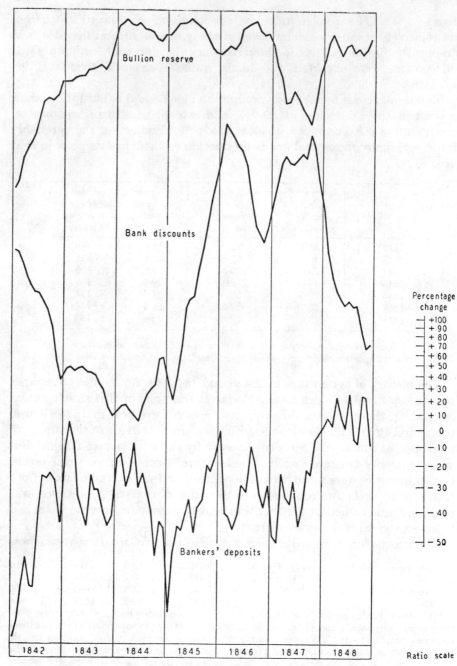

Percentage
change

+100
+ 90
+ 80
+ 70
+ 60
+ 50
+ 40
+ 30
+ 20
+ 10
0
− 10
− 20
− 30
− 40
− 50

Bullion reserve

Bank discounts

Bankers' deposits

| 1842 | 1843 | 1844 | 1845 | 1846 | 1847 | 1848 |

Ratio scale

FIG. 88 a. Finance, 1842–8

virtual panic.[1] The slow beginnings of high farming were set back in the period 1846–52.[2] From June 1847 to February 1850 the wheat price was falling. But better times were at hand, with Caird's pamphlet of 1848 pointing the way—*High Farming . . . the Best Substitute for Protection*.

5. Finance. Financial statistics reveal the minor crisis of 1845, the major crisis of 1847 (in £ millions):

	Bullion in the Bank of England	Bills and notes discounted by the Bank of England	Total bills of exchange created	London bankers' deposits in the Bank of England	Bank-rate of discount	Market-rate of discount
					(per cent.)	
1842.	8·3	4·2	249·4	1·1	4·27	3·33
1843.	11·8	2·5	230·6	1·5	4·00	2·17
1844.	15·4	2·3	246·0	1·5	3·60	2·12
1845.	15·2	4·7	283·3	1·3	3·40	2·96
1846.	14·8	9·1	294·0	1·5	4·10	3·79
1847.	10·4	9·6	293·6	1·5	6·00	5·85
1848.	13·9	4·3	224·6	2·3	4·40	3·21

Unlike the boom of the thirties, when the money market tightened progressively from 1833 to 1836, easy money persisted throughout the first two years of recovery in the forties (1843–4). The annual averages show a continuous tightening of the money market from 1845 to 1847. For the greater part of 1846, however, the Bank's reserve was rising (January to September) and the market-rate of interest declining (February to October). There was, clearly, an interval of relatively easy money between the two financial crises.

A feature of this boom was the continuance of easy money through the first two years of prosperity. The market-rate of interest was at a low point for the entire period (1824–50) in August 1844.[3] The Bank's stock of bullion, which, in general, fluctuated somewhat less violently in this cycle than in the major movements of the twenties and thirties, sagged slightly through most of 1844, but moved to a peak as late as July 1845.[4] The Bank rate was lowered to 3 per cent. in October 1844 and raised to 4 per cent. in March 1845, lagging the upward tendency in the market rate by some months.

The protracted period of easy money (1842–5) was certainly a considerable factor in encouraging the railway boom. It enveloped the long- as well as the short-term capital markets:[5]

as 1845 it was said that half the farmers in the country were insolvent; the other half were paying rents out of their capital (*A.R.* 1845, p. 64).

[1] Ernle, p. 371.

[2] Ibid., p. 370.

[3] In both May and Aug. 1844 the market rate was 1¾ per cent.

[4] The railway share market broke in Aug.,

and the market became gradually more tight until Oct., the month of most severe pressure in 1845.

[5] Quoted by Hunt (p. 103) from the *Morning Chronicle*, 22 Jan. and 12 Oct. 1844. In Feb. Gladstone told the House of Commons that unemployed capital abounded to a degree almost unprecedented and that there could be no doubt that its investment

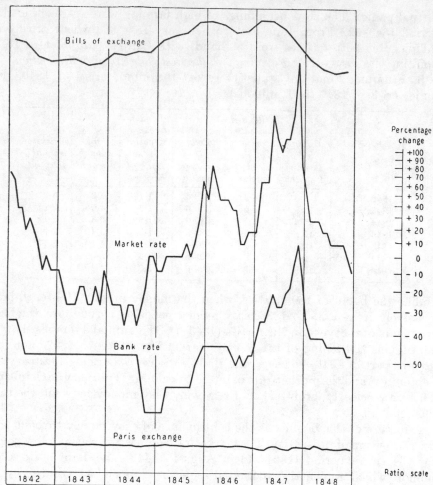

FIG. 88b. Finance, 1842–8.

For two years (January 1844) our capitalists have been anxiously waiting for
a revival of trade and commerce. . . . Profitable investment there seems to be
none. The rate of interest continues to decline. The Funds maintain an unnatural
buoyancy. Deposits in savings banks are rapidly accumulating. . . . Capital
clamours for profitable investment (October, 1844), confidence has become
eager, and may shortly become blind; railroads present the first tangible form of
investment, but anything is acceptable which promises the most ordinary
return. General prosperity begins to bear its prolific brood of speculation . . .
the public which, but the other day buttoned up its pockets is now becoming
eager to embark in any scheme.

On 2 September 1844, at the height of the period of easy money, the

'would take a direction towards the extension of railways' (cf. *Hansard*, 1844, lxxii.
233, quoted by Hunt, p. 103 n.). On the

influence of easy money in the long-term
capital market, see also Tooke, iv. 63–4.

Bank Act came into effect. The crises of 1836 and 1839 had raised the whole issue of credit control and the Bank Act of 1844 was the answer of the Currency School. In a literal version of the tradition of the Bullion Report of 1810, the framers of the Act sought to control the note issue so as 'to ensure that their volume fluctuated automatically with the bullion holding, and, therefore, more or less automatically with the foreign exchanges'.[1] Beyond the regulation of the note issue the Bank was to operate as a private commercial bank. Peel's enunciation of the theory which justified the dichotomy follows:

> The principle of competition, though unsafe in our opinion when applied to issue, ought, we think, to govern the business of banking. After the issue of paper currency has once taken place, it is then important that the public should be enabled to obtain the use of that issue on as favourable terms as possible . . . banking business, as distinguished from Issue, is a matter in respect to which there cannot be too unlimited or unrestricted a competition.

The fatal assumption which underlay this proposition was that the note issue was either the crucial element in the monetary circulation or that loans and deposits would fluctuate with the note issue:[2] 'This, as events have subsequently proved repeatedly, was a vain hope.'

Immediately upon the new act's coming into effect the Bank launched an aggressive campaign for increasing its private discounts.[3] Bills and notes discounted increased from less than £2 million in June 1844 to well over £10 million in March 1846. An incident in the new policy was the alteration, in March 1845, of the Bank's policy with respect to its discount rate: the published figure was to be thereafter a minimum rate. The rate actually charged might vary with the quality of the security, its length, and any other factors that would affect the rate of a private bank.[4]

The new policy coincided with the oncome of the railway speculation. The Bank indirectly aided in financing the payment on the new railway shares. On behalf of the subscribers private and joint-stock banks were required to deposit with agents of the government the necessary sums.[5] This process of converting short- into long-term balances kept the money market almost continuously tight in 1845–7;[6] and the Bank of England

---

[1] King, p. 103. Under the terms of this act, the Bank's note issue was to be segregated from its other business; all Bank of England notes above a fiduciary £14,000,000 were to be backed by their equivalent in bullion; existing private issues were to be limited; and new banks of issue absolutely prohibited.

[2] Idem.

[3] Newmarch before the Committee of 1857 said: 'The effect of that doctrine (the principle of the Act) has been, that the Directors of the Bank of England have considered themselves not merely at liberty, but, to a certain degree, bound, to enter into competition in the way of discount, in times of cheap money, with the houses in Lombard Street.' (Quoted King, p. 106 n.)

[4] Ibid., pp. 109–12. Also Tooke, iv. 63.

[5] Evans, pp. 18–19 and Tooke, iv. 66–7.

[6] Typical of *The Economist*'s general explanation of the panic is the following (1847, pp. 406–7): 'Railway construction means an enormous conversion of floating into fixed capital. By raising capital for railway construction a large command over commodities is transferred into the hands of the railway companies. That means new demand for

was called upon to meet the increased requirements of the financial circulation. The turning-point in railway shares in 1845 (August)[1] and, more especially, the financial panic of the last quarter were precipitated by pressures of this kind :[2]

In the early part of October no doubt was entertained of the increasing value of money, and on the 16th, the Bank directors advanced their rate to 3 per cent. In Lombard Street higher terms were demanded. There the more current quotation on first class paper was $3\frac{1}{4}$ to $3\frac{3}{4}$ per cent.

Although the great host of share speculators at first treated the Bank's advance with indifference, it was not long before the price of securities underwent considerable change. In prospect of the amount of capital to be deposited with the Government under legislative enactment, it was seen that a continuous demand for money would in all probability ensue, and hence arose a cause for substantial anxiety.

The latter end of October, 1845, will be ever memorable for the commencement of the panic in the Share-market. The animation of speculators was suddenly arrested; Consols, which towards the end of September were quoted at $98\frac{1}{4}$ had gradually declined to $96\frac{1}{2}$; and Exchequer Bills from 47s. premium had fallen to 38s. premium, the markets generally presenting an unsatisfactory appearance. At this period the leading journal again addressed its best energies to the exposure of the 'hazardous delusion' which had fallen upon the country, and a prophetic voice advised 'a shortening of sail as the storm was at hand'. Speedily this ominous prediction was verified—many of the schemes dropped as if by fell enchantment to a discount, and the prices of all kinds of shares hourly became further depressed.

The anxiety to 'get out' had not then taken the form of that indiscriminate and spasmodic rush known as panic, but nevertheless it had reached a point sufficiently intense and general to create serious alarm for the future. As was naturally the case, London experienced the first effect of the revulsion; but Liverpool, Manchester, Bristol, Leeds, Edinburgh, and Glasgow, soon evinced sympathetic action. At all these great marts, where share speculation had been encouraged to an extent vastly disproportionate to the means of the parties engaging in it, the failure of confidence was immediately responded to by a heavy declension in prices.

When the question of the Government deposit presented itself in its true light the shock was most terrific. Calculated at a sum which fortunately it never realized, the multitude took alarm—since even the most prudent then saw,

labour, a rise of wages, increased consumption.' This line of argument held that, even without the additional pressure of inadequate harvests, Britain's relatively greater prosperity and high prices would have tended to increase imports, decrease exports, and thus cause a bullion drain and financial panic. See also *The Economist*, 1847, pp. 320, 435, 489, 517, 953, for the relation between railway financing and monetary stringency.

[1] D. M. Evans, p. 19 n.: 'In the month of August, the period when railway prices generally saw what is technically called "the top of the market", the rage for gambling was enormous. The responsibility incurred by parties signing deeds of subscription attracted universal notice. At this particular date, the *furor* was so great, that those who were engaged in railway share business, found a large portion of their time occupied in keeping the necessary appointments for perfecting these documents, which were of vital importance to the existence of the companies.'

[2] Ibid., pp. 18–19.

making allowance for over estimates, that an enormous amount of capital would be temporarily withdrawn from active circulation.

The event so long prognosticated had come to pass. From one end of the kingdom to the other the tocsin of alarm resounded.

From November 1845 to about the middle of September 1846, the exchanges turned favourable to Britain,[1] while bullion in the Bank rose from January to September. The market-rate of interest, declining from February to October, also points to an interval of easy money. It was the need for large grain imports which inaugurated the second wave of stringency,[2] although, from January 1847, railway calls and financial difficulties on the Continent dominated the money market.

The crisis came in two phases during 1847, the first having its climax in the spring, the second in the last quarter: the market-rate of interest reached peaks in May and November. In the early months of the year railway calls, crisis in Paris, and the necessity of grain imports tightened the market and weakened the exchanges.[3] The Bank acted somewhat late, its bullion reserve having begun to decline in October 1846 :[4]

On the 14th of January the minimum rate for discounts at the Bank was raised from 3 to 3½ per cent., and on the 21st to 4 per cent. The rapid diminution of the bullion, and the higher rate of interest current out of doors, afforded an abundant explanation of these steps; yet they excited considerable alarm.

The bullion, which at the end of January had fallen to £12,900,000, continued slowly to decrease, chiefly by exportation to France and the United States, during February and the first three weeks of March. Thenceforward the drain proceeded more rapidly till the week ending the 24th of April, when the bullion in the two departments had fallen to £9,200,000; showing a loss of nearly six millions in four months.

The market rate of interest continued to advance. On the 8th of April the minimum rate at the Bank was raised to 5 per cent.; and during the latter period of the drain the terms of the advances and discounts were gradually restricted, till in the third week of April it was understood that only bills of the first class, due in May and June, were discountable at so low a rate as 5½ per cent.; those running into July being charged 6 per cent., and many being altogether rejected: the Directors having determined that only a limited amount should be

[1] Tooke, iv. 59–61.

[2] Ibid., pp. 70–1 and Evans, p. 58. A speculative movement in cotton, based on 'prospective scarcity', also contributed to the abnormal demand for foreign exchange and bullion.

[3] Tooke, iv. 72–4; Evans, pp. 54–62; Hawtrey, A Century of the Bank Rate, pp. 20–1.

[4] Tooke, iv. 72–4. The pressure on Britain's gold reserve was eased in the spring of 1847 by the Russian purchase of some 50 million francs of 3 per cent. French rentes. The credit raised at St. Petersburg in favour of the Bank of France thus 'became conveniently available for meeting heavy drafts from the north of Europe upon France and England, for corn supplied to both, as well as for large supplies to the latter, at unusually high prices' (ibid., p. 73 n.). The Bank of England benefited indirectly because foreign exchange on the Baltic states was available to the Bank of France in payment of a loan then due to the Bank of England. If bullion had been required to pay London, a further serious derangement of international financial centre would have followed.

discounted, however unexceptionable the bills, and however high the credit of the party offering them. This last circumstance—the entire rejection of bills without reference to their character—it was which brought on the extreme severity of the pressure in April.

The pressure upon the money market in the spring of 1847 may be said to have attained its greatest severity in the last week of April. At this time the effect of the violent contraction of its advances by the Bank was seen in the stoppage of the transmission of bullion to America. A considerable amount in gold, which was on the point of being shipped (and even some that had been actually placed on board) was withdrawn, and applied to the making of payments in this country.

In the following week, however, it was observed that the bullion in the Bank was increasing; and it was understood that the Directors were affording increased accommodation—making advances on Stock and Exchequer Bills, and discounting bills not having more than ninety-five days to run, at 5 and $5\frac{1}{2}$ per cent.

A brief interval of easier money occurred until July, when bullion exports to the United States were renewed.[1] Some £5 million in railway calls then became due, about £1 million on foreign issues.[2] From August to September the market tightened; and the two following months saw a tremendous number of bankruptcies, a 'violent contraction of credit'.[3] As private and joint-stock banks sought to make themselves liquid the demands on Threadneedle Street increased.[4] The minimum bank rate moved, on 7 August, to $5\frac{1}{2}$ per cent.,[5] but the crisis pressures continued with increasing severity through the following two months :[6]

This total revision in the terms of money accommodation granted by the great national establishment, forthwith gave birth to universal panic; the cry that railways with their calls were breaking down mercantile credit, was again

[1] The market rate of interest declined from May to July 1847; the Bank's bullion reserve rose slightly from April to June; the Bank's discounts declined from March to July.

[2] Evans, p. 65.

[3] Tooke, iv. 78. For a list of important failures at this time, see Evans, pp. 68–79.

[4] See especially the statement of the Chancellor of the Exchequer quoted by Macleod, pp. 317–19. Evans (p. 77) lists four major provincial bank failures and many minor ones.

[5] The London banks, however, held firm, although they drew heavily from the Bank of England. The banking failures followed, in general, the wave of mercantile bankruptcies. The defensive action of the provincial bankers was thus described by Samuel Gurney (quoted by Evans, p. 84 n.) from evidence before the Committee on Distress (1848): 'The failures began to take place in August. The number of failures in each week was increased, and was at last followed by a considerable panic. The effect of that panic was to cause very general distrust, and a gradual running down of the reserved fund of the Bank as well as of the bullion. After a little time people began to think, under the influence of this panic, how are we to get circulating medium ? And the wealthy and more powerful took care very largely to over-provide themselves, and drew upon the reserves of the Bank infinitely beyond the real necessities of the case. The consequence was, that the amount of notes in the hands of the public amounted to nearly £21,000,000; and I have not the slightest doubt that at that period at least from four to five millions sterling of the notes issued were locked up and inoperative, in consequence of the alarm and of a fear of not being able to get Bank notes at all.'

[6] Ibid., p. 76.

raised, and with more success than previously, since it was soon seen that the companies, who could not collect sufficient funds to carry on their works, came into the market for loans without delay, almost regardless of the rate of interest so long as they secured the required aid.

On 23 October a group of London bankers went to Downing Street and there petitioned for 'relief by a suspension of the Bank Charter Act': a letter from the Prime Minister of 25 October recommended to the Governor of the Bank of England that the directors 'enlarge the amount of their discounts and advances upon approved security, but that, in order to retain this operation within reasonable limits, a high rate of interest should be charged. In present circumstances, they would suggest that the rate of interest should not be less than 8 per cent.'[1] The suspension of the Bank Charter Act in this manner was designed as an 'extraordinary and temporary measure, to restore confidence to the mercantile and manufacturing community'. In this it succeeded. The Bank's discounts were, in fact, less in November than in October :[2]

Immediately this correspondence was made public, a steady advance in Government securities took place, much of the pervading gloom was dissipated, and from that date henceforward, a gradual but progressive return to confidence was manifested.

The market rate of interest and the Bank's discounts fell steadily from that point throughout 1848, bullion and bankers' deposits returned to the Bank; the Bank rate went to 4 per cent. in January 1848 and was down to 3 per cent. at the end of the year. Despite revolution on the Continent, for Britain 1848 was a year of financial recuperation, although political unrest abroad and at home certainly inhibited a return of long-run confidence.[3]

From the side of the demand for money there had been a variety of pressures on the Bank's reserve : from grain imports, from the competition of crisis situations in continental centres, from abnormal cotton imports, from a measure of capital exports; and, once a panic psychology had gripped banking centres, the Eastern trade revealed itself as 'overextended'. But there seems to be little question that it was the progressive calling up of short-term funds, earlier committed to the railways, that impoverished the market :[4] 'The public had undertaken to make railways

---

[1] Quoted in full, Evans, p. 87 (from Committee on Distress, 1848, p. x).

[2] Ibid., pp. 89–90. Macleod (pp. 314–16) quotes some eighteen major cases of aid granted by the Bank of England to various banking and commercial firms, in difficulty, but able to present good, if illiquid, security: 'The far larger portion of this assistance was given before the 23rd of October.'

[3] See Evans, pp. 109–29, 'Epoch the Third, the French Revolution', which discusses fully the impact of the continental situation on British financial affairs. The most specific effect was the failure, in the spring of 1848, of several houses specializing in trade with France and Belgium. By the end of 1848, however, 'a feeling of confidence sprung up, domestic and foreign politics presenting an ameliorated aspect' (ibid., p. 126). Also The Economist, 1848, p. 254 and A.R., Chr., 1848, p. 31 for the effects of the revolution in Paris on the prices of government securities, and their rally thereafter (p. 45).

[4] The Economist, 1848, p. 1187.

far beyond their means to accomplish.' The external drains were, relatively, far less severe than in 1825 or 1839. But the internal transfer to the new railways left little margin.

From the side of the supply of money, the Bank Act would appear not to have limited significantly the Bank's willingness to lend. The sort of qualitative restriction undertaken in the early stages of panic (spring, 1847) was no more drastic than in the early stages of similar situations in the previous two decades. The reaction of the public to the government's letter to the Bank, late in October, would lead one to suspect that the Bank Act's greatest role was psychological. People feared that the Bank could not lend and the flight to liquidity was accentuated :[1] 'The fear of a rigid refusal of discounts once dispelled, the drain of currency ceased.' In some respects this situation parallels that which occurred after the decision had been taken, in 1819, to return to the gold standard. The fear of credit contraction helped to make it a fact.

6. Labour. Of the measures of labour's position available, textile wages and non-agricultural relief conform best to the expected cyclical pattern

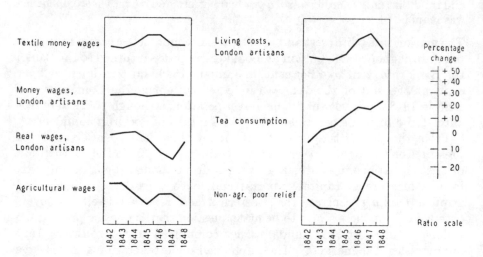

FIG. 89. Labour, 1842–8

(see table opposite). There is no very obvious explanation for the fall in the money wages of London artisans in 1845, their rise in the following year. The fall in their calculated real wage, 1845–7, can, of course, be connected with the high food prices of those years. The decline in poor relief expenditure in 1848 was probably a consequence of lower prices rather than of increased employment. Agricultural wages too, are to be linked to the British wheat price, the sharp decline in 1844 being a partial consequence of the low range of agricultural prices in the year following

[1] Hawtrey, p. 23.

	Tucker's index of		Kondratieff's index of money wages in the textile industry	Bowley's index of agricultural money wages	Poor-relief expenditures in non-agricultural counties of England and Wales (in £ millions)
	Money wages of London artisans	Real wages			
1842 . .	61·6	54·7	49·8	154	3·4
1843 . .	61·7	55·3	49·3	154	3·2
1844 . .	61·9	55·8	50·7	144	3·2
1845 . .	61·2	53·2	53·6	135	3·1
1846 . .	61·6	48·7	53·6	144	3·4
1847 . .	61·6	46·7	50·2	144	4·1
1848 . .	61·6	52·0	50·2	137	3·9

June 1844, as well as an over-supply of agricultural labour.[1] Tooke emphasizes especially the latter :[2]

In the condition of the people, notwithstanding a degree of improvement in the mass which made itself palpable through every medium of observation and inquiry available to the public, there was still, even at the close of 1844, a melancholy and painful exception presented by the state of the labourers in the agricultural districts. This was of course attributed to the abatement of protective duties on agricultural produce in 1842; and more particularly to the low range of the prices of corn during the two following years. But it may be much more clearly traced, in the first instance, to the accumulating results of the interruption of the customary migration from the agricultural to the manufacturing districts, during the long and severe depression of the latter; and secondly, though in a much less degree, to the disheartening effect upon the agricultural mind, of the prophecies of ruin uttered by the advocates of protection, confirmed, as to persons of limited observation these apparently had been, by the fall in the prices of both corn and cattle immediately after the session of 1842.

It is now abundantly obvious as well from the Annual Reports of the Poor Law Commissioners, as from other and not less trustworthy sources of information, that while the manufacturing districts were being again (in 1843–44) brought into a busy and prosperous condition, the purely agricultural parts of the country were still burdened with the population raised to supply the usual stream of migration to the towns, and not drawn off during the three or four previous years.

The rise in agricultural wages (1846–7) and the cessation of complaint from agricultural labour can be traced to the demand for unskilled men in railway construction :[3]

The complaints of want of employment for agricultural labourers would probably have been even louder and more frequent, as they would undoubtedly

[1] See A.R., 1843, p. 24, for reference to the return, during the previous years of depression, of agricultural workers to their home districts, after migration to the cities in the boom of the thirties.

[2] Op. cit. iv. 56–7. Tooke assigns some part to the fall in agricultural prices, although, as usual, he stresses the neglected role of supply conditions. He admits (pp. 57–8) 'that the low prices of produce may have induced many farmers, pressed by high money rents, to pay to those they selected from the crowd competing for employment lower wages than usual'; but it is the 'crowd competing' which engages his main interest.

[3] Ibid., p. 58.

have been longer continued, than they were, had not a new demand for field labour gradually arisen during the summer and autumn of 1844, from the construction of new railways, consequent upon the speculations of that year. This additional demand does not seem to have had much effect upon the purely agricultural districts, whence, chiefly, the complaints were heard, until the beginning of 1845; but after that period these districts appear to have shared completely the renewed activity previously displayed elsewhere.

By 1848 the agricultural prices were low, railway construction had fallen off, and agricultural wages declined.

The figures for wine, tea, tobacco, and rum consumption in the United Kingdom follow:

	Tobacco consumption (in million lb.) in the United Kingdom	Tea consumption	Rum consumption (in million gallons) in the United Kingdom	Wine consumption
1842	22·2	37·4	2·10	48·2
1843	23·0	40·3	2·10	60·7
1844	24·6	41·4	2·20	68·4
1845	26·2	44·2	2·47	67·4
1846	26·9	46·7	2·68	67·4
1847	26·7	46·3	3·33	60·5
1848	27·3	48·7	2·99	61·4

Rum consumption shows the poorest conformity, continuing its rise to 1847, declining in 1848. Tobacco and wine consumption agree in their sharp rise (1842 to 1845), halted in 1846, followed by a clear decline in 1847 and recovery in 1848. This latter increase may represent a direct consequence of the fall in food prices in that year in addition to a reaction from the abnormally low level of imports in the previous year of crisis. Tea consumption moves similarly, except for the sharp rise in 1846, which was due primarily to the fact that tea constituted the most ready means of repayment for previous British exports to the Eastern markets.[1]

Although there were many evidences of general trade recovery in 1843, it was not a good year for labour. Poor Law Commissioners could report, after the first quarter, a steady increase in employment, especially in the cotton textile areas, but woollen, iron, and coal workers were still suffering grave distress.[2] There were bloody riots in South Wales and the Chartists were chronically active.[3] But, by the 'opening of the year 1844 the country was, for the most part, in a thriving and tranquil condition. An increasing revenue and reviving trade reanimated the spirits of the community after the long depression.' The Queen's speech in February 1844 could speak of 'the increased demand for labour', which had improved the condition of

[1] Tooke, iv. 68–9.

[2] P.P. 1843, xxi. 5. The Annual Register (1843, pp. 1–2 and 23) speaks of 'discouragement and perplexity' created by 'the widespread and alarming distress which pervaded the country'.

[3] A.R., 1843, Chr., pp. 10, 22, 36, 53, 179. The most serious difficulties were confined to the early months of the year.

the working classes.[1] Low food prices slackened, for the time, even the strenuous campaign of the Anti-Corn Law League ;[2] and money wages did not decline.[3]

1845 was, of course, an even more thoroughly prosperous year for labour,[4] the crisis in the railway-share market having no immediate or direct consequences on the industrial demand for labour. In the latter months of 1845 and in the following year, however, unemployment appeared, and labour's position in addition was injured by a rise in food prices. In iron and cotton textile areas men were laid off.[5] Poor relief rose sharply, and consumption goods' imports, although larger than in 1845, increased by a lesser amount than in the previous year. 1846 saw a spate of post-crisis strikes, centring in the building, textile, and mining trades.[6] Employers took advantage of their increasing bargaining power in the labour market (due to unemployment) to attempt to destroy newly formed or strengthened unions. The men, however, after some three years of steady employment and high wages, were willing to fight, although, in most cases, they went back to work 'on the master's terms'.

Not until 1847 was serious general distress felt :[7] 'The ebb of commercial prosperity which had succeeded to the high tide of 1845, still continued to operate with depressing influence upon all branches of trade, to check confidence, to retrench expenditure, and, either directly or indirectly, to affect the circumstances of all classes of society.' The raw cotton shortage, and consequent high prices, at a time of declining demand led to a sharp fall in employment in the textile industry,[8] while iron-founders' unemployment, too, increased drastically. Pressure on the poor rates was accentuated by the steady influx of immigrants from impoverished Ireland.[9] Numerous reports of food riots occur in the *Annual Register*.[10]

In the early months of 1848, while revolution raged in western Europe, the Chartists made their last important appearance, in the farce on Kensington Common.[11] The government's grotesque over-preparation was perhaps a better indication of Britain's difficulties than the gathering itself. But it was the fall in food prices rather than the government's repressive

---

[1] *A.R.*, 1844, p. 3.
[2] Ibid., p. 2.
[3] Ibid., pp. 14, 18, and 20.
[4] Ibid., 1845, pp. 1, 84–5.
[5] *P.P.* 1847, xxviii. 8–10; also *The Economist*, 1846, p. 38.
[6] *The Economist*, 1846, pp. 76, 268, 301, 440, 538, 600, 634, 666, 741, 761, 835. A significant commentary on the state of the textile industry in August 1846 was the following incident (ibid., p. 1089). Employers in the Oldham district sought to introduce a 5 per cent. wage cut for spinners. The workers in meeting agreed to work four days a week but on no account to submit to wage reductions. The employers then accepted a

four-day week, maintaining, for the moment, the current wage rate. See also Bowley, p. 136, for a chronicle of major strikes in these years.
[7] *A.R.*, 1847, p. 1.
[8] Ibid., p. 87.
[9] *P.P.* 1847, xxviii. 10.
[10] *A.R.*, Chr., 1847, pp. 32, 40, 58, 126, 145. Among the human incidents included in the chronicle of 1847 is this (p. 98): A stripper in a cotton mill, unemployed for some time, and whose family had been without food for two days, killed the family.
[11] Cole, i. 169–70, and *A.R.*, 1848, p. 125, and Chr. pp. 35, 39, 50, 59–60.

vigour which created the relative tranquillity of the latter months of 1848; although the first signs of recovery could be discerned in some areas.[1]

Aside from the Corn Law, which was not strictly a working-class measure in its origin (though it was in the support it commanded), the Factory Act of 1847 was the principal legislative act affecting labour in these years. This measure prevented the employment of women and children for more than ten hours a day; and, under the technical conditions of production, this involved limitation for men as well. A few years previous (1844) the Act had been rejected, as the manufacturers argued that their entire profit margin would be wiped out. In 1847 the widespread existence of short time eliminated a major argument against the bill and it was passed:[2] a feeble Tory counterblast against the great middle-class triumph of the previous year.[3]

EPILOGUE: 1849-50

The final two years covered by this study were a period of increasing general recovery, in which agriculture alone did not share. In 1849, 'the condition of the country could neither be described as positively prosperous, nor as decidedly the reverse. The commercial and manufacturing interests were rallying, but had not yet effectually revived from the prostration occasioned by the commercial crisis (1847–48).'[4] In the latter six months, however, clear evidences of revival appeared in the northern textile districts.[5] Bankruptcies fell, the Bank rate was lowered, exports increased sharply. Poor-relief expenditure and iron-founders' unemployment declined. By the beginning of 1850 'the domestic affairs of the British nation presented a tranquil and, with partial exceptions, a cheering aspect'.[6]

[1] *The Economist*, 1848, p. 1045 (16 Sept.): 'We do not assert that our manufacturing districts are actually in a prosperous condition; but whether we test their condition by the amount of employment enjoyed by the people, or by the profit obtained by the manufacturer, we have no hesitation in saying that, so far as regards the great leading trades of cotton, linen, silk, and woollen, they have been in a better condition during the last 3 months than at any period since 1846. When the French revolution broke out in February the number of mills in Manchester "working full time" was 153, now the number is 184; then the number "working short time" was 35, now only 15; then the number "stopped" was 17, now only 9.'

[2] *A.R.*, 1847, p. 110.

[3] *The Economist* expresses the bitterness felt in certain quarters over the Factory Act (1848, pp. 711 and 735): 'In a few years the ten hours bill will bring ruin on all the manufacturing interest. . . . Busy demagogues, and zealous, but not prudent, sentimentalists, by false and almost fraudulent representations, induce the legislature to make an unjust law; and then the interest of many individuals making them evade it, the law becomes a scandal, and authority is brought into contempt . . . the sooner such a law is repealed the better.'

[4] *A.R.*, 1849, p. 2.

[5] Tooke, v. 244–9.

[6] *A.R.*, 1850, p. 2. See also City article of the *London Times*, 1 Jan. 1850: 'The year 1849 has realized the anticipation that its commercial history would be one of transition. At its commencement, the ruin consequent upon agricultural, mercantile, and political convulsions, such as in their rapid succession had been without a parallel, had just subsided, and the promise of a reaction as marked as had been the violence of the previous depression was everywhere appa-

The export trade continued to lead in the recovery. The declared value of exports was £52·8 million in 1848, £71·4 million in 1850, with the American and Asiatic markets offering the principal stimuli. The opening of California and the consequent boom in the United States was felt with particular strength. The movement of poor-relief expenditure, iron-founders' unemployment, and bankruptcies, as well, pointed to increasing prosperity.[1] Even shipbuilders ceased to complain and spoke of business in 1850 as being 'of a decidedly healthy kind'.[2] A moderate amount of railway building was undertaken and rail shares at last rose, along with other security prices. An appropriate stage was set for the Crystal Palace Exposition of the following year, and the beginning of the era of Mid-Victorianism.

rent. The prosperity, moreover, was to be tangible and unequivocal, for all faith had been destroyed, except in steady industry.'

[1] The City article of *The Times*, 17 Sept. 1850, reported as follows: 'The accounts of the state of trade in the provinces continue satisfactory from all parts, except Manchester, where there has again been a great tendency to depression, although a favourable reaction seems now to be looked for. The woollen cloth trade is active everywhere, and stocks are still further reduced. The demand in the lace and hosiery markets appears steady, both on home and foreign account.'

[2] Tooke, v. 257.

Appendix A

THE BUSINESS-CYCLE PATTERN IN GREAT BRITAIN, 1790–1850

1. Reference Dates. In terms of the technique of business-cycle analysis developed by the National Bureau of Economic Research, the term 'reference date' is used to denote the turning-points of a business cycle, i.e. its peak and trough. The establishing of accurate reference dates is a preliminary step in the statistical analysis of cyclical behaviour.[1] When turning-points have been defined, one is in a position to state that the economic system was in a state of expansion from date x to date y, in a state of contraction from date y to date z.[2] It is then possible to proceed with the examination of the behaviour of an individual series in the course of a single business cycle, or to discover its typical cyclical pattern of behaviour by a process of averaging.

It is obvious, as well, that reference dates have a more general historical interest. Assuming that business fluctuations were a continuous phenomenon (i.e. that the economic system was always in a state of general expansion or contraction), they serve as a shorthand business history. The reader of this volume will immediately sense the limitations of such simple dating; but as a first approximation it is felt that these dates may serve as a useful framework of reference not only for the statistician but also for the general historian.

Monthly reference dates are, of course, preferable to the cruder annual dating; and we have attempted to define turning-points both in terms of years and months. But, since so much more of the statistical material available is in annual than in monthly form, the monthly dates must be regarded as subject to a considerably greater margin of error than the annual.

A turning-point is not defined in terms of any single variable; e.g. unemployment, production, or *per capita* national income. This is due less to ambiguity in the definition of a business cycle than to a certain caution in relying upon any single existing index purporting to represent such complex aggregates. That caution is observed even in setting recent reference dates; and it is considerably more persuasive in our period, where the data are less complete and less accurate. The reference dates given here represent a judgement based on all relevant statistical and non-statistical evidence examined.

2. Statistical Indicators of Cyclical Turning-points. The criterion that has been employed by the National Bureau of Economic Research is the moment of the turning-point in 'general business activity'. The ambiguity of this concept is more apparent than real; for in the modern period at least there is a variety of over-all series, reflecting the response of many areas within the economic system: freight-car loadings, bank clearings, and general indexes of production and employment. Since, at best, reference dates must be arbitrary—the processes of the turning-point being complicated and extending over a considerable time-period—useful points can be defined by examining such indicators of 'general business activity'.

The only series purporting to represent over-all changes in output, in our

---

[1] For the role of reference dates in this type of analysis, see below, Vol. II, pp. 659ff.

[2] When reference dates are set monthly, expansion is dated from the month following the trough, contraction from the month following the peak.

period, are the Hoffmann and Beveridge production indexes.[1] Since we regard the Hoffmann indexes as inconclusive we were thrown back on a very limited sample of individual production series. The meagreness of information relative to production, however (which, in large measure, explains the imperfection of indexes like Hoffmann's), forced us to rely heavily upon indirect measures of changes in output. The foreign trade data, which are relatively abundant for this period, have served as the most important substitutes for direct production figures.

Among the foreign trade data we have regarded export series as more intimately responsive to the course of business fluctuations than imports.[2] The imported commodity markets were subject to powerful movements which distort the influence of general cyclical fluctuations. They were large and well-organized institutions sensitive to what we have regarded as inventory, rather than production, movements. Raw wool, cotton, silk, &c., were imported and sold to the manufacturers by large-scale firms—much larger than the average manufacturing unit. These large importers held varying amounts of stocks, depending on their expectations with respect to price and money market conditions as well as to the industrial demand. The nature of these raw materials, too, lent themselves to warehousing more easily than the varied manufactured products to which they contributed.

Exports, to some extent, were also subject to a kind of inventory fluctuation with respect to actual output movements. But it is our view that the institutional arrangements for exporting, as well as the more varied nature of the finished export products, made for a more direct relation between physical output and exports than imports. The total volume of imports, further, is distorted as a measure of general business fluctuations by the presence of wheat imports, which exhibit a tremendous amplitude of movement. Although changes in wheat imports are related, and at times importantly related, to business cycles in this period, they distort the volume of imports as a year-to-year measure of general fluctuations.[3]

It probably goes without saying that continuous and inclusive statistical data on *per capita* national income and unemployment are unavailable for this period. From 1830 on statistics on unemployed iron-founders become available, and despite their doubtful representativeness, we have made use of them.

As far as possible we tried to restrict the series employed as statistical indicators of turning-points in general business to measures of physical change. A few financial series were, however, considered relevant—notably our newly constructed indexes of share prices and the value of inland bills of exchange created. Because of the peculiar position of the Bank of England in the British banking structure —which gives to the bullion reserve and Bank discounts a fairly consistent lagging relation to the timing of general business fluctuations—we did not use Bank series in setting annual reference dates. They were, however, carefully consulted.

---

[1] The Beveridge Index is discussed in Vol. II, pp. 616–22.

[2] In this respect our view differs from that of Beveridge who has used import series heavily in the compilation of his index of industrial activity. Kondratieff's index of textile production is weighted almost to the point of identity with raw cotton imports. Hoffmann's index of consumer's goods production uses both import and export series in an effort to establish the movement of textile output.

[3] It is of interest that the National Bureau of Economic Research has found that for modern Britain, as well, exports are more closely related to business cycles than imports.

Our use of the price data as cyclical indicators was also rather limited. Reliance on prices as indexes of general business activity assumes that they will move with rough conformity to monetary demand, and that changes in supply conditions, in the short run, will not obscure that relation. Prices from 1790 to 1850, however, were under constant pressure from the side of supply, and tell a quite different story than do statistics of production and foreign trade. This is not to imply, of course, that price movements were ignored in establishing reference dates, but simply that they were not regarded as definitive.

3. Procedure. Our aim then was to determine when a consensus existed among the movements of these series (all annual), representing many economic activities. The task of establishing the existence of a concentration in their turning-points around certain moments of time was not undertaken until after the bulk of the *History* had been written, and specific cycles[1] in most of our series had been marked off and analysed. We were thus equipped with both qualitative and quantitative evidence bearing on the problem of the identification of general business cycles.

Several procedures were followed in attempting to ascertain the consensus of cyclical turning-points. First we plotted the original data of all our series and compared their specific cycles. On *a priori* grounds we then eliminated those which we did not regard as conforming closely to business cycles, although, of course, we could not know with certainty that our judgement was valid until after we had set reference dates. Next we compiled a table showing the specific highs and lows of a sample group of thirty-six series during the period 1790–1850; a simple count of the number of highs and lows, some of which occurred in every year, was then made. But this was an obviously crude approach, for it gave equal weight to each series in our sample group, and took no account of percentage changes. There is, of course, less scatter in time in the cyclical turns of annual than of monthly time series; but the mere clustering of a maximum number of turnings in one year, for example, as compared with the preceding or following years, was patently an unsatisfactory basis for decision.

We then applied a device used by Dr. Arthur F. Burns[2] to fix the turning-points of 'trend cycles'. He refers to it as 'a technique better adapted than the method of averages to extract a common element from a mass of cyclical data which are only a "sample" of their universe'. We turned the data for a group of twenty series into comparable form by obtaining relatives of their own average value for each of the series over successive periods of from three to thirteen years' duration;[3] then ranked the relatives for each year, and made tables of quartiles,[4] which are shown graphically for each of the time-periods in Fig. 90 (p. 346). The first quartile curve in the chart simply joins the first quartile value in the successive years, and similarly with the other quartile curves. When

---

[1] Specific cycles are the cyclical fluctuations in a series peculiar to itself. They are not to be confused with reference cycles, the cyclical fluctuations in general business, although, of course, series with close conformity to general business movements may well show specific and reference cycles with virtually identical timing.

[2] See his *Production Trends in the United States since 1870*, pp. 182–96.

[3] The periodization was determined largely on the basis of the years in which new series were introduced into or removed from business.

[4] The first quartile is a simple average of the values of the first 25 per cent. of the ranked observations; the second quartile is the average of the values of the next 25 per cent. of the observations, and so on.

all of the quartiles move in the same direction between successive years, a shift common to all portions of the array is indicated. But when there is an irregular arrangement of the quartile lines between successive years, the impulses to cyclical change obviously did not act commonly through all the activities represented.

Table 1 summarizes the extent of the parallelism in the direction of the quartile lines in each of the years in the period. Our first approximation to the final set of reference dates was made on the basis of this evidence.[1]

We then re-examined all the evidence for and against the designation of each year in the period as a turning-point. To some series (like the volume of exports) we gave greater weight than to others because the former appeared representative of wider areas of business activity and their conformity to business-cycle movements seemed to us closer. If only a few relatively unimportant series showed troughs or peaks in a year and no contemporary account referred to a change in business conditions, the existence of a general business turn seemed questionable. The clustering of the turning-points, and the movement of the quartile averages, in conjunction with non-statistical evidence, proved sufficiently consistent to establish our final set of annual reference dates.

On the whole the annual reference dates, for the limited purposes for which they are designed, may be used with some confidence. They represent a carefully considered evaluation of a considerable body of evidence. The monthly reference dates, however, can be regarded as little more than a series of informed guesses. Only commodity and security prices, bankruptcies, interest rates, foreign exchange rates, and Bank of England data exist in monthly form; although the quarterly series representing the value of inland bills of exchange were also helpful in setting the monthly dates. Turning-points in share prices and bankruptcies tended to lead turning-points in the other series, and in several cases where the evidence for the designation of the monthly peak or trough was inconclusive, the mean month between the series which led and the others were chosen. Qualitative evidence, referring to 'the later' or 'the early' months of a year, or, occasionally, to the spring or autumn as being the interval within which a turning-point occurs, was also employed. Although these dates have been given here in monthly form they are perhaps better to be used as indicative of the quarter within which the turning-points took place. Except for the strictly statistical analysis of monthly series, this usage is indicated not only because of the inherent doubt attached to the exact dates given, but also because turning-points can be regarded most usefully as a process covering a considerable time interval rather than as an event taking place within so restricted a period as a month. It is evident, nevertheless, that the monthly dates represent some considerable refinement over the annual figures.

4. **Annual and Monthly Turning-points.** The annual and monthly reference dates that we have selected appear on p. 348. The annual dates do not define necessarily the year within which recovery or depression got under way. The year as a whole is the analytic unit. In the monthly analysis, for example, a trough has been marked off in June 1794. On the whole, however, 1794 has been regarded as a more prosperous year than 1793; and thus 1793, among the annual dates, is a cyclical trough.

[1] The table also shows our final choice of reference turning-points and those which were surrounded with doubt. The latter are discussed further in section 5 below.

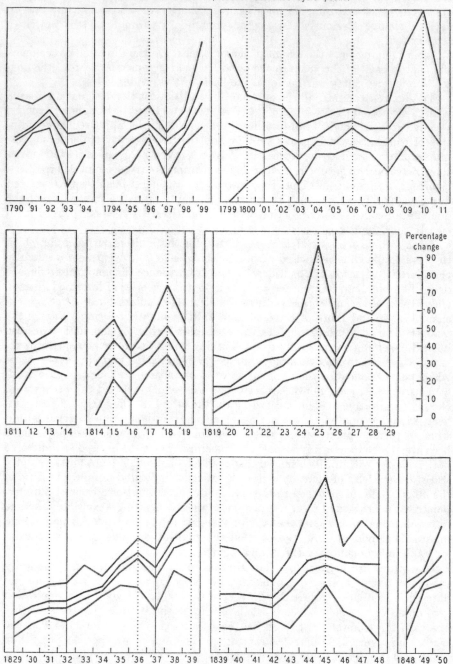

Solid vertical lines represent reference cycle troughs.
Dotted vertical lines represent reference cycle peaks.

Fig. 90. Movements of Quartile Averages of Ranked Relatives of Selected Series, 1790–1850

TABLE 1. *Movements of the Quartile Averages shown in Fig. 90 and Reference Turning-points*

| Year | Number moving | | | Reference dates |
	Upward	Downward	Stationary	
1791 . .	3	1	..	..
2 . .	4	..	..	Peak
3 . .	..	4	..	Trough
4 . .	4	..	..	..
1795 . .	3	1	..	*
6 . .	4	..	..	Peak*
7 . .	..	4	..	Trough
8 . .	4	..	..	..
9 . .	4	..	..	..
1800 . .	2	2	..	Peak
1 . .	1	3	..	Trough
2 . .	3	1	..	Peak
3 . .	..	4	..	Trough
4 . .	4	..	..	..
1805 . .	2	1	1	..
6 . .	4	..	..	Peak
7 . .	..	4	..	..
8 . .	1	2	1	Trough
9 . .	4	..	..	*
1810 . .	3	1	..	Peak*
1 . .	..	4	..	Trough
2 . .	3	1	..	..
3 . .	4	..	..	..
4 . .	2	2	..	..
1815 . .	4	..	..	Peak
6 . .	..	4	..	Trough
7 . .	4	..	..	..
8 . .	4	..	..	Peak
9 . .	..	4	..	Trough
1820 . .	2	1	1	..
1 . .	3	..	1	..
2 . .	4	..	..	..
3 . .	4	..	..	..
4 . .	4	..	..	..
1825 . .	4	..	..	Peak
6 . .	..	4	..	Trough
7 . .	4	..	..	..
8 . .	2	2	..	Peak
9 . .	1	3	..	Trough
1830 . .	4	..	..	*
1 . .	4	..	..	Peak*
2 . .	1	1	2	Trough
3 . .	4	..	..	..
4 . .	3	1	..	..
1835 . .	4	..	..	..
6 . .	3	1	..	Peak
7 . .	..	4	..	Trough
8 . .	4	..	..	*
9 . .	3	1	..	Peak*
1840 . .	1	2	1	..
1 . .	1	2	1	..
2 . .	1	3	..	Trough
3 . .	3	1	..	..
4 . .	4	..	..	..
1845 . .	4	..	..	Peak
6 . .	..	4	..	..
7 . .	1	3	..	..
8 . .	..	3	1	Trough
9 . .	4	..	..	..
1850 . .	4	..	..	..

* The asterisks indicate competing years for final choice as a reference date.

Annual		Monthly	
Peak	Trough	Peak	Trough
1792	1793	1792–Sept.	1794–June
1796	1797	1796–May	1797–Sept.
1800	1801	1800–Sept.	1801–Oct.
1802	1803	1802–Dec.	1804–Mar.
1806	1808	1806–Aug.	1808–May
1810	1811	1810–Mar.	1811–Sept.
1815	1816	1815–Mar.	1816–Sept.
1818	1819	1818–Sept.	1819–Sept.
1825	1826	1825–May	1826–Nov.
1828	1829	1828–Jan.	1829–Dec.
1831	1832	1831–Mar.	1832–July
1836	1837	1836–May	1837–Aug.
1839	1842	1839–Mar.	1842–Nov.
1845	1848	1845–Sept.	1846–Sept.
		1847–Apr.	1848–Sept.

The monthly data revealed only one cycle which did not appear in the annual statistics: that from September 1846 to September 1848. Most annual figures reflect an uninterrupted decline from 1845 to 1848. Although there are no monthly statistics relating to foreign trade, qualitative evidence (largely in Tooke) indicated some general revival from the latter months of 1846 through the early months of 1847. Monthly commodity prices and financial data seemed to reveal this brief recovery; while exports to the United States (annually)—of great importance in cyclical fluctuations in this period—were at a clearly marked peak in 1847. This evidence argued the existence of a slight cyclical movement, although its designation among the annual dates seemed unjustified.

5. Doubtful Cases. Most of the annual dates are unequivocal when the data are even superficially examined; e.g. such peaks as 1792, 1810, 1825, 1836, and such troughs as 1816 and 1826. In general, as one would expect from the nature of the processes involved, peaks were somewhat easier to identify than troughs.[1]

Although serious doubts as to the proper dating arose in relatively few cases, in virtually none of the instances were the statistical data completely unequivocal. This was due, in part, to the fact that some of the series exhibit consistent leads and lags; but even taking this factor into account a certain area of doubt existed. It should be remarked, however, that few of our series reflect total movements of the economic system, and the failure of all industries or branches of industry to respond synchronously was not unexpected.

The following are the annual dates to which the greatest area of doubt attached:[2]

[1] The fact that the peaks were accompanied by, or shortly followed by, severe money market disturbances, and by sharp reversals in the commodity and security markets, often makes their selection easier. Contemporary commentators, too, were more easily moved to comment on the sensational and unpleasant events that accompanied the upper turning-points than the slow and gradual process of depression turning to prosperity.

[2] In several of these instances doubt arose not about the actual timing of the turning-points (i.e. the year within which the turning-point occurred) but rather about the proper year to designate as peak or trough; for there is no need, so far as the requirements of the National Bureau procedure are concerned, to choose the year within which the monthly turning-point occurred. In the case of 1803–4, for example, it was calculated that the turning-point occurred at

Troughs

Date chosen	Date considered
1793	1794
1803	1804
1811	1812
1819	1820

Peaks

1796	1795
1802	1803
1810	1809
1831	1830
1839	1838
1845	1846

The following table presents link relatives between the alternative years in a selected number of the series we have regarded as most relevant to a choice of reference dates in our period. This procedure is designed to indicate not only the direction of movement from year to year but also the percentage amount of movement. For further evidence on these dates and those which we regard as unequivocal the reader is referred to the *History* and to the detailed statistical materials on which it is, in part, based.

The reasons for our final choice are stated below in separate consideration of each of the doubtful cases.

Troughs

1793–4. On a monthly basis it has been calculated that the up-turn came in June 1794. This would explain some of the ambiguity in the annual figures. The substantial rise in the volume of exports, however, principally justified the judgement that 1794, in net, saw some improvement over 1793. The decline in brick production and in the index of producers' goods output was not considered persuasive evidence against our choice, because those series consistently exhibit a lag in their response to recovery. The sharp fall in bankruptcies, a slight rise in broad cloth milled in the West Riding, the increase in tin mined in Cornwall, and the considerable increase in the import of tea and tobacco also supported the case for 1793 as the proper trough. Qualitative evidence pointed to a considerable measure of recovery in the course of 1794; and it was known that by the last quarter of 1793 the liquidation of the previous crisis had been completed in the money market.

1803–4. Again, monthly, it was found that the trough fell in the alternative year (March 1804). But the annual data strongly pointed to substantial net recovery in the latter year; *vide* tin mined, broad cloth milled, raw cotton consumption, the production indexes (excepting, as in 1794, producers' goods output), and several important branches of the export trade, as well as the total figures.

about Mar. 1804; and yet, clearly, 1804, in net, exhibited some considerable improvement over 1803; and 1803 emerges as the proper trough. In other cases the doubt arose not in our data but from the fact that other investigators (notably Thorp) were in disagreement with our first judgements. Such instances were treated as 'doubtful' cases and subjected to special analysis. Disagreements between Thorp's view of the cyclical pattern and ours are presented below, in Appendix C.

TABLE 2. *Link Relatives between Years competing for Choice as Turning-dates in Important British Series*

Series	Troughs				Peaks					
	1794/1793	1804/1803	1812/1811	1820/1819	1796/1795	1803/1802	1810/1809	1831/1830	1839/1838	1846/1845
Production of bricks	79	100	98	86	97	106	110	103	110	112
Production of copper in Cornwall	—	96	109	110	—	107	83	112	108	92
Production of tin	105	103	99	90	89	111	80	97	—	—
Woollen broad cloth milled in the West Riding	100	112	117	—	101	103	88	—	—	—
Woollen narrow cloth milled in the West Riding	97	108	90	—	101	100	104	—	—	—
Consumption of raw cotton	128	117	67	115	124	91	145	101	77	101
Kondratieff's index of textile production	—	113	77	106	—	96	130	102	83	70
Hoffmann's index of total production	100	102	93	103	100	104	108	101	109	100
Hoffmann's index of consumers' goods production	100	105	90	101	99	100	108	101	109	96
Hoffmann's index of producers' goods production	95	97	97	105	100	111	109	103	109	110
Volume of domestic exports	123	111	127	107	104	82	105	102	105	98
Volume of exports of domestic manufactures	—	—	—	107	—	—	—	104	106	98
Volume of exports of brass and copper manufactures	—	—	—	125	—	—	—	96	103	87
Volume of exports of cotton manufactures	141	123	138	123	133	93	98	96	105	100
Volume of exports of linen manufactures	124	141	131	125	140	63	90	118	112	92
Volume of exports of woollen manufactures	102	107	116	95	111	80	106	112	99	86
Volume of exports of iron, hardware, and cutlery	99	120	116	98	125	69	113	111	113	109
Volume of total imports	115	104	99	106	102	89	124	108	105	93
Shipping tonnage in foreign trade, entered	—	—	—	90	—	—	—	110	111	101
Shipping tonnage in foreign trade, cleared	—	—	—	94	—	—	—	112	110	105
Shipping tonnage in coasting trade, entered and cleared	—	—	—	—	—	—	—	100	101	96
Number of bankruptcies	61	100	86	88	109	108	164	110	132	137
Index of share prices	—	—	92	96	—	—	—	90	96	95
Small bills of exchange created	—	—	—	105	—	—	—	98	101	100
Medium bills of exchange created	—	—	—	100	—	—	—	103	110	100
Large bills of exchange created	—	—	—	93	—	—	—	108	119	106
Total bills of exchange created	—	—	—	97	—	—	—	105	114	104
Bullion in the Bank of England	—	132	91	181	43	91	84	74	45	97
Market rate of discount	—	—	—	—	—	—	—	131	171	128
Tea consumption	107	89	109	102	95	98	116	101	109	106
Tobacco consumption	113	98	101	95	91	104	108	101	99	103

1811–12. The argument against placing a trough in 1811 is, superficially, impressive. Although the volume of exports rose and bankruptcies declined sharply, brick production and all available output indexes declined in 1812. As in the two cases considered above, the decline in brick production and in the index of producers' goods output can be ignored as evidence against 1811. The movement of textile and consumers' goods production, however, would seem to argue that the increase in exports came from previously manufactured stocks rather than from current output. In fact their behaviour stems from the movement of raw cotton imports, which fell off drastically owing to the war with the United States. This series is a heavily weighted component in both the Kondratieff and Hoffmann indexes. Qualitative evidence also indicates a considerable recovery in the course of 1812, sharply accentuated in the latter months of the year by the withdrawal of the British Orders in Council (from June 1812). In net, then, we view 1812 as a less depressed year than 1811.

1819–20. The statistical evidence leaves little doubt that there was a considerable net recovery in 1820. The declines in the security index, bills of exchange, and brick production are not inconsistent with the first year of recovery, while the fall in the export of iron and woollen manufactures is easily outweighed by increases elsewhere. Considerable qualitative evidence supports this view.

Peaks

1796–1795. There seems to be no doubt that 1796 was, at best, a year of somewhat restricted prosperity. The monthly turning-point has been designated as early as May 1796, which, in itself, would tend to confuse the annual evidence. The tightness of the money market, at a time when the government was financing a large volume of new war loans, and when the restraints of the bullion standard had not yet been lifted, limited the scope of recovery forces even in the early months. The net movement of the quantitative evidence, however, seems to favour 1796 over 1795 as the appropriate peak. We believe the increases in foreign trade and in woollen cloth milled in the West Riding outweigh in significance the declines in brick production, copper mined in Cornwall, and in tea and tobacco imports. The sharp rise in bankruptcies is not to be taken as evidence of general depression; for that series customarily anticipates reference cycle peaks.

1803–1802. A number of series indicative of activity in the capital goods industries exhibit increase in 1803: brick production, copper and tin mined in Cornwall, and the index of producers' goods output. These movements we have regarded as reflecting the conventional lag of capital goods output. The nature of the depressive forces in 1803—the outbreak of war and the consequent limitation of foreign trade—were such as to affect most immediately the volume of imports and exports. Their impact in that area is evident (excepting tobacco imports). Since the upper turning-point came, in our judgement, as late as December 1802, the lag in certain of the production series (annually) might be expected to be fairly pronounced. Qualitative evidence and the behaviour of the financial data support the view that 1803 was an interval of relative depression when compared with the preceding and following years.

1810–1809. By our monthly calculations an upper turning-point occurred in March 1810. Although the latter months of 1810 were certainly marked by many depression phenomena (witness the extraordinarily sharp rise in bankruptcies) in net, most import series reflecting the position of production and foreign trade exhibit increase over 1809, the most important exceptions being copper mined in Cornwall and broad cloth milled in the West Riding.

1831–1830. 1831 is still another year in which a monthly upper turning-point occurs early (March). Again, however, the overwhelming testimony of foreign trade and production data favours the choice we have made. Their testimony is supported here by the increase in the value of inland bills of exchange, which, despite some slight tendency to lag at the peak, are a good cyclical indicator.

1839–1838. We have designated March 1839 as the monthly upper turning-point; but the evidence favours the later, rather than the earlier year as the proper cyclical peak. An abnormal decline in raw cotton imports (due to the collapse of Anglo-American speculation in that commodity) affects the figures for raw cotton consumption and the textile production index. But those series must be used with considerable caution in all cases. Again a rise in bankruptcies appears, which can be regarded as anticipatory.

1845–6. It is certain that some branches of British industry remained relatively active for some time after the upper turning-point in this cycle (September 1845). The operation of two forces in 1845, however, justify placing it as a peak: a decline in the export trade and the beginnings of the decline of new enterprise in railway floatation (witness the decline in the index of share prices which, at this point, is largely controlled by the movement of railway securities). The falling off in exports, and in the index of consumers' goods output, is clearly marked. The rise in brick production and the index of producers' goods output may be regarded as indicative of a lag, made especially strong in this instance by the scale and long period of gestation of railway construction. The rise in bankruptcies is rather to be expected, while the mild increase in inland bills of exchange has not been judged sufficient evidence for rejecting 1845 as the proper peak. Considerable qualitative evidence supports this view that the year dating from the last quarter of 1845 saw increased industrial depression. If the testimony of the unemployment series for iron-founders is to be relied upon—and, over the period for which it is available, it exhibits a high degree of conformity to our reference dates—then industrial depression extended even to the iron industry which, admittedly, received some abnormal support after the upper turning-point from continued railway construction.

The cyclical movement which, for us, has raised the greatest difficulty in definition and which must be viewed with the most suspicion is that which has been marked off (trough to trough) from 1801 to 1803. For certain purposes, in the analytic chapters of Part I of Vol. II, that cycle has been ignored, the period 1797–1803 being regarded as the proper analytic unit. Although it is clear that the relative depression of 1801 was not as severe, for example, as in 1797 or 1803, there is some evidence pointing to a falling off in that year, as compared to the position in 1800, and to an improvement in 1802 over the position in 1801. The tables indicate the standing of link relatives for significant series in 1800–1 and 1802–1.

There can be little question that the statistical evidence, as a whole, indicates a net improvement from 1801 to 1802. The decline in 1801, however, fails to emerge in several significant series, notably in textile exports and brick produc-

Table 3. *Standing of Link Relatives of Significant Series in 1800 and 1802*

(1801 = 100)

	1802/ 1801	1800/ 1801
Production of bricks	112	89
Production of copper in Cornwall	99	98
Production of tin	113	107
Woollen broad cloth milled in the West Riding . . .	101	106
Woollen narrow cloth milled in the West Riding . . .	104	124
Consumption of raw cotton	106	95
Kondratieff's index of textile production	100	—
Hoffmann's index of total production	104	104
Hoffmann's index of producers' goods production . .	108	108
Hoffmann's index of consumers' goods production . .	104	102
Volume of domestic exports	100	98
Volume of exports of domestic manufactures . .	—	—
Volume of exports of cotton manufactures	107	83
Volume of exports of woollen manufactures . . .	91	94
Volume of exports of linen manufactures	87	78
Volume of exports of brass and copper manufactures . .	—	—
Volume of exports of iron, hardware, and cutlery . .	114	112
Volume of total imports	94	89
Number of bankruptcies	95	84
Bullion in the Bank of England	90	126
Tea consumption	107	98
Tobacco consumption	115	112

tion. The total volume of exports (Schlote) remains constant from 1800 to 1802; but these figures may conceal a brief cycle of slight amplitude. Among the annual figures the strongest evidence for a decline in 1801 appears in the movement of broad cloth milled in the West Riding, the Hoffmann indexes,[1] tonnage entered and cleared, and the number of bankruptcies. The behaviour of the monthly financial data also seems to justify the marking off of a cycle from 1801 to 1803; and there is some qualitative evidence (see Chap. I, Part II of the *History*) which supports this view.

Appendix B

BUSINESS-CYCLE INDEXES

As an indicator of the cyclical pattern—aside from their utility in statistical analysis—reference dates are limited in one important respect. They define the periods during which presumably continuous expansion and contraction processes occurred, but they in no way represent the intensity of those movements or the rate at which they proceeded in different intervals. To supply that lack two business-cycle indexes have been constructed.

[1] The index of general industrial activity, constructed by Beveridge, also exhibits a clearly marked trough in 1801.

The first of these is a weighted geometric index incorporating the following series:

TABLE 4. *Series included in the Index of Business Activity, with Respective Weights*

Series	Weight
Hoffmann's index of total production	1 (1790–1850)
Kondratieff's index of textile production . . .	2 (1801–50)
Number of bankruptcies (inverted)	2 (1790–1850)
Total value of inland bills of exchange created . .	2 (1816–50)
Production of bricks	2 (1790–1850)
Index of share prices (including mining shares, 1811–26; excluding mining shares, 1827–50)	2 (1811–50)
Volume of domestic goods exports	3 (1790–1850)
Percentage of iron-founders unemployed . . .	1 (1831–50)

When the index is expressed in terms of relatives of the period 1821–5, the following series results (see Fig. 91):

TABLE 5. *Index of Business Activity*

(1821–5 = 100)

1790	. .	54·6	1820	. .	80·8
1	. .	58·2	1	. .	81·7
2	. .	61·9	2	. .	89·4
3	. .	46·9	3	. .	97·8
4	. .	55·4	4	. .	105·6
1795	. .	57·5	1825	. .	125·5
6	. .	56·2	6	. .	85·8
7	. .	51·5	7	. .	103·5
8	. .	55·8	8	. .	105·6
9	. .	64·2	9	. .	101·9
1800	. .	65·3	1830	. .	108·8
1	. .	64·2	1	. .	109·0
2	. .	66·6	2	. .	106·6
3	. .	62·4	3	. .	114·4
4	. .	66·2	4	. .	119·5
1805	. .	67·6	1835	. .	129·9
6	. .	68·2	6	. .	148·4
7	. .	66·4	7	. .	119·4
8	. .	62·1	8	. .	140·7
9	. .	75·0	9	. .	137·2
1810	. .	74·8	1840	. .	134·0
1	. .	64·0	1	. .	127·4
2	. .	65·3	2	. .	126·7
3	. .	64·7	3	. .	138·6
4	. .	68·9	4	. .	157·5
1815	. .	72·9	1845	. .	176·0
6	. .	66·5	6	. .	145·9
7	. .	74·4	7	. .	141·1
8	. .	91·1	8	. .	126·0
9	. .	79·8	9	. .	143·0
			1850	. .	159·9

The magnitude of the trend movement contained in this index is spurious and does not reflect the rate of growth of the economy as a whole. And, in the following instances at least, we regard the index as misrepresenting the true cyclical pattern.

1796. The rise in bankruptcies and the fall in brick production outweigh, in the index, the rise in the volume of exports. This produces a decline from 1795

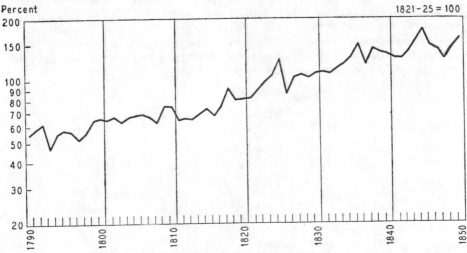

FIG. 91. Index of Business Activity

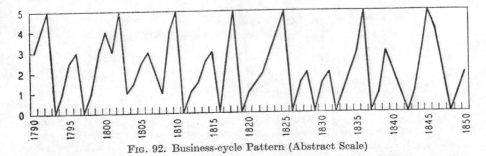

FIG. 92. Business-cycle Pattern (Abstract Scale)

to 1796. As explained above, on fuller evidence 1796 is considered the peak in the cycle 1793–7.

1810. In 1810 a sharp rise in bankruptcies outweighs the upward influence of all other components of the series, yielding a spurious, if slight, net decline.

1813. The abnormal obstruction to raw cotton imports during the War of 1812 results in a fall in the index of textile production sufficient to yield (in conjunction with the movement of brick production and the securities index) a slight decline from 1812 to 1813. There is no reason to believe that the recovery movement begun in 1811 was interrupted in 1813 in a manner sufficient to justify the marking off of an additional cycle.

1839. The rise in bankruptcies and the collapse of the Anglo-American speculation in raw cotton (resulting in an abnormal decline in British imports and in the Kondratieff textile production index) misrepresent the net cyclical movement from 1838 to 1839. As explained earlier, we regard 1839 as the proper peak.

We place no great store by this index. It may, however, serve as a useful summary when used in conjunction with the other evidence available. It fits moderately well our reference dates; and, further, it conforms, in general, to our judgements on the relative intensity of the cyclical movements.[1]

A second and statistically less formal index of general business activity has been constructed. This is designed to fit more accurately our full judgement—statistical and qualitative—on the cyclical pattern. Each year is rated from 0 (deep depression) to 5 (major cycle peak).[2] The peaks and troughs conform, of course, to the annual reference dates, and the figures are designed to reflect the relative cyclical position of each year (see Fig. 92, p. 355):

TABLE 6. *Business-cycle Pattern*

Year	Value	Year	Value	Year	Value
1790	3	1810	5	1830	1½
1	4	1	0	1	2
2	5	2	1	2	0
3	0	3	1½	3	1
4	1	4	2½	4	2
1795	2½	1815	3	1835	3
6	3	6	0	6	5
7	0	7	3	7	0
8	1	8	5	8	1
9	3	9	0	9	3
1800	4	1820	1	1840	2
1	3	1	1½	1	1
2	5	2	2	2	0
3	1	3	3	3	1
4	1½	4	4	4	3
1805	2½	1825	5	1845	5
6	3	6	0	6	4
7	2	7	1½	7	2
8	1	8	2	8	0
9	4	9	0	9	1
				1850	2

[1] In the first three chapters of Part I of Vol. II, a distinction is drawn between major and minor business cycles, largely on the criterion of the relative importance exhibited by domestic investment. Employing evidence other than the index of business activity we arrived at the following division among the cycles:

Major cycles	Minor cycles
1797–1803	1793–7
1808–11	1803–8
1816–19	1811–16
1819–26	1826–9
1832–7	1829–32
1842–8	1837–42

One of the characteristics of major cycles that has been defined is the relatively greater amplitude of aggregate variables in their course, e.g. in total production, credit facilities, bankruptcies, &c. This emerges clearly in the index. It also reveals fairly accurately what we conceive the cyclical pattern to have been in the somewhat obscure interval from 1800 to 1803.

[2] A precedent for this procedure is to be found in G. Haberler's *Prosperity and Depression*, where similar indexes are constructed (for more modern periods) on the basis of Thorp's *Annals*. Haberler's indexes differ from the one presented here only in that he expresses the position of each year as a plus or minus deviation from a central line. Our system of designation has been preferred because it avoids any possible implication that the zero line represents an equilibrium situation.

APPENDIX C

A NOTE ON THORP'S *ANNALS*

In 1926 Willard Thorp published, under the aegis of the National Bureau of Economic Research, a set of business annals covering, over varying periods, the economic fortunes of seventeen nations.[1] For Great Britain his account begins in 1790, thus embracing the whole of our period. Each year is characterized as one of 'depression', 'revival', 'prosperity', 'recession', &c. Supplementary information is given with respect to foreign trade, industrial activity, price movements, harvest yields, the state of the money market, and important political events of economic significance.

The following are the more flagrant differences in judgement between Thorp's view and our own:

1794. This year is characterized by Thorp as one of 'depression', with 'industry at a standstill'. We have dated recovery from June 1794, and, in net, considered 1794 a year of revival as compared to the position in 1793.

1798–1800. Thorp fails to represent a cyclical expansion from 1797 to 1800. Each of the years 1798, 1799, and 1800 is characterized by him as an interval of 'depression'. Since the export markets were in a state of rapid expansion in these years, and all statistical indicators of production exhibit increase, it is difficult to understand why Thorp put forward this view. It stems, perhaps, from the fact that the period was marked by serious unrest, due largely to high living costs, but not, so far as one can establish, to unemployment.

1817. Thorp dates revival from the spring of 1817. We have marked off the beginnings of recovery from September 1816.

1831. Thorp characterizes 1830 as 'depression; revival', 1831 as 'recession; depression'. This would imply that the peak in this slight cyclical movement occurred in 1830, probably late in the year. We have dated the peak in March 1831.

1838–9. Thorp fails to represent the clearly marked revival in 1838 and part of 1839 (peak, March 1839). Both years are described unequivocally as intervals of 'depression', whereas statistical and qualitative evidence attest to a considerable recovery from the latter months of 1837 through the first quarter of 1839.

1843. Thorp dates a trough as late as March 1843. At the latest, we would place the trough in November 1842.

1845–7. Thorp marks off no turning-point until the financial panic of April 1847. 1845 and 1846 are described as years of 'prosperity'; 1847, as of 'prosperity; panic; recession'. We have placed the major upper turning-point in September 1845, and, thereafter, can find evidence of an upward movement only from September 1846 to April 1847. On the basis of annual data even this brief revival cannot be discerned: 1846 and 1847 have, on the whole, been regarded by us as years of increasing depression.

[1] Willard Thorp, *Business Annals*. The annals for England from 1790 to 1850 are to   be found on pp. 150–62.

PART II
BRITISH SHARE PRICES AND JOINT-STOCK ENTERPRISE
Chapter I
CONSTRUCTION OF THE INDEX NUMBERS

1. Introduction. The purpose of Chapters I and II of this portion of the text is to present monthly index numbers of British share prices from 1811 to 1850, and to analyse their movements. Chapter III contains a series of brief summary sections describing the institutional setting in which the share market and joint-stock companies operated, as well as the origin, nature, and fortunes of the various types of enterprises represented on the Exchange. Throughout Chapter II an attempt is made to relate the sequence of events affecting the share market and its constituents to the movements of the index numbers.

The indexes begin with the year 1811. In that year prices for shares other than government and quasi-public issues first appeared in the official list of quotations. The London Stock Exchange at that time was a market-place for transactions chiefly in the Funds (i.e., Consols and other government bonds), and in Bank of England Stock, South Sea Stock, &c.— the private issues of government-established monopolies. In 1811 prices of American securities and of canal, dock, insurance, and waterworks shares were quoted for the first time. At later dates prices of shares of bridges, mines, gas-light and coke companies, banks, railways, and miscellaneous companies, were added to the list of quotations. It is evident from the types of undertakings named that the securities dealt in during the early nineteenth century were, unlike those of today, mainly 'non-industrial' in character. They were rather what are today regarded as public utilities.

The advantages of incorporation for enterprises requiring large capital investment were clearly recognized before the turn of the nineteenth century, as is indicated by successive parliamentary acts authorizing the raising of funds to finance canal companies. Popular prejudice, however, effectively retarded the general spread of the joint-stock principle in English industry until the middle of the nineteenth century.[1] This prejudice stemmed from the disappointments of the South Sea Bubble of 1720, and found official expression in the law, passed in the same year, prohibiting public subscriptions without specific parliamentary sanction. Even the

---

[1] Elie Halévy, *A History of the English People in 1815*, p. 272: 'Joint stock companies were unknown in the branches of manufacture really representative of the industrial revolution such as the manufacture of cloth, metal-working and mining.' Also see below, pp. 410–17.

removal of the legal obstructions to incorporation, however, did not accelerate markedly the growth of corporate business organization in Great Britain, for a number of reasons : the relative smallness in size of the average English firm ; the considerable wealth of private owners of many firms ; and the underwriting procedure, which was geared to the special necessities of large governmental issues. To this day the role played by British industrial shares on the London Stock Exchange is relatively limited.[1]

Thus the indexes cannot reasonably be expected to reflect the conditions of all British industry in a strict sense. At best they summarize the changing fortunes of those selected companies that were quoted on the Stock Exchange. The security market would have had to be representative of a larger and more diversified area of the British economy, inclusive of textiles and other manufactures, to reflect the profitability of industry as a whole.

2. Sources of Data and Adjustments made. The original prices were obtained from the current official price list, called *Course of the Exchange*. This was published in London on Tuesdays and Fridays until 1843 (when it became daily) by the stockbroker, James Wetenhall, under the authority of the Stock Exchange Committee. One quotation each month, as near as possible to the 15th, was copied for those groups which exhibited little intra-monthly variation. The prices of mines and railways were obtained as often as they appeared. Additional sources, publishing share quotations, that were consulted include the *Gentleman's Magazine* in the early period, and, for the later years, the *Railway Magazine* and the *Quarterly Mining Review*.

Certain adjustments in the data were necessary. Occasional blanks in a series were interpolated by taking into account the direction of this series' prices, the movements of other securities in the sub-group, and whatever other relevant information was available. In the case of a number of securities, chiefly those of mines, gas-light and coke companies, and railways, adjustments had to be made because of frequent changes in the amount of the paid-up capital per share. It was a common practice for certain companies when issuing shares to require that only a part of their face value be paid for at the time of purchase, the remainder being subject to future call. For the period prior to a call, the amount that was subsequently called was added to the quoted prices in order to correct for changes in capitalization. The reason it seems proper (at least as an approximation) to add to the earlier quoted prices the number of pounds that later came into the company through a call that was answered is that the answering of the call might be assumed to have increased the value of the stock by that amount.[2] In cases

[1] See *Report of the Committee on Finance and Industry*, H. P. Macmillan, Chairman, 1931, pp. 161–2, 166–74.

[2] The exact wording of a typical mine company prospectus with respect to calls may be of interest. The prospectus of the

United Mexican Mining Company, which had a nominal capital of £240,000 divided into 6,000 shares of £40 each, read as follows: 'The first instalment of £5 per share to be paid forthwith, into the hands of the Bankers of the Association, to the

where there were successive calls, an attempt was made to avoid following this procedure, that is, adding to the previous market price of the share a figure equal to the total of the later measurements. Instead, when the amount to be added was a large percentage of the current price, the share was treated exactly as if it were that of a new company, its paid-up value at that time representing the total paid-up value.[1]

No adjustment was made to offset the effect of the payment of dividends on the prices of shares. Between two dividend dates, if the stock partakes somewhat of the nature of a bond, in that the investor has confidence that a dividend payment of a known amount will be made, then the slowly accruing dividend tends to cause a rise in the share value to the amount of the dividend. Following the dividend payment, the value is likely to fall abruptly to the same extent. Since the amplitude of this fluctuation was quite small in all cases, an adjustment did not seem to be necessary.

3. Sampling Procedure. Before constructing an index number it is important that the investigator set before himself a purpose that can be translated into concrete statistical terms. In a sense, almost any index number will reflect 'general movements on the Stock Exchange' because the expression itself is so vague. Whatever meaning attaches to an index number obviously stems not from the total data available that might have been used, but from the data which actually were used, as determined by the sampling procedure, and from the methods of averaging and weighting chosen. It is therefore of prime importance that the sampling procedure, and the methods of averaging and weighting, be chosen in the light of the purpose that the index is designed to serve.

Definite answers to a variety of definite questions may be sought from index numbers, each question requiring a different index. For example, it may be desired to secure a measure of changes in the total cost of a fixed portfolio of securities, or, more inclusively, of variations in the value of all securities held by the public; or the objective may be to arrive at a sensitive index for forecasting other economic series; or to discover changes in the prices of shares that are traded in.

A 'general purpose' index frequently used is a simple arithmetic average of relatives on a fixed base; yet, in fact, this index too has its own special implications. It would reflect the changing fortunes of an investor who, in the base year, spent the same number of pounds on each of the stocks which is included in the indexes, purchasing as many shares of each stock as could be bought for that fixed sum of money.

Our index is designed to represent the total price movement (i.e. net changes in value) of shares quoted on the London Stock Exchange from 1811 to 1850. It should therefore include, theoretically, every security for

account of the Directors. The second instalment of £5 per share, to be paid on signing the Deed of Settlement, and the remaining sum of £30 per share, to be advanced from time to time, as may be required by the Court of Directors, the calls to be made at not less than 21 days notice.'

[1] These corrections are made clear in the tables of the adjusted and unadjusted data, to be separately microfilmed.

which prices are given, and the actual prices should ideally be weighted by the number of shares outstanding in each case. It was, however, necessary to limit our component series to a sample group. Table 7 represents a list of the eight sub-groups included in the index and the individual companies they comprise, together with a statement of the period during which each

TABLE 7. *List of Companies included in the Total Share Index*

Canals

1. Ellesmere, Feb. 1811–Dec. 1850
2. Grand Junction, Feb. 1811–Dec. 1850
3. Leeds and Liverpool, Feb. 1811–Dec. 1850
4. Coventry, Feb. 1811–Dec. 1845
5. Monmouthshire, Feb. 1811–Dec. 1845
6. Trent and Mersey, Feb. 1811–Dec. 1845
7. Worcester and Birmingham, Jan. 1815–Dec. 1850

Docks

1. East India, Feb. 1811–July 1838
2. West India, Feb. 1811–July 1838
3. East and West India, Aug. 1838–Dec. 1850
4. London, Feb. 1811–Dec. 1850
5. Saint Katharine, Nov. 1828–Dec. 1850

Waterworks

1. East London, Feb. 1811–Dec. 1850
2. Grand Junction, Feb. 1811–Dec. 1850
3. West Middlesex, Feb. 1811–Dec. 1850
4. Kent, Feb. 1811–Dec. 1850
5. Manchester and Salford, Jan. 1815–Dec. 1842

Insurance companies

1. Globe, Feb. 1811–Dec. 1850
2. Imperial Fire, Feb. 1811–Dec. 1850
3. Eagle, Feb. 1811–Dec. 1850
4. Rock Life, Feb. 1811–Dec. 1850
5. Royal Exchange, Feb. 1811–Dec. 1850
6. Albion, Feb. 1811–Dec. 1850
7. Imperial Life, Jan. 1821–Dec. 1850
8. Atlas, Jan. 1821–Dec. 1850

Gas-light and coke companies

1. Bristol, Jan. 1819–Dec. 1846
2. City, Jan. 1819–Dec. 1839
3. Westminster Chartered, Jan. 1819–Dec. 1850
4. Phoenix, Jan. 1825–Dec. 1850
5. United General, Jan. 1825–Dec. 1850
6. British, Apr. 1830–Dec. 1850
7. British Provincial, Jan. 1831–Dec. 1850

Mines

1. Brazilian Imperial, Jan. 1825–Dec. 1850
2. Bolanos, Jan. 1825–Dec. 1844

Mines (cont.)

3. Real del Monte, Nov. 1824–Sept. 1840
4. United Mexican, Oct. 1824–Dec. 1840
5. Anglo-Mexican, Oct. 1824–Dec. 1838
6. Colombian, Jan. 1825–Dec. 1835
7. Mexican Mining, Oct. 1827–Nov. 1836
8. General Mining, Jan. 1825–Dec. 1850
9. British Iron, Jan. 1826–Dec. 1839
10. Hibernian, Nov. 1824–Dec. 1834
11. Alten, Oct. 1833–Dec. 1838

Railways

1. Liverpool and Manchester, May 1827–Mar. 1836
2. Stockton and Darlington, Jan. 1828–Dec. 1834
3. Cheltenham, May 1827–Mar. 1836
4. Forest of Dean, May 1827–Feb. 1832
5. London and Birmingham, June 1833–Aug. 1846
6. Great Western, Sept. 1835–Dec. 1850
7. London and Greenwich, Jan. 1835–Dec. 1850
8. Bristol and Exeter, Mar. 1836–Dec. 1850
9. Manchester and Leeds, Nov. 1836–July 1847
10. North Eastern, Jan. 1838–July 1847
11. London and Southwestern, Nov. 1839–Dec. 1850
12. Midland Counties, Jan. 1841–Dec. 1850
13. Edinburgh and Glasgow, Jan. 1842–Dec. 1850
14. Great North of England, Jan. 1841–Dec. 1850

Banks

1. Provincial Bank of Ireland, Jan. 1831–Dec. 1850
2. Royal of Scotland, Jan. 1831–Dec. 1845
3. National Provincial of England, June, 1833–Dec. 1850
4. National of Ireland, July 1835–Dec. 1850
5. London and Westminster, Mar. 1835–Dec. 1850
6. London Joint Stock Bank, Jan. 1837–Dec. 1850

is included in the index. This sample was chosen following a close study of the entire list at three-year intervals. In addition to the price quotations, the record gave details about the number of shares outstanding, the par value, and the amount paid up.

An ideal sample for the index would have been based on due representation for all significant categories into which the universe could have been subdivided. Principles for such classification would have been the geographic distribution, type of enterprise, size, financial position, and stability of the companies. It was not always possible, however, to represent adequately all these categories. Difficulties arose under practically every one of these heads, making it necessary for us at times somewhat to relax our principles of selection. It soon became apparent, for example, that it would not be feasible to obtain an adequate representation with respect to size; because, for the most part, the smaller companies in each type of enterprise passed out of existence as separate entities in a comparatively short time. Moreover, transactions in securities of small companies were relatively infrequent, and their quotations consequently too sporadic. Thus while there were approximately one hundred companies officially listed in 1811, at the start of the index, and slightly more than two hundred in 1850, when the index ends, the shares of only one-third of the companies listed in any one group had a continuous existence from the date of their first appearance in the list. Shares of companies with small capitalization were those most frequently found among the inactive group, and the mortality rate of these companies was highest. It can thus be seen that of the total number of companies available, under the circumstances, for inclusion in a continuous index, a very large proportion has, in fact, been represented.

It might, of course, have been possible to include more small companies by constructing separate indexes for very short intervals and then chaining the separate periods. But this method would have resulted in a cumulative error. Each link involves the tacit assumption that the new item to be included would have affected the index prior to its inclusion in the same manner and degree as its influence during the arbitrary period chosen for computing the adjustment coefficient. The greater the number of adjustments of this kind, the less the homogeneity of the index, and the more dubious become comparisons over widely separated dates; as Professor Mitchell has said, 'no refinement of methods can mend the fundamental defect of the data'.[1] Thus, in order to avoid the necessity for making frequent interpolations for non-existent prices, or numerous adjustments for changes in the composition of the index, the representation of small companies was of necessity reduced.

Yet the reader should be aware that by restricting the sample to companies for which continuous quotations are available over a period of years the index is over-weighted in favour of the more successful companies, and the representativeness of the sample with respect to companies with poor financial records is thereby weakened. It is not unlikely that an element of some upward bias is introduced because of this factor.[2] With respect to the

[1] W. C. Mitchell, 'A Critique of Index Numbers of the Prices of Stocks', *Journal of Political Economy*, xxiv (1916), 693.

[2] See Alfred Cowles, 3rd, and Associates, *Common Stock Indexes, 1871–1937*, p. 34:

'With regard to various methods of sampling, the most common defects are due to employing hindsight in the selection of the sample. In extending a stock index back through early years, authors are apt to include only

geographical criterion, an attempt was made to include companies from all sections of Great Britain, in proportion to their capitalization. Further, no company was excluded or dropped because it had not yet achieved financial stability, or because it was on the decline following a period of maturity. Nor were erratic fluctuations or inflexible prices *per se* regarded as ground for exclusion.

All types of enterprises quoted were included except bridges and those falling in the miscellaneous group. For a few bridges the quotations given were not for common stock but for annuities, and were omitted for that reason; and for the remainder the shares were uniformly quoted at such a considerable discount as to suggest some special circumstance without knowledge of which their inclusion would have been justified. The omission of this sub-group, however, while regrettable from the angle of complete coverage of the share market, cannot be considered very serious.

The group of companies listed as 'Miscellaneous' in *Course of the Exchange*—including a wide variety of enterprises, such as Golden Lane Brewery, Covent Garden, General Steam Navigation, Literary Institutions, and so on—also had to be omitted from the index because none of the companies was listed for long; and it was not possible to obtain regular quotations even for the short periods that the companies were in existence.

It will be noted that not all of the companies in the sample are British. Most of the mines included, though financed by British capital, were located in Mexico and South America. If the index had been designed to reflect conditions of British industry, it is obvious these foreign mines would have no place in it. Since, however, the purpose was to ascertain the total price movement of shares traded on the London Stock Exchange, the behaviour of foreign mine shares, which were widely held, especially during periods of speculative excess, was of great significance; and, accordingly, such shares were, we feel, rightly included in the sample.

4. Techniques employed. Our objective in measuring net changes in the total value of shares was best achieved by assigning to each company an importance in proportion to its total market valuation. The sub-indexes were therefore computed from averages of actual prices weighted by the number of shares outstanding. The final share price index is a weighted arithmetic average of the sub-index numbers. It was clearly desirable, in combining the sub-groups to form the total index, to weight them. The inclusion of a larger or smaller number of items in a sub-group was purely fortuitous. It was not determined by the importance of that type of undertaking in the segment of the British economy represented on the Exchange, so that weights based on the numbers in each group obviously had to be ruled out. Fortunately there were data at hand that could be employed to

"stocks that are outstanding today", or "stocks on which substantially complete quotations exist". Such a procedure is likely to impart an upward bias . . . since an investor in one of the early years repre- sented by the index would have no way of knowing which stocks would subsequently be the most important or which would later afford a complete record of quotations.'

give greater effect to movements of the more important sub-groups than
to those of the less important ones. The index purports to measure the
total changes in the market-value of an investment in a representative
group of shares over a period of time. For this reason the weights used were
based on the ratios of the paid-up capital invested in each of the groups to
the total paid-up capitalization of all the groups. Since these ratios changed
during the course of the period, it was desirable to use more than one set
of weights. Table 8 presents a list of the weights assigned to each of the
sub-groups.

TABLE 8. *Weights used in computing the Total Share Index*[a]

Group	Feb. 1811– Dec. 1818	Jan. 1819– Sept. 1824	Oct. 1824– Apr. 1827	May 1827– Dec. 1830	Jan. 1831– Dec. 1833	Jan. 1834– Dec. 1850
Canals	45	43	37	29	28	16
Docks	20	19	17	13	12	9
Insurance companies	25	23	21	16	16	9
Waterworks	10	10	8	6	6	2
Gas-light and coke companies	..	5	4	3	3	2
Mines	..	..	13	10	9	9
Railways	..	..	..	23	23	44
Banks	..	..	..	..	3	9
Total	100	100	100	100	100	100

[a] The weights represent the percentages of the total paid-up capital invested in each of
the several groups. The weights were determined on the basis of information given in the
following sources: (a) Henry English, *A Complete View of the Joint Stock Companies Formed
During the Years 1824 and 1825*, pp. 29 ff., which lists the numbers of companies, by groups,
existing before 1824, the number of shares outstanding and the capitalization, the companies
floated in 1824–5 and those of this number existing in 1827, with their authorized and paid-up
capital; (b) Parliamentary Report of 1844, on Joint Stock Companies, vii, Appendix 4, which
summarizes capitalization during the period 1834–6; (c) W. F. Spackman, *Statistical Tables
of the United Kingdom*, p. 157, which contains a 'Summary (for 1843) of the Investment of
British Capital in Foreign Loans and Public Companies, so far as the same is known on the
London Market'; (d) *Course of the Exchange*—the lists used in choosing our sample—at three-
year intervals; (e) P.P. 1854–5 (1965), xlviii, Report to the Lords of the Proceedings of the
Department relating to Railways for the Year 1854, dated 13 July 1855, p. xvii, which lists
the paid-up capital of railways annually during the preceding decade.

The aggregates of the sub-indexes were expressed as relatives of the
June 1840 aggregate. The year 1840 was neither a period of depression nor
of boom and may perhaps be designated as 'normal'. But the choice of a
base is always an arbitrary matter, and no special significance attaches to
this selection. The base of the sub-indexes, and consequently of the final
index, too, may be shifted at will to any month or period desired.

In view of the above discussion of the technique employed, it is clear
that no correction was needed for stock splits, since these had no effect on
the market valuation represented by the product of price and number of
shares.

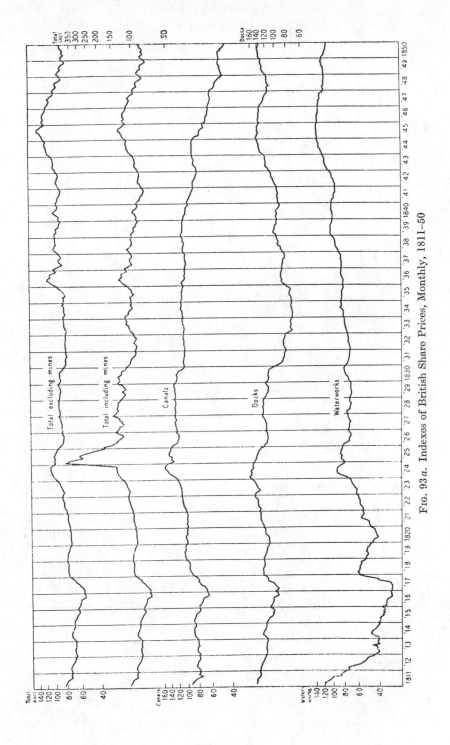

Fig. 93a. Indexes of British Share Prices, Monthly, 1811–50

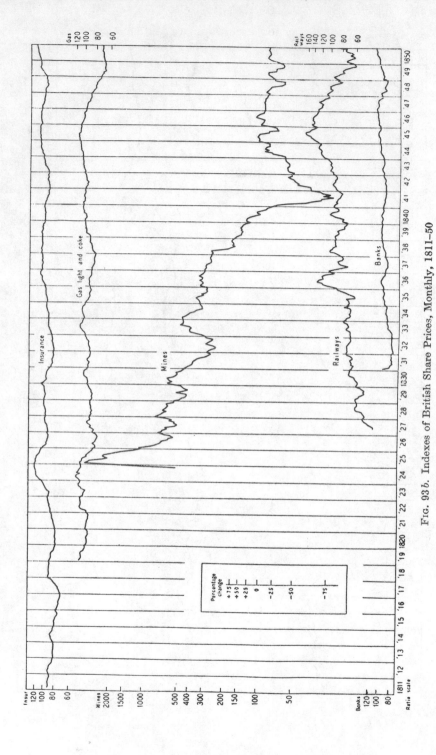

Fig. 93 b. Indexes of British Share Prices, Monthly, 1811–50

When a new security or a new sub-group was introduced in any given year, a simple chaining procedure was used to maintain the continuity of the index. The index was computed for a period of months up to a year following its introduction, first excluding and then including the new security or sub-group, and the ratio between the averages of the two resultant indexes was computed. The index numbers in all the months prior to the introduction of the additional item were changed in accordance with this ratio. A similar adjustment was made when a security was dropped from the index. When there was a change in the number of shares, not arising from a stock split, the index was computed for an overlapping period, first with the old weights and then with the new, and an adjustment was made on the basis of the two averages. The net effect of this adjustment was to raise or lower the level of the index for those years without affecting relative movements from month to month. The method is not to be regarded as a 'correction', but merely as a device for smoothing out discontinuities arising from a break in the homogeneity of the components.

5. The Total Indexes. An examination of the curves of sub-indexes (Fig. 93) reveals a striking degree of consilience among them with the important exception of mine shares. Mine shares are so far out of line with those of other companies' shares that it was advisable to present the total index in two forms—one including mine shares, the other excluding them (see Tables 9 and 10). The latter index is, in one sense, more 'typical' than the former. Mine shares were, at certain periods, subject to such wide fluctuations that their movements dominate changes in the total index. On one occasion at least mine shares moved inversely to all the other sub-indexes (see Tables 11–18). The peak in share prices, exclusive of mines, in the early twenties occurs in the last quarter of 1824, ending an expansion of some years' duration; there is no boom observable in that index during 1825. Yet a peak late in 1824 inaccurately represents the true course of share prices in general;[1] contemporary sources are unanimous in describing the early months of 1825 as an interval of unprecedented boom prices on the stock market, with heaviest concentration of activity in mines. Thus, despite the fact that the other enterprises did not share the 1825 peak, a truer picture of contemporary market conditions is given by the index including mines. The point is discussed further in the following chapter.

[1] See Tooke, *History of Prices*, ii. 159; *A. R.*, 1825, 'General History', p. 2.

TABLE 9. *Total Index of Share Prices, inclusive of Mines*

(June 1840 = 100)

Year	Jan.	Feb.	Mar.	Apr.	May	June	July	Aug.	Sept.	Oct.	Nov.	Dec.
1811	..	111·3	110·8	108·9	107·0	105·9	102·4	96·5	97·7	98·5	98·3	96·5
2	96·9	97·9	99·4	98·6	97·0	95·9	94·3	92·4	91·0	90·2	89·4	89·3
3	87·9	88·5	90·3	89·9	90·3	90·3	88·9	88·7	88·9	89·3	88·8	89·1
4	90·8	93·2	95·7	96·0	96·2	95·9	94·8	93·8	92·8	91·8	91·5	91·2
1815	91·4	91·5	91·1	90·0	87·7	87·3	86·0	84·7	82·7	82·0	83·7	85·5
6	84·5	83·7	81·3	80·9	79·8	79·8	79·4	75·4	72·5	72·8	73·6	75·1
7	74·3	74·3	76·4	77·3	80·6	81·7	84·3	88·6	88·0	90·0	94·1	99·6
8	100·2	100·8	101·5	102·3	102·7	102·7	101·8	101·9	101·3	102·3	102·9	105·1
9	104·5	104·8	103·4	103·3	103·6	103·4	101·3	100·6	100·3	99·4	97·8	96·4
1820	95·5	95·8	95·9	96·7	96·7	97·6	97·0	97·6	97·6	97·1	97·6	99·5
1	97·9	98·9	100·2	100·1	100·7	102·3	101·9	102·3	102·3	101·8	103·0	104·0
2	104·5	104·4	106·6	108·5	109·4	109·4	109·7	110·3	111·0	112·2	113·2	113·8
3	112·9	112·4	110·1	109·7	112·7	114·3	115·3	117·0	118·1	119·2	122·1	124·3
4	128·2	132·2	134·7	137·3	138·9	141·5	141·4	142·8	143·8	143·2	186·1	237·0
1825	404·8	381·0	371·2	307·5	284·7	308·1	302·5	282·5	253·5	234·4	206·2	183·1
6	186·3	161·2	150·9	143·1	140·0	138·8	130·4	129·1	124·3	127·3	136·8	146·3
7	139·9	138·7	133·5	136·6	124·7	123·4	128·1	127·1	133·5	131·5	137·6	153·1
8	148·0	142·9	140·6	136·9	141·9	140·1	138·7	137·1	138·3	139·3	131·1	130·9
9	125·7	123·4	120·3	117·9	119·0	126·5	120·1	116·9	120·1	122·7	125·0	135·2
1830	136·5	130·9	133·2	134·4	137·3	131·1	127·1	127·2	127·6	120·6	116·8	115·2
1	111·2	108·3	105·5	106·0	105·2	104·2	102·3	98·9	96·2	95·5	95·2	97·1
2	95·9	94·7	93·5	93·6	95·5	99·0	97·3	95·6	94·4	94·5	98·1	99·2
3	99·4	103·5	106·3	107·2	108·4	108·6	110·0	116·6	114·8	114·7	115·7	115·6
4	116·9	117·0	111·5	109·2	110·2	106·3	105·0	101·3	101·7	105·7	103·3	104·8
1835	104·0	104·1	105·1	107·6	101·8	98·9	101·8	101·9	102·1	106·2	108·8	110·0
6	117·9	123·5	125·2	125·9	133·7	129·9	124·5	128·1	126·7	122·0	112·9	115·7
7	117·1	110·6	106·1	101·4	103·6	105·0	105·5	105·4	102·4	101·8	102·0	105·9
8	106·7	109·8	113·9	107·2	105·0	102·7	101·1	101·7	102·1	103·1	103·5	102·1
9	102·5	102·5	100·5	97·9	97·4	99·4	97·7	93·9	93·5	92·7	90·7	89·1
1840	93·2	93·6	91·9	94·2	96·8	100·0	99·6	96·6	92·3	90·7	90·2	91·9
1	92·5	89·8	86·3	86·4	85·0	84·1	81·5	81·4	80·6	79·8	80·7	83·0
2	84·5	85·5	86·1	88·6	89·4	88·9	87·7	87·9	86·8	87·0	87·1	88·9
3	90·5	91·2	94·7	94·9	95·0	93·9	94·7	95·7	95·1	96·2	98·2	99·8
4	103·5	106·2	109·0	109·4	112·1	111·0	112·2	114·7	114·1	113·4	111·9	116·3
1845	118·9	121·5	121·4	125·2	125·0	132·1	131·4	130·5	122·8	121·4	115·7	113·9
6	120·5	121·6	117·9	117·7	120·3	119·4	120·6	119·3	116·3	113·9	113·4	111·9
7	112·2	109·6	106·7	106·2	104·6	106·8	108·6	104·5	102·6	96·9	96·9	96·4
8	97·8	96·7	93·5	89·8	93·0	91·9	91·3	87·3	83·1	80·3	84·6	83·4
9	88·1	90·4	87·7	87·0	83·2	83·6	84·0	82·7	78·9	75·3	76·1	77·3
1850	82·4	83·5	81·9	78·9	80·1	82·2	79·7	80·8	84·2	85·0	84·1	88·4

TABLE 10. *Total Index of Share Prices, exclusive of Mines*

(June 1840 = 100)

Year	Jan.	Feb.	Mar.	Apr.	May	June	July	Aug.	Sept.	Oct.	Nov.	Dec.
1811	..	84·1	83·7	82·3	80·9	80·0	77·4	72·9	73·9	74·4	74·3	72·9
2	73·2	74·0	75·1	74·5	73·3	72·5	71·3	69·8	68·8	68·2	67·5	67·5
3	66·4	66·9	68·2	68·0	68·2	68·3	67·1	67·0	67·2	67·5	67·1	67·3
4	68·6	70·4	72·3	72·6	72·7	72·5	71·6	70·8	70·1	69·4	69·1	68·9
1815	69·0	69·2	68·8	68·0	66·3	65·9	65·0	64·0	62·5	61·9	63·2	64·6
6	63·8	63·2	61·4	61·2	60·3	60·3	60·0	57·0	54·8	55·1	55·7	56·8
7	56·2	56·2	57·7	58·4	60·9	61·7	63·7	66·9	66·5	68·0	71·1	75·2
8	75·7	76·2	76·7	77·3	77·6	77·6	77·0	77·0	76·6	77·3	77·7	79·4
9	79·0	79·2	78·2	78·1	78·3	78·1	76·6	76·0	75·8	75·1	73·9	72·9
1820	72·2	72·4	72·4	73·1	73·0	73·8	73·3	73·7	73·7	73·4	73·7	75·2
1	74·0	74·7	75·7	75·7	76·1	77·3	77·0	77·3	77·3	76·9	77·8	78·6
2	79·0	78·9	80·5	82·0	82·7	82·7	82·9	83·3	83·9	84·8	85·5	86·0
3	85·3	84·9	83·2	82·9	85·1	86·4	87·1	88·4	89·2	90·1	92·3	94·0
4	96·9	99·9	101·8	103·8	105·0	107·0	106·9	107·9	108·7	108·2	106·6	104·0
1825	98·8	98·6	100·6	99·7	98·8	101·5	100·7	99·5	98·0	96·1	95·7	93·8
6	92·0	88·2	85·1	84·2	83·7	83·0	82·6	82·2	82·2	82·6	85·0	85·9
7	84·5	84·3	84·9	86·0	84·4	85·3	86·8	86·4	87·2	88·5	89·6	90·0
8	88·7	88·2	88·3	88·5	89·2	90·8	90·3	90·5	90·7	90·3	90·6	90·7
9	89·7	89·6	89·4	88·2	88·3	87·5	87·2	87·5	87·9	89·1	90·4	91·4
1830	89·0	87·9	87·0	87·3	88·8	89·3	88·3	89·2	88·5	85·6	83·3	82·3
1	80·3	79·5	78·1	79·0	78·3	79·0	78·1	77·0	77·0	77·5	78·2	78·2
2	78·0	78·0	78·5	78·9	79·3	79·6	79·1	78·8	78·4	78·5	78·8	78·8
3	78·2	77·8	77·6	78·3	79·7	80·9	80·8	80·4	80·8	80·9	82·1	81·2
4	82·4	82·0	79·8	79·6	81·1	80·7	80·8	80·6	80·5	84·8	81·0	82·5
1835	81·8	81·3	81·5	82·9	78·3	78·6	80·2	82·8	84·2	88·1	91·3	91·6
6	97·1	103·5	107·0	107·8	113·6	111·4	105·7	107·1	107·0	103·1	94·1	97·6
7	98·8	92·8	87·5	82·5	85·5	89·1	89·7	89·7	86·0	85·3	86·1	90·1
8	92·0	94·5	99·1	98·8	97·3	96·6	93·9	95·0	95·3	95·7	96·4	95·5
9	96·5	97·3	96·0	93·2	93·2	94·7	93·0	88·4	88·6	87·9	86·3	85·9
1840	89·3	89·8	88·1	91·2	95·3	100·0	98·9	95·5	92·0	90·9	90·6	93·0
1	94·6	93·0	90·8	91·4	90·4	89·5	87·2	86·6	86·2	84·9	85·7	87·6
2	89·3	90·3	91·0	92·6	03·7	92·8	91·4	91·4	89·9	89·8	90·4	92·4
3	94·4	94·5	98·2	98·5	98·6	97·6	98·4	99·5	98·6	99·7	101·9	103·5
4	107·6	110·1	111·8	112·2	113·9	113·6	114·1	117·1	117·1	116·1	114·6	118·4
1845	120·2	123·2	123·1	126·8	126·9	134·9	135·9	134·9	128·0	126·1	119·9	117·3
6	122·4	123·9	120·1	119·9	122·8	121·1	121·5	120·4	117·5	115·7	115·1	113·7
7	114·0	111·1	108·0	107·4	105·6	107·9	110·1	105·7	103·6	97·7	97·7	97·4
8	99·1	97·1	94·0	90·3	94·0	93·0	93·6	89·8	85·0	82·1	85·4	84·1
9	88·7	91·1	87·7	87·0	82·8	84·5	85·0	83·6	80·3	76·5	77·1	78·1
1850	83·3	83·5	81·6	77·9	79·5	81·9	79·3	80·5	84·1	84·9	84·0	88·6

TABLE 11. *Sub-index of Prices of Canal Shares*

(June 1840 = 100)

Year	Jan.	Feb.	Mar.	Apr.	May	June	July	Aug.	Sept.	Oct.	Nov.	Dec.
1811	..	93·3	92·9	90·9	87·4	85·7	81·7	74·0	77·4	80·8	78·6	77·8
2	78·1	79·6	83·8	85·2	83·3	82·5	82·0	80·3	79·1	78·5	78·9	79·7
3	78·3	80·0	83·4	82·8	82·6	82·6	79·3	80·2	80·8	81·4	81·4	81·9
4	83·2	84·7	87·0	87·4	88·1	87·8	88·1	87·4	87·2	85·4	85·5	85·6
1815	86·9	88·1	87·9	86·9	85·9	85·5	84·6	81·7	79·0	77·4	78·7	79·2
6	79·2	79·2	75·4	75·4	73·7	73·7	73·7	67·4	64·3	64·2	65·5	66·9
7	67·6	67·9	70·0	70·2	76·9	77·0	78·1	80·2	79·2	80·7	83·1	88·5
8	89·9	91·0	92·7	94·4	95·5	96·3	95·6	96·0	95·4	97·4	99·0	103·1
9	102·7	104·2	104·5	104·2	105·5	105·9	102·3	102·5	102·8	102·9	102·5	100·8
1820	99·4	99·7	100·1	103·0	101·8	102·2	99·1	100·5	100·2	99·5	99·8	100·2
1	97·9	99·0	100·1	99·6	99·3	99·8	99·9	99·7	99·8	99·6	100·4	101·0
2	102·2	102·6	104·4	107·3	107·7	107·8	107·9	109·2	109·5	109·7	110·1	110·8
3	111·4	111·1	110·6	110·8	112·0	113·2	113·7	114·4	115·4	116·4	119·5	120·2
4	122·9	127·5	133·9	137·2	143·2	145·9	147·4	153·0	154·7	154·1	150·2	143·6
1825	129·4	129·8	136·3	133·8	134·5	143·1	142·8	142·3	139·6	136·9	137·5	136·4
6	133·8	126·2	122·0	118·4	118·3	117·3	116·6	116·5	116·4	117·6	122·3	122·3
7	120·8	121·0	121·9	124·0	123·0	125·3	125·6	121·9	123·4	124·3	125·3	126·5
8	124·5	123·8	124·0	124·4	125·2	125·5	123·2	123·5	123·4	123·6	124·7	125·2
9	123·8	124·1	123·9	124·0	125·5	125·8	125·0	125·0	126·6	127·9	127·4	123·9
1830	121·4	121·0	120·2	119·5	120·4	121·5	118·8	117·3	114·7	106·7	104·3	103·9
1	103·6	104·3	104·7	105·1	103·8	104·6	102·9	102·8	102·8	102·9	102·0	102·1
2	101·8	101·7	102·3	103·2	103·5	103·7	103·6	104·3	104·2	104·7	104·6	104·6
3	103·7	104·0	102·7	102·7	103·9	105·0	105·9	106·1	106·4	106·6	106·6	104·7
4	106·7	106·6	107·0	107·2	107·6	110·1	110·2	109·7	109·5	109·3	109·5	109·6
1835	109·3	107·5	107·6	107·6	108·4	108·0	108·0	107·2	107·2	106·3	104·9	106·3
6	106·0	109·9	105·1	103·1	101·3	102·3	102·4	100·6	101·0	101·7	100·9	100·9
7	101·4	100·2	99·5	99·4	100·0	101·2	101·2	101·3	101·2	101·0	101·0	105·1
8	104·7	104·9	105·4	104·2	103·7	103·2	103·2	106·4	105·6	105·4	107·2	108·2
9	108·7	108·1	106·9	106·2	106·1	106·2	105·7	105·9	106·1	105·9	105·6	105·2
1840	103·9	104·1	102·7	100·8	99·8	100·0	99·9	98·5	98·5	97·1	94·6	96·0
1	97·5	94·9	94·7	92·0	91·7	90·6	89·6	88·8	87·7	86·7	85·7	85·1
2	85·3	86·0	85·3	85·5	84·9	83·6	81·6	80·9	80·1	79·4	79·3	79·0
3	79·3	79·4	80·3	82·7	84·4	84·7	84·0	83·8	84·8	86·0	86·1	86·5
4	86·7	87·3	87·0	87·0	87·4	87·5	86·9	86·7	86·7	86·5	86·2	85·8
1845	84·2	81·0	74·9	75·3	75·3	74·9	74·0	71·7	68·3	70·4	70·4	70·4
6	65·7	65·5	65·5	65·7	65·0	63·4	63·3	63·0	62·6	62·6	61·9	62·2
7	62·0	61·5	60·4	60·2	59·8	59·4	59·4	59·7	60·0	60·0	60·0	59·4
8	59·0	54·6	54·7	53·9	53·9	53·2	52·6	51·3	50·0	48·5	46·7	45·3
9	46·1	46·4	47·0	47·4	47·5	48·1	47·6	49·1	49·3	49·2	49·3	48·5
1850	48·5	48·6	49·0	49·0	49·0	49·1	46·4	47·6	45·4	44·2	43·7	43·1

TABLE 12. *Sub-index of Prices of Dock Shares*

(June 1840 = 100)

Year	Jan.	Feb.	Mar.	Apr.	May	June	July	Aug.	Sept.	Oct.	Nov.	Dec.
1811	..	151·3	150·4	149·2	150·4	149·7	144·1	140·9	140·3	139·4	143·7	140·7
2	140·4	140·9	139·6	137·7	137·1	135·5	132·7	130·9	129·9	128·2	125·6	125·1
3	123·4	123·0	123·2	122·9	124·7	125·4	123·8	124·1	123·4	122·9	121·4	121·3
4	124·7	128·8	133·5	133·5	131·8	130·2	127·3	126·6	125·2	124·9	124·3	124·6
1815	123·1	121·4	119·3	116·5	110·5	109·1	107·0	109·2	106·6	107·0	109·4	116·0
6	113·7	111·8	109·3	108·2	107·5	107·3	107·5	103·7	97·6	99·5	99·9	105·0
7	98·6	97·1	101·3	103·1	104·1	105·5	112·7	121·2	119·4	121·1	124·8	132·2
8	132·4	131·7	133·1	133·1	133·1	130·9	129·2	129·2	127·8	128·8	129·8	131·5
9	129·9	130·0	126·1	126·1	124·4	124·1	123·0	122·4	122·1	118·8	118·8	116·7
1820	116·9	117·5	117·3	116·7	118·4	121·7	125·9	126·2	126·6	125·4	126·3	131·7
1	130·0	130·8	134·2	134·4	136·1	139·7	138·0	138·4	139·1	137·1	139·8	141·0
2	139·7	138·5	142·1	143·5	145·0	145·3	145·3	145·0	146·5	151·7	155·3	154·5
3	152·0	150·2	141·1	139·9	145·7	147·7	148·0	150·9	152·5	154·0	160·3	165·2
4	169·8	172·8	162·8	165·8	162·5	167·4	164·3	157·5	158·9	159·2	158·4	157·2
1825	153·8	151·0	149·6	149·2	147·0	146·1	144·5	143·0	142·3	137·9	136·3	128·8
6	127·6	126·1	120·0	121·4	119·6	118·9	118·9	119·0	119·7	119·9	121·9	124·1
7	121·8	121·8	122·3	122·5	122·3	123·5	124·2	125·5	127·3	128·8	132·1	132·9
8	130·9	130·2	130·4	130·2	130·5	131·8	129·6	129·3	130·4	130·0	129·8	129·4
9	124·3	123·6	122·6	120·8	117·9	118·4	118·3	117·2	118·3	120·0	123·0	125·5
1830	118·8	118·4	117·4	117·9	119·7	119·0	117·6	117·4	116·6	115·4	108·0	105·2
1	96·3	92·8	88·7	88·0	87·3	87·2	85·7	85·4	85·5	85·4	83·0	82·8
2	83·5	85·2	86·2	86·4	86·4	87·9	87·6	86·5	85·4	85·4	84·7	84·0
3	79·4	73·1	72·8	75·2	76·1	75·7	74·5	75·3	76·4	75·6	74·2	72·3
4	72·3	72·2	72·3	72·2	73·8	73·6	74·5	75·2	74·7	74·6	74·0	74·3
1835	74·5	74·4	75·4	76·0	77·7	77·2	76·9	76·6	75·3	78·5	82·1	83·4
6	88·2	90·4	90·2	89·8	90·1	91·8	91·4	91·2	91·4	90·1	89·8	89·0
7	89·0	89·6	88·8	88·3	88·0	87·4	87·4	84·8	85·4	84·9	85·3	87·1
8	88·4	91·5	91·5	91·6	96·3	97·3	96·4	95·6	97·3	98·1	98·5	99·6
9	99·9	105·1	105·3	103·3	102·2	103·2	102·2	101·5	98·6	98·8	98·6	98·4
1840	98·4	100·7	98·8	97·2	98·9	100·0	99·2	95·6	94·2	93·0	92·6	94·3
1	95·3	95·4	95·2	95·7	96·9	97·2	95·6	95·8	97·0	97·6	97·8	98·2
2	99·4	101·4	102·3	103·7	105·9	105·2	107·3	108·8	109·1	109·1	110·8	112·8
3	114·5	117·8	121·2	122·3	121·6	120·8	121·6	122·2	123·2	123·0	124·0	125·6
4	130·3	135·8	136·1	136·4	137·7	133·6	139·1	138·7	140·3	140·4	141·6	144·8
1845	144·9	142·2	141·4	141·9	138·5	142·1	141·0	141·6	141·6	141·1	139·7	135·5
6	139·9	139·1	139·0	138·0	137·7	138·1	137·6	137·5	136·7	136·8	137·0	136·5
7	134·8	131·6	128·6	126·2	125·2	125·0	123·0	122·0	121·3	117·7	115·5	116·0
8	115·6	116·6	116·4	110·8	114·2	115·8	115·9	117·0	117·0	117·0	117·0	117·5
9	119·1	123·8	125·3	127·9	128·3	127·3	127·2	129·8	131·5	131·3	130·0	132·9
1850	133·6	135·9	135·7	135·1	136·3	136·6	136·0	138·0	136·7	136·5	135·6	136·3

TABLE 13. *Sub-index of Prices of Waterworks Shares*

(June 1840 = 100)

Year	Jan.	Feb.	Mar.	Apr.	May	June	July	Aug.	Sept.	Oct.	Nov.	Dec.
1811	..	118·5	117·2	110·6	105·3	102·4	100·2	85·8	86·3	82·3	80·6	74·1
2	73·5	73·5	69·5	63·0	56·7	55·4	52·8	51·6	50·6	49·3	44·7	42·8
3	41·6	40·0	40·3	41·1	41·4	41·4	45·5	39·8	41·2	41·2	40·1	40·6
4	40·2	44·0	45·7	46·7	45·9	45·1	43·3	42·0	41·0	40·1	39·7	40·1
1815	39·1	39·1	39·1	39·1	37·1	36·8	36·8	35·5	36·5	35·7	35·8	37·2
6	34·6	34·4	34·3	34·2	34·1	33·9	31·6	30·2	31·1	30·7	31·8	30·7
7	30·7	30·7	30·7	30·7	31·3	31·3	33·2	40·5	40·9	47·9	54·1	58·7
8	58·6	61·3	58·6	58·8	57·7	58·5	57·3	57·0	56·1	56·8	52·9	51·7
9	51·2	51·3	49·5	49·6	50·0	51·5	50·6	50·3	48·9	47·1	47·5	45·6
1820	44·8	44·3	43·1	40·5	40·8	41·8	42·1	42·6	42·8	43·2	44·2	47·3
1	47·1	48·1	48·3	48·2	50·7	56·0	56·0	55·1	53·4	53·3	53·9	54·7
2	54·6	54·6	55·2	57·2	57·3	57·9	57·6	57·7	59·0	58·6	59·9	61·5
3	61·7	61·7	61·3	63·7	64·1	65·8	67·1	67·8	68·7	69·1	72·5
4	76·3	82·6	89·0	90·9	91·3	92·3	91·1	91·2	87·5	84·4	81·6	78·9
1825	79·3	82·2	84·9	83·8	82·6	85·2	85·1	84·7	84·0	82·8	82·5	82·4
6	80·2	78·0	74·5	70·8	72·0	71·7	70·1	69·0	68·7	69·4	71·1	73·7
7	72·0	70·6	71·4	71·0	70·4	69·2	70·0	71·1	72·5	72·1	74·1	73·4
8	74·0	75·5	71·2	69·9	69·8	69·5	68·5	68·3	70·2	70·6	70·0	70·2
9	69·8	68·5	68·2	67·7	68·2	68·5	68·6	68·7	68·7	68·4	68·6	69·4
1830	71·0	72·5	73·0	73·7	76·5	77·8	77·6	78·2	78·5	79·4	78·4	76·9
1	74·1	73·1	72·0	71·8	70·9	70·8	70·3	70·1	70·1	69·6	69·8	69·4
2	69·2	69·7	70·1	70·7	71·9	72·4	71·5	71·3	72·0	72·4	73·0	73·5
3	73·6	74·9	75·9	75·9	76·8	77·3	77·5	78·0	78·1	78·1	78·3	79·5
4	79·5	79·5	79·6	79·6	80·3	81·6	85·0	82·4	82·4	82·4	83·3	82·9
1835	82·9	82·6	82·6	82·6	82·6	82·6	82·6	80·9	79·3	80·6	80·6	80·6
6	80·6	79·8	79·8	80·2	81·6	82·7	83·8	83·8	83·4	83·4	83·3	82·9
7	83·0	82·5	82·3	82·3	82·4	83·5	83·5	83·5	83·6	83·6	85·2	87·3
8	88·0	89·0	90·9	92·9	92·5	93·1	93·1	94·0	94·3	95·2	98·2	102·0
9	102·0	102·1	101·9	101·7	101·9	102·0	102·0	100·5	100·0	99·1	98·6	98·6
1840	98·3	97·7	98·1	98·3	98·3	100·0	100·6	100·3	100·5	100·5	100·3	99·5
1	99·5	99·5	95·5	95·2	95·1	95·1	94·4	92·1	92·4	92·4	92·7	92·7
2	92·8	92·7	93·6	95·0	94·9	97·7	99·3	100·0	100·0	100·2	101·7	105·5
3	108·5	109·5	111·2	113·1	113·1	114·2	114·9	113·9	114·6	116·3	117·1	118·9
4	119·5	121·2	122·5	122·5	127·7	127·6	127·7	127·7	129·0	130·3	131·3	131·3
1845	130·9	132·0	132·4	132·4	132·4	132·8	133·9	133·9	133·9	134·1	134·1	129·2
6	131·6	131·6	130·6	130·6	131·0	129·7	129·1	128·4	128·4	128·4	128·4	128·4
7	128·0	128·2	126·6	126·4	124·5	123·2	124·6	123·6	123·8	123·0	116·3	115·4
8	114·5	115·8	116·5	114·6	114·3	114·4	114·8	114·1	113·7	113·7	113·5	113·4
9	114·4	113·9	114·8	115·1	114·7	116·7	117·3	117·4	117·8	119·3	117·8	118·2
1850	118·2	114·2	112·9	112·9	110·8	110·8	109·9	108·8	107·3	107·1	107·3	106·4

TABLE 14. *Sub-index of Prices of Insurance Shares*

(June 1840 = 100)

Year	Jan.	Feb.	Mar.	Apr.	May	June	July	Aug.	Sept.	Oct.	Nov.	Dec.
1811	..	90·1	89·9	90·0	90·1	90·7	89·9	89·4	88·3	87·6	87·8	87·9
2	89·0	89·7	90·3	89·0	88·9	88·0	86·2	84·0	82·3	82·2	82·1	81·9
3	80·8	81·2	81·4	81·2	81·4	80·9	80·8	80·6	80·5	80·9	80·8	80·8
4	82·5	83·8	85·0	85·2	86·1	87·0	85·2	83·6	81·8	81·8	81·2	79·7
1815	79·4	79·3	79·6	79·5	78·1	78·3	77·0	75·8	74·5	74·6	76·7	77·1
6	76·0	74·9	74·4	74·0	73·4	74·0	73·1	72·4	71·5	71·5	71·5	71·1
7	71·9	72·6	73·2	75·2	74·2	76·3	77·8	81·1	81·9	82·7	87·2	90·6
8	90·3	90·2	89·7	89·8	89·8	89·9	89·7	89·5	89·6	89·0	89·1	89·8
9	89·0	87·6	86·1	86·1	86·1	86·0	83·4	81·8	81·1	81·0	79·6	79·5
1820	79·0	79·8	79·8	79·6	79·8	79·9	79·8	79·5	79·6	79·6	79·8	80·4
1	79·8	80·8	81·5	82·2	82·6	83·2	83·4	85·3	85·2	85·4	86·0	87·5
2	88·2	88·1	88·2	88·7	90·2	89·9	91·0	91·5	92·0	92·3	92·5	93·4
3	91·9	91·8	91·0	90·2	95·1	96·3	98·2	99·7	100·9	102·0	103·7	106·2
4	111·3	113·7	117·0	118·7	118·6	118·7	119·0	120·3	122·1	122·5	122·3	122·3
1825	122·2	121·5	121·0	121·4	118·4	118·1	115·2	112·1	110·3	109·6	108·1	106·0
6	103·8	99·1	96·1	97·0	96·5	95·6	95·4	93·9	93·9	93·1	94·9	95·9
7	93·7	93·7	94·0	95·0	95·6	96·1	98·6	98·9	99·4	99·6	99·5	99·0
8	98·4	98·7	97·8	98·2	99·2	99·8	100·7	101·7	101·9	101·6	101·9	101·5
9	100·9	100·2	99·5	99·1	99·0	100·1	100·3	101·1	101·8	101·7	105·5	108·1
1830	103·7	100·1	96·6	97·2	98·4	98·2	97·7	96·7	96·3	95·7	93·4	91·2
1	89·0	88·4	86·3	86·4	87·3	87·7	86·1	85·0	84·7	84·7	85·4	85·2
2	84·0	84·0	84·4	85·0	85·5	85·5	86·6	86·6	85·8	86·2	86·8	87·0
3	88·7	89·0	89·3	91·4	91·3	93·9	93·9	93·4	93·7	93·4	93·3	93·4
4	93·9	93·1	93·3	93·4	95·0	95·7	96·0	96·8	96·6	97·7	97·0	97·1
1835	95·8	96·1	96·3	96·4	98·4	98·8	98·6	99·3	98·8	99·7	100·2	101·1
6	101·3	103·3	105·3	107·5	107·4	107·4	106·8	110·4	110·6	110·1	109·5	106·6
7	106·7	107·1	106·8	105·7	104·6	106·5	106·7	105·8	106·7	106·6	106·7	108·4
8	108·7	107·8	108·4	108·5	107·8	107·5	106·7	107·4	107·6	107·7	107·3	108·0
9	107·6	107·5	108·7	107·7	105·8	106·0	106·1	105·7	105·8	102·6	101·7	101·3
1840	101·9	101·2	100·9	100·7	100·2	100·0	101·8	101·2	101·8	104·0	103·4	101·6
1	101·9	100·2	98·5	98·4	97·7	97·3	95·7	94·7	94·8	95·7	93·0	93·6
2	93·7	93·7	94·5	94·5	95·7	96·8	96·7	95·4	96·8	96·6	94·6	94·9
3	96·0	97·6	98·4	101·6	103·5	101·4	103·6	102·8	103·7	104·0	104·6	104·5
4	105·3	108·5	109·7	108·2	111·3	112·2	112·2	112·0	111·9	113·3	112·8	112·8
1845	113·3	114·7	113·9	114·0	114·6	114·8	114·7	114·8	114·6	115·1	114·6	111·2
6	110·8	112·7	113·0	113·6	113·6	113·5	112·9	113·8	113·5	112·1	111·5	110·3
7	110·2	110·8	108·7	107·6	106·6	105·9	106·3	106·0	105·6	105·4	105·2	102·4
8	104·8	104·5	104·2	100·9	99·3	98·6	100·7	100·1	101·4	102·0	100·5	101·6
9	105·1	106·8	109·6	111·0	113·1	114·8	116·3	114·6	113·9	114·0	114·0	114·7
1850	115·8	116·9	118·4	119·2	121·4	121·5	121·4	121·8	122·1	123·2	124·0	124·3

TABLE 15. *Sub-index of Prices of Gas-light and Coke Company Shares*

(June 1840 = 100)

Year	Jan.	Feb.	Mar.	Apr.	May	June	July	Aug.	Sept.	Oct.	Nov.	Dec.
1819	106·3	103·9	101·2	101·2	101·1	103·5	102·3	96·3	96·3	94·4	94·4	94·4
1820	91·8	90·5	90·5	90·6	91·6	91·3	90·1	88·4	88·8	88·8	89·4	93·6
1	92·7	92·1	91·5	91·1	90·6	90·6	88·5	88·5	88·5	88·0	89·1	·91·6
2	92·7	92·7	102·6	104·0	105·1	104·0	103·6	102·8	103·7	103·7	103·3	104·1
3	98·7	98·4	97·2	95·9	93·4	101·2	102·8	108·0	108·2	108·5	104·9	104·9
4	108·3	110·7	115·0	114·2	104·9	112·3	109·5	108·6	105·4	102·3	103·8	103·6
1825	104·2	105·6	101·9	101·3	99·1	92·1	94·6	90·0	87·2	84·8	82·5	81·3
6	77·6	77·8	78·8	82·9	77·5	77·8	76·2	75·0	74·7	75·1	77·2	82·1
7	81·9	79·6	82·2	87·0	85·0	89·2	91·8	92·0	87·2	86·2	87·7	87·0
8	85·9	84·4	84·7	83·8	84·6	85·8	84·9	85·6	86·2	86·3	86·5	86·0
9	83·0	83·1	83·9	83·4	83·0	85·0	84·2	87·1	88·2	88·6	90·0	92·1
1830	90·9	91·1	91·5	92·1	94·7	98·4	98·8	98·3	98·0	96·4	92·2	90·1
1	90·1	90·6	89·4	88·5	91·4	92·2	89·0	87·3	87·5	87·3	87·0	86·8
2	88·8	87·5	88·6	89·6	90·3	90·1	89·7	91·6	94·0	94·5	96·6	96·4
3	96·9	97·9	102·1	104·4	106·1	106·1	105·7	105·6	102·6	100·8	100·3	99·2
4	97·8	99·2	100·6	100·8	102·0	103·3	101·9	101·2	100·3	97·0	96·6	96·0
1835	94·6	91·0	90·2	88·5	88·1	88·4	88·1	87·0	85·3	86·9	87·8	88·2
6	89·1	89·4	88·7	89·3	89·7	89·5	86·8	85·2	85·2	85·2	85·4	84·9
7	85·0	84·3	82·1	81·6	80·3	80·6	80·6	80·8	80·3	79·3	79·2	78·3
8	81·1	83·3	83·5	84·1	84·1	85·4	85·0	88·9	87·9	87·9	87·6	87·6
9	87·3	89·5	95·4	94·5	94·4	94·6	96·0	96·6	97·3	97·3	97·2	97·8
1840	97·9	97·2	93·9	95·1	95·1	100·0	99·0	99·2	100·7	100·5	101·1	99·5
1	100·1	100·1	97·4	98·1	97·8	99·7	99·4	97·8	96·5	96·2	97·2	95·6
2	96·7	93·7	92·9	92·9	90·8	95·4	95·6	95·9	95·9	96·3	96·9	99·7
3	97·4	98·9	100·0	100·9	100·8	101·4	100·0	100·6	100·8	101·8	102·7	103·5
4	102·9	103·2	102·7	104·3	105·9	106·4	106·4	108·3	107·9	109·4	109·1	110·5
1845	111·4	110·9	111·2	111·2	111·8	108·6	108·2	108·2	108·2	106·4	106·4	106·4
6	106·0	105·0	104·5	102·7	101·3	100·6	100·5	101·2	101·0	98·3	97·7	97·0
7	96·4	96·4	95·9	95·1	94·0	90·3	90·3	90·3	89·3	88·0	88·8	88·3
8	85·8	84·2	82·2	80·8	80·8	79·7	78·9	79·4	77·6	76·1	72·8	72·9
9	72·2	71·2	69·3	70·1	66·0	67·7	67·7	67·0	67·0	67·0	67·6	67·7
1850	68·7	68·1	69·5	69·8	69·8	69·8	70·0	71·1	70·9	70·0	70·0	69·7

TABLE 16. *Sub-index of Prices of Mining Company Shares*

(June 1840 = 100)

Year	Jan.	Feb.	Mar.	Apr.	May	June	July	Aug.	Sept.	Oct.	Nov.	Dec.
1824	..	..	..	..	..	..	..	..	..	525·1	989·2	1,546·4
1825	3,326·6	3,080·0	2,960·7	2,307·0	2,077·0	2,296·2	2,245·4	2,047·7	1,759·3	1,577·9	1,287·7	1,065·2
6	1,114·4	886·7	807·3	734·9	707·4	700·5	617·1	607·7	556·7	585·1	662·2	752·8
7	698·9	687·4	628·4	651·2	536·7	512·3	550·8	542·8	606·8	571·1	629·1	798·6
8	753·7	701·8	675·1	631·8	680·9	644·5	633·7	614·0	625·7	641·1	545·2	541·6
9	494·4	469·1	436·5	421·1	434·0	524·8	456·7	418·1	449·4	465·6	479·6	582·8
1830	622·3	570·5	605·9	616·2	633·7	558·8	524·0	516·1	527·1	478·6	459·3	452·1
1	428·5	403·5	386·9	383·2	380·4	362·7	350·2	322·4	291·2	278·2	267·4	289·1
2	277·9	264·7	245·2	241·4	259·6	296·4	281·9	266·4	256·4	256·3	295·9	306·8
3	315·0	367·8	401·2	403·7	403·7	393·1	410·2	489·8	464·4	463·4	462·1	469·3
4	470·5	475·7	435·8	413·6	408·6	369·3	353·4	313·6	319·4	319·1	331·5	333·7
1835	332·3	338·2	346·3	361·0	342·9	307·8	322·9	297·6	285·7	292·0	287·9	299·1
6	331·0	328·4	311·2	312·2	339·8	319·3	317·1	342·6	329·0	315·1	305·3	301·5
7	304·8	293·6	296·0	294·3	288·3	268·1	267·0	267·0	270·7	270·4	264·5	267·3
8	257·3	266·7	266·0	193·0	183·8	165·4	175·2	170·3	172·2	179·1	176·3	170·0
9	164·6	155·3	146·4	146·7	141·1	147·5	145·6	149·8	143·7	141·9	135·9	122·0
1840	133·0	132·6	131·0	125·2	111·6	100·0	106·6	107·5	96·2	88·6	86·8	81·4
1	71·1	57·5	39·8	35·4	29·3	29·3	22·7	28·3	24·1	28·3	29·8	36·1
2	36·1	36·3	36·3	47·6	46·2	49·0	50·5	51·9	54·7	58·3	53·9	53·9
3	51·0	57·4	58·1	58·1	58·7	56·3	56·3	56·3	58·8	60·5	60·5	61·2
4	61·2	66·2	79·7	80·4	93·1	84·6	93·1	90·3	83·2	85·0	84·2	95·5
1845	105·5	103·3	104·0	108·4	105·5	104·0	85·0	85·0	70·3	73·2	73·2	79·1
6	101·1	98·2	95·2	95·2	93·8	102·5	111·3	108·4	104·0	95·2	95·2	93·8
7	93·8	93·8	93·8	93·8	93·8	95·2	92·8	92·8	92·8	88·9	88·9	86·3
8	85·0	92·1	88·3	84·4	83·1	80·5	67·5	62·3	63·6	62·3	76·6	76·1
9	81·3	83·1	87·6	87·6	87·6	74·0	74·0	74·0	64·9	63·6	64·9	68·8
1850	72·7	83·1	85·7	88·9	87·0	84·4	83·1	84·4	85·7	87·0	85·7	85·7

TABLE 17. *Sub-index of Prices of Railway Shares*

(June 1840 = 100)

Year	Jan.	Feb.	Mar.	Apr.	May	June	July	Aug.	Sept.	Oct.	Nov.	Dec.
1827	..	..	..	..	40·5	40·5	43·5	45·5	46·1	49·5	50·5	50·8
8	49·5	48·3	49·9	50·7	51·9	57·1	58·8	58·8	58·3	56·6	56·8	57·0
9	58·3	58·9	59·1	55·4	55·3	50·2	49·7	50·7	49·4	52·1	53·4	58·8
1830	58·0	56·1	56·1	57·2	59·4	60·1	60·1	66·7	68·0	66·7	66·2	66·2
1	63·8	63·8	61·4	65·6	64·1	65·4	66·5	62·8	62·8	65·4	70·2	70·5
2	70·8	69·7	70·1	70·1	70·4	70·4	67·9	66·1	65·0	64·7	65·5	65·8
3	65·5	65·9	65·9	65·9	69·2	71·5	70·1	67·9	69·0	69·7	75·8	75·4
4	71·8	71·0	66·1	65·5	67·5	65·3	65·5	65·2	65·2	74·4	66·7	69·0
1835	67·7	67·5	67·8	70·4	59·6	60·2	64·0	69·7	73·2	80·4	86·4	86·1
6	96·4	107·2	115·7	117·0	129·4	124·2	112·9	116·1	116·0	108·8	90·8	98·8
7	101·1	89·2	79·1	69·9	76·1	82·7	83·9	84·4	76·5	75·2	76·3	82·2
8	85·8	90·2	99·2	98·7	94·5	92·9	87·5	88·5	88·9	89·6	90·0	87·1
9	88·9	89·8	86·9	82·1	82·6	85·4	82·2	73·0	74·0	73·3	70·5	69·9
1840	76·9	77·7	75·4	83·0	91·2	100·0	97·7	92·5	85·4	83·9	84·0	88·5
1	91·2	89·2	85·8	88·0	85·9	84·2	80·8	80·4	79·7	77·3	79·8	83·6
2	86·7	88·2	89·5	92·6	94·2	92·0	89·4	89·9	86·5	86·2	87·2	90·5
3	94·1	93·3	99·0	97·8	96·9	95·7	97·2	99·8	97·3	98·8	102·8	105·5
4	112·7	115·6	118·7	119·1	120·8	119·6	121·1	127·1	126·8	124·6	121·2	128·1
1845	132·1	140·0	142·1	149·4	149·4	165·3	167·9	166·6	153·8	149·8	137·5	133·9
6	145·1	147·3	139·8	139·7	145·9	142·6	143·8	141·0	135·6	132·2	131·4	128·5
7	129·6	124·3	119·9	120·1	117·0	122·0	126·4	117·6	113·9	103·7	105·1	105·3
8	108·2	105·1	100·2	96·0	102·6	100·2	101·5	94·3	85·0	79·7	87·8	85·0
9	91·8	95·6	87·9	85·0	76·0	79·1	79·7	75·8	68·5	60·5	61·9	63·3
1850	73·5	73·5	69·1	61·4	63·9	68·3	63·8	65·2	73·7	75·4	73·7	83·1

TABLE 18. *Sub-index of Prices of Joint-stock Bank Shares*

(June 1840 = 100)

Year	Jan.	Feb.	Mar.	Apr.	May	June	July	Aug.	Sept.	Oct.	Nov.	Dec.
1831	97·5	84·7	83·9	82·4	80·0	81·4	80·9	82·1	81·4	81·4	81·8	81·8
2	78·0	79·6	79·9	80·3	80·5	81·4	81·6	81·4	81·4	81·4	81·8	81·0
3	81·4	81·4	81·0	81·4	83·6	84·8	88·4	87·9	87·7	88·5	89·8	89·2
4	88·7	89·1	90·0	89·6	90·8	92·0	90·4	90·6	90·3	89·2	89·3	92·9
1835	93·6	93·9	93·4	93·9	95·8	96·6	95·2	94·3	94·0	94·9	96·2	95·4
6	95·6	96·4	97·1	99·6	99·9	99·5	99·0	97·6	95·8	92·9	92·3	92·2
7	91·9	91·4	90·0	87·5	88·1	88·1	87·8	88·1	89·1	89·7	91·4	91·9
8	91·6	91·3	91·6	92·5	93·8	94·8	96·5	96·6	96·6	97·0	98·0	98·9
9	99·2	98·9	99·1	98·5	99·2	99·9	99·2	99·6	98·8	98·2	97·6	98·2
1840	99·6	99·1	98·3	97·4	99·0	100·0	99·9	97·6	97·0	95·3	96·6	96·6
1	95·9	95·3	94·5	93·4	93·9	94·4	93·9	92·3	92·1	91·3	91·3	92·4
2	91·7	92·0	92·1	91·4	92·5	94·4	93·9	92·9	93·7	96·0	96·6	97·0
3	96·1	96·0	98·9	98·9	99·5	97·7	96·5	95·7	95·3	95·4	96·4	96·5
4	96·6	97·7	98·6	101·5	103·4	103·9	102·3	103·2	103·0	102·5	103·4	104·4
1845	105·0	103·9	104·4	104·6	107·4	107·7	108·1	107·7	106·4	103·8	103·5	103·8
6	104·4	107·8	106·8	105·9	106·5	107·7	107·8	109·8	109·6	109·6	109·8	111·1
7	110·4	111·1	108·9	106·3	106·6	107·6	109·9	109·4	107·4	102·2	98·7	98·7
8	100·6	103·4	96·7	91·2	94·1	96·5	94·9	93·6	92·2	91·2	90·7	91·7
9	99·0	98·2	96·5	98·1	98·5	98·5	99·8	101·2	102·3	103·4	104·6	105·3
1850	105·4	105·4	105·1	106·0	106·5	109·3	110·5	110·7	110·4	111·4	111·7	113·0

Chapter II

CYCLICAL AND SECULAR CHANGES IN SHARE PRICES

1. Behaviour of the Indexes. In examining the behaviour of the indexes an attempt has been made to indicate briefly the underlying historical developments which bear directly on their course. An important example of such a connexion is the following. The immediate impression conveyed by even a casual glance at the graph of the index inclusive of the mines is that there is a fundamental qualitative alteration in the character of share-price fluctuations after 1824. The mild, undulating movements that characterized the curve from 1811 to 1824 stand out in sharp contrast to the choppy oscillations thereafter. What circumstances were responsible for this change in the pattern of the index ? It is important to bear in mind that at the beginning of the nineteenth century transactions on the Stock Exchange were confined exclusively to the public funds.[1] Although prices of shares were given in the authorized list of quotations by 1811, there was really no widespread interest in them as an outlet for savings until the decade of the twenties. Such shares as there were on the market at the outset probably had no special attraction either for investors or for speculators.

For the investor, most of the shares then available had neither the advantage of security offered by Consols nor a compensating differential in yield for greater risk elements. On the other hand, speculators—eager to realize on capital gains rather than to draw a steady and modest return—could not expect to reap windfalls from the types of shares then on the market. In the Consol market, however, rumours relating to England's fortunes in the war provided ready opportunities for price manipulation. Though there are no statistics on daily share turnover, indirect evidence suggests that it was very limited.[2]

As was said at the outset, the curve of the index inclusive of mines before 1823 illustrates the languid state of the share market. This curve,

---

[1] Moreover, even Consols had achieved public acceptance as a safe investment only in the preceding decades. The notorious speculation of the beginning of the eighteenth century culminating in the Bubble Act of 1720 had effectively checked any widespread public support for securities except for an occasional flurry like that of 1807 (see Tooke, i. 278). Although there always remained a professional group in London that carried on an active trade in securities, the habit of turning over hard cash in return for a piece of paper that promised a safe and steady income was for the public at large a relatively new development. Joseph Lowe points out that it was not until the end of the Napoleonic Wars that the public funds were resorted to as an outlet for savings by people in the provinces. See Joseph Lowe, *The Present State of England with a Comparison of the Prospects of England and France*, p. 326.

[2] Until the railway boom, in 1843, four or five brokers were able to handle the entire trade in shares (E. T. Powell, *The Evolution of the Money Market*, p. 535).

however, assumes after 1823 a considerable degree of volatility which may be accounted for almost *in toto* by the presence of the mine shares, the first area of the share market where extensive and general speculation occurred. The alteration in the character of the curve exclusive of mines does not take place until the early thirties, when railways introduce another speculative area in the capital market.

This extended example, although of considerable intrinsic interest, has been cited to illustrate the need for constant reference to the historical meaning of movements in the indexes. The latter have been constructed primarily as tools for further historical and cyclical analysis.

2. Individual Cycles in Share Prices. Until 1824 both the index inclusive of mines and that exclusive of mines are, of course, identical, since the mine group is not introduced until the last quarter of 1824. As indicated in Tables 19 and 21 (which will be discussed below), there are two cycles in this period with peaks in May 1814 and December 1818. Both cycles, which are relatively small in amplitude and about average in duration, attracted little notice in contemporary literature so far as the share market was concerned. Perhaps one reason for the mildness of these swings is the fact that neither expansion was accompanied by promotional activity of any substantial proportions. In this connexion the limited nature of the share market at this time should be recalled. There is, however, a clear downward movement from 1811 to 1816, only slightly interrupted by a revival culminating in May 1814. This fall may be regarded as a combination of cyclical contraction following upon the boom which culminated in 1810 and post-war deflation after 1815. The cyclical movements of the index throughout the decade seem remarkably similar in all the components.

The year 1820 ushers in a prolonged period of revival in share prices, gradual at the beginning, but gathering momentum during 1823 and 1824. The post-Napoleonic War deflation had run its course, heavy taxation had been reduced, capital was abundant, and a strong need was felt for new outlets. The yield on Consols reached a high point in 1820 and fell almost continuously during the next few years. Towards the close of 1822, 5 per cent. stock (government funds) had been converted into 4 and the old 4 per cents. were reduced to $3\frac{1}{2}$ per cent. stock. The smaller return on Consols strengthened the position of shares and foreign holdings, the yield on which then appeared much higher in relation to other investment opportunities.

The contemporary literature abounds with evidence of an increasing, widespread demand for shares by the middle and upper classes. Newspapers began to publish daily articles on the condition of the stock market. Not since the South Sea Bubble had a boom psychology gripped the public's imagination on a comparable scale.

Promoters were quick to meet the eagerness of the public to get in on the bull market. The time was ripe for promotional activity on a large scale; new issues were readily subscribed and the prices of outstanding shares were bid up. In the case of most new issues only a small amount, usually about £5, was required to be paid at the outset, further instalments being callable at a later date. Thus a moderate increase in the prices of shares often produced a huge percentage profit in the sum actually invested. Henry English lists the various types of companies projected during the boom period of 1824–5: mining companies, gas companies, insurance and investment enterprises, canals, railways, steam companies, trading corporations, building companies, and others. Gas-light and mine companies —especially the latter—enjoyed the best reception. The former, in these years, were putting in their first appearance, and were regarded as an exceedingly sound investment. Not only was the new illuminant superior to oil and candlelight in brilliancy, but the promoters claimed that it could be produced at half the price. In 1824–5, however, a series of promotions of mines in foreign countries completely eclipsed the attraction of all other forms of share investment.

The sub-index of mine share prices leaped more than 500 per cent. from October 1824 to January 1825, a period of only three months, during which speculation was frenzied. It was noted earlier that the climax of the boom in other shares was reached in 1824, while the peak in mine shares did not occur until the first months of 1825. The probable explanation for this discrepancy is the shifting of funds from the less speculative issues. These, to be sure, had, up to this point, undergone a sizeable appreciation of their own. But investors sought to unload them towards the end of 1824 in order to get in on the bull market in mines. A sagging in the prices of the more conservative stocks resulted, while mines continued to boom.

Beginning in March 1825, the index including mine shares records a catastrophic and almost uninterrupted drop until September 1826. But it was not only mine shares that suffered from the wave of liquidation; for, by October 1826, the index exclusive of mines had also fallen to its pre-boom level of the beginning of 1823.[1]

During the period between the peaks of 1824–5 and 1836 the inclusive index is highly volatile, whereas only one mild cyclical movement can be detected in the index exclusive of mines. In the same years three distinct cycles appear in the inclusive index, with peaks in 1827, 1830, and 1834. The sharpness of fluctuations in the total index, then, is to be attributed essentially to the movement of mine shares. More broadly, the decade under examination was one of relative quiescence in the stock market. The most clearly defined movement (before 1835) is the decline in both indexes

[1] Tooke, ii. 158, describes the process by which the fall took place: '. . . a general deficiency of means among the subscribers to pay up the succeeding instalments, as they had relied for the most part upon a continued rise, to enable them to realise a profit before another instalment should be called for, or upon the same facility as had before existed, of raising money for the purpose at a low rate of interest;—and as applied to foreign loans, the absence of security for some of them, and the rise of the rate of interest in this country, which had the same depressing effect upon all of them'.

during the greater part of 1830 and 1831. This can probably be explained by the violent political agitation which distinguished the period before the Reform Bill went through.

In the middle of 1827 railways enter the index and their effect is to exert an upward influence, counter to the general trend as measured from the peak in 1824–5. Similarly, banks, which are introduced in 1831, rise continuously for a number of years thereafter.

The boom in the share market in 1835–6 was based largely on the formation of numerous railways. It foreshadowed the more intense railway speculation which dominated the stock market a decade later. In the single year from June 1835 to May 1836 the sub-index of railway shares was more than doubled; at the former date it was 60·2, at the latter, 129·4. This increase in market values was even more remarkable than any such simple comparison would indicate, since at no time prior to 1835 had the index reached a level as high as 80.[1] Moreover, the sums which Parliament authorized to be raised in 1836 for railway construction exceeded the total amount authorized for that purpose during all preceding years.[2]

There was also substantial activity in the shares of joint-stock banks, a number of which had been formed upon the passage of the Bank Charter Act a few years earlier. Especially towards the close of 1835 and in the first part of 1836 new joint-stock banks and branches were established in large numbers. Bank shares were sold at considerable premiums, which further encouraged speculative activity.[3] The extent of the concentration of activity in banks and railways may be judged from the fact that total new investment in these two fields during 1834–6 constituted almost three-quarters of all new joint-stock capital issues.[4]

Although there were tremendous capital exports to the United States, so far as the share market was concerned, the speculation of this period was directed towards domestic undertakings. It thus contrasts with the boom of 1824–5, when large sums were invested abroad, both in foreign governments and mines; and, moreover, these foreign investments constituted the focus of speculation in the whole market.[5] The speculation of 1835–6

---

[1] Of course, the absolute levels are in themselves no indication of the condition of the railway share market. In fact the general trend of railway share prices was rising from 1827, the year in which the sub-index begins. The index figures referred to are based on the value for the single month of June 1840, which happens to be relatively high.

[2] G. R. Porter, *Progress of the Nation*, p. 332. The bullish atmosphere of the time is thus described by John Francis, *History of the English Railway*, i. 290: 'The press supported the mania; the government sanctioned it; the people paid for it. Railways were at once a fashion and a frenzy. England was mapped out for iron roads. The

profits and percentage of the Liverpool and Manchester were largely quoted. The prospects and power of the London and Birmingham were as freely prophesied.'

[3] Tooke, ii. 274.

[4] Report of Select Committee on Joint Stock Companies, *P.P.* 1844, vii, Appendix 4, p. 345.

[5] There was, however, considerable investment and speculation in foreign bonds in the thirties during the years preceding the share boom. Prices of foreign bonds broke in May 1835. See John Francis, *Chronicles and Characters of the Stock Exchange*, pp. 312 ff., for a description of the state of the market then.

differs, further, in that it never reached the intensity of 1825; nor was it carried on over as long a period of time. In 1835–6 the upward movement lasted just about a year, whereas the liquidation occurred over an even shorter period. The steepness of the fall in the index during the early months of 1837 may reflect the general lack of confidence caused by the aftermath of crisis, and, more particularly, the precarious position of three leading banks, which resulted from their over-extension of credit to the American trade.[1]

From 1836 on the mine group is of negligible importance and the two curves (inclusive and exclusive of mines) closely parallel each other. There are three cycles from 1837 to the end of our period, with peaks in 1838, 1840, and 1845. However, except for railways, only a single cycle can be marked off in the sub-indexes prior to 1845. It is because of the presence of clear cycles in the railway index in 1838 and 1840 (railways carry 44 per cent. of the total weight during this period) that the total index shows such a cyclical pattern.

The sub-indexes of the older types of companies suffered a prolonged, though mild, decline following the 1837 liquidation. Relatively little new capital was invested even in railway enterprise until 1844;[2] but the reluctance of promoters to project new lines did not affect the valuation of existing securities which were rising in price during this period.

In 1841 the longest cyclical movement in our index (and the one with greatest total amplitude) got under way. It is noteworthy that the movement culminating in a peak in 1845 is common to all the sub-indexes with the exception of banks; prices of the latter's shares do not slump until 1847.

The story of the cycle from 1841 to 1849 is really an account of the mania for railway shares which culminated in 1845. The early stages of the railway boom, as reflected in security quotations, were probably a natural response to real increases in revenues enjoyed by the leading lines. The Liverpool and Manchester, the London and Birmingham, and the Grand Junction paid dividends of about 10 per cent. in 1844 while a few others paid even more.[3] The profitable returns of these companies not only reacted on the prices of almost all existing railway shares, but attracted promoters with new projects, eager to share in the gains from traffic by laying down competitive lines.

It is difficult to represent the cumulative nature of railway speculation during these years in terms of numerical magnitudes alone. Two parliamentary reports issued in 1846 contain the names of persons who subscribed to railway capital in 1845, and the sums subscribed by each. The contrast in occupational descriptions affords an illuminating commentary on the manner in which the middle classes participated *en masse*.

[1] Tooke, ii. 306.
[2] Edward Cleveland-Stevens, *English Railways*, p. 24, and Porter, p. 332.
[3] Wetenhall's *Course of the Exchange* (see p. 359 above for an account of this basic source).

The railway share index, which had averaged 98·2 in 1843 and 121·3 in 1844, continued its speculative climb through the first half of 1845, reaching a peak figure of 167·9 in July. In August, trading in railway shares still exhibited all the symptoms of frenzied speculation. They were seldom bought as permanent investments, but rather in the hope of quickly netting large profits by resale. After the middle of the month the only real buyers of shares were persons of limited means and still more limited information; and from this point forward the speculation degenerated into the worst sort of gambling. The anxiety to sell at the high prices prevalent was so great as to constitute an actual panic. Prices fell headlong as speculators made feverish haste to sell.[1]

The total index records an almost continuous decline for four years beginning with 1846. In 1850, the last year of the index, what appears to be a recovery movement is discernible.

3. The Nature of the Analysis. Our aim is to illuminate two types of fluctuations characterizing the movements of the indexes : first, the cyclical expansions and contractions in share prices which are more or less closely related to general fluctuations in business activity, and second, the secular trends in share prices which supply evidence as to the changing profitability of particular investment outlets.[2] For this purpose numerical measures were computed according to the technique of analysis devised by the National Bureau of Economic Research. This technique is explained in some detail in Part II of Vol. II, and the reader is advised to turn to that volume for a more complete description of the nature of the analysis that is here presented.

The National Bureau attempts to learn how different economic processes behave with reference to business cycles by observing their movements during the time periods occupied by revivals, expansions, recessions, and contractions in general business activity. The first task then is to mark off these time periods. A table of 'reference dates' showing the months and years of the troughs and peaks of successive business cycles has been compiled by us, and appears below (see Table 19). A full explanation of the reasons for our choice of these dates is given in Appendix A of Vol. I, Part I. We compute the average of the monthly values during each 'reference cycle' and convert the data into percentages of this base; we call these percentages 'reference cycle relatives'.

It is well known that cyclical fluctuations in diverse economic processes differ from one another in timing, amplitude, and relationship to the expansions and contractions of general business. The cyclical movements found in a series may have timing dates that differ little from our reference dates, or that usually lead or lag behind the reference dates by brief or by considerable intervals, or that have no regular relationship to the reference dates. The course of business cycles is influenced by cyclical fluctuations

[1] D. M. Evans, pp. 11–18.
[2] No regular seasonal variation was ob-   served in the fluctuations of the indexes.

in every economic process, whether or not these fluctuations harmonize with the general tides of activity. Hence supplementing our analysis based upon business-cycle time-periods, we observe the movements of a series during 'specific cycles', the wave-like movements of the same order of magnitude as that of business cycles, peculiar to each series. We mark off the specific cycles by the dates of their turning-points, and compute the average value of the data during each cycle. This second set of relatives corresponds in character to the reference-cycle relatives, except that the new set shows movements during specific cycles.

On the basis of this twofold schematization of the data, in terms of reference-cycle dates and specific-cycle turning-points, various cyclical attributes of a series are measured. The timing and duration of specific cycles, the amplitude of expansion and contraction, secular change from cycle to cycle, the pattern of behaviour and the rates of change during successive stages of cycles, and measures of conformity to general business cycles are computed for each cycle; and, by a process of averaging, the typical cyclical character of a series in the course of successive cycles is determined. A detailed explanation of the derivation of the measures computed will not be presented here, but as each measure is introduced into the analysis, the accompanying discussion will enable the reader to grasp its essential character.

4. The Timing and Duration of Cycles in Share Prices. Our tables of 'reference' dates yield measures of the duration of business cycles and of their phases of expansion and contraction. The dates of the 'specific' cycle turning-points yield similar measures. Table 19 presents this information for individual specific cycles of the two total indexes, and for individual reference cycles. Table 20 shows the average durations for the total indexes, and for the sub-indexes as well. By comparing the turning-points of specific cycles with the reference dates we determine how regularly the specific cycles of a given series correspond in time to business cycles. The differences in months between the turning-dates of the specific cycles and the reference dates are also shown in these tables.

Several points of interest may be noted. The cycles in none of the indexes show one-to-one correspondence with reference cycles; but three of the sub-indexes, docks, railways, and mines, contain the same number of specific and reference cycles. With the exception of the gas-light company and joint-stock bank subgroups, all the indexes exhibit some tendency to anticipate reference peaks. This tendency is most pronounced in the waterworks, canal, and dock sub-indexes, and in the two total indexes. Regularity of relationship to reference troughs is less marked in all the indexes. In sum, the timing measures reveal that, on the average, share prices from 1813 to 1849 began to fall some months before a decline in general business activity set in, but reversed the direction of their movement earlier, later, or at the same time as the upturn occurred in business generally, with no great consistency of behaviour. The analytic and historical significance of

TABLE 19. *Timing and Duration of Specific Cycles in Total Share Price Indexes compared with Reference Cycles*

| Specific cycles, total index of share prices, including mines | | | | | | | | | Reference cycles | | | | | | |
| Expansion | | Contraction | | Duration in months | | | Lead (−) or lag (+) | | Expansion | | Contraction | | Duration in months | | |
Revival	Peak	Recession	Trough	Expansion	Contraction	Full cycle	At reference peak	At reference trough (+)	Revival	Peak	Recession	Trough	Expansion	Contraction	Full cycle
Feb. 1813	May 1814	June 1814	Sept. 1816	16	28	44	−10	+16	Oct. 1811	Mar. 1815	Apr. 1815	Sept. 1816	42	18	60
Oct. 1816	Dec. 1818	Jan. 1819	Jan. 1820	27	13	40	+3	0	Oct. 1816	Sept. 1818	Oct. 1818	Sept. 1819	24	12	36
Feb. 1820	Jan. 1825	Feb. 1825	June 1827	60	29	89	−4	+4	Oct. 1819	May 1825	June 1825	Nov. 1826	68	18	86
July 1827	Dec. 1827	Jan. 1828	Aug. 1829	6	20	26	−13	+7	Dec. 1826	Jan. 1829	Feb. 1829	Dec. 1829	26	11	37
Sept. 1829	May 1830	June 1830	Apr. 1832	9	23	32	(−10)[a]	−4	Jan. 1830	Mar. 1831	Apr. 1831	July 1832	15	16	31
May 1832	Feb. 1834	Mar. 1834	June 1835	22	16	38	[b]	−3							
July 1835	May 1836	June 1836	Apr. 1837	11	11	22	0		Aug. 1832	May 1836	June 1836	Aug. 1837	46	15	61
May 1837	Mar. 1838	Apr. 1838	Dec. 1839	11	21	32	−12	−4	Sept. 1837	Mar. 1839	Apr. 1839	Nov. 1842	19	44	63
Jan. 1840	June 1840	July 1840	Oct. 1841	6	16	22		−13[c]	Dec. 1842	Sept. 1845	Oct. 1845	Sept. 1846	34	12	46
Nov. 1841	June 1845	July 1845	Oct. 1849	44	52	96	−3	+13[d]	Oct. 1846	Apr. 1847	May 1847	Sept. 1848	7	17	24
AVERAGE				21.2	22.9	44.1	−5.6	+1.8	..	..	..	..	31.2	18.1	49.3
AVERAGE DEVIATION				13.6	8.1	19.4	5.2	7.3	..	..	..	..	14.5	5.7	16.1

[a] Leads or lags that do not correspond closely to reference turns are enclosed in parentheses. A turning-point of a specific cycle is judged to correspond closely to a reference turn when it deviates from the corresponding reference turns by no more than half the duration of the reference phase within which it falls. In striking averages of leads or lags, parenthesis entries are generally omitted.

[b] A blank indicates that a turn of the specific cycles is considered as not corresponding to a reference turn.

[c] The specific cycle troughs correspond to the reference trough in November 1842.

[Continued

TABLE 19 (continued)

Specific cycles, total index of share prices, excluding mines

Lead (−) or lag (+)		Duration in months			Expansion		Contraction	
At reference peak	At reference trough	Expansion	Contraction	Full cycle	Revival	Peak	Recession	Trough
−10	+16	16	28	44	Feb. 1813	May 1814	June 1814	Sept. 1816
+3	0	27	13	40	Oct. 1816	Dec. 1818	Jan. 1819	Jan. 1820
−8	+4	56	24	80	Feb. 1820	Sept. 1824	Oct. 1824	Sept. 1826
(+11)	(−10)[e]	39	21	60	Oct. 1826	Dec. 1829	Jan. 1830	Sept. 1831
0	−4	56	11	67	Oct. 1831	May 1836	June 1836	Apr. 1837
−12		11	21	32	May 1837	Mar. 1838	Apr. 1838	Dec. 1839
−2	−13[c]	6	16	22	Jan. 1840	June 1840	July 1840	Oct. 1841
	+13[d]	45	51	96	Nov. 1841	July 1845	Aug. 1845	Oct. 1849
−4·8	+2·0	32·0	23·1	55·1				
5·2	7·7	17·0	8·4	20·6				

[d] The specific cycle troughs correspond to the reference trough in September 1848.

[e] The specific cycle trough corresponds to the reference trough in July 1832.

TABLE 20. *Average Timing and Duration of Specific Cycles in the Share Price Indexes*

	(1) Total, including mines	(2) Total, excluding mines	(3) Canals	(4) Water-works	(5) Docks	(6) Insurance	(7) Gas-light	(8) Railways	(9) Banks	(10) Mines
PERIOD COVERED BY REFERENCE CYCLES	1811–48	1811–48	1811–48	1811–48	1811–48	1811–48	1819–48	1830–48	1832–48	1826–48
NUMBER OF REFERENCE CYCLES	9	9	9	9	9	9	7	5	4	6
PERIOD COVERED BY SPECIFIC CYCLES	1813–49	1813–49	1811–48	1813–48	1813–48	1813–48	1821–49	1829–49	1832–48	1827–49
NUMBER OF SPECIFIC CYCLES	10	8	8	8	9	6	8	5	3	6
TIMING OF SPECIFIC CYCLES AT:										
Reference Peaks										
No. of leads, lags, coincidences	5, 1, 1	4, 1, 1	5, 0, 0	7, 1, 0	5, 1, 1	3, 2, 0	2, 1, 1	1, 0, 1	1, 1, 1	3, 1, 0
Av. lead (−) or lag (+) in months	−5·6 (5·2)ᵃ	−4·8 (5·2)	−9·6 (7·1)	−8·2 (5·5)	−7·1 (5·3)	−4·0 (5·2)	+0·5 (9·8)	−1·0 (1·0)	+4·3 (7·1)	−6·2 (5·2)
Reference Troughs										
No. of leads, lags, coincidences	4, 4, 1	3, 3, 1	4, 4, 0	4, 2, 0	2, 3, 1	4, 2, 0	4, 3, 0	3, 1, 0	3, 1, 0	3, 2, 0
Av. lead (−) or lag (+) in months	+1·8 (7·3)	+2·0 (7·7)	+1·0 (4·2)	−2·3 (5·4)	+3·3 (6·4)	−2·3 (8·7)	+2·1 (8·7)	−1·8 (7·4)	−5·4 (4·0)	−0·6 (8·5)
AVERAGE DURATION OF SPECIFIC CYCLES (in months)										
Expansion	21·2 (13·6)	32·0 (17·0)	26·8 (9·0)	29·1 (13·9)	20·2 (11·2)	36·3 (17·2)	17·4 (9·2)	24·8 (18·2)	51·0 (8·7)	16·2 (9·6)
Contraction	22·9 (8·1)	23·1 (8·4)	29·2 (11·8)	23·9 (7·2)	25·6 (10·6)	33·2 (9·6)	24·0 (8·2)	23·4 (11·0)	16·3 (3·6)	28·5 (13·7)
Full cycle	44·1 (19·4)	55·1 (20·6)	56·0 (13·8)	53·0 (19·2)	45·8 (13·9)	69·5 (22·8)	41·4 (14·5)	48·2 (27·0)	67·3 (11·1)	44·7 (11·7)

ᵃ The figures in parentheses show the mean deviation measured from the averages given to their left. The size of the mean deviation as compared with the average serves as a measure of the degree of dispersion of the individual items around the mean, and therefore is an indicator of the extent of uniformity of behaviour from cycle to cycle.

this characteristic is discussed further below; but it may be stated briefly that it stems simply from the conservative, non-speculative nature of most of the shares included in the index.

A comparison of the measures of duration reveals specific cycles somewhat shorter in duration than reference cycles in the index inclusive of mine shares, and somewhat longer in the exclusive index. This difference exists because the index exclusive of mines has two cycles fewer than the inclusive index. The two additional specific cycles appear during the period between the peaks of 1824–5 and 1836. Only one mild cyclical movement with a peak in December 1829 can be detected in the index exclusive of mines during this period. Three distinct cycles, however, with peaks in December 1827, May 1830, and February 1834 appear in the inclusive index. The addition of the mine-share subgroup to the total index introduces a component with cycles which are shorter in duration than the average of the other subgroups, and the effect of the inclusion is to lower the average duration of the index including mine shares to 44 (19)[1] months compared to a figure of 55 (21) when mines are excluded. In the decade after 1825, although mining shares had already begun their long decline, they were still the object of occasional, ill-fated speculative revivals; and these explain the shorter average duration of cycles in the inclusive index.

The inclusive index has longer contractions relative to expansions than the exclusive index, reflecting the downward pressure exerted by mine shares after 1825. Excluding mine shares, share prices tended to rise on the average over as many months as business in general was expanding, but fell over a somewhat longer period than reference contractions.

The duration of cycles in the subgroup indexes varies in length from 41 months, in the case of gas-light companies, to 70 months, in the case of insurance companies. Shares which sold in a bear market over a greater part of the period typically were, of course, falling in price for more months than their prices were rising. Mine, gas-light company, dock, and canal share prices had longer periods of contractions than expansions. Insurance company share prices, which exhibited cycles of the longest duration, typically were declining over more months than any other subgroup, while cycles in bank share prices, with the longest duration next to insurance shares, were characterized by expansion of greater absolute duration than any other subgroup.

5. **Cyclical Amplitude and Secular Change in Share Prices.** The amplitudes of cyclical swings are measured by finding the rise of the specific-cycle relatives from the initial trough of a cycle to the peak, and the fall from the peak to the terminal trough. The results show rise and fall in percentages of the average value of the series during the specific cycle that is being measured. Table 21 presents the percentage figures for the

---

[1] The figures in parentheses represent the average deviation of the individual cycle durations around the mean given to the left. When compared with the size of the mean itself the measure of deviation serves as a check on the reliability of the average.

TABLE 21. Amplitude of Specific Cycles in Total Share Price Indexes

Total index of share prices, inclusive of mines

Expansion		Contraction	Total movement			Movement per month		
			Rise	Fall	Rise and fall	Rise	Fall	Rise and fall
Feb. 1813	June 1814	Sept. 1816	8	25	33	0·5	0·9	0·8
Oct. 1816	Jan. 1819	Jan. 1820	33	9	42	1·2	0·7	1·0
Feb. 1820	Feb. 1825	June 1827	170	149	319	2·8	5·1	3·6
July 1827	Jan. 1828	Aug. 1829	15	20	35	2·5	1·0	1·3
Sept. 1829	June 1830	Apr. 1832	14	35	49	1·6	1·5	1·5
May 1832	Mar. 1834	June 1835	20	13	33	0·9	0·8	0·9
July 1835	June 1836	Apr. 1837	25	23	48	2·3	2·1	2·2
May 1837	Apr. 1838	Dec. 1839	7	19	26	0·6	0·9	0·8
Jan. 1840	July 1840	Oct. 1841	9	21	30	1·5	1·3	1·4
Nov. 1841	July 1845	Oct. 1849	49	52	101	1·1	1·0	1·1
AVERAGE . . .			35·0	36·6	71·6	1·5	1·5	1·5
AVERAGE DEVIATION .			(29·8)	(25·6)	(55·4)	(0·6)	(0·8)	(0·6)

Total index of share prices, exclusive of mines

Expansion		Contraction	Total movement			Movement per month		
			Rise	Fall	Rise and fall	Rise	Fall	Rise and fall
Feb. 1813	May 1814	Sept. 1816	8	25	33	0·5	0·9	0·8
Oct. 1816	Dec. 1818	Jan. 1820	32	8	40	1·2	0·6	1·0
Feb. 1820	Oct. 1824	Sept. 1826	41	30	71	0·7	1·2	0·9
Oct. 1826	Dec. 1829	Sept. 1831	9	15	24	0·2	0·7	0·4
Oct. 1831	May 1836	Apr. 1837	40	30	70	0·7	2·7	1·0
May 1837	Mar. 1838	Dec. 1839	14	11	25	1·3	0·5	0·8
Jan. 1840	June 1840	Oct. 1841	12	13	25	2·0	0·8	1·1
Nov. 1841	July 1845	Oct. 1849	48	55	103	1·1	1·1	1·1
. .		. .	25·5	23·4	48·9	1·0	1·1	0·9
. .		. .	(14·8)	(11·6)	(24·4)	(0·4)	(0·5)	(0·2)

individual specific cycles in the two total indexes. Another set of measures shows the amplitude per month. These per-month amplitudes are a resultant of the relation between the absolute amplitude and the duration of specific cycles. Now, in general, there is a much wider degree of variation among the absolute amplitude measures of the various series than among the measures of duration. The duration of cycles in the subgroup indexes varies in length, it will be recalled, from 41 months to 70 months. The amplitude variation is much greater, ranging from 30 in the case of banks to 122 for mines. Even if mines are excluded, the amplitude variation is much greater than the variation in duration.

Share prices of financial institutions—banks and insurance companies—reveal the smallest degree of volatility on the basis of per-month amplitude, while prices of railway and mine shares show the greatest oscillation. The latter are the only types of securities included in our indexes which, in the course of this period, were the objects of large-scale public speculation. Since railways and foreign mines were relatively new types of enterprise, offering the investor no record of past earnings by which to judge future prospects, promoters were able to arouse expectations far in excess of reasonable hopes. Moreover, when an industry is new and promises to expand in response to an unsatisfied demand, it is not difficult to understand why the public should be susceptible to the arts of promotion. Of course, when the actual achievements of these companies fell short of expectations, there was an inevitable reaction. On the other hand, banks and insurance companies, because of the nature of their business, were characterized by relatively more stable incomes, and their share prices more closely reflected actual earnings. It should be remembered, too, that our indexes include only those banking and insurance enterprises whose shares were quoted continuously. If firms which had failed were included, the average amplitude of the subgroups might well have been greater.

Measures of average percentage changes from cycle to cycle indicate the net trend movement over the entire period. Table 22 presents these measures. There is a slight but clear-cut upward trend in the exclusive index, but no significant secular movement appears when the influence of mining shares is present. The inclusive index rises sharply to 1825, and, in net, falls in the following twenty-five years, at a decelerating rate.

The most spectacular trend of all is the steep fall in mine shares until 1841 from their peak in January 1825. The frenzy in the mine share market which reached its zenith in the latter year could not be sustained after mining operations were actually begun and the expected rich veins proved a mirage. The depreciation in the prices of mine securities after 1825 reflected, then, the thorough disillusionment of shareholders in this field of investment.

In contrast to the direction of the secular trend of mine shares, waterworks reveal a most pronounced upward movement. In 1818 the waterworks companies arrived at a monopolistic agreement which arbitrarily

TABLE 22. *Average Cyclical Amplitude and Secular Change in the Share Price Indexes*[a]

	(1) Total, including mines	(2) Total, excluding mines	(3) Canals	(4) Waterworks	(5) Docks	(6) Insurance	(7) Gas-light	(8) Railways	(9) Banks	(10) Mines
AVERAGE AMPLITUDE OF RELATIVES										
Total movement										
Rise	35·0 (29·8)	25·5 (14·8)	18·1 (12·9)	30·5 (19·9)	19·7 (8·5)	21·7 (8·9)	16·5 (3·4)	46·0 (20·0)	17·0 (4·0)	50·8 (25·1)
Fall	36·6 (25·6)	23·4 (11·6)	24·0 (13·0)	20·2 (12·8)	21·3 (9·9)	18·5 (4·8)	18·9 (11·6)	41·8 (24·2)	13·0 (4·0)	71·0 (31·3)
Rise and fall	71·6 (55·4)	48·9 (24·4)	42·1 (17·4)	50·8 (27·2)	41·0 (10·4)	40·2 (11·6)	35·4 (12·7)	87·7 (44·2)	30·0 (7·3)	121·8 (31·1)
Movement per month										
Rise	1·5 (0·6)	1·0 (0·4)	0·7 (0·3)	1·2 (0·7)	1·1 (0·4)	0·8 (0·4)	0·2 (0·5)	2·9 (1·6)	0·3 (0·0)	3·6 (0·9)
Fall	1·5 (0·8)	1·1 (0·5)	0·8 (0·3)	0·8 (0·4)	0·9 (0·2)	0·6 (0·2)	0·7 (0·2)	2·0 (1·1)	0·8 (0·2)	3·5 (1·9)
Rise and fall	1·5 (0·6)	0·9 (0·2)	0·8 (0·2)	1·0 (0·5)	0·9 (0·1)	0·6 (0·2)	0·9 (0·2)	2·3 (1·1)	0·4 (0·1)	2·8 (0·6)
SECULAR MOVEMENTS (in percentages)										
Av. change from cycle to cycle	+1·8 (14·2)	+6·4 (6·4)	-2·0 (13·1)	+16·0 (9·1)	+1·2 (15·9)	+6·0 (4·0)	-0·6 (7·8)	+13·0 (21·0)	+6·0 (0·0)	-35·6 (34·7)
Weighted av. change per month from cycle to cycle	-0·04	+0·12	-0·03	+0·31	+0·03	+0·08	-0·01	+0·33	+0·09	-0·77

[a] See note to Table 20.

shared the markets and eliminated competition. In the face of London's
rapid growth, and a correspondingly expanding demand, they were enabled
by virtue of this agreement to raise their rates. The rising trend of railway
share prices, however, is attributable to the sound appraisal by investors
of the prospects of the new mode of transportation, which was rapidly
superseding rival forms of carriage. Even the sharp deflation following
upon the crisis of 1836 constituted only a temporary interruption in the
upward trend, which was resumed in the following year. It is difficult to
judge with confidence, on the basis of our index which terminates in 1850,
whether the decline after the railway mania of 1845 represents more than
prolonged cyclical contraction. In any case, the trend from 1827 until 1845
is unmistakably positive.

There is also a rising trend—slight but consistent—in the share prices
of joint-stock banks and insurance companies, a natural outcome of the
growing need for the type of accommodation that these institutions provided. On the other hand, no significant trend movements can be detected
in the indexes of dock or gas-light shares.

The figure for average intercycle change in canal share prices does not
adequately represent the true secular movement of this index. It appears
as only −0·03 per cent. But the bulk of the decline is concentrated in the
period beginning in February 1839, after which it is much steeper than the
average figure for the whole period. The over-all average figures for intercycle change are not true reflectors of secular movements wherever those
movements change direction within the period for which the average is
constructed. There is actually a rising trend in canal share prices until
1824, indicating that the form of inland transportation they provided was
still an essential element in the economy. It is not until after 1824 that
threatened railway competition begins to depress the canal share market;
and by the late thirties this competition becomes an active reality.

In the light of these trend movements, how did the investor, who
throughout the period held a representative group of securities, fare? If
an investor had spent any given number of pounds, k, in 1811 on a portfolio
of securities which in miniature included proportionately all shares listed
on the Exchange; and if subsequently he had bought and sold shares in
such a manner that the representativeness of his portfolio was maintained
intact, would the market value of his portfolio in 1850 have been less than,
equal to, or greater than k? On the basis of our index it appears that such
an investor would have been 20 per cent. worse off in 1850 than he was in
1811 in terms of pounds sterling.[1] But perhaps the comparison should not
be made for the initial and terminal years of the index but for the two
points of time that represent similar phases of cycles. Thus, if the index at

[1] However, if he had been conservative
and steered clear of mine shares, the cash
value of his investment would in 1850 have
been just about equal to its value in 1811.
On the other hand, in so far as the index is
overweighted with better-than-average securities, investors would have been worse
off in 1850 than this comparison shows. See
above, pp. 363–7, on techniques employed
in constructing the index.

the trough of the first cycle (1816) is compared with its value at the trough of the last cycle (1849), the position of our investor would not have altered materially between the two years.

6. Rates of Change in Share Prices. To show the behaviour of a series during the course of its specific cycles in detail, each specific cycle is segmented into nine stages. Stages I, V, and IX cover the three months centred on the initial revival, the recession, and the terminal revival, respectively. Stages II to IV cover successive thirds of the phase of expansion, and stages VI to VIII successive thirds of the phase of contraction. By averaging the specific-cycle relatives for the months included in each of these stages, we get the standing of the series at nine points during the course of the cycle. When charted, the 'specific-cycle patterns' are vividly represented. 'Reference-cycle patterns' are made on a similar plan, but the nine stages are marked off by the turning-dates of general business.

Next the rates of change per month from stage to stage in each specific and reference cycle are computed, to learn the changing pace of rise and fall. Table 23 presents the average percentage rates of change from stage to stage of specific and reference cycles for each of the indexes. Before analysing the significance of the average patterns, the relationships revealed by average rates of change will first be explained.

It is clear from Table 23 that the rate of change in share prices was far from steady during successive stages of specific-cycle expansion and contraction. The impulse to buy strengthened and weakened in the course of the price rise, while the urge to sell also manifested itself with varying intensity at different stages during the course of the price fall. A concentration of the maxima in the rates of change of the various indexes occurs in stage III–IV, from the middle to the last third of expansion. Prices of canal, waterworks, insurance, gas-light, and railway shares were bid up most strongly during the latter stages of their rise. The two total indexes also share this characteristic. The most violent movements, as might be expected, tend to occur in the two speculative groups, mines and railways.

Although the rates of rise exceeded the rates of fall in five of the subgroups, both total indexes tended to decline at a steeper rate than that of their rise. The most violent declines in share prices appear to have occurred during stage V–VI, the interval of transition from recession to contraction. The highest average rate of change in any stage in all of the indexes occurs in mine shares during stage VI–VII, but the size of the average deviation reduces the significance of the figure. The momentum of unloading mine shares evidently increased as soon as the first seeds of suspicion regarding the soundness of the investment had been sown. In most of the indexes a second concentration of high rates of decline occurs in stage VII–VIII, indicating that the desire to sell shares was not spent in the first stage of reaction.

In discussing the rates of change in share prices during specific cycles, the timing of the successive stages varies for each series. A comparison of

TABLE 23. *Average Percentage Rates of Change from Stage to Stage of Specific and Reference Cycles in the Share Price Indexes*[a]

	(1) Total, including mines	(2) Total, excluding mines	(3) Canals	(4) Waterworks	(5) Docks	(6) Insurance	(7) Gas-light	(8) Railways	(9) Banks	(10) Mines
Specific cycles										
AVERAGE RATES OF CHANGE (per month)										
From I to II	+1·2 (0·6)	+0·7 (0·4)	+0·8 (0·6)	+0·5 (0·3)	+1·0 (0·6)	+0·4 (0·3)	+1·6 (1·0)	+2·9 (1·1)	+0·4 (0·1)	+3·4 (1·7)
,, II to III	+1·2 (1·3)	+0·3 (0·6)	+0·4 (0·6)	+0·4 (0·5)	+1·4 (1·0)	+0·7 (0·4)	+0·9 (0·4)	+1·0 (2·0)	+0·5 (0·1)	+4·8 (2·4)
,, III to IV	+2·0 (1·2)	+1·5 (1·0)	+0·8 (0·6)	+2·4 (2·1)	+1·1 (0·6)	+1·0 (0·6)	+1·4 (0·9)	+4·8 (3·1)	+0·3 (0·1)	+4·1 (2·3)
,, IV to V	+1·9 (2·7)	+1·0 (0·8)	+0·6 (0·4)	+1·0 (1·2)	+0·2 (0·7)	+0·7 (0·8)	+0·2 (0·5)	+2·2 (1·1)	+0·1 (0·1)	+1·7 (2·8)
,, V to VI	−2·8 (2·2)	−1·2 (0·6)	−1·2 (0·6)	−1·4 (0·8)	−0·7 (0·4)	−0·6 (0·5)	−1·0 (0·2)	−3·0 (0·4)	−0·9 (0·4)	−3·2 (1·2)
,, VI to VII	−2·3 (1·8)	−0·9 (0·6)	−0·7 (0·6)	−0·5 (0·5)	−0·8 (0·5)	−0·7 (0·5)	−0·5 (0·4)	−1·6 (1·6)	−1·2 (0·5)	−7·3 (7·3)
,, VII to VIII	−1·1 (0·4)	−1·3 (0·5)	−0·8 (0·5)	−0·7 (0·4)	−1·3 (0·8)	−0·7 (0·4)	−1·0 (0·4)	−1·9 (1·0)	−0·6 (0·2)	−2·8 (1·8)
,, VIII to IX	−1·8 (1·8)	−0·8 (0·7)	−0·4 (0·6)	−0·8 (0·5)	−0·5 (0·7)	−0·3 (0·1)	0·0 (0·5)	−1·7 (1·3)	−0·4 (0·5)	−2·1 (1·4)
Reference cycles										
AVERAGE RATES OF CHANGE (per month)										
From I to II	0·0 (0·8)	0·0 (0·6)	+0·2 (0·5)	−0·4 (1·5)	0·0 (0·6)	−0·1 (0·7)	+0·3 (0·6)	+0·1 (1·1)	+0·4 (0·3)	−0·1 (2·3)
,, II to III	+0·1 (0·9)	+0·5 (0·7)	+0·3 (0·4)	+0·6 (1·1)	+0·3 (0·9)	+0·3 (0·5)	+0·4 (0·5)	+0·8 (1·2)	+0·5 (0·1)	−2·3 (4·2)
,, III to IV	0·0 (0·2)	+0·1 (0·9)	−0·1 (1·0)	+0·5 (1·0)	−0·3 (1·2)	+0·1 (0·6)	−0·2 (0·7)	0·0 (1·4)	0·0 (0·7)	−1·2 (1·4)
,, IV to V	+0·2 (1·8)	0·0 (0·7)	−0·2 (0·5)	−0·6 (0·9)	−0·6 (0·9)	−0·3 (0·5)	−0·3 (0·8)	+0·8 (2·0)	0·0 (0·4)	−2·8 (2·2)
,, V to VI	−1·9 (1·8)	−0·9 (0·7)	−0·1 (0·6)	−0·9 (0·8)	−0·7 (0·5)	−0·5 (0·6)	−0·9 (0·8)	−1·9 (1·7)	−0·5 (0·5)	−0·2 (2·6)
,, VI to VII	−1·8 (2·4)	−0·8 (1·0)	−0·5 (0·7)	−0·6 (0·6)	−0·7 (0·5)	−0·5 (0·5)	−0·3 (0·6)	−1·0 (2·5)	−0·5 (0·8)	−0·7 (2·4)
,, VII to VIII	−0·8 (0·9)	−0·5 (0·6)	−0·6 (0·6)	−0·3 (0·5)	−0·1 (0·5)	−0·2 (0·5)	−0·3 (0·7)	−1·0 (1·0)	−0·4 (0·6)	−0·2 (1·8)
,, VIII to IX	−0·2 (1·2)	−0·6 (0·7)	−0·7 (0·9)	0·0 (0·7)	−0·2 (0·7)	−0·2 (0·4)	+0·2 (0·8)	−1·4 (1·3)	+0·2 (0·4)	+0·2 (2·6)

a See footnote to Table 20.

the rates of change during reference cycles, however, gives a picture of the relations among the movements of the different series during the same time periods, i.e. the stages of cyclical expansion and contraction in general business. Two significant characteristics of the cyclical behaviour of share prices are revealed by the rate of change from stage to stage of the reference cycles. In the first place it is noteworthy that every subgroup, on the average, has more stages with negative than with positive rates of change. Gas-light companies, railways, and banks tended to have three stages with rising rates; canals, waterworks, and insurance companies, two stages; and docks and mines, only one stage each. The two total indexes show only two stages with rising rates of change. During most business cycles, then, share prices were largely falling away. A corollary to the absence of a preponderance of positive rates of change in share prices is their low numerical values, when they are positive. The highest average positive rate in the inclusive index is $+0·2$; the highest average negative rate, $-1·9$. In the exclusive index, the two comparable figures are $+0·5$ and $-0·9$. The maximum average positive rate in the sub-indexes is $+0·8$. The maximum average negative rate is $-2·8$. The next highest positive rate is $+0·6$, the next highest negative rate, $-2·3$.[1]

A second feature of the behaviour of share prices clearly revealed by the average rates of change is the nature of the process of rise. There seems to be a tendency towards a slow recovery in share prices, which rapidly gathers momentum, and tails off before general business reaches its peak. Thus the total index exclusive of mines shows its greatest average rate of expansion in stage II–III, a lower positive rate in stage III–IV, and a negative rate in stage IV–V.[2] In four of the sub-indexes the rate of change is zero or negative in stage I–II, and in seven of the subgroups the downturn, on the average, in the rate comes not later than stage III–IV.[3]

In general, then, share prices did not exhibit a strong upward tendency during reference cycles. And once a rise in share prices did get under way, it tended to collapse rather earlier than did general business expansions.

Share prices fall most rapidly between the first and middle thirds of reference contraction, although the rate of decline slackens only slightly

[1] Both these high negative rates are found in mine shares. This sub-index, however, may not be considered representative. The next highest rates are found in the railway sub-index ($-1·9$). It is true that if these two sub-groups are excluded there is little difference between the size of the positive and negative rates of change in the other sub-indexes.

[2] This process of rise does not manifest itself so clearly in the average rates of change of the index inclusive of mines, principally because of the concentration of the price increase in mine shares in stages III–V of the reference cycle from 1819 to 1826. As a result the average rates of change of the inclusive index exhibit a maximum in stage IV–V.

[3] In the railway sub-index the average rate of change from stage IV–V is positive, but the figure is unrepresentative. In the reference cycle from 1832 to 1837, during which the early railway boom occurred, shares surged upward tremendously during the interval from the last third of reference expansion to the onset of contraction. This movement produces an uncharacteristically high positive average rate of change during the stage IV–V of railway shares.

during the interval between the middle and last thirds of the contraction phase. In the two total indexes as well as in waterworks, docks, banks, insurance, and gas-light companies, the rate of fall is abated as reference contraction comes to a close. The opposite progression seems to character-ize the movements of canal share prices, which fall more sharply, on the average, as reference contraction proceeds. The average rates of change for railways and mines during reference contraction do not move so regularly as in the other sub-indexes. The rate of fall in these two subgroups is at a maximum early in reference contraction, declines, and then increases again.

Although for most purposes we consider each business cycle as one unit of observation, disregarding variations in duration and amplitude between different cycles, we have noted at least one distinction between the succes-sive cycles from 1793 to 1848. In Part I of Vol. II the reference cycles are classified according to the magnitude of domestic investment during their course. All cycles, it is here argued, were characterized by increases in the volume of exports, but the relative movement of domestic investment offers a criterion for dividing the cycles into two groups. Cycles marked by large increases in domestic investment as well as in the volume of exports are designated major ; while cycles during which such investment cannot be traced, but during which the volume of exports and other over-all variables increased, are designated minor. The following grouping results :[1]

Business-cycle Classification

Major cycles	Minor cycles
1816–19	1811–16
1819–26	1826–9
1832–7	1829–32
1842–8	1837–42

When the rates of change are averaged for major and minor cycles respectively, a marked difference in the behaviour of the share indexes during the two types of cycles is brought to light (see Table 24). The total inclusive index exhibits average rise only in the course of major-cycle expansions, and that rise occurs principally late in the expansion phase. The exclusive index, while rising somewhat in minor cycles, shows a pro-nounced upswing only in major cycles. And here the pattern of a slow rise in share prices in stage I–II succeeded by a more rapid rate of rise between stages II–IV, and a lower rate of rise in stage IV–V, emerges most clearly. The minor cycles do not share in this process of rise. The later stages of expansion of minor cycles, however, do exhibit either larger rates of decline or smaller rates of rise than do the early stages. The absence of speculative

---

[1] In Vol. II the annual dating of cycles is employed. Only one reference cycle could be detected in the annual data from 1842 to 1848, whereas two have been marked off on the monthly basis. For purposes of this classification the two monthly cycles 1842–6 and 1846–8 have been treated as a single unit here, with the peak in September 1845.

spirit in minor cycles is attested to by this behaviour. The average rates of decline during major-cycle contractions are, also, considerably greater than for the minor cycle contractions.

TABLE 24. *Average Rates of Change (per month) from Stage to Stage of Major and Minor Reference Cycles in the Total Share Price Indexes*[a]

Stages	Major cycles		Minor cycles	
	Total index, including mines	Total index, excluding mines	Total index, including mines	Total index, excluding mines
I–II	+0·7 (0·4)	+0·4 (0·4)	−0·3 (0·8)	0·0 (0·6)
II–III	+1·0 (0·8)	+1·0 (0·7)	−0·4 (0·6)	+0·3 (0·4)
III–IV	+1·3 (0·6)	+1·0 (0·2)	−0·7 (0·9)	−0·3 (0·7)
IV–V	+2·1 (2·3)	+0·7 (1·1)	−1·4 (0·6)	−0·6 (0·2)
V–VI	−2·7 (3·6)	−0·6 (0·9)	−1·1 (0·3)	−0·8 (0·5)
VI–VII	−3·8 (4·1)	−1·6 (1·0)	−0·4 (0·5)	−0·2 (0·2)
VII–VIII	−1·8 (0·9)	−1·1 (0·3)	0·0 (0·6)	0·0 (0·6)
VIII–IX	−0·1 (1·1)	−0·4 (0·7)	+0·3 (1·1)	−0·5 (0·6)

[a] See footnote to Table 20.

Major cycles thus appear to have been characterized by more intense activity in the share market than minor cycles. This conclusion bears out the distinction drawn between the two types of cycles, in terms of the more important role of domestic investment in major cycles. It would be only reasonable to expect share prices to respond to the same sort of long-term confidence which induced large-scale new investment. The fact that the share indexes have such mild movements relative to the violent sweeps in investment is only another indication of their limited coverage of domestic industry.

7. The Cyclical Patterns of the Indexes. In trying to determine whether the cycles in share prices did or did not conform regularly to the waves in general business activity, an important aid is the observation of the similarity or the difference between the specific-cycle and the reference-cycle patterns of the series. The closer the turns in specific cycles conform in timing to business cycles, the closer the identity of the two patterns. If the specific cycles have no systematic relationship in time to the turns of business cycles, however, the clear-cut pattern of the specific cycles is obscured or disappears on a reference-cycle basis.

Fig. 94 presents the average specific and reference-cycle patterns for each of the share indexes. The chief impression conveyed by the average patterns is that share prices bore a rather irregular relationship to business cycles. The most striking difference between the two total indexes is the downward tilt of the cyclical patterns of the inclusive index, indicative of its declining secular trend. The charts picture the longer expansion phase of specific cycles in the exclusive index, and the large amplitude of specific cycles in the inclusive index. The one pattern in which the reference dates

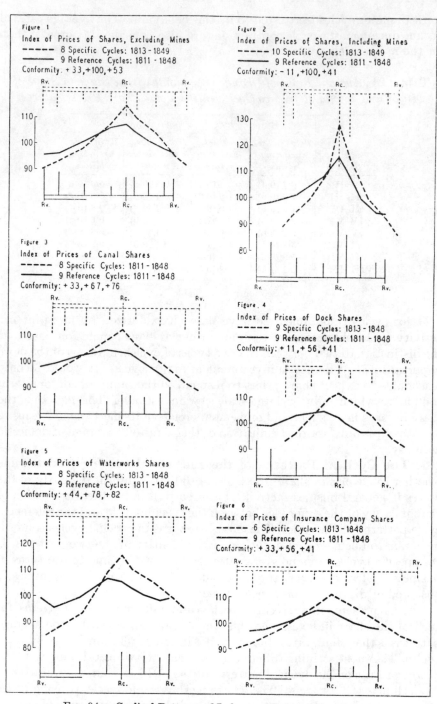

FIG. 94 a. Cyclical Patterns of Indexes of British Share Prices

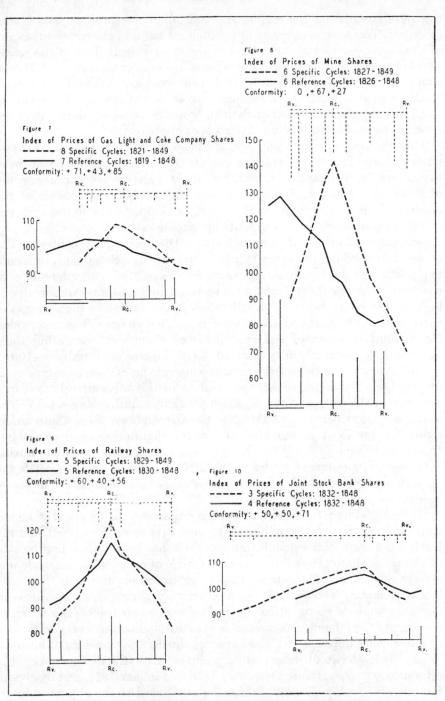

FIG. 94b. Cyclical Patterns of Indexes of British Share Prices

completely obliterate the regular rise and fall of the specific cycles is that for mines. The enormous range of the fluctuations and the conspicuous size of the average deviations overshadow the cyclical behaviour of the series. The behaviour of mine shares during one business cycle had so little relation to its behaviour during another that the averages of the reference-cycle relatives over a number of business cycles reveal mainly the declining secular trend. In all the other figures, however, some similarity between specific- and reference-cycle patterns is easily perceived.

Though it is possible to judge on the basis of the comparison of the two patterns, whether or not the movements of share prices match business cycles closely, a numerical expression of the degree of conformity would obviously be superior. For this purpose, following the procedure of the National Bureau of Economic Research, we divide the reference cycles of the share price series into segments of 'expansion' and 'contraction', by determining during what reference stages they commonly contract. The stages during which the series typically rise are 'associated with reference expansion', while the remaining stages are 'associated with reference contraction'. Indexes of conformity are then computed to show uniformity or lack of uniformity between the direction of movement in the segment of expansion and contraction and the corresponding phases of business cycles. No account is taken of the magnitude of change in calculating these indexes. Positive conformity is rated +100, inverse conformity, −100.

Table 25 presents the standings at the nine stages of each reference cycle for the two total indexes. An examination of this table reveals that in a majority of the reference cycles, share prices rose during stages I–IV. The average reference-cycle patterns for the two indexes show share prices rising in stage IV–V as well; but the average figure is not representative. In six out of nine cycles (in both indexes) share prices were falling during this stage. The reference cycles of the exclusive index, however, show the pattern of rise in stages I–IV more consistently than those of the inclusive index.

Matching stages I–IV with reference expansion yields slightly higher conformity for the exclusive than for the inclusive total index (see Table 26). Both series show perfect conformity to reference contraction, i.e. the rate of change of share prices during stages IV–IX of every reference cycle was always downward. The relationship to reference expansion is, however, less systematic. The inclusive index actually shows more instances of declining than of rising prices during reference expansion. The index of conformity for reference expansion is negative, indicating a preponderance of movements opposite to those expected during the upswings of business cycles. At least two of these contrary movements—the decline during the reference expansions from December 1826 to January 1829, and from September 1837 to March 1839—are to be attributed to the almost uninterrupted deflation to which mining shares were subject for over fifteen years after the end of the 1824–5 speculation.

TABLE 25. *Average Standings during Nine Stages of Successive Reference Cycles in the Share Price Indexes*

(a) Index of Prices of Shares, including Mines

Stages[a]	1811–16		1816–19		1819–26		1826–9		1829–32		1832–7		1837–42		1842–6		1846–8	
	Period covered	Average standing	Period covered	Average standing	Period covered	Average standing	Period covered	Average standing	Period covered	Average standing	Period covered	Average standing	Period covered	Average standing	Period covered	Average standing	Period covered	Average standing
I Revival	Oct. 1811	109	Oct. 1816	78	Oct. 1819	70	Dec. 1826	107	Jan. 1830	121	Aug. 1832	87	Sept. 1837	110	Dec. 1842	80	Oct. 1846	114
II	Nov. 1811–Nov. 1812	106	Nov. 1816–June 1817	81	Nov. 1819–Aug. 1821	69	Jan. 1827–Aug. 1827	99	Feb. 1830–May 1830	121	Sept. 1832–Nov. 1833	97	Oct. 1837–Mar. 1838	113	Jan. 1843–Nov. 1843	85	Nov. 1846–Dec. 1846	112
III	Dec. 1812–Jan. 1814	100	July 1817–Jan. 1818	97	Sept. 1821–June 1823	76	Sept. 1827–Apr. 1828	106	June 1830–Oct. 1830	114	Dec. 1833–Feb. 1835	98	Apr. 1838–Sept. 1838	110	Dec. 1843–Oct. 1844	99	Jan. 1847–Mar. 1847	110
IV	Feb. 1814–Mar. 1815	104	Feb. 1818–Sept. 1818	108	July 1823–May 1825	130	May 1828–Jan. 1829	103	Nov. 1830–Mar. 1831	101	Mar. 1835–May 1836	102	Oct. 1838–Mar. 1839	109	Nov. 1844–Sept. 1845	111	Apr. 1847	106
V Recession	Apr. 1815	100	Oct. 1818	109	June 1825	209	Feb. 1829	93	Apr. 1831	95	June 1836	118	Apr. 1839	105	Oct. 1845	108	May 1847	105
VI	May 1815–Sept. 1815	96	Nov. 1818–Jan. 1819	111	July 1825–Nov. 1825	179	Mar. 1829–May 1829	90	May 1831–Sept. 1831	92	July 1836–Oct. 1836	114	May 1839–June 1840	100	Nov. 1845–Jan. 1846	105	June 1847–Oct. 1847	103
VII	Oct. 1815–Mar. 1816	93	Feb. 1819–May 1819	111	Dec. 1825–May 1826	113	June 1829–Aug. 1829	92	Oct. 1831–Feb. 1832	86	Nov. 1836–Apr. 1837	103	July 1840–Aug. 1841	95	Feb. 1846–June 1846	107	Nov. 1847–Mar. 1848	96
VIII	Apr. 1816–Sept. 1816	87	June 1819–Sept. 1819	108	June 1826–Nov. 1826	92	Sept. 1829–Dec. 1829	95	Mar. 1832–July 1832	87	Apr. 1837–Aug. 1837	95	Sept. 1841–Nov. 1842	91	June 1846–Sept. 1846	107	Apr. 1848–Sept. 1848	89
IX Revival	Oct. 1816	81	Oct. 1819	106	Dec. 1826	99	Jan. 1830	101	Aug. 1832	87	Sept. 1837	94	Dec. 1842	94	Oct. 1846	103	Oct. 1848	82

ᵃ The standings at stages I, V, and IX are averages of the three months centred on the month of the initial revival, the recession, and the terminal revival.

TABLE 25 (cont.)

(b) Index of Prices of Shares, excluding Mines

Stages[a]	1811–16 Period covered	Average standing	1816–19 Period covered	Average standing	1819–26 Period covered	Average standing	1826–9 Period covered	Average standing	1829–32 Period covered	Average standing	1832–7 Period covered	Average standing	1837–42 Period covered	Average standing	1842–6 Period covered	Average standing	1846–8 Period covered	Average standing
I Revival	Oct. 1811	109	Oct. 1816	78	Oct. 1819	87	Dec. 1826	96	Jan. 1830	109	Aug. 1832	91	Sept. 1837	95	Dec. 1842	81	Oct. 1846	114
II	Nov. 1811–Nov. 1812	106	Nov. 1816–May 1817	81	Nov. 1819–Aug. 1821	86	Jan. 1827–Aug. 1827	97	Feb. 1830–May 1830	107	Sept. 1832–Nov. 1833	91	Oct. 1837–Mar. 1838	99	Jan. 1843–Nov. 1843	86	Nov. 1846–Dec. 1846	112
III	Dec. 1812–Jan. 1814	100	June 1817–Jan. 1818	97	Sept. 1821–June 1823	95	Sept. 1827–Apr. 1828	100	June 1830–Oct. 1830	108	Dec. 1833–Feb. 1835	94	Apr. 1838–Sept. 1838	105	Dec. 1843–Oct. 1844	99	Jan. 1847–Feb. 1847	110
IV	Feb. 1814–Mar. 1815	104	Feb. 1818–Sept. 1818	108	July 1823–May 1825	116	May 1828–Jan. 1829	102	Nov. 1830–Mar. 1831	99	Mar. 1835–May 1836	105	Oct. 1838–Mar. 1839	105	Nov. 1844–Sept. 1845	111	Mar. 1847–Apr. 1847	106
V Recession	Apr. 1815	100	Oct. 1818	109	June 1825	116	Feb. 1829	101	Apr. 1831	96	June 1836	127	Apr. 1839	103	Oct. 1845	109	May 1847	105
VI	May 1815–Sept. 1815	95	Nov. 1818–Jan. 1819	111	July 1825–Nov. 1825	113	Mar. 1829–May 1829	100	May 1831–Sept. 1831	95	July 1836–Oct. 1836	122	May 1839–June 1840	99	Nov. 1845–Jan. 1846	105	June 1847–Oct. 1847	103
VII	Oct. 1815–Mar. 1816	93	Feb. 1819–May 1819	110	Dec. 1825–May 1826	102	June 1829–Aug. 1829	99	Oct. 1831–Mar. 1832	95	Nov. 1836–Mar. 1837	108	July 1840–Aug. 1841	100	Feb. 1846–May 1846	107	Nov. 1847–Mar. 1848	95
VIII	Apr. 1816–Sept. 1816	87	June 1819–Sept. 1819	108	June 1826–Nov. 1826	96	Sept. 1829–Dec. 1829	102	Mar. 1832–July 1832	97	Apr. 1837–Aug. 1837	100	Sept. 1841–Nov. 1842	98	June 1846–Sept. 1846	105	Apr. 1848–Sept. 1848	89
IX Revival	Oct. 1816	81	Oct. 1819	106	Dec. 1826	98	Jan. 1830	101	July 1832	96	Sept. 1837	100	Dec. 1842	101	Oct. 1846	102	Oct. 1848	83

[a] The standings at stages I, V, and IX are averages of the three months centred on the month of the initial revival, the recession, and the terminal revival.

Three cases of decline during the stages matched with reference expansion are common to both the exclusive and inclusive indexes. During the reference expansion from October 1811 to March 1815, share prices fall, except for a brief revival in the first quarter of 1814.[1] The final stages of the war were marked by government expenditures on a larger scale than

TABLE 26. *Conformity of Share Price Indexes to Business Cycles*

| | | Index of conformity to | | |
Index	Expansion stages	Reference expansion	Reference contraction	Business cycles
Total index including mines . .	I–IV	−11	+100	+41
Total index excluding mines . .	I–IV	+33	+100	+53
Canals	I–IV	+33	+67	+76
Waterworks . . .	VIII–IV	+44	+78	+82
Docks	I–IV	+11	+56	+41
Insurance. . . .	I–IV	+33	+56	+41
Gas-light	VIII–III	+71	+43	+85
Railways	I–IV	+60	+40	+56
Banks	VIII–IV	+50	+50	+71
Mines	VIII–III	0	+67	+27

at any other period.[2] The government's demands on the capital market limited, of course, the flow of investment in other directions; while the general political and military uncertainty was a further depressant force.[3] There were, of course, special influences affecting each of the subgroups which were not related to the general political or business environment. The most pronounced fall in price for 1811 to 1815 is registered by the waterworks sub-index. The London waterworks experienced a period of intensified competition during these years, induced by parliamentary action in an effort to protect the consumer. Rivalry for control of districts which the companies supplied in common led to rate-cutting and a severe depreciation in the value of their equities. Fire insurance companies also appear to have been subject to pressures, peculiar to them alone, from 1813 to 1815. Too much stress must not, then, be placed on generalization from political and economic conditions in the large to the particular movements of the share indexes. The fact that canal share prices, the one exception, actually rose during this reference expansion bears out this need for caution.

[1] This upswing coincided with rising commodity prices, accounted for by speculation in the re-export trade. Continental buying, it was expected, would greatly expand upon the break-up of the Napoleonic hegemony and the coming of peace. These hopes were disappointed and there followed a sharp curtailment of activity from the time of Waterloo until late in 1816.

[2] See above, pp. 131–2.

[3] It can hardly be stated for this period that the share index is directly sensitive to year-by-year changes in those political or military events that, on *a priori* grounds, might be expected to affect security prices. Some correspondence is, however, evident. The precipitate drop in 1815, accompanying Napoleon's hundred days' return, is to be noted.

The second instance of declining share prices during general business expansion (December 1829 to March 1831) occurred in the period of unrest preceding the passage of the Reform Bill. Actually the index began declining before the first agitation over the reform question started. Canal, dock, and insurance share prices reached a peak late in 1829 and fell through 1830. It is because of their movements that the total index declines during 1830. The reform issue, however, was not raised until November 1830. The decline in all share prices (with the exception of railways) after that month undoubtedly was a consequence of the alarm felt in conservative quarters over the outcome of political reform. Earlier in 1830, the revolution in France and Belgium, and the Russo-Polish War may have had depressing repercussions on the share market, but their influence was not so generally felt as was the agitation for reform. More likely the lack of new investment during this reference expansion was responsible for the sag in the total share index, although railway, gas-light company, and waterworks shares did evidence some increase in price during 1830. The upward movement in output and employment in 1830 appears to have been very modest, and largely confined to textiles. The type of business confidence associated with rising share prices was missing. Finally, share prices moved counter-cyclically during the reference expansion from September 1846 to April 1847. Every one of the subgroups except banks shared in the decline during these months, but the downward movement is strongest in railways. The business contraction following the collapse of the railway boom in 1845 was relieved towards the close of 1846 and early in 1847 by large exports to the United States, by an interval of easy money in the short-term market, and by the persistence of railway construction inaugurated in the previous boom.[1] No recovery, however, occurred in the share market. As in the case of mines after 1825, the calling up of payments on railway shares, purchased with a small initial outlay, continued after the peak of prices in 1845. The pressure to dispose of the shares, now that they were depreciating, and holding them involved further outlays, served to bring their prices even lower. The government, moreover, stipulated that a certain portion of the funds raised by the railways be placed on deposit with its agents. This action, by converting short- into long-term balances, kept the money market almost continuously tight in 1845–7.[2] More immediately, the cause of financial stringency during the last quarter of 1846, and the consequent further fall in share prices, was the need for large grain imports. From January 1847, however, railways calls and the crisis in Paris added to the pressure on the money market. Amidst these disturbing financial difficulties, it is not surprising that the share market failed to participate in that measure of business recovery which was experienced.

The typical cyclical patterns of the sub-indexes are essentially homologous. Four of the subgroups—canals, docks, insurance companies, and railways—show expansion in stages I–IV, like the total indexes. Water-

[1] See above, pp. 304–5.   [2] See above, pp. 329–36.

works and banks tend to anticipate the lower as well as the upper turning-point and their prices describe an VIII–IV pattern, while gas-light companies and mines have been designated as showing expansion in stages VIII–III. The average and the typical patterns coincide only in the cases of canals, insurance, and gas-light companies.

Arraying the subgroups in the order of magnitude of their indexes of conformity, beginning with the highest, yields the following results: gas-light companies, waterworks, canals, banks, railways, docks, insurance companies, mines.

On the basis of the numerical value of their indexes of conformity, the first five of the sub-indexes listed may be considered to have conformed rather well to business cycles. The index of gas-light companies shares is one of the two subgroups which conformed better to reference expansion than to contraction. The one instance of countercyclical behaviour during reference expansion occurred during the financial stringency of the last cycle which has just been described. Waterworks shares show two countercyclical movements not present in the total index. During the reference expansion from December 1826 to January 1829, the index exhibits, in net, no movement. This behaviour results from the decisive downward movement in the first half of 1828, which probably reflected shareholders' fears that some form of regulation of the industry would follow the parliamentary investigation then under way.[1] The reference contraction from May 1836 to August 1837 also did not affect waterworks shares. The explanation may be sought in the secure economic and legal position enjoyed by an industry of monopolists in the years from 1828 to 1845.

The sub-index of canal share prices and the total index excluding mines have the same numerical index of conformity to reference expansion. Canal share prices, however, moved in the expected direction during the war cycle when, it will be recalled, the total index was declining, but exhibited a contrary movement, not found in any of the other subgroups, including mines, during the reference expansion from December 1842 to September 1845. The reason for the decline in canal shares during this period is obvious. The encroachment of railway transportation, in some cases parallel to the water-ways, resulted not only in a diversion of traffic but also a forced reduction of rates on the canals. The railway boom was, by the same token, the canal slump. Before the advent of railway competition, however, the canals were a thriving investment. Trading in canal shares was brisk, and in two reference contractions their prices did not fall. Next among the well-conforming share sub-indexes is the group of joint-stock banks. During the four reference cycles covered by the sub-index, one contrary movement appears in reference expansion and contraction respectively. Bank shares rose from September 1845, when reference contraction began, although the rise was at a lesser rate than in the preceding

[1] See below, p. 428.

reference expansion. Possibly the effect of the Bank Charter Act of 1844 in sheltering the existing joint-stock banks from new competition[1] was to keep their share prices high, although the rest of the market was caught up in the liquidation which followed the break in railway share prices. Bank share prices did, however, fall off during the succeeding reference expansion when the money market was so unfavourable. Last in this group are the railways. Like the banks, railway shares declined in the last reference expansion, and rose during one reference contraction (March 1831 to July 1832). The success of the early railway ventures so far exceeded expectations that the shares were immune to the cyclical turns in general business. Even in the reference contraction from 1839 to 1842 there was no net downward movement in railway shares.

The remaining three subgroups behave even less regularly with respect to our reference dates than those thus far examined. In addition to the three countercyclical movements during reference expansion found in the total index, docks decline during the major business upswing from 1832 to 1836. Competition, excess capacity, and the falling profits of the industry from 1832 to 1835 (reference stages I–III) chiefly explain this behaviour. During stages III–V of this cycle (March 1835–June 1836) and the following one (October 1838–April 1839), however, dock shares stage a strong recovery. Because stage IV–V in dock share prices typically falls in reference contraction, the rising movement in this stage during these two cycles yields a net positive change in the contraction phase, although stages VI–IX actually do show declines.[2] The substantial increase during 1836–9 over the preceding years in total foreign tonnage entered and cleared at the Port of London appears to have brought fuller utilization of dock facilities, and to have enhanced the value of dock shares. Insurance shares move upward during two reference contractions, but in each case at a lesser rate than during the preceding, though not the following, expansion. The case of the mine shares calls for no special comment, the reasons for its irregular cyclical character having been sufficiently indicated above.

8. **Conclusions.** We have here surveyed the cyclical characteristics of two general indexes of share prices and of their eight component subindexes. In a sense any such analysis, from the perspective of business-cycle theory, must be unsatisfactory for Britain in the years 1811–50; for only two types of shares—those of mines and railways—were subject to the type of short-run influence that one associates contemporaneously with equities. And mine shares are so special a story that their behaviour contributes little to general analysis. It must be remembered that the long-term capital market was dominated by government floatations, even towards the end of our period. The bulk of our share prices represent rather safe and predictable investments in well-established firms. Their trend movements, of course, are clearly indicative of the long-run forces playing upon the

---

[1] See below, p. 441.

[2] In the reference contraction from Apr. 1839 to Nov. 1842, however, the price of dock shares moves upward in stages VII–IX.

respective industries, e.g. the rise and then the decline of canal shares. Several significant conclusions, nevertheless, about the shares included and about the role of the capital market generally may be drawn when the measures of cyclical behaviour are viewed in the light of other evidence.

The prevailing I–IV expansion pattern among the sub-indexes, for example, proceeds directly from the fact that our shares are closer to bond than to stock prices. Their upper turning-point anticipated the business-cycle peak simply because in the final, speculative stage of expansion their prices were bid down in competition with the more speculative types of investment then available: in 1824–5, mine shares; in 1835–6, railways and American securities; in 1844–5, railways. Like the anticipatory rise in the yield on Consols in stage IV–V, this typical movement represents truly a rise in the expected return from long-term capital investment in that stage.

We have discovered, further, that periods of rise in share prices were concentrated almost exclusively in what we have called 'major' expansions cycles, i.e. those characterized by considerable increases in new capital investment. The behaviour of our indexes thus fits this broad hypothesis. Share prices could be expected to decline in periods when the general incentives to invest were weak; when the supply of long-term investible funds was limited, and opportunities for profitable investment scarce. They could be expected to rise when those supply and demand conditions had changed, until the moment, at least, when there appeared in the capital market some type or types of new speculative security calculated to capture the imagination of Britain's relatively small investing class. At such moments Consols and most of the shares represented in our indexes were dumped on the market to an extent sufficient to lower their prices.

We have been dealing, then, with security prices which, in their cyclical behaviour, fall somewhere between bond and stock prices of today. With the exception of mines and rails, which most closely approximate modern industrial securities, they move less than stocks and exhibit a marked weakening at a moment during the business cycle when the upward movement of stocks might be expected to be most strong. But, like Consols, which share this mixed character, they continue to rise until a later stage of the business cycle than bond prices. This, of course, is indicative of the limited role of the capital market in a system where industrial investment was preponderantly financed out of individual or corporative hoards, and where the typical investor in the capital market was searching for security rather than speculative profit.

Chapter III

THE INSTITUTIONAL BACKGROUND TO THE
SHARE INDEXES

Introduction

THE period covered by the new share price indexes (1811–50) saw an important transition in British capital market and floatation institutions. At the turn of the century the Stock Exchange in London was almost wholly concerned with government issues, and a relatively small proportion of total investment took the form of company floatations. In the railway boom of the forties Consols were firmly pushed from the centre of Stock-Exchange activity and company floatation was, for a time at least, the instrument for the most substantial form of investment within the economy. It is the purpose of the first two sections of this chapter briefly to outline the course of this institutional transition. The final eight sections briefly sketch the main historical lines of the activities reflected in the share sub-indexes and the impact on the sub-indexes of their unique features. These sections cover canals, docks, waterworks, gasworks, mines, railways, banks, and insurance companies. The fluctuations, and especially the trends in share prices, often result from events and institutional changes special to particular segments of the British economy, for which the *History* alone provides an inadequate background.

1. The London Stock Exchange. When, in 1802, the five hundred members of the Stock Exchange transferred to their own building, more than a century of operations lay behind them. From the time of William and Mary at least, when the Bank of England lent its capital to the Exchequer in return for the privilege of incorporation,[1] a market for stocks had existed in London. And, almost from the beginning, forms of regulation were applied to its operations, reflecting a continuing public suspicion.[2] The scale of government issues and dealings in them during the war years at the close of the eighteenth century gave the Stock Exchange enhanced importance. The transition from coffee-house days was completed with the erection of a building solely devoted to transactions in securities.[3]

At this stage the Stock Exchange was governed by nine managers, who looked after the building, collected the fee and subscription of membership,

---

[1] 5 & 6 William and Mary, c. 20, passed in 1694.

[2] An act of 1697 (8 & 9 William III, c. 32) 'to restrain the numbers and ill practices of Brokers and Stock-jobbers' was the first public regulation. A further act of 1733 (7 Geo. II, c. 8) 'to prevent the infamous practice of stock-jobbing' was designed to stamp out speculative dealings in stock for future delivery. Although strengthened in 1746 and 1756, this act, associated with the name of Sir John Barnard, was mainly ineffective. See especially A. P. Poley and F. H. C. Gould, *History, Law, and Practice of the Stock Exchange*, pp. 6–8; E. T. Powell, pp. 154 and 157; J. Francis, *Stock Exchange*, pp. 81 and 213; and E. McDermott, *The London Stock Exchange*, p. 32.

[3] C. Duguid, *Story of the Stock Exchange*, pp. 61 and 87–8. In 1773 the transition was begun with the inscription of 'Stock Exchange' over the coffee-house door.

as well as by a Committee for General Purposes, consisting of thirty, who were elected annually by ballot of the membership. The committee controlled membership, held powers of suspension and expulsion, settled disputes, and enforced rules. In 1812 the committee codified and printed its rules for the first time.

The London Exchange had for long been distinguished by the separation of function between broker and jobber.[1] The broker received orders from the public but carried out all purchases and sales through jobbers. His income was derived from commission. The jobber, working on the floor of the Exchange, usually specialized in a particular kind of security, which, in theory at least, he was always prepared to buy or to sell. He offered, at any moment, a high and a low price, for sale or purchase, the margin being determined by the activity of the security, the size of the order, and the competition from other jobbers, as well as by the expected movement of the price. The jobber's was a gambler's income.

This division of function roughly insured a continuous competitive market, although the jobber simply disappeared from the market when he did not wish to enter a transaction, and would not 'make a price' for securities when he was not certain of being able to balance the transaction. In securities of local companies, with limited markets, for example, better prices could often be obtained on the provincial exchanges than in London.[2]

Dealings on the London Exchange were mainly on account although cash transactions were, of course, also permitted. Contracts to buy or sell were generally settled monthly in the Consol market and fortnightly (i.e. eleven to fourteen days) for other securities. Dealings on account were useful for several reasons. In the first place, they permitted a flexible market to operate in inscribed or registered stocks whose actual legal transfer was a cumbersome and expensive clerical process. Second, they gave the foreigner, operating through his broker, an opportunity to choose an appropriate moment for purchase or sale without making prior remittance to London. Third, and perhaps most important, they allowed a large volume of transactions to proceed without recourse to bank credit; for the banks were generally shy of the Stock Exchange, although they often helped brokers to carry over their accounts from one settlement day to the next.[3]

This system worked reasonably well, although periodic settlement led to more failures than would have occurred under, for example, daily settlement. A broker, knowing his position bankrupt, might indulge, in the period before settlement day, in wild gambles, with everything to gain and nothing to lose.[4] The Committee for General Purposes was for this reason usually severe on defaulters, although a later Royal Commission had occasion to complain of its laxity in readmitting them.[5]

[1] See, especially, F. Hirst, *The Stock Exchange*, pp. 47–50.

[2] The provincial exchanges date from about 1830 onwards. See, especially, E. T. Powell, pp. 538 ff.

[3] Ibid., pp. 572–3 and W. C. Van Antwerp, *The Stock Exchange from Within*, pp. 353–4.

[4] J. Hedges, *Commercial Banking*, p. 98, and Van Antwerp, p. 351.

[5] *P.P.* 1878, xix, Report, p. 23.

In effect the Stock Exchange sustained its unofficial monopoly in London throughout the years considered here. In 1821, however, the committee was successfully challenged, when it forbade 'option' dealings, a fairly pure form of gambling. The threat of setting up a rival exchange from some of the members induced it to rescind the ruling.[1] There was, as well, a recurrent public feeling that transactions openly arrived at in the presence of the principals would be more honest than the subtle and faintly mysterious interplay of broker and jobber. A bill, introduced in Parliament by Sir William Curtis, which would have created a public market for dealing in funds, was defeated in the House of Lords.[2] Rival exchanges, on a small scale, were in fact set up, but failed because their market was too limited and their facilities too slow.[3]

When the new Stock Exchange building opened the list of quotations included prices for only twenty securities, all government loans or issues of public corporations: Bank Stock, Consols, Navy Bills, Long and Short Annuities, Exchequer Bills, South Sea Stock, and so forth. Although there was a brief company floatation boom in 1807–8,[4] such issues dominated the Exchange over the war years. In 1817–18 foreign governments came to London for funds on a considerable scale;[5] but it is with the reduction in interest rates on funds in 1823, at a time when general business expansion was gathering momentum, that a major turning-point in the history of the Exchange occurred. There was a prompt shift into foreign government issues and gas-light shares were taken up with interest. And the Exchange was prepared to make the most of the foreign mining shares and South American government loans when they flooded into the market over the next two years. The boom and collapse of these years is considered elsewhere.[6] As Britain's greatest effort since the South Sea Bubble it involved not only excessive share-price increases, but a variety of dubious practices.[7] By 1827 the new foreign floatations, excepting Brazil, were mainly in default of interest.[8] Nevertheless London had moved a step towards the position of international capital centre which was not wholly reversed in the post-1825 disillusion. Public participation and interest in the Stock Exchange was permanently enlarged.[9]

The succeeding boom, of the next decade, saw repeated, over a wider range of issues, something of the same sequence. Not only foreign governments and the American states drew funds from London, but at home joint-stock banks, the early railways, and a variety of other companies floated their issues. As early as 1835 the market weakened and losses were

[1] Duguid, pp. 72 ff. and 122.
[2] Ibid., p. 105.
[3] McDermott, p. 39.
[4] See above, pp. 94–5.
[5] See above, p. 162.
[6] See above, pp. 185–92.
[7] See, for example, Duguid, p. 127 and the discussion and warnings in *The Times*, especially during July 1825.

[8] Jenks, p. 58. Between 1818 and 1823, twenty-six foreign government loans were floated in England, of which only 10 continued to pay interest in 1832. The nominal value of these loans was £57 million, which London houses contracted at £43 million. *P.P.* 1831–2, vi, Appendix No. 95, p. 98.
[9] Duguid, p. 131; and E. T. Powell, p. 600 n.

exceedingly heavy in the crisis of 1837.[1] Although it was some fifteen years before substantial American borrowing in London was again feasible, the Stock Exchange grew further as an institution and, in a sense, prepared itself for its central role in the railway floatations of the forties.

Not only were the dealings in rail shares on a larger scale and more widespread than previous Exchange operations,[2] but they involved qualitative changes as well in Stock Exchange practice. The rail boom of the forties was the first occasion when the Stock Exchange dealt seriously in joint-stock shares as opposed to bonds; and, in fact, became heavily involved in the machinery of their floatation. The Exchange role in joint-stock floatations, as opposed to government issues, had hitherto been, almost certainly, unimportant.[3] But the letter of allotment (which an applicant for shares normally received to certify his allotment, payment of deposit, and future payment liabilities) became itself an important object of speculation during the railway boom. Since liability for future assessments on the shares was incurred only by the investor who paid the deposit and signed the deed of covenant of the new company, preliminary speculation in the letters of allotment could proceed with relatively little risk.[4]

Until about 1843 four or five brokers and an even smaller number of jobbers were able to handle the entire trade in shares,[5] and this at a time when the membership of the Stock Exchange was getting on towards 800.[6] In 1850 the National Debt was about £830 million; foreign security holdings, about £125 million; Bank of England Stock, £11 million; joint-stock bank shares, £34 million; East India and South Sea Company Stock, £10 million; and shares in all companies except railways, about £100 million.[7] Although, at times, shares were unusually active on the Stock Exchange, it is clear that the National Debt in the long run overshadowed all other dealings. In the forties, railway shares evidently diminished the predominance the debt held in the market. Capital issues for railways, which amounted to £60 million in 1843, had quadrupled by 1850.[8] But it is important not to over-emphasize even the railways.

Writing in 1822, Joseph Lowe noted that, as late as the beginning of the Napoleonic Wars, 'in the provincial parts of Britain, the public funds were comparatively little resorted to as a deposit for private property', because 'the inhabitants are little acquainted with the security conferred on property by public register, the power of transfer, and the steady observance and good faith towards the public creditor'.[9] By 1815, however, Lowe remarks that public funds were in the hands not only of Londoners and

---

[1] See above, pp. 257–8.
[2] See Hirst, p. 58, on the exclusion of other interests at the height of the rail boom; and Duguid, pp. 147, 149, on the extraordinary volume of transactions by previous standards.
[3] G. H. Evans, *British Corporation Finance*, pp. 15 ff.
[4] Duguid, pp. 149 ff.
[5] E. T. Powell, p. 535.
[6] In 1850 there were 864 members. Duguid, p. 144.
[7] W. F. Spackman, p. 157. Spackman's figures are here given in round numbers.
[8] *P.P.* 1854–5, xlviii (1965), p. xvii.
[9] Op. cit., p. 326.

residents of other principal towns but also of people 'in every district and in every variety of occupation'. In 1752 Hume estimated that there were 17,000 fund holders including foreign holders of British funds; in 1829 their number is estimated by Doubleday as 275,839.[1]

The three post-war decades, and notably the railway floatations of the forties, much expanded the spread of fund and share holding. Tooke wrote: 'In every street of every town, persons were to be found who were holders of Railway Shares. Elderly men and women of small realised fortunes, tradesmen of every order, pensioners, public functionaries, professional men, merchants, country gentlemen . . . the mania had affected all.'[2]

As an economic institution it is difficult to measure the over-all importance of the Stock Exchange in the British economy. It would appear, however, that the Stock Exchange, until the forties, was not the most important channel for new British investment. Direct investment in the iron, textile, and other industries, as well as in the expansion of foreign trade, was almost certainly more substantial. But the course of events on the Exchange partly reflected and, in turn, partly influenced developments elsewhere. The timing of the floatation of new issues and of rises in yield were closely related to waves of enterprise elsewhere in the economy, and were undoubtedly influenced by the general forces affecting the view of the future. In turn, waves of optimism on the Stock Exchange accompanied by rising share prices or yields tended to reinforce general optimism and to draw into the market funds from all other lines of investment. Jenks takes the view that 'from any important connection with the industrial life of Great Britain the stock market was entirely divorced'.[3] Leaving aside the railway floatations, his view over these years has considerable force. The shares of companies first traded in were hardly of strategic industrial importance. Nevertheless, the prices of Consols and of shares appear to reflect in post-war years factors other than the credit standing of the government and the history of particular firms and industries; while the indirect consequences for foreign trade and industry of the large foreign investments channelled through the Exchange in the twenties and thirties were, obviously, considerable.

2. The Business Corporation. The shadow of the South Sea Bubble and the Bubble Act of 1720 still lay across British corporate enterprise over the first half of the nineteenth century, despite important parliamentary modifications in 1825 and later. The Bubble itself was a climax to some thirty years of expanding joint-stock activity. Up to 1688 there had been less than two dozen companies formed in England and Scotland.[4] After the wave of promotion during the early 1690's, partly stimulated, like that of 1807–8, by a war-time frustration of foreign trade, the number of companies was close to 150 in 1695. The South Sea Company, formed in 1711 on hold-

---

[1] D. Hume, *Essays*, i. 373 n.; T. Doubleday, *History of England*, p. 264.
[2] Op. cit. v. 234.
[3] Op. cit., p. 14.
[4] W. R. Scott, *Joint-Stock Companies*, i. 327–8.

ings of the National Debt, carried forward the new method of organization. The collapse in the latter half of 1720 brought South Sea shares down to a ninth of their mid-year price level, and even halved the value of Bank of England Stock. Whether the Bubble Act, formulated and passed in the midst of the wreckage, was justly aimed,[1] it effectively retarded the spread of joint-stock companies for more than a century. Insurance companies, in principle regarded even by Adam Smith as suitable for charter, increased in number only from three to six in the period 1720–1800.[2]

The spirit if not the letter of the Bubble Act was nevertheless successfully evaded on occasion, especially towards the close of the eighteenth century.[3] Unincorporated companies were set up, in legal form large partnerships, but possessing many qualities of the corporation. And, as well, the scale and character of investment required in canals and waterworks, and, later, gas-works and railways accelerated the use of formal parliamentary incorporation.

The mechanism of early-nineteenth-century company promotion is described by G. H. Evans.[4] When the idea for a business requiring a considerable investment of capital (say, a canal) was conceived, the original projectors would have made a preliminary engineering survey and would then announce to prominent citizens residing in the neighbourhood their intention of issuing a prospectus. Only occasionally did the promoters have sufficient resources or connexions to undertake the project themselves. At a public meeting of interested persons an investigating committee would be appointed, and, if the latter's findings were approved at a second meeting, it would be decided

that a company be formed with a certain capital divided into a specified number of shares; that subscription books be opened at a certain time and that the deposits (that is, initial payments) on the shares be of a certain amount; that an act of incorporation be sought from Parliament; that particular individuals or firms be appointed engineers, bankers, and solicitors to the company; and finally that certain persons be named a committee of management to carry out the resolutions and run the company until incorporation should have been attained and a board of directors elected to succeed them.[5]

The actual raising of the money was not carried through actively by investment bankers. There was no organized market for new floatations, and those who sold shares comprised a variety of different groups among whom were included principally sharebrokers, engineers, and manufacturers. It was common practice for the solicitor to appeal first to a selected group of prospective customers and then to try the general public through advertisements and public meetings. Evans concludes from a study of official lists of canal shareholders that, in general, they were widely distributed.[6]

[1] For a critical evaluation of the act see W. S. Holdsworth, *A History of English Law*, p. 220.

[2] J. Francis, *Life Assurance*, p. 185.

[3] See, especially, A. B. Du Bois, *English*

Business Company, for an account of joint-stock operations in the latter part of the eighteenth century.

[4] Chapter II.

[5] Ibid., p. 14.   [6] Ibid., chap. iii.

The boom in domestic enterprise in 1807–8, when other avenues were temporarily blocked, was the first of the discontinuous stages which marked the evolution of the joint-stock company in the nineteenth century. A wide variety of unincorporated companies were promoted and financed, but never reached operation. These included some industrial projects of a type relatively new to public promotion, e.g. textile companies, breweries, and distilleries. The Attorney-General appears to have bestirred himself, viewing some of the companies as in violation of the Bubble Act.[1] But the opening of Brazil soon drew British enterprise in other directions, certainly not less speculative, although well within law and convention.

The floatation boom of the twenties was a more serious affair. As early as 1821 the first of the foreign loans was floated in London, on behalf of Spain.[2] In all, nominal lending of this type, heavily directed towards Latin American countries, amounted to £46 million by 1825. In addition there were the large Mexican and Colombian mine floatations which are briefly considered below, as their shares form one component of the new index.[3]

Further, of course, there were heavy joint-stock floatations. The best available, and perhaps the most complete, statistical account of the promotions of this period is given in *A Complete View of Joint Stock Companies formed during the Years 1824 and 1825*, a pamphlet compiled by Henry English in 1827 chiefly on the basis of original prospectuses.[4] In sum, 624 companies were formed or projected in 1824–5 with a total capitalization of £372,173,000:

I. *Companies formed or projected in 1824–5*

	Capital	Shares
	£	
74 Mining companies	38,370,000	537,200
29 Gas companies.	12,077,000	200,940
20 Insurance companies	35,820,000	651,000
28 Investment companies	52,600,000	686,500
54 Canal, railway, &c. companies	44,051,000	542,210
67 Steam companies	8,555,500	125,220
11 Trading companies	10,450,000	85,000
26 Building companies	13,781,000	164,900
23 Provision companies.	8,360,000	674,000
292 Miscellaneous companies	148,108,600	2,294,350
624	£372,173,100	5,961,320

[1] *Rex* v. *Dodd*, 9 East 516–27 (1808).

[2] See Spackman, p. 111, for a full listing of foreign loans floated. Similar, though not identical, lists may be found in the *Fifth Annual Report of the Council of the Corporation of Foreign Bondholders* (1877), p. 52, and in *Statistical Illustrations of the British Empire*, London Statistical Society, p. 112. The latter's list includes, for 1822, a loan of £160,000 for the country of 'Poyais'. Jenks

(p. 47), in commenting on the wild speculation of this period, remarks in this connexion that 'the comedy turned burlesque when a loan was eagerly taken up for the "Kingdom of Poyais", a fictitious political entity on the Mosquito Coast of which a Scotch officer had assumed the title of "Cazique"'.

[3] See below, section 7.

[4] Preface; also tables, pp. 29–31. Some discrepancies have been corrected by us.

Of these 624 companies, 127 were in existence in 1827:

II. *Companies in Existence in 1827*

	Capital	Amount paid	Present value	No. of shares
	£	£	£	
44 Mines	26,776,000	5,455,100	2,927,350	358,700
20 Gas	9,061,000	2,162,000	1,504,625	152,140
14 Insurance . . .	28,120,000	2,247,000	1,606,000	545,000
49 Miscellaneous . .	38,824,600	5,321,850	3,265,975	562,500
127	£102,781,600	£15,185,950	£9,303,950	1,618,340

A second group consisted of 118 companies which were abandoned after their shares were issued and sold on the market:

III. *Companies abandoned*

	Capital	Amount paid	No. of shares
	£	£	
16 Mines	5,585,000	400,900	98,200
9 Investment	8,550,000	746,000	78,500
20 Canal, railway, &c. . .	19,135,000	393,375	246,000
30 Steam.	2,927,500	79,900	35,650
43 Miscellaneous . . .	20,409,000	799,500	390,250
118	£56,606,500	£2,419,675	848,600

Thirdly, there was a group of 236 companies which were officially projected —i.e. either prospectuses were issued or announcements made in the press—but had not, so far as information is available, issued shares:

IV. *Companies projected*

	Capital	No. of shares
	£	
14 Mines	6,009,000	80,300
9 Gas	3,016,000	48,800
19 Investment . . .	44,050,000	608,000
6 Insurance . . .	7,700,000	106,000
11 Trading	10,450,000	85,000
26 Building . . .	13,781,000	164,900
18 Dock, canal, &c. . .	13,851,000	164,410
16 Railway . . .	11,065,000	131,800
37 Steam	5,628,000	89,570
23 Provision . . .	8,360,000	674,000
57 Miscellaneous . . .	19,700,000	382,600
236	£143,610,000	2,535,380

And lastly, there were an additional 143 companies which issued prospectuses or gave notice through the newspapers, but of which no particulars were given. Their capital was estimated as £69,175,000, divided up among 959,000 shares.

In addition to the 127 companies established during the boom and existing in 1827, there were 156 companies formed prior to the year 1824, which withstood the crisis:

V. *Companies in Existence prior to 1824*

	Capital	Amount advanced	No. of shares
	£	£	
63 Canals . . .	12,202,096	12,202,096	175,374
7 Docks	6,164,591	6,164,591	57,582
25 Insurance . .	20,488,948	7,548,948	399,841
16 Waterworks . .	2,973,170	2,973,170	39,760
4 Bridges . . .	2,452,017	1,952,017	31,731
27 Gas	1,630,700	1,215,300	35,194
7 Roads	494,965	479,815	7,472
7 Miscellaneous . .	1,530,000	1,530,000	17,580
156	£47,936,487	£34,065,937	764,534

When the totals of Table II are added to Table V, a fairly complete statistical summary is obtained of the status of joint-stock companies after the 1824–5 crisis. There were, in all, 283 companies with a grand capitalization of £150,718,086, divided among 2,382,874 shares, on which £49,251,887 was paid.

This period also saw several significant legal changes which affected joint-stock practice. In June 1825 the Bubble Act was repealed in response to complaint of its ambiguity, its growing separation from accepted practice, and the heavy and arbitrary penalties it would impose.[1] In the future fraudulent practices were to be dealt with under the common law, and the degree of individual liability was to be left to the discretion of the Crown. A further Act of 1834 empowered the Crown to grant to trading companies by letter patent 'some of the privileges of and incident to corporations created by royal charter', and especially the privilege of suing and being sued in the name of a principal officer.[2] Perhaps most directly relevant to the events of the thirties, however, was the Banking Act of 1826, which permitted the establishment of joint-stock banks beyond a sixty-five-mile radius of London without limitation as to the number of partners. This opened a channel for joint-stock enterprise fully exploited in the expansive years preceding 1836.

The latter stages of the general expansion which started in 1833 saw joint-stock banking draw substantial funds, although second in volume to railways among company floatations:[3]

[1] *P.P.* 1825, i. 253 and 407.
[2] 4 & 5 Will. IV, c. 94 and *P.P.* 1834, ii. (441).
[3] *Report of Select Committee on Joint Stock Companies, P.P.* 1844, vii, App. 4, p. 345.

Type of company	No.	Nominal capital	No. of shares
		£	
Railway	88	69,666,000	590,920
Mining	71	7,035,200	447,730
Packet and navigation . .	17	3,533,000	127,390
Banking	20	23,750,000	670,000
Conveyance	9	500,000	50,500
Insurance	11	7,600,000	68,000
Investment	5	1,730,000	23,900
Newspaper	6	350,000	46,000
Canal	4	3,655,000	14,400
Gas	7	890,000	72,400
Cemetery	7	435,000	24,000
Miscellaneous	55	16,104,500	403,450
	300	£135,248,700	2,538,690

Among 'miscellaneous' floatations were included a number of manufacturing companies, e.g. a flax and canvas company, firms planning to produce cement, railway locomotives and carriages, rails, hats, &c. Joint-stock organization in the woollen industry also appears to have grown to some importance.[1] On the whole, despite the scale of the American loans, the boom of the thirties can be regarded as a more heavily domestic affair than that of the twenties, marking a distinct advance in the institutional importance of the joint-stock company.

This advance induced, in the aftermath of crisis (1837), a general reconsideration of company law. The advisability of introducing the limited partnership was considered, but in the end rejected as a stimulant to industrial investment unnecessary in England, whatever its virtues in France.[2] The only legal change made at this time was an act, superseding that of 1834, which made the due recording of shareholders and transfers a condition for the granting by the Crown of corporate privileges by letters patent. In addition, provision was made for terminating a shareholder's liability on the transfer of stock.

Economic doctrine and prejudice still stood firm against limited liability;[3] and Shannon's classification of companies in 1844 (see p. 416) reveals the extent to which, on balance, Adam Smith's conception of the proper province of the joint-stock company had thus far been honoured in practice.[4] Spackman estimated that there were in 1843 not less than 612 companies quoted on the London market with a nominal capitalization of about £225 million, in addition to investments in foreign securities totalling over £120 million.[5]

[1] Ibid., App. 5, p. 348; but see also J. Clapham, *Woollen and Worsted Industries*, pp. 152–3.
[2] The final report of this inquiry conducted by H. Bellenden Ker, is summarized in *P.P.* 1844, vii, App. 1.
[3] See Lord Brougham, *Hansard*, 1833,

xliv, col. 840, on the opposition of 'all the great luminaries of political science' to the principle of limited partnership.
[4] H. A. Shannon, 'The First Five Thousand Limited Companies and their Duration', *Economic History*, Jan. 1932; based upon *P.P.* 1846, xliii. 3–24.   [5] p. 157.

Type of company					No. existing in Sept. 1844
Coal and iron mines	.	.	.	.	19
Lead, copper, &c., mines		.	.	.	32
Quarries	.	.	.	.	9
Smelting, manufacturing ores			.	.	8
Railway, rolling-stock	.		.	.	1
Briquette and coal by-products			.	.	1
Bricks, tiles, pottery	.		.	.	1
Shipping: coastal	.	.	.	.	46
,, ocean	.		.	.	5
Omnibuses, &c.	.	.	.	.	4
Cotton manufacturing	.		.	.	1
Woollen manufacturing		.	.	.	24
Miscellaneous industries		.	.	.	14
Breweries	.	.	.	.	9
Other food and drink	.		.	.	14
Houses, land, and buildings	.		.	.	14
Market and public halls		.	.	.	31
Colonial railways	.	.	.	.	1
Colonial mines and lands		.	.	.	21
Foreign gas and water	.		.	.	1
,, mines and lands		.	.	.	22
Petty lending	.	.	.	.	48
Insurance	.	.	.	.	172
Gas and water	.	.	.	.	224
Railways	.	.	.	.	108
Other public utilities and works			.	.	84
Unclassified	.	.	.	.	33
					947

It was against a background of joint-stock activity on this scale, and in the midst of another wave of heavy investment at home, that the Select Committee on Joint Stock Companies sat in 1844. Typical of the views expressed before it was the testimony of John Duncan: 'Inasmuch . . . as transferable shares become in a measure part of the circulation of the country, and as there will always be an extensive class of buyers and sellers of shares thus made publicly vendible by sanction of the law, . . . it is the duty of the legislature to keep some degree of control over the birth and course of life of joint stock companies. . . .'[1]

The Act of 1844 provided for full registration, including submission of prospectuses and subscription contracts, annual balance-sheets and auditors' reports, as well as the right of inspection of accounts by the shareholders.[2] Thus companies which complied with the tightened registration requirements were permitted to carry on business with full corporate rights except limited liability. And, just as over the previous decades practice had anticipated legislation, considerable elements of limited liability existed for some time before its legal recognition in the fifties.[3]

[1] 1844, vii, Q. 2256.
[2] 7 & 8 Vict. c. 110. Joint-stock banks were separately provided for in 7 & 8 Vict. c. 113.
[3] For some of the loopholes by which limited liability was practised, see P.P. 1844,

vii, Q. 2073 and, especially, Geoffrey Todd, 'Some Aspects of Joint Stock Companies, 1844–1900', Economic History Review, iv, Oct. 1932, p. 61.

The joint-stock company was, of course, placed on a new level by the rail floatations of the forties, whose influence on the character and status of the Stock Exchange was briefly considered above. As one of the elements in the share index, the railways are examined at somewhat greater length in a subsequent section.[1]

3. Canals. The period covered by the canal shares index (1811–1850) includes the years of greatest importance and profitability for British canals as well as the beginnings of their decline in the face of the railways, which can be dated from the thirties. The seven canal companies included in the index are believed to constitute a fair sample with respect to size, region, and return on capital.

The great canal building boom of the early 1790's[2] had been preceded by some forty years of canal development. Perhaps the most important initial impulse to the canal movement was the high cost of coal transport. The Duke of Bridgewater's early link between Worsley and Manchester halved the price of coal in the latter town. The success of the early ventures and the general growth of industry in these years soon suggested more ambitious projects. The extent to which transport rates declined following the construction of inland waterways is revealed in the following figures, which compare the rates per ton by land carriage before the opening of the Trent and Mersey Canal with the rates charged by it :[3]

Transport Rates per Ton

	By land	By Trent and Mersey Canal
	£ s. d.	£ s. d.
From Liverpool to Etruria	2 10 0	0 13 4
,, ,, Wolverhampton . .	5 0 0	1 5 0
,, ,, Birmingham . . .	5 0 0	1 10 0
,, Manchester to Lichfield . . .	4 0 0	1 0 0
,, ,, Derby . . .	3 0 0	1 10 0
,, ,, Newark . . .	5 6 8	2 0 0
,, ,, Nottingham . .	4 0 0	2 0 0
,, ,, Wolverhampton . .	4 13 4	1 5 0
,, ,, Birmingham . .	4 0 0	1 10 0
,, ,, Leicester . . .	6 0 0	1 10 0
,, ,, Shardlaw . . .	3 0 0	1 10 0

Thus the cost of transportation in the region of the Trent and Mersey Canal was cut to about one-third of its previous figure. On the basis of much more diverse information, it would seem that this figure is roughly correct for canals as a whole.[4]

By the turn of the century the pre-eminence of canals in the internal

---

[1] See below, section 8.

[2] See above, p. 14.

[3] Quoted in Thomas Baines, *History of Liverpool*, p. 440, from Williamson's *Liver-pool Advertiser*, 8 Aug. 1777.

[4] See W. J. Jackman, *Transportation in Modern England*, ii, App. 8.

movement of merchandise and heavy raw materials was securely established:

Throughout the country, stone for building, paving and roadmaking; bricks, tiles and timber; limestone for the builder, farmer or blast furnace owner; beasts and cattle; corn, hay and straw; manure from the London mews and the mountainous London dustheaps; the heavy castings which were coming into use for bridge-building and other structural purposes—all these, and whatever other bulky wares there may be, moved along the new waterways over what, half a century earlier, had been impossible routes or impossible distances.[1]

There is a fine symmetry in the story of the canals. Their battle against the coasting trade, against land-holders who feared that the canals would drain water off their estates, and against the road-transport interests, was only matched by the canal's later and, in the end, equally unsuccessful fight against the railways.[2]

The canal development of the early 1790's holds a place similar to the boom of the forties in British railways.[3] In the four years 1791–4 a total of eighty-one canal acts were passed.[4] As many canals were projected and planned in 1792 as the total number previously in existence.[5] Shares were oversubscribed several times, as in the case of the Ellesmere Canal.[6] In fact it was seriously suggested that a reasonable upper limit of 10 or 12 per cent. be set on returns from canal investments.[7] Trading in canal shares had become something in the nature of a lottery. Though many uneconomical projects were set in motion and heavy losses incurred by individual investors, the boom was neither as prolonged nor as intense as the railway mania fifty years later. It marked, however, the first time that the shares of canal companies were floated by public rather than private subscription.

Whether even at their peak the canals were, on the average, a profitable form of investment has been questioned by several historians.[8] Jackman estimates, on the basis of figures in Fenn's *English and Foreign Funds*, that in the period before 1850, at least one-half and possibly two-thirds of the canals in England earned dividends below what was recognized as a reasonable minimum.[9] From the point of view of return to capital, both good and

[1] Clapham, *Economic History*, i. 79. For a vivid account of the effect of canals on the midlands see G. C. Allen, *The Industrial Development of Birmingham and the Black Country*, pp. 30–1.

[2] See especially, F. C. Clifford, *History of Private Bill Legislation*, i. 34; Jackman, i. 368, quoting from Brit. Mus. 214.1.4 (119) 'Letter from Yarmouth regarding the Canal from Coventry to Oxford now depending in Parliament'. Landowners' petitions against the passage of canal bills in *Journals of the House of Commons*, xxx. 627, 683, 707–8.

[3] Baines, p. 488, states: 'The canal share market in 1792 very much resembled the railway share market in 1845. At a sale of canal shares in October, 1792, the shares in

the Trent navigation sold for 175 guineas each; those in the river Soar Canal . . . for 765 guineas; . . . one share in the Oxford Canal for 156 guineas . . . ; ten shares in the Grand Junction Canal, of which not a sod was dug, sold for 355 guineas premium.'

[4] E. A. Pratt, *Inland Transport and Communications*, p. 183.

[5] Baines, p. 488.

[6] Pratt, p. 183.

[7] *Gentleman's Magazine*, lxii (1792), pt. 2, p. 1162.

[8] See Clapham, i. 82 ff.; Jackman, i. 369, 416–18; also *Quarterly Review*, xxxii. 170–1, anonymous article.

[9] Op. cit. i. 420.

bad companies are included in the new index. The Ellesmere and Chester and the Worcester and Birmingham might be taken as representative of the latter. The geographical distribution covers the north (Ellesmere and Chester, Leeds and Liverpool, and Trent and Mersey), the midlands (Grand Junction, Coventry, Worcester and Birmingham), and the south-west (Monmouthshire). As to size, Coventry and Trent and Mersey represent rather small capitalizations, the remainder large.

With the improvement of the locomotive in the thirties rail competition was significantly felt by the canals. No new inland canal, as distinct from ship canals, was constructed in England after 1834.[1] The following table indicates the character of the comparative advantage enjoyed by the railways over alternative means of transport.[2]

Bristol to London, Rates per Ton

Article	Rates charged by carriers			Rates charged by railway
	1820	1830	1840	1866
	s. d.	s. d.	s. d.	s. d.
Drapery . .	66 0	60 6	47 6	40 0
Hops . .	68 0	63 0	49 6	40 0
Oil . . .	60 6	47 0	42 0	20 0
Tobacco . .	66 0	66 0	47 6	26 8

Birmingham to London, Rates per Ton

	Canal		Railway
	1836	1842	1866
	s. d.	s. d.	s. d.
Undamageable iron . .	25 0	..	15 0
Hardware	60 0	40 0	27 6
Sugar	40 0	37 6	21 8
Tallow	35 0	30 0	21 8
Drapery	70 0	45 0	40 0
Glass	70 0	..	27 6

Since the London and Birmingham railway was opened in 1837–8, its effect on canal charges is indicated by the difference between the rate in 1836 and 1842. The report also reveals the following changes in rates on bales of grain shipped from Manchester to London:

> By quick vans, 1833 at £20 a ton.
> „ canal   1834 at £4 a ton.
> „ railway   1840 at £3. 4s. 8d. a ton.

Jackman concludes that a conservative estimate of the effects of railway competition is that it caused a reduction of at least one-third to one-half of the previous navigation rates.[3]

The manner in which the canal companies fought the railway encroach-

---

[1] Pratt, p. 296.
[2] P.P. 1867 (3844), xxxviii, Pt. 1, p. lxv.
[3] Jackman, p. 635. His estimate is based on additional data given in App. 10.

ment was suggestive of the tactics used by river navigation carriers to ward off canal competition sixty years earlier. In some cases, by threatening opposition to railway bills, the canal proprietors hoped to force the railway companies either to buy them out or to guarantee them against loss. For example, in order to overcome the opposition of the Severn Canal commissioners, the directors of the Oxford, Worcester, and Wolverhampton Railway Company (which afterwards amalgamated with the Great Western) were forced to pay the commissioners £6,000 a year for many years. The sum was claimed to be the difference between the anticipated revenue of the canal and the actual revenue, a deficit presumably caused by the introduction of the railway. Without this subsidy the railway promoters feared a long delay of their act by a Parliament sympathetic to the interests of the waterways.[1]

Competition between railways and canals led, in the late thirties, to working agreements of various kinds with respect to rates and traffic and to amalgamation in some cases.[2] By 1845 the possible evils of the growing control and absorption of canals by railway companies had become evident, and Parliament decided to take measures to strengthen the competitive position of the waterways. An Act was passed in 1845 rescinding the law which prohibited canals from engaging in the carrying trade.[3] In addition, canals were given powers to vary their tolls and to lease their tolls to each other.[4] These privileges made it possible for the canal companies to adjust their rates to one another and enter into agreements which would place them on a more equal competitive footing with the railways, which had already been granted similar privileges by the Railway Clauses Consolidation Act of 1845.

The Canal Acts of 1845, though designed to strengthen the position of navigation, served, in fact, to increase the dominance of railways. Railway companies that owned canals could now, in their capacity as navigation companies, gain control over other canals through the liberal traffic arrangements permitted under these acts. The terms of these agreements were, almost invariably, more favourable to the railways, which, of course, had the upper hand in bargaining. During 1845–7 a total canal mileage of 948 was bought or leased by the railway companies, leaving some 2,750 miles of independent canals in Great Britain.[5]

The secular decline in canals is graphically revealed by a comparison of the total securities index (exclusive of mines) and the canal sub-index. In the years up to about 1831 canal shares fluctuate more often and more

[1] Pratt, p. 297.

[2] The Second Report from the Select Committee on Railways and Canals Amalgamation (P.P. 1846 (275), xiii) states, 'That there are about 32 bills before Parliament in which power is sought to effect the amalgamation of Canals with Railways'. These bills are grouped in three classes: (1) bills for the amalgamation, by lease, purchase, or otherwise, of entire lines of canals with competing railway lines; (2) bills for the amalgamation of some canal forming a link in a chain of water communications with a railway line competing with the whole chain; (3) bills for converting canals into railways.

[3] Act 8 & 9 Vict., c. 42.

[4] Ibid., c. 28.   [5] Clapham, i. 398.

sharply than the total index, indicating a considerable volume of trading. In the period from 1811 to 1815, while the total index falls, the sub-group rises; its peak, moreover, in the following cycle, extends to June 1819, whereas the total index declines from December 1818. These facts, and the exuberant rise in canal shares to the latter months of 1824, supplement the view of canals as an active, and, on the whole, prosperous branch of British industry. In the failure of the canals to share the rise of the total index in 1832–6, the first signs of serious weakness are evident. The sharp peak in the total index in May 1836 does not appear in the canal shares, which had been declining from July 1834. That decline continued, with only mild interruptions, to 1850. The major peaks in 1824, 1836, and 1845 are successively higher in the total index; for canal shares, the level of 1824 was never again attained. The lack of frequent fluctuations, in the latter years, probably representing desultory as well as pessimistic trading, further reflects the closing of the canal era.

4. Docks. The docks represented in the index are all London companies, since those of other ports were not actively traded in during the period ending in 1850.

At the beginning of the nineteenth century London had no docks at all. Lighters would unload ships moored or anchored some distance from the shore and land their cargo at legal quays. The inadequacy of the system led to much controversy over the best method of improving the port.[1] Chief opposition to any change in the existing system stemmed from various vested interests, notably the lightermen and proprietors of the legal quays.

In 1799 the West India Dock Act was passed,[2] giving the company a twenty-one year monopoly which compelled all vessels bound for or coming from the West Indies to load or land their cargoes at the dock. The dock interests were assessed by the commissioners to compensate the wharfingers and the lightermen for their losses—which were substantial, because the West India trade was then the largest single trade of the port. In addition, the act set rates to be charged vessels for entering and leaving the dock, and for cargo landed; the one exception was the 'free water clause' which stated that no lighter delivering goods at the dock was to be subject to these charges, a clause which proved a severe handicap to the dock when its monopoly lapsed.[3]

In 1805 the West India Docks and the London Docks were completed, the latter having been given a twenty-one-year monopoly of the imports of tobacco, rice, wine, and brandy, except from the East and West Indies. The East India Docks, the third great system erected during this period, were completed in 1806 with a twenty-one-year monopoly over the East India trade.

---

[1] *P.P.* 1796 (129), Appendix A, for Memorial of the Committee of Merchants on the state of the legal quays.

[2] 39 Geo. III, c. 69.

[3] See J. G. Broodbank, *History of the Port of London*, i. 98 and D. Owen, *Ports and Docks*, p. 94.

For the duration of their monopolies the three companies were quite prosperous, except the London Docks, whose trade suffered during the Napoleonic Wars. The accompanying table summarizes the accounts of the West India Dock Company for the fourteen years beginning in 1811. After 1815 a competitive reduction of rates impaired the revenues of all the companies. Again the London Docks suffered most, owing to the opening, in

TABLE 27. *Annual Accounts of West India Dock Company, 1811–23*

(in £000)

Year ending 1 Feb.	Receipts		Expenditures			Balance	Total^k
	Rates	Interest	Dividends^h	Capital improvements	All other expenditures^l		
1811 . .	34^a	5	108	74	135	66	383
	291	..	..	..	..	..	..
2 . .	290	8	108	36	165	55	364
3 . .	446	3	108	3	186	207	504
4 . .	443	23	108	74	200	292	673
1815 . .	434	36	108	5	249	398	761
6 . .	337	—^b	108	3	207^l	418	735
7 . .	333	24	120	—	172	483	775
8 . .	285^c	13	120	68	144	449	781
9 . .	266	23	120	91	159	368	738
1820 . .	227	22	120	21	141	335	617
1 . .	244	21	120	4	137	414	675
	..	74^d	..	..	..	..	..
2 . .	249	42^e	..	..	..	..	..
	..	23	..	..	..	..	..
3 . .	193^f	21	..	..	..	..	..
	..	16^e	..	..	..	..	..
	..	1^g	..	..	..	..	..

a Arrears collected.

b Loss in value of funded property since January 1815.

c Reduction of rates, Mar. 1817.

d Gain on funded property sold; increase in value since 31 Dec. 1815 on remainder, taken at price on 1 Jan. 1821.

e Increase in value of funded property since previous year.

f Reduction of rates, Apr. 1822.

g Naval school, received more than expended.

h From 1811 to 1816, less property tax deducted.

i Includes expenditure on wages, salaries, donations, taxes, insurance, stores, repairs, losses, incidental charges, and naval school.

k If the balance remaining from 1810 (£53—the figure does not appear in the table) is added to the receipts for 1811, and the balance for 1811 added to the expenditures for 1811, both sums equal the figure £383 for 1811 in the 'Total' column. Similarly, if the balance remaining from 1811 (£66) is added to the receipts for 1812, and the balance for 1812 added to the expenditures for 1812, both sums equal the total £364 for 1812. There may be a slight discrepancy in the totals because of the omission of thousands.

l Includes loss in value of funded property.

Source: *P.P.* 1823 (411), iv. App. 2. The figures published by Broodbank, p. 139, do not agree with those given here. He does not state his source, nor does he define what is included under each of the headings of the columns.

1828, of the St. Katharine Dock close to their site. The rivalry between the East and West India Docks was also intense, ending only in 1838 with the amalgamation of the two companies. Even the amalgamated company, however, never succeeded in returning a dividend higher than 6 per cent. Dock company revenues were further reduced by the passage of the Warehousing Act of 1832, which terminated the exclusive advantage they had enjoyed in the warehousing trade because of the limitations of the bonded warehouse system.

The adjustment of rates to the new competitive situation occurred in the early thirties. Our share index reaches its trough in 1834, but it is significant that there is no corresponding decline in tonnage figures. Indeed the upward trend of the tonnage of the Port was, despite cyclical set-backs, relatively unchanged during this period.[1] The peak in the share index reached in 1824, when, under conditions of general prosperity, at least two of the docks still enjoyed monopoly privileges, was never again attained. The trend was unmistakably downward for the ten years after the opening of the St. Katharine Dock.

To be sure, from the mid-thirties onward the trend of the share index is once again upward; and the return on capital invested in the dock industry, while considerably less than it had been in the days of monopoly, was still substantial. Every subsequent decline in the share index occurs on a rising trend, and, as the movements of the tonnage curve suggest, in response to pervasive cyclical forces. Since both St. Katharine's and the East and West India Dock companies were paying 5 per cent. by 1840, and the London Docks reached that level during the next decade, it can hardly be argued that capital invested in docks was not yielding a good return. It was largely for this reason that the bill sponsored by the dock companies in 1855 for the abolition of the 'free water clause' did not receive parliamentary sanction.[2]

The annual tonnage of ships entered and cleared at all ports of the United Kingdom and the tonnage entered and cleared at the Port of London are shown on Fig. 95 with the share index, although the index measures only the prices of shares of London docks.[3] There is, as might be expected, a

---

[1] See below, Fig. 95, comparing the index of dock share prices and the tonnage of ships entered and cleared at the Port of London. It is true, however, that the rate of growth maintained in the period before and after the early thirties fell off from 1830 to 1834, as the tabulation below shows:

Percentage Change in Total Foreign Tonnage entered and cleared at Port of London in each Quinquennial Period on the Preceding Period

Periods	Per cent.
1825–9 on 1820–4	+27·8
1830–4 on 1825–9	−2·4
1835–9 on 1830–4	+20·2
1840–4 on 1835–9	+14·8
1845–9 on 1840–4	+28·3

Source: Report of His Majesty's Commissioners, appointed to inquire into the subject of the Administration of the Port of London, and other matters connected therewith, *P.P.* 1902, xliii. 17.

[2] Owen, p. 95.

[3] Tonnage figures are given at the close of this section.

considerable similarity between the tonnage curve for London and that for the United Kingdom. The Port of London handled from one-quarter to one-third of the total trade of the kingdom during the first half of the nineteenth century. For this reason, too, such similarity as the index shows

Fig. 95. Shipping Tonnage entered and cleared and the Index of Prices of Dock Shares, 1811–50

with movements of tonnage in and out of London is also present with respect to the movements of the total tonnage curve. Since, as we have seen, a great many other factors besides general business conditions, as reflected in the tonnage figures, affected the prosperity of the docks, it is not surprising that there is not a very high degree of conformity between the dock share index and the London Port tonnage curve. The conformity is somewhat better from 1835 to 1850, except for the peak in the forties, which occurs in 1845 in the share index and in 1847 in the tonnage totals. The more general forces of depression affecting the capital market and the economy as a whole appear to outweigh the influence of a high volume of traffic at this period. In earlier years the lack of similarity is no doubt due to the fact that the companies at first possessed exclusive control over certain types of tonnage, and then faced a difficult adjustment to new competitive conditions.

The sharp decline of the dock index in 1830–1 (over 30 per cent.) constitutes the principal divergence of the sub-index from the total index (exclusive of mines). In 1824, 1836,[1] and 1845 dock shares exhibited a tendency to decline some months before the turning-point for securities as a whole was reached. As in the case of the shares of the waterworks, that characteristic may reflect the competition of more attractive speculative issues in the latter stages of Stock Exchange booms. The smooth movement of the sub-index, from 1834 to 1850, supports this view of docks as a conservative type of investment in the latter decades of the period.

TABLE 28. *Tonnage of Vessels with Cargoes and Ballast entered and cleared Annually at Ports in the United Kingdom, 1814–50*

Year	Tonnage of vessels entered and cleared (000's)	Year	Tonnage of vessels entered and cleared (000's)
1814 . .	3,765	1835 . .	6,635
5 . .	4,269	6 . .	7,061
6 . .	3,534	7 . .	7,207
7 . .	4,069	8 . .	8,096
8 . .	5,099	9 . .	8,928
9 . .	4,471	1840 . .	9,440
1820 . .	4,099	1 . .	9,418
1 . .	3,868	2 . .	9,127
2 . .	4,130	3 . .	9,824
3 . .	4,435	4 . .	10,347
4 . .	4,961	1845 . .	12,078
1825 . .	5,803	6 . .	12,416
6 . .	5,075	7 . .	14,279
7 . .	5,495	8 . .	13,307
8 . .	5,344	9 . .	14,004
9 . .	5,688	1850 . .	14,504
1830 . .	5,800		
1 . .	6,439		
2 . .	5,706		
3 . .	5,949		
4 . .	6,281		

Source: *P.P.*, Annual Finance Accounts for the United Kingdom.

[1] Although the mathematical peak in dock shares came in June 1836, one month after that in the total index, the rise had virtually ended in Feb. From then until May the total index rises sharply, the sub-index for dock companies sags.

TABLE 29. *Tonnage of Vessels in Foreign Trade entered and cleared Annually at the Port of London,*[a] *1816–50*

Year	Tonnage of vessels entered and cleared (000's)	Year	Tonnage of vessels entered and cleared (000's)
1816 . .	1,248	1835 . .	1,758
7 . .	1,427	6 . .	1,947
8 . .	1,858	7 . .	1,965
9 . .	1,496	8 . .	2,230
1820 . .	1,400	9 . .	2,505
1 . .	1,251	1840 . .	2,441
2 . .	1,262	1 . .	2,382
3 . .	1,420	2 . .	2,286
4 . .	1,608	3 . .	2,361
1825 . .	1,829	4 . .	2,470
6 . .	1,592	1845 . .	2,689
7 . .	1,772	6 . .	2,768
8 . .	1,780	7 . .	3,443
9 . .	1,896	8 . .	3,164
1830 . .	1,744	9 . .	3,256
1 . .	1,976	1850 . .	3,290
2 . .	1,545		
3 . .	1,618		
4 . .	1,779		

Source: *P.P.* 1851 (656), lii.

[a] No data available for the period before 1816.

5. Waterworks.

Like the course of the dock index, the shares of waterworks companies are much affected by the changing character of market organization and monopolistic practices, from 1811 to 1850. Provision of a water supply in England remained a municipal function until the establishment of the London Bridge Waterworks at the end of the sixteenth century.[1] Thereafter, at least until the middle of the nineteenth century, waterworks were established as private enterprises. With the exception of the Manchester and Salford, the waterworks included in the index are London companies, since their shares were quoted more fully than English waterworks as a whole.

During the seventeenth and eighteenth centuries the companies were granted district monopolies by parliamentary act. But in the early nineteenth century Parliament, prompted by a desire to improve service and reduce rates, began to sanction competitive companies and, on occasion, to insert clauses requiring that rates be reasonable.[2] The ensuing intense competition among the London companies for the control of common districts caused severe financial set-backs and substantially depreciated share prices.

Competitive rate cutting had, by 1817, so impoverished the London companies that some method of eliminating the intense rivalry was sought. The device resorted to was that of sharing the market.[3] The territory was

[1] Scott, iii. 3–5; also Clifford, i. 9–10, 249.
[2] See, for example, 46 Geo. III, c. 119 (West Middlesex Waterworks).
[3] See, for example, *P.P.* 1821 (706), v,

App. C, pp. 202–5, for agreement between New River and East London Waterworks companies.

divided, assuring to each company an allotted rental. Thus the consumers were confronted by district water monopolies which almost immediately increased rates by about 25 per cent. Though consumer protest was widespread, attempts at government regulation and the setting of maximum rates failed.[1]

From 1828 until 1845 the waterworks share index shows an almost continuous rise; and, though declining during the next five years, it was still high. The Waterworks Clause Act of 1847, setting 10 per cent. as the maximum dividend a water company could declare, merely embodied in a general act clauses already found in many of the companies' charters.[2] Furthermore, its provisions were in fact inoperative, since, as indicated in Tables 30 and 31 below, water companies never paid dividends greater than 8 per cent.[3] During most of this period official attention was centred less on the rates charged than on the purity of the water supply.

TABLE 30. *Dividends per Share paid by various Waterworks Companies, 1811–28*

Company	London Bridge	Chelsea	New River	York Buildings	West[c] Middlesex	Grand Junction	East[c] London
No. of shares	1,500	2,000 2,000	72	84	7,542	4,500	3,800
Par value .	£100	£20 £10	No par, capital in 1815, £850,000; 1821, £925,000	£100	£100	£50	£100
Year	£	s.	£	£	£	£	£
1811 . .	3	12	283	None	None	None	5
2 . .	$2\frac{3}{4}$	12	221	1 out of cap.	None	None	2
3 . .	$2\frac{1}{2}$	12	114	None	None	None	None
4 . .	$2\frac{1}{2}$	12	23	None	None	None	None
1815 . .	$2\frac{1}{2}$	12	60	None	None	None	2
6 . .	$2\frac{3}{4}$	12	85	None	None	None	2
7 . .	$2\frac{3}{4}$	12	120	None	None	None	$2\frac{1}{2}$
8 . .	$2\frac{1}{2}$	12	159	None	None	None	3
9 . .	$2\frac{1}{2}$	12	200	b	$1\frac{3}{4}$	$1\frac{1}{4}$	$3\frac{1}{2}$
1820 . .	$2\frac{1}{2}$	12	266	..	2	$\frac{5}{8}$	$1\frac{3}{4}$
1 . .	$2\frac{1}{2}$	12	342	..	2	$2\frac{1}{2}$	None
2 . .	$2\frac{1}{2}$	12	402	..	$2\frac{1}{4}$	$2\frac{1}{2}$	1
3 . .	a	14	448	..	$2\frac{1}{2}$	$2\frac{1}{2}$	$3\frac{1}{2}$
4 . .	..	14	489	..	$2\frac{1}{2}$	$2\frac{3}{4}$	5
1825 . .	..	14	502	..	$2\frac{5}{8}$	3	$5\frac{1}{2}$
6 . .	..	14	491	..	$2\frac{3}{4}$	3	$5\frac{1}{4}$
7 . .	..	14	517	..	$2\frac{7}{8}$	3	5
8 . .	..	14	..	..	3	3	5

a Dividend guaranteed by New River Company after 1822.
b Acquired by New River Company.
c For dividend payments after 1828, see Table 31.

Source: *P.P.* 1828 (567), viii, Appendix.

[1] G. Turnbull, p. 360 in W. Besant (ed.), *London in the Nineteenth Century*; also Clifford, ii. 142.

[2] 10 & 11 Vict., c. 17.
[3] Clifford, i. 250.

TABLE 31. *Dividends per Share paid by two Waterworks Companies, 1829–50*

	West Middlesex	East London
	(in £)	
1829–36 . .	3	5
1837 . . .	$3\frac{1}{2}$	6
1838–9 . .	4	6
1840 . . .	$4\frac{1}{4}$	7
1841 . . .	$4\frac{1}{2}$	7
1842 . . .	$4\frac{1}{2}$	$7\frac{1}{2}$
1843 . . .	$4\frac{3}{4}$	8
1844–5 . .	$4\frac{4}{5}$	8
1846 . . .	$5\frac{1}{4}$	8
1847 . . .	$5\frac{5}{8}$	8
1848 . . .	$5\frac{3}{4}$	8
1849–50 . .	6	8

Data on the dividends paid by other waterworks are not available.
Source: Wetenhall's *Course of the Exchange.*

The major features of the history of the companies are quickly revealed by a comparison of the waterworks' share index with the total index (exclusive of mines). The sub-index declines much more sharply than the total index, from 1811 to the third quarter of 1816, clearly reflecting the period of unrestricted competition.[1] From June 1817 to February 1818 waterworks' shares rose more than 95 per cent., the total index less than 45 per cent. In these months the framework was laid for the market-sharing agreements which made the companies once again profitable. The sub-index fully reflects the general rise to the 1824 peak. That high point comes somewhat earlier in waterworks than in the index as a whole: June as opposed to September. This may indicate that the waterworks' shares were among the first to suffer the competition of the new mining shares, which, in 1824, began to dominate the security market.

The brief but decisive downward movement in waterworks' shares, in the first half of 1828, probably represents the market's fears that some form of parliamentary regulation would result from the investigation then under way. From its low point in 1829, however, the index moves steadily to a peak in November 1845. The boom and slump of 1836, clearly evident in the total index, barely disturb the smooth upward course of the sub-index. From 1837 to 1842, while the total index fluctuates erratically, well below the 1836 peak, waterworks' shares moved to a new, higher level, despite a mild decline from February 1839 to August 1841. The general upward movement of securities, from 1841 to 1845, appears as well in the sub-index. The turning-point in waterworks' shares, however, comes later in the year, November as opposed to August; and the decline to the end of 1848 is relatively mild.

In the early years of the period, waterworks' shares fluctuated more erratically than the index as a whole. From about 1828, however, the

---

[1] Adjustment to the new competitive conditions appears to have taken place in 1811–12. From 1813 to 1816, waterworks' shares fluctuate with the total index, at a new and lower level.

movements of the sub-index are more regular than those of the total index. It is probable that, with their legal position secure, and with more speculative investments available for the daring investor, waterworks' shares acquired a status closer to that of debentures than equities. Their mild amplitude of movement, relative to the sharp cycles in other shares, tends to support this view.

   6. Gas-light Companies. The first coal gas company in England was incorporated, after considerable parliamentary vicissitudes, in 1810 under the name London Gas Light and Coke Company.[1] Early in the history of this enterprise, which came to be known as the 'Chartered Company', it encountered opposition from various sources: oil-lamp manufacturers, brass and metal workers, the whale-fishery interests—all of whom regarded the substitution of coal for oil in lighting as a threat to their means of existence; road authorities who faced the task of laying mains and pipes; and those gas companies which had been operating without statutory powers. By 1820 the superiority of gas over oil as an illuminant was widely urged. Investment in gas-light enterprises was further stimulated by prospective economies which were thought to be possible from the sale of coke and tar by-products of gas manufacture.

   Gas-light companies sprang up throughout England.[2] Costs were greater than anticipated, the technique of manufacture and distribution was crude, management was inexperienced, and consumer use was inaccurately checked. The relative prosperity of the City of London Gas Light and Coke Company, which consistently paid the highest dividends, was due chiefly to the fact that it was formed out of two unprofitable companies which were purchased at bankruptcy prices. The speculative character of the industry until 1830 was further increased by the development of oil gas companies and portable coal gas companies. Their effective competition was, however, shortlived.

   In 1823 a bill was introduced providing for the fixing of exclusive districts for each of the London companies, and for the regulation of public lighting rates, as well as for compulsory safety measures.[3] From the time when this bill, after much controversy, failed of enactment, until the middle of the century, competition characterized the gas industry. Together with a fall in the price of coal and various technical economies, this environment contributed to the decline in gas rates during this period.[4]

   Despite the decline in rates, however, fair dividends were paid, at least by the London gas companies (see Tables 32 and 33). According to the index, the years from 1837 to 1845 were rather prosperous; thereafter a sharp decline set in. Effective regulation of the industry by general statute did not take place until after 1850.[5]

---

[1] 50 Geo. III, c. 163. Frederick Albert Winsor was the organiser. See S. Hughes, *A Treatise on Gas Works*; W. Matthews, *A Historical Sketch of Gas Lighting*; F. Accum, *Gas Light*.

[2] Hughes, p. 21; Matthews, p. 226.

[3] See *P.P.* 1823 (428), i.

[4] *P.P.* 1847 (734), xliv; 1850 (399), xlix, for rates from 1820 to 1850.

[5] The movement towards control began with the Gas-Works Clauses Act of 1847 (10 & 11 Vict., c. 15), the provisions of which were largely evaded. See Clifford, pp. 224–5.

TABLE 32. *Annual Rates per 1,000 Cubic Feet of Gas charged by Eleven Chartered London Gas Companies, 1821–50*

Name of company	Chartered	City	Poplar	Imperial	British	Ratcliff	Phoenix	Independent	Equitable	London	South Metropolitan
Year											
1821	a	15s.	15s.	..	..	b	..	..	..	..	..
2	..	15s.	15s.	..	..	..	..	..	..	..	..
3	15s.	15s.	15s.	..	..	..	..	..	..	..	..
4	15s.	15s.	15s.	17s.	..	..	15s.	..	..	..	..
1825	15s.	15s.	15s.	17s.	..	..	15s.	..	..	..	..
6	15s.	15s.	15s.	15s.	..	..	15s.	..	..	..	..
7	15s.	15s.	15s.	15s.	..	..	15s.	..	..	..	..
8	15s., 13s. 6d.	13s. 6d.	15s.	15s.	..	..	15s.	12s.	..	..	..
9	13s. 6d.	13s. 6d.	15s.	15s.	13s. 9d.	12s. 6d.	15s.	12s.	..	..	..
1830	13s. 6d.	13s. 6d.	15s.	13s. 6d.	13s. 9d.	12s. 6d.	15s.	12s.	12s.	..	..
1	13s. 6d., 12s. 6d., 11s. 3d.	12s. 6d.	15s.	13s. 6d.	13s. 9d.	12s. 6d.	13s. 6d.	11s.	12s.	..	..
2	12s. 6d., 11s. 3d.	12s. 6d.	12s.	13s. 6d.	13s. 9d.	12s. 6d.	13s.	11s.	12s.	..	..
3	12s. 6d., 11s. 3d., 10s.	10s.	10s.	12s.	13s. 9d.	12s. 6d.	11s.	9s.	12s.	..	..
4	10s.	10s.	10s.	10s.	11s. 3d.	10s.	9s.	9s.	10s.	..	11s.
1835	10s.	10s.	10s.	10s.	11s. 3d.	9s.	9s.	9s.	10s.	..	11s.
6	10s., 9s.	9s.	10s.	10s.	9s. 6d.	9s.	9s.	9s.	9s.	9s.	11s.
7	9s.	9s.	10s.	10s.	9s. 6d.	9s.	9s.	8s.	9s.	9s.	11s.
8	9s.	9s.	10s.	9s.	9s. 6d.	9s.	9s.	8s.	9s.	9s.	11s.
9	9s.	9s.	9s.	9s.	9s. 6d.	8s.	9s.	8s.	9s.	9s.	9s.
1840	9s.	9s.	9s.	9s.	7s. 10d.	8s.	9s.	8s.	9s.	9s.	9s.
1	9s.	9s.	9s.	9s.	7s. 10d.	8s.	9s.	8s.	9s.	9s.	9s.
2	9s.	8s.	9s.	9s.	7s. 10½d.	8s.	9s.	8s.	9s., 8s.	9s.	9s.
3	9s., 8s.	8s.	9s.	8s.	7s. 6d.	8s.	8s.	7s.	7s.	9s., 8s.	8s.
4	8s.	7s.	8s.	8s.	6s. 6d.	7s.	8s.	6s.	7s.	7s.	8s.
1845	8s., 7s., 6s.	7s.	7s.	7s.	6s.	7s.	8s.	6s.	7s.	7s.	8s.
6	7s., 6s.	7s.	6s.	7s.	6s.	7s.	8s.	6s.	7s., 6s.	8s., 7s.	8s.
7	7s., 6s.	6s.	6s.	7s.	6s.	7s., 6s.	7s., 6s.	6s.	6s.	7s., 6s.	8s.
8	6s.	5s., 4s.	6s.	7s., 6s.	6s.	6s.	6s.	..	..	6s.	7s., 6s.
9	6s., 5s.	..	..	6s.	..	..	..	..	..	..	6s.
1850	5s., 4s.	..	..	..	..	..	..	..	..	..	..

a Previously to 1823 gas was not supplied by meter, so price is not available.
b Previously to 1829 gas was not supplied by meter, so price is not available.

Source: *P.P.* 1847 (734), xliv; 1850 (399), xlix.

TABLE 33. *Annual Dividends Paid, Per Cent. per Annum, by Eleven Chartered London Gas Companies, 1820–50*

Name of company	Chartered	City	Poplar	Imperial	British	Ratcliff	Phoenix	Independent	Equitable	London	South Metropolitan
Capital 1850a (£000)	£300	£200	£20	£665	£140	£90	£441	£120	£200	£550	£200
Year											
1820	8	10	..	..	..	..	..	..	..	..	..
1	8	7	No	No	..	..	..	..	..	..	..
2	8	8·5	No	No	..	..	..	..	..	..	..
3	7	8	No	No	No	No	No	..	..	..	..
4	7	9·5	No	6	No	No	5	..	..	..	..
1825	6	10	No	6	No	No	5	..	..	..	..
6	6	10	No	6	No	No	5·5	..	..	..	..
7	6	10	No	3	1	No	6	..	..	..	..
8	6	10	No	No	No	No	6	5	..	..	..
9	6	10	No	5·5	No	4	6	6	..	..	..
1830	6	10	No	5	5	3·5	6	6	..	..	..
1	6	10	No	5	5	4	6	6	..	..	..
2	6	10	No	5	6·1	4	6	6	No	..	..
3	6	10	No	5	6·25	4	4·5	6	No	..	..
4	6	10	No	5	6·4	4	3	6	4	No	No
1835	5	10	4	5	6·66	4	3	6	4	No	No
6	6	10	4	5	6·95	4	3	6	4·5	No	1·5
7	6	10	4	5	6·95	4	3·5	6	4·5	4	2·5
8	6	10	4	5	6·95	5	4	6	7·5	4	2·5
9	6	10	5	5	6·95	5	5	6	3	4	4
1840	6	10	5	5·5	6·95	5	5	6	No	5	4·5
1	6	10	No	6	6·95	5	5	6	No	5	5
2	6	10	1·5	6	6·95	5	5	6	8	5	6
3	6	10	3·5	6	6·95	5	5	6	4	6	6
4	6	10	5	6	6·95	5	5	6	4	6	6
1845	6	10	5	6	6·95	5	5	6	4·5	6	6
6	6	10	4	6	5·55	5	5	6	4·5	6	6
7	6	10	4	6	5	5	5	6	5	3	6
8	6	10	No	6	5	5	4·5	6	2·5	No	6
9	6	8	No	6	5	5	4·5	6	No	No	6
1850	6	..	..	6	5	5	4·5	6	..	..	6

a The figures given do not in all cases agree with those shown in Wetenhall's *Course of the Exchange*.

Source: *P.P.* 1847 (734), xliv; 1850 (399), xlix.

The index of the share prices of gas-light companies begins in 1819, when quotations for the industry become generally available. It reveals at least three broad movements in the fortunes of the gas-light companies. From a peak in 1824 the index declines for two years, and rises to one peak in 1830 and another in 1833. A long slow decline then begins and lasts until the end of 1837. From that point the index rises in 1845, to the highest point since 1824, after which a decline sets in. This brings the index to its low point for the entire period, in 1848. This latter decline is possibly to be connected with the legislation of 1847. The index, it is to be noted, fails to share substantially the boom of 1836. It declines almost steadily from 1833 to the end of 1837; and it fails (except from 1837 to 1845) to exhibit the general upward tendency of the total index (exclusive of mines). Competition probably affected earnings relative to those in other industries, where more monopolistic conditions were maintained, or where stronger secular forces of expansion operated.

7. Mine Companies. The heavy investment in mining companies shares during 1824 and 1825 was largely speculative. Most of the mines were located in Mexico and South America and little basis existed for the extraordinary expectations which these ventures aroused in the minds of investors. Their optimism was based principally on two assumptions which later proved false: that the abandonment of the Mexican and South American mines after 1810 was due entirely to political turmoil and not mineral exhaustion; and that, with the application of English capital and superior technical skills, the mines would yield more profits than they had before the revolutions.[1] Additional pressure to support the undertakings came from political propaganda urging the British public to support the newly acquired liberty of the South American colonies. There was also believed to be an increased demand for the precious metals, due to the simultaneous resumption of specie payments on the part of a number of countries.[2]

The intense speculation in mine shares, which reached its high point in 1825, could not be sustained after actual mining operations were begun and the first results were known. The initial decline of that year was a short-period reaction from the previous excesses, but the continued downward trend thereafter, until 1841, was a reflection of the demonstrable failure of the ventures to yield profitable returns. The depression of the mine share market was reinforced by the fact that the companies had originally required that only a part of the capital be paid up. When the serious decline began in August 1825, more capital was called in and shareholders were forced either to borrow money or sell the shares, thus further depressing the market.

The high prices of mining shares in 1825 can only be explained in terms of the expectations that characterized the period. A *Times* correspondent observed, 'What . . . could be more preposterous than the rise in January,

---

[1] Sir William Adams, *The Actual State of the Mexican Mines*, p. 23 n., and English, p. 5.

[2] Jenks, pp. 27–8, 53–4.

to 100 per cent. premium, of the mining shares of companies which had then only begun their career, and did not themselves know the terms on which the chief part of their contracts were likely to be concluded.'[1] A contemporary writer, John Taylor, pictures the public attitude towards mining ventures as follows : 'The public seemed to think mining a certain source of immeasurable wealth, to be obtained by everyone who was lucky enough to get a share in any mine, in any place, and under any kind of management.'[2]

There were some who looked upon the huge capital investments of the time with suspicion. One writer states : 'You ask my friendly opinion as to the multitudinous schemes that have of late been set on foot here. . . . My honest opinion is, that some good may possibly arise out of the present schemes, but a much greater amount of evil. The projectors may, at the outset, deceive themselves only, but may yet have to make a scapegoat of the first man they meet with ; and, in the course of time and the progress of events, one wide-sweeping destruction may overtake a great portion of the community.'[3]

Since nearly all the mining companies originally called in only a part of their capital, it was possible, while prices were rising, to sell at a profit before a further call was made. However, once the serious decline in prices occurred, from August 1825 on, this was impossible. Shareholders, who had never expected to be called on for more capital, were forced, as noted above, to borrow money or to sell the shares.

The public's attitude towards mining ventures changed from one of confidence to suspicion in the last few months of 1825.

The extraordinary revolution in public opinion, with respect to mining speculation which we have witnessed in the course of a few months, presents a remarkable instance of ill-advised confidence and temerity having been followed by excessive alarm and doubt, while in reality neither one nor the other, except in a few cases, has been founded on a knowledge of the subject. Shares in undertakings of this description have been sought after with the utmost eagerness at prices the most extravagant, without much inquiry into the merits of the enterprise and this has been followed by ignorant or unjust denunciation of the whole.[4]

Taylor attributed the fluctuations not to 'any just appreciation of the adventures of the sort, but to the fact that the shareholders considered it a game on the price of shares and the chance of premiums'.[5]

In the early years eleven companies are included in the index ; Anglo-Mexican, Bolanos, Real Del Monte, United Mexican Mining Company, Mexican Mining Company, Imperial Brazilian, Colombian, Alten, General, Hibernian, and British Iron. Because of failures and absence of quotations only two are quoted by 1850. During the period from 1841 to 1850 there are at most three companies in the index, none of which paid dividends.

[1] *The Times*, 28 Oct. 1825.

[2] *Profits of Mining in England, Prospects in Mexico*, p. 50.

[3] A. Romney, *Three Letters on the Speculative Schemes of the Present Times*, pp. 2, 3, 20.

[4] Taylor, p. 1.   [5] p. 55.

They somehow managed to limp along and occasional transactions in their shares were recorded. The history of the individual companies are extraordinarily similar in their pattern of initial disappointments, additional calls for capital, continued failure, and final disillusionment of shareholders. They do not justify extended consideration here. Only the relatively small Alten Company, which mined copper in Norway, can be said to have achieved any measure of success.

8. Railways. The pace and scale of railway development during the period 1825–50 stand out in marked contrast to the long and slow growth that preceded. The origin of the railway can be traced as far back as the first half of the seventeenth century, when parallel courses of wood were laid on dirt roads to facilitate the carting of coal from the pit's mouth to the river. By 1750 cast-iron rails had come into use and proved so successful that there was hardly a colliery without its adjacent tramway.[1]

The act which in 1801 authorized the construction of the Surrey Iron Railway was the first strictly railway act, in the sense that the proposed road was not connected with any particular canal company or mine.[2] The significance of the statute lies in the fact that it served as a model for many early railway statutes. Chief among its provisions was the requirement that the tracks be open to the vehicles of anyone who paid the prescribed tolls, and the latter could not exceed certain stipulated maxima.

From 1801 until 1821, a total of only nineteen new tramway companies were sanctioned by Parliament.[3] The capital of the largest of these companies was £125,000, but most were considerably smaller. The year 1821 marks the passage of the act for the Stockton and Darlington Railway which, at its opening in 1825, was the first to use (though not exclusively) steam locomotion.[4]

Neither the Surrey Iron Railway nor the Stockton and Darlington, though both were independent of canal companies, was in direct competition with the waterways. They were, rather, supplementary to inland navigation facilities. Practically all other railways established before 1825 were either private roads or feeder lines for canals. The Liverpool and Manchester line, however, was launched in 1826 as the first road designed to compete with and eventually to supplant existing water facilities. The background for the establishment of this line is an example of the manner in which the canals had exploited their monopoly position; and it serves to illustrate the types of opposition which the development of the new form of locomotion aroused.

Railways shared in the booms of 1825 and 1836, especially the latter. From the beginning of the century until 1824 an average of one railway

---

[1] A 'tramway' refers exclusively to a horse-drawn vehicle on tracks as opposed to a 'railway' which implies automatic locomotion. The latter term, however, is used in a generic sense, inclusive of tramways, during the early railway era.

[2] 41 Geo. III, c. 33.

[3] J. Francis, *A History of the English Railway*, i. 57–62.

[4] 1 & 2 Geo. IV, c. 44; also amended Act of 1823, 4 Geo. IV, c. 33.

act was passed each year; in 1825–6, Parliament sanctioned nineteen new lines. Thereafter about five new railways were authorized in each year until 1836, when twenty-nine were sanctioned, followed by fifteen in the next year. The boom of 1836–7 was also reflected in a volume of authorized railway capital far in excess of the total in all preceding years and in the considerable heights to which share prices were pushed. The reaction to the 1836–7 boom was evidenced in the relatively smaller volume of new railway issues from 1838 to 1843. Share prices, however, held firm, maintaining steadily a higher level than that which preceded the boom. The years from 1843 to 1848 mark the period of greatest concentration of railway activity in British history. In the single year 1846 almost £133 million of new capital were authorized, easily surpassing all other types of new investment at that time.

The story of the railway boom of the mid-forties is thoroughly familiar. It remains here merely to summarize a few of its features that bear on the course of the rail share index.

The boom in railway enterprise which took place in 1836, a decade earlier, appeared at the time to be one of major magnitude. In a single year, from June 1835 to May 1836, the index of the prices of railway shares more than doubles: at the former date it stands at 60·2, at the latter, 129·4. This increase in market values was even more remarkable than any such simple comparison would indicate, since at no time prior to 1835 does the index reach a level as high as 80.[1] Moreover, the sums which Parliament authorized to be raised in 1836 for railway construction exceeded the total amount authorized for that purpose during all preceding years.

It is interesting to note the character of the reaction that followed the 1836 boom. There was an immediate deflation of share prices fully revealed in the index, which dips as low as 70, in April 1837; but in every year following the boom the index showed a higher average level than in any year before 1836. The major post-boom reaction in railways apparently took place not in the valuation of existing securities but in the reluctance of promoters to project new lines and to raise new capital. As contrasted with capital powers of £23 million awarded in 1836 and £13·5 million in 1837, only £2 million were authorized by Parliament in 1838. This sum was a smaller total than in any year since 1833. There was an increase in new railway enterprise in 1839; but from 1840 through 1843 the sums authorized by Parliament ranged from £2·5 million to £5·3 million.[2] Most of the acts passed during the period were either amending statutes or awards of additional capital powers to lines already in existence rather than authorization of new railways. In sum, the length of railway lines authorized by Parliament to the end of 1843 was 2,390 miles, of which

[1] Of course, the absolute levels are in themselves no indication of the condition of the railway share market. In fact, the general trend of railway share prices was rising from 1827, the year in which the index begins. The index figures referred to are based on the value for the single month of June 1840, which happened to be relatively high.

[2] Porter, p. 332.

2,036 had been opened for traffic. The total authorized capital of these lines amounted to £82 million, of which about £66 million had been raised.[1]

Share prices had already begun to move up rapidly at the end of 1843, and, for the first time since 1836, the index rises well above 100. These increases were probably a reaction to the large earnings realized by the more important railways. The Liverpool and Manchester, the London and Birmingham, and the Grand Junction paid dividends of about 10 per cent. in 1844, while a few others paid even more.[2] The profitability of these established companies had the effect not only of boosting the prices of existing railway shares, but of encouraging the promotion of new projects as well. At this point absence of parliamentary machinery for handling railway petitions on a long-run, non-speculative basis was important. Clifford in his *History of Private Bill Legislation* described the struggle in 1844, a year in which the boom had only begun to gather momentum:

Existing companies . . . made strenuous efforts to hold possession of the ground already allotted to them. First, they alleged vested interests, insisting that their capital had been spent upon the implied condition that Parliament had granted them certain rights which were not to be taken away, even in part, by similar concessions to competitive undertakings, except upon clear proof of neglect or inability to accommodate the traffic. They did not, however, rely wholly upon this defence, but wisely prepared a second line of entrenchments, on which they might fall back, and asked Parliament to sanction branches, subsidiary to their main lines, or railways intended chiefly to block out intruders. Possession, and a command of almost unlimited resources, gave to existing companies great power in the Committee rooms, but Committees were not always swayed in their favour, and sometimes, indeed, sanctioned competing lines as the best remedy against threatened monopoly. The result was that, in the year 1844 alone, some fifty new lines, more than 800 miles long, were approved by the Legislature, with capital powers amounting to twenty millions and a half.[3]

There followed in the next few years a fever of railway speculation. Attracted by a bull market and the irresistible appeals in the financial press, groups of middle-class folk, who hitherto had never known the Stock Exchange, hurried to place their small accumulations in securities. The public funds and foreign government bonds were now eclipsed as the chief objects of a speculation, and their brokers and jobbers were crowded out by the specialists in railway securities.

The railway share index, which averages 98·2 in 1843 and 121·3 in 1844, climbs to a peak figure of 167·9 in July 1845, then slumps, but remains at a level above 140 through most of 1846. Even more spectacular is the manner in which the boom was reflected in railway legislation. The number of acts for new lines, and for alterations and extensions of the facilities of existing companies, rose to 120 in 1845, authorizing £59,479,500 for the construction of 2,700 miles of railway.[4] This mileage, though authorized in

---

[1] *P.P.* 1867, xxxviii, Report of the Royal Commission on Railways, Pt. I, p. 10.
[2] Wetenhall's *Course of Exchange.*

[3] i. 87.
[4] Report of the Royal Commission on Railways, 1867, Pt. I, p. 17.

a single year, exceeded the total mileage authorized for all the railways of Great Britain down to the end of 1843.[1] But the next year produced a deluge of railway activity that dwarfed even that of 1845 and marked 1846 as the outstanding year in the whole history of British railways. The number of miles authorized in 1846 reached 4,538, and capital powers were granted to the extent of £132,617,000. These magnitudes can best be appreciated in the light of the figures for the preceding and the following years, which are presented in the following tabulation and Fig. 96. The tabulation also gives the average annual value of our railway share price index, making possible a comparison of the course of the share market with new promotional activity.

Year	Capital authorized[a]	Railway share price index (June 1840 = 100)
	£	
1826 . .	1,687,653	. .
7 . .	251,608	45·9
8 . .	424,000	54·5
9 . .	904,125	54·3
1830 . .	735,650	61·7
1 . .	1,799,875	65·2
2 . .	567,685	68·0
3 . .	5,525,333	69·3
4 . .	2,312,053	67·8
1835 . .	4,812,833	71·1
6 . .	22,874,998	111·1
7 . .	13,521,799	81·4
8 . .	2,096,198	91·1
9 . .	6,455,797	79·9
1840 . .	2,495,032	86·4
1 . .	3,410,686	83·8
2 . .	5,311,642	89·4
3 . .	3,861,350	98·2
4 . .	20,454,000	121·3
1845 . .	59,479,000	149·0
6 . .	132,617,000	139·4
7 . .	39,460,000	117·1
8 . .	15,274,000	95·5
9 . .	3,911,000	77·1
1850 . .	4,116,000	70·4

Mileage open Dec. 1843: 1,952. Mileage open Dec. 1850: 6,621

a The figures for capital authorized until 1843 are taken from Porter, p. 332; thereafter from Cleveland-Stevens, p. 24. Figures for 1844 and 1845 overlap in the two sources, but only those for the latter year are in agreement. Since Cleveland-Stevens's figures are based on parliamentary reports issued after the publication of Porter's work, his figure for 1844 is taken. The figures on mileage open are also from Cleveland-Stevens. For the construction and composition of the railway share index, see above, pp. 361–4.

1 See table in E. Cleveland-Stevens, *English Railways*, p. 24. The figures are taken from the Report of the Commissioners of Railways for 1848 (p. 45), and the Report of the Railway Department for 1854 (p. vii).

Though no neat covariation between the two series is revealed from year to year, the major fluctuations of the mid-thirties and forties are clearly reflected in both (see Fig. 96). In the case of the latter boom, the peak in

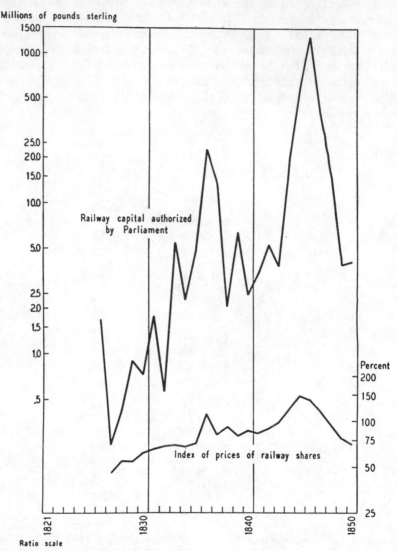

Fig. 96. Railway Capital Authorized and the Index of Prices of Railway Shares, 1826–50

capital authorized appears in 1846 while the high point in prices comes in 1845. This type of discrepancy might be due to the fact that the figures are in annual form and therefore make possible only very crude comparisons. A lag of one year in the high or low points of the two annual series is not inconsistent with closer monthly coincidence. But even monthly figures would probably show some lag in the capital authorized series, since the temporal sequence is from high share prices to increases in new issues; and, most important, the latter received parliamentary authorization only after the lapse of the considerable time necessary for applications to be put through the legal processes.

Until 1847 railway share prices had remained on a comparatively high level. But by the end of the year the public, only recently initiated into the share market, had invested far beyond its means. This was especially hazardous because at this time, when many new enterprises were being projected, the purchase of a share for a small initial payment involved the obligation of meeting a long series of future calls. The effects of repeated calls upon shareholders whose funds were already exhausted were thus described in *The Economist*: 'Either the shares themselves upon which the "call" had been made were sold, in order to avoid its payment; or some other shares were sold, in order to raise money for that purpose. But whichever plan was adopted, there was a constantly increasing number of sellers, and a constantly diminishing number of buyers.'[1] When, in the early part of 1849, mismanagement and fraud were first disclosed in the companies of George Hudson, the 'railway king', share prices fell to new lows : 'The year 1849 was probably the period of greatest disaster and distress to those persons who were embarked in railway enterprises.'[2]

In 1850 an act was passed 'to facilitate the abandonment of railways and the dissolution of railway companies'.[3] This act enabled companies to abandon the whole or parts of their enterprises and released them from the conditions under which their powers had been granted. Of a total of 8,592 miles sanctioned by Parliament in 1845, 1846, and 1847, 1,560 miles were abandoned by the promoters under the powers of this act.[4] Mr. G. C. Glyn, chairman of the London and North Western Railway, probably touched the heart of the matter when he laid the blame for the collapse 'on those who, in 1845 and 1846, opened the door of the Legislature to projects designed simply for the purpose of competition . . . who forced us in defence . . . to undertake schemes which otherwise I take upon myself and my colleagues to say would never have entered into our heads.'[5]

The very intensity of competition during the forties acted as an impetus to the amalgamation movement. Especially at the height of the railway mania, combinations were incident to the struggle of rival companies to improve their position. The establishment of the Railway Clearing House in 1847 was further evidence of the movement towards co-operation and integration. By 1850 the era of intensely competitive railway enterprise, carried on with a minimum of government regulation, had already passed.

9. Joint-stock Banks. The act of 1694 incorporating the Bank of

[1] 21 Oct. 1848, p. 1187.
[2] Tooke and Newmarch, v. 361.
[3] 13 & 14 Vict., c. 83.
[4] Report of the Royal Commission on

Railways, 1867, Pt. I, p. 17.
[5] *Railway Times*, 19 Feb. 1848, p. 203; quoted by Cleveland-Stevens, p. 166.

England did not confer monopoly privileges.[1] Successive renewals of the Bank's charter throughout the eighteenth century, however, established the principle of its exclusive right to joint-stock organization among English banks.[2] In fact, the clause on which this principle was based merely forbade a joint-stock bank or partnership of more than six persons from issuing notes payable to bearer on demand, or from discounting short-term commercial paper. Since the clause was falsely interpreted—on the view of a later generation—as a prohibition of further joint-stock banking, every English bank other than the Bank of England was either a one-man firm or a partnership with no more than six members.

Throughout the eighteenth century, therefore, two types of banks predominated in England : the wealthy London private banks which soon surrendered their note-issuing privilege, and the country banks, carrying on a lucrative business of note issue.

The suspension of specie payment by the Bank of England in 1797 was followed by a tremendous growth of country banks and country bank issues. Numerous bank failures reflected a fundamental weakness of structure : the uneconomical size of the banking unit. The effect of the Bank of England's monopoly was to foster the formation of small banks, whose capitalizations were necessarily limited by the combined investment of a few proprietors not exceeding six in number. Such small, local banks found it difficult to spread their risks. Over-trading was common, public suspicion widespread, and runs upon them not infrequent.

It was not, however, until the great collapse in 1825, when bank failures were general, that positive action was taken. In 1826 an act was passed prohibiting the issue of any further notes under £5 after 1829, thus curbing the tendency towards over-issue of banknotes of small denominations by country bankers.[3] Of greater significance was the enactment, in the same year, of the Banking Co-Partnerships Act, which, by legalizing the establishment of banks of issue with any number of shareholders outside a radius of sixty-five miles from London, diluted the Bank of England's monopoly.[4] As *quid pro quo*, the Bank was permitted to establish branches throughout England.

By 1832 the best legal opinion in England confirmed the fallaciousness of the view that the Bank's charter prohibited joint-stock banks in London. Accordingly, when it was time to renew the charter in 1833, a clause was inserted in the Bank Charter Act removing all doubts that joint-stock banks might legally be established in London or within sixty-five miles radius thereof, provided they did not issue notes.[5] This Act marked the beginning of the period of modern banking in England. And, as noted above, joint-stock bank floatations figured significantly among the categories of long-term investment in the thirties.[6]

---

[1] 5 & 6 Will. and Mary, c. 20.
[2] See 7 Anne, c. 30 (1708); also W. T. C. King, *History of the London Discount Market*, p. 7.
[3] 7 Geo. IV, c. 6.
[4] Ibid. c. 46.
[5] 3 & 4 William IV, c. 98.
[6] See above, p. 255.

The occasion of the renewal of the Bank's charter was seized upon as an opportunity to study the whole problem of the existing system of note circulation. One result was the passage of the Bank Charter Act of 1844, which, besides dividing the Bank into separate issue and deposit departments, imposed a number of restrictions upon note issues of private and joint-stock banks, with the aim of concentrating this function in the hands of the Bank of England. These provisions also had the effect of discouraging the amalgamation movement in banking and the further development of provincial banks. Another result of the banking investigation was the passage of the Joint Stock Bank Act of 1844, which provided for the regulation of all new joint-stock banks. The failure of seven joint-stock banks in the single year 1847 attests, however, to the continued existence of elements of bad management and insecurity in the banking structure.

In considering the relevance of the general evolution of English joint-stock banking to the new sub-index of bank shares, it is well to bear in mind that none of the banks which failed was quoted consistently enough to permit its inclusion in our index. It is, therefore, an index of successful joint-stock banks. It should be further noted that the sub-index includes two Irish banks and one Scottish bank, whose special features are briefly discussed below.

The curve of the joint-stock bank index shows a steady rise from its start, despite set-backs in 1836–7, 1840–1, and 1847–8. Ranging in the 80's in 1831, the index reaches a level between 100 and 110 in 1850. Brief accounts of the banks included in the index follow, designed to assist in the interpretation of movements of the index.

At its start in 1831, the index includes no English bank, because shares of the provincial banks, formed under the Act of 1826, were not quoted on the London exchange. An Irish bank, however, was quoted, since the capital of the *Provincial Bank of Ireland* was largely raised in London. The circumstances of the establishment of this bank in some ways parallel the story of the first joint-stock banks in England. Banking in Ireland was patterned on English lines. The Bank of Ireland was chartered in 1783 with the exclusive privilege of joint-stock banking in Ireland.[1] In 1821, however, the Bank surrendered its monopoly in places farther than fifty miles from Dublin (the equivalent of sixty-five English miles). Only in 1845 was the whole of Ireland thrown open to joint-stock banking.[2]

The Provincial Bank of Ireland, the first great joint-stock bank in Ireland other than the chartered Bank, was projected in 1824 by Joplin and others,[3] but not until late in 1825 did its branches, located in all the principal provincial towns in Ireland, begin to function. A clause in the Act of 1822, compelling every partner in an Irish joint-stock bank to reside in Ireland, was chiefly responsible for delay in the opening of the bank until 1825, when an amendment was passed. This clause was a serious handicap.

---

[1] J. W. Gilbart, *The History and Principles of Banking*, pp. 175 ff.

[2] 8 & 9 Vict., c. 37.

[3] Clapham, i. 512.

Ireland was short of capital and depended on English investors for its long-term funds. The amendment, by abolishing the residence requirement for investors in Irish joint-stock banks, opened the way for the flow of English investment; and, as indicated above, it was in London that the capital for the Provincial Bank was chiefly raised.

The Bank was established with a nominal capital of £2,000,000, of which £500,000 was paid up. The only addition to the paid-up capital made before 1850 was a sum of £40,000 taken from the surplus in 1836.[1]

The Provincial Bank was directed from London, because the Bank of Ireland's monopoly prohibited the maintenance of a Dublin office. The success of the bank has been traced to this circumstance. The directorate obtainable in London was evidently superior to that available in other parts of the country; and the distance between the board and the actual banking operations apears to have increased the soundness and objectivity of the decisions of the directors. The bank had fifteen branches by 1831 and more than twice that number by 1850.

Its early years were marked by considerable difficulties. Like the new joint-stock banks in England, the Provincial Bank had to meet the spirited competition of the branches of the chartered bank, as well as lawsuits by the Bank of Ireland because of infringements of the letter of the law with respect to its privileges.[2] There were a number of runs upon the Provincial Bank in its early days. It dealt with a public ignorant of banking methods; and the failure of any one bank would create general panic. A run in January 1831—when our index begins, however, barely affected the price of its shares. Runs in March 1833, November 1836, February 1839,[3] also had no noticeable effect on the market price of the bank's shares. Their level was steadily upward, from 1831 on, fluctuating around £40 per share when only £25 had been paid up.

The hostility between the Provincial Bank and the Bank of Ireland was shortlived. There is evidence of collaboration with the chartered institution in opposition to competing joint-stock banks.[4] According to a witness before the Committee of 1837 in England,[5] the officers of the Provincial Bank deliberately spread rumours about the soundness of a rival bank, the Agricultural and Commercial Bank of Ireland, which failed in 1836. The Provincial Bank was also accused of acting with the Bank of Ireland in a scheme to reduce the rate of discount on English bills to such a low point as to make the return unremunerative—this solely to drive the Agricultural and Commercial Bank from business.

The Provincial Bank, at any rate, was successful during our period. The

---

[1] M. Dillon, *Banking in Ireland*, p. 52.
[2] Ibid., p. 50.
[3] Ibid., pp. 56–7.
[4] S. E. Thomas, *Joint Stock Banking*, p. 271, n. 5, says: 'This bank was one of the first joint stock banks to be established in Ireland, and from the outset worked hand-in-glove with the Bank of Ireland. Hence it was always hostile to the new joint stock institutions not only because its own interests were threatened, but also because it wished to back up the Bank of Ireland.'
[5] *P.P.* 1837 (531), xiv. See James Dwyer's testimony, Q. 3135–8, 3144.

following statement shows the net profits and dividends per share, in percentages, of the bank from the first year for which there are returns through 1850 :[1]

Year	Net profits	Dividend and bonus	Year	Net profits	Dividend and bonus
	£	per cent.		£	per cent.
1827 . .	28,700	4	1840 . .	59,531	8
8 . .	22,200	4	1 . .	47,514	8
9 . .	22,600	4	2 . .	51,908	10
			3 . .	49,402	8
1830 . .	21,800	4	4 . .	47,413	8
1 . .	21,800	5			
2 . .	34,063	5	1845 . .	49,721	8
3 . .	42,971	6	6 . .	53,989	8
4 . .	56,317	7	7 . .	54,473	10
			8 . .	46,109	8
1835 . .	61,049	8	9 . .	45,733	8
6 . .	61,791	8			
7 . .	45,943	8	1850 . .	43,344	8
8 . .	47,375	8			
9 . .	56,774	10			

The other Irish bank included in our index, the *National Bank of Ireland*, was established in 1834 by the Nationalist Party, with its main office in London.[2] It began operations in 1835 with a nominal capital of £500,000. There were 10,000 shares of which £10 was paid, £40 being subject to call. At the beginning there were two distinct bodies of proprietors, the English and Irish shareholders, one group matching the other's subscription of capital and sharing profits equally.[3] In 1837 this arrangement was terminated because of the inconvenience involved, and the shares of both groups consolidated, except in two branches where the local shareholders were unwilling to let the entire body of stockholders share their profits. The bank was successful at its start because the patriot, Daniel O'Connell, was the first Governor, and, thanks to his popularity, its note-issue increased rapidly. By 1850 £22½ per share had been paid but the market price was at a discount from the paid-up value from 1837 on. The dividend rate was substantial, however, fluctuating between 5 and 6 per cent. In 1847, on O'Connell's death, a rumour spread that he was heavily indebted to the bank ; but no substance was established and the price of its shares was not affected.[4]

The other component of the joint-stock bank index at its start is the *Royal Bank of Scotland*, an institution of greater antiquity than any of the others included. Unlike the others, which were commercial banks, it was more in the nature of a banker's bank. The Bank of Scotland was founded with privileges similar to those of the Bank of England, except that it was formed by private persons to promote trade, and not to support the credit

[1] Dillon, p. 58.
[2] Gilbart, p. 235.
[3] Dillon, p. 63.
[4] Ibid., p. 64.

of the government.[1] It differed in that it lost its monopoly of joint-stock banking in 1727. That very year the Royal Bank of Scotland was established with a charter from the Crown, and public funds were deposited with it.[2]

After 1727 there was no monopolistic banking legislation in Scotland, and a joint-stock banking system developed without difficulty. The reluctance of the older banks, like the Royal, to open branches led to the establishment of many local private and joint-stock banks in Scotland, from which was evolved a well-organized system of branch banking, national in scope. This system had not yet been achieved by the time our index begins; but banking in Scotland was then in a far more advanced stage than it was in England. It had already achieved a sound currency in which notes of small denominations played an important role; but these were not, as in England, periodically over-issued. In this system the business of the Royal Bank, as also of the other chartered banks, was largely with the private bankers of Edinburgh, who in turn financed manufacturers and merchants.

In 1831 the Royal Bank had a capital of £2,000,000 on which it was paying a dividend of $5\frac{1}{2}$ per cent. There was a considerable decline in the price of its shares in February 1831[3] as a result of the changes in its charter on its eighth renewal.[4] Its capital until August 1831 was £1,500,000 and the dividend rate 6 per cent. By the terms of its new charter the capital was increased by £500,000, although it appears that the increase was not essential.[5] The dividend rate subsequently declined $\frac{1}{2}$ per cent. The capital and dividend thereafter remained unchanged until 1850.

In 1833 the bank opened a branch in Greenock, fifty years after it had established its first and only branch in Glasgow; but it still made no effort to follow in the footsteps of its competitors who were opening branches widely.

The prices of shares of the Royal Bank throughout the period of its inclusion in our index were at high premiums. Without doubt, the bank was a more stable institution than the average Scottish bank, but from 1830, the average joint-stock bank in Scotland was hardly less safe an investment.[6] In this sense the Royal Bank may well be considered a representative firm. There are no quotations for this bank after 1845.

The first English bank to be included in our index is the *National Provincial Bank of England*, fathered by Thomas Joplin. Joplin, one of its directors from 1833 to 1836, had also founded the Provincial Bank of Ireland in 1824. The National Provincial was established in 1833 under the

[1] C. A. Conant, *Modern Banks of Issue*, p. 143.

[2] A. W. Kerr, *History of Banking in Scotland*, *passim*, from which this account is drawn.

[3] Our index clearly registers this decline.

[4] N. Munro, *History of the Royal Bank of Scotland*, pp. 198–9.

[5] Idem. 'It was an old office tradition of the Royal that this increase of capital, though hardly justified on principles of financial expediency, was dictated by an apprehension that the Government contemplated the abolition of bank-note issues and the substitution of a State issue, in which case a large capital might secure special privileges in the conduct of the new system.'

[6] Kerr, p. 162, gives the dividends of joint-stock banks in Scotland, showing their stability.

provisions of the Act of 1826, and began operations in Gloucester in 1834.[1] While the National Provincial had an office in London which administered the affairs of its branches, it did no banking business there until 1866, because of the exclusion of banks of issue from the metropolis.[2] The issue of its own notes in the provinces was a mainstay of the National Provincial during its early years.

As in the case of the National Bank of Ireland, it was proposed that the National Provincial consist of a grouping of local banks, with local share-holders 'deriving their profits, or incurring their losses (as the case may be) from or at and by means of such separate banks'.[3] The scheme, strongly favoured by Joplin, was given a trial in which it proved impracticable and was abandoned. Joplin quit the Board of Directors following this decision.

The bank had a nominal capitalization of £1,000,000, divided into 10,000 shares of a par value of £100 each. Only £5 was paid up the first year and the maximum reached before 1850 was £35, which was paid up in 1837. From 1835 on the dividend fluctuated between 5 and 6 per cent. per share. The price of the bank's shares was always very close to par.

An example of the extraordinary hostility existing between the private and joint-stock banks during this period is afforded by the experience of the National Provincial. In 1837 it withdrew part of its business from a private London banking firm which had been its agent in the metropolis and made the London Joint Stock Bank part agent. The private bank thereupon refused to accept bills of the National Provincial, and for a time endangered the credit standing of the bank.[4]

National Provincial played an important part in the controversy between the Bank of England and the joint-stock banks on the matter of the pro-hibition of the joint-stock banks from accepting bills at shorter dates than six months.[5] The bank was one of those which drew bills payable at less than six months' date without acceptance on its London agents, the Lon-don Joint Stock Bank.

The branches of the National Provincial were established very rapidly throughout England. There was some question whether this policy was not being pursued to the detriment of the interests of the shareholders.[6] In the first place, any branch which did not prove successful involved an increase in the burden of the unlimited liability borne by the shareholders; and, in the second place, building up the business of a new branch, by diverting some of the reserves of established branches, meant that present dividends were lower than they otherwise would have been. Shareholders complained that smaller banks were paying higher dividends than the large National Provincial and that, for 1850, the profits of this bank equalled only £350

---

[1] H. Withers, *Nat. Prov. Bank*, pp. 1–2, 44.
[2] W. R. Crick and J. E. Wadsworth, *Joint Stock Banking*, p. 309.
[3] Quoted by Withers, p. 44, from the notice of the first Yearly General Meeting in *The Times* of 25 Apr. 1834.

[4] H. Burgess, *Circular to Bankers*, 13 Jan. 1837.
[5] Thomas, pp. 241 ff.
[6] 'Profits of English Joint Stock Banks.' Letter in *Banker's Magazine*, July 1851, p. 436.

per branch, whereas the bigger branches of National Provincial must have been yielding more than this average return. Some of the joint-stock banks which failed during our period had, indeed, over-extended their branch facilities. Even though the directors of National Provincial may have opened certain branches out of enthusiasm for the growth of the institution, and without due consideration of the business prospects of the branches, on the whole their decisions, as reflected in the steady prosperity of the firm, seem to have been sound.

National Provincial was one of the few joint-stock banks of issue which accepted with good grace the provisions of the Bank Charter Act, which limited a bank's circulation to the amount of its notes outstanding in 1844. The directors seemed to believe that the improvement in communication afforded by the railway system would operate to reduce the number of notes needed in the provinces, and thus mitigate any injurious effects of the legal restriction of the circulation.[1]

The first London joint-stock bank established under the Act of 1833 is also included in our index. This was the *London and Westminster Bank*, which began business in 1834 under the management of J. W. Gilbart.[2] The bank started with a decided handicap. Contemporary newspaper accounts were sceptical of its chances for success, and the reaction of the investing public to the new enterprise was unfavourable. While the task of obtaining subscribers for 10,000 shares for which the bank first advertised applications proved relatively easy, collecting the first call of £5 per share was much more arduous. There were many shareholders in and about London who did not answer the call promptly, the Secretary to the Committee of the London and Westminster Bank reported in November 1833, and 'the small amount of the payment . . . could only be attributed to misrepresentations out of doors'.[3]

As soon as the bank began to function, however, all doubts about its future were dispelled, and its shares were widely sought after. The number of shares was increased to 18,000 in 1835, to 30,000 in the following year, to 40,000 in 1843, and to 50,000 in 1850. £20 was paid up by March 1836, and until 1850 there were no more calls. The par value of each share was £100. Except for a few months in 1837 London and Westminster shares sold at a premium from the time of the last call in 1836 until 1850.

It was this bank which initiated in London the custom of paying interest on all time deposits, even in small amounts,[4] and which developed facilities for small customers, keeping their accounts for a fixed annual or commission charge.

The impediments to joint-stock banking in London at this time have already been discussed. The pioneering London and Westminster Bank

---

[1] See the 1845 'Report of the National Provincial Bank' in *Banker's Magazine*, June 1845, pp. 180–1.

[2] T. E. Gregory, *The London and Westminster Bank*, i. chap. 3.

[3] Ibid., p. 85.

[4] 2 per cent. was paid on all deposits under £1,000, interest on larger amounts being settled between the parties at the time of deposit.

suffered many set-backs during its early days in seeking recognition for the new type of enterprise it represented. Not until the same year were joint-stock banks allowed to accept bills drawn on them at short dates; not until 1842 did the Bank of England open a drawing account for the London and Westminster Bank; and not until 1854 were the joint-stock banks admitted to the London Clearing House.[1]

Long before the disabilities of the London joint-stock banks were removed, however, the London and Westminster Bank had won its spurs. It had established connexions with country banks and with institutions overseas by the end of the thirties, and was a formidable competitor of the London private banks. A policy of granting shares to large country banking establishments in order to extend the London and Westminster Bank's connexions was pursued from the start.[2] Country banks, which had only a local business, relied on a correspondent bank in London to handle their London transactions, and to assist them in times of pressure. The London and Westminster Bank was the regular agent for a number of important country banks,[3] for which it discounted bills to an agreed amount, at a specified rate, and accepted deposit accounts for investment, at a set brokerage charge, &c. The banking operations of a great number of country firms during this period are revealed in the course of an examination of their applications to the London and Westminster Bank for discount facilities. Not all of them were in a satisfactory position, and some, when granted facilities, sought to use them beyond the agreed limits. By 1837 the London and Westminster Bank had overseas agencies in three French cities, and by 1845 in South Africa as well.[4]

Until 1850 the bank's growth may be traced to increases in its capital and reserves and the business of its head office and branches, and not to the amalgamation characteristic of a later period. Nor did it attempt to establish an extensive network of branches. The bank had six establishments by June 1836, and the number remained unchanged until 1855.[5]

An impression of the progress of the London and Westminster Bank may be obtained from Table 34, showing the assets and liabilities of the bank until 1850, and the dividends paid (see p. 448).

The remaining bank included in our index is the *London Joint Stock Bank*, founded in 1836 on the wave of general prosperity, with a nominal capital of £3 million divided into 60,000 shares of £50 each. Though by this time its predecessor, the London and Westminster, had gained a firm foothold, the new bank found it difficult to induce investors to purchase shares.[6] £7 was paid up per share at the outset, but the market price was at a discount until 1837. The directors attempted to rig the price by purchasing shares on behalf of the bank, 'provided that on no account are so many . . .

---

[1] Gregory, i. chap. 4.
[2] Ibid., chap. 6, especially pp. 236–7.
[3] Ibid. See pp. 298–301 for a list of the banks for which the London and Westminster Bank was agent.
[4] Ibid., pp. 300–1.
[5] Ibid., p. 291.
[6] Crick and Wadsworth, pp. 281–2.

purchased as will reduce the remaining number issued below 30,000'.[1] By this time the peak of prosperity had passed so that the poor showing of the bank in the share market may have been due to the condition of the capital market in general rather than to its inherent weakness. In May 1838 £10 was paid up, and no more calls were made thereafter. After 1837 the price of the shares was always quoted at a considerable premium.

TABLE 34. *Assets and Liabilities of the London and Westminster Bank, 1834–50*

	Liabilities (£000)				Assets (£000)			
31 Dec.	Capital paid-up	Reserve	Deposits	Net profits	Cash in hand and money at call	Loans and discounts	Invest-ments (Govt. securities)	Dividend and bonus
								per cent.
1834	182	1	180[a]	4	..	..	..	5
5	267	2	267	12	..	..	..	5
6	597	5	643	32	..	..	..	5
7	597	7	793	32	..	..	..	6
8	597	21	1,388	44	..	..	..	6
9	597	33	1,267	48	..	..	..	6
1840	597	46	1,362	49	..	..	..	6
1	786	56	1,499	51	..	..	..	6
2	800	63	2,088	55	..	..	..	6
3	800	67	2,220	52	..	..	..	6
4	800	70	2,677	51	..	..	..	6
1845	800	70	3,594	66	563	2,928[b]	1,040	8
6	800	88	3,288	72	635	2,677[b]	939	6
7	989	96	2,747	58	721	2,378[b]	792	6
8	999	95	3,090	62	645	2,386[c]	1,189	6
9	1,000	105	3,681	65	687	3,158[c]	974	6
1850	1,000	111	3,970	67	566	3,459[c]	1,090	6

[a] Deposits include Circular Notes.   [b] 'Other Securities.'
[c] 'Other Securities, including bills discounted and loans.'

Source: Gregory, ii. 304–5, and Thomas, pp. 188 and 663, for reserves 1834–44, and for dividend and bonus figures. In a few cases there are slight discrepancies between the figures as given in the two sources. The Gregory figures have been used in those instances.

The bank set out to do business on lines which speedily attracted customers. In the first place it offered interest on both current and deposit accounts, while the London and Westminster allowed interest only on the latter. Secondly the rate of interest fixed was $2\frac{1}{2}$ per cent. per annum on sums not exceeding £2,000, a rate $\frac{1}{2}$ per cent. higher than that offered by the London and Westminster.

The London Joint Stock Bank thus challenged not only the old bankers but the new ones as well. It was not long before the effectiveness of its challenge was revealed. In 1839 the bank obtained an important railway account, hitherto kept by a private banking firm, by offering it better

[1] Quoted, Crick and Wadsworth, p. 283.

terms.[1] The concern felt by the London and Westminster Bank over the competition of the newcomer is revealed in reports by Gilbart to the directors in 1838 and 1849, on the reasons for the failure of the City office to maintain its position relative to the branches.[2] He ascribed the success of the London Joint Stock Bank in acquiring a City business much larger than theirs to the fact that 'their Directors are commercial men and though not of a higher social rank than our own, they have from their City connections more City influence, which they have used energetically for the interest of their Bank'.[3]

The London Joint Stock Bank also acquired the London agency of various provincial banks, and had mutual correspondent relations with banks in Canada and the United States.[4] The rapid development of London's international financing during this period derives to a certain extent from the joint-stock banks' activity in establishing overseas connexions.

Within two years of its establishment the Bank had considered opening a branch office in the West End of London, but found no opportunity to do so until 1840, when the business of an old firm of private bankers, which had suspended payment, was transferred to it.[5] This was the only branch the bank opened before 1850.

The importance of the policy of paying interest on current and deposit accounts in contributing to the early success of the London Joint Stock Bank, while great, was proved not to be decisive. The decline in the general level of interest rates in 1843 and 1844 reduced the bank's margin of profits to such an extent that in 1844 interest on current accounts was fixed at 1 per cent., to be paid only on accounts with an average minimum monthly balance of £200. Nevertheless, there was no decrease in outstanding balances. It was only after the middle of the century, when even the reduced cost of interest became too burdensome, that the bank abolished all interest on current accounts, and the distinction between non-interest-earning current accounts and interest-earning deposit accounts became common.

Compared with the dividends paid by some of the provincial banks, the returns received by shareholders of the London Joint Stock Bank were rather modest. One reason for this was that the deed of settlement of the London Joint Stock Bank provided that the directors were to maintain and add to a reserve fund until it had grown to a million pounds sterling, despite the fact that the total paid-up capital of the Bank was only £600,000.[6] The ratio of its reserves to its liabilities tended therefore to be much higher than was the case with the other London banks, and its dividends to be lower than they otherwise might have been.[7] Shareholders complained that their interests were being sacrificed for the sake of future

[1] Crick and Wadsworth, p. 288.
[2] Gregory, i. 253 ff.
[3] Ibid., p. 259.
[4] Crick and Wadsworth, pp. 285 and 307-8.

[5] Ibid., pp. 286-8.
[6] Thomas, pp. 591-2.
[7] Actually the dividends were no lower than those of any other London joint-stock bank.

shareholders who, it was argued, would obtain larger dividends, once the required fund had been accumulated and whose equity would be more valuable because of the bank's strong position.[1] The conservative reserve practice of the London Joint Stock Bank was, however, a bulwark of strength for the institution in times of panic and crisis. Only the generous size of its guarantee fund permitted the bank to pay its usual dividend and a bonus in 1848 when the bank suffered considerable losses on account of bad debts and defalcation.[2]

A table showing the capital, reserve, deposits, and dividend and bonus paid by the London Joint Stock Bank from 1837 to 1850 follows:

TABLE 35. *London Joint Stock Bank*

		Capital (£000)	Reserve (£000)	Deposits (£000)	Dividend and bonus per cent.
1837	. .	218	3	594	4
8	. .	311	11	1,145	5
9	. .	311	21	1,035	5
1840	. .	445	50	1,171	5
1	. .	590	82	1,403	5
2	. .	600	94	1,772	6
3	. .	600	91	2,046	6
4	. .	600	91	2,245	6
1845	. .	600	96	2,460	6
6	. .	600	120	2,446	6+2s.
7	. .	600	124	1,972	6+7s. 6d.
8	. .	600	124	2,238	6
9	. .	600	133	2,793	6
1850	. .	600	134	2,950	6

Source: Thomas, p. 664.

10. Insurance Companies. The three basic forms of insurance from which all others grew were life, fire, and marine insurance.[3] Each developed quite independently of the other two, although in their later stages of development we find companies handling two or all three types. Companies underwriting all these kinds of insurance are included in our index.

Marine insurance is the oldest form of insurance, dating from the fourteenth century. By the early eighteenth century private underwriters would gather at Lloyd's Coffee House, which became the centre of marine insurance business. Two of the first companies to engage in this field were granted a monopoly of marine insurance in England, save for the individual underwriters.[4] Despite the monopoly, however, the private underwriters

[1] Thomas, p. 592.
[2] Crick and Wadsworth, p. 289.
[3] The terms insurance and assurance are commonly used interchangeably, no clear distinction being drawn between them. Cornelius Walford, in his *Insurance Cyclopaedia* (i. 206), suggests that 'assurance' denotes the principle, and 'insurance' the practice, but this differentiation has seldom been observed. We shall follow common usage and regard the terms as identical in meaning.
[4] H. G. Lay, *History of Marine Insurance*, p. 29.

of Lloyd's retained a major share of all marine underwriting. In the decades following 1720, they joined the two chartered companies in resisting intrusions of new companies into their business.

The years of the Napoleonic Wars were especially prosperous for marine insurance both because of the increased demand for this service and the advance in the premium rates.[1] After 1815 a severe depression was suffered until 1824, when a revival of trade resulted in a temporary increase in the amount of marine insurance underwritten. It was also in 1824 that the monopoly of the two oldest companies was finally terminated.[2] Of the many new companies formed, however, only a few survived more than a short while. The depression in marine insurance was halted in 1846 by the repeal of the Corn Laws and the adoption of a free-trade policy in England.

In 1800 there were only eight life offices in existence. Many new life insurance companies, however, were established during the first few decades of the nineteenth century. Of the three types, the proprietary, the mixed type, and the mutual, only the first two are included in the index since mutual companies have no shares. Though there was much poor management in life insurance, a margin between receipts and disbursements was often realized because the premium charges were based on an under-estimation of the going rate of interest at which money could be invested and excessively high mortality schedules.

Notorious failures during the thirties led to a Parliamentary Committee investigation from 1841 to 1843, which resulted in the enactment of the Joint Stock Registration Act, the purpose of which was closer supervision of all joint-stock companies other than banks.[3] The many new life insurance companies formed thereafter were at a competitive disadvantage compared with those established earlier due to the falling interest rates after 1815.

The increase in the number of fire insurance companies in the early nineteenth century brought about a reduction in the rates of premium, which caused the sums insured to increase nearly 50 per cent., 1804–12.[4] A period of stagnation in fire insurance until 1820 was followed by some improvement thereafter.[5] But competitive bidding and a relaxation of standards led to the failure of a number of fire offices in 1823 and 1827. For the majority of offices there was no real prosperity during this period.[6] Of the forty in existence in Great Britain in 1831, six made more than half the total sales of fire insurance. The remaining business had to be shared by thirty-four offices, most of which could barely cover costs. This skewed distribution was accentuated in the next decade as more companies were attracted to fire insurance and the two largest companies grew relatively even larger. The steady entry of new firms, despite the mortality rate of fire offices, is explained by the success of the few larger offices, and the secular

---

[1] See *Royal Exchange Assurance Magazine*, ii, Nov. 1905, pp. 62, 63, for income fluctuations, 1795–1824.
[2] 5 Geo. IV, c. 114.

[3] *P.P.*, 1844, vii (119), Report.
[4] *P.P.*, 1863, xxvi (3118), p. 2.
[5] Walford, iii. 493.
[6] Ibid., pp. 574–5.

growth in total insurance outstanding. The proportion of uncovered insurable property in the country was a powerful inducement to new enterprise.

A proposal was made to tabulate the record of the experience of all the offices with different classes of fire risk. Thus, a statistical basis for estimating risks would be established and competitive underbidding of risks restrained. The companies, however, refused to divulge the necessary information.

Insurance of private homes was more profitable than mercantile insurance; i.e., wharfs, docks, tradesmen's premises and stock. Competition for the latter business kept rates below the level required by the risk involved.

The index consists of price quotations for the following eight companies :[1]

Company	Paid-up capitalization	Type of insurance handled
	£	
Globe Insurance	1,000,000	Life and Fire
Royal Exchange Assurance . .	750,000	Life, Fire, and Marine
Atlas Assurance	125,000	Life and Fire
Imperial Fire Insurance . .	120,000	Fire
Albion Fire and Life . .	100,000	Life (Fire until 1826)
Eagle Insurance . . .	100,000	Life (Fire until 1826)
Rock Life Assurance . .	100,000	Life
Imperial Life Insurance . .	75,000	Life

Seven of them maintained life offices, six fire offices (four after 1826), and one a marine insurance office. The advantage of amalgamating the different branches of insurance does not appear to have been very great. Aside from the saving that was made by using only one set of premises, and by managing the affairs of all the branches with only one board of directors, the joint handling of two or three types of insurance did not confer any special benefit. One branch of business did not bring custom to the others; the books as well as the premium incomes, and the capitals of the different branches were generally kept separate.[2] Nevertheless, insurance companies, more often than not, engaged in more than one type of underwriting.

The apparent neglect of marine insurance companies in the index is explained, as noted above, by the circumstance that individual underwriters, chiefly at Lloyd's, did the great bulk of all marine insurance. Though many marine offices did come into existence after the abolition of the monopoly of the Royal Exchange and London Assurance Corporations, they did such a small part of the business, and were so shortlived, that it was impossible to obtain quotations for them. Royal Exchange's marine department was one of the larger company offices, but even its business was trifling compared with the underwriting transactions of the individual insurers.

---

[1] For years during which included, and importance relative to all listed companies, see above, pp. 361–4.

[2] See *P.P.*, 1844, vii (119), Committee on

Joint Stock Companies (1843), Evidence of Charles Ansell and Griffith Davies, Qq. 1920–5.

The life and fire offices included in the index are among the larger, more successful offices[1] and they are not representative of the scores of smaller companies that attempted to gain a foothold during this period, and failed.[2] There was little choice available to us, however, in selecting our sample, for, as has been said above, shares of unsuccessful and smaller companies simply were not quoted regularly. There can be no question, therefore, that our index of share prices is more stable, especially after 1826, than the level of shares of all companies must have been.

The index shows a clear upward trend, which is perfectly reasonable so far as our sample of companies is concerned. The insurance business was expanding throughout this period, and of course share values would be expected to move upward so long as the offices continued to insure lives and property for larger and larger sums.

From 1811 to 1850 there may be marked off six cyclical movements in the curve of the index. The price of shares was declining when the index begins, reaching a low in 1813. The peak in 1814 is followed, in 1816, by the deepest trough the index shows for the full 40-year period. The explanation for this initial period of decline is somewhat obscure. Marine insurance, as was noted above, expanded until 1815. Fire insurance, on the other hand, seems to have suffered a definite reversal during this period, although there is no clear contemporary discussion of the reasons for such a movement. As for life insurance, information of any kind is lacking. The obvious explanation for the fall in share prices during this period is the general crisis of 1816, affecting almost all commodity and security prices. The reaction of share prices to post-war conditions, in any case, was shortlived and relatively mild.

In 1817 share prices rose again, reaching a new peak at the end of the year, from which there was no real decline until 1819. From 1820 until the spring of 1825 a slow revival gradually gathered momentum until it achieved boom proportions. The history of this period is a little better known. Despite the set-back to marine insurance in the post-Napoleonic decade, the insurance business as a whole was flourishing. Whether the profits were real or merely anticipated, new capital flowed into the industry, and security speculation was rife. With the government no longer absorbing the savings of the public, new investment outlets were scarce, and insurance appears to have offered a promising alternative channel.

The collapse in 1825 lasted through the following year. Though most of

---

[1] There are, of course, no data on the actual or relative size and profits of the life offices during this period. From the returns of the duty collected by the fire insurance companies it is possible to rank the fire offices according to the amount of insurance they sold. The four fire offices rank among the first 10 or so London companies. There are no country offices included, because their shares were not quoted on the London exchange.

[2] This statement is subject to the qualification that two companies in the index were forced to relinquish their fire offices, and to this extent some representation of unsuccessful offices might be claimed. However, the shares of neither the Albion nor the Eagle Company seemed to show any decline in the years before the closing of their fire departments.

the insurance company failures occurred in 1826, it is interesting to note that the greatest part of the decline in the index in this period of contraction is concentrated in the latter months of 1825. After 1826 the index becomes very stable and shows no signs of a repetition of the speculative mania of 1825. The cyclical movements are very mild. There is a peak in 1829 followed by a trough in 1832. This was a period of acute competition in all branches of insurance, and was characterized by frequent failures of firms. A long, slow rise culminated in a peak in 1836, and an equally slow decline followed. Not only were fire and life offices again experiencing a widening market for their policies, but marine insurance companies were also enjoying a brief period of prosperity. The final peak during this period is reached in 1845, 1848 marking the bottom of the cycle.

The dearth of any data on the profits of the insurance companies during this period makes the interpretation of specific movements of the curve difficult. Dividend payments were very stable, and hence are not very useful in this connexion, especially since they may have been drawn from reserves and not current earnings. A table of the dividends paid by the insurance companies included in our index follows (Table 36). Where there are blanks in the table, figures were not given, but it is not certain that this means that no dividends were paid.

TABLE 36. *Dividends paid by Insurance Companies, 1811–50*

Year	Albion	Atlas	Eagle	Globe	Imperial Fire	Imperial Life	Rock Life	Royal Exchange
	£	s.	s.	£	£	s.	s.	£
1811	..	..	..	6	..	..	..	10
2	..	..	..	6	..	..	2	10
3	..	..	..	6	..	..	2	10
4	..	..	..	6	..	..	2	
1815	..	..	..	6	..	..	2	
6	..	..	..	6	..	..	2	
7	5 from Aug.	..	..	6	..	..	2	
8	5	6	..	6	..	..	2	10
9	5	6	..	6	..	..	2 and bonus	10
1820	2·5	6	5	6	1·5 to Sept. 4·5 from Oct.	..	2	10
1	2·5	6	5 to Aug.	6	4·5	..	2	10
2	2·5	6		6	4·5	..	2	10
3	2·5	6		6 to Apr. 7 from May	4·5 to July 5 from Aug.	8 from Aug.	2	10
4	2·5	6 to July 9 from Aug.	5 from May	7	5	8	2 and bonus	10
1825	2·5	9	5	7	5	8	2 and bonus	10 to July 8 from Aug.
6	2·5	9 to June 10 from July	5	7	5	8	2, bonus to Nov. 3 from Dec.	8
7	2·5	10	5	7	5	8	3	8
8	2·5	10	5	7	5	8	3	8
9	2·5 to Feb. 3 from Mar.	10	5	7	5 to Sept. 5·25 from Oct.	8	3	8

TABLE 36 (cont.)

Year	Albion	Atlas	Eagle	Globe	Imperial Fire	Imperial Life	Rock Life	Royal Exchange
	£	s.	s.	£	£	s.	s.	£
1830	3 to Oct. 3·5 from Nov.	10	5	7	5·25	8	3	5
1	3·5	10	5	7	5·25	8 to June 9 from July	3	5
2	3·5	10	5	7	5·25	9	3	5
3	3·5	10	5	7	5·25 to July 5·35 from Aug.	9	3	5
4	3·5	10	5	7	5·35	9	3 to Oct. 5 from Nov.	5
1835	3·5	10 to June 12 from July	5	7	5·35	9	5	5
6	3·5	12	5	7	5·35	9	5	5
7	3·5	12	5	7	5·35	9	5	5
8	3·5	12	5	7	5·35 to July 5·6 from Aug.	9	5	5
9	3·5	12	5	7 to Apr. 6 from May	5·6	9	5	5
1840	3·5	12	5	6	5·6	9	5 to Aug. 7 from Sept.	5
1	3·5	12·6	5 to May 6 from June	6	5·63	9 to Sept. 10·6 to Nov. 12 from Dec.	3·6 to Aug. 4 from Sept.	5
2	3·5	12·6	6	6	5·63	12	4	5
3	3·5	12·6	6	6	6 to Oct. 12 from Nov.	12	4	5 and bonus
4	3·5	12·6	6	6	12	12	4	5 and bonus
1845	3·5	12·6	6	6	12 to June 6, bonus from July	12	4	5
6	3·5	12·6	6	6	6 and bonus	12	4	5
7	3·5	12·6	6	6	6, bonus to Apr. 12 from May	12	4	5
8	3·5	12·6	6	6	12	12	4	5
9	3·5	12·6	6	6	12	12	5	5 to June 6, bonus from July
1850	3·5	12·6 and bonus	6 to Oct. 5 from Nov.	6	12	12	5	6 and bonus

Source: Wetenhall's *Course of the Exchange.*

APPENDIX

OTHER INDEXES OF BRITISH SHARE PRICES, COVERING PORTIONS OF THE PERIOD

This Appendix presents two indexes of security prices which relate to the period following the terminal date of this study, and which overlap the years considered here. By bringing together Hayek's unpublished index (the only monthly index to fill the gap between 1850 and 1867) along with that of Rousseaux (1825–67), a continuous view of the course of British security prices is made possible from 1811, the initial date of our indexes, down to the present time. For, after 1867 there are available the London and Cambridge Economic Service Index, 1867–1914; the *Bankers', Insurance Managers' and Agents' Magazine* Index, 1887 to date; and the London and Cambridge Economic Service New Index, 1925 to date.

TABLE 37. *Hayek's Index of Share Prices, 1820–68*

Base: 1841 average = 100

Year	Jan.	Feb.	Mar.	Apr.	May	June	July	Aug.	Sept.	Oct.	Nov.	Dec.
1820	121·0	121·0	120·2	121·4	120·0	118·3	117·4	117·8	118·6	116·9	117·6	121·3
1	125·4	126·8	127·6	128·1	129·2	132·4	132·0	132·1	128·8	128·6	128·7	125·7
2	118·7	118·7	117·7	121·6	122·0	119·9	117·6	118·8	119·3	119·9	121·4	122·2
3	122·3	122·8	121·7	118·9	120·6	122·0	124·7	125·7	125·1	125·1	127·1	131·2
4	132·7	136·2	137·2	139·3	140·4	141·7	143·5	144·2	143·3	141·6	140·6	137·6
1825	168·0	203·7	217·8	196·5	183·1	195·9	193·3	170·9	154·0	145·3	132·3	136·5
6	131·6	114·4	118·7	101·2	99·9	97·7	84·8	89·1	86·2	88·4	92·5	101·2
7	97·4	94·9	94·9	93·9	95·7	94·8	92·6	94·5	93·7	94·5	95·0	94·8
8	91·7	88·5	88·1	88·9	89·9	94·2	89·2	92·3	92·7	90·9	90·5	89·6
9	88·1	88·1	87·5	86·4	86·8	87·4	87·5	87·7	88·1	88·3	89·2	89·5
1830	88·6	88·8	90·3	91·0	94·3	95·2	94·8	94·5	94·5	92·5	89·2	85·5
1	83·7	83·1	81·2	81·4	82·0	82·8	82·4	81·9	82·1	82·8	83·1	83·2
2	83·9	84·5	85·2	86·0	86·4	87·4	87·2	87·8	89·1	89·8	95·7	97·5
3	97·6	97·2	99·4	101·7	102·3	101·6	102·0	103·4	106·2	105·9	105·6	105·8
4	106·6	108·9	109·4	111·0	108·8	108·8	110·8	108·9	108·8	109·2	109·5	110·4
1835	109·4	108·4	108·5	108·9	108·2	107·8	109·1	108·6	109·1	112·1	115·2	117·7
6	130·2	135·0	136·4	136·5	133·6	132·6	128·3	126·7	129·8	122·8	118·0	118·3
7	125·8	122·4	118·3	113·0	114·8	113·4	114·5	112·9	115·3	113·5	114·4	112·9
8	117·4	119·5	122·3	122·1	121·8	120·7	115·9	116·6	118·3	119·9	122·8	121·8
9	123·3	126·4	126·4	125·7	125·4	123·2	122·1	120·5	120·4	121·3	120·9	119·9
1840	120·8	120·8	120·0	118·1	119·8	122·0	116·4	115·0	114·3	112·6	111·7	112·1
1	110·3	109·4	103·4	101·1	101·0	99·8	99·2	98·6	95·2	95·0	95·1	96·3
2	96·8	99·7	100·5	101·5	103·0	104·4	103·6	103·5	103·1	103·8	104·6	106·5
3	108·0	108·6	109·9	111·5	112·1	112·2	112·0	112·1	113·5	115·1	116·5	118·2
4	117·6	119·0	120·5	123·1	124·2	125·2	125·1	126·3	126·7	126·7	128·0	129·4
1845	136·2	137·1	139·8	142·4	141·8	145·0	145·4	147·2	148·2	147·1	140·1	139·6
6	138·5	136·9	132·8	130·0	131·4	131·3	130·1	130·0	129·4	127·7	127·7	127·0
7	125·6	124·3	121·3	119·4	117·7	116·6	117·4	114·3	112·1	108·1	105·5	104·5
8	106·1	104·2	100·7	97·7	98·7	98·3	97·9	96·9	95·8	92·4	96·9	100·0
9	106·7	109·8	109·6	109·8	108·6	108·1	108·5	108·9	108·2	107·1	107·0	108·3
1850	111·6	111·9	110·8	109·5	109·9	110·3	109·6	109·7	111·1	112·3	112·5	114·8
1	113·5	113·7	114·8	115·3	115·3	114·5	113·3	112·7	113·1	113·5	114·4	114·6
2	114·2	113·8	115·3	116·6	117·3	119·6	122·1	122·7	122·8	123·9	124·9	125·6
3	126·3	126·1	126·2	125·4	127·2	126·8	126·5	124·4	121·5	117·1	117·0	117·0
4	115·1	112·3	110·7	108·7	107·8	108·7	109·1	110·1	111·6	113·2	113·6	113·2
1855	113·2	112·3	112·4	113·2	112·8	114·3	114·4	112·6	111·3	109·6	109·0	109·4
6	109·3	110·7	112·0	114·1	114·3	114·9	116·0	116·1	115·4	114·3	114·8	115·3
7	116·1	116·2	119·5	119·5	117·9	116·3	114·2	112·9	111·4	109·5	107·5	108·5
8	111·2	114·6	114·1	113·3	113·6	113·6	112·9	113·3	113·4	114·5	115·4	115·6
9	113·8	113·2	113·5	113·3	109·8	111·1	112·9	115·5	114·9	115·4	113·3	113·3
1860	113·8	110·2	109·5	111·3	111·6	111·6	112·8	115·2	118·9	122·5	123·6	125·9
1	126·0	125·4	123·5	122·1	122·9	124·0	123·2	122·0	125·4	125·6	127·5	129·8
2	132·4	136·9	138·9	139·6	140·9	141·0	140·8	141·3	144·4	150·9	150·0	151·4
3	150·8	157·2	168·6	170·0	167·1	168·5	175·7	174·8	172·3	173·4	174·0	170·8
4	172·9	175·7	175·7	172·7	170·4	169·2	166·2	167·9	165·4	163·2	163·4	179·4
1865	177·4	176·6	177·4	176·8	180·6	180·0	179·6	180·9	182·3	178·3	188·6	182·0
6	178·2	172·0	168·8	165·0	153·2	142·4	148·4	147·4	148·2	143·0	137·7	141·2
7	150·2	149·5	149·6	146·4	144·9	148·0	144·2	142·1	145·3	144·8	140·5	138·6
8	141·0	142·9	142·9	141·7	140·1	141·6	139·1	139·5	135·9	138·6	141·6	139·6

1. Hayek's Monthly Index of Share Prices, 1820–67. Professor Hayek's hitherto unpublished index covers the period from 1820 to 1867, at which point the intention is to link it with the London and Cambridge Economic Service index covering the period from 1867 onwards.[1] The index was constructed in connexion with a research project financed by General Dawes and carried out on his commission. The basic data were taken, as for our indexes, from Wetenhall's *Course of the Exchange.*

Professor Hayek's purpose is to show how British ordinary industrial shares reacted to cyclical movements of trade and industrial production. Therefore he excludes banks, insurance companies, and bridges. The sub-groups making up his index are canals, docks, waterworks, gas light and coke companies, British mines, railways, and miscellaneous companies.

The sample was chosen according to the following criteria: those shares were included which had continuous quotations, were issued by companies with large capitalization, and were active.

The sub-indexes are unweighted arithmetic averages of relatives on a fixed base—the average of the monthly prices of 1841. The group indexes are also combined on an unweighted basis.

Hayek claims to have adjusted his index for marked discontinuities arising out of the introduction into or disappearance from the index of a company or a group. Our examination of his figures, however, reveals frequent cases where no correction is made for such a sudden rise or decline of considerable amplitude.

There is some question, moreover, whether Hayek's index can legitimately be linked to the London and Cambridge Economic Service Index, in view of the fact that the former is heavily weighted with railway shares at the time of their overlapping, whereas the latter deliberately excludes railway shares because of 'their specialized character'.

2. Rousseaux's Annual Index of Share Prices, 1825–67. Dr. Rousseaux has constructed an annual index of share prices in connexion with a study of long waves in Great Britain published in 1938.[2] He, too, links his index with that of the London and Cambridge Economic Service for the period after 1867, though he is aware of the 'profound difference in composition between the two'. The composition of his index is somewhat different from Hayek's in that it includes insurance companies and banks, and also bridges, but excludes mines, without any explanation. There is no statement as to the number and dates of the quotations obtained from which the annual averages were struck. Separate sub-indexes for the component groups listed by Rousseaux were not constructed.

From Rousseaux's description of methods of sampling and construction, it appears on the whole to be a workmanlike job. He discusses the various problems arising in the selection of a sample along the lines noted in the account of our index, and his solution was to construct chain index numbers for five-year intervals with overlapping terminal and initial years. The difficulties connected with changing paid-up capitals resulting from successive 'calls' were ingeniously resolved by expressing the quotations of each stock as a percentage of the sum total actually paid up at a given time. These percentages were then averaged

---

[1] We are indebted to Professor F. A. von Hayek and his assistant, Mr. A. Maizels, for permission to publish their index and for providing us with a special memorandum describing its composition and construction.

[2] Paul Rousseaux, *Les Mouvements de Fond de l'Économie Anglaise, 1800–1913,* pp. 143–56.

geometrically. No further discussion of the method of averaging is to be found. Aside from possible technical objections to the geometric mean, it is somewhat surprising that he used it in view of the linking of his index with the London and Cambridge index, which is an arithmetic average of relatives. Evidently no consideration was given to the problem of weighting, for there is no mention of it.

Rousseaux's index may be adequate for his special purpose of revealing the broad movements significant for a study of long waves in speculation. But, in view of the foregoing comments, this index must be considered a rather rough measure of total changes in share values, and cannot be confidently used for short-period comparisons.

TABLE 38. *Rousseaux's Index of Share Prices, 1825–67*

Base: Average of 1884 and 1896 = 100

Year	Index	Year	Index
1825	69	1850	53
6	57	1	55
7	61	2	56
8	62	3	60
9	62	4	60
1830	60	1855	62
1	52	6	66
2	52	7	65
3	56	8	65
4	59	9	72
1835	61	1860	73
6	59	1	73
7	56	2	85
8	59	3	90
9	61	4	102
1840	60	1865	94
1	56	6	87
2	56	7	74[a]
3	57		
4	63		
1845	65		
6	62		
7	56		
8	52		
9	51		

Source: Rousseaux, p. 272.

[a] The index after 1867 is the London and Cambridge index linked to this one.

PART III

BRITISH COMMODITY PRICES

INTRODUCTION

PART III of this volume presents for the first time in monthly form three new indexes of commodity prices, comprising imported, domestic, and all commodity prices. The raw data from which they have been constructed were obtained from the collection of over 100 individual monthly series, originally transcribed under the direction of Professor Norman J. Silberling, and now in the possession of the Harvard University Committee on Economic Research. The basic data are to be microfilmed for those who may be interested in the movements of particular series, or who may desire to examine the behaviour of sub-groups other than those constructed by us.

In general, our preference has been to analyse individual series rather than indexes; for such composites merely show net resultants, but not necessarily similar or typical movements in the several series. The use of indexes, however, seemed justifiable to us in this instance, because it was beyond our resources to analyse any very large number of individual prices in monthly form; thirteen of the more important individual prices, however, have been analysed in Part II of Vol. II. A reasonable alternative to a more detailed study of individual prices appeared to be the analysis of indexes representing average changes in sub-groups of prices most relevant to a study of business fluctuations. The several existing commodity price indexes fell short of our needs, and we felt constrained to construct new ones. The number of sub-groups constructed was, again, limited by the time and funds at our disposal. It is to be hoped that later investigators will be in a position to exploit more fully than we have the wealth of monthly price data here made available.

Chapter I of this portion of the text is similar in character to Part II, Chapters I and II. The methods used in constructing the indexes are described; the statistical characteristics of the cyclical and secular behaviour of the indexes are examined; the course of prices is traced through successive cycles, with some explanation of their movements; and finally some comparisons are made between the behaviour of our total index and existing indexes of British prices. A section of background material similar to Part II, Chapter III, was not, however, undertaken for commodity prices. To examine the nature of each of the commodity markets in which prices were set was obviously a bypath we could not afford to pursue.

In Part I of this volume, which presents an historical account of the short-run movements of the economy, the course of commodity prices is related to general business fluctuations. The forces producing the net movements of the indexes (and of agricultural prices) are treated there in separate *Price* sections; while the course of the more important industrial prices is traced in conjunction with data on output, employment, and changes in costs, in the sections devoted to *Industry and Agriculture*. In Part I of Vol. II (*Business Cycles and Trends*) the cyclical and trend behaviour of commodity prices is subjected to theoretical analysis; while Part II, Chapter IV of that volume presents the results of a statistical analysis of the cyclical and trend behaviour of certain individual prices and group indexes.[1]

The series used in the indexes exhaust the monthly price data available for this period. They cover virtually all British commodity imports, i.e. imported industrial raw materials, and foodstuffs. The coverage of domestic commodities—specifically, of manufactured goods—is much less adequate. The reason the price statistics for imports are more abundant than for domestic commodities lies in the difference in organization of the markets for goods of foreign and domestic origin. Monthly, and even weekly prices are available for the trade in home-grown foodstuffs—wheat, oats, peas, &c.—and in coal, which was conducted under highly organized market conditions. Most domestic commodities, however, were not sold under such conditions, and thus lack records of continuous price quotations. Imports, on the other hand, were standardized in quality; they were dealt in by merchants who were generally large-scale distributors for whom it was feasible to keep records of prices paid on importation. In contrast with the centralized character of the import trade, the organization of the export trade was loose and decentralized. The average British manufacturer who produced for export was a small business man. The manufactures included a variety of unstandardized goods. These were generally sold on a system of advances from a local factor, who resold them to a London factor, who in turn was dependent on the resources of some strong mercantile house which actually disposed of the goods abroad. Some of the firms in this chain of middlemen undoubtedly recorded the prices of goods which passed through their hands, and, it is to be hoped, these data will one day be brought to light. At the moment, however, the lack of detailed statistical information on the prices of domestic manufactured goods constitutes a serious gap in the data.

[1] A supplementary section on *annual* price data will be found in the microfilmed volume of basic British statistical data. The principal sources of such material are there described, and individual series are presented.

Chapter I

THREE NEW INDEXES OF BRITISH COMMODITY PRICES, MONTHLY, 1790–1850

1. Introduction. For several decades the best approximation of changes in British prices from 1790 to 1850 has been the quarterly index constructed by Norman J. Silberling.[1] Although Jevons's index for the same period was available and widely used, Silberling's is in a very real sense a pioneering work. A critical examination of Jevons's index with respect to the nature of the original prices, its composition, and the methods of construction used brought Silberling to a recognition of its serious shortcomings,[2] and led him to explore the possibilities of gathering new data and constructing an improved index. But for a number of reasons to be discussed below, Silberling's index seemed to be open to certain basic technical objections; although there is no doubt that it is markedly superior to Jevons's.

The first refinement on Silberling's use of the data was the construction of the price indexes in monthly as opposed to quarterly form. The number of continuous monthly series for the period 1790–1850 is small, indeed. For the purposes of business-cycle analysis on general historical grounds it was felt that such data as were available should be used fully. The added labour involved, it was hoped, would be justified, in cyclical analysis, by the greater degree of accuracy which such figures make possible in establishing turning-points.

Our monthly index of British wholesale prices from 1790 to 1850 is subgrouped into prices of domestic and imported commodities. For the purpose of computing these indexes the raw data painstakingly gathered by Silberling have been employed. Most of this material was not used in his index, and none of it has ever been published in monthly form.[3] The eleven-year period before 1790, for which Silberling collected prices, has not been included in our index for two reasons. First, the data, although serviceable in quarterly form, were not complete monthly; and second, these early years fall outside the limits of the period of our investigation. In a number of cases Silberling did not include a series in his index because it was incomplete before 1790; but this, of course, was no ground for excluding the series from our index.

---

[1] 'British Prices and Business Cycles, 1779–1850', *Review of Economic Statistics*, 1923, pp. 223 ff.

[2] 'British Financial Experience, 1790–1830', *Review of Economic Statistics*, 1919, pp. 282 ff.

[3] Thanks to Dr. Silberling and the Harvard Committee on Economic Research, all the data were made available to us, and it is with their kind permission that we publish the original prices. We wish to acknowledge a special debt to Professor Arthur H. Cole and Miss Dorothy Wescott for their helpfulness in extending the committee's facilities to us.

2. Sources and Nature of Data. A description of the sources of the data and the methods of collection, as given by Silberling in his 1923 article, follows:

It has been generally assumed that little first-hand material for the study of prices beginning at so early a date remained in existence, beyond what has been preserved in such publications as Tooke's *History of Prices*, which was the principal source of the well-known index numbers of Jevons. A careful search of the principal libraries of London, made by the writer in 1920, resulted in the discovery that there is still available a virtually continuous set of publications, from which ample and trustworthy price data, beginning in the latter part of the eighteenth century, may be secured. These are the various editions of *Price Current* lists, which were issued by several private agencies in London for the use of business men. They contain the high and low wholesale quotations during each week (in later years twice a week) for a vast number of commodities, mainly imported raw materials of industrial or commercial consequence. They contain, as well, precise indications of the unit, grade, and variety of each article; information regarding the bonding, import duties, and drawbacks affecting the articles; the rates of marine insurance and of foreign exchange; and even, in some later issues, the stocks of various commodities held in warehouses.

The editions of the *Price Current* lists which were used in obtaining the materials for the present study, and the collections containing them, are as follows:

1779–1785: Prince's *London Price Current*
(Guildhall Library, Corporation of London).
1786–1795: *Universal London Price Current*
(Library of the Board of Trade).
1796–1817: Prince's *London Price Current*
(Library of the Board of Trade).
1818–1831 (third quarter): *The New London Price Current*
(British Museum).
1831 (last quarter)–1850: *London Mercantile Price Current* (British Museum),
with occasional use of the *New Price Current*.

Although the first number of Prince's *Price Current* appears to have been published as early as 1775, no copies of the list prior to the Guildhall volume of 1779 could be discovered, either in London or elsewhere. Files of the *Universal Price Current* for 1787–1789, which happened to be missing from the Board of Trade collection, were found in the Library of the British Museum, although in somewhat defective condition. During these three years a set of quotations was, nevertheless, secured at least once in every quarter. For all the other years practically perfect copies of price lists have been preserved.[1] No transcription of data was made beyond the year 1850, although the British Museum files of the lists run well beyond that year.

The first task was naturally a selection from this wealth of material of those commodities for which prices happened to be quoted continuously throughout

---

[1] 'It is said that the volumes now in the Board of Trade collection were saved years ago from the waste-paper heap by the merest accident.'

the period in all the lists used. A preliminary selection of articles was drawn up, based upon the items included in existing index numbers and also upon a study of such sources of information as McCulloch's *Dictionary of Commerce*. A preliminary examination of occasional price-lists between 1786 and 1830[1] resulted in the selection of about 140 commodities for which transcription was undertaken. It was found necessary from time to time to discontinue the transcription of articles which proved to be quoted irregularly or which were omitted from later issues of the available lists. It also became necessary in some cases to replace articles originally selected with others of a slightly different variety or different origin. This was done only after a careful study had been made of the various articles and the meaning of the quotations.

After the selection of what seemed to be a representative list of articles, averages were made directly of the weekly high and low prices as printed. This practice was followed until 1818, when, in view of the greater stability of the general level, a single monthly quotation for most articles was considered sufficient, and this was taken as close as possible to the middle of the month, the high and low for that date being averaged. No attempt was made to enter the rates of duty pertaining to some imported articles,[2] but careful note was made as to whether the articles were or were not quoted 'in bond' or 'warehoused'.

. . . . Interpolation was accomplished, in most instances, by observing the movement in the periods of omission in the prices of related articles or other varieties of the article whose movements in general were observed to be similar to those of the article in question. In a few cases, where such guides were lacking, it was necessary to interpolate roughly by extending a fixed quotation through a number of years. The individual price curve, furthermore, indicated points where unsuspected sudden changes of quality or method of quotation had occurred. In the relatively few cases where such a break proved of material consequence, the several parts of the series were adjusted. In order to obtain a continuous series of quotations of that variety of an article which appeared to be commercially predominant and hence most significant, it was sometimes necessary to join together portions of several series, again with adjustment for any marked discrepancy at the point of juncture. In rare cases a point could be safely located for making a direct passage from one series to another very similar one, as, for example, from West Indies cotton to Georgia cotton in 1817.

3. Critique of Silberling's Index. Silberling included 35 commodities in his index and listed 80[3] which he rejected on one or more of the following grounds: (*a*) prices were constant for years at a time; (*b*) there were extreme and irregular fluctuations in the price movements; (*c*) the commodity was represented by another series with similar fluctuations; (*d*) quotations were not given for the whole period; (*e*) the commodity was not homogeneous over time. The first two reasons recommended themselves to Silberling as grounds for exclusion, since his purpose was to arrive at 'an

---

[1] 'It was originally planned to cover only the years 1786–1830. The volumes of Prince's *Price Current* for 1779–1785 were not found until after the anlysis of the period 1786–1830 had been completed, and later still it was decided to carry the whole work down to 1850.'

[2] 'Sufficient material of this nature was available in Parliamentary Papers.'

[3] There are, in fact, 132 series in this collection of data. Frequently several varieties of the same commodity were listed together under one head.

indicator sensitive to the play' of general business movements. The use of a price index as a barometer of fluctuations in output and employment involves at least one important assumption, which Silberling leaves implicit; i.e. that the movement of prices included in the barometric index results from changes on the demand side of the markets in which those prices are set, or, in other words, from monetary forces. That assumption ignores, in Marshallian terms, the movement of long-run supply curves; and it dismisses the possibility that the shape of cost curves will, in the short run, permit considerable movements in output and employment (i.e. shifts in the demand curves of individual markets) without any equivalent change in prices. The obvious defence of a price index as a barometer of business fluctuations is the empirical observation that, in fact, some prices do usually rise sometime, to some degree, in the course of a cyclical upswing, and fall during the downswing: cyclical fluctuations in demand do, in short, have some effect on prices in many markets. Certain prices, moreover, set in large markets, sensitive to changes in general expectations, might, *a priori*, be expected to have turning-points closely related to the turning-points in other sections of the economy. But at best, prices must be regarded as a crude, and often treacherous, measure of business fluctuations.

It is, nevertheless, possible that Silberling using some other, more reliable index of business fluctuations, might have selected a group of prices which seemed to conform to that index. It is clear that, for such an objective, a small and selected group of commodities, from which both inflexible and extremely fluctuating prices are excluded, and only those which reflect movements typical of general activity are retained, is sufficient. Yet, even if Silberling's index were to be interpreted solely as a business barometer rather than as a measure of changes in the general price level, one is inclined to question its validity on the basis of other considerations. In the first place, if more or less 'typical movements' are a criterion for the inclusion of a price series in the index, the implication is plain that one is using some outside standard of reference with respect to which one seeks general conformity in the series. According to his description of the manner in which the sample was chosen, Silberling possessed no such standard. Instead, he regarded the preponderating movements of the prices themselves as a standard. But if this method is pursued, one wonders whether the preponderating movements of a group of price series, two-thirds of which represent imported commodities, can truly be taken to reflect business conditions in Great Britain.[1] Similarly, food products included, which respond erratically to outside non-economic factors—such as weather conditions—have no place in a sensitive index. The point is clear that if the index under construction is to be a 'sensitive' one, it does

---

[1] Of course, if it can be shown that of the total output of these foreign commodities, a very large part was consumed in Great Britain, then it may validly be inferred that British business conditions decisively affected their prices.

not matter which commodities or how many commodities are included, provided those which are included have been shown to fluctuate closely with some separate index of business activity.

Although his stated purpose was to construct a business barometer, Silberling proceeds to use his index as if it were a measure of changes in the general price level.[1] The objections to this interpretation of his index are even more serious than its limitations as a 'sensitive' index. The primary characteristic of a general commodity price index should be its inclusiveness. Any index which purports to measure changes in the level of prices as a whole cannot logically exclude commodities whose price movements are sluggish or whose fluctuations are erratic or irregular. On the contrary, if it is to be a faithful index of average movements of commodity prices in general, it must give due representation to all groups—sluggish prices and sensitive ones, prices of farm products, animal products, minerals and textiles, prices of raw materials and semi-processed goods, and so forth; and each group must be weighted in accordance with some criterion of importance.

In attempting to isolate the action of general business forces, Silberling makes clear that he wants to eliminate all factors peculiar to the demand and supply conditions of the markets for the individual articles. Because his average is unweighted, he holds that these special variations, which are not representative of the general drift, tend to be offset, one against another, without arbitrary bias. This will be true, he claims, only in so far as the commodities admitted into the average are economically 'independent types'. Therefore it would not do to admit more than one of several cognate articles, such as turpentine and rosin, because this would give double weight to the special circumstances of the turpentine-rosin industry.

Silberling here reverts to the traditional conception of price index numbers, which lay at the basis of much of the work of Jevons, Edgeworth, and others. The assumption implied in these unweighted index numbers is that the prices of commodities are subject to two sets of forces: (1) monetary factors which affect all prices equally and in the same direction; and (2) special factors, arising out of shifts in the demand and supply curves for individual commodities, which produce differential changes in their prices. Silberling hoped that by not weighting the individual items in his index, and by carefully selecting 'independent types', the second set of influences would be averaged out, leaving a residual which truly reflected

---

[1] Hawtrey and Viner also somewhat loosely quote Silberling's figures as quantitative measures of the general British price level. It is probably the divergence between Silberling's avowed purpose and method of construction which accounts for the loose interpretation given to the index by these writers. R. G. Hawtrey, *Currency and Credit*, p. 329, 'According to Professor Silberling's index number, prices, which had risen from a level represented by 102 in 1792 to 109 in 1793, had stopped short at 107 in 1794, and then sprang up to 126 in 1795 and 136 in 1796.' Jacob Viner, *Studies in the Theory of International Trade*, p. 174, 'From a peak according to Silberling's index of 198 in 1814, the English price level fell to 136 in 1819, to 114 in 1822, to 106 in 1824, and to 93 in 1830.'

the general level of prices at different points in time. It is reasonable to suppose, therefore, that on this view the general drift which is thus isolated represents the influence of monetary factors.

Aside from the more basic objections to this grouping of the factors influencing prices, there seems to be little reason for supposing, as Silberling does, that price changes arising from factors peculiar to individual commodities are normally distributed in a sample which includes only thirty-five commodities. Moreover, the assumption that these price changes are independent of one another can hardly be substantiated; and hence normality of distribution is an unwarranted assumption even for large samples. This interdependence of price changes lends special significance to the problem of weighting, since the number of commodities secondarily affected by a fluctuation in one price, and the size of these secondary changes, depend on the relative weights of the different commodities. It is unnecessary to labour the point that the commodities included in Silberling's index are treated as of equal importance, despite the fact that the value of the home consumption of wheat, one of its components, is over 700 times greater than the value of sal-ammoniac, another component. The really basic theoretical objection to Silberling's procedure is the assumption that there are two distinct sets of forces acting on prices and that the non-monetary influences merely affect the relative prices of individual commodities and not the general level. As Keynes clearly points out, 'the price level is itself a function of relative prices and liable to change its value whenever, and merely because, relative prices have changed'.[1] It is, further, erroneous to suppose, as this theory does, that a change arising from the side of money has no effect on relative prices. In this day and age it is almost platitudinous to remark that it is just this differential effect of monetary changes on the various elements in the price structure that makes those changes so significant in their social consequences.

There is a further and more practical difficulty in interpreting Silberling's index as a measure of the general commodity price level. In constructing the index customs duties were eliminated from the prices of imports whenever they happened to be quoted inclusive of duty. By this procedure he eliminated the dampening effect of adding a fairly constant amount to his presumably sensitive price indicators. There may be some justification for such a deduction for the restricted purposes of a 'sensitive' or 'business barometer' index; though, as has been pointed out above, this interpretation of the index is itself open to serious objections. In any case, under no circumstances is the subtraction of duty warranted for the purpose of an index of the British price level. For what in fact do prices quoted in bond denote? They are, in a sense, nobody's price in England, because practically no imported commodity could enter British channels of trade unless the duty were paid. Especially during the first half of the period the amount of duty was so considerable as to make the price without it un-

[1] J. M. Keynes, *A Treatise on Money*, i. 87.

recognizable; and the changes in the rates levied occurred so frequently as to alter the relations between prices over time. It is obvious, therefore, that the character of the movement of the index might be appreciably changed by the inclusion of duty.

It is important, moreover, to distinguish the movement of prices of domestic commodities from those of imported commodities. (See Tables 39–41 and Chart 97.) Without constructing such sub-indexes,[1] Silberling lumps the 24 imported and 11 domestic commodities together in one index. This over-weighting with imported prices has been raised, by Viner, as an objection against the use of Silberling's index as a valid measure for the comparison of fluctuations in the English price level with changes in foreign price levels.[2] For Britain, from 1790 to 1850, foreign trade played an important, often an overwhelming, role in business fluctuations. A strict differentiation of domestic and imported prices was, for that reason, thought advisable; and, finally, the domestic index seems to meet the objections raised by Viner to Silberling's index as a tool for the study of comparative price levels.

The reasons, then, for which it was felt proper to calculate a new index may be summarized as follows:

1. For purposes of cyclical analysis, and because of greater general precision, a monthly rather than a quarterly index was deemed superior.
2. To construct a proper index of the general price level weighting was required.
3. The attempt by Silberling to make his index sensitive to cyclical fluctuations had led to the exclusion of many prices for which data were available.
4. Silberling had used the prices of imported commodities in bond, i.e. without duty. This, it was believed, misrepresented the level of import prices, and distorted their movement over long periods, because of numerous and considerable alterations in import duties.
5. Finally, a strict separation of domestic and import prices was thought necessary for the analysis of international factors in British business fluctuations.

4. Classification and Description of the Individual Commodities. From the group of 132 series examined 54 were eliminated, because data were scanty, or the commodity was not homogeneous. A small minority of the series does not extend over the entire period of the index, and, in such cases, the conventional chaining procedure was followed.

The commodities were grouped according to whether they were domestic or imported. The classified list is shown in Table 42. There were, in all, 78 commodities, of which 26 were domestic and 52 foreign. To the prices of

[1] Silberling did construct a pair of sub-indexes, but his subdivision of commodities was based on the size of the freight charges.

[2] Viner, p. 170.

TABLE 39. *Index of Wholesale Prices of Domestic and Imported Commodities,*
1790–1850

Base: Monthly average 1821–5 = 100

Year	Jan.	Feb.	Mar.	Apr.	May	June	July	Aug.	Sept.	Oct.	Nov.	Dec.
1790	87·5	86·4	85·2	86·2	91·6	92·4	91·4	91·6	92·4	89·9	88·2	89·2
1	89·4	90·1	90·1	91·1	88·9	88·9	89·2	88·7	88·7	88·9	90·6	91·6
2	90·9	88·7	87·5	85·5	84·0	84·7	85·9	87·5	88·0	92·7	91·1	90·1
3	91·6	92·9	95·1	96·5	97·6	97·8	99·0	99·7	98·1	96·0	96·5	98·1
4	99·3	100·0	100·5	99·0	97·6	97·6	97·8	98·1	97·0	97·2	99·0	99·0
1795	101·9	104·9	107·3	109·8	111·7	114·2	121·3	130·9	118·3	116·2	121·1	121·3
6	121·5	123·2	125·7	120·0	115·6	115·1	116·5	116·1	111·3	109·9	110·1	108·7
7	110·6	106·6	104·9	104·2	103·4	103·0	101·4	102·4	107·3	111·6	109·6	109·1
8	108·2	107·3	106·8	108·2	108·4	109·1	108·4	109·1	107·6	108·7	105·6	107·6
9	109·6	111·3	110·8	118·6	124·0	125·7	127·4	132·4	130·7	132·9	135·4	136·6
1800	141·3	143·7	148·2	152·5	157·9	155·7	159·1	146·0	145·8	146·0	154·4	161·2
1	168·6	175·8	181·1	170·6	159·4	157·4	160·1	154·7	144·2	134·6	130·3	131·5
2	131·0	128·5	126·8	122·0	119·1	118·3	118·6	120·3	122·0	118·0	121·1	120·6
3	120·6	121·3	119·1	120·1	123·3	127·5	126·0	124·3	124·1	124·6	127·3	125·1
4	124·3	120·8	120·6	117·8	118·6	117·3	121·1	123·7	128·7	128·7	133·2	136·3
1805	134·8	139·4	139·0	137·0	135·8	137·5	137·5	140·0	137·5	131·8	131·3	133·0
6	134·0	132·5	132·7	136·3	139·0	135·0	135·8	134·8	134·6	133·7	131·8	133·7
7	132·5	132·5	132·5	132·5	131·0	130·8	131·5	130·8	130·3	128·5	129·3	132·5
8	133·0	134·6	136·3	138·0	141·0	145·0	147·2	148·4	150·7	149·4	154·2	156·5
9	155·7	159·6	159·9	156·5	152·7	147·2	147·7	151·2	156·7	158·2	157·2	157·2
1810	158·2	153·3	156·0	155·2	156·0	154·5	155·6	155·8	154·3	147·3	149·0	145·9
1	147·6	145·9	145·7	141·5	142·0	141·3	141·8	142·0	143·2	148·3	151·4	153·8
2	153·1	153·1	151·7	160·9	168·8	167·3	171·1	175·3	173·4	161·6	163·7	164·4
3	168·8	172·9	173·6	175·5	177·0	171·7	170·7	169·7	164·9	162·8	160·5	158·6
4	161·3	166·2	168·1	162·3	151·0	148·3	141·8	146·4	152·4	151·2	146·4	149·0
1815	136·0	131·6	133·3	134·6	134·6	134·0	129·5	130·7	128·7	125·6	122·0	118·7
6	113·6	110·9	110·2	111·4	117·9	117·4	116·7	119·9	123·2	123·6	126·3	132·3
7	131·6	133·5	133·8	130·2	133·3	136·2	136·0	132·3	130·2	128·7	128·7	127·8
8	136·5	137·7	139·9	142·5	138·4	135·5	135·8	137·4	139·5	141·8	140·6	139·3
9	138·1	136·9	137·9	132·8	127·3	122·5	124·9	125·9	124·7	122·9	123·2	120·3
1820	119·1	119·6	120·6	120·6	122·2	118·3	118·1	118·1	114·3	106·5	104·4	103·5
1	103·7	103·0	101·7	100·3	98·4	98·2	97·5	98·6	102·2	100·8	97·1	94·3
2	94·2	92·5	91·1	88·9	84·9	88·2	87·3	85·8	84·2	86·1	85·1	86·3
3	86·8	92·3	97·4	98·6	101·9	103·6	100·3	102·7	99·3	93·0	96·0	99·8
4	99·3	105·0	103·6	101·5	101·9	102·4	101·2	100·5	97·2	98·1	104·6	106·9
1825	109·1	111·9	115·5	115·5	116·6	113·8	111·7	112·7	112·9	113·1	112·7	110·5
6	108·1	102·7	100·7	101·0	99·6	96·9	96·0	98·8	100·7	96·9	99·8	99·1
7	98·6	99·8	102·9	103·6	101·5	100·5	101·2	99·3	97·4	94·9	95·5	96·0
8	94·0	94·7	95·3	94·9	93·0	92·5	93·2	95·8	94·7	101·5	102·7	104·3
9	106·2	102·0	97·2	95·1	97·0	93·0	95·1	94·7	94·7	92·8	89·9	91·8
1830	90·9	92·3	90·4	91·6	94·9	94·9	98·1	99·3	95·1	94·2	94·9	96·9
1	96·7	98·8	99·8	98·6	93·5	97·2	91·6	94·7	92·3	93·0	94·9	92·5
2	93·7	92·0	94·2	92·7	93·	93·9	92·0	90·6	89·4	89·2	88·0	88·7
3	88·7	87·3	86·6	87·5	86·8	87·5	87·7	90·8	92·7	89·2	90·4	88·0
4	87·3	86·6	88·7	87·0	86·3	89·2	86·6	86·6	86·1	83·7	84·9	84·6
1835	83·9	83·0	84·6	84·9	86·6	83·9	85·6	88·2	83·7	82·5	82·5	84·9
6	83·7	88·9	93·0	98·4	96·7	98·4	96·7	96·0	95·3	95·7	98·1	101·2
7	100·7	99·3	96·9	94·7	93·2	94·9	91·8	93·5	93·2	90·4	90·8	91·8
8	92·3	94·7	95·1	96·2	96·9	97·4	98·1	101·0	98·1	97·6	101·0	105·5
9	107·2	105·5	104·1	104·6	103·4	103·8	103·8	104·6	105·0	104·3	103·1	102·4
1840	102·2	101·7	102·4	103·6	102·4	103·6	104·8	105·3	105·0	100·7	99·3	98·1
1	98·8	99·3	99·8	99·3	97·4	96·7	96·2	100·3	97·9	95·5	95·7	95·5
2	95·3	93·9	91·1	90·6	90·4	90·4	90·6	87·7	85·6	84·9	82·7	82·3
3	81·1	78·9	78·7	77·5	77·3	79·6	81·1	84·2	79·4	79·2	80·4	79·2
4	80·4	79·4	82·5	82·7	83·7	83·5	82·5	79·9	78·9	78·7	79·4	81·3
1845	81·5	80·6	81·3	79·9	79·9	82·7	82·7	84·6	84·8	87·7	88·4	86·0
6	84·6	84·6	85·3	85·1	84·8	82·7	82·5	81·3	84·1	90·1	93·2	93·7
7	99·3	99·8	99·3	98·7	104·2	107·4	101·9	98·0	91·1	89·8	87·0	85·4
8	84·7	84·9	84·0	82·6	82·2	81·5	80·1	81·2	82·2	80·5	80·1	78·0
9	75·2	75·0	73·9	73·9	73·5	73·0	75·0	75·0	73·3	73·7	72·8	72·3
1850	73·3	72·6	71·6	74·2	71·2	71·2	75·7	75·5	73·9	73·5	73·0	76·2

TABLE 40. *Index of Wholesale Prices of Domestic Commodities, 1790–1850*

Base: Monthly average 1821–5 = 100

Year	Jan.	Feb.	Mar.	Apr.	May	June	July	Aug.	Sept.	Oct.	Nov.	Dec.
1790	85·4	83·5	81·9	83·1	90·5	91·2	89·7	90·0	91·4	87·6	85·0	86·4
1	85·9	86·4	85·7	87·4	84·5	84·5	84·5	83·3	82·1	82·1	83·8	84·2
2	83·3	80·2	79·0	76·9	75·7	77·1	78·3	80·4	80·9	86·9	85·2	83·5
3	85·0	85·9	88·3	90·2	91·6	92·8	95·0	96·4	94·5	92·1	92·4	94·5
4	95·9	97·1	97·4	96·7	95·2	95·9	96·2	96·7	95·0	94·8	96·7	98·1
1795	100·0	101·2	103·1	105·7	108·6	111·9	122·2	136·5	117·7	115·0	120·5	120·5
6	122·6	124·8	128·0	120·5	115·3	114·6	116·6	116·1	109·7	107·3	108·3	106·1
7	106·6	101·2	99·3	98·8	97·8	96·9	96·4	97·3	102·0	106·1	103·9	102·7
8	101·2	100·3	99·5	100·7	101·0	100·7	101·7	102·9	99·8	99·8	96·1	98·6
9	101·0	102·4	101·7	110·7	117·8	119·5	120·9	127·5	126·8	131·9	137·2	140·9
1800	145·3	148·0	154·0	159·6	167·2	163·5	167·4	148·9	148·4	148·7	159·4	168·4
1	176·7	185·9	193·5	179·3	165·0	163·5	168·4	161·8	148·0	134·8	130·4	132·6
2	132·4	129·5	127·8	122·2	118·0	117·0	118·0	121·4	122·6	117·0	121·4	120·0
3	118·0	118·8	115·6	116·6	120·2	124·6	122·4	120·7	120·7	121·2	124·6	121·4
4	120·5	115·6	114·9	111·9	112·7	110·7	115·3	118·8	126·1	125·8	130·7	133·8
1805	131·4	136·5	136·0	133·6	132·1	135·1	135·8	139·0	135·8	128·7	128·0	130·2
6	131·9	129·9	130·4	133·6	137·2	132·4	133·6	131·7	131·7	131·2	128·7	130·9
7	129·2	129·2	129·7	129·5	128·2	127·8	128·7	127·5	127·0	125·1	126·5	130·9
8	131·4	132·4	133·8	134·8	138·0	142·1	144·3	145·8	147·2	145·3	148·9	151·4
9	149·9	155·0	156·5	155·3	152·3	146·7	148·2	152·1	157·0	158·2	157·7	157·2
1810	155·7	149·5	152·8	152·8	156·2	155·0	156·9	157·6	157·1	148·0	151·6	148·5
1	150·7	148·3	148·3	143·2	144·9	144·4	146·4	147·1	148·0	154·0	156·9	158·3
2	157·4	156·9	154·7	167·9	179·4	178·0	183·2	189·0	186·1	169·1	171·5	173·4
3	174·9	179·2	180·8	183·0	184·4	178·2	176·8	175·6	167·2	163·4	159·5	154·5
4	156·4	160·5	163·8	156·6	144·7	142·8	136·5	141·6	147·5	146·6	140·4	144·2
1815	129·1	125·5	129·3	130·1	130·3	129·8	125·0	125·5	123·1	119·3	115·7	112·3
6	107·1	104·4	102·8	104·0	112·6	113·5	113·3	118·1	121·9	122·4	126·0	133·7
7	132·5	134·9	135·3	130·5	134·6	138·7	138·4	132·5	128·4	125·8	125·3	124·3
8	136·3	138·4	140·1	144·4	138·7	135·3	136·5	138·2	140·8	144·4	142·5	142·0
9	140·1	140·1	142·8	136·3	129·8	123·8	127·2	128·4	126·7	124·3	124·6	121·2
1820	120·0	121·2	123·8	123·8	126·2	121·2	120·7	121·4	116·9	106·8	103·7	103·2
1	103·5	103·2	101·3	98·9	96·5	96·3	95·8	97·2	102·0	99·6	95·3	91·3
2	91·3	89·1	87·4	84·8	79·2	83·8	83·3	82·1	79·7	82·1	81·2	82·4
3	82·9	89·4	96·4	97·8	103·1	106·0	101·0	104·1	99·3	90·8	94·7	99·0
4	99·5	107·5	105·6	103·6	104·8	105·3	103·6	103·1	98·8	100·0	107·7	110·6
1825	112·3	115·5	117·4	117·9	118·6	116·9	115·2	115·2	117·4	117·6	117·9	115·7
6	114·7	108·2	106·5	108·0	106·5	103·1	102·4	106·5	108·7	103·1	107·2	106·0
7	105·2	106·6	110·7	112·2	109·8	108·8	109·3	106·4	103·0	99·9	100·8	101·3
8	98·6	99·6	100·8	100·6	98·6	97·9	98·9	102·5	100·8	110·7	112·4	113·9
9	116·5	110·5	103·7	100·8	104·0	98·9	102·8	101·8	102·0	99·1	95·0	98·4
1830	96·7	98·4	96·0	97·7	102·0	102·3	107·6	109·0	102·0	100·8	102·0	105·4
1	104·7	107·6	108·6	107·1	99·6	105·9	98·2	102·8	99·1	100·1	102·8	99·6
2	101·1	98·9	101·1	99·6	100·1	101·5	99·1	97·2	95·5	94·8	92·8	93·6
3	94·1	91·9	90·9	92·1	91·1	91·4	90·9	93·6	95·5	90·9	92·8	90·7
4	89·5	88·3	91·3	89·5	88·8	92·4	88·8	88·5	87·8	84·7	85·6	85·1
1835	83·7	82·5	84·7	84·9	86·8	83·5	85·6	89·3	82·7	81·5	81·8	84·7
6	83·2	90·5	94·8	101·8	99·7	102·8	100·1	98·9	98·0	98·9	103·3	108·6
7	107·9	106·2	103·8	102·1	101·6	104·3	100·1	102·3	100·9	96·8	96·8	96·8
8	97·2	100·6	101·3	103·8	105·5	105·7	106·9	111·5	106·9	105·9	110·3	116·1
9	118·0	115·6	113·4	113·2	111·5	112·5	113·4	113·9	113·9	113·4	111·8	110·5
1840	109·8	109·3	112·0	112·7	110·8	112·5	113·7	113·9	113·4	107·2	105·5	104·5
1	105·7	106·7	108·4	107·4	105·2	104·0	103·8	110·1	106·9	103·5	104·5	104·0
2	103·3	101·3	97·5	97·2	97·2	98·4	98·2	94·1	90·9	90·7	87·6	87·1
3	85·6	83·5	83·0	81·5	81·3	84·4	86·8	91·2	84·4	83·5	85·4	83·9
4	85·6	83·9	87·8	89·0	89·3	89·7	88·8	84·7	84·2	83·9	85·1	87·8
1845	88·3	86·8	87·6	87·6	87·6	91·7	91·7	94·3	93·9	98·2	99·7	96·8
6	95·3	95·1	96·3	96·3	95·5	92·4	91·9	90·5	95·1	102·8	107·4	107·4
7	116·3	116·5	116·8	116·1	126·0	130·9	121·6	115·1	104·3	103·8	100·8	99·2
8	98·0	98·0	96·2	95·7	95·2	94·6	92·7	94·6	96·4	93·6	92·7	89·5
9	84·8	84·4	82·3	82·3	81·8	81·1	84·2	83·0	79·3	79·5	77·4	76·8
1850	77·9	76·1	74·7	78·6	74·7	74·4	80·5	80·0	77·7	77·0	76·3	80·7

TABLE 41. *Index of Wholesale Prices of Imported Commodities, 1790–1850*

Base: Monthly average 1821–5 = 100

Year	Jan.	Feb.	Mar.	Apr.	May	June	July	Aug.	Sept.	Oct.	Nov.	Dec.
1790	85·4	86·2	85·7	87·1	87·6	88·4	88·4	88·1	87·6	88·6	88·4	88·8
1	90·1	91·8	93·2	93·2	92·0	92·0	92·5	94·1	96·9	98·3	99·8	101·5
2	102·0	103·0	100·9	99·2	97·5	96·6	97·9	97·5	97·9	98·3	98·1	98·6
3	100·0	102·2	103·4	103·9	103·2	101·5	100·3	99·6	98·3	97·3	98·1	98·8
4	99·0	99·0	99·2	96·4	95·2	93·5	93·9	93·7	94·7	95·8	96·6	93·9
1795	98·2	105·0	108·6	110·0	110·3	110·3	110·7	111·3	111·5	110·5	113·2	114·3
6	109·6	110·5	110·7	110·5	107·9	108·1	108·1	107·6	107·3	108·6	107·1	107·1
7	113·2	114·9	113·7	113·0	112·6	113·2	108·1	109·8	114·9	119·4	118·5	119·4
8	120·4	120·4	121·4	122·4	122·1	122·1	120·2	119·8	125·5	128·7	128·7	128·7
9	128·5	129·9	130·6	133·8	133·3	134·6	136·9	135·9	132·5	126·0	120·2	115·8
1800	117·7	119·7	119·7	119·2	120·0	120·9	122·9	124·6	125·6	125·3	127·0	127·5
1	133·2	135·4	134·9	133·9	131·5	128·5	125·3	123·3	122·7	122·3	119·0	117·6
2	117·2	116·7	114·9	113·7	114·1	113·2	111·2	108·5	111·5	113·0	111·9	113·0
3	120·5	121·5	122·7	123·3	125·0	128·6	129·6	128·3	127·3	127·5	128·1	128·3
4	130·0	132·0	133·5	131·5	132·0	133·5	134·0	133·5	130·7	131·7	134·2	136·8
1805	138·8	142·6	142·4	141·9	140·8	138·5	137·0	136·8	136·8	136·3	135·7	135·7
6	135·6	135·4	134·9	139·0	139·2	138·2	138·0	139·0	138·2	138·0	136·7	137·7
7	139·4	139·1	138·6	138·2	137·1	136·6	137·1	137·3	137·1	136·0	133·9	133·7
8	135·4	138·3	141·5	145·9	148·3	151·1	153·8	153·8	159·0	160·1	168·5	169·8
9	173·9	173·2	169·4	158·8	152·2	147·4	144·8	146·9	153·5	155·9	154·0	154·9
1810	162·6	162·8	163·6	160·0	153·7	151·5	149·3	148·1	144·9	143·5	140·1	137·2
1	137·8	137·4	136·5	135·2	132·8	130·6	128·2	127·2	128·7	131·4	135·2	139·9
2	140·1	141·8	141·0	141·0	140·3	139·1	139·1	140·3	140·5	140·1	142·2	147·6
3	150·5	154·3	152·6	153·4	155·8	153·0	152·4	152·4	156·0	158·5	161·4	168·7
4	173·5	180·3	178·6	176·5	168·2	162·4	155·8	158·1	164·8	162·4	162·1	160·7
1815	154·9	148·6	143·7	145·9	145·6	144·2	140·8	143·9	144·2	143·5	140·3	136·1
6	132·3	129·7	131·8	132·8	131·8	127·4	125·8	123·4	125·3	125·8	126·0	127·2
7	127·2	128·7	128·0	128·2	128·0	127·4	127·4	130·7	134·2	135·7	136·7	135·7
8	135·5	133·3	136·9	135·9	135·2	133·5	131·8	133·3	134·2	132·8	133·5	130·8
9	130·6	126·5	124·1	122·1	118·7	116·8	117·5	118·1	117·5	117·7	117·5	116·4
1820	115·4	113·2	110·3	109·8	110·3	109·6	109·6	107·9	105·9	104·5	105·0	102·5
1	102·7	101·0	101·0	102·2	102·2	102·5	101·0	101·6	101·8	102·2	101·3	102·5
2	102·5	102·1	102·5	101·8	102·8	101·6	99·0	97·8	98·3	98·3	97·2	98·3
3	99·0	100·6	100·6	100·1	98·5	96·7	98·1	98·8	99·0	99·2	99·7	101·6
4	98·5	98·5	97·8	95·1	94·1	94·1	93·8	93·4	92·7	92·7	96·2	96·5
1825	100·3	102·1	109·5	108·6	110·6	104·6	102·1	105·5	100·8	100·8	98·8	96·7
6	91·1	88·2	86·4	83·7	81·9	81·1	79·7	80·4	81·1	80·8	81·1	81·5
7	81·9	82·1	83·2	82·8	81·5	80·4	81·9	81·5	83·0	82·1	82·3	82·1
8	82·1	81·7	81·1	79·9	79·0	78·5	79·0	79·0	79·2	79·7	79·5	81·5
9	81·5	81·5	80·8	80·6	79·7	77·6	76·5	76·3	76·0	76·5	76·3	75·1
1830	76·0	76·7	76·0	76·0	76·5	76·3	75·8	76·3	77·6	77·4	77·4	76·5
1	77·4	78·1	78·3	77·6	77·6	75·8	75·0	75·1	75·3	75·3	75·1	75·0
2	75·0	75·3	76·7	76·0	75·1	74·8	74·3	74·3	74·1	75·0	75·3	76·2
3	75·1	75·3	75·0	75·3	75·1	76·9	79·2	83·4	85·0	85·0	83·0	80·8
4	81·8	81·7	81·0	80·6	79·9	80·3	80·1	80·8	81·3	81·3	82·5	83·9
1835	84·3	84·8	85·0	85·0	85·7	85·3	85·3	85·0	86·4	85·5	85·3	85·0
6	85·0	85·3	87·8	89·7	89·3	87·3	87·8	88·3	88·0	87·8	85·3	83·2
7	83·0	81·8	79·7	76·0	73·2	72·5	71·3	72·0	74·1	74·5	76·0	78·3
8	79·4	79·7	79·2	77·8	76·7	77·4	76·7	76·0	76·9	77·4	78·5	80·3
9	81·0	81·0	81·7	83·9	83·7	83·0	80·8	81·8	83·2	82·1	81·7	82·3
1840	83·7	83·2	82·1	81·7	82·3	82·1	83·0	84·1	84·6	84·3	83·9	82·5
1	82·1	81·0	79·4	79·4	78·5	78·3	77·6	77·4	75·8	75·6	75·1	75·1
2	75·3	75·3	75·1	74·3	73·4	70·9	71·6	71·8	72·0	70·2	70·4	70·2
3	69·3	68·0	67·3	67·3	66·9	67·1	66·9	66·9	67·1	68·2	67·8	67·8
4	67·1	67·6	68·6	67·3	70·2	68·0	67·3	67·3	66·2	66·2	65·1	65·3
1845	65·3	64·8	66·2	61·5	61·7	61·7	61·8	62·1	63·3	63·3	62·2	61·2
6	60·7	60·9	60·5	59·6	60·7	60·7	60·3	59·8	59·6	61·8	61·8	63·6
7	63·8	64·5	62·9	62·7	60·9	61·8	61·8	62·1	62·4	59·3	57·5	56·2
8	56·2	56·8	56·8	54·7	54·0	53·8	52·8	52·6	52·4	52·6	53·1	53·1
9	53·3	53·8	54·2	54·4	54·0	54·0	54·0	56·2	58·2	59·3	60·7	60·9
1850	61·4	63·1	63·3	62·7	62·4	62·4	63·1	64·0	64·0	64·5	64·2	64·7

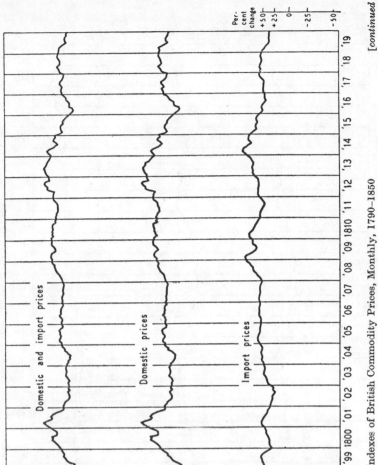

FIG. 97a. Indexes of British Commodity Prices, Monthly, 1790–1850

[continued]

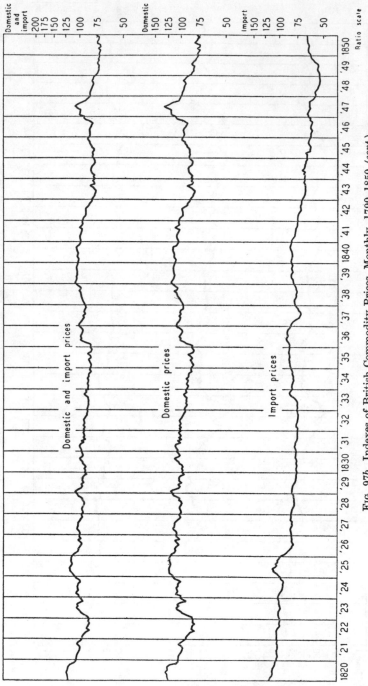

FIG. 97b. Indexes of British Commodity Prices, Monthly, 1790–1850 (cont.)

the latter group the customs duties, gathered from various official sources, were added.

Tables 43 and 44, in sum, present a list of all commodities for which prices were collected by Silberling, including a brief description of each commodity. Table 43 consists of the 78 commodities included in our index. Table 44, Part A, lists 28 series which might be used, even though, in some cases, they are not complete for the entire period. These were excluded because they represent additional varieties of commodities, the dominant variety of which was already included. Since, with few exceptions, only total weights could be obtained, without differentiation as to variety, only the dominant one was included. Table 44, Part B, lists the remainder of the commodities for which prices were obtained but not used. In the case of the latter the accuracy of the data is questionable, or the series are not homogeneous; or else the data are fragmentary. Table 45 presents a classification of all commodities included in our final index according to their nature and use. Separate sub-indexes, corresponding to this breakdown, have not been computed.[1]

5. Import Duties. The first adjustment of the raw monthly data was the addition of the relevant import duties. The Parliamentary Report on Customs Tariffs of the United Kingdom from 1800 to 1897[2] contains full tables of duties established by the tariff laws subsequent to 1823, but it is not a complete source for specific duties levied on articles prior to 1823. There exists no comprehensive and detailed study of the tariff for the first quarter of the century, although such a study would fill an evident need.[3]

It was thus necessary to consult the numerous statutes themselves. The tariff acts passed during the Napoleonic Wars listed hundreds of articles on which duties of various kinds and amounts were levied; permanent, war, additional as well as excise. Imports were subject to different levies according to the grade of the commodity, its place of origin, or the country of transhipment; whether it entered a bonded warehouse or the channels of trade directly; and whether it was conveyed in British owned, or British built, or British manned ships, or ships of other nationalities. The frequent and often confusing changes in duty further complicated this laborious work. Differences between the unit in which a price was quoted and the unit of the commodity in which the duty was expressed, and changes in the tariff unit itself, involved numerous adjustments before the duty could be added to the price. On a few commodities both import and excise duties were levied, and both had to be added to the price in bond.

---

[1] In addition to the price indexes, analysis has been completed of a number of the more important individual series. In the case of the share prices, analysis of the movements of the separate shares was never contemplated and hence the sub-indexes were computed at the outset.

[2] *P.P.*, 1898, lxxxv.

[3] It may be added that the tables of duties in Tooke [and Newmarch], *History of Prices*, should be used with great caution, inasmuch as there are errors both of omission and commission.

TABLE 42. *List of Seventy-eight Commodities included in Index*

26 domestic commodities

No.	Commodity	Period
1.	Alum	Jan. 1790–Dec. 1850
2.	Beef	Jan. 1790–Dec. 1850
3.	Butter	Jan. 1790–Dec. 1850
4.	Camphor	Jan. 1790–Dec. 1850
5.	Coal	Jan. 1796–Dec. 1850
6.	Copper	Jan. 1790–Dec. 1850
7.	Hides	Jan. 1790–Dec. 1809
8.	Iron, bars	Jan. 1822–Dec. 1850
9.	Iron, pigs	Jan. 1790–Dec. 1850
10.	Lead, pigs	Jan. 1790–Dec. 1846
11.	Leather butts	Jan. 1790–Dec. 1850
12.	Mutton	Jan. 1790–Dec. 1850
13.	Oats	Jan. 1796–Dec. 1850
14.	Oil, linseed	Jan. 1790–Dec. 1850
15.	Oil, rape	Jan. 1790–Dec. 1850
16.	Oil, vitriol	Jan. 1790–Dec. 1821 / Jan. 1834–Dec. 1850
17.	Pork	Jan. 1790–Dec. 1850
18.	Sal-ammoniac	Jan. 1790–Dec. 1850
19.	Seeds, clover, red	Jan. 1790–Dec. 1850
20.	Soap, hard yellow	Jan. 1790–Dec. 1850
21.	Soap, mottled	Jan. 1790–Dec. 1850
22.	Starch, common	Jan. 1790–Dec. 1850
23.	Tallow	Jan. 1790–Dec. 1850
24.	Tin	Jan. 1810–Dec. 1821
25.	Tin plates	Jan. 1827–Dec. 1850
26.	Wheat	Jan. 1790–Dec. 1850

52 imported commodities

No.	Commodity	Period
1.	Annatto	Jan. 1790–Dec. 1850
2.	Ashes, pearl	Jan. 1790–Dec. 1850
3.	Balsam	Jan. 1790–Dec. 1850
4.	Barilla	Jan. 1790–Dec. 1850
5.	Barwood	Jan. 1790–June 1845
6.	Beeswax	Jan. 1790–Dec. 1850
7.	Brandy	Jan. 1790–Dec. 1850
8.	Brazilwood	Jan. 1790–Dec. 1850
9.	Brimstone	Jan. 1790–Dec. 1850
10.	Bristles	Jan. 1790–Dec. 1850
11.	Cinnamon	Jan. 1790–Dec. 1850
12.	Cochineal	Jan. 1790–Dec. 1850
13.	Cocoa	Jan. 1790–Dec. 1850
14.	Coffee	Jan. 1790–Dec. 1850
15.	Cotton	Jan. 1790–Dec. 1850
16.	Flax	Jan. 1790–Dec. 1850
17.	Fustic	Jan. 1790–Dec. 1850
18.	Geneva Spirits	Jan. 1795–Dec. 1850
19.	Ginger	Jan. 1790–Dec. 1850
20.	Hemp	Jan. 1790–Dec. 1850
21.	Hides	Jan. 1790–Dec. 1850
22.	Indigo	Jan. 1790–Dec. 1850
23.	Iron	Oct. 1822–Dec. 1850
24.	Isinglass	Jan. 1790–Dec. 1850
25.	Jalap	Jan. 1790–Dec. 1850
26.	Linseed	Jan. 1790–Dec. 1850
27.	Liquorice	Jan. 1790–Dec. 1850
28.	Logwood	Jan. 1790–Dec. 1850
29.	Madder Root	Jan. 1790–Dec. 1850
30.	Mahogany	Jan. 1790–Dec. 1850
31.	Oil, castor	Jan. 1790–Sept. 1830
32.	Oil, olive	Jan. 1790–Dec. 1850
33.	Opium	Jan. 1790–Dec. 1850
34.	Pepper	Jan. 1790–Dec. 1850
35.	Quicksilver	Jan. 1790–Dec. 1850
36.	Quinine	Jan. 1790–Dec. 1850
37.	Rum	Jan. 1790–Dec. 1850
38.	Saltpetre	Jan. 1790–Dec. 1850
39.	Silk, raw	Jan. 1790–Dec. 1850
40.	Silk, thrown	Jan. 1790–Dec. 1850
41.	Staves	Jan. 1790–Dec. 1850
42.	Sugar	Jan. 1790–Dec. 1850
43.	Sumac	Jan. 1790–Dec. 1850
44.	Tar	Jan. 1790–Dec. 1850
45.	Tea	Jan. 1790–Dec. 1850
46.	Timber: Memel fir	Jan. 1790–Dec. 1807
	Amer. pine	Jan. 1808–Dec. 1850
47.	Tobacco	Jan. 1790–Dec. 1850
48.	Turpentine	Jan. 1790–Dec. 1850
49.	Whale Fins: Greenland	Jan. 1790–Sept. 1822
	Southern	Oct. 1822–Dec. 1850
50.	Whale Oil	Jan. 1790–Dec. 1850
51.	Wine	Jan. 1790–Dec. 1850
52.	Wool: Spanish	Jan. 1790–Dec. 1799
	Spanish	Jan. 1810–Dec. 1821
	Saxon	Jan. 1822–Dec. 1850

TABLE 43. *Description of Commodities included in Index*

A. Twenty-six Domestic Commodities

1. *Alum*: British, an astringent mineral salt, produced under monopoly conditions (prices constant for years at a time); per ton, 1790–1850.
2. *Beef*: Irish, cured mess; per tierce, 1790–1850.
3. *Butter*: Waterford (Ireland), full, 1st; per cwt. 1790–1850.
4. *Camphor*: British, refined (from E.I. crude); per lb., 1790–1850.
5. *Coal*: Sunderland, for 1796–1809 interpolated from average of high and low for each month given in the *Gentleman's Magazine*; for 1810–31 from various *Price Current* sources; for 1832–50 from the Newcastle–Sunderland average monthly prices given in *Memoirs of the Geological Survey, Mineral Statistics*, 1865; all adjusted to form a continuous series; per chaldron.
6. *Copper*: British, manufactured, adjusted for change from plates to cakes in Jan. 1792 and from cakes to sheets in Nov. 1821; per lb., 1790–1850.
7. *Hides*: British, for dressing; per lb., 1790–1809; 1822–50.
8. *Iron, bars*: British; data for 1847–50 obtained from *The Economist*; per ton.
9. *Iron, pigs*: (Prices apparently controlled between 1804 and 1816, during which period no changes whatever occurred.) Included in index: 1790–1846. Data for 1847–50, iron pigs, No. 1 Wales (in microfilmed table), obtained from *The Economist*; per ton.
10. *Lead, pigs*: British, on board; per ton, 1790–1850.
11. *Leather butts*: British (tanned heavy ox-hide), 60–66 lb. prior to 1828, thenceforward 45–50 lb. (adjusted); per lb., 1790–1850.
12. *Mutton*: (fresh) Smithfield market; 1796–1849 from averages of the mean, high, and low monthly quotations in the *Gentleman's Magazine*; 1850 from *Annual Register*; per stone of 8 lb.
13. *Oats*: British (*Gazette* average of England and Wales); per quarter, 1790–1850.
14. *Oil, linseed*: British; per ton, 1790–1850.
15. *Oil, rape seed*: British, important for domestic illumination; per ton, 1790–1850.
16. *Oil, vitriol*: British (sulphuric acid); per lb., 1790–1821; 1834–50.
17. *Pork*: Irish mess, salted, in barrels; per barrel, 1790–1850.
18. *Sal-ammoniac*: British (ammonium chloride); per cwt., 1790–1850.
19. *Seeds, clover*: red, British; per cwt., 1790–1850.
20. *Soap, hard yellow*: British, for consumer use; per cwt., 1790–1850.
21. *Soap, mottled*: British; for industrial use, especially in textiles; per cwt., 1790–1850.
22. *Starch, common*: English, made principally from wheat in this period; per cwt., 1790–1850.
23. *Tallow*: English, town, not melted; per cwt., 1790–1850.
24. *Tin*: British block, on board; per cwt., 1790–1850.
25. *Tin plates*: British, No. IC; per box of 225 sheets, 1827–50.
26. *Wheat*: *Gazette* average of England and Wales. Adjustment made for change in 1793 in method of quotation from pence per bushel to shillings per quarter (of 8 bushels). Average weekly quotations prior to 1834 taken directly from the *London Gazette*; beginning 1834, from monthly average quotations in *Gentleman's Magazine* (based on *Gazette*); per quarter, 1790–1850.

B. Fifty-two Imported Commodities

1. *Annatto*: West Indies, flag (a red dye); per lb., 1790–1850.
2. *Ashes, pearl*: Canadian, crude potassium carbonate; per cwt., 1790–1850.
3. *Balsam of Tolu*: Peru; per lb., 1790–1850.
4. *Barilla, ashes*: Spanish or Carthagenian, crude soda bicarbonate; per cwt., 1790–1850.
5. *Barwood*: Angola, a dyewood; per ton, 1790–June 1845.
6. *Beeswax*: Hamburg, white or manufactured; per lb., 1790–1850.
7. *Brandy, Cognac*: (Prices violently affected by commercial depression during war period.) Per gallon, 1790–1850.
8. *Brazilwood*: A dyewood (fluctuations extreme and irregular); per ton, 1790–1850.
9. *Brimstone*: Sicily; per ton, 1790–1850.

10. *Bristles, hog*: St. Petersburg, first sort, rough; per cwt., 1790–1850.
11. *Cinnamon*: East Indies, second quality; per lb., 1790–1850.
12. *Cochineal*: Middling; Spanish, garbled; after 1817, West Indies, silver; per lb., 1790–1850.
13. *Cocoa*: Granada; per cwt., 1790–1850.
14. *Coffee*: Jamaica ordinary; per cwt., 1790–1850.
15. *Cotton, raw*: Berbice (West Indies), to 1812; from 1813, Georgia bowed; from 1832, Georgia upland; per lb., 1790–1850.
16. *Flax*: St. Petersburg, 12 head; after 1834, 9 head; quotations for 1833–5, 1840, 1847–50 interpolated on basis of Riga (P.T.R. grade); per ton, 1790–1850.
17. *Fustic*: Jamaica, a dyewood; per ton, 1790–1850.
18. *Geneva Spirits*: Holland; per gallon, 1795–1850.
19. *Ginger*: Barbados, white; per cwt., 1790–1850.
20. *Hemp*: St. Petersburg, clean; per ton, 1790–1850.
21. *Hides*: Buenos Ayres, 'B'; per lb., 1790–1850.
22. *Indigo*: East Indies, blue; after 1817, blue violet. Interpolated on basis of East Indian copper indigo in 1832–3, 1835, and 1848–50; per lb., 1790–1850.
23. *Iron, wrought bars*: Swedish, first sort, used for manufacture of most steel in early part of period; per ton, 1790–1850.
24. *Isinglass*: Baltic, long staple; per lb., 1790–1850.
25. *Jalap*: West Indies; per lb., 1790–1850.
26. *Linseed*: Russia; per quarter, 1790–1850.
27. *Liquorice*: Spanish to 1796, thereafter Italian (Sicily); per cwt., 1790–1850.
28. *Logwood*: Campeachy (West Indies), a dyewood; per ton, 1790–1850.
29. *Madder Root*: Smyrna or Turkey; used as a red dye; per cwt., 1790–1850.
30. *Mahogany*: Honduras, used largely as a dye; per foot, 1790–1850.
31. *Oil, castor*: West Indies, per bottle of 1½ lb.; 1790–Sept. 1830.
32. *Oil, olive*: Gallipoli, used especially in the wool manufacture; per ton, 1790–1850.
33. *Opium*: Turkey (fluctuations violent and irregular); per lb., 1790–1850.
34 *Pepper*: East Indies, white (fluctuations extreme and irregular); per lb., 1790–1850.
35. *Quicksilver*: Spanish; per lb., 1790–1850.
36. *Quinine*: South America, Jesuits or yellow bark (extreme fluctuations during years 1803–8); per lb., 1790–1850.
37. *Rum*: Jamaica, 27–32 per cent. over proof; per gallon, 1790–1850.
38. *Saltpetre*: East Indies, nitre, rough (fluctuations extreme and irregular); per cwt., 1790–1850.
39. *Silk, raw*: China, data for 1828–9 interpolated; per lb., 1790–1850.
40. *Silk, thrown*: Piedmont, white; per lb., 1790–1850.
41. *Staves*: Danzig, oak crown pipe (enormous fluctuations in 1808–10 due to interruption of shipments); per 1,200 pieces, 1790–1850.
42. *Sugar*: Jamaica, brown; per cwt., 1790–1850.
43. *Sumac*: Sicily, used in tanning, dyeing, and calico printing; per cwt., 1790–1850.
44. *Tar*: Stockholm; per barrel, 1790–1850.
45. *Tea*: Congou, middling; per lb., 1790–1850.
46. *Timber*: Memel fir, American pine. (Prices subject to extreme variation 1795–1815.) Memel fir from 1790 to 1807, American pine from 1808 to 1850; per last of 50 cubic feet.
47. *Tobacco*: Maryland, brown, middling (prices 1818 to 1832 adjusted for slight change in quality); per lb., 1790–1850.
48. *Turpentine*: American, rough; per cwt., 1790–1850.
49. *Whale fins*: A joint product of whale oil. (Fluctuations irregular. During peace the price varied with the oil, during war the general trend was inverse to that of oil.) Greenland for 1790–Sept. 1822; Southern for Oct. 1822–50; per ton, 1790–1850.
50. *Whale Oil*: British fishery up to third quarter of 1830; thenceforward British South Sea fishery; per ton, 1790–1850.
51. *Wine, Port*: Red; per 138 gallons of 231 cubic inches, 1790–1850.
52. *Wool*: Spanish, Leonesa, 1790–99; 1810–21 (market considerably narrowed after that, owing to increased use of other wools). Saxon, 'Electoral', 1822–50, per lb.

TABLE 44. *List of Fifty-four Price Series not included in Index*

A. TWENTY-EIGHT SERIES WHICH ARE USABLE BUT WERE REJECTED FOR REASONS
GIVEN BELOW

1. *Ashes, pot*: Canada (crude potassium hydrate) ⎫ represented by Canadian pearl ash.
2. *Ashes, pearl*: Russia ⎭
3. *Beeswax*: America; series incomplete; represented by Hamburg beeswax.
4. *Cotton*: Pernambuco (Brazil) ⎫
5. *Cotton*: Surat (East Indies) ⎬ represented by Berbice-Georgia series used
6. *Cotton*: Smyrna ⎭
7. *Flax*: Dutch, series incomplete.
8. *Flax*: Riga, or Druana; series incomplete.
9. *Hemp*: Riga, series incomplete, represented by St. Petersburg hemp.
10. *Lead*: British red ⎫ represented by pig-lead.
11. *Lead*: British white ⎭
12. *Madder*: Dutch crop; largely displaced in commerce by madder root in latter part of period.
13. *Oil, cod*: Newfoundland, represented by whale oil.
14. *Oil, turpentine*: British, refined, fluctuated like American crude turpentine; problem of weighting, hence not used in index of domestic prices.
15. *Rosin*: English, yellow; a joint product of refined turpentine; fluctuations very similar to those of imported turpentine. Hence excluded from index.
16. *Rye*: English (*Gazette* average); series incomplete.
17. *Silk, raw*: Bengal skein until 1822; after 1822, Novi ⎫ same general type as China silk,
18. *Silk, raw*: Brutia ⎭ but series less complete.
19. *Sugar*: St. Kitts or Demerare; middling ⎫ represented by
20. *Sugar*: Bengal; East India loaves ⎬ Jamaica brown
21. *Sugar*: Barbados; cloyed until 1804; Savannah, white, 1805–50 ⎭ sugar.
22. *Tallow*: Russian ⎫ represented by English tallow.
23. *Tallow*: Siberian soap ⎭
24. *Tobacco*: Virginia, York River, or partly fine block; series less complete than Maryland brown, which sufficiently represents the tobacco group.
25. *Turpentine*: British, refined spirits, represented by American crude.
26. *Whalebone*: Southern, 1790–1821; Greenland, 1822–50; series incomplete.
27. *Wool*: Australian superior; prices from 1834 only. Represented by Saxon wool.
28. *Wool*: Southdown, quarterly prices, 1790–1, as given by Mr. Lagge before the Wool Committee of 1828; 1792–1824 as given by Mr. Nottage before the same committee; 1825–34 as quoted in Bischoff, *Comprehensive History of Wool*, ii. 125; for 1833–50 from McCulloch's *Dictionary of Commerce*, art. 'Wool'. Represented by Saxon wool.

B. TWENTY-SIX SERIES WHICH ARE NOT USABLE FOR REASONS GIVEN BELOW

1. *Almonds*: Bitter, Barbary; series not homogeneous.
2. *Borax*: British, refined (from East Indies crude); erratic movements, homogeneity of data doubtful.
3. *Clover seed*: white, Dutch (or foreign); doubtful; represented by British clover seed.
4. *Coffee*: Mocha; fluctuations extreme, quality not homogeneous.
5. *Copperas*: British, green (sulphate of iron); price movements inelastic and irregular; accuracy of data questionable.
6. *Currents*: Zante (Levant); extreme fluctuations; frequent changes in quality.
7. *Figs*: Turkey: series incomplete; seasonal changes in quality.
8. *Gum*: Arabic, Turkey; accuracy of data questionable.
9. *Ivory*: ('elephant's teeth'); several important changes in quality; in general erratic movements.
10. *Oak*: Timber, American, white; series fragmentary.
11. *Oak*: Plank; Danzig; series fragmentary.
12. *Opium*: East Indies; data fragmentary.
13. *Pitch*: New England; data fragmentary.
14. *Raisins*: Smyrna, red; seasonal changes in quality.
15. *Rhubarb*: Russia; series incomplete and of doubtful accuracy.

16. *Rice*: Carolina; frequent changes in quality.
17. *Skins*: Goat; German and Barbary ⎫
18. *Skins*: Kid; Sicily or Naples ⎭ data fragmentary; seasonal changes in quality.
19. *Spirits*: British malt; data fragmentary.
20. *Tar*: Carolina, data fragmentary; represented by Baltic Tar.
21. *Tea*: Bohea, best (black)⎫ Series of little value for the purpose in hand due to irregular
22. *Tea*: Nipon, best (green)⎬ movements, to extensive changes in marketing conditions
23. *Tea*: Ceylon (black) ⎭ and in quality.
24. *Tobacco*: Maryland, yellow; data fragmentary.
25. *Wine, sherry*: Data not homogeneous after 1831.
26. *Wine, claret*: Data fragmentary.

TABLE 45. *Classification of Commodities included in Index*

Farm Products
1. Clover seeds
2. Hides, British
3. Hides, Buenos Ayres
4. Linseed
5. Oats
6. Tobacco
7. Wheat

Lumber and Building Materials
1. Oil, linseed
2. Staves
3. Tar
4. Timber
5. Turpentine

Wines and Spirits
1. Brandy
2. Geneva Spirits
3. Rum
4. Wine

Chemicals
1. Alum
2. Ashes, pearl
3. Barilla
4. Brimstone
5. Camphor
6. Oil of vitriol
7. Sal-ammoniac
8. Saltpetre

Drugs
1. Balsam of Tolu
2. Castor oil
3. Jalap
4. Liquorice
5. Opium
6. Quinine

Fuel and Lighting
1. Coal
2. Tallow
3. Whale oil
4. Rape seed oil

Food, &c.
1. Beef
2. Butter
3. Cinnamon
4. Cocoa
5. Coffee
6. Ginger
7. Mutton
8. Pepper
9. Pork
10. Sugar
11. Tea

Miscellaneous
1. Beeswax
2. Bristles
3. Isinglass
4. Starch, common
5. Soap, hard yellow
6. Whale fins

Metals
1. Copper
2. Iron, bars, domestic
3. Iron, pigs, domestic
4. Iron, bars, Swedish
5. Lead, pigs
6. Quicksilver
7. Tin
8. Tin plates

Textiles and Auxiliary Materials
1. Annatto
2. Barwood
3. Brazilwood
4. Cochineal
5. Cotton
6. Flax
7. Fustic
8. Hemp
9. Indigo
10. Leather butts
11. Logwood
12. Madder root
13. Mahogany
14. Olive oil
15. Silk, raw
16. Silk, thrown
17. Soap, mottled
18. Sumac
19. Wool

To some extent the Parliamentary Report was useful for the period before 1823. It contains special sections on wines, foreign and colonial spirits, tobacco, tea, sugar, corn, and wood, which list the duties on these articles chronologically from the earliest date of their levy.

In some cases the original prices Silberling obtained included duty, and these were used as they were. The list of these commodities and the dates for which their prices included duty follow:

Annatto.	. . .	1790–June 1814
Barwood	. . .	1790–Dec. 1818
Brandy cognac	. .	1790–Aug. 1809
Brazilwood	. . .	1790–Dec. 1817
Brimstone	. . .	1790–Dec. 1818
Cinnamon, E.I.	. .	1790–Dec. 1798
Geneva Spirits	. .	1795–July 1809
Jalap	. . . .	1790–Dec. 1817
Opium	. . .	1790–Dec. 1817
Quicksilver	. . .	1790–Dec. 1818
Sugar	. . . .	1790–Dec. 1850
Wine, port	. . .	1790–Dec. 1810

Silberling also added duties to the prices of tea and tobacco for use in an annual cost-of-living index which he computed.

A list of the principal tariff acts passed between 1787 and 1819, the dates of their enactment, and a brief description of each act, follow in Table 46 :

TABLE 46. *List of Principal Tariff Acts, 1787–1819*

Act	Date passed	Nature[a]
27 Geo. III, c. 13	Mar. 1787	Consolidated duties.
37 Geo. III, c. 15	31 Dec. 1796	Increase on 1787 duties: 10% increase on brimstone, hemp, iron, staves, 5% on every other article except wine.
37 Geo. III, c. 110	15 July 1797	Increase on 1787 duties in additon to increase in 1796: 5% on every article, except olive-oil, sugar, wine, tobacco.
38 Geo. III, c. 76	July 1798	Addition to previous increases: convoy duties which were levied to defray cost of preventing capture of British merchantmen.
42 Geo. III, c. 43	May 1802	Addition to previous increases: new duties taking place of convoy.
43 Geo. III, c. 68	June 1803	Consolidated duties imposed between 1787 and 1803.
43 Geo. III, c. 70	July 1803	Increase on June 1803 duties: 12% on every article.
44 Geo. III, c. 53	June 1804	Increase on June 1803 duties, in addition to increase in July 1803: 12½% on every article.
45 Geo. III, c. 18	Apr. 1805	Increase on June 1803 duties, in addition to increases in July 1803 and June 1804: 10% on barilla, brimstone, bristles; 5% on iron, turpentine; 2½% on every other article.
46 Geo. III, c. 42	19 May 1806	Increase on June 1803 duties, in addition to increases in July 1803, June 1804, and Apr. 1805: 8⅓% on every article except cotton, tobacco, wine, timber of Norway.
49 Geo. III, c. 98	July 1809	Consolidated duties imposed between June 1803 and 1809, distinguishing permanent from temporary duties of war.
53 Geo. III, c. 33	May 1813	Increase on June 1809 permanent duties: 25% on every article except silk and cotton wool.
59 Geo. III, c. 52	July 1819	Consolidated duties imposed between July 1809 and 1819.

a All the exceptions to the general tariffs are not here listed, but only those involving commodities used in the index. Several commodities for a decade or so after 1790 were on the free list, and imports from the East Indies were in a special category. After 1819 complete details of tariff acts are available in the Parliamentary Report on Customs Tariffs of the United Kingdom, 1898, lxxxv.

6. Techniques employed. The prices of the items listed in Table 42 were geometrically averaged[1] and the mean of the prices from 1821 to 1825, inclusive, was taken as the base. These years were used as a base for the index of wholesale prices in Philadelphia from 1784 to 1861[2] and we adopted them as our base for the sake of immediate comparability.

Weights are assigned to each commodity in proportion to values consumed in Great Britain. 'Value consumed in Great Britain' or 'home consumption' refers to the portion of a commodity which was 'consumed' in Great Britain either in the sense of conversion to a semi-fabricated or fabricated state, or in the sense of actually reaching the final consumer.

During the period under consideration England assumed the role of what amounted to general wholesaler or distributor of 'colonial' foods and raw materials for the Continent, and hence quantities of these goods (e.g. coffee, sugar, indigo) were imported, sometimes far in excess of British requirements. Such excess consignments were not 'consumed' in Great Britain but were merely warehoused near the docks and then exported at some later date without any duty having been paid. These 're-exports' were, therefore, not included in the weights assigned to the respective imported commodities. In general, weights could be more accurately ascertained for imported goods than for domestic goods, though even in the former group they are to be regarded only as rough approximations.

In the case of the imported group, figures on quantities consumed at home are not available for all commodities for each year of our period. Import data, moreover, though more complete, bear no very consistent relation to the volume of home consumption. For each year the quantity consumed at home does not equal the difference between total imports and re-exports.[3] For our purposes, however, an adequate approximation to home

---

[1] It seems worth while to comment that in constructing an index based on a geometric average, it is unnecessary to go through the labour of first converting actual prices into relatives, unless the relatives are required in some other connexion. Both Silberling and the authors of *Wholesale Prices in Philadelphia 1784–1861* obtained relatives as a preliminary to computing their geometric indexes. It can easily be demonstrated that computing the index from the logarithms of the actual prices must give the same results as computing it from the logarithms of relatives:

Let $p_1, p_2,..., p_n$ represent the actual prices of n commodities in a given year.

Let $b_1, b_2,..., b_n$ represent the actual prices of the same commodities in the base year.

Let $w_1, w_2,..., w_n$ represent the weights of the respective commodities.

Then M, the weighted geometric average of the price relatives, is:

$$M = \left[\left(\frac{p_1}{b_1} \right)^{w_1} \left(\frac{p_2}{b_2} \right)^{w_2} ... \left(\frac{p_n}{b_n} \right)^{w_n} \right]^{1/\Sigma w}.$$

The latter expression is equal to:

$$\frac{(p_1^{w_1} p_2^{w_2} ... p_n^{w_n})^{1/\Sigma w}}{(b_1^{w_1} b_2^{w_2} ... b_n^{w_n})^{1/\Sigma w}}.$$

Therefore the geometric average of price relatives is equal to the ratio of the geometric average of the actual prices in the given year to the geometric average of the actual prices in the base year. The fact that the weights are, in the case of an unweighted index, equal to 1 for each commodity, obviously does not affect the validity of this proof.

[2] Anne Bezanson, Robert D. Gray, Miriam Hussey, *Wholesale Prices in Philadelphia 1784–1861.*

[3] At times, home consumption during a given year may even exceed imports owing to the drawing upon warehoused stock.

consumption can be arrived at on the basis of the former quantities. From 1820 on, Porter's tables, presented in the *Parliamentary Papers*, are fairly complete; and for most commodities figures were secured for the quantity of home consumption for the years 1820, 1830, and 1840.[1] In addition, consumption data are available for years prior to 1820 in the case of about twenty commodities. But these latter data were not used because, in assigning weights, it was thought preferable to use figures for the same time period for all commodities.[2] Except for balsam, barwood, and brazilwood, each commodity is represented by at least one home consumption figure in the years 1820, 1830, and 1840, and for forty commodities figures were obtained for all three years. The home consumption figure for each commodity in the given years was multiplied by its average price during that year, and in this way a table was constructed giving the average value of the home consumption for each commodity over the period 1820 through 1840. Weights were assigned to each commodity on the basis of these values by giving the weight of *one* to the item, the home consumption of which was smallest, and assigning proportionately larger weights to the others. In the case of the three import commodities for which no home consumption figures could be secured, the commodities were assigned weights of *one* each, on the assumption that the lack of data for these commodities is attributable to their slight importance.

The quantities used for weighting the domestic commodities are production figures. They may, however, also be regarded as consumption figures, because all the items in the domestic index are foods and raw materials, virtually all the home production of which was domestically consumed.

The weighting of the twenty-six domestic commodities presented more difficult problems than those encountered in the import group. There simply are no continuous production series for any of these commodities for the period before 1850.[3] Even for such staples as wheat, coal, and beef there exist, at best, rough approximations for scattered years. Moreover, it would be desirable to deduct from the production figures of such foods as wheat, oats, mutton, beef, butter, and pork the quantities which never entered the market, but were consumed directly on the farm. Since no price was paid for that portion of the output, it should ideally be excluded in arriving at appropriate weights.[4] There is, however, no direct information

[1] *P.P.* 1835, xlix, Part 2; 1842, xxxix; 1870, lxviii. In the case of jalap and isinglass the figures were taken from McCulloch's *Dictionary of Commerce*, 1839 edition.

[2] The fact that consumption data for the imported price index before 1820 are only fragmentary, and are even more unsatisfactory for the domestic index, ruled out the use of more than one set of weights for the period. However, what figures we do have for the earlier period suggest that the use of our single set of weights does not involve any serious error in the relative magnitudes of the respective weights even for the years prior to 1820.

[3] For a few commodities partial production series for a restricted locality are available; e.g. tin mined at Cornwall. G. R. Porter, *Progress of the Nation*, p. 273.

[4] The United States Bureau of Labor Statistics also follows the procedure in its commodity price indexes of including in its weights only that portion of the commodity which is actually marketed. See Bulletin No. 440, p. 3.

of a quantitative sort on this point, and indirect clues, such as data on the degree of diversification of agriculture, are imprecise and incomplete. Any scaling down of weights in order to correct for this circumstance would, therefore, have to be applied uniformly to all relevant commodities. But since the weights of those commodities (i.e. the six foods mentioned above) are extremely large, the net effect of this rough correction would be very slight.[1] The same proportions among these items would still be retained, and, in sum, they would continue to overshadow in importance almost all other commodities. It was therefore decided not to introduce any arbitrary correction factor to the production estimates on account of output consumed by the producer.

For most of the domestic commodities production estimates in Mulhall's *Dictionary of Statistics*, for years prior to 1850, have been used. Where there was any choice, estimates of annual production for years falling within the period 1820 to 1840 were taken, in order to make the weighting base cover the same period for the domestic as for the imported commodities.

Mulhall's figures have been supplemented with an estimate for the production of camphor in 1831, taken from McCulloch's *Dictionary of Commerce*, and figures for starch, taken from both McCulloch and an unpublished dissertation by Dr. Selma Fine.[2] The latter also furnished figures for hard and soft soap production. Mulhall does not present estimates of oat production for any period before the 1890's. However, the quantity of various types of grains produced, including wheat and oats, is estimated for 1812 by Colquhoun.[3] The ratio between the quantity of wheat and oat production for that year does not differ much from the ratios obtained for the latter part of the century. Because of the relative constancy of this ratio over time, it was made the basis for estimating the production of oats in the years 1820, 1830, and 1840 from the estimated wheat production for those years. The production figure for bar-iron was derived from Swank's estimates for pig-iron[4] by assuming, on the basis of McCulloch's calculation,[5] that seven-tenths of the pig-iron was converted into bar-iron. Alum production was roughly estimated on the basis of figures for the 1870's presented in the *Mineral Industry*.[6] Despite the fact that these figures may be somewhat large for our period, they do not bring the weight of alum above the minimum figure of *one*.

From these sources we were able to derive estimates for the production

[1] See Table 47.

[2] Selma Fine, *Excise and Production*, unpublished dissertation in the Radcliffe College Library. Dr. Fine uses the annual figures on excise returns from which she derives production series for some 15 domestic commodities for the period from 1790 to 1825. The accuracy of the production estimates is somewhat open to question because of widespread evasion of duties, as Dr. Fine points out.

[3] Patrick Colquhoun, *Wealth of the British Empire*, p. 89.

[4] T. M. Swank, *Iron in All Ages*, p. 520, corrected by W. Page, *Commerce and Industry*, ii. 180.

[5] McCulloch's *Dictionary of Commerce*, p. 736.

[6] *The Mineral Industry*, i. 1892, p. 596 (ed. R. P. Rothwell).

of each of the domestic commodities, with the exception of the three oils and sal-ammoniac. No information whatsoever for our purpose is supplied in the Board of Trade's *Statistical Abstract of the United Kingdom*, which presents miscellaneous annual statistical data from 1840 on.[1] As in the case of the imported commodities, the quantity figures were multiplied by their appropriate prices, and weights assigned to each commodity in proportion to the resulting value figures. Again in accordance with the procedure in the import index, weights of *one* each were assigned to those commodities for which data were lacking.

From Table 47 it will be seen that in the total index the weight assigned to domestic commodities is almost three times the weight given the imported commodities, though the latter are twice as numerous as the former. The value of wheat, moreover, is more than one-quarter that of all domestic items; and the value of the six most important home-produced foods—wheat, oats, mutton, beef, butter, and pork—constitute over three-quarters the value of the whole domestic group and well over one-half the weight of the total index. Within the sub-group of imported commodities, there is a similarly skewed distribution of weights, though not quite as spectacular as in the domestic group. Here the four largest items— sugar, cotton, wool, and tea—loom greater in importance than the other forty-eight imported commodities combined. And if the weights of those four imported items are added to the total weight of the six above-mentioned domestic foods, plus the weights of coal and tallow, we find that these twelve largest items have a weight of 3,081 out of a total weight of 3,861 for all seventy-eight commodities. It is apparent, therefore, that the net effect on the final weighted index of the movements of the remaining sixty-six commodities is almost negligible.

Certain theoretical objections may be raised with respect to this weighting procedure. Our selection of commodities includes practically all of the important raw materials and foods which were then traded in Great Britain. Because this is a sample group, however, it does not include a large number of small and relatively unimportant items in these categories. It would therefore seem that by assigning weights proportionate to value to such large items as wheat, oats, beef, coal, cotton, wool, and sugar, the importance of these commodities relative to all raw materials and food traded in Great Britain is somewhat exaggerated. Obviously the percentage weight assigned to wheat in the index would be somewhat less, if, instead of a total of seventy-eight commodities, it had been possible to include two or three times that number. In view of this fact there might be some justification for dampening down the weights of the larger items, relative to those of the smaller, in order that the large sector of relatively unimportant commodities not included in the index should not be left out of the picture. But such a procedure would be warranted only on the assumption that the large number of items not represented in the index fluctuated in the same

---

[1] *P.P.* 1854, xxxix.

manner as the smaller items that *are* represented in the index. But since there are no empirical grounds for making this assumption, whatever downward adjustment of weighting we undertook would have to be applied equally to all commodities. Of course, if this were done, the net effect of the adjustment would be nil.

TABLE 47. *Weights used in computing the Commodity Price Indexes*

Domestic commodities	Weights	Imported commodities	Weights		Weights
Wheat	745	Sugar	166	Pepper	3
Oats	497	Cotton	163	Beeswax	2
Mutton	461	Wool	119	Brimstone	2
Beef	239	Tea	111	Cochineal	2
Coal	216	Silk, raw	61	Isinglass	2
Tallow	132	Tobacco	58	Liquorice	2
Butter	116	Timber	38	Logwood	2
Pork	116	Rum	28	Madder root	2
Iron, bars	83	Flax	27	Mahogany	2
Iron, pigs	66	Brandy	22	Sumac	2
Leather, butts	41	Wine, port	22	Annatto	1
Soap, hard	41	Staves	20	Balsam	1
Hides	38	Indigo	19	Barwood	1
Tin plates	21	Hemp	18	Brazilwood	1
Copper	16	Hides	18	Cinnamon	1
Lead, pigs	13	Coffee	18	Cocoa	1
Tin	6	Silk, thrown	13	Fustic	1
Soap, mottled	4	Linseed	11	Geneva Spirits	1
Starch	3	Oil, olive	5	Ginger	1
Alum	1	Ashes, pearl	4	Jalap	1
Camphor	1	Bristles	4	Oil, castor	1
Oil, linseed	1	Saltpetre	4	Opium	1
Oil, rape	1	Tar	4	Quicksilver	1
Oil, vitriol	1	Turpentine	4	Whale fins	1
Sal-ammoniac	1	Barilla	3	Whale oil	1
Clover seeds	1	Iron	3	Quinine	1
	2,861				**1,000**[a]

[a] It will be noticed that the sum of the weights of the imported items equals 1,000. The total value of their home consumption was equated to this round figure in order to save one arithmetical operation, namely, the division of the sum of the weighted logarithms by the sum of the weights. Needless to say, this economy could be effected for only one of the three indexes, since the choice of any arbitrary total weight for one of the indexes predetermined the sum of the weights for the other two.

There is yet another limitation to this direct system of weighting which reduces the precision of the index as a measure of the 'wholesale' price level. Take the case of iron pigs and iron bars. Both are included in the domestic index, and weights are assigned to each roughly in proportion to the value of the output. Yet bar-iron is fabricated from pig-iron and merely represents a later stage of production. The prices of both irons could be expected to move roughly together. Iron therefore receives a weight greater than it would have if only the basic material were included. Ideally the weight to each commodity should represent not only the value of the material in its earliest stage of production but also in each subsequent stage of partial fabrication. In this way a weight might be secured which would more closely approximate the importance of the commodity in the average wholesale price level, in so far as each stage through which the commodity passes involves a price transaction. However, if one departs from the direct weighting basis (namely, value of home consumption or value of production), and proceeds to impute weights to commodities, taking into account the later stages through which they pass, one enters a realm where the statistical foundation is exceedingly tenuous and where the major reliance must be put on broad speculation. It was only after a full consideration of the alternatives that we decided to adhere to the restricted weighting criteria as outlined above.

It is important that the reader bear in mind precisely what our index is and precisely what it is not. It represents, in fact, the changing valuation over time of a fixed set of goods consisting entirely of raw materials and foods. Though indexes of this and similar types have been loosely referred to in the past as 'general wholesale commodity price', they may more correctly be regarded as reflecting the price level of working capital and foods. The common reference to such wholesale price index numbers as measures which register changes in the purchasing power of the consumers' monetary unit is an interpretation of very questionable validity. It is strictly valid only for index numbers which include exclusively finished goods and services in proportion to the expenditure of final consumers on them. In presenting our index, which includes no completely fabricated goods, and, of course, no services, we can merely urge that due caution be exercised in its use to take account of its composition and manner of construction.

Chapter II

BEHAVIOUR OF THE COMMODITY
PRICE INDEXES

1. Trends in Prices. An examination of the broad movements of the
total price index reveals a long-period rise culminating in the second quarter
of the year 1813,[1] followed by a secular decline, the low point of which
appears to be reached in 1850 (see Fig. 97). But it cannot be definitely
stated that this is actually the trough unless the index is extended several
years beyond 1850.[2]

Viewing the period as a whole, the index exhibits a net downward trend
from 1790 to 1850. On the base 1821–5 the index rises from a low point of
85 in March 1790 to a peak of 177 in May 1813, from which point it declines to a low of 71 in June 1850. The curve shows a pronounced hump in
the upward secular movement from the end of 1798 until the middle of
1802. In the two and a half years following the last quarter of 1798 the
curve rises 70 points, as compared with a net rise of 20 points in the nine
preceding years. The fall from March 1801 to October 1802, though briefer,
is even more precipitous, wiping out 60 points of the earlier rise. The shape
of the total price index during this period is largely determined by the
fluctuations of the domestic price index which, in turn, is dominated by the
price of wheat. Several years of bad harvests, during which grain imports
were obstructed by war conditions, were followed by a year of an abundant
wheat crop. The atypical movement from 1799 to 1802 was thus produced.
Thereafter, until 1813, when the second phase of the war with France was
in progress, the cycles are milder and the trend movement more continuous.

In the period of decline the rate of fall is greatest until 1822, by which
time the index falls to its 1790 level, completely erasing the advance before
1813. From 1822 until the end of the period the movement is gradual but
unmistakably downward in its general direction.

Both sub-indexes are characterized by a rising trend during the war
period, and a secular decline thereafter, but the difference in the amplitude
of the movement, as between imported and domestic commodities, is con-

---

[1] In point of fact the index reaches its
highest value in March 1801, at which time
it is actually 4 points greater than in 1813.
But the 1801 figure is clearly a cyclical peak
and not the crest of a secular movement.
This view is confirmed by the curve of the
annual averages, which is higher in 1813
than in 1801. In this context, the term
'cycles' refers merely to the movement of
the series under examination, not to fluctuations of the economy as a whole.

[2] The timing of the long wave revealed by

our index corresponds in general to the
dating of the first long wave in British prices
pointed out by Kondratieff on the basis of
Silberling's index. According to the latter,
the initial trough comes in 1789, the year
prior to the beginning of our index. The
crest of Silberling's index follows ours by
one year, and its terminal trough leads by
one year. (See N. D. Kondratieff, 'Die
langen Wellen der Konjunktur', *Archiv für
Sozialwissenschaft und Sozialpolitik*, Dec.
1926, lvi. 573–609.)

siderable. The timing of the turning-points of the trend pattern in the two series also differs. Prices of domestic goods rise from a low of 76 in May 1792 to a peak of 189 in August 1812; they fall to 79 in May 1822, but are never below this average until November 1849; the lowest point reached by domestic prices during the whole period 1790–1850 is 74, in June 1850.

The secular rise in the prices of imported commodities during the war period, although slightly less steep, is more continuous than for domestic prices. Prices of imports are at their lowest in January 1790 when the index stands at 85. The secular peak in prices occurs eighteen months later in imported than in domestic commodities. The import price index in February 1814 registers 180, its highest point for the whole period. The secular decline in import prices is more gradual than in the domestic index during the years when the latter is falling, but prices of imports move steadily downward over a greater part of the period after 1814 than do domestic prices. The net secular decline in import prices is greater than for domestic prices. In October 1824 the import index is at a low of 92, in comparison with a much steeper fall undergone by domestic prices by that time. By September 1848, however, prices of imports had declined further, by more than half as much as their fall from February 1814 to October 1824, while, it will be recalled, domestic prices showed virtually no secular change from 1822 to 1848. The import index reads 52 in September 1848, and thereafter seems to be moving to a new level of trend, but the inauguration of no similar long-period change is perceptible in domestic prices. For the whole period 1790–1850 the negative trend is most pronounced in the import price index, weakest in the domestic price index, and only slightly stronger in the total index.

2. Characteristics of Specific Cycles in the Indexes. Nineteen specific cycles[1] can be distinguished in the movements of the total index during the entire period, some more clearly defined than others. For the period 1790–1850 we have chosen a set of 'reference dates', marking the months and years of the troughs and peaks of successive business cycles (see Table 48). By comparing the timing of the specific cycles in commodity prices with our reference dates it is possible to determine with what regularity the turning-points in prices preceded, coincided with, or lagged behind the turning-points in general business.

Only fourteen cycles in general business activity have been noted by us during the period under investigation. The greater number of specific cycles in prices is indicative of the speculative character of commodity markets. Most of the prices in our index were set in large markets which tended to experience frequent movements. One-to-one correspondence between cycles in the total commodity price index and the reference dates

[1] 'Specific cycles' are the cycles peculiar to an individual series. It is important not to confuse them with business cycles in general. The methods used in dating and measuring various attributes of the specific cycles were devised by the National Bureau of Economic Research.

TABLE 48. Timing and Duration of Specific Cycles in Total Commodity Price Index compared with Reference Cycles

Specific cycles, Index of prices of domestic and imported commodities

Expansion		Contraction		Duration in months			Lead (−) or lag (+)	
Revival	Peak	Recession	Trough	Expansion	Contraction	Full cycle	At reference peak	At reference trough
June 1792	Mar. 1794	Apr. 1794	Sept. 1794	22	6	28	b	+3
Oct. 1794	Aug. 1795	Sept. 1795	July 1797	11	23	34	−9	−2
Aug. 1797	Oct. 1797	Nov. 1797	Nov. 1798	3	13	16		(+12)a
Dec. 1798	Mar. 1801	Apr. 1801	Oct. 1802	28	19	47	+6	+3
Nov. 1802	June 1803	July 1803	June 1804	8	12	20	+6	−7
July 1804	Aug. 1805	Sept. 1805	Oct. 1807	14	26	40	−12	−3
Nov. 1807	Mar. 1809	Apr. 1809	June 1811	17	27	44	(−12)	(+36)
July 1811	May 1813	June 1813	Mar. 1816	23	34	57	(−22)	
Apr. 1816	Apr. 1818	May 1818	Sept. 1822	25	53	78	−5	
Oct. 1822	Feb. 1824	Mar. 1824	Sept. 1824	17	7	24		
Oct. 1824	May 1825	June 1825	July 1826	8	14	22	0	−4
Aug. 1826	Apr. 1827	May 1827	June 1828	9	14	23	0	
July 1828	Jan. 1829	Feb. 1829	Nov. 1829	7	10	17	0	−1
Dec. 1829	Mar. 1831	Apr. 1831	Mar. 1833	16	24	40	0	+8
Apr. 1833	Sept. 1833	Oct. 1833	Nov. 1835	6	26	32		
Dec. 1835	Dec. 1836	Jan. 1837	Oct. 1837	13	10	23	+7	+2
Nov. 1837	Jan. 1839	Feb. 1839	May 1843	15	52	67	−2	+6
June 1843	Nov. 1845	Dec. 1845	Aug. 1846	30	9	39	+2	−1
Sept. 1846	June 1847	July 1847	June 1850	10	36	46	+2	(+21)
AVERAGE				14·8	21·8	36·7	−0·4	−0·2
AVERAGE DEVIATION				6·3	11·0	13·5	4·4	3·8

Reference cycles

Expansion		Contraction		Duration in months		
Revival	Peak	Recession	Trough	Expansion	Contraction	Full cycle
July 1794	May 1796	June 1796	Sept. 1797	23	16	39
Oct. 1797	Sept. 1800	Oct. 1800	Oct. 1801	36	13	49
Nov. 1801	Dec. 1802	Jan. 1803	Mar. 1804	14	15	29
Apr. 1804	Aug. 1806	Sept. 1806	May 1808	29	21	50
June 1808	Mar. 1810	Apr. 1810	Sept. 1811	22	18	40
Oct. 1811	Mar. 1815	Apr. 1815	Sept. 1816	42	18	60
Oct. 1816	Sept. 1818	Oct. 1818	Sept. 1819	24	12	36
Oct. 1819	May 1825	June 1825	Nov. 1826	68	18	86
Dec. 1826	Jan. 1829	Feb. 1829	Dec. 1829	26	11	37
Jan. 1830	Mar. 1831	Apr. 1831	July 1832	15	16	31
Aug. 1832	May 1836	June 1836	Aug. 1837	46	15	61
Sept. 1837	Mar. 1839	Apr. 1839	Nov. 1842	19	44	63
Dec. 1842	Sept. 1845	Oct. 1845	Sept. 1846	34	12	46
Oct. 1846	Apr. 1847	May 1847	Sept. 1848	7	17	24
AVERAGE				28·9	17·6	46·5
AVERAGE DEVIATION				11·6	4·5	12·9

a Leads or lags that do not correspond closely to reference turns are enclosed in parentheses. A turning-point of a specific cycle is judged to correspond closely to a reference turn when it deviates from the corresponding reference turns by no more than half the duration of the reference phase within which it falls. In striking averages of leads or lags, parenthesis entries are generally omitted.

b A blank indicates that a turn of the specific cycles is considered as not corresponding to a reference turn.

TABLE 49. *Timing and Duration of Specific Cycles in the Domestic and Import Price Indexes*

Index of prices of domestic commodities

Expansion		Contraction		Duration in months			Lead (−) or lag (+)	
Revival	Peak	Recession	Trough	Expansion	Contraction	Full cycle	At reference peak	At reference trough
June 1792	Aug. 1795	Sept. 1795	July 1797	39	23	62	−9	(−25)a
Aug. 1797	Oct. 1797	Nov. 1797	Nov. 1798	3	13	16	b	−2
Dec. 1798	Mar. 1801	Apr. 1801	Mar. 1803	28	24	52	+6	(+17)
Apr. 1803	Nov. 1803	Dec. 1803	June 1804	8	7	15	(+11)	+3
July 1804	Aug. 1805	Sept. 1805	Oct. 1807	14	26	40	−12	−7
Nov. 1807	Oct. 1809	Nov. 1809	Apr. 1811	24	18	42	−5	−5
May 1811	Aug. 1812		Mar. 1816	16	43	59	(−3½)	−6
Apr. 1816	June 1817	July 1817	Dec. 1817	15	6	21	+1	+32
Jan. 1818	Oct. 1818	Nov. 1818	May 1822	10	43	53		−4
June 1822	May 1825	July 1823	Oct. 1823	13	4	17	0	−1
Nov. 1823	Apr. 1827	June 1825	July 1826	19	14	33		
July 1828	Jan. 1829	May 1827	June 1828	9	14	23	−7	(+39)
Dec. 1829	Aug. 1830	Feb. 1829	Nov. 1829	7	10	17	+7	+4
Nov. 1835	Dec. 1836	Sept. 1830	Oct. 1835	9	62	71	+2	+1
Jan. 1838	Jan. 1839	Jan. 1837	Dec. 1837	14	12	26	+2	−1
June 1843	Nov. 1845	Feb. 1839	May 1843	13	52	65		
Sept. 1846	June 1847	Dec. 1845	Aug. 1846	30	9	39		(+21)
		July 1847	June 1850	10	36	46		
AVERAGE				15·6	23·1	38·7	−1·4	+1·7
AVERAGE DEVIATION				6·9	13·8	15·8	4·6	6·9

Index of prices of imported commodities

Expansion		Contraction		Duration in months			Lead (−) or lag (+)	
Revival	Peak	Recession	Trough	Expansion	Contraction	Full cycle	At reference peak	At reference trough
July 1792	Apr. 1793	May 1793	June 1794	10	14	24		0
July 1794	Dec. 1795	Jan. 1796	Dec. 1796	18	12	30	−5	(−9)
Jan. 1797	July 1799	Aug. 1799	Dec. 1799	31	5	36	+5	(+10)
Jan. 1800	Feb. 1801	Mar. 1801	Aug. 1802	14	18	32	(−18)	−5
Sept. 1802	Feb. 1805	Mar. 1805	Dec. 1807	30	34	64	0	−1
Jan. 1808	Mar. 1809	Feb. 1809	July 1809	13	6	19		−1
Aug. 1809	Mar. 1810	Apr. 1810	Aug. 1811	8	17	25	−13	(+61)
Sept. 1811	Feb. 1814	Mar. 1814	Aug. 1816	30	30	60	−6	+2
Sept. 1816	Mar. 1818	Apr. 1818	Oct. 1824	19	79	98	0	
Nov. 1824	May 1825	June 1825	Sept. 1832	7	88	95		−1
Oct. 1832	Oct. 1833	Nov. 1833	May 1834	13	7	20	−1	0
June 1834	Apr. 1836	May 1836	July 1837	23	15	38		0
Aug. 1837	Sept. 1840	Oct. 1840	Sept. 1846	38	72	110	+18	
Oct. 1846	Feb. 1847	Mar. 1847	Sept. 1848	5	19	24	−2	
AVERAGE				18·5	29·7	48·2	−0·4	−0·8
AVERAGE DEVIATION				8·6	22·1	26·6	5·5	1·2

a See note to Table 48.
b See note to Table 48.

is obviously lacking. Commodity prices showed no regular relation in time either to reference peaks or troughs. Where specific peaks could be matched with reference peaks, there were four cases of leads, five of lag, and three of coincidence. The timing at reference troughs was almost equally indecisive. Seven specific troughs preceded reference troughs, five lagged behind.

Marked dissimilarities are revealed in a comparison of the curves of the two sub-indexes. The domestic price index at times moves in a most erratic manner, often showing little relation to the course of import prices. Its movements are generally more abrupt and precipitous than those of the index of imported commodity prices. This lack of conformity between the two sub-indexes is emphasized by the fact that while the import index contains fourteen complete cycles, the domestic index contains eighteen (see Table 49). Only one peak (May 1825) coincides in both indexes; none of the troughs is identical. There are, however, a number of roughly similar cycles.

Despite the fact that the import price index contains the same number of specific and reference cycles, there is no one-to-one correspondence in their dating. The domestic price index exhibits four more specific cycles than there are reference cycles. Again, the distribution of leads and lags, in both sub-indexes, at reference peaks and troughs reveals no significant timing behaviour.

The duration of specific cycles in the index of prices of imported commodities is the greatest of all three indexes and closest to the duration of reference cycles. All three indexes are characterized by longer phases of contraction than of expansion.

Domestic prices show the greatest amplitude of movement, in total, and on a per month basis (see Table 50). But while the total index and the prices of imports tended to exhibit a greater amplitude of fall than of rise, the total movement of rise in domestic prices was no smaller than that of fall. The amplitude of movement per month, however, was greater in contraction than in expansion only for import prices.

Of the nineteen cycles in the total index, seven and a half cycles are included in the period of rise until 1813; eleven and a half fall within the ensuing period of declining prices. The cycles falling within the period of secular decline are both of longer average duration and of greater average amplitude than those included within the years of secular rise, before 1813. On the average, cycles during the first period lasted 33 (10)[1] months as compared with 39 (16) months for the second period. During both periods, it will be recalled, the mean duration of the contraction phases was greater than that of the expansion phases, though the difference between the duration of contraction and expansion is greater in the second period. The expansion phases were longer on the average during the period of secular

---

[1] The figures in parentheses show the mean deviation, measured from the averages given to their left. The size of the mean deviation as compared with the average serves as a measure of the degree of dis- persion of the individual items around the mean. It is, therefore, an indicator of the extent of uniformity of behaviour from cycle to cycle.

rise in prices than they were during the years of secular decline. Likewise, the contraction phases were briefer for the first period than for the second.

With one major exception the relations between the average amplitude of the cyclical phases are similar to the relations between the mean duration: i.e., in the period of positive trend, the amplitude of rise is greater

TABLE 50. *Average Cyclical Amplitude of the Commodity Price Indexes*

	Total	Import	Domestic
PERIOD COVERED . .	1792–1850	1792–1848	1792–1850
NUMBER OF CYCLES . .	19	14	18
AVERAGE AMPLITUDE OF RELATIVES			
Period of rising prices			
Total movement			
Rise	19·4 (9·2)	18·6 (6·9)	27·0 (16·6)
Fall	12·6 (9·7)	13·1 (6·4)	18·0 (14·0)
Rise and fall. . .	31·6 (19·7)	32·1 (6·8)	45·7 (33·9)
Movement per month			
Rise	1·3 (0·5)	1·0 (0·3)	1·5 (0·6)
Fall	0·7 (0·4)	1·3 (0·9)	0·9 (0·5)
Rise and fall. . .	0·9 (0·4)	1·1 (0·4)	1·2 (0·5)
Period of falling prices			
Total movement			
Rise	14·3 (5·7)	12·0 (3·7)	19·1 (6·5)
Fall	19·8 (12·9)	27·3 (10·8)	24·2 (16·0)
Rise and fall. . .	34·8 (17·8)	40·5 (13·5)	43·6 (7·6)
Movement per month			
Rise	1·2 (0·5)	1·0 (0·5)	1·6 (0·6)
Fall	0·8 (0·3)	0·8 (0·3)	1·1 (0·4)
Rise and fall. . .	0·9 (0·3)	0·8 (0·2)	1·3 (0·4)
Full Period			
Total movement			
Rise	16·4 (7·3)	15·8 (6·1)	22·2 (10·4)
Fall	17·2 (11·9)	20·2 (9·8)	22·2 (15·5)
Rise and fall. . .	33·6 (18·6)	36·0 (12·3)	44·3 (23·1)
Movement per month			
Rise	1·2 (0·5)	1·0 (0·4)	1·5 (0·6)
Fall	0·8 (0·4)	1·1 (0·6)	1·1 (0·4)
Rise and fall. . .	0·9 (0·4)	0·9 (0·3)	1·2 (0·4)

than in the period of negative trend, the amplitude of fall, less; within the period of negative trend, the amplitude of the contraction phases is greater than that of the expansion phases. The exception occurs during the period of secularly rising prices, 1790–1813. Here the average movement from trough to peak was greater than the average movement from peak to trough, although the mean duration of the expansion phases was smaller than that of the contraction phases. In point of fact, it is a mathematical necessity that the average expansion *amplitudes* be greater than the average contraction *amplitudes* during a rising trend period, if, as is the case, the average *duration* of the expansion phase is smaller than that of the contraction phase; otherwise the trend could not be upward. For the period of generally declining prices after 1813, the mean amplitude of the contractions was larger than that of the expansions. For prices from 1790 to 1850 there seems to be a tendency for an upward trend to increase the average amplitude of the expansion phase relative to the contraction phase, and for a downward trend to increase the average amplitude of the contraction relative to that of expansion. But for the period 1813–50 these relations are not maintained when amplitudes are converted to a per month basis. This is due to the fact that the average *duration* of the downward phases, when related to the average *amplitude* of the downward phases, is smaller than the relation between the same variables in their upward phases during these years:

Total Commodity Price Index
(June 1813–June 1850)

Duration in months		Amplitude		Per month movement (in per cent.)	
Expansion	Contraction	Rise	Fall	Rise	Fall
14	24	14	20	1·2	0·8

The decline in each contraction period was, in other words, spread so widely that the per month fall was *less* than the per month rise in each expansion; although the total fall per cycle was *greater* than the rise.

From this view of the variation in the behaviour of the total price index during the two periods of secular trend, we turn to a more detailed examination of the character of the rise and fall in the specific cycles of prices over the whole period. By breaking down each cycle into nine stages and computing the average level of the indexes at these points, and then averaging the standings at each stage for all the cycles, average patterns of the specific cycles in the indexes are obtained. These average patterns show prices rising in stages I–V, and declining in stages V to IX, and by their tilts they picture the secular trend which characterizes the series (see Fig. 98). Thus the domestic price index is at the same level in stage IX as in stage I, indicative of the absence of any clear-cut trend in the series over the whole period. The average standing in stage IX of the total index is somewhat lower than in stage I, as might be expected with a very slight downward trend. And the downward tilt of the average pattern of the price index of imported commodities is unmistakable. The average patterns also show that the rises and falls are not continuous during successive stages of expansion and contraction. The sub-indexes exhibit little change in the rates of rise during stages I–IV, but from IV to V the rate of rise falls off practically to the vanishing point. In the total index the rate of rise slackens as early as the last third of expansion. Similarly the rates of decline in the sub-indexes are substantially the same during stages V–VIII, although in the total index there is a marked decline in the rate of fall in stages VI–VIII. But in stage VIII–IX the fall in prices tapers off. In this stage in the domestic index, the rate is actually positive. This irregularity may be ascribed to a peculiarity of technique of analysis according to which we make cyclical patterns on a revival-to-revival basis instead of a trough-to-trough basis. If a series flattens out some months before the terminal trough and then rises sharply, it may show a rise from stages VIII to IX by the method we have used.[1]

3. The Conformity of Commodity Prices to Business Cycles. The behaviour of prices during the periods occupied by successive business cycles may be studied by transferring our measurements from specific cycles, which vary in timing for each of the indexes, to reference cycles, which cover a uniform period of time for all series. By dividing the reference cycles into eight segments (nine points), and computing the levels of the indexes during each of these stages for successive reference cycles, average reference-cycle patterns are obtained (see Table 51).

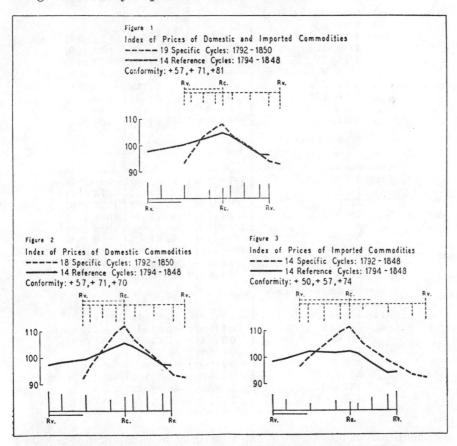

FIG. 98. Cyclical Patterns of Monthly Indexes of British Commodity Prices

[1] See Vol. II, Part II, Chap. I.

From the average standings of the series during the nine stages of each reference cycle, and the duration in months of each stage, rates of change,

TABLE 51. *Average Standings and Average Percentage Rates of Change from Stage to Stage of Specific and Reference Cycles in the Commodity Price Indexes*

Specific cycles	Total	Domestic	Import
Average standings of relatives in			
Stage I	93·3 (4·8)	92·3 (7·9)	96·6 (7·0)
,,　　II . . .	97·2 (3·7)	97·1 (6·4)	99·9 (7·0)
,,　　III . . .	103·3 (3·8)	103·1 (4·9)	104·5 (6·5)
,,　　IV . . .	106·7 (4·2)	109·6 (6·2)	109·8 (5·8)
,,　　V . . .	108·1 (5·0)	112·1 (7·2)	111·5 (5·7)
,,　　VI . . .	103·9 (2·7)	106·7 (4·5)	105·4 (2·2)
,,　　VII . . .	99·5 (2·9)	100·4 (4·4)	98·6 (3·1)
,,　　VIII . . .	94·1 (5·1)	93·5 (6·1)	93·4 (4·6)
,,　. IX . . .	92·9 (6·5)	92·4 (8·9)	92·4 (5·8)
Average rates of change (per month)			
From I to II . . .	+1·5 (1·1)	+1·9 (1·2)	+1·1 (0·6)
,,　　II to III .	+1·5 (0·8)	+1·4 (1·2)	+1·1 (1·0)
,,　　III to IV .	+1·1 (0·9)	+1·6 (1·1)	+1·2 (0·7)
,,　　IV to V .	+0·2 (0·8)	+0·3 (1·0)	+0·1 (0·9)
,,　　V to VI .	−1·2 (0·7)	−1·5 (1·2)	−1·3 (0·5)
,,　　VI to VII .	−0·6 (0·6)	−1·2 (1·0)	−1·4 (1·2)
,,　　VII to VIII .	−0·8 (0·4)	−1·4 (1·0)	−1·1 (0·9)
,,　　VIII to IX .	−0·1 (0·5)	+0·4 (1·3)	−0·1 (0·5)
Reference cycles			
Average standings of relatives in			
Stage I	97·8 (6·2)	97·4 (7·6)	98·5 (6·1)
,,　　II . . .	98·7 (5·2)	98·4 (6·4)	99·7 (4·1)
,,　　III . . .	100·2 (5·0)	99·6 (6·1)	102·2 (2·6)
,,　　IV . . .	103·1 (3·3)	103·4 (4·3)	101·6 (3·6)
,,　　V . . .	104·9 (4·0)	105·6 (5·2)	102·2 (3·0)
,,　　VI . . .	103·6 (5·1)	104·6 (6·4)	101·4 (2·5)
,,　　VII . . .	100·5 (6·0)	101·4 (8·0)	97·9 (4·7)
,,　　VIII . . .	96·5 (5·4)	97·4 (6·6)	94·1 (5·9)
,,　　IX . . .	96·4 (5·6)	97·1 (7·3)	94·6 (6·9)
Average rates of change (per month)			
From I to II . . .	+0·5 (0·9)	+0·5 (1·0)	+0·4 (0·7)
,,　　II to III .	+0·4 (0·9)	+0·5 (1·1)	+0·3 (0·6)
,,　　III to IV .	+0·3 (0·4)	+0·4 (0·5)	−0·1 (0·4)
,,　　IV to V .	+0·4 (0·8)	+0·5 (1·1)	+0·1 (0·7)
,,　　V to VI .	−0·4 (1·0)	−0·4 (1·2)	−0·3 (0·7)
,,　　VI to VII .	−0·6 (0·8)	−0·6 (0·9)	−0·7 (0·9)
,,　　VII to VIII .	−0·8 (0·6)	−0·8 (0·7)	−0·7 (0·6)
,,　　VIII to IX .	0·0 (1·3)	−0·1 (1·6)	+0·1 (0·7)

per month, from one stage to the next may be computed. The rate of change, in the indexes, on the average, was moderate, but, of course, in-dividual prices fluctuated much more violently than the indexes. The only noteworthy change in the rate of rise characterizes prices of import which increased at the most rapid rate in stages I–III, and show almost no average rate of increase in stages III–IV. Prices tended to fall at their maximum rate during stages VI–VIII. If monthly production or foreign trade data were available for this period, a comparison, which would be highly suggestive, could be made of the rates of change in these series with the rates of change in prices during the course of business cycles. We are not, however, in a position to state whether the price of imports rose faster than in I–III, or whether the quantity of imports declined during the latter stages of expansion as does the price rise. We can only state our rather limited findings.

The fluctuations of the average nine-point pattern on a reference-cycle basis when compared with the average specific-cycle pattern give a picture of the degree of relationship between cycles in prices and general cyclical movements. In Fig. 98 the average patterns are presented. Their inspection reveals a fair degree of similarity between reference and specific cycles, but the numerical measures of conformity we compute give more exact knowledge of the closeness of the relationship.

The average reference-cycle patterns do not show prices rising continuously from stage I to V and falling continuously from stage V to IX, as do the specific-cycle patterns. Domestic prices, on the average, move in this way, but the total index tends to remain unchanged from stage VIII to IX, and the index of imported commodities to rise from stage I to III, and from stage IV to V. When the patterns for individual reference cycles are scrutinized, however, the diverse behaviour concealed by the average pattern emerges. The domestic index, for example, declines (rises) in the following number of reference cycles in each of the four stages when the average pattern is rising (falling):

Number of Reference Cycles

Showing declines		Showing rises	
I–II. . .	6	V–VI . . .	2
II–III . .	5	VI–VII . .	3
III–IV . .	3	VII–VIII . .	2
IV–V . .	7	VIII–IX . .	6

Despite these instances of movements contrary to the average, it is obvious that in the majority of the reference cycles, domestic prices were rising during stages I–V and falling during stages V–IX. The total index shows even fewer cases of contrary movements. Both these indexes are best described as rising typically during stages I–V. The index of imported commodities, however, is less regular. The distribution of cycles showing rises and falls in the successive stages is as follows:

	Number of Reference Cycles[a]	
	Showing declines	*Showing rises*
I–II . . .	3	9
II–III . .	4	8
III–IV . .	7	6
IV–V . .	5	8
V–VI . .	9	2
VI–VII . .	11	3
VII–VIII . .	9	2
VIII–IX . .	5	7

[a] When the sum of the two columns is less than 14 (the total count of reference cycles), the remainder are to be understood to have shown no movement during the stage in question.

The most consistent rises occur only in stages VIII–III and IV–V. The series, nevertheless, has been designated as showing rise during stages VIII–V (see Table 52). The prices of imported commodities thus appear to have anticipated somewhat the upturn in general business, inasmuch as they typically began to rise in the interval from the last third of expansion to the terminal revival in business activity. If this relation in time were really

TABLE 52. *Conformity of Commodity Price Indexes to Business Cycles*

	Total	Domestic	Import
Expansion stages covered . .	I–V	I–V	VIII–V
Index of conformity to			
Reference expansion . .	+57	+57	+50
Reference contraction . .	+71	+71	+57
Business cycles . . .	+81	+70	+74

pervasive, however, it would have emerged in a fairly consistent lead in prices of imports at reference troughs. Since the timing measures do not reveal any such regularity, the significance of the lead in the average pattern is circumscribed. The total index is more nearly like the domestic than the import series, as might be expected in view of the fact that the former received a weight of 75 per cent., on the basis of the value of the commodities represented.

Having determined during what reference stages the series commonly expand, and during what stages they commonly contract, we then compute indexes of conformity to show the uniformity or lack of uniformity between the direction of movement in the segment of expansion and contraction and the corresponding phases of business cycles. Positive conformity is scored +100, inverse conformity, −100.

The highest numerical index of conformity among the price indexes is that for the total. Next in order of magnitude is the conformity index of imported commodities. The import price index thus appears to reflect the course of business activity in Britain better than the index of domestic prices. This result may seem contrary to expectations, since the imported commodities not only originated in a variety of places, with peculiar and changing local supply conditions, but they include in their prices changing tariff charges. Our domestic price index, however, because it is so heavily weighted with foodstuffs (they constitute over three-quarters of the total weight of the index), fluctuates more in accordance with the mercurial supply conditions for agricultural produce than with general business activity. Wheat and oats comprise over 40 per cent. of the total weight of the domestic index, causing the latter's movement to be largely dependent upon British harvests. Despite this preponderance of agricultural commodities in the domestic index, the numerical value of its index of conformity is not significantly smaller than is that of the index of imports. In point of fact, the domestic index shows higher conformity to reference expansions and contractions than does the index of imports. The fact that the rates of movement conformed in cycles where the direction of movement was contrary yields a higher index of conformity to all business cycles for imports than for domestic commodities. This circumstance also explains why the index of conformity to all business cycles is higher for the total than for the domestic index when their indexes of conformity to reference expansion and contraction have the same numerical values.

The principal failures of the domestic index to conform may be traced to the movements of the wheat price. Three cases of declining prices occur during reference expansion, two of rising prices during reference contraction. The decline in the domestic index during the reference expansion from November 1801 to December 1802 is almost wholly to be explained in terms of the harvest. Following an extraordinary succession of bad harvests which pushed the wheat price and the domestic index in March 1801 to a peak point for the entire period 1790–1850, the good harvest in 1801 produced a falling wheat price and a decline in the index. The amplitude of this rise until 1801 is attributable, in part at least, to the difficulties in the way of obtaining cheap grain imports, created by the war. The decline thereafter was likewise aided by the abatement of war activity towards the end of 1801, which produced some fall in freight rates.

The next movement contrary to expectations appears in the domestic index during the reference contraction from August 1806 to May 1808. The index was falling during 1806 and 1807, when the harvests were about average, but a short supply in 1808, when the Continent was virtually shut off as a source of supply, resulted in a sharp rise in the wheat price. As a consequence, a net rise manifests itself in the domestic index during this reference contraction.

The failure of the domestic index to reveal net rise during the reference expansion from September 1811 to March 1815 also stems from variations in the domestic grain yield. The short harvests of 1811 and 1812 were succeeded by three bumper crops during 1813–15, and a headlong fall in agricultural prices ensued. Non-agricultural domestic prices, on the other hand, were rising during 1812–14, but not sufficiently to outweigh the fall in agricultural prices.

Although the domestic index was rising during the latter stages of the reference expansion from October 1819 to May 1825, its fall during 1819–22 yields a net downward movement over the whole phase. Again abundant harvests largely account for the price fall. Non-agricultural domestic prices, however, affected by the depression which extended from the latter months of 1818, continued to decline beyond the lower turning-point in business in general. Non-agricultural domestic prices did not recover earlier principally because the increase in business activity during 1820–1 did not result from a resumption of internal investment. The specific-cycle low in the domestic index comes in May 1822. The movement of non-agricultural domestic commodities, which coincides with the development of a speculative spirit in the business community directed to domestic long-term commitments, determines this turning-point. For the rest, the fluctuations in the grain market contribute to the rise in the index.

During the reference contraction from September 1845 to September 1846, the domestic index exhibits a two-month lag behind the reference peak, and a one-month lead at the reference trough. The effect of this timing is to produce a slight net rise during the reference contraction phase. Both the lag and the lead were caused by high grain prices. From September 1845, and from August 1846, the price of wheat was rising.

All the contrary movements exhibited by the domestic index occur also in the total index. None of the contrary movements in the index of imported commodities, however, is repeated in the total, with the exception of three instances of lack of conformity which are common to both domestic and imported commodities.

In the period from 1794 to 1806 there is a rise in the prices of imports during each reference contraction, except that from September 1800 to October 1801. The forces tending to raise import prices in 1796–7, 1802–4, and 1807–8 are all traceable to special war conditions. The increase in the cost of transporting goods from the Baltic and from America on account of rising freight, insurance, and interest rates, and the unfavourable exchange, served to push prices of imports upward even against a tide of business contraction. The resumption of the war early in 1803 reinforced these price-raising factors throughout 1804 and the early part of 1805. The abrupt rise in import prices from December 1807 continuing throughout 1808, which yields a net increase in the index during the reference contraction, was caused by concern over possible shortages of raw materials as a result of the combination of the Napoleonic blockade of the Continent and the American embargo.

After 1808 the index of conformity to reference contractions is perfect, but the net fall during the reference expansions from November 1801 to December 1802, October 1819 to May 1825, and December 1842 to December 1845 and the net absence of movement from December 1826 to January 1829, reduce the numerical value of the conformity index for reference expansions. The slump in prices of imports during 1801–2 was caused by the movements of colonial produce. A slackening in the demand for these imports developed in 1801, and in 1802 peace-time conditions caused a depression in prices.

Except for a brief but fairly strong recovery from the end of 1824 through the first half of 1825, when business prosperity was reaching its climax, the prices of imports fell steadily during the reference expansion beginning in 1819. This continued fall appears to have been produced by the extension of the sources of supply of the principal raw materials imported by Britain, accompanied by a diminution in their cost of production. Towards the end of 1824, however, when the stock market and industry were pervaded with optimism, a boom in commodity imports was fostered by a supposed deficiency in stocks. Speculation in commodities drove up prices through the spring of the following years, but the high prices both repelled buyers and attracted too great a supply. At this point a severe decline set in.

The decline in import prices during the reference expansion from 1842 to 1845 reflects the relative depression in British foreign trade until the middle of 1843, accentuated by the downward influence of tariff reforms. From May 1843 through the first half of 1844, the fall was halted, in response to the extraordinary activity resulting from the large-scale investment in and construction of railways. Supplies of imports during these years, however, were always available in excess of demand, despite its increase, and prices were falling again from May 1844 to September 1845, the reference peak.

The final instance when the prices of imports failed to exhibit net rise during a reference expansion occurs in 1826–9. The absence of a sustained upward movement in the commodity markets is reflected in the relative steadiness of prices. Foreign trade increased, but there was no boom. Domestic investment was at a minimum. In such an atmosphere a rally of the markets was easily discouraged.

4. Conclusions. Summing up the behaviour of the price indexes in relation to fluctuations in general business, it seems clear that they are not completely satisfactory indicators of reference expansion and contraction. Considering the nature of the disturbing influences to which prices were subject during this period, it is perhaps fairer to say that the conformity of the indexes is remarkably good. War conditions produced counter-cyclical movements, although prices were generally responsive to reference expansion during these years. In the period of secular decline the upward pressures on prices during business prosperity tended to make themselves felt, against the supply factors pushing prices down, only in the latter stages of general prosperity, if at all.

The influence of harvest fluctuations on the domestic index may, on first thought, suggest only a tenuous connexion between the index and our reference cycles. Evidence presented in Vol. II, Part I, however, indicates an important, though indirect, relationship between harvests, imports of wheat, the balance of trade, the state of the money market, and general confidence. Similarly, fluctuations in the prices of imports, which may seem some steps removed from the condition of British industry, were intertwined at many points, through the complex of the international money markets (of which London was the centre), with domestic prosperity and depression.

These observations on the movements of the price indexes are designed merely to state verbally some of the statistical results given in the tables above. They do not pretend to explain either the short-run or the secular movements of import and domestic prices. The immediate background to their short-run fluctuations is given, in some detail, in the following chapter, and in the *Price* sections of the *History*, while the course of various important individual prices is described and explained in the sections devoted to *Agriculture and Industry*. A more full perspective on the forces influencing prices is afforded by the *History* as a whole. Secular trends are discussed in Chap. IV of Vol. II. The general implications of the measures of cycle duration, timing, and amplitude are, as well, examined there.

The price index has been regarded as a necessary but not a sufficient tool in examining the relations of prices to business cycles and trends. The index, in itself, tells little. As nearly as the data and techniques available permit, it measures movements in the 'British Price Level'. Even for this purpose, its limitations, as outlined above, are many.

In the analysis of business cycles it is necessary to break down the economic system into its various interrelated markets: the markets for money, long-term capital, exported, imported, and domestic commodities, labour, and so forth. Only after these segments have been examined in the light of their interrelations can significant generalization be made about the economic system as a whole. Similarly, the full significance of the price index and its relation to business fluctuations will not be apparent until the average it represents is broken down, and the principal, often divergent, movements of which it is made up are revealed and explained. The construction of separate sub-indexes for domestic and imported commodities has been a step in that direction. The *History* and the essays of Vol. II represent a further, but by no means, final development of this approach.

Chapter III

THE COURSE OF THE PRICE INDEXES

1. Introduction. In Part II, Chapter III, of this volume there is presented a group of historical sections designed to contribute a broad institutional background to the newly constructed indexes of share prices. Symmetrical chapters for this portion of the text would have required, perhaps, a description of the markets within which the commodity prices here presented were set. Since these prices cover materials relating to all of Britain's major industries, sections of this type would have called for a survey of the price-setting procedure throughout the economy. In part, the descriptions of particular markets to be found in Clapham and other institutional historians fulfil that need. But it is clearly a task outside the scope of this study.

We shall present, rather, a brief survey of the factors that produced the principal movements in the two commodity price indexes. All of this material is to be found treated at greater length in the *History*, for the most part in its *Price* sections. The periodization employed in this brief account will follow that used in the *History*, permitting the reader to search out easily the more detailed account of the forces summarized here.

2. 1790-3. The cyclical trough before 1790 is calculated to have occurred in 1788. It is not surprising, then, that we find the import index in the process of fairly continuous increase from January 1790 to February 1792. The boom which reached a peak in 1792 was marked by rapid increases in foreign trade and the rather sensitive import index responds accordingly. After weakening briefly the import index moves to a second high point in April 1793, some time after the general cyclical peak. This latter movement was partially produced by the fears of raw-material shortage engendered by the outbreak of war with France early in 1793. Throughout 1793, however, a year of general depression, supply and demand conditions were such as to yield falling import prices. A trough in this movement was reached in June 1794. The level of the index at that point, however, indicates that some of the factors at least which were to make for rising import prices in the following two decades were already operative: the depression level of June 1794 is about the same as that for the second quarter of 1791.

From 1790 to 1792 (May) the domestic index declines. This movement is attributable to the fact that the domestic harvest yield, in addition to considerable grain imports, made for a falling wheat price. The harvest of 1792, however, was relatively inadequate, as was that of the following year; and the domestic index rises without any important break. From 1790 to 1793 non-agricultural domestic prices, in net, rose considerably even in the interval (1790–2) when grain prices and the total domestic

index were falling. Their net upward movement is reflected in the fact that
the domestic index is at a higher point in 1793 than in 1790, although the
wheat price, taken annually, is somewhat lower.

3. 1794–1801. The movement of the domestic commodity price index
in this period results principally from the fact of bad harvests in the years
1795–6 and 1799–1800. There are two clearly pronounced cyclical movements, neither of which is closely connected with the pattern of business
cycles. The peaks occur in August 1795 and March 1801. The latter peak
represents the highest point reached by the domestic price index throughout our period, although the annual average for the year 1812 is higher
than that for 1801. The extraordinary net rise which occurred from 1794
to 1801 stems largely from inadequate harvests and obstructed and costly
grain imports. Non-agricultural domestic commodities, however, also rose
sharply in this interval, although their movement was in no instance comparable to that in the price of wheat.

The import index exhibits a sharp and almost continuous trend rise
with peaks occurring in 1799 and in 1801. There is also a slight break in the
course of 1796, largely in response to tight money market conditions which
preceded Britain's departure from a bullion standard. The sharp decline
from July to December 1799 resulted from the brief but severe crisis in the
Hamburg trade. That city had been serving as the principal entrepôt for
trade between Britain and the Continent, and a tremendous speculation
in commodity imports (especially colonial commodities) had led to a credit
expansion and collapse. The second break, in 1801, is attributed by Tooke
to favourable harvests on the Continent affecting the British import prices
of silk, wine, oils, &c. There are, however, evidences of some slight commercial depression in that year; and, as well, the war slackened in its intensity
in the latter months, causing some decline in freight rates. The continued
decline of the import index through most of 1802 took place in the face of
substantial increases in Britain's foreign trade; the fall resulting from a
sharp decline in freight, insurance, and interest rates that accompanied
that brief interval of peace.

The trend rise in import prices in the period 1794–1801 stemmed most
directly from a tremendous increase in the cost of transporting goods, both
from the Baltic and from colonial America. In many cases freight rates
more than doubled, and the uncertainty of war contributed substantial
increases in the cost of insurance as well. From the side of demand the fact
that Britain was serving as a monopolist with respect to the Continent's
supply of such commodities as sugar, coffee, &c., also contributed to the
trend increase in such prices, along with the increased cost in pounds
sterling of foreign exchange, after the bullion standard had been abandoned.

4. 1802-6. Good harvests in Britain yielded, until March 1804, a falling
wheat price which is clearly reflected in the domestic index. The resumption of war in 1803 caused, in some cases, a slight rise in non-agricultural

domestic commodities; but even when their upward movement was bol-
stered (1804–6) by a return to moderate prosperity, no very sharp price
rises resulted. With respect to government expenditure in excess of revenue,
domestic investment, and foreign trade, the interval from 1802 to 1808 was
quiescent as compared with the previous decade. Even the inadequate
harvests of 1804–6 were abundant when compared with those of 1795–6
and 1799–1800.

From its trough in August 1802 the import index rises to a new high
point in February 1805. The resumption of war early in 1803 brought into
play, with perhaps lesser intensity, the factors that had made for the import
price increase in 1793–1801. The rate of increase of neither the volume of
imports nor re-exports was equivalent, however, in 1804–6, to its previous
expansion rate; and the peak level of the import price index in 1805 was
only slightly above that in 1799 and 1801. In the course of 1806 the operation of Napoleon's continental blockade began to make itself significantly
felt. It served both to obstruct the supply of such articles as Baltic timber
(tending to raise their prices) and to block off important re-export markets
(tending to lower British import prices). These contrary consequences may
be traced among the individual commodities. Their net effect in the course
of 1805–6 was to yield a very slight fall in the total import index.

5. 1807-11. The English harvest of 1807 was slightly above the average,
and the wheat price fell, despite the fact that the Baltic grain supply had
been virtually eliminated by the continental blockade. Under these circumstances a short supply in 1808 caused a very rapid rise in the wheat price,
which appears in the domestic index. Although the harvest of 1809 was not
abundant, the imports which Napoleon made available to Britain prevented
any substantial further increase in the price of wheat. A continuation of
this policy until the middle of 1811 explains the rather stagnant level of the
domestic index; the abundant harvest of 1810, in fact, permitted some
falling away in grain prices. From the latter months of 1811, however,
Napoleon reversed his previous mercantilist policy with respect to grain
exports from the Continent to Britain, and the bad harvests of 1811–12
produced a rise in grain prices second only to that in 1799–1801 and, later,
in 1847.

Non-agricultural domestic commodities respond clearly to the movement of general business fluctuations, rising with expansion from low
points in 1808–9 to peaks in 1809–10. The depression of the latter months
of 1810–11 can be even more clearly discerned than the previous cyclical
expansion.

Throughout 1807 the import price index remains virtually stagnant,
with a slight declining tendency. From December 1807 to August 1811,
however, it exhibits two clearly marked cycles. The sharp rise in the course
of 1808 was compounded of fears of raw-material shortage engendered
both by the blockade of the Continent and by the American embargo. The
latter months saw also the beginnings of the Latin American boom which

followed upon the freeing of the Spanish colonies. The decline in the early months of 1809 does not represent a slackening in commercial activity, but rather an easing of supply conditions, especially in the Baltic. The final phase of the price expansion, ending in March 1810, is a speculative boom in import commodities typical of those which accompanied most of the substantial business expansions in this period. The decline in the import index through the latter months of 1810 until August 1811 is to be accounted for by the collapse of the South American boom and Napoleon's tightening of the blockade from the summer of 1810. For about the year previous some, at least, of the important continental trade centres had been open to British trade.

6. 1812–16. The movement of the domestic index is again controlled primarily by the domestic harvest yield: the harvests of 1811 and 1812 were inadequate; those of the following three years were abundant. By 1815 the catastrophic fall in agricultural prices was sufficient to induce drastic parliamentary intervention in the form of the Corn Law of that year.

Non-agricultural domestic prices follow a pattern quite different from that of the domestic index. Most of them rise somewhat in the period 1812–14, exhibiting peaks in the first two quarters of 1814. Since the main impulses to expansion in the boom of 1811–15 came from the side of foreign trade, it is not surprising that their net increase in this period was, in most cases, relatively slight.

As the war drew to its close, and the continental blockade disintegrated, a considerable revival in trade with the Continent, and thus in re-exports, took place. Especially in its final phase (August 1813–February 1814), the commodity markets were dominated by extravagant expectations with respect to the commercial possibilities of peace on the Continent. It was hoped that the markets which had been only irregularly available over the previous twenty years would be able to absorb a tremendous supply of both British manufactures and colonial foods and raw materials. From the early months of 1814 it was clear that such hopes were doomed to disappointment; and prices fell despite large British shipments in the course of that year. The availability of American markets in 1815 partially compensated for the complete depression on the Continent, although import and domestic prices continued the fall begun in the early months of 1814.

All prices continued to fall throughout most of 1816 with the exception of those of agricultural produce. The harvest of 1816 was bad, and a sharp rise in the price of wheat and foodstuffs generally contributed to the serious unrest which severe unemployment had already created.

7. 1817-21. In 1817–18 both agricultural and non-agricultural domestic prices rose. The domestic harvest of 1817 was fairly abundant, but the demand from an almost famine-ridden Continent kept grain prices from any important relapse. At that point, too, non-agricultural domestic prices began to rise, and the average level of domestic prices was somewhat higher in 1818 than in 1817. The latter months of that year were marked by the onset of severe depression, while fears of a drought proved unwarranted at about the same time. The general price decline continued on through 1819–21. The harvests were adequate, and such revival in commercial and industrial activity as occurred was found incapable of reversing the downward price trend. It is significant of the nature of the revival that took place between 1819 and 1821 that the downward course of import prices was arrested sooner than for non-agricultural prices. The increases in business activity that justify one in regarding 1820 and 1821 as years of revival resulted from an expanding volume of trade rather than from internal investment activity.

The course of import prices from 1816 to 1821 follows a neat cyclical pattern with a peak in March 1818 and a decisive fall beginning with the last few months of that year. Although a trough in that decline cannot be marked off until October 1824, the rate of decline perceptibly slackens after the close of 1820. The rise of import prices in the course of 1817–18 is a typical inventory movement accompanying general increases in both export markets and domestic investment. Stocks of imported commodities were found to be severely depleted by the close of the depression year 1816, and, as usual, the process of restocking was carried on at a rate which could not be indefinitely sustained.

8. 1822–6. The index of domestic prices reaches a low point, in its decline from 1818, in May 1822. It then moves up in three irregular surges to a peak in May 1825. The subsequent decline to a low point in July 1826 leaves the index well above the level of 1822. In the rise to 1825 both agricultural and non-agricultural price increases contributed to the movement of the domestic index. The harvests of 1823–4 were less abundant than their three predecessors, while those of 1825–6 were seriously inadequate. In fact, the downward movement in the domestic index to 1826 results primarily from the course of non-agricultural domestic prices.

Such prices responded to general recovery at different dates. But in most cases some modest rise occurred in the course of 1822 and the early months of 1823. In response to fears of a general European war a minor relapse took place in the spring of the latter year, after which the mild upward trend was resumed. Not until the final quarter of 1824 did very substantial price increases take place in non-agricultural domestic commodities. Then, as full employment situations developed throughout the principal British industries, a brief but spectacular rise occurred. The relapse which followed the beginnings of general depression brought non-agricultural domestic prices, in some cases, to new low levels. Their decline was much more marked than the behaviour of the domestic index in that interval would indicate.

The import index behaves, on the whole, much like non-agricultural domestic prices, although there is, as noted earlier, no sustained rising tendency until the latter months of 1824. The speculative commodity boom which then occurred, paralleling the final stage of general business expansion, reached its peak in May 1825. By July 1826 the price fall virtually ceased, as a revival in some of the export markets began to get slowly under way. But after 1825 no clear trough in the import price index can be marked off until September 1832.

9. 1827-32. In this period there were no sustained upward movements in the commodity markets. The trend in both import and non-agricultural domestic prices was steadily downward, interrupted only by brief and abortive upward surges, occurring towards the close of 1828 and the first month of 1829 and in 1831. This was a period when there was little new domestic investment and when those branches of domestic industry dependent on such investment were chronically depressed. The substantial increases in the volume of exports, furthermore, did not yield price increases, largely because of the heritage of the expanded and improved plant from the boom of 1819–25, and because of the continued fall in the prices of raw materials.

Agricultural prices, however, were more active. Harvests, in this interval, were on the whole inadequate, and the large and well-organized grain markets were in constant movement, guessing about the degree of inadequacy and the extent of the foreign grain supply available for Britain. Not until the summer of 1832 was there a decisive fall in the price of wheat, the good harvest which produced it ushering in another interval, like 1819–22, of agricultural distress.

10. 1833-7. The domestic price index falls irregularly from January 1833 to October 1835. This net movement conceals a divergence between the course of agricultural and non-agricultural commodities. Non-agricultural commodities rose, in response to general recovery through 1833, continuing generally upward until the middle of 1834. This mild movement was broken by a slight relapse; and in 1835–6 a rise developed much like that in 1824–5. The expansion from 1832–6, in its latter stages especially, involved full employment in most of Britain's major industries, and industrial prices reflect that fact. Their subsequent fall in the latter months of 1836 through most of 1837 was more severe than the domestic index as a whole would indicate, although the limited nature of the liquidation of 1836–7 caused a lesser price liquidation than that which followed immediately upon the collapse of prices in 1825.

The domestic harvest yield, as in the other cases, strongly influences the pattern of the total domestic price index. The abundant harvests of 1832–5 prevent the appearance of any sustained price rise. The wheat price was successively lower in 1833, 1834, and 1835; while parliamentary committees on agriculture sat in almost constant session. The harvests of 1836 and 1837 were, however, inadequate and the domestic index moves accordingly. Its mild declining tendency in the course of 1837 results not only from the fall of non-agricultural domestic prices in that interval, but also from a slight decline in the wheat price, due to the availability of an unexpectedly large foreign grain supply.

Like non-agricultural domestic prices, the import price index moved upward in two waves in the course of the 1832–6 expansion. The mild relapse from October 1833 to May 1834 represents a typical inventory movement which tended to occur sometime in the course of a prolonged general business expansion. Although the subsequent rise to a peak in April–May 1836 was considerable, it was the opinion of contemporaries that it did not proceed to the same speculative lengths as that of 1824–5. The decline, however, to a low point in July 1837, brings the import index to a trough for the whole period 1790–1837. The mechanics of this commodity boom and collapse seem to have been typical: beginning with a real or alleged raw-material shortage in domestic industry; breaking when stocks were believed to be adequate and when short-term financing proved difficult; ending when stocks were again depleted and the money market easy.

11. 1838-42. The domestic price index, which, despite general depression, fell only slightly in 1837, owing to a second consecutive bad harvest, rises again sharply in 1838. It then falls away slowly and irregularly to July 1842, precipitately to a low point in May 1843. Only at its nadir in 1843 does it return to the level of late 1835, before the speculative stage of the previous boom and the coming of inadequate crops.

A poor harvest in 1838 caused a considerable rise in the wheat price, which gave way slightly through the following year as foreign grain poured into Britain. Not until the summer of 1842, however, did Britain enjoy a truly abundant harvest; and throughout the period 1839–42 the domestic index is sustained by a relatively high level of grain prices.

Non-agricultural domestic commodities responded irregularly to the general expansion of 1838–9, but fell away in most cases to new low points in 1842. As in the equally stagnant and difficult period 1826–32, there are occasional breaks in the downward movement; but the trend is unmistakable.

From a low point in July 1837, the import price index rises irregularly to a peak in September 1840, declining steadily thereafter, without any interruption, to the end of 1842, when it finds a new low point. The rise in 1838–9 results in large part from the movement of the price of cotton. There was a deficient American crop in 1838, and cotton served as the basis for the medium-term bills by which American financiers sustained the cracking Anglo-American credit structure, which had been erected in 1832–6. This latter factor added an unnatural speculative upward tendency to the existing deficiency in supply.

The price of cotton and most other imported commodities broke in the course of the early months of 1839; but the index as a whole continues on up slightly to a peak in 1840. This movement resulted from speculations in the markets for tea and sugar, whose supply was obstructed by influences operative in China and the West Indies, respectively. On the whole the commodity markets from early in 1839 to the latter half of 1843 were dull and declining; and, from 1840 on, the import price index reflects this interval of depression in Britain's foreign trade. The tariff reforms of the early forties, of course, accentuate this downward price movement.

12. 1843-8. The domestic price index describes two clear-cut cycles from 1842 to 1850. These have peaks in November 1845 and June 1847. The first of these movements is dependent on a rise in non-agricultural domestic prices at a time when the fall, at least in agricultural prices, had ceased. This upward movement, of course, paralleled the general business expansion of 1842–5, and is reflected in almost all industrial prices, particularly those directly affected by the large-scale railway construction of that period. The second upward movement in the domestic price index, dating from August 1846 to June 1847, stems almost completely from the behaviour of agricultural prices. Despite relatively free access to the international grain supply and consequently enormous imports, the deficient harvest of 1846–7 yielded an immense increase in agricultural prices. Some non-agricultural prices also rose slightly from 1846 to 1847 in response to several general impulses to business expansion; but the sharp movement of the total domestic price index is to be traced almost completely to the grain markets.

The import price index exhibits a less clear-cut movement in the course of the business cycle 1842–8 than in any other major cycle in our period. Except for a brief upward surge, extending from September 1846 to February 1847, there is virtually no break in the decline which began in September 1840. A slackening in the rate of the decline from about May 1843 to May 1844 is the only response of this index to the powerful domestic boom. This is to be attributed primarily to the extraordinary channelling of enterprise into railway construction in this period. Among Britain's foreign markets only those of China and India inspired any considerable speculative activity. And although a large volume of raw materials was required for the expanded output of domestic industry, no commodity speculation occurred. The brief upward surge that ended early in 1847 seems to have been inspired by a real shortage of raw materials whose supply had probably been impeded by the tight money conditions that existed in the latter months of 1845 and the early months of 1846. The decline in the import index through most of 1847, until September 1848, represents the severe general depression of that interval. The resumption of a rise in the following two years reflects the beginnings of general international recovery.

Chapter IV

COMPARISON OF THE NEW INDEXES WITH EXISTING INDEXES

WE have compared our commodity price index with five existing indexes of British wholesale prices in annual form, covering all or part of the period from 1790 to 1850: Jevons's, 1790–1850, Sauerbeck's, 1818–50, Silberling's, 1790–1850, Kondratieff's, 1790–1850, and Rousseaux's, 1800–50[1] (see Fig. 99). The comparison, of necessity, was made on an annual basis, because, with the exception of Silberling's, the indexes were not constructed for shorter intervals (see Tables 53–4). Though all these indexes are referred to as wholesale commodity price indexes, certain important differences in their behaviour belie their common designation.

Each of the indexes, with the exception of Sauerbeck's, which falls entirely within the period of declining prices, divides into two periods, one of rising trend culminating either in 1809 or 1813–14, and one of falling trend. The Jevons,[2] Kondratieff, and Rousseaux indexes reach their high point in 1809, whereas our total index attains its peak in 1813, and Silberling's index a year later.[3] The explanation for this disagreement lies in the different composition of the indexes. It has been alleged[4] that the reason for the decline of Jevons's index from 1809 to 1814 is that it was too much influenced by the inclusion of a relatively large number of oriental products whose prices fell to an extraordinary extent after 1811. This explanation does not hold in the case of Kondratieff's index, in which there is a relatively small number of oriental products, nor for Rousseaux's index.

It will be recalled that the secular peak in our index of domestic commodities was reached in 1812, and in our index of imports in 1814. The years of the turning-points in individual prices within these sub-groups were even more widely divergent. The harvests indeed were at their worst during the season of 1812 and elevated domestic agricultural prices in that year, but there was no concentration of peaks in domestic industrial prices in 1812. The distribution of the turning-points in domestic prices is as given on p. 512.

---

[1] See Appendix below, 'Other Indexes of British Wholesale Commodity Prices, 1790–1850', for a description of these indexes.

[2] The index usually ascribed to Jevons was reduced by him to a gold standard basis for the years Britain was off gold. In this index the figure for 1809 is considerably higher than that for 1813, being 157 at the former, and 115 at the latter date. When the original paper-standard index comparable to our own is considered, the discrepancy between the two years is not nearly so great,

being 161 and 153 respectively. The peak actually comes in 1810 in the paper-standard index, so the ratio between the two competing peak years is even closer to 100.

[3] Silberling also mentions an index by John Taylor, a nineteenth-century statistician, who combined approximately 90 prices at seven-year intervals which reached their highest point in the period around 1814.

[4] N. J. Silberling, 'British Financial Experience, 1790–1830', *Review of Economic Statistics*, 1919, pp. 282 ff.

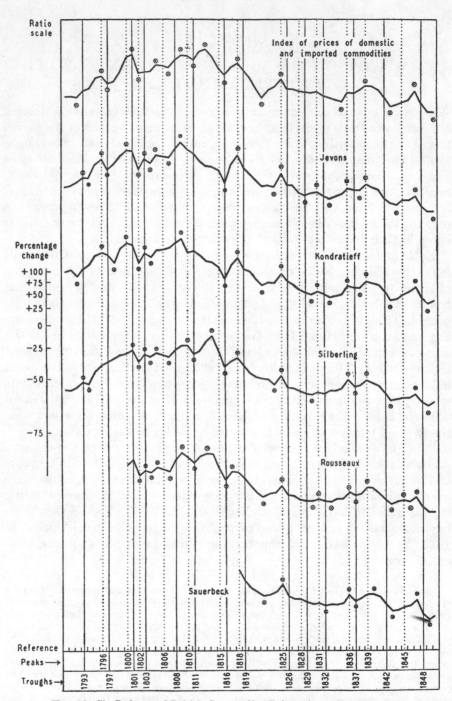

FIG. 99. Six Indexes of British Commodity Prices, Annually, 1790–1850

TABLE 53. *Comparison of Specific-cycle Measures of Six British Commodity Price Indexes*

Specific-cycle measures	Jevons	Sauerbeck	Silberling	Kondratieff	Rousseaux	Total index
Full Period						
PERIOD COVERED .	1789–1850	1822–49	1789–1849	1789–1849	1802–51	1792–1850
NUMBER OF CYCLES .	12	4	11	11	11	9
AVERAGE DURATION						
Expansion . .	25 (9)	..	37 (19)	30 (14)	21 (8)	37 (10)
Contraction . .	36 (20)	..	28 (17)	35 (18)	33 (16)	40 (21)
Full cycle . .	61 (17)	..	66 (18)	66 (23)	54 (17)	77 (23)
AVERAGE AMPLITUDE OF RELATIVES Total Movement						
Rise . . .	17 (7)	..	15 (7)	18 (7)	10 (5)	22 (6)
Fall . . .	19 (14)	..	17 (10)	20 (12)	15 (10)	23 (11)
Rise and fall . .	37 (18)	..	32 (14)	38 (17)	25 (13)	45 (14)
Movement per month						
Rise . . .	0·8 (0·4)	..	0·5 (0·2)	0·6 (0·3)	0·5 (0·2)	0·6 (0·2)
Fall . . .	0·6 (0·4)	..	0·6 (0·3)	0·6 (0·2)	0·4 (0·2)	0·7 (0·4)
Rise and fall . .	0·7 (0·3)	..	0·5 (0·1)	0·6 (0·2)	0·4 (0·2)	0·6 (0·2)
Secular movement in %: weighted average change per month from cycle to cycle .	−0·04	−0·07	−0·03	−0·05	−0·08	−0·01
Period of Rising Prices						
AVERAGE DURATION						
Expansion . .	26 (11)	..	38 (19)	34 (16)	16 (5)	36 (10)
Contraction . .	17 (6)	..	14 (4)	18 (6)	18 (6)	18 (6)
Full cycle . .	44 (16)	..	54 (22)	53 (17)	34 (9)	56 (12)
AVERAGE AMPLITUDE OF RELATIVES Total movement						
Rise . . .	18 (6)	..	18 (10)	21 (8)	12 (8)	22 (9)
Fall . . .	9 (8)	..	7 (5)	13 (7)	4 (2)	11 (7)
Rise and fall . .	29 (13)	..	26 (14)	35 (16)	17 (9)	34 (18)
Movement per month						
Rise . . .	0·8 (0·2)	..	0·5 (0·2)	0·7 (0·3)	0·7 (0·2)	0·6 (0·1)
Fall . . .	0·5 (0·4)	..	0·6 (0·4)	0·7 (0·2)	0·2 (0·0)	0·8 (0·6)
Rise and fall . .	0·8 (0·2)	..	0·5 (0·1)	0·7 (0·3)	0·6 (0·4)	0·7 (0·3)
Period of Falling Prices						
AVERAGE DURATION						
Expansion . .	24 (8)	42 (6)	36 (19)	28 (12)	22 (8)	44 (9)
Contraction . .	50 (19)	39 (22)	40 (20)	45 (18)	36 (16)	58 (25)
Full cycle . .	76 (15)	81 (20)	76 (17)	74 (16)	59 (18)	99 (36)
AVERAGE AMPLITUDE OF RELATIVES Total movement						
Rise . . .	16 (8)	14 (2)	12 (3)	15 (6)	10 (4)	22 (3)
Fall . . .	26 (13)	21 (6)	24 (8)	24 (12)	17 (10)	32 (5)
Rise and fall . .	43 (19)	35 (8)	38 (7)	40 (15)	28 (13)	55 (9)
Movement per month						
Rise . . .	0·8 (0·5)	0·3 (0·1)	0·5 (0·2)	0·6 (0·2)	0·5 (0·2)	0·6 (0·2)
Fall . . .	0·7 (0·4)	0·7 (0·2)	0·7 (0·3)	0·5 (0·2)	0·4 (0·2)	0·7 (0·2)
Rise and fall . .	0·8 (0·4)	0·4 (0·0)	0·7 (0·4)	0·6 (0·2)	0·5 (0·2)	0·7 (0·2)

TABLE 54. *Comparison of Reference-cycle Measures of Six British Commodity Price Indexes*

	Jevons	Sauerbeck	Silberling	Kondratieff	Rousseaux	Total index
Period covered . . .	1793–1848	1819–48	1793–1848	1793–1848	1801–48	1793–1848
Number of cycles. . .	13	6	13	13	11	13
Average standing of relatives in stage						
I	100·4 (8·5)	102·3 (4·3)	99·4 (5·7)	101·4 (7·4)	101·5 (5·5)	99·8 (7·4)
III	99·8 (3·2)	98·5 (1·8)	99·9 (2·5)	98·7 (4·0)	101·3 (4·1)	99·2 (4·6)
V.	103·4 (6·7)	104·0 (3·7)	102·5 (4·2)	101·8 (6·3)	100·9 (4·5)	102·7 (5·7)
VII	100·6 (5·3)	102·0 (3·0)	100·2 (4·1)	100·8 (5·4)	98·1 (4·1)	101·2 (5·2)
IX	97·5 (6·3)	95·0 (3·3)	97·8 (6·8)	98·5 (6·0)	95·7 (5·4)	98·5 (6·3)
Average change per month of relatives in						
I–III	0·0 (0·6)	−0·1 (0·3)	0·0 (0·4)	−0·2 (0·5)	0·0 (0·5)	−0·1 (0·6)
III–V	+0·1 (0·6)	+0·2 (0·2)	+0·1 (0·4)	0·0 (0·7)	−0·1 (0·5)	+0·1 (0·6)
V–VII	−0·4 (0·5)	−0·4 (0·4)	−0·3 (0·5)	−0·2 (0·4)	−0·4 (0·4)	−0·3 (0·4)
VII–IX	−0·4 (0·6)	−0·7 (0·3)	−0·3 (0·6)	−0·3 (0·5)	−0·3 (0·5)	−0·3 (0·4)
Index of conformity to						
Reference expansions . .	+15	−17	+23	+38	+18	+15
Reference contractions .	+62	+100	+38	+54	+64	+46
All business cycles .	+44	+100	+44	+36	+57	+48
Expansion covers stages .	I–V	I–V	I–V	III–VII	I–V	I–V

Domestic Commodities and Peak Years of their Prices

1809	1810	1811	1812	1813	1814
Copper	Camphor	Iron bars	Wheat	Leather	Alum
Lead pigs	Oil of		Oats	butts	Beef
Linseed oil	vitriol		Rape oil	Mutton	Butter
Soft soap	Clover		Starch	Pork	Coal
	seeds				Sal-ammoniac
					Hard soap
					Tallow
					Tin

Pig-iron: no movement between 1809 and 1814.

In the group of imports, prices of commodities which originated on the Continent, more especially in the Baltic area, tended to be at peak levels around 1809, during the period of the Napoleonic blockade. Imports (especially of American origin) from other parts of the world, except the East, tended to be higher priced in 1814 than in any other year during the period. The peak in 1809 in three existing indexes can thus be accounted for by the predominance of Baltic and oriental commodities among their component series. And the close correspondence[1] between our index and that of Silberling with respect to the timing of the peak results from the fact that almost 50 per cent. of our commodities were also included in Silberling's index. One factor contributing to a later peak in our index, not operative for other indexes, is the inclusion of the duty in the prices of

[1] The peak in the total index comes in 1813, representing a kind of average of the turning-points in 1812 and 1814 in the sub-groups. The peak in Silberling's index, in which agricultural commodities have only a small weight, coincides with the turning-point of our index of imports.

imports used by us. The amount of the duty levied, in general, had a pronounced upward tendency from the first years of the index until the early twenties, and this circumstance raises the level of our 1814 prices of imports as compared with those in 1809.

The indexes of Jevons, Silberling, and Kondratieff, as well as that compiled in the course of this study, cover a comparable period, and a direct comparison of their measures of cyclical behaviour is possible. All of the price indexes, except Silberling's, exhibit a longer duration for specific-cycle contraction than for expansion. The specific cycle in Jevons's index from 1804 to 1807, which cannot be satisfactorily marked off in the other series (except Rousseaux's), makes for a somewhat shorter average specific cycle than in the case of Silberling's or Kondratieff's indexes. Without exception the amplitude of contraction is greater than for expansion and the net secular trend is downward. The heavy weight assigned to grain prices in our index accounts both for the lesser number of specific cycles and the slightness of the net downward trend.

When cyclical behaviour is compared for the intervals of rising and falling trend, the relative duration and amplitude of expansion and contraction move as one would expect. The most striking phenomenon, perhaps, is the universally greater duration and total amplitude of specific cycles in the period of declining general prices. During this period our total price index shows cycles, on the average, of longer duration and wider amplitude than any existing index. The failure of our index to exhibit a net decline in 1837 sufficient to justify the marking off of a specific cycle trough at that point accounts for its larger average duration.

The Sauerbeck index, available only during the period of declining trend, behaves much like the other series in that interval, although the net downward movement (and both the amplitude and duration of specific cycle contractions) is relatively less, since a considerable part of the trend decline had already occurred by 1822, when the first specific-cycle trough is delineated. Rousseaux's series, because of the tremendous amplitude of the decline between 1814 and 1816, shows a lesser average amplitude of movement from 1816 to 1851 than any of the others in that period. The marking off of a specific cycle from 1843 to 1846 lowers, as well, the average duration of specific cycle in Rousseaux's index as compared to the others.

An average I–V expansion pattern best describes the cyclical behaviour of all the price indexes except Kondratieff's. A III–VII pattern best describes its typical behaviour, but that sequence of movement with respect to the reference dates is actually identifiable in only one cycle (1842–8). Except for the three cycles from 1801 to 1811, when the index rises in the course of the cyclical contractions, a I–V pattern is as good a description of its cyclical behaviour as a III–VII pattern. In all instances the contraction index is higher than the index for expansion, indicating that in a number of instances the net movement in the course of expansion was negative. Such cases, except for the notable instance of the decline in

1802 (due to a brief return to peace and abundant harvests), occurred, for the most part, in the period of secular price decline (1816–50). The instances of net expansion in the course of cyclical contraction, however, tended to occur during the earlier years of warfare. With the exception of the Sauerbeck index, the numerical measures of conformity to all business cycles are only moderately high. The perfect conformity of the Sauerbeck index (analysed from 1819 to 1848) to contractions, and its negative conformity to expansions, are clearly indicative of the character of cyclical behaviour in the two trend periods.

In all cases but that of Rousseaux's index a greater average rate of movement appears in stage III–V than I–III; none of the indexes, in fact, records average expansion in stage I–III. The net decline in III–V in Rousseaux's series stems principally from the enormous fall in 1815.

In general, then, these price series emerge as indifferent indexes of general business fluctuations (see Fig. 100a, b, pp. 515–16). After 1816 they consistently reflect contraction, but the early stages of expansion, and, in some cases, the later stages as well, are not represented by absolute increases. The existence of divergent trend forces within their span also reduces their usefulness as a short-hand measure of general cyclical movements.

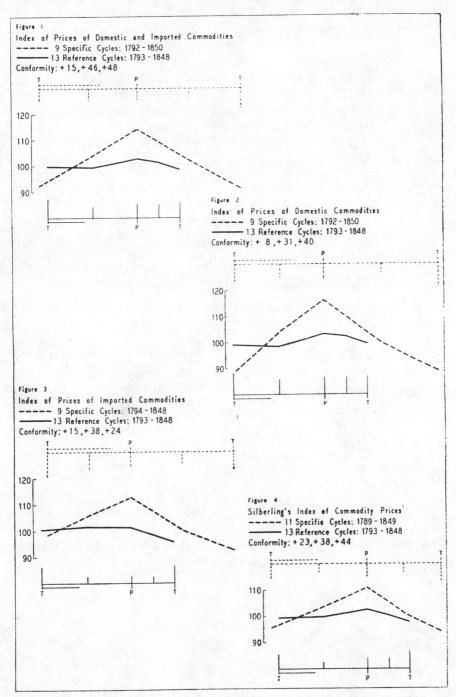

Figure 1

Index of Prices of Domestic and Imported Commodities
----- 9 Specific Cycles: 1792 - 1850
——— 13 Reference Cycles: 1793 - 1848
Conformity: + 15, + 46, +48

Figure 2

Index of Prices of Domestic Commodities
----- 9 Specific Cycles: 1792 - 1850
——— 13 Reference Cycles: 1793 - 1848
Conformity: + 8 , + 31, +40

Figure 3

Index of Prices of Imported Commodities
----- 9 Specific Cycles: 1794 - 1848
——— 13 Reference Cycles: 1793 - 1848
Conformity: + 15 , + 38 , + 24

Figure 4

Silberling's Index of Commodity Prices
----- 11 Specific Cycles: 1789 - 1849
——— 13 Reference Cycles: 1793 - 1848
Conformity: + 23, + 38, +44

FIG. 100 a. Cyclical Patterns of Six Annual Indexes of British Commodity Prices

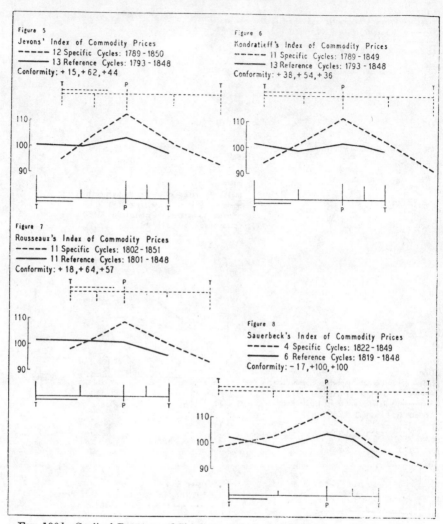

FIG. 100*b*. Cyclical Patterns of Six Annual Indexes of British Commodity Prices

Appendix

OTHER INDEXES OF BRITISH WHOLESALE
COMMODITY PRICES, 1790–1850

1. Early Indexes. A considerable part of the economic literature of the second part of the nineteenth century is devoted to the problem of the changing value of gold and its economic and social repercussions. The interest in this problem led to the development of a statistical technique for measuring the value of money over a period of time. The practical application of this technique yielded index numbers which traced the course of the general price level as far back as data were then available.

The construction of price index numbers, however, was known at least half a century earlier, and even their use as guides for monetary policy under a managed currency was then understood. The early contributors to the subject, nevertheless, were hardly more than forerunners of the main body of index-number statisticians, among whom the names of Jevons and Sauerbeck are outstanding.

The most important of these forerunners is Joseph Lowe who conceived a 'plan for lessening the injury arising from the fluctuation of prices'.[1] Lowe proposed that price ratios of corn, sugar, woollen, and linen manufactures, and other prices from the books of the Victualling Office, of the Commissariat Department, and of Public Hospitals be combined. The plan contains all the elements of a price index. The chief application of such a measure according to Lowe would be in long-term contracts in order to confer 'on a specified sum a uniformity and permanency of value, by changing the numerical amount in proportion to the changes in the power of purchase'.[2]

Lowe's plan derived from some ideas of Sir George Shuckburgh,[3] who at the end of the eighteenth century had already constructed a series which measured the changing value of money in England since 1550, at intervals of fifty years for the early period, and thereafter at shorter intervals. He apologizes for his two-page treatment of price index numbers as follows: 'However I may appear to descend below the dignity of philosophy in such economical researches, I trust 1 shall find favour with the historian, at least, and the antiquary.' The index, based on 1550 = 100, is the arithmetic average of the prices of twelve miscellaneous articles including five species of domestic animals, three varieties of poultry, butter, cheese, ale, and beer, plus the price of day labour and the price of beef and mutton. The values for 1790, 1795, and 1800[4] are 496, 531, and 562. Shuckburgh says that 'the various changes that have taken place, by authority in different reigns, either in the weight or alloy of our coins, are allowed for in the subsequent table'.[5]

Dissatisfaction with Shuckburgh's tables, because of alleged inaccuracy of the

[1] Joseph Lowe, *The Present State of England*, pp. 298 ff.

[2] Ibid., p. 302.

[3] Sir George Shuckburgh-Evelyn, Bt., An Account of Some Endeavours to Ascertain a Standard of Weight and Measure', *Philosophical Transactions of the Royal Society of London*, 1798, pp. 175–6.

[4] Ibid., p. 176. This paper was written in 1798, but Shuckburgh estimated the figure for 1800.

[5] Ibid., p. 176.

data, led Arthur Young to construct an index of his own.[1] Some of his prices he gathered by dispatching 'a circular letter to many respectable correspondents throughout England and Wales'.[2] He also obtained prices of manufactured articles, which Sir George excluded. Of chief interest is the fact that he weighted his index by 'repeating wheat five times, on account of its importance, barley and oats twice, provisions four times, labour five times, and reckoning wool, coal, and iron, each but once'.[3]

The name of G. P. Scrope[4] must also be added to this group of early authors who contributed to the literature on index numbers. His analysis of monetary problems led him to the view that no commodity can claim to be invariable in value, but that changes in the price level could be measured by a large list of about one hundred fairly representative commodities, which would be combined in proportion to their total consumption. Whether price ratios should be formed from the original figures is inconclusively discussed: he regards variations 'in the sum' simply, as a measure of the varying value of gold. Also, Scrope suggests the employment of such an index for a tabular standard in order to balance the debtor-creditor relations in long-term private contracts, but specifically disapproves of using an index number as the basis for the regulation of a paper currency system.[5]

It is unclear whether the figures Scrope presents are calculated in the manner outlined above, or whether they are rough estimates. Prices published in the *Report of a Select Committee on the Bank Charter*, 1832, are used for a comparison of the general price level of 1830 with that of 1819. It appears that in that period prices of home-produced raw materials fell by about 35 per cent., foreign raw materials by some 40 per cent. on the average, and the prices of manufactured goods by more than 60 per cent. or an average fall of about 50 per cent. This appears to be the first example of a subdivision of a price index according to the nature of the commodities included.[6]

2. Jevons's Indexes. The first of the indexes constructed by Jevons appeared in 1863. It was an arithmetic average of thirty-nine monthly prices taken from *The Economist*, computed on base 1845–50. The index covered the period from 1845 to 1862 inclusive. Sub-groups for silver (1), metals (6), timber (1), oils (2), tallow, &c., (3), cotton (3), wool, &c. (3), corn (6), hay (3), meat (4), sugar, &c. (4), and dyes (2) were also calculated. The figures in parentheses indicate the number of items in each sub-group.[7] (A sub-group for hemp was not calculated.)

The index numbers follow:

Year	Index
1845	104·4
1846	105·4
1847	110·8
1848	94·1
1849	89·6
1850	92·1

---

[1] Arthur Young, *An Enquiry into the Progressive Value of Money in England.*
[2] Op. cit., p. iv.
[3] Ibid., p. 72.
[4] *Principles of Political Economy.*
[5] Loc. cit., pp. 405–6.

[6] Loc. cit., p. 408.
[7] 'A Serious Fall in the Value of Gold Ascertained, and its Social Effects Set Forth' (1863), reprinted in *Investigations in Currency and Finance*, pp. 15 ff.

Jevons made a second provisional study of the price movements for the years 1833–43. He states that he formed 'hasty averages'[1] of twenty-four commodities taken from Tooke's *History of Prices*, the *Annual Register*, and other sources which are not specified. Thirdly, Jevons published in a letter to *The Economist* an index based upon about fifty commodities, the prices of which were published in *The Economist*.[2] The index covers the period from 1847 to 1869 with the base in 1849, the year of lowest prices. The following are the index numbers for the first four years: 1847 = 122, 1848 = 106, 1849 = 100, 1850 = 101.

3. Weighting and Averaging of the Main Jevons Index, 1782–1850.

The main index constructed by Jevons formed part of a paper read before the Statistical Society of London in May 1865.[3] It is based upon price ratios and is probably the first to be constructed by geometric averaging. The averaging procedure had been a subject of discussion between Jevons and Laspeyres,[4] who made a case for simple arithmetic averages. Jevons used the example of a rise of 100 per cent. in the price of one commodity and a reduction of 50 per cent. in another commodity without further explanation, to state, that 'on the average ... there has been no alteration of price whatsoever'.[5] Laspeyres described an index number as a means of measuring the changing value of gold. According to his contention, an identical quantity of gold would buy in the second year, after the changes in prices mentioned above, a smaller quantity of the two commodities, the amount of reduction being measured by the change in the arithmetic average.[6]

Jevons, while granting 'some ground for the argument', adds that equally cogent points could be made in favour of the harmonic mean. He finally adopts the geometric average, for reasons which have little to do with the logic of the case: first, because it lies between the arithmetic and the harmonic mean, and secondly, on account of the convenience of using logarithms in forming geometric means. The third reason, which is somewhat difficult to comprehend, is that the geometric average 'seems likely to give in the most accurate manner such general change in prices as is due to a change on the part of gold'.[7]

No weights are used in this index. Some commodities, however, are represented in the index by more than one variety and, to that extent, are indirectly weighted.

[1] *Investigations in Currency and Finance*, p. 109.

[2] *The Economist*, 8 May 1869. Reprinted in *Investigation in Currency and Finance*, p. 153.

[3] *Journal of the Statistical Society*, xxviii, 1865, pp. 294–320. Reprinted in *Investigations in Currency and Finance*, pp. 119–50, under the title, 'The Variations of Prices and the Value of the Currency since 1782'.

[4] Laspeyres, E., 'Hamburger Waaren-preise 1851–1863 und die californisch-austra-lischen Goldentdeckungen seit 1848', in *Jahrbücher für Nationalökonomie und Statistik*, iii. 81–118, 209–36.

[5] *Investigations in Currency and Finance*, p. 24.

[6] 'Hamburger Waarenpreise', p. 97: 'If a certain quantity of cocoa (1 cwt.) formerly cost 100 thalers and a certain quantity of clover (1 cwt.) also 100 thalers, and if the price of cocoa rises from 100 to 200, while that of the clover decreases from 100 to 50, 200 thalers no longer have the same power of purchasing cocoa and clover. For 200 thalers the buyer receives only $\frac{3}{4}$ cwts. of cocoa (= 150 thalers) and 1 cwt. of clover (= 50 thalers), or he receives 1 cwt. of cocoa (= 200) and no clover at all. The purchasing power is one fifth less. In order to get the same quantities, the buyer has to add another quarter (50 thalers), as the 250 thalers are now worth one fifth less than formerly. This is exactly what is expressed by the arithmetic mean.'

[7] *Investigations in Currency and Finance*, p. 121.

For the additional sub-groups 'comparative' index figures are constructed showing the extent to which these series have risen or fallen as compared with the total index in each year. From 1800 to 1820 the index is expressed both in terms of paper and in terms of gold. The original figures in paper are multiplied by a factor representing the ratio of the actual price of gold to the standard price, taken from tables of Lord Lauderdale and other authors.

Jevons then plotted the logarithmic ratios. The fact is of some historic interest inasmuch as Jevons claims[1] that his was the first attempt in economics to use the logarithmic scale for charting.

The year 1782 was selected as base year, not for any considerations of normality, but because this was the first year of Tooke's tables.

For the calculation of the index no direct price ratios based on 1782 were formed. Instead, differences between logarithms of the prices for consecutive years were obtained and the subgroups were combined by taking the arithmetic mean of these differences of the individual items of the group. In order to get the final index each of these logarithms was added to the chain of additions of all preceding logarithms beginning with 1783.

4. Composition of Jevons's Index. For the period from 1782 to 1844 the main source was Tooke's *History of Prices*. For the following years most of the prices were taken from the price lists of *The Economist*, mainly from the annual review of trade. Other sources used were: Matthews' *Report of Commission on Manufactures*; McCulloch's *Dictionary, Exchange Magazine, Journal of the Statistical Society, Gentleman's Magazine*, and the *London Gazette*.

In some instances annual averages were used, without explanation as to how they were formed. In general, however, the average of the highest and lowest quotations for March, as shown by Tooke, was obtained.

The total consists of forty commodities which are grouped in several ways: first, differentiated according to their origin, as (a) tropical products, and (b) oriental products; and second, according to their nature.

The attempt to use weights did not result in any considerable change in the index, according to Jevons.[2] The exclusion of commodities which showed exceptionally great changes in price also did not make a noticeable difference.[3] The index is shown in Table 55.

5. Jevons's Practical Use of the Index. In a fragment written to form the conclusion of a book on money, which was never completed, Jevons tries to apply the index to practical questions of monetary policy.[4] He held the separation of the different functions of money to be indispensable, arguing that gold be used as a common denominator of money and temporary standard of value, while long-term debts should be regulated by a tabular standard with the help of price indexes.

6. Sauerbeck's Indexes. Sauerbeck constructed two indexes, covering two different periods. One series runs from 1846 until 1885.[5] The second series constructed by Sauerbeck is an arithmetic average of thirty-one commodities,

---

[1] *Investigations in Currency and Finance*, p. 128. [2] Ibid., p. 57. [3] Ibid., p. 58.
[4] Reprinted in *Investigations in Currency and Finance*, pp. 297 ff., under the title 'An Ideally Perfect System of Currency'.
[5] See Augustus Sauerbeck, 'Prices of Commodities and the Precious Metals',

Journal of the Statistical Society, 1886. A graph on an unnumbered page between pp. 648–9 shows the series together with a ten-year moving average of it. The index is brought up to date monthly in the *Journal of the Statistical Society*, now the *Journal of the Royal Statistical Society*.

TABLE 55. *Jevons's Index of Wholesale Commodity Prices*

Annually, 1782–1850

Base: 1782 = 100

Year	Index	Year	Index
1782 . .	100	1820 . .	103
3 . .	100	1 . .	94
4 . .	93	2 . .	88
1785 . .	90	3 . .	89
6 . .	85	4 . .	88
7 . .	87	1825 . .	103
8 . .	87	6 . .	90
9 . .	85	7 . .	90
1790 . .	87	8 . .	81
1 . .	89	9 . .	79
2 . .	93	1830 . .	81
3 . .	99	1 . .	82
4 . .	98	2 . .	78
1795 . .	117	3 . .	75
6 . .	125	4 . .	78
7 . .	110	1835 . .	80
8 . .	118	6 . .	86
9 . .	130	7 . .	84
1800 . .	141	8 . .	84
1 . .	140	9 . .	92
2 . .	110	1840 . .	87
3 . .	125	1 . .	85
4 . .	119	2 . .	75
1805 . .	132	3 . .	71
6 . .	130	4 . .	69
7 . .	129	1845 . .	74
8 . .	145	6 . .	74
9 . .	157	7 . .	78
1810 . .	142	8 . .	68
11 . .	136	9 . .	64
12 . .	121	1850 . .	64
13 . .	115		
14 . .	114		
1815 . .	109		
16 . .	91		
17 . .	117		
18 . .	132		
19 . .	112		

Source: *Investigations in Currency and Finance*, pp. 144–5.

for the period from 1818 to 1850. Data for the values of the components from year to year are not published, nor is the composition of this index explained. The base of the index is the average of prices from 1867 to 1877. The numbers are presented in Table 56.

The data for 1818–20 are reduced to a gold basis.

7. Indexes constructed by Tidman and Giffen. Some other indexes, covering at least some years of the period of this study, are published in the

TABLE 56. *Sauerbeck's Index of Wholesale Commodity Prices*

Annually, 1818–50

Base: 1867–77 = 100

Year	Index	Year	Index
1818 . .	142	1838 . .	99
19 . .	121	9 . .	103
1820 . .	112	1840 . .	103
1 . .	106	1 . .	100
2 . .	101	2 . .	91
3 . .	103	3 . .	83
4 . .	106	4 . .	84
1825 . .	117	1845 . .	87
6 . .	100	6 . .	89
7 . .	97	7 . .	95
8 . .	97	8 . .	78
9 . .	93	9 . .	74
1830 . .	91	1850 . .	77
1 . .	92		
2 . .	89		
3 . .	91		
4 . .	90		
1835 . .	92		
6 . .	102		
7 . .	94		

Source: *Journal of the Statistical Society*, 1886, pp. 634 and 648.

report of a Royal Commission that investigated the causes of the prolonged depression of the seventies and eighties.[1] The first of these, by Paul F. Tidman, is contained in one of the many memoranda which accompany the Commission's Report.[2] The index in question covers the period from 1845 to 1885, and is an average of fifty of the 'principal articles of commerce'. Its composition in detail is not given. The year 1849 is the base, and nothing else is told about the index except that the table 'has been constructed on the principle of averages shown by "index numbers" adopted by Professor Jevons, and the prices have been collected from the best statistical sources'.

The index numbers are as follows:

1845 .	.	100	1850 .	.	101
6 .	.	100	1 .	.	103
7 .	.	122	2 .	.	101
8 .	.	106			
9 .	.	100			

A second index number constructed was one for export prices calculated by Robert Giffen[3] from the declared export quantities and export values of individual commodities. Giffen does not explain the composition of the extended

[1] Report of the Royal Commission, Depression of Trade and Industry, Third Report, *P.P.*, 1886, xxiii.

[2] Ibid., p. 433.

[3] The index, originally constructed for the years 1861–77, was published in the *Journal of the Statistical Society*, 1879, in Robert Giffen's paper, 'On the Fall of Prices of Commodities in Recent Years'. A short description of the technique used is given on p. 41. The series was continued backwards to 1840, and published in an appendix to the Report of the Royal Commission in *P.P.*, 1886, xxiii. 329. The author of the appendix in which the index is given is Palgrave.

index, the base for which is 1840. The components are weighted according to the relative importance of the different items in British export trade, though it is not stated whether constant or shifting weights were used. The index numbers are as follows:

Year		Index	Year		Index
1840	.	. 100	1848	.	. 80
1841	.	. 97	1849	.	. 76
1845	.	. 91	1852	.	. 75

8. Porter's Index. Porter's index is the only contemporary index on a monthly basis. It covers the short period of five years, beginning January 1833, and consists of prices of fifty 'articles of commerce, including wheat', quoted at the beginning of each month. The base is the average of the prices prevailing in the first week of January 1833.

The commodities entering the index comprise the 'principal kinds of goods that enter into foreign commerce'. They are combined in the form of an un-weighted arithmetic average.[1] Further details on individual items, and sources, &c., are not given. The index differs considerably from the one constructed in this study. It oscillates with much greater amplitude, although the general direction of both indexes is the same. Porter's index numbers follow:

Month			1833	1834	1835	1836	1837
Jan.	.	.	1·0000	1·1094	1·1503	1·2555	1·2682
Feb.	.	.	1·0034	1·0996	1·1606	1·2640	1·2477
Mar.	.	.	0·9999	1·1026	1·1681	1·2762	1·2494
Apr.	.	.	0·9995	1·1014	1·1637	1·2915	1·2255
May	.	.	0·9933	1·0900	1·1580	1·2990	1·1865
June	.	.	0·9977	1·1029	1·1672	1·3120	1·1591
July	.	.	1·0360	1·1087	1·1686	1·3290	1·1422
Aug.	.	.	1·0717	1·1102	1·1697	1·3460	1·1336
Sept.	.	.	1·0996	1·1191	1·1855	1·3287	1·1321
Oct.	.	.	1·0951	1·1267	1·1892	1·3233	1·1450
Nov.	.	.	1·0932	1·1307	1·2198	1·3289	1·1586
Dec.	.	.	1·0863	1·1470	1·2327	1·2920	1·1689

9. Silberling's Index. Professor Norman J. Silberling's article in the *Review of Economic Statistics* (1923), 'British Prices and Business Cycles, 1779 to 1850', mentioned above, presented his quarterly index of British wholesale prices for this period, based upon thirty-five commodities. These commodities were sub-grouped into Group A, consisting of eleven British and six imported articles bearing relatively low freight charges, and Group B, consisting of eighteen imported articles bearing relatively heavy freight charges. These commodities were chosen, as pointed out above, because of their fitness, on Silberling's view, to serve 'as barometers of general business movements'.[2]

It will be recalled that, in forming the index, Silberling deducts duties where included in the imported prices, deliberately refrains from weighting the individual prices, and excludes commodities with rigid or erratic price movements.

[1] This is mentioned in Porter, *Progress of the Nation* (1838 ed.), Section 3, p. 228; index, pp. 236–7. Jevons, *Investigations in Currency and Finance*, p. 123, speaks of this index as being 'probably the arithmetic average'.

[2] See above, pp. 464 ff., for further discussion of the barometer idea in Silberling's index.

The index is a geometric average of price relatives on the base 1790. It is shown in Table 57.

TABLE 57. *Silberling's Index of Wholesale Commodity Prices*
Annually and quarterly, 1790–1850

Quarterly average 1790 = 100

Year	Annual Index	Quarterly Index			
		I	II	III	IV
1790 . .	100	97	99	102	101
1 . .	99	99	99	97	101
2 . .	102	103	101	101	102
3 . .	109	109	112	108	108
4 . .	107	109	106	105	108
1795 . .	126	115	125	129	135
6 . .	136	135	134	135	138
7 . .	141	143	142	136	144
8 . .	149	148	148	149	152
9 . .	156	152	157	158	155
1800 . .	159	154	156	161	164
1 . .	166	173	172	164	155
2 . .	143	147	144	141	141
3 . .	156	149	156	159	158
4 . .	153	156	151	149	156
1805 . .	160	162	161	158	158
6 . .	157	159	160	155	153
7 . .	152	155	153	150	149
8 . .	166	156	164	169	175
9 . .	176	183	173	169	178
1810 . .	176	184	182	173	166
11 . .	158	166	159	152	157
12 . .	163	161	160	162	168
13 . .	185	178	180	183	198
14 . .	198	211	203	190	189
1815 . .	166	170	169	165	157
16 . .	135	142	134	130	135
17 . .	143	142	140	141	149
18 . .	150	153	150	148	150
19 . .	136	146	138	132	130
1820 . .	124	128	126	123	120
1 . .	117	120	118	116	116
2 . .	114	117	114	112	113
3 . .	113	115	116	112	109
4 . .	106	108	106	104	106
1825 . .	118	115	122	118	117
6 . .	103	111	102	99	101
7 . .	101	104	102	100	99
8 . .	97	99	96	96	96
9 . .	94	98	95	92	91
1830 . .	93	92	91	92	96
1 . .	95	97	95	92	95
2 . .	94	95	95	93	94
3 . .	97	94	95	99	100
4 . .	97	99	96	95	96

TABLE 57 (cont.)

Year	Annual Index	Quarterly Index			
		I	II	III	IV
1835 . .	100	98	98	99	103
6 . .	112	106	116	112	113
7 . .	102	109	101	96	101
8 . .	104	102	102	104	108
9 . .	111	112	112	110	110
1840 . .	108	110	108	108	108
1 . .	103	108	104	100	100
2 . .	94	97	95	92	90
3 . .	86	88	86	84	85
4 . .	87	87	88	86	87
1845 . .	88	88	87	87	91
6 . .	88	90	87	86	90
7 . .	93	94	96	93	90
8 . .	84	89	86	81	81
9 . .	80	80	80	79	80
1850 . .	84	84	84	83	85

Source: 'British Prices and Business Cycles, 1779 to 1850', *Review of Economic Statistics*, 1923, pp. 232–3.

10. Kondratieff's Indexes. In his paper on long waves[1] Kondratieff uses a combination of Silberling's index for 1780 to 1846, and Sauerbeck's from 1846 to 1922, spliced together during 1846–50, and recalculated on the base of the average of 1901 to 1910. For the period 1914–22, as well as for 1801–20, paper values are expressed in terms of gold.

For his articles on price dynamics,[2] Kondratieff constructed his own price index, from 1786 to 1924 inclusive, on an annual basis. It consists of twenty-five products, as follows: rye, wheat, oats, barley, peas, beans, rice, butter, meat, wool, cotton, silk, linen, hemp, tobacco, linseed-oil, palm-oil, olive-oil, cotton goods (from 1814), iron, copper, tin, zinc, coal (from 1804), and forest products. Index numbers were calculated for each of the series on the base of the arithmetic average of prices from 1901 to 1910.

Two sub-indexes, one of agricultural goods (including all the commodities listed beginning with rye and ending with tobacco), and the other of industrial goods (inclusive of all commodities listed beginning with linseed-oil and ending with forest products), were formed as unweighted geometric averages of these items. The sub-indexes are also combined geometrically to form the total index, with equal weight given to each group index.

The sources are: Tooke's *History of Prices*, Tooke's *Thoughts and Details on the High and Low Prices*, Mulhall's *Dictionary*, Mulhall's *History of Prices*, Jevons's *Investigations in Currency and Finance*, McCulloch's *Statistical Account*, *Journal of the Statistical Society*, and the *Statistical Abstract of the United Kingdom*.

[1] 'Die langen Wellen der Konjunktur', *Archiv für Sozialwissenschaft und Sozialpolitik*, lvi. 573–609. The index is on p. 600.

[2] 'Die Preisdynamik der industriellen und landwirtschaftlichen Waren', ibid. lx. 1–85. The method is described on p. 14; the index appears on p. 72.

In addition to the actual index series the deviations from a calculated trend are given in the text.

TABLE 58. *Kondratieff's Index of Wholesale Commodity Prices*

Annually, 1786–1850

Base: 1901–10 = 100

Year	Index	Year	Index
1786 . .	148·6	1820 . .	143·0
7 . .	144·6	1 . .	129·4
8 . .	140·4	2 . .	118·0
9 . .	134·5	3 . .	123·4
1790 . .	141·6	4 . .	122·7
1 . .	145·8	1825 . .	138·8
2 . .	134·6	6 . .	125·1
3 . .	147·8	7 . .	120·8
4 . .	155·4	8 . .	112·6
1795 . .	176·5	9 . .	109·7
6 . .	181·1	1830 . .	105·1
7 . .	176·9	1 . .	110·7
8 . .	158·7	2 . .	106·0
9 . .	192·3	3 . .	102·5
1800 . .	208·6	4 . .	104·4
1 . .	201·8	1835 . .	106·0
2 . .	159·6	6 . .	117·6
3 . .	181·3	7 . .	116·0
4 . .	173·1	8 . .	115·1
1805 . .	187·3	9 . .	125·6
6 . .	189·9	1840 . .	121·1
7 . .	194·0	1 . .	120·3
8 . .	208·4	2 . .	110·3
9 . .	219·4	3 . .	98·0
1810 . .	184·3	4 . .	99·4
11 . .	187·3	1845 . .	105·7
12 . .	175·7	6 . .	108·9
13 . .	163·3	7 . .	116·8
14 . .	161·6	8 . .	100·0
1815 . .	152·3	9 . .	93·8
16 . .	130·2	1850 . .	97·5
17 . .	154·5		
18 . .	168·7		
19 . .	147·5		

Source: 'Die Preisdynamik der industriellen und landwirtschaftlichen Waren', *Archiv für Sozialwissenschaft und Sozialpolitik*, lx, p. 72.

11. Paul Rousseaux's Indexes. Rousseaux's recent investigation into long waves in England includes a section in which he presents new annual indexes of British commodity prices from 1800 to 1913.[1] Though all of his basic data were obtained from the well-known sources and have been readily available, Rousseaux's work is unique in that it presents a breakdown of his material into a number of sub-groups for which separate indexes are presented.

[1] Paul Rousseaux, *Les Mouvements de Fond de l'Économie Anglaise, 1800–1913,* pp. 72–9, 262–7.

Rousseaux's price data were drawn largely from the quotations published by Jevons, those gathered by Silberling and used in the latter's index, and finally from those of Sauerbeck which were continued by the editor of the *Statist* and presented regularly in the *Journal of the Royal Statistical Society*. In order to make the representation of commodities in each of the sub-groups more complete, these series were supplemented by quotations obtained from Tooke, the price currents of *The Economist*, and the *Report on Wholesale and Retail Prices in the United Kingdom* of 1903. The latter report includes some valuable annual data beginning for the most part with the first years of the nineteenth century, and obtained chiefly at certain large poor-houses near London. In addition to these sources, Rousseaux used figures obtained from various books and articles for the purpose of filling in gaps in the above series or of serving as a check on their accuracy.

Rousseaux's indexes break into two periods: the first, from 1800 to 1850, based on forty-two commodities, and the second, from 1846 to 1913, based on sixty-one items. These quotations were divided into two major groups, agricultural and industrial. The agricultural group comprises the following categories: (1) domestic farm products; (2) imported farm products; (3) imported farm food products, a sub-group of (2); (4) total farm products, consisting of the sum of (1) and (2); (5) animal products, and (6) domestic agricultural products, consisting of (1) and part of (5). The index for total agricultural products comprises the sum of the items in sub-groups (4) and (5) above.

As for the industrial products, only a single index was constructed which includes the principal industrial materials exclusive of chemicals. This exclusion was dictated by the general aim which Rousseaux had in mind in choosing the type of sub-groups for which indexes were to be constructed: namely, to distinguish as far as possible the same categories as were presented in the analysis of Belgian prices by F. Loots.[1] The Belgian list is divided into principal industrial products and chemical products. Since Rousseaux found too scanty quotations to construct a separate index for the latter group, he excluded them altogether in order to obtain an index which would be strictly comparable to the Belgian industrial group. Considerations of comparability with the Loots indexes also explain the subdivision of agricultural products.

The total index 'is simply the average of the agricultural and the industrial index'. In no case is there any mention of the type of average used, nor of the question of weighting, though it is perhaps reasonable to suppose that in these matters too the methods of Loots have been followed. Loots used a simple geometric average.

The indexes for each of the two periods (1800–50, 1846–1913) were constructed on the base of the average of two rather widely separated dates 'in order to diminish as much as possible the dispersion of the quotations at the extremities of the period'. Thus the series for the first period were constructed with the average of the years 1820 and 1840 as base; the average of the years 1865 and 1885 served as base for the second period. The indexes for the two periods were chained by the use of a correction coefficient based on the ratio between their averages during the overlapping years 1849 and 1850.

---

[1] François Loots, 'Les Mouvements Fondamentaux des Prix de Gros en Belgique de 1822 à 1913', *Bulletin de l'Institut des Sciences Économiques*, viii, Nov. 1936, p. 23.

The figures for the two major subgroups and the total index are presented in Table 59.[1]

TABLE 59. *Rousseaux's Indexes of Wholesale Commodity Prices*

Annually, 1800–50

Base: Average of 1865 and 1885 = 100

Year	Agricultural products	Industrial products	Total index
1800	188	163	175
1	210	166	188
2	158	146	152
3	160	162	161
4	157	160	159
1805	175	166	170
6	162	170	166
7	155	167	161
8	176	202	189
9	184	229	206
1810	190	196	193
11	170	186	178
12	207	186	196
13	216	189	203
14	210	195	202
1815	164	164	164
16	152	136	144
17	184	137	161
18	182	138	160
19	160	134	147
1820	143	121	132
1	127	115	121
2	116	116	116
3	125	116	120
4	122	122	122
1825	144	121	133
6	126	107	117
7	128	106	117
8	122	102	112
9	122	98	110
1830	124	94	109
1	126	97	112
2	125	93	109
3	121	92	107
4	119	104	112
1835	118	106	112
6	129	116	123
7	129	107	118
8	133	105	119
9	143	116	130
1840	141	115	128
1	131	110	121
2	122	100	111
3	113	96	105
4	119	96	108
1845	120	99	110
6	118	99	109
7	125	104	115
8	107	92	100
9	102	87	95
1850	98	93	95

Source: Paul Rousseaux, *Les Mouvements de Fond de l' Économie Anglaise, 1800–1913*, pp. 266–7.

[1] The base is that of the second period, the average of the years 1865 and 1885.